Diversity and Society

3

2011/2012 UPDATE

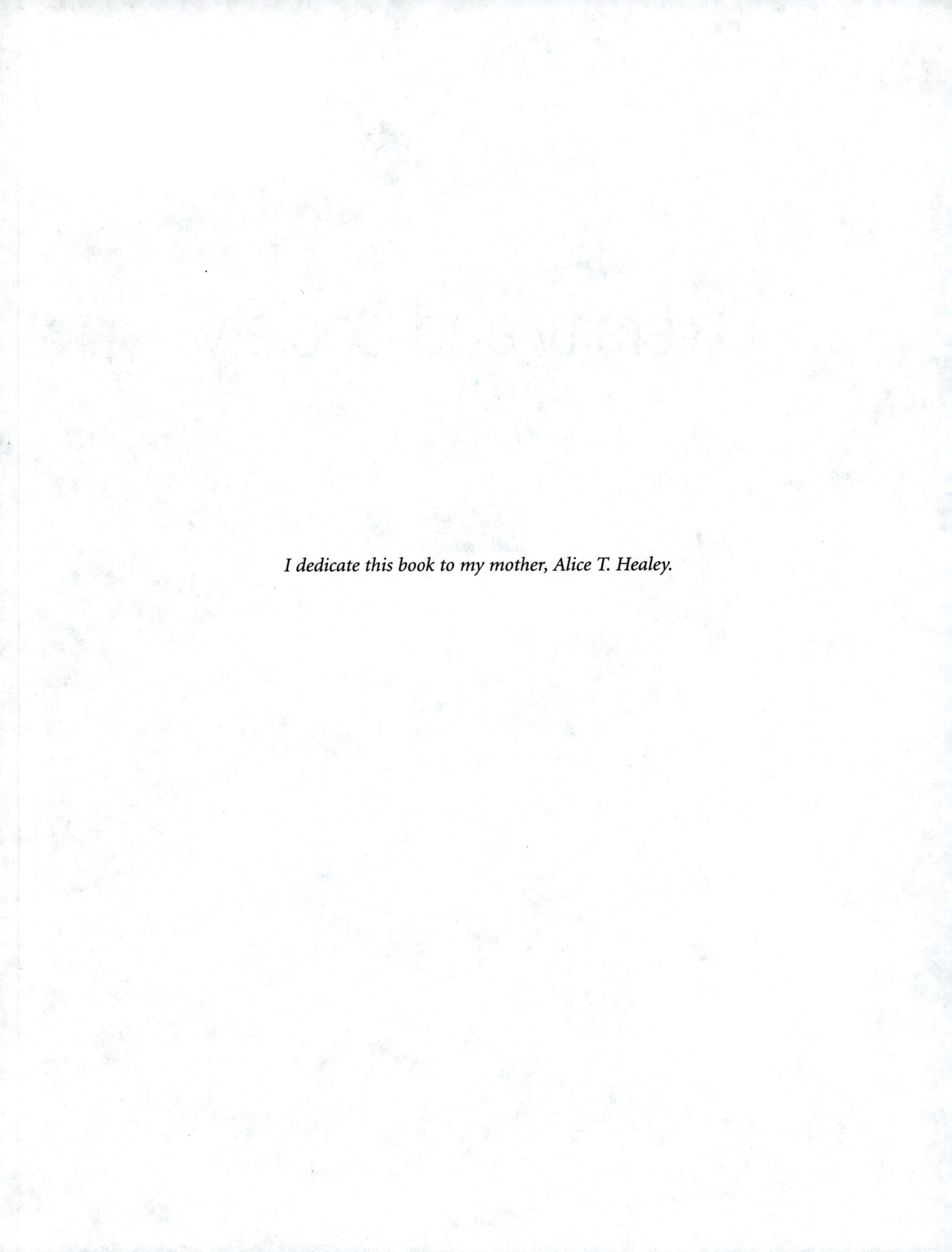

I dedicate this book to my mother, Alice T. Healey.

Diversity and Society

Race, Ethnicity, and Gender

Joseph F. Healey
Christopher Newport University

Los Angeles | London | New Delhi
Singapore | Washington DC

Los Angeles | London | New Delhi
Singapore | Washington DC

FOR INFORMATION:

Pine Forge Press
An Imprint of SAGE Publications, Inc.
2455 Teller Road
Thousand Oaks, California 91320
E-mail: order@sagepub.com

SAGE Publications Ltd.
1 Oliver's Yard
55 City Road
London EC1Y 1SP
United Kingdom

SAGE Publications India Pvt. Ltd.
B 1/I 1 Mohan Cooperative Industrial Area
Mathura Road, New Delhi 110 044
India

SAGE Publications Asia-Pacific Pte. Ltd.
33 Pekin Street #02-01
Far East Square
Singapore 048763

Acquisitions Editor: David Repetto
Editorial Assistant: Maggie Stanley
Production Editor: Laureen Gleason
Copy Editors: Teresa Herlinger/Amy Rosenstein
Typesetter: C&M Digitals (P) Ltd.
Proofreaders: Gretchen Treadwell/Laura Webb
Indexer: Jeanne Busemeyer
Cover Designer: Bryan Fishman
Marketing Manager: Erica DeLuca

Printed in the United States of America

Cataloging-in-Publication Data is on file with the Library of Congress

Paperback ISBN 978-1-4129-9433-0

This book is printed on acid-free paper.

11 12 13 14 15 10 9 8 7 6 5 4 3 2

Contents

Preface

Of all the challenges confronting the United States today, those relating to minority groups continue to be among the most urgent and the most daunting. Discrimination and racial inequality are part of our national heritage and—along with equality, freedom, and justice—prejudice and racism are among our oldest values. Minority-group issues penetrate every aspect of society, and virtually every item on the national agenda—health care reform, crime and punishment, safety in the streets, the future of the family, even defense spending, foreign policy, and the war on terrorism—has some connection with dominant–minority relations.

These issues will not be resolved easily or quickly. Feelings are intense, and controversy and bitter debate often swamp dispassionate analysis and calm reason. For example, in the summer of 2009, Professor Henry Louis Gates, an African American, was arrested by a white police officer who was responding to a report of a possible break-in at Gates's house. Professor Gates, a widely known scholar and distinguished member of the faculty at Harvard University, was arrested inside his own house, even after he produced identification. The police officer, Sergeant Crowley, argued that Gates was being belligerent and uncooperative. The incident made headlines across the nation; was prominently featured on TV news outlets; and was the subject of seemingly endless discussions, accusations, and counteraccusations for weeks. Were the police once again singling out a member of the black community for special and unequal treatment? Was this another instance of racial profiling? Regardless, the volume of accusations and rejoinders showed once again that issues of race and inequality remain at the top of the national agenda, and the fury and emotion of the charges and countercharges demonstrated the intense feelings that color our national discussions of these matters. As a society, we have little hope of resolving these dilemmas unless we confront them openly and honestly; they will not disappear, and they will not resolve themselves.

This textbook contributes to the ongoing discussion by presenting information, raising questions, and probing issues. My intent is to help students increase their fund of information, improve their understanding of the issues, and clarify their thinking regarding matters of race and ethnicity. This text has been written for undergraduate students—sociology majors and nonmajors alike. It makes minimal assumptions about students' knowledge of history or sociological concepts, and the material is presented in a way that students will find accessible and coherent.

For example, a unified set of themes and concepts is used throughout the text. The analysis is consistent and continuous, even as multiple perspectives and various points of view are examined. The bulk of the conceptual framework is introduced in the first four chapters. These concepts and analytical themes are then used in a series of case studies of minority groups in contemporary America and are also used to investigate group relations in various societies around the globe. In the final chapter, main points and themes are summarized and reviewed, the analysis is brought to a conclusion, and some speculations are made regarding the future.

This textbook is written in the tradition of conflict theory, but does not aspire to be a comprehensive statement of that tradition. Other perspectives are introduced and applied, but no attempt is made to give equal attention to all current sociological paradigms. The text does not try to explain everything, nor does it attempt to include all possible analytical points of view. Rather, the goals are (a) to present the sociology of minority-group relations in a way that students will find understandable as well as intellectually challenging and (b) to deal with the issues and tell the stories behind them in a textbook that is both highly readable and a demonstration of the power and importance of thinking sociologically.

Every chapter (except the last) begins with a recounting of personal experiences that foreshadow the material compellingly and dramatically. These introductions include the personal experiences and thoughts of a wide variety of people: immigrants, minority-group members, journalists, sociologists, and slaves, among others. Also, each chapter (except the last) includes a section called "Focus on Contemporary Issues," which addresses a specific issue in U.S. society that readers will find current and relevant to everyday life.

This text also explores the diversity of experiences within each minority group, particularly gender differences. Too often, minority groups (and the dominant group, for that matter) are seen by nonmembers as single, undifferentiated entities. The text acknowledges the variety of experiences within each group and, in particular, explores differences in the experiences of minority-group males and females. The analysis explores the ways in which gender differences cut across ethnic and racial differences and stresses that these sources of inequality and injustice are independent of each other. Solving one set of problems (e.g., prejudice and racial discrimination) will not automatically or directly solve the other (e.g., sexism and gender inequalities).

I focus on the experiences of minority groups in the United States, but a considerable amount of comparative, cross-national material has also been included. Every chapter but the final one includes a section called "Comparative Focus" that explores group relations in other societies.

Finally, this text stresses the ways in which American minority groups are inseparable from American society. The relative success of this society is due no less to the contributions of minority groups than to those of the dominant group. The nature of the minority-group experience has changed as the larger society has changed, and to understand America's minority groups is to understand some elemental truths about America. To raise the issues of race and ethnicity is to ask what it means—and what it has meant—to be an American.

This text is an abridged and updated version of *Race, Ethnicity, Gender, and Class: The Sociology of Group Conflict and Change* (5th edition), also published by Pine Forge

Press. The larger volume includes a number of additional features, more detail and explanation, and a separate chapter on prejudice. This volume takes a more macro approach and deemphasizes individual prejudice but retains the overall format, case study approach, and conceptual framework of the larger text.

A companion volume entitled *Race, Ethnicity, and Gender* (3rd edition) is available that includes readings and other features. The readings are organized in chapters that parallel this text and are drawn from a variety of sources and represent a wealth of viewpoints. The companion volume also includes current debates on topics such as reparations for slavery, and immigration, as well as personal narratives written by people who have experienced (and sometimes triumphed over) racism and discrimination.

Changes in This Edition of *Diversity and Society*

Many changes have been made in the third edition of *Diversity and Society,* most of them designed to decrease length and sharpen the focus:

- Research findings and all data have been updated. In particular, this edition relies on the 2007 American Community Survey of the U.S. Bureau of the Census for the latest background information on America's minority groups.
- The number of chapters has been shortened from 12 to 10. The case study chapter on White Ethnics has been merged into Chapter 2. The cross-national material formerly in Chapter 11 has been distributed throughout the text and integrated into other chapters.
- The chapter on "New Americans" has been shortened by moving most new immigrant groups into the case study chapters. That is, the smaller Hispanic groups are now covered in Chapter 7, and the smaller Asian groups in Chapter 8. This allows Chapter 9 to be more focused on recent immigrants and immigration issues in general.
- Each chapter except the last begins with a vignette or incident that seeks to personalize the subject matter of the chapter and draw students into the narrative that is unfolding throughout the text.
- New sections labeled "Focus on Contemporary Issues" have been added to all chapters except the last. These address a range of topics including slavery in the contemporary world, the racial and gender implications of Hurricane Katrina, and other matters of widespread interest and concern. These sections are integrated into the flow of the chapters and, generally, apply or relate to the specific material in that chapter.
- New sections labeled "Comparative Focus" have been added to all chapters except the last. These address group relations in other nations, make explicit comparisons to the United States, and seek to widen the perspective of students. Like the new "Focus on Contemporary Issues" feature, these sections are integrated into the flow of the chapters.
- An appendix comparing the status of all groups covered in this text on a number of variables has been added to the study site at **www.pineforge.com/healeyds3e.** The information for these graphs comes from the 2007 American Community Survey conducted by the U.S. Bureau of the Census.
- Maps and other graphics have been added to increase the visual appeal of the text and to convey information in a more easily comprehensible way.
- A new type of graph displaying the distribution of income for groups—not just the averages—has been added to the case study chapters.

Part I

An Introduction to the Study of Minority Groups in the United States

The United States is a nation of groups as well as individuals. These groups vary along a number of dimensions, including size, wealth, education, race, culture, religion, and language. Some of these groups have been part of American society since colonial days, and others have formed as recently as the past few years.

How should all these groups relate to one another? Who should be considered American? Should we preserve the multitude of cultural heritages and languages that currently exists and stress our diversity? Should we encourage everyone to adopt Anglo-American culture and strive to become more similar and unified? Should we emphasize our similarities or celebrate our differences? Is it possible to do both?

Questions of unity and diversity are among the most pressing to face the United States today. In this text, we will analyze these and many other questions. Our goal is to develop a broader, more informed understanding of the past and present forces that have created and sustained the groups that compose U.S. society.

1

Diversity in the United States

Questions and Concepts

Who am I? . . . Where do I fit into American society? . . . For most of my 47 years, I have struggled to find answers to these questions. I am an American of multiracial descent and culture [Native American, African American, Italian American, and Puerto Rican]. In this aspect, I am not very different from many Americans [but] I have always felt an urge to feel and live the intermingling of blood that runs through my veins. American society has a way of forcing multiracial and biracial people to choose one race over the other. I personally feel this pressure every time I have to complete an application form with instructions to check just one box for race category.

—A 47-year-old male[1]

Actually, I don't feel comfortable being around Asians except for my family. . . . I couldn't relate to . . . other Asians [because] they grew up in [wealthier neighborhoods]. I couldn't relate to the whole "I live in a mansion" [attitude]. This summer, I worked in a media company and it was kind of hard to relate to them [other Asians] because we all grew up in a different place. . . . [T]he look I would get when I say "Yeah, I'm from [a less affluent neighborhood"] they're like, "Oh, Oh" like, "That's unfortunate for your parents, I'm sorry they didn't make it."

—A 19-year-old Macanese-Chinese-Portuguese female[2]

Yeah, my people came from all over—Italy, Ireland, Poland, and others too. I don't really know when they got here or why they came and, really, it doesn't matter much to me. I mean, I'm just an American. . . . I'm from everywhere. . . . I'm from here!

—A 25-year-old white American female[3]

(Continued)

(Continued)

What do these people have in common? How do they differ? They think about their place in U.S. society in very different ways. All are connected to a multitude of groups and traditions, but not all find this fact interesting or important. One feels alienated from the more affluent members of her group, one seeks to embrace his multiple memberships, and one dismisses the issue of ancestry as irrelevant and is comfortable and at ease being "just an American."

Today, the United States is growing more diverse in culture, race, religion, and language. The number of people who can connect themselves to different cultural traditions is increasing, as is the number of Americans of mixed race. Where will this lead us? Will increasing diversity lead to greater tolerance and respect for one another? Can we overcome the legacies of racism and inequality that stretch back to colonial days? Will we fragment along these lines of difference and dissolve into warring ethnic enclaves (the fate of more than one modern, apparently unified nation)?

This text raises a multitude of questions about the past, present, and future of group relationships in U.S. society. What historical, social, political, and economic forces shaped those relationships in the past? How do racial and ethnic groups relate to each other today? What issues and problems can we expect in the years to come? Why do some people struggle with their identity? What is an American?

Introduction

The United States is a nation of immigrants and we have been arguing, often passionately, about who we are and who we should be, about inclusion and exclusion, and about unity and diversity since the infancy of American society. Every member of our society is in some sense an immigrant or the descendant of immigrants. Even Native Americans "immigrated" to this continent, albeit thousands of years ago. We are all from someplace else, with roots in another part of the world. Some came here in chains, others came on ocean liners or 747s, and some came on foot. Some arrived last week, and others have had family here for centuries. Each wave of newcomers has in some way altered the social landscape of the United States. As many have observed, American society is continually becoming and is permanently unfinished.

Today, the United States is remaking itself yet again. Large numbers of immigrants are entering the nation from, literally, all over the world and, once again, questions are being raised about who belongs, what it means to be a U.S. citizen, and how much cultural and linguistic variety we can tolerate. Our growing diversity means that many will struggle to find a place, to conceptualize what kind of American they are.

Even as we debate the consequences and implications of high rates of immigration, other long-standing issues of belonging, fairness, and justice remain unresolved. American Indians and African Americans have been a part of this society since its inception but as "others," slaves and enemies, victims of genocide, servants, and laborers—groups outside the mainstream, not "true Americans" or full citizens. The legacies of **racism** and exclusion continue to affect these groups today and, as we shall see in chapters to come, they and other American minority groups continue to suffer from inequality, discrimination, and marginalization.

Today, the definition of *American* seems up for grabs. After all, we have elected Barack Obama—a black man—to the most powerful position in the society (and, arguably, in the world). To many Americans, this is proof that America has finally become what it has so often proclaimed itself to be: a truly open and just society and the last, best hope for all of humanity. Yet, even a casual glance at our schools, courts, neighborhoods, churches, corporate boardrooms—indeed, any nook or cranny of our society—reveals pervasive patterns of inequality, differential opportunity, injustice, and unfairness. Which is the real America: the land of tolerance and opportunity or the sink hole of narrow-mindedness and inequity?

Are we at a crossroads in this era of growing diversity? Do we have an opportunity to reexamine the fundamental questions of citizenship and inclusion in this society: What is an American? Can we incorporate all groups while avoiding fragmentation and chaotic disunity? What can hold us together? Should we celebrate our diversity or stress the need for unity?

Our understanding of these issues and our answers to these questions are partly affected by the groups to which we belong. Some of us feel intensely connected to our people and identify closely with our heritage. Others are uncertain about who they are exactly, where they fit in the social landscape. Still others feel no particular connection with any tradition, group, or homeland. However, these elements of our identity still influence our lives and perceptions. They help to shape who we are and how we relate to the larger society. They affect the ways others perceive us, the opportunities available to us, the way we think about ourselves, and our view of American society and the larger world. They affect our perception of what it means to be American.

The Increasing Variety of American Minority Groups

Our group memberships also shape the choices we make in the voting booth and in other areas of social life. As a society, we face important decisions about what we are becoming, and we need to contemplate these choices systematically and thoroughly. We also need to be aware that members of different groups will evaluate these decisions in different ways. The issues will be filtered through the screens of divergent experiences, group histories, and present situations. The debates over which direction our society should take are unlikely to be meaningful or even mutually intelligible without some understanding of the variety of ways of being American.

These choices about the future of our society are especially urgent because of our increasing diversity. Since the 1960s, the number of immigrants arriving in the United States each year has more than tripled and includes groups from all over the globe (U.S. Department of Homeland Security, 2008). Concerns about increasing diversity are compounded by other long-standing minority issues and grievances that remain unresolved.

In many ways, the problems of African Americans, Native Americans, Hispanic Americans, and Asian Americans today are just as formidable as they were a generation ago.

As one way of gauging the dimensions of diversity in our nation, consider the changing group structure of U.S. society. Exhibit 1.1 presents the percentage of the total U.S. population in each of five groups. Before examining the data in the exhibit, consider the groups themselves and the labels used to designate them. All of the category names are arbitrary, and none of these groups have clear or unambiguous boundaries. Two people within one of these categories might be as different from each other as any two people selected from different categories. The people included in a category may share some general physical or cultural traits, but they will also vary by social class, religion, gender, and in thousands of other ways. People classified as "Asian and Pacific Islander" represent scores of different national and linguistic backgrounds (Japanese, Samoan, Vietnamese, Pakistani, and so forth), and "American Indian" includes people from hundreds of different tribal groups. The racial and ethnic categories, as stated in Exhibit 1.1, frequently appear in government reports and in the professional literature of the social sciences, but they are arbitrary and should never be mistaken for unchanging or "natural" divisions between people.

Exhibit 1.1 Groups in U.S. Society, Percentage of Total Population, 1980 to 2050

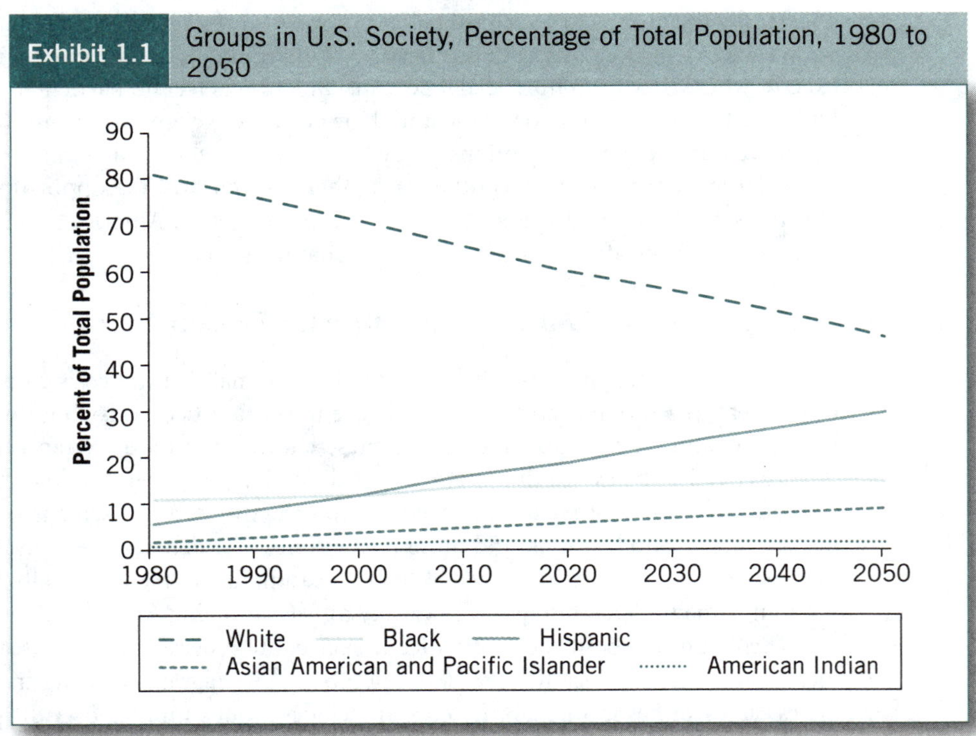

SOURCE: Based on data from U.S. Bureau of the Census, 2008a.

NOTES: "White" refers to non-Hispanics only. "Hispanic" may be of any Latin race.

Exhibit 1.1 reports the actual relative sizes of the groups for 1980, 1990, and 2000, and the projected or estimated relative sizes through 2050. The increasing diversity of U.S. society is reflected in the declining numerical predominance of non-Hispanic whites, who are projected to fall to less than half of the population by the middle of the century. Several states (Texas, California, Hawaii, and New Mexico) are already "majority-minority," and this will be true of the entire nation within several decades.

African Americans and Native Americans will grow in numbers but are projected to remain stable in their relative size. In contrast, the populations of Hispanic Americans and Asian Americans and Pacific Islanders will grow dramatically. Asian American and Pacific Islander groups made up only 2% of the population in 1980 but will grow to nearly 10% by mid-century. The most dramatic growth, however, will be for Hispanic American groups. Hispanic Americans became the largest minority group in 2002, surpassing African Americans, and will grow to 30% of the population by mid-century.

The projections into the future are only educated guesses, but they presage profound change for the United States. As this century unfolds, our society will become less white, less European, and more like the world as a whole. Some see these changes as threats to traditional, white, middle-class American values and lifestyles. Others see them as providing an opportunity for other equally attractive and legitimate value systems and lifestyles to emerge.

Even though the categories in Exhibit 1.1 are broad, they still provide no place for a number of groups. For example, where should we place Arab Americans and recent immigrants from Africa? Although these groups are relatively small in size (about 1 million people each), there is no clear place for them in Exhibit 1.1. Should Arab Americans be classified as "Asian"? Should recent immigrants from Africa be placed in the same category as African Americans? Of course, there is no particular need to have a category for every single group, but we should recognize that classification schemes like the one used in this exhibit (and in many other contexts) have limited utility and application.

A further limitation of classification schemes like the one used in Exhibit 1.1 will become increasingly apparent in the years to come: There are no categories for the growing number of mixed-race individuals, mentioned in the introduction to this chapter. The number of people who identify themselves as belonging to "two or more races" is relatively small today, about 2% of the population in 2007 (U.S. Bureau of the Census, 2007), but is likely to increase rapidly because of the growing number of marriages across group lines. The number of these marriages has multiplied by more than 10 since 1960 and by 3.5 between 1980 and 2007 (U.S. Bureau of the Census, 2009b, p. 52). Obviously, the greater the number of marriages that cross group lines, the greater the number of mixed-race Americans. One study estimates that 21% of the population will claim membership in this category by the 2050 census (Smith & Edmonston, 1997, p. 119).

What are the implications of these numbers? What kind of society are we becoming? What should it mean to be American? How inclusive should the definition of American be? How wide can the limits be stretched before national unity is threatened? How narrow can they be before the desire to preserve cultural and linguistic diversity is unjustly and unnecessarily stifled?

These first few paragraphs have raised a lot of questions. The purpose of this book is to help you develop some answers and some thoughtful, informed positions on these issues. You should be aware from the beginning that the questions addressed here are complex and that the answers we seek are not obvious or easy. Indeed, there is no guarantee that we as a society will be able or willing to resolve all the problems of intergroup relations in the United States. However, we will never make progress in this area unless we confront the issues honestly and with an accurate base of knowledge and understanding. Certainly these issues will not resolve themselves or disappear if they are ignored.

In the course of our investigation, we will rely on sociology and other social sciences for concepts, theory, and information. Chapters 1 to 3 introduce and define many of the ideas that will guide our investigation. Part II explores how relations between the dominant group and minority groups have evolved in American society. Part III analyzes the current situation of U.S. minority groups. In Part IV, the final section of the book, we explore many of the challenges and issues facing our society (and the world) and see what conclusions we can glean from our investigations and how they might shape the future.

What Is a Minority Group?

Before we can begin to sort out the issues, we need common definitions and a common vocabulary for discussion. We begin with the term **minority group.**[4] Taken literally, the mathematical connotation of this term is misleading because it implies that minority groups are small. In reality, a minority group can be quite large and can even be a numerical majority of the population. Women, for example, are sometimes considered to be a separate minority group, but they are a numerical majority of U.S. citizens. In South Africa, as in many nations created by European colonization, whites are a numerical minority (less than 10% of the population), but despite recent changes, they remain the most powerful and affluent group.

Minority status has more to do with the distribution of resources and power than with simple numbers. The definition of minority group used in this book is based on Wagley and Harris (1958). According to this definition, a minority group has five characteristics:

1. The members of the group experience a pattern of disadvantage or inequality.
2. The members of the group share a visible trait or characteristic that differentiates them from other groups.
3. The minority group is a self-conscious social unit.
4. Membership in the group is usually determined at birth.
5. Members tend to marry within the group.

We will examine each of the defining characteristics here and, a bit later, we will return to examine the first two—inequality and visibility—in greater detail, because they are the more important characteristics of minority groups. The first and most important defining characteristic of a minority group is *inequality,* or a pattern of disability and disadvantage. The nature of the disability and the degree of disadvantage are variable and can range from exploitation, slavery, and genocide to slight irritants such as a lack of desks for left-handed students or a policy of racial exclusion at an expensive country club. (Note, however, that you might not agree that the irritant is slight if you are a left-handed student awkwardly taking notes at a right-handed desk or if you are a golf aficionado who happens to be African American.)

Whatever its scope or severity—whether it extends to wealth, jobs, housing, political power, police protection, or health care—the pattern of disadvantage is the key characteristic of a minority group. Because the group has less of what is valued by society, the term **subordinate group** is sometimes used instead of minority group.

The pattern of disadvantage is the result of the actions of another group, often in the distant past, that benefits from and tries to sustain the unequal arrangement. This group can be called the core group or the **dominant group.** The latter term is used most frequently in this book because it reflects the patterns of inequality and the power realities of minority group status.

The second defining characteristic of a minority group is *visibility:* some trait or characteristic that sets members of the group apart and that the dominant group holds in low esteem. The trait can be cultural (language, religion, speech patterns, or dress styles), physical (skin color, stature, or facial features), or both. Groups that are defined primarily by their cultural characteristics are called **ethnic minority groups.** Examples of such groups are Irish Americans and Jewish Americans. Groups defined primarily by their physical characteristics are **racial minority groups,** such as African Americans or Native Americans. Note that these categories overlap, as reflected in several of the quotations that opened this chapter. People may confuse the terms or equate one with the other. So-called ethnic groups may have (or may be thought to have) distinguishing physical characteristics (for example, the stereotypical Irish red hair or Jewish nose), and racial groups commonly have (or are thought to have) cultural traits that differ from the dominant group (for example, differences in dialect, religious values, or cuisine).

These distinguishing traits set boundaries and separate people into distinct groups. The traits are outward signs that identify minority group members and help to maintain the patterns of disadvantage. The dominant group has (or at one time, had) sufficient power to create the distinction between groups and thus solidify a higher position for itself. These markers of group membership are crucial: Without these visible signs, it would be difficult or impossible to identify who was in which group, and the system of minority group oppression would soon collapse.

It is important to realize that the characteristics that mark the boundaries between groups usually are not significant in and of themselves. They are selected for their visibility and convenience, and objectively, they may be quite trivial and unimportant. For example, scientists have concluded that skin color and other so-called racial traits have little scientific, evolutionary, medical, or biological importance. As we shall see, skin color is an important marker of group membership in our society because it was selected during a complex and lengthy historical process, not because it has any inherent significance. These markers become important because we attribute significance to them.

A third characteristic of minority groups is *awareness:* Minority groups recognize their differentiation from the dominant group and their shared disabilities. This shared social status can provide the basis for strong intragroup bonds and a sense of solidarity and can lead to views of the world that are quite different from those of the dominant group and other minority groups. For example, public opinion polls frequently show vast differences between dominant and minority groups in their views of the seriousness and extent of discrimination in American society. Exhibit 1.2 displays one result of an August 2008 *USA Today*/Gallup poll and shows that, while 78% of blacks thought that racism is widespread in the United States, only 51% of whites (and 59% of Hispanics) agreed, a difference of 27 percentage points (Jones, 2008).

Exhibit 1.2 Percentage of Whites, Blacks, and Hispanics Agreeing That Racism Is Widespread Against Blacks Today

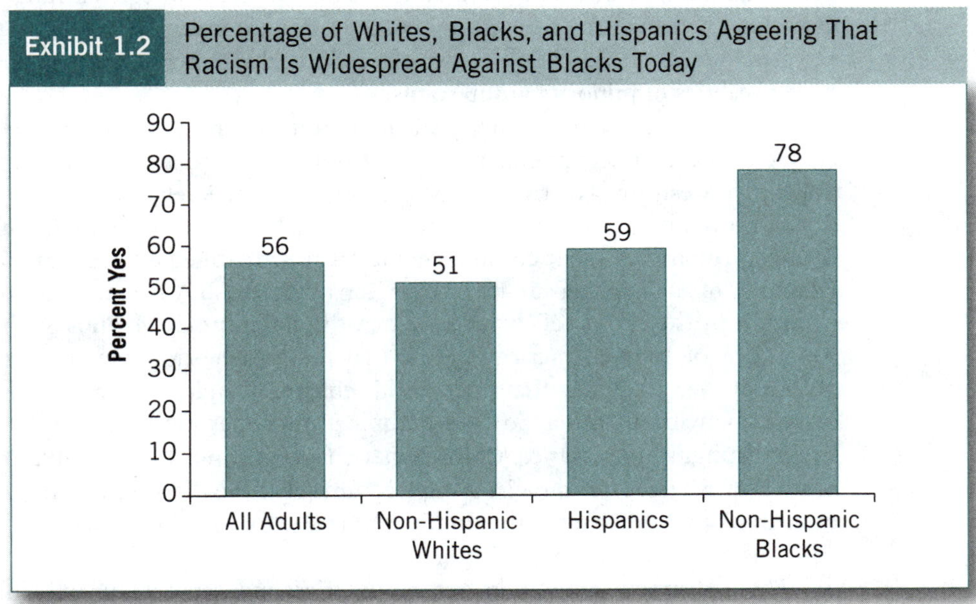

SOURCE: From "Majority of Americans Say Racism Against Blacks Widespread," Jeffrey M. Jones, August 4, 2008. Copyright © 2008 Gallup. Reprinted with permission.

The differences in perception are further illustrated by a poll taken just before the inauguration of President Barack Obama in January 2009. When asked if they believed that Obama's election meant that the United States had achieved the vision of America articulated by Martin Luther King in his famous "I Have a Dream" speech—a society in which people are judged "by the content of their character," not the color of their skin—the great majority (70%) of black Americans said "yes" versus only 46% of whites ("Most Blacks Say MLK's Vision Fulfilled," 2009). These results reverse the usual pattern of greater pessimism among the minority group and probably reflect the (temporary?) euphoria among African Americans stimulated by the dazzling success of a member of the group. Still, they illustrate the vast differences in worldview between the two groups.

A fourth characteristic of a minority group is that membership is, in general, *permanent.* Membership is an **ascribed status,** or a status that is acquired at birth. The traits that identify minority group membership typically cannot be easily changed, and minority group status is usually involuntary and for life.

Finally, minority group members tend to be *endogamous:* They tend to marry within their own groups. This pattern can be voluntary, or the dominant group can dictate it. In fact, interracial marriages were illegal in many U.S. states until the late 1960s, only 40 years ago, when laws against **miscegenation** were declared unconstitutional by the U.S. Supreme Court (Derrick Bell, 1992).

This is a lengthy definition, but note how inclusive it is. Although it encompasses "traditional" minority groups such as African Americans and Native Americans, it also could be applied to other groups (with perhaps a little stretching). For instance, women arguably fit the first four criteria and can be analyzed with many of the same concepts and ideas that guide the analysis of other minority groups. Also, gay, lesbian, and transgendered Americans; Americans with disabilities; left-handed Americans; elderly Americans; and very short, very tall, or very obese Americans could fit the definition of minority group without much difficulty. Although we should not be whimsical or capricious about matters of definition, it is important to note that the analyses developed in this book can be applied more generally than you might realize at first and may lead to some fresh insights about a wide variety of groups and people.

The Pattern of Inequality

As mentioned earlier, the most important defining characteristic of minority group status is inequality. As will be documented in later chapters, minority group membership can affect access to jobs, education, wealth, health care, and housing. It is associated with a lower (often much lower) proportional share of valued goods and services and more limited (often much more limited) opportunities for upward mobility.

Stratification, or the unequal distribution of valued goods and services, is a basic feature of society. Every human society, except perhaps the simplest hunter-gatherer societies, is stratified to some degree; that is, the resources of the society are distributed so that some get more and others less of whatever is valued. Societies are divided into horizontal layers (or strata), often called **social classes,** which differ from one another by the amount of resources they command. Many criteria (such as education, age, gender, and talent) may affect a person's social class position and his or her access to goods and services. Minority group membership is one of these criteria, and it has had a powerful impact on the distribution of resources in the United States and many other societies.

This section begins with a brief consideration of theories about the nature and important dimensions of stratification. It then focuses on how minority group status relates to stratification. During the discussion, I identify several concepts and themes that will be used throughout this book.

Theoretical Perspectives

Sociology and the other social sciences have been concerned with stratification and human inequality since the formation of the discipline in the 19th century. An early and important contributor to our understanding of the nature and significance of social inequality was Karl Marx, the noted social philosopher and revolutionary. Half a century later, a sociologist named Max Weber, a central figure in the development of the discipline, critiqued and elaborated on Marx's view of social inequality. Here, we will also consider the views of Gerhard Lenski, a contemporary sociologist whose ideas about the influence of economic and technological development on social stratification have considerable relevance when comparing societies and understanding the evolution of intergroup relations. The section ends with another contemporary sociologist, Patricia Hill Collins, who argues that we need to view class, racial, gender, and other inequalities as a single, interlocking system.

Karl Marx

Although best known as the father of modern communism, Karl Marx was also the primary architect of a political, economic, and social philosophy that has played a major role in world affairs for over 150 years. *Marxism* is a complex theory of history and social change in which inequality is a central concept and concern.

Marx argued that the most important source of inequality in society was the system of economic production. More specifically, he focused on the **means of production,** or the materials, tools, resources, and organizations by which the society produces and distributes goods and services. In an agricultural society, the means of production include land, draft animals, and plows. In an industrial society, the means of production include factories, commercial enterprises, banks, and transportation systems such as railroads.

All societies include two main social classes that struggle over the means of production. One class owns or controls the means of production, and in the case of an industrial society, Marx called this elite or ruling class the **bourgeoisie.** The other class is the working class, or the **proletariat.** Marx believed that conflict between these classes was inevitable and that the ultimate result of this class struggle would be the victory of the working class, followed by the creation of a utopian society without exploitation, coercion, or inequality—in other words, a classless society.

Marxism has been extensively revised and updated over the past century and a half. Still, modern social science owes a great deal to Marx's views on inequality and his insights on class struggle and social conflict. As you shall see, Marxism remains an important body of work and a rich source of insight into group relations in industrial society.

Max Weber

One of Marx's major critics was Max Weber, a German sociologist who did most of his work around the turn of the 20th century. Weber thought that Marx's view of inequality was too narrow. Whereas Marx saw social class as a matter of economic position or relationship to the means of production, Weber noted that inequality was more complex than this and included dimensions other than just the economic. Individuals could be members of the elite in some ways but not in others. For example, an aristocratic family that has fallen on hard financial times might belong to the elite in terms of family lineage but not in terms of wealth. To use a more contemporary example, a major figure in the illegal drug trade could enjoy substantial wealth but be held in low esteem otherwise.

Weber expanded on Marx's view of inequality by identifying three separate stratification systems. First, economic inequality is based on ownership or control of property, wealth, and income. This is similar to Marx's concept of class, and in fact, Weber used the term class to identify this form of inequality.

A second system of stratification revolves around differences in **prestige** between groups, or the amount of honor, esteem, or respect given to people by others. Class position is one factor that affects the amount of prestige enjoyed by a person. Other factors might include family lineage, athletic ability, and physical appearance. In the United States and other societies, prestige is affected by the groups to which people belong, and members of minority groups typically receive less prestige than members of the dominant group.

Weber's third stratification system is **power,** or the ability to influence others, have an impact on the decision-making process of society, and pursue and protect one's self-interest and achieve one's goals. One source of power is a person's standing in politically active organizations, such as labor unions or pressure groups, which lobby state and federal legislatures. Some politically active groups have access to great wealth and can use their riches to promote their causes. Other groups may rely more on their size and their ability to mobilize large demonstrations to achieve their goals. Political groups and the people they represent vary in their abilities to affect the political process and control decision making; that is, they vary in the amount of power they can mobilize.

Typically, these three dimensions of stratification go together: Wealthy, prestigious groups will be more powerful (more likely to achieve their goals or protect their self-interest) than low-income groups or groups with little prestige. It is important to realize, however, that power is a separate dimension: Even very impoverished groups that enjoy little respect have sometimes found ways to express their concerns and pursue their goals.

Gerhard Lenski

Gerhard Lenski is a contemporary sociologist who follows Weber and distinguishes among class (or property), prestige, and power. Lenski (2005) expands on Weber's ideas, however, by analyzing stratification in the context of societal evolution, or the **level of development** of a society. He argues that the nature of inequality (the degree of inequality or the specific criteria affecting a group's position) is closely related to **subsistence technology,** the means by which the society satisfies basic needs such as hunger and thirst. A preindustrial agricultural society relies on human and animal labor to generate the energy necessary to sustain life. Inequality in this type of society centers on control of land and labor because they are the most important means of production at that level of development.

In a modern industrial society, however, land ownership is not as crucial as ownership of manufacturing and commercial enterprises. At the industrial level of development, control of capital is more important than control of land, and the nature of inequality will change accordingly.

The United States and other societies have recently entered still another stage of development, often referred to as *postindustrial society.* In this type of society, economic growth is powered by developments in new technology, computer-related fields, information processing, and scientific research. It seems fairly safe to speculate that economic success in the postindustrial era will be closely related to specialized knowledge, familiarity with new technologies, and education in general (Chirot, 1994, p. 88; see also Daniel Bell, 1973).

These changes in subsistence technology, from agriculture to industrialization to the "information society," alter the stratification system. As the sources of wealth, success, and power change, so do the relationships between minority and dominant groups. For example, the shift to an information-based, "hi-tech," postindustrial society means that the advantages conferred by higher levels of education will be magnified and that groups that have less access to schooling are likely to fall even lower in the stratification system.

Patricia Hill Collins

Sociologist Patricia Hill Collins calls for a new approach to the study of inequality and group relations. She argues that it is insufficient to examine the dimensions of inequality—class, race, and gender—separately, or one at a time. Rather, they need to be seen as interlocked and mutually reinforcing. Traditionally, inequality has been viewed by social scientists as a series of dichotomies: elite versus masses, powerful versus powerless, men versus women, blacks versus whites, and so forth. **Intersectionality** theorists urge us to analyze how these statuses are linked to each other and form a "matrix of domination." For example, white Americans should not be seen as simply the "dominant group," undifferentiated and homogenous. Some segments of this group, such as women or poor whites, may occupy a privileged status in terms of their race and a subordinate status in other areas, as defined by their gender or economic status. In the same way, minority groups are internally differentiated along lines of class and gender, and members of some segments are more privileged than others. Who is oppressed and who is the oppressor changes across social contexts, and people can occupy both statuses simultaneously.

All groups experience some relative degree of advantage and disadvantage, and Hill urges us to focus on how the separate systems of domination and subordination crosscut and overlap each other, how opportunity and individual experience is shaped by the matrix of domination. In this text, one of our main concerns will be to explore how minority group experience is mediated by class and gender, but be aware that this approach can be applied to many other dimensions of power and inequality including disability, sexual preference, and religion.

Minority Group Status and Stratification

The theoretical perspectives we have just reviewed raise three important points about the connections between minority group status and stratification. First, as already noted, minority group status affects access to wealth and income, prestige, and power. A society in which minority groups systematically receive less of these valued goods is stratified, at least partly, by race and ethnicity. In the United States, minority group status has been and continues to be one of the most important and powerful determinants of life chances, health and wealth, and success. These patterns of inequality are documented and explored in Part III of this book, but even casual observation of U.S. society will reveal that minority groups control proportionately fewer resources and that minority group status and stratification are intimately and complexly intertwined.

Second, although social classes and minority groups are correlated, they are separate social realities. The degree to which one is dependent on the other varies from group to group. Some groups, such as Irish or Italian Americans, enjoy considerable **social mobility** or easy access to opportunities today, even though they faced considerable discrimination in the past. Furthermore, as stressed by the intersectionality approach, degrees of domination and subordination are variable, and all groups are subdivided by crosscutting lines of differentiation. Because social classes and minority groups are different dimensions of social life, they can vary independently. Some members of a minority group can be successful economically, wield great political power, or enjoy high prestige, even though the vast majority of their group languishes in poverty and powerlessness. Each minority group is internally divided by systems of inequality based on class, status, or power, and in the same way, members of the same social class may be separated by ethnic or racial differences. The dimensions of inequality and group identity crisscross each other in complex and variable ways, as stressed by the intersectionality approach.

The third point concerning the connections between stratification and minority groups brings us back to group conflict. Dominant–minority group relationships are created by struggle over the control of valued goods and services. Minority group structures (such as slavery) emerge so that the dominant group can control commodities such as land or labor, maintain its position in the stratification system, or eliminate a perceived threat to its well-being. Struggles over property, wealth, prestige, and power lie at the heart of every dominant–minority relationship. Karl Marx believed that all aspects of society and culture were shaped to benefit the elite or ruling class and sustain the economic system that underlies its privileged position. The treatment of minority groups throughout American history provides a good deal of evidence to support Marx's point.

Visible Distinguishing Traits

In this section, we focus on the second defining characteristic of minority groups: the visible traits that denote membership. The boundaries between dominant and minority groups have been established along a wide variety of lines, including religion, language, and occupation. Here we consider race and gender, two of the more physical and permanent—and thus more socially visible—markers of group membership.

Race

In the past, race has been widely misunderstood. The false ideas and exaggerated importance attached to race have not been mere errors of logic, subject to debate and refutation. At various times and places, they have been associated with some of the greatest tragedies in human history: massive exploitation and mistreatment, slavery, and genocide. Many myths about race survive in the present, although perhaps in diluted or muted form, and it is important to cultivate an accurate understanding of the concept (although the scientific knowledge that has accumulated about race is no guarantee that the concept will not be used to instigate or justify further tragedies in the future).

Thanks to advances in the sciences of genetics, biology, and physical anthropology, we know more about what race is and, more importantly, what it is not. We cannot address all of the confusion in these few pages, but we can establish a basic framework and use the latest scientific research to dispel some of the myths.

Race and Human Evolution

The human species first appeared in East Africa about 100,000 year ago. Our ancient ancestors were hunters and gatherers who slowly drifted away from their ancestral regions in search of food and other resources. Over the next 90,000 years, our ancestors wandered across the entire globe, first to what is now the Middle East and then to Asia, Europe, Australia, and North and South America.

Human "racial" differences evolved during this period of dispersion, as our ancestors adapted, physically as well as culturally, to different environments and ecological conditions. For example, consider skin color, the most visible "racial" characteristic. Skin color is derived from a pigment called *melanin.* In areas with intense sunlight, at or near the equator, melanin screens out the ultraviolet rays of the sun that cause sunburn and, more significantly, protects against skin cancer. Thus, higher levels of melanin and darker skin colors are found in peoples who are adapted to equatorial ecologies.

In peoples who have adapted to areas with less intense sunlight, the amount of melanin is lower, and skin color is lighter. The lower concentration of melanin may also be an adaptation to a particular ecology. It maximizes the synthesis of vitamin D, which is important for the absorption of calcium and protection against disorders such as rickets. Thus, the skin color (amount of melanin) of any group balances the need for vitamin D and the need to protect against ultraviolet rays.

The map in Exhibit 1.3 shows the distribution of skin color prior to the mass population movements of the past several centuries. Note the rough correlation between skin color and proximity to the equator: Peoples with darker skin color were generally found within 20 degrees of the equator, while peoples with lighter skin were found primarily in the Northern Hemisphere, in locales distant from tropical sunlight. Note also that our oldest ancestors were adapted to the equatorial sun of Africa. This almost certainly means that they were dark skinned (had a high concentration of melanin), and that lighter skin colors are the more recent adaptation.

The period of dispersion and differentiation began to come to a close about 10,000 years ago when some of our hunting and gathering ancestors developed a new subsistence technology and settled down in permanent agricultural villages. Over the

Exhibit 1.3 The Distribution of Skin Color

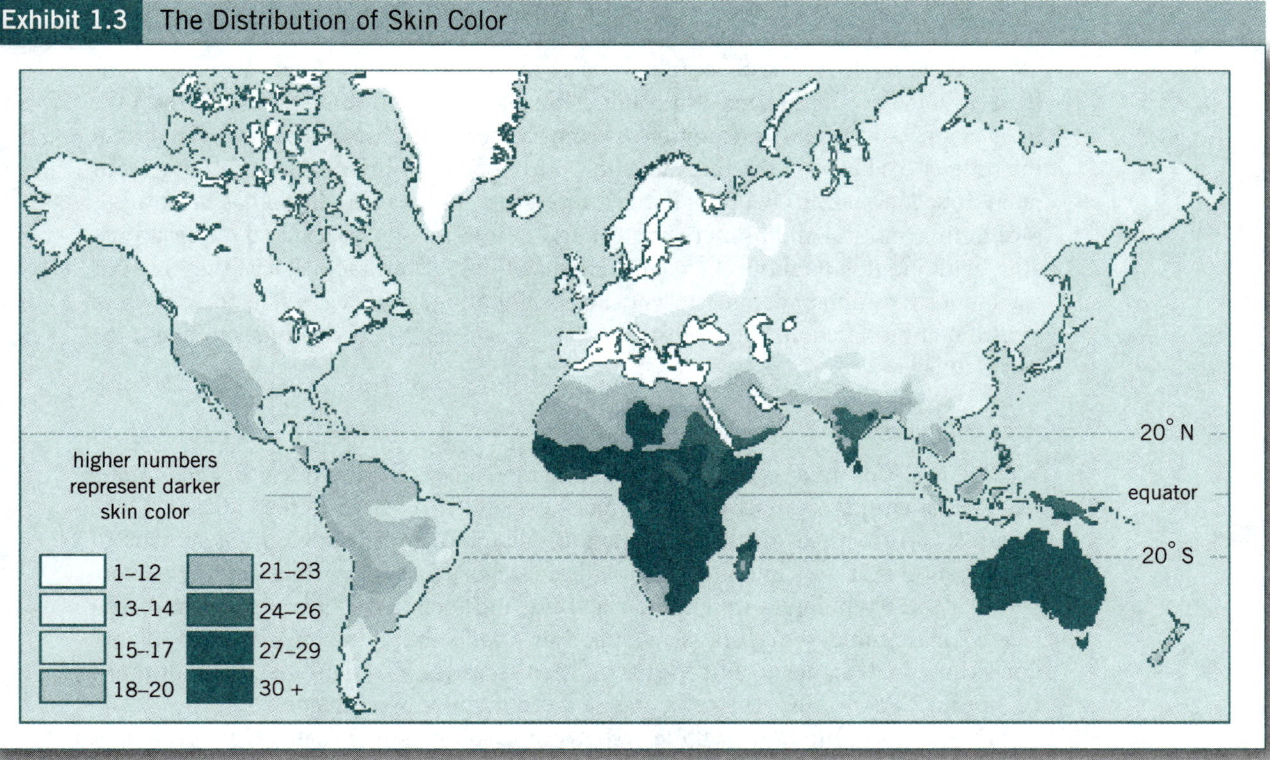

SOURCE: O'Neil, Dennis (n.d.).

NOTE: Data for native populations collected by R. Biasutti prior to 1940.

centuries, some of these settlements grew into larger societies and kingdoms and empires that conquered and absorbed neighboring societies, some of which differed culturally, linguistically, and racially from each other. The great agricultural empires of the past—Roman, Egyptian, Chinese, Aztec—united different peoples, reversed the process of dispersion and differentiation, and began a phase of consolidation and merging of human cultures and genetics. Over the next 10,000 years, human genes were intermixed and spread around the globe, eliminating any "pure" races (if such ever existed). The differentiation created during the 90,000 years of dispersion was swamped by the consolidation that continues in the present. In U.S. society, consolidation manifests itself in the increasing numbers of mixed-race people, but similar patterns are common across the globe and throughout more recent human history. The consolidation phase accelerated, beginning about 500 years ago, with the expansion of European power that resulted in the exploration and conquest of much of the rest of the world.

Race and Western Traditions

The U.S. concept of race has it origins in Western Europe. Race became a matter of concern in the Western European tradition beginning in the 1400s when Europeans, aided by breakthroughs in navigation and ship design, began to travel to Africa, Asia, and eventually North and South America. They came into continuous contact with the peoples of these continents and became more aware of and curious about the physical differences they saw. Europeans also conquered, colonized, and sometimes destroyed the peoples and cultures they encountered. From the beginning, the European awareness of the differences between the races was linked to notions of inferior and superior (conquered vs. conquering) peoples. For centuries, the European tradition has been to see race in this political and military context and to intermix biological and physical variation with judgments about the relative merits of the various races. Racist thinking was used to justify military conquest, genocide, exploitation, and slavery. The toxic form of racism that bloomed during the expansion of European power continues to haunt the world today.

Race and Biology

While Europeans used race primarily to denigrate, reject, and exclude nonwhites, there were also attempts to apply the principles of scientific research to the concept. These investigations focused on the construction of typologies or taxonomies, systems of classification that were intended to provide a category for every race and every person. Some of these typologies were quite elaborate and included scores of races and subraces. For example, the "Caucasian" race was often subdivided into Nordics (blond, fair-skinned Northern Europeans), Mediterraneans (dark-haired Southern Europeans), and Alpines (those falling between the first two categories).

One major limitation of these systems of classification is that the dividing lines between the so-called racial groups are arbitrary and blurred. There is no clear or definite point where, for example, "black" skin color stops and "white" skin color begins. The characteristics used to define race blend imperceptibly into each other, and one racial trait (e.g., skin color) can be blended with another (e.g., hair texture) in an infinite variety of ways. A given individual might have a skin color that is associated with one race, the hair texture of a second, the nasal shape of a third, and so forth. Even the most elaborate racial typologies could not handle the fact that many individuals fit into more than one category or none at all. Although people undeniably vary in their physical appearance, these differences do not sort themselves out in a way that permits us to divide people up like species of animals: The differences between the so-called human races are not at all like the differences between elephants and butterflies. The ambiguous and continuous nature of racial characteristics makes it impossible to establish categories that have clear, non-arbitrary boundaries.

Over the past several decades, dramatic advances in the science of genetics have provided additional information and new insights into race that continue to refute many racial myths and further undermine the usefulness of racial typologies. Perhaps the most important single finding of modern research is that genetic variation *within* the "traditional" racial groups is greater than the variation *between* those groups (American Sociological Association, 2003). In other words, any two randomly selected members of, say, the "black" race are likely to vary genetically from each other at least as much as they do from a randomly selected member of the "white" race. No single finding could be more destructive of traditional racial categories which are, after all, supposed to place people into homogenous groupings.

The Social Construction of Race

Despite its very limited scientific usefulness, race continues to animate intergroup relations in the United States and around the world. It continues to be socially important and a significant way of differentiating among people. Race, along with gender, is one of the first things people notice about one another. In the United States, we still tend to see race as a simple, unambiguous matter of skin color alone and to judge everyone as belonging to one and only one group, ignoring the realities of multiple ancestry and ambiguous classification.

How can this unimportant scientific concept retain its relevance? Because of the way it developed, Western concepts of race have a social as well as a biological or scientific dimension. To sociologists, race is a **social construction** and its meaning has been created and sustained not by science but by historical, social, and political processes (see Omi & Winant, 1986; Smedley, 1999). For example, in Chapter 3, we will analyze the role of race in the creation of American slavery and will see that the physical differences between blacks and whites became important as a *result of* the system of inequality. The elites of colonial society felt a need to justify their unequal treatment of Africans and seized on the obvious difference in skin color, elevating it to a matter of supreme importance, and used it to justify the enslavement of blacks. In other words, the importance of race was socially constructed as the result of a particular historical conflict, and it remains important not because of objective realities but because of the widespread, shared social perception that it is important.

Gender

We have already seen that gender is a primary dimension in the matrix of domination, an important distinction in the experiences of dominant and minority group members alike. Like race, gender has both a biological and a social component and can be a highly visible and convenient way of judging and sorting people. From birth, the biological differences between the sexes form the basis for different **gender roles,** or societal expectations about proper behavior, attitudes, and personality traits of males and females. In virtually all societies, including those at the advanced industrial stage, adult work roles tend to be separated by gender, and boys and girls are socialized differently in preparation for these roles. In simple hunter-gatherer societies, for example, boys typically train for the role of hunter, whereas girls learn the skills necessary for the successful gathering of vegetables, fruit, and other foodstuffs. In advanced industrial societies, girls tend to learn nurturing skills that will help them take primary responsibility for the well-being of family and community members, and boys learn aggressiveness, which is considered necessary for their expected roles as leaders, combatants, and providers in a highly competitive society.

Gender roles and relationships vary across time and from society to society, but gender and inequality have usually been closely related, and men typically claim more property, prestige, and power. Exhibit 1.4 provides some perspective on the variation in gender inequality across the globe. The map shows the distribution of a statistic called the *gender development index,* which measures the amount of inequality between men and women across a range of variables, including education, health, and income. As you can see, gender equality is generally highest in the more developed, industrialized nations of North America and Western Europe and lowest in the less developed, more agricultural nations of sub-Saharan Africa.

Exhibit 1.4 Map of Gender Development Index Scores

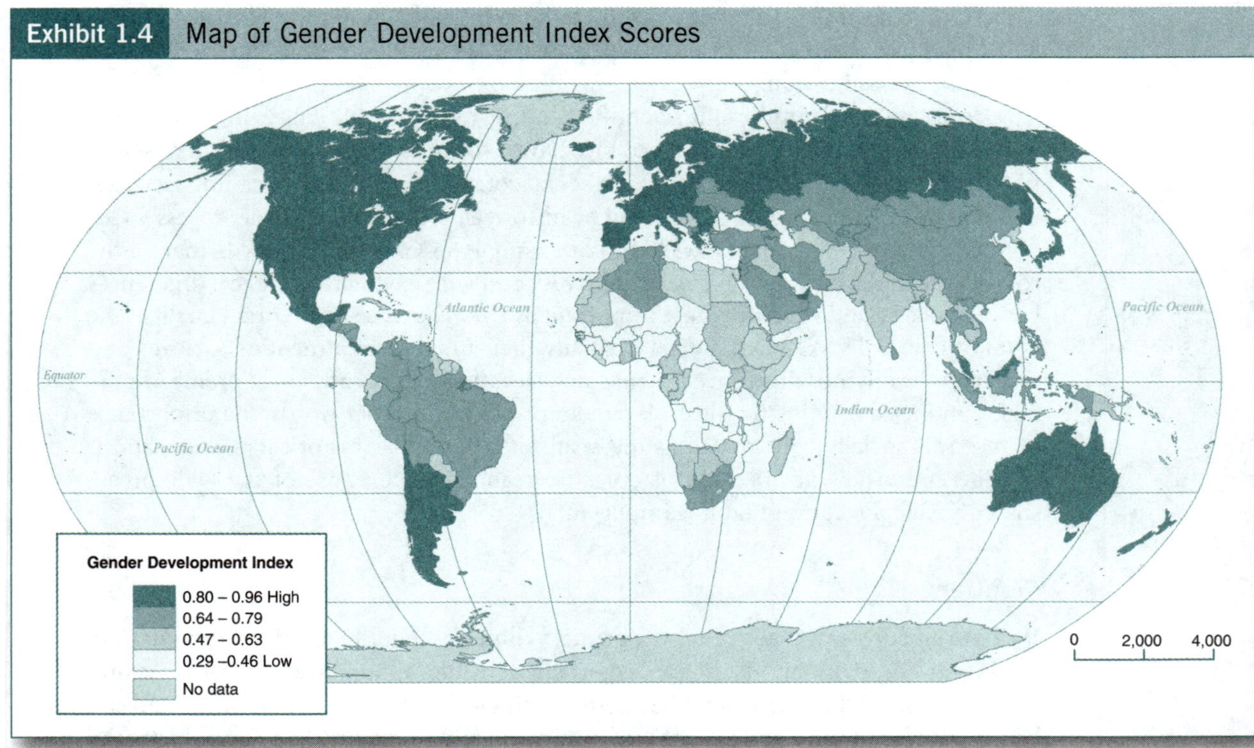

SOURCE: Nationmaster.com

Despite their high score on gender equality, the societies of Western Europe and the United States have strong traditions of **patriarchy,** or male dominance. In a patriarchal society, men have more control over the economy and more access to leadership roles in religion, politics, and other institutions. In these societies, women possess many characteristics of a minority group (namely, a pattern of disadvantage based on group membership marked by a physical trait). Thus, women could be, and in many ways should be, treated as a separate minority group.

History generally has been and is written from the standpoint of the "winners," that is, those in power. The voices of minority groups have generally been repressed, ignored, forgotten, or trivialized. Much of the history of slavery in America, for instance, has been told from the viewpoint of the slave owners. Slaves were illiterate by law and had few mechanisms for recording their thoughts or experiences. A more balanced and accurate picture of slavery began to emerge only in the past few decades, when scholars began to dig beneath the written records and memoirs of the slave owners and reconstruct the experiences of African Americans from non-written materials such as oral traditions and the physical artifacts left by the slaves.

Furthermore, our understanding of the experiences of minority groups is often based on the experiences of minority group males, and the experiences of minority group females are much less well-known and documented. If the voices of minority groups have been hushed, those of *female* minority group members have been virtually silenced. One of the important trends in contemporary scholarship is to adjust this skewed focus and systematically incorporate gender as a factor in the minority group experience (Espiritu, 1997; Zinn & Dill, 1994).

The Social Construction of Gender

In the social sciences, race is conceptualized as a social construction formulated in certain historical circumstances (such as the era of European colonialism) when it was needed to help justify the unequal treatment of nonwhite groups. What about gender? Is it also merely a social creation designed to rationalize the higher status of men and their easier access to power, prestige, and property? People commonly believe that boys and men are more aggressive and independent and that girls and women are more emotional and expressive. (Or, in the words of a recent best-seller, "men are from Mars and women are from Venus.") What is the basis of these distinctions? What connection, if any, do they have with biology and genetics?

First of all, the traits commonly seen as "typical" of men or women—aggressiveness or emotional expressiveness, for example—are not discrete, separate categories. Every person has them to some degree and, to the extent that gender differences exist at all, they are manifested not in absolutes but in averages, tendencies, and probabilities. Aggressiveness is often thought of as a male characteristic, but many women are more aggressive than many men. Likewise, emotionality tends to be associated with women, but many males are more expressive and emotional than many females. As was the case with racial differences, research has shown that there is more variation *within* categories than between, a finding that seriously undermines the view that the gender differences are genetic or biological (Basow, cited in Rosenblum & Travis, 2002).

Secondly, the social construction of gender roles is illustrated by the fact that what is thought to be "appropriate" gender behavior varies from one historical period to another and from society to society. The behavior expected of a female in Victorian England would be thoroughly out of place in 21st-century America, and the typical behavior of a contemporary male would be regarded as outrageously scandalous in Puritan America. This variability makes it difficult to argue that the differences between the genders are "hard-wired" in the genetic code: If they were, the variations would be nonexistent.

To be sure, biology and genetics shape the production of personality in some ways (e.g., see Udry, 2000), but the key to understanding gender is social and experiential (Booth, Granger, Mazur, & Kivlighan, 2006, pp. 167–191). Gender, like race, is a social construction, especially when the supposed differences between men and women are treated as categorical and fixed and then used to deny opportunity and equality to women.

Key Concepts in Dominant–Minority Relations

Whenever sensitive issues such as dominant–minority group relations are raised, the discussion turns to (or on) matters of prejudice and discrimination. As we will be very concerned with these subjects in this book, we need to clarify what we mean by these terms. This section introduces and defines four concepts to help you understand dominant–minority relations in the United States.

This book addresses how individuals from different groups interact, as well as relations among groups. Thus, we need to distinguish between what is true for individuals (a more psychological level of analysis) and what is true for groups or society as a whole (a more sociological level of analysis). Beyond that, we must attempt to trace the connections between the two levels of analysis.

We also need to make a further distinction on both the individual and the group levels. At the individual level, what people think and feel about other groups and how they actually behave toward members of that group may differ. A person might express negative feelings about another group in private but deal fairly with members of the group in face-to-face interactions. Groups and entire societies may display this same kind of inconsistency. A society may express support for equality in its official documents or formal codes of law and simultaneously treat minority groups in unfair and destructive ways. An example of this kind of inconsistency is the contrast between the commitment to equality stated in the Declaration of Independence ("All men are created equal") and the actual treatment of black slaves, Anglo-American women, and Native Americans at the time the document was written.

At the individual level, social scientists refer to the "thinking/feeling" part of this dichotomy as *prejudice* and the "doing" part as *discrimination.* At the group level, the term *ideological racism* describes the "thinking/feeling" dimension and *institutional discrimination* describes the "doing" dimension. Exhibit 1.5 depicts the differences among these four concepts.

Exhibit 1.5 Four Key Concepts in Dominant–Minority Relations

Dimension	Individual	Group or Societal
Thinking/feeling	Prejudice	Ideological racism
Doing	Discrimination	Institutional discrimination

Prejudice

Prejudice is the tendency of an individual to think about other groups in negative ways, to attach negative emotions to those groups, and to prejudge individuals on the basis of their group memberships. Individual prejudice has two aspects: the *cognitive* or thinking aspect, and the *affective* or feeling part. A prejudiced person thinks about other groups in terms of **stereotypes (cognitive prejudice),** generalizations that are thought to apply to group members. Examples of familiar stereotypes include notions such as "women are emotional," "Jews are stingy," "Blacks are lazy," "the Irish are drunks," and "Germans are authoritarian." A prejudiced person also experiences negative emotional responses to other groups **(affective prejudice),** including contempt, disgust, arrogance, and hatred. People vary in their levels of prejudice, and levels of prejudice vary in the same person from one time to another and from one group to another. We can say that a person is prejudiced to the extent that he or she uses stereotypes in his or her thinking about other groups and has negative emotional reactions to other groups.

Generally, the two dimensions of prejudice are highly correlated with each other. However, they are also distinct and separate aspects of prejudice and can vary independently. One person may think entirely in stereotypes but feel no particular negative emotional response to any group. Another person may feel a very strong aversion toward a group but be unable to articulate a clear or detailed stereotype of that group.

Causes of Prejudice

American social scientists of all disciplines have made prejudice a primary concern and have produced literally thousands of articles and books on the topic. They have approached the subject from a variety of theoretical perspectives and have asked a wide array of different questions. One firm conclusion that has emerged is that prejudice is not a single, unitary phenomenon. It has a variety of possible causes (some more psychological and individual, others more sociological and cultural) and can present itself in a variety of forms (some blatant and vicious, others subtle and indirect). No single theory has emerged that can explain prejudice in all its complexity. In keeping with the macrosociological approach of this text, we will focus primarily on the theories that stress the causes of prejudice that are related to culture, social structure, and group relationships.

Competition between groups and the origins of prejudice. Every form of prejudice—even the most ancient—started at some specific point in history. If we go back far enough in time, we can find a moment that predates anti-black prejudice, anti-Semitism, negative stereotypes about Native Americans or Hispanic Americans, or antipathy against Asian Americans. What sorts of conditions create prejudice?

The common factor that seems to play a crucial role in the origin of all prejudices is competition between groups: Prejudice originates in the heat of that competition and is used to justify and rationalize the privileged status of the winning group. If we go back far enough, we can always find some episode in which one group successfully dominates, takes resources from, or eliminates a threat from some other group. The successful group becomes the dominant group, and the other group becomes the minority group. Why is group competition associated with the emergence of prejudice? Typically, prejudice is more a *result* of the competition than a cause. Its role is to help mobilize emotional energy for the contest; justify rejection and attack; and rationalize the structures of domination, like slavery or segregation, which result from the competition. Groups react to the competition and to the threat presented by other groups with antipathy and stereotypes about the "enemy" group. Prejudice emerges from the heat of the contest but then can solidify and persist for years (even centuries) after the end of the conflict.

The relationship between prejudice and competition has been demonstrated in a variety of settings and situations ranging from labor strikes to international war to social psychology labs. In the chapters to come, we will examine the role of prejudice during the creation of slavery in North America, as a reaction to periods of high immigration, and as an accompaniment to myriad forms of group competition. Here, to illustrate our central point about group competition and prejudice, we will examine a classic experiment from the sociological literature. The experiment was conducted in the 1950s at a summer camp for 11- and 12-year-old boys known as Robber's Cave.

The camp director, social psychologist Muzafer Sherif divided the campers into two groups, the Rattlers and the Eagles (Sherif, Harvey, White, Hood, & Sherif, 1961). The groups lived in different cabins and were continually pitted against each other in a wide range of activities. Games, sports, and even housekeeping chores were set up on a competitive basis. The boys in each group developed and expressed negative feelings (prejudice) against the other group. Competition and prejudicial feelings grew quite intense and were manifested in episodes of name-calling and raids on the "enemy" group.

Sherif attempted to reduce the harsh feelings he had created by bringing the campers together in various pleasant situations featuring food, movies, and other treats. But the rival groups only used these opportunities to express their enmity. Sherif then came up with some activities that required the members of the rival groups to work cooperatively with each other. For example, the researchers deliberately sabotaged some plumbing to create an emergency that required the efforts of everyone to resolve. As a result of these cooperative activities, intergroup "prejudice" was observed to decline and, eventually, friendships were formed across groups (Sherif et al., 1961).

In the Robber's Cave experiment, as in many actual group relationships, prejudice (negative feelings and stereotypes about other campers) arose to help mobilize feelings and to justify rejection and attacks, both verbal and physical, against the out-group. When group competition was reduced, the levels of prejudice abated and eventually disappeared, again demonstrating that prejudice is caused by competition, not the other way around.

Although the Robber's Cave experiment illustrates our central point, we must be cautious in generalizing from these results. The experiment was conducted in an artificial environment with young boys (all white) who had no previous acquaintance with each other and no history of grievances or animosity. Thus, these results may be only partially generalizable to group conflicts in the "real world." Nonetheless, Robber's Cave illustrates a fundamental connection between group competition and prejudice that we will observe repeatedly in the chapters to come. Competition and the desire to protect resources and status and to defend against threats—perceived as well as real—from other groups are the primary motivations for the construction of traditions of prejudice and structures of inequality that benefit the dominant group.

Culture, socialization, and the persistence of prejudice. Prejudice originates in group competition of some sort but often outlives the conditions of its creation. It can persist, full-blown and intense, long after the episode that sparked its creation has faded from memory. How does prejudice persist through time? How is it passed on to succeeding generations?

In his classic analysis of American race relations, *An American Dilemma,* Swedish economist Gunnar Myrdal (1944/1962) proposed the idea that prejudice is perpetuated through time by a self-fulfilling prophecy or a **vicious cycle,** as illustrated in Exhibit 1.6. The dominant group uses its power to force the minority group into an inferior status, such as slavery, as shown in the diagram in area (1). Partly to motivate the construction of a system of racial stratification and partly to justify its existence, individual prejudice and racist belief systems are invented and accepted by the dominant group, as shown in area (2). Individual prejudices are reinforced by the everyday observation of the inferior status of the minority group. The fact that the minority group is in fact impoverished, enslaved, or otherwise exploited confirms and strengthens the attribution of inferiority. The belief in inferiority motivates further discrimination and unequal treatment, as shown in area (3) of the diagram, which reinforces the inferior status, which validates the prejudice and racism, which justifies further discrimination, and so on. Over just a few generations, a stable, internally reinforced system of racial inferiority and an elaborate, widespread set of prejudiced beliefs and feelings can become an integral, unremarkable, and (at least for the dominant group) accepted part of everyday life.

Exhibit 1.6 Myrdal's Vicious Cycle

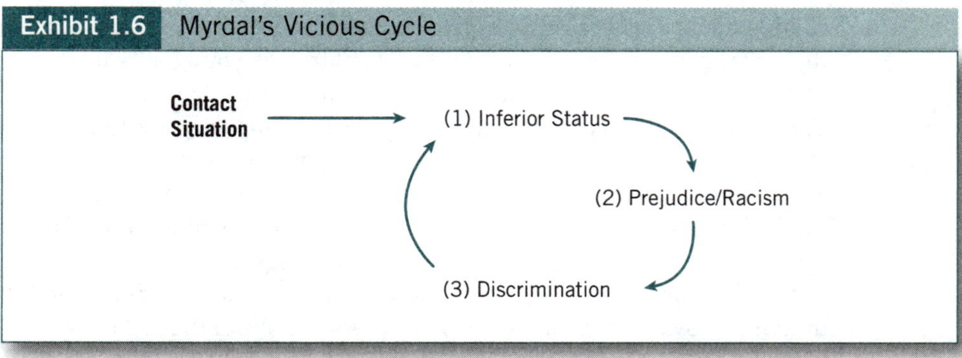

Culture is conservative, and, once created, prejudice will be sustained over time just like any set of attitudes, values, and beliefs. Future generations will learn prejudice in the same way and for the same reasons that they learn any other aspect of their culture. Thus, prejudice and racism come to us through our cultural heritage as a package of stereotypes, emotions, and ideas. We learn which groups are "good" and which are "bad" in the same way we learn table manners and religious beliefs (Pettigrew, 1958, 1971, p. 137; Simpson & Yinger, 1985, pp. 107, 108). When prejudice is part of the cultural heritage, individuals learn to think and feel negatively toward other groups as a routine part of socialization. Much of the prejudice expressed by Americans—and the people of many other societies—is the normal result of a typical socialization in families, communities, and societies that are, to some degree, racist. Given the long history of intense racial and ethnic exploitation in America, it is not surprising that Americans continue to manifest antipathy toward and stereotypical ideas about other groups.

The idea that prejudice is learned during socialization is reinforced by studies of the development of prejudice in children. Research generally shows that people are born without bias and have to be taught whom to like and dislike. Children become aware of group differences (e.g., black vs. white) at a very early age. By age 3 or younger, they recognize the significance and the permanence of racial groups and can accurately classify people on the basis of skin color and other cues (Brown, 1995, pp. 121–136; Katz, 1976, p. 126). Once the racial or group categories are mentally established, the child begins the process of learning the "proper" attitudes and stereotypes to associate with the various groups, and both affective and cognitive prejudice begins to grow at an early age.

It is important to note that children can acquire prejudice even when parents and other caregivers do not teach it overtly or directly. Adults control the socialization process and valuable resources (food, shelter, praise), and children are motivated to seek their approval and conform to their expectations (at least in the early years). There are strong pressures on the child to learn and internalize the perceptions of the older generation, and even a casual comment or an overheard remark can establish or reinforce negative beliefs or feelings about members of other groups (Ashmore & DelBoca, 1976). Children need not be directly instructed about presumed minority group characteristics; it is often said that racial attitudes are "caught and not taught."

A somewhat different line of research on the development of prejudice argues that children are actively engaged in their learning and that their levels of prejudice reflect their changing intellectual capabilities. Children as young as 5 to 6 months old can make some simple distinctions (e.g., by gender or race) between categories of people. The fact that this capability emerges so early in life suggests that it is not simply a response to adult teaching. "Adults use categories to simplify and make sense of their environment; apparently children do the same" (Brown, 1995, p. 126). Gross, simplistic distinctions between people may help very young children organize and understand the world around them. The need for such primitive categorizations may decline as the child becomes more experienced in life and more sophisticated in his or her thinking. Doyle and Aboud (1995), for example, found that prejudice was highest for younger children and actually decreased between kindergarten and the third grade.

The decline was related to increased awareness of racial similarities (as well as differences) and diverse perspectives on race (see also Black-Gutman & Hickson, 1996; Brown, 1995; Powlishta, Serbin, Doyle, & White, 1994). Thus, changing levels of prejudice in children may reflect an interaction between children's changing mental capacities and their environment rather than a simple or straightforward learning of racist cultural beliefs or values.

Further evidence for the cultural nature of prejudice is provided by research on the concept of social distance, which is related to prejudice but is not quite the same thing. *Social distance* is defined as the degree of intimacy that a person is willing to accept in his or her relations with members of other groups. The most intimate relationship would be close kinship, and the most distant relationship is exclusion from the country. The inventor of the **social distance scale** was Emory Bogardus (1933), who specified a total of seven degrees of social distance:

1. To close kinship by marriage
2. To my club as personal chums
3. To my street as neighbors
4. To employment in my occupation
5. To citizenship in my country
6. As visitors only to my country
7. Would exclude from my country

Research using social distance scales demonstrates that Americans rank other groups in similar ways across time and space. The consistency indicates a common frame of reference or set of perceptions, a continuity of vision possible only if perceptions have been standardized by socialization in a common culture.

Exhibit 1.7 Rank on Social Distance for Selected Groups, 1926–2001

Group	1926	1946	1956	1966	1977	1993	2001
English	1	3	3	2	2	2	4
American Whites	2	1	1	1	1	—	1
Canadians	3	2	2	3	3	—	3
Irish	5	4	5	5	7	1	5
Germans	7	10	8	10	11	10	8
Norwegians	10	7	10	7	12	8	—

(Continued)

Exhibit 1.7 (Continued)

Group	1926	1946	1956	1966	1977	1993	2001
Russians	13	13	24	24	29	13	20
Italians	14	16	12	8	5	3	2
Poles	15	14	13	16	18	12	14
American Indians	18	20	18	18	10	16	12
Jews	19	19	16	15	15	15	11
Mexicans	21	24	28	28	26	18	25
Japanese	22	30	26	25	25	19	22
Filipinos	23	23	21	21	24	—	16
African Americans	24	29	27	29	17	17	9
Turks	25	25	23	26	28	22	—
Chinese	26	21	25	22	23	20	17
Koreans	27	27	30	27	30	21	24
Asian Indians	28	28	29	30	27	—	26
Vietnamese	—	—	—	—	—	—	28
Muslims	—	—	—	—	—	—	29
Arabs	—	—	—	—	—	—	30
Mean (all scores)	2.14	2.12	2.08	1.92	1.93	1.43	1.44
Range	2.85	2.57	1.75	1.56	1.38	1.07	0.87
Total number of groups included	28	30	30	30	30	24	30
Correlation with 1926 rankings	—	.95	.93	.90	.84	.92	.76

SOURCES: 1926 through 1977, Smith & Dempsey (1983, p. 588); 1993, Kleg & Yamamoto (1998); 2001, Parrillo (2003).

NOTES: Scores are the group's rank for the year in question. For example, the Irish were ranked fifth of 28 groups in 1926, rose to fourth of 30 in 1946, and so forth. To conserve space, some groups and ranks have been eliminated.

Exhibit 1.7 presents some results of seven administrations of the scale to samples of Americans from 1926 to 2001. The groups are listed by the rank order of their scores for 1926. In that year, the sample expressed the least social distance from the English and the most distance from Asian Indians. While the average social distance score for the English was 1.02, indicating virtually no sense of distance, the average score for

Asian Indians was 3.91, indicating a distance between "to employment in my occupation" and "to my street as neighbors."

Note, first of all, the stability in the rankings. The actual *scores* (not shown) generally decrease from decade to decade, indicating less social distance and presumably a decline in prejudice over the years. The *rankings* of the various groups, however, tend to be the same year after year. This stability is clearly displayed in the bottom row of the table, which shows correlations between the group rankings for each year and the 1926 ranking. If any of the lists of scores had been identical, the statistic in this row would have shown its maximum value of 1.00. Although they weaken over time, the actual correlations approach that maximum value and indicate that the rank order of the groups from year to year has been substantially the same. Considering the changes that society has experienced between 1926 and 2001 (the Great Depression; World War II, the Korean War, and other wars; the Cold War with the USSR, the civil rights movement, the resumption of large-scale immigration, etc.), this overall continuity in group rankings is remarkable.

Second, note the nature of the ranking: Groups with origins in Northern and Western Europe are ranked highest, followed by groups from Southern and Eastern Europe, with racial minorities near the bottom. These preferences reflect the relative status of these groups in the U.S. hierarchy of racial and ethnic groups. The rankings also reflect the relative amount of exploitation and prejudice directed at each group over the course of U.S. history.

Although these patterns of social distance scores support the general point that prejudice is cultural, this body of research has some important limitations. The respondents were generally college students from a variety of campuses, not representative samples of the population, and the differences in scores from group to group are sometimes very small. Still, the stability of the patterns cannot be ignored: The top two or three groups are always Northern European, Poles and Jews are always ranked in the middle third of the groups, and Koreans and Japanese always fall in the bottom third. African Americans and American Indians were also ranked toward the bottom until the most recent rankings.

Finally, note how the relative positions of some groups change with international and domestic relations. For example, both Japanese and Germans fell in the rankings at the end of World War II (1946). Comparing 1966 with 1946, Russians fell and Japanese rose, reflecting changing patterns of alliance and enmity in the global system of societies. The dramatic rise of Native American and African Americans since the 1966 ranking may reflect declining levels of overt prejudice in American society. In 2001, the scale was administered in the weeks following the terrorist attacks on 9/11, and the low ranking of Arabs reflects the societal reaction toward those traumatic events.

How do we explain the fact that group rankings generally remain stable from the 1920s to 2001? The stability strongly suggests that Americans view the various groups through the same culturally shaped lens. A sense of social distance, a perception of some groups as "higher" or "better" than others, is part of the cultural package of intergroup prejudices we acquire from socialization into American society. The social distance patterns illustrate the power of culture to shape individual perceptions and preferences and attest to the deep streak of prejudice and racism built into American culture.

Modern racism. A large and growing body of research demonstrates that prejudice evolves as group relations and cultural beliefs and information change. The harsh, blatant forms of prejudice that typified U.S. society in its first several centuries have become muted in recent decades, leading some people to conclude that individual prejudice is no longer a significant problem in American life. However, sociological research clearly demonstrates that prejudice has not disappeared. Rather, it has assumed a more subtle and indirect form, consistent with the growing sensitivity of Americans, the success of the civil rights campaign of the 1950s and 1960s and the resultant societal rejection of blatant prejudice, and the growing resources of minority groups and their enhanced ability to protect themselves from attacks.

The new forms of prejudice have been described with a variety of terms including **modern racism, color-blind racism,** and **symbolic racism.** People who are prejudiced in these ways typically reject "old-fashioned" blatant prejudice and the traditional view that racial inferiority is innate or biological. They often proclaim their allegiance to the ideals of equality of opportunity and treatment for all. Analysis of their thinking, however, reveals prejudice lurking just beneath the surface of these egalitarian sentiments and powerfully influencing their views of racial issues.

To illustrate, Eduardo Bonilla-Silva (2001, 2006) has been investigating what he calls "racism without racists," or perceptual frameworks that allow people to express and act on prejudiced ideas without appearing to be prejudiced. He refers to one such framework as "naturalization," or the idea that some forms of racial inequality—such as residential or school segregation—are "natural" and reflect the presumed fact that people prefer to be with "their own kind." Using this framework, people can accept even the most blatant and extreme manifestations of racial segregation with no qualms or questions because it's seen as natural and even inevitable for people to choose to be with people like themselves. Furthermore, the naturalization framework allows dominant group members to participate in these patterns—to live in segregated neighborhoods and send their children to segregated schools—without guilt or hesitation because, after all, everyone prefers their own group (Bonilla-Silva, 2006, p. 28).

What makes this belief system racist? First, it encourages people to take for granted the realities around them—the legacies of centuries of segregation, racism, and exclusion—much like the way, in earlier times, Americans were encouraged to accept ideas about innate racial inferiority as an explanation for black slavery or segregation. More importantly, this framework obscures the myriad, not-so-subtle social forces that created segregated schools, neighborhoods, and other manifestations of racial inequality in the first place and maintain them in the present. That is, residential and school segregation are not the results of some abstract and benign tendency of people to seek out others like themselves. Rather, these patterns were *created* by the deliberate, conscious actions of real estate boards; school boards; city councils; zoning boards; and other local, state, and national institutions (see Satter, 2009, for an example of how black "ghettoes" in Chicago were created). The naturalization framework permits people to ignore the social, political, and economic realities that actually create and sustain racial inequality and, by this selective perception, to support a kind of racism without appearing to be a racist. We will return to the subject of modern racism frequently and especially in Chapter 5.

The sociology of individual prejudice. The sociological approach to prejudice used in this text stresses several points. Individual prejudice has its origins in competition between groups, but it is more a result of that competition than a cause. It is created at a certain time in history to help mobilize feelings and emotional energy for competition and to rationalize the consignment of a group to minority status. It then becomes a part of the cultural heritage and is passed on to later generations as part of their "taken for granted" world, where it helps to shape their perceptions and reinforce the very group inferiority that was its original cause. Although it has evolved into a more subtle form, prejudice remains an important force in U.S. society and will continue as long as there are patterns of inequality and systems of group privilege and disadvantage that require justification.

Discrimination

Discrimination is defined as the unequal treatment of a person or persons based on group membership. An example of discrimination is an employer deciding not to hire an individual because he or she is African American (or Puerto Rican, Jewish, Chinese, etc.). If the unequal treatment is based on the group membership of the individual, the act is discriminatory.

One obvious and common cause of discrimination is prejudice. However, just as the cognitive and affective aspects of prejudice can be independent, discrimination and prejudice do not necessarily occur together. For example, the social situation surrounding the individual may encourage or discourage discrimination, regardless of the level of prejudice. Social situations in which prejudice is strongly approved of and supported might evoke discrimination in otherwise unprejudiced individuals. In the southern United States during the height of segregation, or in South Africa during the period of state-sanctioned racial inequality, it was usual and customary for whites to treat blacks in discriminatory ways. Regardless of their actual level of prejudice, white people in these situations faced strong social pressure to conform to the commonly accepted patterns of racial superiority and participate in acts of discrimination.

On the other hand, situations in which there are strong norms of equal and fair treatment may stifle the tendency of even the most bigoted individual to discriminate. For example, if a community vigorously enforces antidiscrimination laws, even the most prejudiced merchant might refrain from treating minority-group customers unequally. Highly prejudiced individuals may not discriminate so that they can "do business" (or, at least, avoid penalties or sanctions) in an environment in which discrimination is not tolerated or is too costly. Also, people normally subscribe to many different value systems, some of which may be mutually contradictory. Even people who are devout racists may also believe in and be guided by democratic, egalitarian values.

One of the earliest demonstrations of the difference between what people think and feel (prejudice) and what they actually do (discrimination) was provided by sociologist Robert LaPiere (1934). In the 1930s, he escorted a Chinese couple on a tour of the United States. At that time, Chinese and other Asian peoples were the victims of widespread discrimination and exclusion, and anti-Chinese prejudice was quite high, as demonstrated by the scores in Exhibit 1.7. However, LaPiere and his companions dined in restaurants and stayed in hotels without incident for the entire trip and experienced discrimination only once. Six months later, LaPiere wrote to every establishment the group had patronized and inquired about reservations. He indicated that some of the party were Chinese and asked if that would be a problem. Of those establishments that replied (about half), 92% said that they would not serve Chinese and would be unable to accommodate the party.

Why the difference? On LaPiere's original visit, anti-Asian prejudice may well have been present but was not expressed to avoid making a scene. In a different situation—the more distant interaction of letters and correspondence—the restaurant and hotel staff may have allowed their prejudice to be expressed in open discrimination because the potential for embarrassment was much less.

To summarize, discrimination and individual prejudice tend to be found together, but they are not the same thing. Discrimination can be motivated by negative feelings and stereotypes, but it also can be a response to social pressures exerted by others.

Ideological Racism

Ideological racism is a belief system that asserts the inferiority of a group or groups. It is embedded in culture and exists apart from the people who inhabit a society at any particular time (Andersen, 1993, p. 75; see O'Sullivan & Wilson, 1988, p. 227). We saw earlier that individual prejudice is created in a particular historical era and can then be incorporated into a society's culture. Members of succeeding generations acquire prejudiced views as a result of being exposed to ideological racism and being socialized to a culture that teaches stereotypes and negative emotions about other groups. Thus, prejudice has a cultural as well as an individual dimension and is passed from generation to generation just as other components of culture, including religious and spiritual beliefs, codes of etiquette, and norms of proper behavior. An example of ideological racism was the elaborate system of beliefs and ideas that were used to justify slavery in the American South (see Chapter 3). The exploitation of slaves was "explained" in terms of the innate racial inferiority of blacks, and this cluster of beliefs was absorbed by each new generation of southern whites (and whites from other regions as well) during the socialization process. For centuries, Americans were encouraged to accept the institutionalized racial inequality that surrounded them as an inevitable part of the natural order of the universe.

The founders of the United States established an American Creed that enshrined the values of freedom, liberty, and individualism—ideals that have inspired people around the world in scores of struggles for democracy and justice. At the same time, American culture was created in the midst of conflict among whites from Europe, blacks from Africa, and Native Americans. The prejudiced beliefs, values, and emotions that were created during the early days of this society and that became institutionalized as ideological racism are just as central to the culture as the more positive and inspiring elements of the American Creed. Some of America's oldest and strongest traditions include Eurocentric views and a belief in a racial and group hierarchy that places whites at the top. The sense of group hierarchy is documented and demonstrated by the social distance scales mentioned earlier in this chapter (see Exhibit 1.7).

Along with racist belief systems, American culture also incorporated ideologies that asserted the innate inferiority of women. Consistent with European traditions of patriarchy and male domination, *misogynistic* (woman-hating) views were embedded in our cultural traditions from the start. When Thomas Jefferson wrote, "All men are created equal" in the Declaration of Independence, he was not using the word *men* as a generic term for "all people" but was referring specifically to white men. Nonwhites were not regarded as equals (Jefferson and many other "founding fathers" owned slaves), and women didn't earn the right to vote until 1920, after a lengthy and protracted struggle for equal political rights.

Ideological racism, like individual prejudice, has grown and evolved over the years but it persists today, along with, to be sure, notions of liberty, equality, and democracy. It continues to shape perceptions, support notions of white superiority, and reinforce the structures that sustain the dominance of whites. We will return to this perceptual framework frequently in the chapters to come and especially in Chapter 5.

Ideological racism and individual prejudice. Distinguishing between individual prejudice and societal racist ideologies naturally leads to a consideration of the relationship between these two phenomena. We will explore this relationship in later chapters, but for now here is what is probably an obvious point: People socialized into societies with strong racist ideologies are very likely to absorb racist ideas and be highly prejudiced. It should not be surprising that a high level of personal prejudice existed among whites in the antebellum American South or in other highly racist societies, such as South Africa. At the same time, it is important to remember that ideological racism and individual prejudice are different things with different causes and different locations in the society. Racism is not a prerequisite for prejudice; prejudice may exist even in the absence of an ideology of racism.

Ideological racism, white racial identity, and white privilege. Besides individual prejudice, another result of being socialized into a culture with a strong racist ideology is racial identity: the part of the self-image linked to racial group membership. For dominant group members, **white racial identity** includes the set of perceptions that places whites at the top of a system of racial hierarchy and ranks all other groups in descending layers of acceptability (see Exhibit 1.7 for one version of this racial hierarchy).

For members of minority groups, racial identity is often manifested as a sense of limitations imposed by the larger society and an awareness of the negative expectations of others, especially in highly race-conscious societies like South Africa under apartheid or the United States during the era of slavery. In contrast, white racial identity is largely unspoken and unconscious. It is not experienced as a constraint or a limitation, as minority racial identities are, so it does not generally provoke or reinforce awareness.

One of the ironies of white racial identity is that white Americans tend to see themselves in non-racial terms, as the norm against which all other groups are compared. This perception of whiteness as "normal" distances all other groups and reinforces the power relationships that have been embedded in U.S. society since colonial days. Whites regard themselves as "just people" and see only "others" as having race. For example, in casual discussions and everyday conversations, whites often mention the race of non-whites, even when racial identities are not relevant to the story. For example, a white American might say, "This black guy asked me for directions to city hall," identifying race even though it plays no particular role in the anecdote. When people are *not* identified by their race ("This guy asked me for directions to city hall"), the assumption is that they are white: normal people who need no further description. This view places whites in a highly privileged status. "Other people are raced, *we* are just people. . . . There is no more powerful position than that of being 'just' human. The claim to power is the claim to speak for the commonality of humanity. Raced people can't do that—they only speak for their own race" (Dyer, 2002).

Just as whites tend to be unaware of their racial identity, they also tend to be unaware of the privileges that attend "whiteness." Sociologist Peggy McIntosh (1988), in a now-classic article, outlined some of the privileges of white racial identity. She notes that whites (like men) are reluctant to acknowledge their privileged status vis-à-vis non-whites (or women). This denial is a way of protecting the privilege—if it doesn't exist, it doesn't have to be explained, examined, or defended—and her checklist attempts to expose the realities of white privilege and make them explicit. The list is too long to be reproduced here,[5] but here are some representative examples of the ways in which whites are privileged:

1. I can, if I wish, arrange to be in the company of people of my race most of the time.
2. I can go shopping most of the time, pretty well assured that I will not be followed or harassed.
3. When I am told about our national heritage or about "civilization," I am shown that people of my color made it what it is.
4. I can arrange to protect my children most of the time from people who might not like them.
5. I can do well in challenging situations without being called a credit to my race.
6. I can choose public accommodation without fearing that people of my race cannot get in or will be mistreated in the place I have chosen.
7. I can choose blemish cover or bandages in "flesh" color and have them more or less match my skin.

In summary, ideological racism is a component of culture that helps reproduce individual prejudice across time. It also helps to create white racial identity and preserve the system of white privilege.

Institutional Discrimination

The final of our four key concepts is the societal equivalent of individual discrimination. **Institutional discrimination** refers to a pattern of unequal treatment based on group membership that is built into the daily operations of society, whether or not it is consciously intended. The public schools, the criminal justice system, and political and economic institutions can operate in ways that put members of some groups at a disadvantage.

Institutional discrimination can be obvious and overt. For many years following the Civil War, African Americans in the American South were prevented from voting by practices such as poll taxes and rigged literacy tests. For nearly a century, well into the 1960s, elections and elected offices in the South were confined to whites only. The purpose of this blatant pattern of institutional discrimination was widely understood by African American and white Southerners alike: It existed to disenfranchise the African American community and keep it politically powerless.

At other times, institutional discrimination may operate more subtly and without conscious intent. If public schools use aptitude tests that are biased in favor of the dominant group, decisions about who does and who does not take college preparatory courses may be made on racist grounds, even if everyone involved sincerely believes that they are merely applying objective criteria in a rational way. If a decision-making process has unequal consequences for dominant and minority groups, institutional discrimination may well be at work.

Note that although a particular discriminatory policy may be implemented and enforced by individuals, the policy is more appropriately thought of as an aspect of the operation of the institution as a whole. Election officials in the South during segregation did not have to be personally prejudiced themselves to implement discriminatory policies, and neither do public school administrators today.

A major thesis of this book is that both racist ideologies and institutional discrimination are created to sustain the positions of dominant and minority groups in the stratification system. The relative advantage of the dominant group is maintained from day to day by widespread institutional discrimination. Members of the dominant group who are socialized into communities with strong racist ideologies and a great deal of institutional discrimination are likely to be personally prejudiced—either in the more blatant and traditional or the more modern and subtle forms—and to routinely practice acts of individual discrimination. The respective positions of dominant and minority groups are preserved over time through the mutually reinforcing patterns of prejudice, racism, and discrimination on both individual and institutional levels. Institutional discrimination is but one way in which members of a minority group can be denied access to valued goods and services, opportunities, and rights (such as voting). That is, institutional discrimination helps to sustain and reinforce the unequal positions of racial and ethnic groups in the stratification system.

FOCUS ON CONTEMPORARY ISSUES: Intersecting Inequalities, Racism, and Hurricane Katrina

Exhibit 1.8 Hurricane Katrina

© NASA.

In late August 2005, there was plenty of warning that a monster storm was approaching the Gulf Coast and threatening the city of New Orleans. People did what they could to protect themselves and their property, and many boarded up their houses and evacuated or moved to shelters. But there is little a person can do in the face of the 120 mph winds and storm surge of a Category 3 hurricane.

When Katrina made landfall on the morning of August 29, its winds were felt along a 200-mile stretch of the Gulf Coast. The storm affected almost 6 million people and killed over 1,800 (Gabe, Falk, & McCarthy, 2005). Katrina obliterated houses, stores, shopping malls, hospitals, and entire towns. When the cost of all the damage was finally totaled up, many months later, Katrina became the most expensive natural disaster in U.S. history.

The city of New Orleans was heavily damaged by the storm, but the real problems began when the levee system failed the day after Katrina passed, flooding virtually the entire city. The combination of hurricane winds and floodwaters nearly annihilated New Orleans, wrecked its infrastructure, killed over 700 of its citizens, and displaced almost the entire population. The city ceased to function and may never again be home for hundreds of thousands of its former residents or return to its status as one of America's premier cities and tourist attractions.

In the days and weeks that followed Katrina, the disaster of late August was compounded by the massive failure of the governmental relief response. Americans watched in horror as the people of New Orleans cried out for help—any kind of help—and the government (especially the Federal Emergency Management Agency, or FEMA) failed to rescue people and provide food, water, or safe shelter. The people of New Orleans were victimized twice, first by the storm and the flooding and then by the colossal ineptitude of the governmental response.

What relevance could Hurricane Katrina have for the concerns of this text? Aren't natural disasters—earthquakes, tornados, floods, and tsunamis as well as hurricanes—blind to race, ethnicity, class, and gender? Even though hurricanes don't care who lies in their path, they do not affect everyone equally, and class, race, ethnicity, and gender are prime factors in determining who becomes a victim and who walks away relatively unscathed. At the time of the disaster, television reports gave the impression that Katrina's victims in New Orleans were poor, black, and disproportionately female, and research since has confirmed the accuracy of this impression. For example, a 2006 Gallup poll reported that 53% of black residents of New Orleans had lost everything versus only 19% of white residents (Lavelle & Feagin, 2006, p. 60).[6] Although the damage was widespread and affected nearly everyone, black neighborhoods—for example the Lower 9th Ward—suffered disproportionately. Virtually every predominantly black New Orleans neighborhood suffered from the storm and the flooding (Logan, 2007).

What could explain the multiple victimizations of the poor black citizens of New Orleans? Why did these racial and class differentials develop? Was it simply prejudice and racism? Was it because, in the famous words of rapper Kanye West, "George Bush just doesn't care about black people" (Moraes, 2005, p. C1). Or were more subtle and less visible forces at work? The underlying principles that explain the racial and class pattern of victimization are consistent with many of the themes of this text, and we will take some time now to begin to explore them, apply them to the disaster in New Orleans, and preview their importance in chapters to come.

The first point we can make is that vulnerability to natural (and many manmade) disasters is closely related to social class and minority group status. Hurricanes don't seek out specific groups, but people with fewer resources (a defining characteristic of a minority group) are more vulnerable to the initial catastrophe and less able to recover in its aftermath. Consider, for example, the ability to evacuate in the hours before the storm struck. Who got out, and who was left behind to face the fury of the storm and the flooding? A general evacuation order was issued for the city, but twice as many poor whites as poor blacks (83% versus 40%) had access to a car to help them escape (Lavelle & Feagin, 2006, p. 59).

A consideration of vulnerability leads to a deeper issue: Why was such a large percentage of the vulnerable population of New Orleans both poor and black? Let's start with a basic sociological profile of the city prior to the storm. Blacks were a majority of the population of New Orleans, but, as was pointed out earlier in this chapter, minority groups are defined by the distribution of resources, power, wealth, and opportunity, not by relative numbers. New Orleans was 67% black when the hurricane hit, but, to consider only one dimension of minority group status, blacks had much higher rates of poverty and much lower incomes, as demonstrated in Exhibit 1.9, which presents five summary statistics for

Exhibit 1.9 Racial Differentials in Poverty and Income in New Orleans, 2000

	Blacks	**Whites**
Median income, all families*	$26,110	$54,008
Median income, female-headed households	$15,684	$28,941
Percent of all families with incomes less than $10,000	20.0%	4.0%
Percent of all families with incomes below the poverty line	29.8%	6.0%
Percent of all female-headed households with incomes below the poverty line	46.8%	17.9%

*Median income is the income that divides a group in half: Half earn more than this figure and half earn less.

SOURCE: U.S. Bureau of the Census (2000h), *Summary File 4.*

(Continued)

(Continued)

the year 2000, the date of the last census. Note that median income for blacks was less than half that of whites and was especially low (for both blacks and whites) for female-headed households. Also, 20% of black families lived on incomes of less than $10,000, while only 4% of white families did the same. These income patterns are consistent with racial differences in poverty. Nearly 30% of the black families in New Orleans lived in poverty, almost 5 times as many as white families. Female-headed households of both races were more likely to be poor, but nearly half of black, female-headed families lived in poverty, a rate 2½ times that of white female-headed households.

These simple statistics clearly demonstrate the greater economic vulnerability of black New Orleans, but how can we account for these huge racial differences? We can begin with a consideration of some of the themes of this text:

- The situation of a minority group in the present is a result of its experiences in the past.
- Minority groups are created in response to the fundamental forces shaping the larger society, especially the subsistence technology.
- Minority–dominant group relations change as the larger society evolves and develops.

We will explore these themes in the chapters to come, but we can point to the centuries of racial oppression and exclusion, institutional discrimination, and racism that preceded the arrival of Katrina as one powerful explanation for the gaps displayed in Exhibit 1.9. Present-day racial inequalities began centuries ago, during the days of slavery (see Chapter 3), when the pre-industrial agricultural technology of the day stimulated the demand for slave labor. In the era before labor-saving machines were developed to do the bulk of farm work, the elite groups that dominated southern society developed slavery to supply a large, highly controlled labor force. Slavery ended in 1865 but was quickly followed by a system of race relations called *de jure segregation* (or segregation by law; see Chapter 4), in which state and local laws were used to continue the powerlessness and economic disadvantages of blacks and to perpetuate their economic and political control by whites. Racial inequality was massive during this era and included separate and distinctly lower positions for blacks in housing, schooling, jobs, and access to political power. To cite only one example of the racial oppression characteristic of segregation, the state of Louisiana passed an amendment to the state constitution in 1898 that effectively denied the right to vote to the black community. African Americans were deprived of their most fundamental political resource and their ability to use the political institution to protect their self-interests.

The formal, legal barriers to equality in the United States were abolished as a result of the civil rights revolution of the 1960s (see Chapter 5), only four decades ago. While progress toward racial equality has been made since that time—at least nationally—we, as a society, are only two generations removed from a system that dictated racial inequality by law and by custom. Furthermore, class inequalities have been hardening throughout the nation over the past several decades as the United States moves into the post-industrial era (see Chapter 4).

The experiences of black Americans during slavery and de jure segregation varied by class (e.g., house slaves vs. field hands) and by gender. Some of these differences are explored in chapters to come, but one dimension of continuing gender differences within the system of racial oppression is reflected in Exhibit 1.9. Minority-group females are the most vulnerable and oppressed segment of the society on many dimensions. Continuing sexism combined with racism often results in black females having the lowest position in the job market. Also, joblessness for minority males is common, leaving women with the responsibility for the care of the children and other family members. Combined, these forces led to high rates of female-centered households and, ultimately, to women being vastly overrepresented in the shelters after Katrina struck (Strolovitch, Warren, & Frymer, 2006).

The status of the black community in New Orleans in the early 21st century was the product of centuries-long processes of institutional discrimination, exclusion, and oppression. The differences in financial resources and social class status documented in Exhibit 1.9 weren't created overnight, and they will not disappear without a concerted struggle, even under the most favorable economic conditions. In modern, post-industrial society, we should note, the key to financial security and upward mobility is education, and access to quality schooling also varies by race. Some of the differences in educational achievement are presented in Exhibit 1.10. The New Orleans school system was in poor shape before Katrina and fell into absolute shambles, a reality that is likely to reinforce the lower educational levels of the black community for years to come.

Exhibit 1.10 Racial Differentials in Educational Attainment in New Orleans, 2000

	Blacks	**Whites**
Percent 25 years of age and older who are high school graduates or higher	67.6%	83.6%
College graduates or higher	12.7%	27.4%
Percent 18–24 years of age with less than a high school degree		
Males	40.1%	26.0%
Females	28.6%	19.0%

SOURCE: U.S. Bureau of the Census (2000h), *Summary File 4.*

The situation of poor blacks in New Orleans took centuries to create and reflects how recently blacks were formerly and legally excluded from the opportunity structure of the larger society. As then-Senator Barack Obama famously remarked at the time of the disaster, the poor black people of New Orleans were "abandoned long before the hurricane" (quoted in Ivey, 2005, p. 1).

A Global Perspective

In the chapters that follow, we will focus on developing a number of concepts and theories and applying those ideas to the minority groups of the United States. However, it is important to expand our perspective beyond the experiences of just a single nation. Just as you would not accept an interview with a single person as an adequate test of a psychological theory, you should not accept the experiences of a single nation as proof for the sociological perspective developed in this text. Thus, we will take time, throughout this text, to apply our ideas to other societies, other historical eras, and a variety of non-American minority groups. If the ideas and concepts developed in this text can help us make sense of these other situations, we will have some assurance that they have general applicability and that the dynamics of intergroup relations in the United States are not unique.

MAIN POINTS

- The United States faces enormous problems in dominant–minority relationships. Although many historic grievances of minority groups remain unresolved, our society is becoming increasingly diverse.
- The United States is a nation of immigrants, and many different groups and cultures are represented in its population.
- A minority group has five defining characteristics: a pattern of disadvantage, identification by some visible mark, awareness of its disadvantaged status, a membership determined at birth, and a tendency to marry within the group.
- A stratification system has three different dimensions (class, prestige, and power), and the nature of inequality in a society varies by its level of development. Minority groups and social class are correlated in numerous and complex ways.
- Race is a criterion widely used to identify minority group members. As a biological concept, race has been largely abandoned, but as a social category, race maintains a powerful influence on the way we think about one another.
- Minority groups are internally differentiated by social class, age, region of residence, and many other variables. In this book, the focus is on gender as a source of variation within minority groups.
- Four crucial concepts for analyzing dominant–minority relations are prejudice, discrimination, ideological racism, and institutional discrimination.

STUDY SITE ON THE WEB

Don't forget the interactive quizzes and other resources and learning aids at **www.pineforge.com/healeyds3e**

FOR FURTHER READING

The following is a classic work on prejudice:

Allport, Gordon. 1954. *The Nature of Prejudice.* Reading, MA: Addison-Wesley.

Here are two analyses of the social and political uses of race:

Omi, Michael, & Winant, Howard. 1986. *Racial Formation in the United States From the 1960s to the 1980s.* New York: Routledge/Kegan Paul.

Smedley, Audrey. 1999. *Race in North America: Origin and Evolution of a Worldview.* Boulder, CO: Westview Press.

The following works offer wide-ranging analyses of the intersecting forces of race, class, and gender:

Anderson, Margaret, & Collins, Patricia Hill. 2007. *Race, Class, and Gender: An Anthology* (6th ed.). Belmont, CA: Cengage.

Rosenblum, Karen, & Travis, Toni-Michelle. 2008. *The Meaning of Difference.* New York: McGraw-Hill.

This is one of the most important treatments of modern or "color-blind" racism:

Bonilla-Silva, Eduardo. 2006. *Racism Without Racists: Color-Blind Racism and the Persistence of Racial Inequality in the United States* (2nd ed.). Lanham, MD: Rowman & Littlefield.

Here is a passionate analysis of the pervasiveness of racism and anti-black prejudice in America:

Feagin, Joseph. 2001. *Racist America.* New York: Routledge.

For a highly readable look at minority groups and cultural diversity in American life, see this work:

Takaki, Ronald. 1993. *A Different Mirror: A History of Multicultural America.* Boston: Little, Brown.

QUESTIONS FOR REVIEW AND STUDY

1. What kind of society should the United States strive to become? In your view, does the increasing diversity of American society represent a threat or an opportunity? Should we acknowledge and celebrate our differences, or should we strive for more unity and conformity? What possible dangers and opportunities are inherent in increasing diversity? What are the advantages and disadvantages of stressing unity and conformity?

2. What groups should be considered "minorities"? Using each of the five criteria included in the definition presented in this chapter, should gay and lesbian Americans be considered a minority group? How about left-handed people or people who are very overweight? Explain and justify your answers.

3. What is a social construction? How do race and gender differ in this regard? How are they the same?

4. Define and explain each of the terms in Exhibit 1.5. Cite an example of each from your own experiences. How does "ideological racism" differ from prejudice? Which concept is more

sociological? Why? How does institutional discrimination differ from discrimination? Which concept is more sociological? Why?

5. What is "white racial identity"? How does it differ from minority-group racial identity? Explain and cite examples of "privilege" associated with white racial identity.

6. Explain how the concepts developed in this chapter can be applied to the impact of Hurricane Katrina on New Orleans. Was this a "natural" disaster? What are its racial, class, and gender dimensions?

INTERNET RESEARCH PROJECT

Additional information and a list of relevant Web sites are included in the Appendix (www.pineforge.com/healeyds3e).

A. Updating Data on Diversity

Update Exhibit 1.1, "Groups in U.S. Society." Visit the Web site of the U.S. Census Bureau (http://www.census.gov) to get the latest estimates on the sizes of minority groups in the United States. Good places to begin the search for data include "Minority Links," "Statistical Abstract," and the list at "Subjects A to Z."

B. How Does the U.S. Government Define Race?

In this chapter, I stressed the point that race is at least as much a social construction as a biological reality. Does the federal government see race as a biological reality or a social convention? Search the Census Bureau Web site for information on the federal definition of race. How was a person's race defined in the 2000 census? How does this differ from previous censuses? Who determines a person's race, the government or the person filling out the census form? Is this treatment of race based on a biological approach or a more arbitrary social perspective? Given the goals of the census (e.g., to accurately count the number and types of people in the U.S. population), is this a reasonable approach to classifying race? Why or why not?

C. Exploring White Privilege

Access Professor Peggy McIntosh's list of white privileges at www.case.edu/president/aaction/UnpackingTheKnapsack.pdf. For any 10 items from the list, cite examples of white privilege from your own experiences. The examples can be situations you have experienced personally or through the media. Conduct a search of the Internet using the phrase "white racial privilege." What additional information and examples can you develop? Summarize and evaluate any criticisms of the concept you find.

Notes

1. From Schwarzbaum, Sarah E., & Thomas, Anita Jones. 2008. *Dimensions of Multicultural Counseling.* Thousand Oaks, CA: Sage Publications, p. 92.
2. From O'Brien, Eileen. 2008. *The Racial Middle: Latinos and Asian Americans Living Beyond the Racial Divide.* New York: New York University Press, p. 45.
3. Personal communication, June 2009.
4. Boldface terms in the text are defined in the glossary at the end of the book.
5. McIntosh's list can be accessed at www.case.edu/president/aaction/UnpackingTheKnapsack.pdf.
6. The percentages are almost certainly gross underestimates because the poll taker contacted only people with active New Orleans phone numbers.

2 Assimilation and Pluralism

From Immigrants to White Ethnics to White Americans

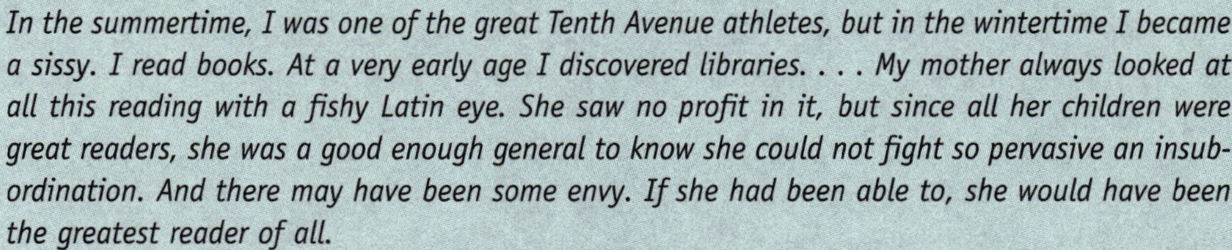

In the summertime, I was one of the great Tenth Avenue athletes, but in the wintertime I became a sissy. I read books. At a very early age I discovered libraries. . . . My mother always looked at all this reading with a fishy Latin eye. She saw no profit in it, but since all her children were great readers, she was a good enough general to know she could not fight so pervasive an insubordination. And there may have been some envy. If she had been able to, she would have been the greatest reader of all.

My direct ancestors for a thousand years have most probably been illiterate. Italy, the golden land . . . so majestic in its language and cultural treasures . . . has never cared for its poor people. My father and mother were both illiterates. Both grew up on rocky, hilly farms in the countryside adjoining Naples. . . . My mother was told that the family could not afford the traditional family gift of linens when she married, and it was this that decided her to emigrate to America. . . . My mother never heard of Michelangelo; the great deeds of the Caesars had not reached her ears. She never heard the great music of her native land. She could not sign her name.

And so it was hard for my mother to believe that her son could become an artist. After all, her one dream in coming to America had been to earn her daily bread, a wild dream in itself. And looking back, she was dead right. Her son an artist? To this day she shakes her head. I shake mine with her. America may be a . . . warmongering, racially prejudiced country today [in the 1970s] . . . but what a miracle it once was!

(Continued)

(Continued)

What has happened here has never happened in any other country in any other time. The poor, who have been poor for centuries . . . whose children had inherited their poverty, their illiteracy, their hopelessness, achieved some economic dignity and freedom. You didn't get it for nothing, you had to pay a price in tears, in suffering, but why not? And some even became artists.

—Mario Puzo[1]

Mark Keppel High School was a Depression-era structure with a brick and art deco facade and small, army-type bungalows in the back. Friction filled its hallways. The Anglo and Asian upper-class students from Monterey Park and Alhambra attended the school. They were tracked into the "A" classes; they were in the school clubs; they were the varsity team members and lettermen. They were the pep squad and cheerleaders.

But the school also took in the people from the Hills and surrounding community who somehow made it past junior high. They were mostly Mexican, in the "C" track (what were called the "stupid" classes). Only a few of these students participated in school government, in sports, or in the various clubs.

The school had two principal languages. Two skin tones and two cultures. It revolved around class differences. The white and Asian kids . . . were from professional, two-car households with watered lawns and trimmed trees. The laboring class, the sons and daughters of service workers, janitors, and factory hands, lived in and around the Hills (or a section of Monterey Park called "Poor Side"). The school separated these two groups by levels of education: The professional-class kids were provided with college-preparatory classes; the blue-collar students were pushed into "industrial arts." . . .

If you came from the Hills, you were labeled from the start. I'd walk into the counselor's office and looks of disdain greeted me—one meant for a criminal, alien, to be feared. Already a thug. It was harder to defy this expectation than just accept it and fall into the trappings. It was a jacket I could try to take off, but they kept putting it back on. The first hint of trouble and the preconceptions proved true. So why not be an outlaw? Why not make it our own?

—Luis Rodriquez[2]

Mario Puzo and Luis Rodriguez are both sons of immigrants, but they grew up in two very different Americas. Puzo, best known as the author of *The Godfather,* grew up in an Italian American community, and his memoir of life in New York City in the 1930s, "Choosing a Dream" (1993), illustrates the patterns that are at the heart of some of the theories presented in this chapter. Writing in the 1970s, Puzo remembers the days of his boyhood and his certainty that he would escape the poverty that surrounded him. Note also his view of (and gratitude for) an America that gave people (or at least white people) the opportunity to rise above the circumstances of their birth.

Rodriguez paints a rather different picture of U.S. society. He grew up in the Los Angeles area in the 1950s and 1960s and was a veteran of gang warfare by the time he reached high school. His memoir, *Always Running: La Vida Loca* (1993), illustrates a world that labels and sorts people and fast-tracks some of them for failure. What kind of life was his high school preparing him for? Contrast his despair ("why not be an outlaw?") with Puzo's gratitude. Which sector of American society was Rodriguez being prepared to enter?

These brief vignettes raise a number of questions about immigrants and U.S. society. How do immigrants adjust to the United States? How does the United States adjust to them? What kind of future, what opportunities, can immigrants and their children expect? Which view is more justified: Puzo's glowing optimism or Rodriguez's dour pessimism? Can both be true?

Introduction

This chapter continues to look at the ways in which ethnic and racial groups in the United States relate to each other. We focus on the experiences of the first mass wave of immigrants to the United States: the millions of Europeans who arrived between the 1820s and 1920s. We follow the descendents of these groups to the present, analyze the ways in which they adjusted to American society, and conclude by considering the emerging sense of "whiteness," or racial identity, that they have come to share with other white Americans.

Before we consider the immigrants themselves, we should deal with the dominant group and core culture to which the immigrants adjusted. The territory that became the United States was colonized and conquered by Northern and Western Europeans, particularly by the English (although the Dutch, Germans, and French also wielded considerable influence). The colonists created a social structure dominated by white Anglo-Saxon Protestants (WASPs) and a culture that stressed a distinctive set of values, beliefs, and norms. As we saw in our consideration of ideological racism in Chapter 1, American culture incorporated both sexism and racism along with the values of liberty, equality, individualism, freedom, and democracy at its core. Thus, the experiences of the immigrants considered in this chapter (and more recent immigrants) have been largely a story of their adjustment to a society dominated by WASPs and to a culture that privileged the English language, British-based traditions, men, and whites. Over the generations, the descendents of the immigrants absorbed this culture, entered this society, and adopted the racial and ethnic identity of the dominant group.

Assimilation and Pluralism

Two concepts, assimilation and pluralism, are at the core of the discussion of the experience of these groups. Each includes a variety of possible group relations and pathways along which group relations might develop.

Assimilation is a process in which formerly distinct and separate groups come to share a common culture and merge together socially. As a society undergoes assimilation, differences among groups decrease. **Pluralism,** on the other hand, exists when groups maintain their individual identities. In a pluralistic society, groups remain separate, and their cultural and social differences persist over time.

In some ways, assimilation and pluralism are contrary processes, but they are not mutually exclusive. They may occur together in a variety of combinations within a particular society or group. Some groups in a society may be assimilating as others are maintaining (or even increasing) their differences. As we shall see in Part III, virtually every minority group in the United States has, at any given time, some members who are assimilating and others who are preserving or reviving traditional cultures. Some Native Americans, for example, are pluralistic. They live on or near reservations, are strongly connected to their heritage, and speak their native language. Other Native Americans are very much assimilated into the dominant society: They live in urban areas, speak English only, and know relatively little about their traditional cultures. Both assimilation and pluralism are important forces in the everyday lives of Native Americans and most other minority groups.

American sociologists have been very concerned with these processes, especially assimilation. This concern was, in fact, stimulated by the massive immigration from Europe to the United States that was mentioned earlier. Over 31 million people crossed the Atlantic during this time, and a great deal of energy has been devoted to documenting, describing, and understanding the experiences of these immigrants and their descendants. These efforts have resulted in the development of a rich and complex literature that I will refer to as the "traditional" perspective on how newcomers are incorporated in U.S. society.

This chapter begins with a consideration of the traditional perspective on both assimilation and pluralism and a brief examination of several other possible group relationships. The concepts and theories of the traditional perspective are then applied to European immigrants and their descendents, and we develop a model of American assimilation based on these experiences. This model will be used in our analysis of other minority groups throughout the text and especially in Part III.

A particularly important issue is whether the theories, concepts, and models based on the first mass immigration to the United States (from the 1820s to the 1920s) apply to the second (post-1965) mass immigration. The newest arrivals differ in many ways and ideas, and theories based on the earlier experiences will not necessarily apply to the present. We will briefly note some of the issues in this chapter and explore them in more detail in the case study chapters in Part III.

Finally, at the end of this chapter, I briefly consider the implications of these first two chapters for the exploration of intergroup relations. By the end of this chapter, you will be familiar with many of the concepts that will guide us throughout this text as we examine the variety of possible dominant–minority group situations and the directions our society (and the groups within it) can take.

Assimilation

We begin with assimilation because the emphasis in U.S. group relations has historically been on this goal rather than on pluralism. This section presents some of the most important sociological theories and concepts that have been used to describe and analyze the assimilation of the 19th-century immigrants from Europe.

Types of Assimilation

Assimilation is a general term for a process that can follow a number of different pathways. One form of assimilation is expressed in the metaphor of the **melting pot,** a process in which different groups come together and contribute in roughly equal amounts to create a common culture and a new, unique society. People often think of the American experience of assimilation in terms of the melting pot. This view stresses the ways in which diverse peoples helped to construct U.S. society and made contributions to American culture. The melting pot metaphor sees assimilation as benign and egalitarian, a process that emphasizes sharing and inclusion.

Although it is a powerful image in our society, the melting pot is not an accurate description of how assimilation actually proceeded for American minority groups (Abrahamson, 1980). Some groups—especially the racial minority groups—have been largely excluded from the "melting" process. Furthermore, the melting pot brew has had a distinctly Anglocentric flavor: "For better or worse, the white Anglo-Saxon Protestant tradition was for two centuries—and in crucial respects still is—the dominant influence on American culture and society" (Schlesinger, 1992, p. 28). Contrary to the melting pot image, assimilation in the United States generally has been a coercive and largely one-sided process better described by the terms **Americanization** or **Anglo-conformity.** Rather than an equal sharing of elements and a gradual blending of diverse peoples, assimilation in the United States was designed to maintain the predominance of the English language and the British-type institutional patterns created during the early years of American society.

Under Anglo-conformity, immigrant and minority groups are expected to adapt to Anglo-American culture as a precondition to acceptance and access to better jobs, education, and other opportunities. Assimilation has meant that minority groups have had to give up their traditions and adopt Anglo-American culture. To be sure, many groups and individuals were (and continue to be) eager to undergo Anglo-conformity, even if it meant losing much or all of their heritage. For other groups, Americanization created conflict, anxiety, demoralization, and resentment. We assess these varied reactions in our examination of America's minority groups in Part III.

The "Traditional" Perspective on Assimilation: Theories and Concepts

American sociologists have developed a rich body of theories and concepts based on the assimilation experiences of the immigrants who came from Europe from the 1820s to the 1920s, and we shall refer to this body of work as the *traditional perspective* on assimilation. As you will see, the scholars working in this tradition have made invaluable contributions, and their thinking is impressively complex and comprehensive. This does not mean, of course, that they have exhausted the possibilities or answered (or asked) all the questions. Theorists working in the pluralist tradition and contemporary scholars studying the experiences of more recent immigrants have questioned many aspects of traditional assimilation theory and have made a number of important contributions of their own.

Robert Park

Many theories of assimilation are grounded in the work of Robert Park. He was one of a group of scholars who had a major hand in establishing sociology as a discipline in the United States in the 1920s and 1930s. Park felt that intergroup relations go through a predictable set of phases that he called a **race relations cycle.** When groups first come into contact (through immigration, conquest, etc.), relations are conflictual and competitive. Eventually, however, the process, or cycle, moves toward assimilation, or the "interpenetration and fusion" of groups (Park & Burgess, 1924, p. 735).

Park argued further that assimilation is inevitable in a democratic and industrial society. In a political system based on democracy, fairness, and impartial justice, all groups will eventually secure equal treatment under the law. In an industrial economy, people tend to be judged on rational grounds—that is, on the basis of their abilities and talents—and not by ethnicity or race. Park believed that as American society continued to modernize, urbanize, and industrialize, ethnic and racial groups would gradually lose their importance. The boundaries between groups would eventually dissolve, and a more "rational" and unified society would emerge (see also Geschwender, 1978; Hirschman, 1983).

Social scientists have examined, analyzed, and criticized Park's conclusions for nearly 80 years. One frequently voiced criticism is that he did not specify a time frame for the completion of assimilation, and therefore his idea that assimilation is "inevitable" cannot be tested. Until the exact point in time when assimilation is deemed complete, we will not know whether the theory is wrong or whether we just have not waited long enough.

An additional criticism of Park's theory is that he does not describe the nature of the assimilation process in much detail. How would assimilation proceed? How would everyday life change? Which aspects of the group would change first?

Milton Gordon

To clarify some of the issues left unresolved by Park, we turn to the works of sociologist Milton Gordon, who made a major contribution to theories of assimilation in his book *Assimilation in American Life* (1964). Gordon broke down the overall process of assimilation into seven sub-processes; we will focus on the first three. However, before considering these phases of assimilation, we need to consider some new concepts and terms.

Gordon makes a distinction between the cultural and the structural components of society. **Culture** encompasses all aspects of the way of life associated with a group of people. It includes language, religious beliefs, customs and rules of etiquette, and the values and ideas people use to organize their lives and interpret their existence. The **social structure,** or structural components of a society, includes networks of social relationships, groups, organizations, stratification systems, communities, and families. The social structure organizes the work of the society and connects individuals to one another and to the larger society.

It is common in sociology to separate the social structure into primary and secondary sectors. The **primary sector** includes interpersonal relationships that are intimate and personal, such as families and groups of friends. Groups in the primary sector are small. The **secondary sector** consists of groups and organizations that are more public, task oriented, and impersonal. Organizations in the secondary sector are often very large and include businesses, factories, schools and colleges, and bureaucracies.

Now we can examine Gordon's first three stages of assimilation, which are summarized in Exhibit 2.1.

Exhibit 2.1 Gordon's Stages of Assimilation

Stage	Process
1. Acculturation (cultural assimilation)	The group learns the culture, language, and value system of the dominant group.
2. Integration (structural assimilation)	
a. At the secondary level	Members of the group enter the public institutions and organizations of the dominant society.
b. At the primary level	Members of the group enter the cliques, clubs, and friendship groups of the dominant society.
3. Intermarriage (marital assimilation)	Members of the group intermarry with members of the dominant group in large numbers.

SOURCE: From Gordon (1964). Copyright ©1964. Reprinted by permission of Oxford University Press, Inc.

1. Cultural Assimilation, or **Acculturation.** Members of the minority group learn the culture of the dominant group. For groups that immigrate to the United States, acculturation to the dominant Anglo-American culture may include (as necessary) learning the English language, changing eating habits, adopting new value systems, and altering the spelling of the family surname.

2. Structural Assimilation, or **Integration.** The minority group enters the social structure of the larger society. Integration typically begins in the secondary sector and gradually moves into the primary sector. That is, before people can form friendships with members of other groups (integration into the primary sector), they must first become acquaintances. The initial contact between groups often occurs in public institutions such as schools and workplaces (integration into the secondary sector). The greater their integration into the secondary sector, the more nearly equal the minority group will be to the dominant group in income, education, and occupational prestige. Once a group has entered the institutions and public sectors of the larger society, according to Gordon, integration into the primary sector and the other stages of assimilation will follow inevitably (although not necessarily quickly). Measures of integration into the primary sector include the extent to which people have acquaintances, close friends, or neighbors from other groups.

3. **Marital Assimilation**, or **Intermarriage**. When integration into the primary sector becomes substantial, the basis for Gordon's third stage of assimilation is established. People are most likely to select spouses from among their primary relations, and thus, in Gordon's view, primary structural integration typically precedes intermarriage.

Gordon argued that acculturation was a prerequisite for integration. Given the stress on Anglo-conformity, a member of an immigrant or minority group would not be able to compete for jobs or other opportunities in the secondary sector of the social structure until he or she had learned the dominant group's culture. Gordon recognized, however, that successful acculturation does not automatically ensure that a group will begin the integration phase. The dominant group may still exclude the minority group from its institutions and limit the opportunities available to the group. Gordon argued that "acculturation without integration" (or Americanization without equality) is a common situation in the United States for many minority groups, especially the racial minority groups.

In Gordon's theory, movement from acculturation to integration is the crucial step in the assimilation process. Once that step is taken, all the other sub-processes will occur inevitably, although movement through the different stages can be quite slow. Gordon's idea that assimilation runs a certain course in a certain order echoes Park's conclusion regarding the inevitability of the process.

More than 40 years after Gordon published his analysis of assimilation, some of his conclusions have been called into question. For example, the individual sub-processes of assimilation that Gordon saw as linked in a certain order are often found to occur independently of one another (Yinger, 1985). A group may integrate before acculturating or combine the sub-processes in other ways. Also, many researchers no longer think of the process of assimilation as necessarily linear or one-way (Greeley, 1974). Groups (or segments thereof) may "reverse direction" and become less assimilated over time, revive their traditional cultures, relearn the old language, or revitalize ethnic organizations or associations.

Nonetheless, Gordon's overall model continues to guide our understanding of the process of assimilation, to the point that a large part of the research agenda for contemporary studies of immigrants involves assessment of the extent to which their experiences can be described in Gordon's terms (Alba & Nee, 1997). In fact, Gordon's model will provide a major organizational framework for the case study chapters presented in Part III of this text.

Human Capital Theory

Why did some European immigrant groups acculturate and integrate more rapidly than others? Although not a theory of assimilation per se, **human capital theory** offers one possible answer to this question. This theory argues that status attainment, or the level of success achieved by an individual in society, is a direct result of educational levels, personal values and skills, and other individual characteristics and abilities. Education is seen as an investment in human capital, not unlike the investment a business might make in machinery or new technology. The greater the investment in a person's human capital, the higher the probability of success. Blau and Duncan (1967), in their pioneering statement of status attainment theory, found that even the relative advantage conferred by having a high-status father is largely mediated through education. In other words, high levels of affluence and occupational prestige are not so much a result of being born into a privileged status as they are the result of the superior education that affluence makes possible.

Why did some immigrant groups achieve upward mobility more rapidly than others? Human capital theory answers questions such as these in terms of the resources and cultural characteristics of the members of the groups, especially their levels of education and familiarity with English. Success is seen as a direct result of individual effort and the wise investment of personal resources. People or groups who fail have not tried hard enough, have not made the right kinds of educational investments, or have values or habits that limit their ability to compete.

More than most sociological theories, human capital theory is quite consistent with traditional American culture and values. Both tend to see success as an individual phenomenon, a reward for hard work, sustained effort, and good character. Both tend to assume that success is equally available to all and that the larger society is open and neutral in its distribution of rewards and opportunity. Both tend to see assimilation as a highly desirable, benign process that blends diverse peoples and cultures into a strong, unified whole. Thus, people or groups that resist Americanization or question its benefits are seen as threatening or illegitimate.

On one level, human capital theory is an important theory of success and upward mobility, and we will use the theory on occasion to analyze the experiences of minority and immigrant groups. On another level, the theory is so resonant with American "commonsensical" views of success and failure that we may tend to use it uncritically.

A final judgment on the validity of the theory will be more appropriately made at the end of the text, but you should be aware of the major limitations of the theory from the beginning. First of all, as an explanation of minority group experience, human capital theory is not so much "wrong" as it is incomplete. In other words, it does not take account of all the factors that affect mobility and assimilation. Second, as we shall see, the assumption that U.S. society is equally open and fair to all groups is simply incorrect. We will point out other strengths and limitations of this perspective as we move through the text.

Pluralism

Sociological discussions of pluralism often begin with a consideration of the work of Horace Kallen. In articles published in the *Nation* magazine in 1915, Kallen argued that people should not have to surrender their culture and traditions to become full participants in American society. He rejected the Anglo-conformist, assimilationist model and contended that the existence of separate ethnic groups, even with separate cultures, religions, and languages, was consistent with democracy and other core American values. In Gordon's terms, Kallen believed that integration and equality were possible without extensive acculturation and that American society could be a federation of diverse groups, a mosaic of harmonious and interdependent cultures and peoples (Kallen, 1915a, 1915b; see also Abrahamson, 1980; Gleason, 1980).

Assimilation has been such a powerful theme in U.S. history that, in the decades following the publication of Kallen's analysis, support for pluralism remained somewhat marginalized. In more recent decades, however, interest in pluralism and ethnic diversity has increased, in part because the assimilation predicted by Park (and implicit in the conventional wisdom of many Americans) has not fully materialized. Perhaps we simply have not waited long enough, but as the 21st century unfolds, distinctions among the racial minority groups in our society show few signs of disappearing, and in fact, some members of these groups are questioning the very desirability of assimilation. Also, more surprising perhaps is that white ethnicity maintains a stubborn persistence, even as it continues to change in form and decrease in strength.

An additional reason for the growing interest in pluralism, no doubt, is the everyday reality of the increasing diversity of U.S. society, as reflected in Exhibit 1.1. Controversies over issues such as "English-only" policies, bilingual education, and welfare rights for immigrants are common and often bitter. Many Americans feel that diversity or pluralism has exceeded acceptable limits and that the unity of the nation is at risk (for example, visit www.us-english.org, the home page of a group that advocates for making English the official U.S. language).

Finally, interest in pluralism and ethnicity in general has been stimulated by developments around the globe. Several nation-states have disintegrated into smaller units based on language, culture, race, and ethnicity. Recent events in India, the Middle East, Eastern Europe, the former Soviet Union, Canada, and Africa, just to mention a few, have provided dramatic and often tragic evidence of how ethnic identities and enmities can persist across decades or even centuries of submergence and suppression in larger national units.

In contemporary debates, discussions of diversity and pluralism are often couched in the language of **multiculturalism,** a general term for a variety of programs and ideas that stress mutual respect for all groups and for the multiple heritages that have shaped the United States. Some aspects of multiculturalism are controversial and have evoked strong opposition. In many ways, however, these debates merely echo a recurring argument about the character of American society, a debate that will be revisited throughout this text.

Types of Pluralism

We can distinguish various types of pluralism by using some of the concepts introduced in the discussion of assimilation. **Cultural pluralism** exists when groups have not acculturated and each maintains its own identity. The groups might speak different languages, practice different religions, and have different value systems. The groups are part of the same society and might even live in adjacent areas, but in some ways, they live in different worlds. Many Native Americans are culturally pluralistic, maintaining their traditional languages and cultures and living on isolated reservations. The Amish, a religious community sometimes called the Pennsylvania Dutch, are also a culturally pluralistic group. They are committed to a way of life organized around farming, and they maintain a culture and an institutional life—a system of group and organizational memberships and interpersonal networks that is separate from the dominant culture (see Hostetler, 1980; Kephart & Zellner, 1994; Kraybill & Bowman, 2001).

Following Gordon's sub-processes, a second type of pluralism exists when a group has acculturated but not integrated. That is, the group has adopted the Anglo-American culture but does not have full and equal access to the institutions of the larger society. In this situation, called **structural pluralism,** cultural differences are minimal, but the groups occupy different locations in the social structure. The groups may speak with the same accent, eat the same food, pursue the same goals, and subscribe to the same values, but they may also maintain separate organizational systems, including different churches, clubs, schools, and neighborhoods. Under structural pluralism, groups practice a common way of life but do so in different places and with minimal interaction across group boundaries. An example of structural pluralism can be found on any Sunday morning in the Christian churches of the United States. Not only are local parishes separated by denomination, they are also often identified with specific ethnic groups or races. What happens in the various churches—the rituals, expressions of faith, statements of core values and beliefs—is similar and expresses a common, shared culture. Structurally, however, this common culture is expressed in separate buildings and by separate congregations.

A third type of pluralism reverses the order of Gordon's first two phases: integration without acculturation. This situation is exemplified by a group that has had some material success (measured by wealth or income, for example) but has not become Americanized (learned English, adopted American values and norms, etc.). Some immigrant groups have found niches in American society in which they can survive and occasionally prosper economically without acculturating very much.

Two different situations can be used to illustrate this pattern. An **enclave minority** establishes its own neighborhood and relies on a set of interconnected businesses, each of which is usually small in scope, for its economic survival. Some of these businesses serve the group, whereas others serve the larger society. The Cuban American community in South Florida and Chinatowns in many larger American cities are examples of ethnic enclaves. A group with a similar pattern of adjustment, the **middleman minority,** also relies on small shops and retail firms, but the businesses are more dispersed throughout a large area rather than concentrated in a specific locale. Some Chinese American communities fit this second pattern, as do Korean American greengroceries and Indian American–owned motels (Portes & Manning, 1986). These types of minority groups are discussed further in Part III.

The economic success of enclave and middleman minorities is partly due to the strong ties of cooperation and mutual aid within their groups. The ties are based, in turn, on cultural bonds that would weaken if acculturation took place. In contrast with Gordon's idea that acculturation is a prerequisite to integration, whatever success these groups enjoy is due in part to the fact that they have not Americanized. At various times and places, Jewish, Chinese, Japanese, Korean, and Cuban Americans have been enclave or middleman minorities (see Bonacich & Modell, 1980; Kitano & Daniels, 2001).

The situation of enclave and middleman minorities, integration without acculturation, can be considered either a type of pluralism (emphasizing the absence of acculturation) or a type of assimilation (emphasizing a high level of economic equality). Keep in mind that assimilation and pluralism are not opposites but can occur in a variety of combinations. It is best to think of acculturation, integration, and the other stages of assimilation (or pluralism) as independent processes.

Other Group Relationships

This book concentrates on assimilation and pluralism, but there are, of course, other possible group relationships and goals. Two commonly noted goals for minority group are separatism and revolution (Wirth, 1945). The goal of **separatism** is for the group to sever all ties (political, cultural, and geographic) with the larger society. Thus, separatism goes well beyond pluralism. Native Americans have expressed both separatist and pluralist goals, and separatism has also been pursued by some African American organizations, such as the Black Muslims. In the contemporary world, there are separatist movements among groups in French Canada, Scotland, Chechnya, Cyprus, southern Mexico, Hawaii, and scores of other places.

A minority group promoting **revolution** seeks to switch places with the dominant group and become the ruling elite or create a new social order, perhaps in alliance with members of the dominant group. Although revolutionary activity can be found among some American minority groups (e.g., the Black Panthers), this goal has been relatively rare for minority groups in the United States. Revolutionary minority groups are more commonly found in situations such as those in colonial Africa, in which one nation conquered and controlled another racially or culturally different nation.

The dominant group may also pursue goals other than assimilation and pluralism, including forced migration or expulsion, extermination or genocide, and continued subjugation of the minority group. Chinese immigrants in the United States were the victims of a policy of expulsion, beginning in the 1880s, when the Chinese Exclusion Act (1882) closed the door on further immigration and concerted efforts were made to encourage those Chinese in the country to leave (see Chapter 9). Native Americans have also been the victims of expulsion. In 1830, all tribes living east of the Mississippi were forced to migrate to a new territory in the West (see Chapter 4). The most infamous example of genocide is the Holocaust in Nazi Germany, during which 6 million Jews were murdered. The dominant group pursues *continued subjugation* when, as with slavery in the antebellum South, it attempts to maintain a powerless and exploited position for the minority group. A dominant group may simultaneously pursue different policies with different minority groups and may, of course, change policies over time.

From Immigrants to White Ethnics

In this section, we will explore the experiences of the minority groups that stimulated the development of the traditional perspective. A massive emigration from Europe began in the 1820s, and over the next century, millions of people made the journey from the Old World to the New. They came from every corner of the continent: Ireland, Greece, Germany, Italy, Poland, Portugal, Ukraine, Russia, and scores of other nations and provinces. They came as young men and women seeking jobs, as families fleeing religious persecution, as political radicals fleeing the police, as farmers seeking land and a fresh start, and as paupers barely able to scrape together the cost of the passage. They came as immigrants, became minority groups upon their arrival, experienced discrimination and prejudice in all its forms, went through all the varieties and stages of assimilation and pluralism, and eventually merged into the society that had rejected them so viciously upon their arrival. Exhibit 2.2 shows the major European sending nations.

Exhibit 2.2 Major European Sending Nations, Immigration to the United States, 1820–1920

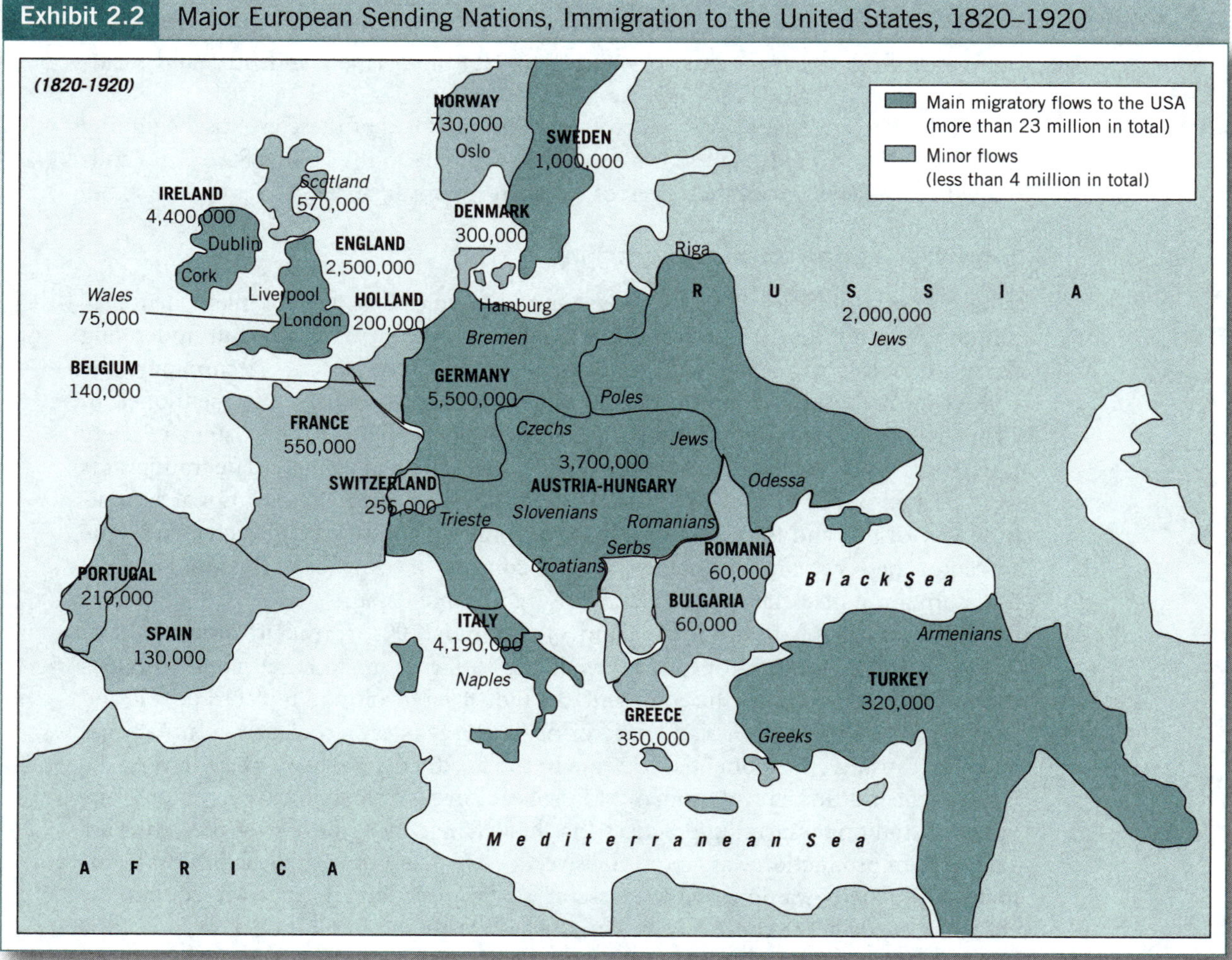

This massive wave of immigrants shaped the United States in countless ways. When the immigration started in the 1820s, the United States was not yet 50 years old, an agricultural nation clustered along the East Coast. The nation was just coming into contact with Mexicans in the Southwest, emigration from China had not begun, slavery was flourishing in the South, and conflict with American Indians was intense and brutal. When the immigration to the United States ended in the 1920s, the U.S. population had increased from fewer than 10 million to more than 100 million, and the society had industrialized, become a world power, and stretched from coast to coast, with colonies in the Pacific and the Caribbean.

It was no coincidence that European immigration, American industrialization, and the rise to global prominence occurred simultaneously. These changes were intimately interlinked—the mutual causes and effects of each other. Industrialization fueled the growth of U.S. military and political power, and the industrial machinery of the nation depended heavily on the flow of labor from Europe. By World War I, for example, 25% of the nation's total labor force was foreign born, and more than half of the workforce in New York, Detroit, and Chicago consisted of immigrant men. Immigrants were the majority of the workers in many important sectors of the economy, including coal mining, steel manufacturing, the garment industry, and meatpacking (Martin & Midgley, 1999; Steinberg, 1981).

In the sections that follow, we explore the experiences of these groups, beginning with forces that caused them to leave Europe and come to the United States and ending with an assessment of their present status in American society.

Industrialization and Immigration

What forces stimulated this mass movement of people? Like any complex phenomenon, immigration to the U.S. from Europe had a multitude of causes, but underlying the process was a massive and fundamental shift in subsistence technology: the **industrial revolution.** The importance of subsistence technology was mentioned in Chapter 1. Dominant–minority relations are intimately related to the system a society uses to satisfy its basic needs, and they change as that system changes. The immigrants were pushed out of Europe as industrial technology wrecked the traditional agricultural way of life, and they were drawn to the United States by the jobs created by the spread of the very same technology. We will consider the impact of this fundamental transformation of social structure and culture in some detail.

Industrialization began in England in the mid-1700s, spread to other parts of Northern and Western Europe, and then, in the 19th century, to Eastern and Southern Europe. As it rolled across the continent, the industrial revolution replaced people and animal power with machines and new forms of energy (steam, coal, and eventually gas and oil), causing an exponential increase in the productive capacity of society. At the dawn of the industrial revolution, most Europeans lived in small, rural villages and survived by traditional farming practices that had changed very little over the centuries. The work of production was labor intensive, done by hand or with the aid of draft animals. Productivity was low, and the tasks of food production and survival required the efforts of virtually the entire family working ceaselessly throughout the year.

Industrialization destroyed this traditional way of life as it introduced new technology, machines, and new sources of energy to the tasks of production. The new technology was *capital intensive,* meaning that much capital had to be invested in machines, equipment, and processes of production, and it reduced the need for human labor in rural areas as it modernized agriculture. Also, farmland was consolidated into larger and larger tracts for the sake of efficiency, further decreasing the need for human laborers. At the same time, even as survival in the rapidly changing rural economy became more difficult, the rural population began to grow.

In response to industrialization, peasants began to leave their home villages and move toward urban areas. Factories were being built in or near the cities, opening up opportunities for employment. The urban population tended to increase faster than the job supply, however, and many migrants had to move on. Many of these former peasants responded to opportunities available in the New World, especially in the United States, where the abundance of farmland on the frontier kept people moving out of the cities and away from the East Coast, thereby sustaining a fairly constant demand for labor in the very areas that were easiest for Europeans to reach. As industrialization took hold on both continents, the population movement to European cities and then to North America eventually grew to become the largest in human history (so far).

The timing of immigration to the United States from Europe followed that of industrialization. The first waves of immigrants, often called the **Old Immigration,** came from Northern and Western Europe in the 1820s. A second wave, the **New Immigration,** began arriving from Southern and Eastern Europe in the 1880s. Exhibit 2.3 shows both

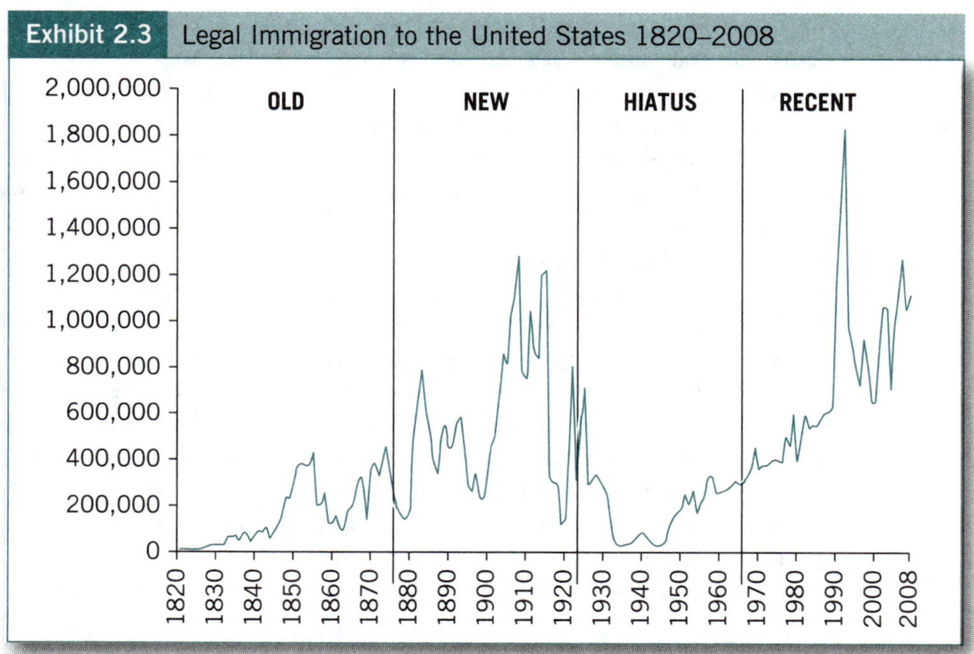

Exhibit 2.3 Legal Immigration to the United States 1820–2008

SOURCE: U.S. Department of Homeland Security (2008).

waves and the number of legal immigrants up to 2006. Note that the "new" immigration was much more voluminous than the "old" and that the number of immigrants declined drastically after the 1920s. We will explore the reasons for this decline later in this chapter and discuss in detail the more recent (post-1965) increase in immigration in Chapters 8 through 10.

European Origins and Conditions of Entry

The immigrants from Europe varied from each other in innumerable ways. They followed a variety of pathways into the United States, and their experiences were shaped by their cultural and class characteristics, their countries of origin, and the timing of their arrival. Some groups encountered much more resistance than others, and different groups played different roles in the industrialization and urbanization of America. To discuss these diverse patterns systematically, I distinguish among three subgroups of European immigrants: Protestants from Northern and Western Europe, the largely Catholic immigrant laborers from Ireland and from Southern and Eastern Europe, and Jewish immigrants from Eastern Europe. We will look at these subgroups in roughly the order of their arrival. In later sections, we will consider other sociological variables (social class, gender) that further differentiated these groups.

Northern and Western Protestant Europeans

Northern and Western European immigrants included English, Germans, Norwegians, Swedes, Welsh, French, Dutch, and Danes. These groups were similar to the dominant group in their racial and religious characteristics and also shared many cultural values with the host society, including the *Protestant ethic*—which stressed hard work, success, and individualism—and support for the principles of democratic government. These similarities eased their acceptance into a society that was highly intolerant of religious and racial differences until well into the 20th century, and these immigrant groups generally experienced a lower degree of ethnocentric rejection and racist disparagement than did the Irish and immigrants from Southern and Eastern Europe.

Northern and Western European immigrants came from nations that were just as developed as the United States. Thus, these immigrants tended to be more skilled and educated than other immigrant groups, and they often brought money and other resources with which to secure a comfortable place for themselves in their new society. Many settled in the sparsely populated Midwest and in other frontier areas, where they farmed the fertile land that had become available after the conquest and removal of American Indians and Mexican Americans (see Chapter 3). By dispersing throughout the midsection of the country, they lowered their visibility and their degree of competition with dominant group members. Two brief case studies, first of Norwegian immigrants and then of Germans, outline the experiences of these groups.

Immigrants from Norway. Norway had a small population base, and immigration to the United States from this Scandinavian nation was never sizable in absolute numbers. However, "America Fever" struck here as it did elsewhere in Europe, and on a per capita basis, Norway sent more immigrants to the United States before 1890 than any European nation except Ireland (Chan, 1990, p. 41).

The first Norwegian immigrants were moderately prosperous farmers searching for cheap land. They found abundant acreage in upper-Midwest states, such as Minnesota and Wisconsin, and then found that the local labor supply was too small to effectively cultivate the available land. Many turned to their homeland for assistance and used their relatives and friends to create networks and recruit a labor force. Thus, chains of communication and migration linking Norway to the Northern Plains were established, supplying immigrants to these areas for decades (Chan, 1990). Today, a strong Scandinavian heritage is still evident in the farms, towns, and cities of the upper Midwest.

Immigrants from Germany. The stream of immigration to the United States from Germany was much larger than that from Norway, and German Americans left their mark on the economy, the political structure, and the cultural life of their new land. In the last half of the 19th century, at least 25% of the immigrants each year were German (Conzen, 1980, p. 406), and today more Americans (about 15%) trace their ancestry to Germany than to any other country (Brittingham & de la Cruz, 2004).

The German immigrants who arrived earlier in the 1800s moved into the newly opened farmland and the rapidly growing cities of the Midwest, as had many Scandinavians. By 1850, large German communities could be found in Milwaukee, St. Louis, and other midwestern cities (Conzen, 1980). Some German immigrants followed the transatlantic route of the cotton trade between Europe and the southern United States and entered through the port of New Orleans, moving from there to the Midwest and Southwest.

German immigrants arriving later in the century were more likely to settle in urban areas, in part because fertile land was less available. Many of the city-bound German immigrants were skilled workers and artisans, and others found work as laborers in the rapidly expanding industrial sector. The double penetration of German immigrants into the rural economy and the higher sectors of the urban economy is reflected by the fact that by 1870, most employed German Americans were involved in skilled labor (37%) or farming (25%) (Conzen, 1980, p. 413).

German immigrants took relatively high occupational positions in the U.S. labor force, and their sons and daughters were able to translate that relative affluence into economic mobility. By the dawn of the 20th century, large numbers of second-generation German Americans were finding their way into white-collar and professional careers. Within a few generations, German Americans had achieved parity with national norms in education, income, and occupational prestige.

Assimilation patterns. By and large, assimilation for Norwegian, German, and other Protestant immigrants from Northern and Western Europe was consistent with the traditional views discussed earlier in this chapter. Although members of these groups felt the sting of rejection, prejudice, and discrimination, their movement from acculturation to integration and equality was relatively smooth, especially when compared with the experiences of racial minority groups. Their relative success and high degree of assimilation are suggested in Exhibits 2.6 and 2.7, presented later in this chapter.

Immigrant Laborers From Ireland and Southern and Eastern Europe

The relative ease of assimilation for Northern and Western Europeans contrasted sharply with the experiences of non-Protestant, less educated and skilled immigrants. These "immigrant laborers" came in two waves. The Irish were part of the Old Immigration that began in the 1820s, but the bulk of this group—Italians, Poles, Russians, Hungarians, Greeks, Serbs, Ukrainians, Slovaks, Bulgarians, and scores of other Southern and Eastern European groups—made up the New Immigration that began in the 1880s. Most of the immigrants in these nationality groups (like many recent immigrants to the United States) were peasants or unskilled laborers, with few resources other than their willingness to work. They came from rural, village-oriented cultures in which family and kin took precedence over individual needs or desires. Family life for them tended to be autocratic and male dominated, and children were expected to subordinate their personal desires and to work for the good of the family as a whole. Arranged marriages were common. This cultural background was less consistent with the industrializing, capitalistic, individualistic, Protestant, Anglo-American culture of the United States and was a major reason that these immigrant laborers experienced a higher level of rejection and discrimination than the immigrants from Northern and Western Europe.

The immigrant laborers were much less likely to enter the rural economy than were the Northern and Western European immigrants. Much of the better frontier land had already been claimed by the time most new immigrant groups began to arrive, and a large number of them had been permanently soured on farming by the oppressive and exploitative agrarian economies from which they were trying to escape. They settled in the cities of the industrializing Northeast and found work in plants, mills, mines, and factories. They supplied the armies of laborers needed to power the industrial revolution in the United States, although their view of this process was generally from the bottom looking up. They arrived during the decades in which the American industrial and urban infrastructure was being constructed. They built roads, canals, and railroads, as well as the buildings that housed the machinery of industrialization. For example, the first tunnels of the New York City subway system were dug, largely by hand, by laborers from Italy. Other immigrants found work in the coal fields of Pennsylvania and West Virginia and the steel mills of Pittsburgh, and they flocked by the millions to the factories of the Northeast.

Like other low-skill immigrant groups, these newcomers took jobs in which strength and stamina were more important than literacy or skilled craftsmanship. In fact, the minimum level of skill required for employment actually declined as industrialization proceeded through its early phases. To keep wages low and take advantage of what seemed like an inexhaustible supply of cheap labor, industrialists and factory owners developed technologies and machines that required few skills and little knowledge of English to operate. As mechanization proceeded, unskilled workers replaced skilled workers in the workforce. Not infrequently, women and children replaced men because they could be hired for lower wages (Steinberg, 1981).

Eventually, as the generations passed, the prejudice, systematic discrimination, and other barriers to upward mobility for the immigrant laborer groups weakened, and their descendants began to rise out of the working class. Although the first and second generations of these groups were largely limited to jobs at the unskilled or semiskilled level, the third and later generations rose in the American social class system. As Exhibits 2.6 and 2.7 show, the descendants of the immigrant laborers achieved parity with national norms by the latter half of the 20th century.

Eastern European Jewish Immigrants and the Ethnic Enclave

Jewish immigrants from Russia and other parts of Eastern Europe followed a third pathway into U.S. society. They were a part of the New Immigration and began arriving in the 1880s. Unlike the immigrant laborer groups, who were generally economic refugees and included many young, single males, Eastern European Jews were fleeing religious persecution and generally arrived as family units intending to settle permanently and become citizens. They settled in the urban areas of the Northeast and Midwest. New York City was the most common destination, and the Lower East Side became the best-known Jewish American neighborhood. By 1920, about 60% of all Jewish Americans lived in the urban areas between Boston and Philadelphia, with almost 50% living in New York City alone. Another 30% lived in the urban areas of the Midwest, particularly in Chicago (Goren, 1980, p. 581).

In Russia and other parts of Eastern Europe, Jews had been barred from agrarian occupations and had come to rely on the urban economy for their livelihoods. When they immigrated to the United States, they brought these urban skills and job experiences with them. For example, almost two-thirds of the immigrant Jewish men had been tailors and other skilled laborers in Eastern Europe (Goren, 1980, p. 581). In the rapidly industrializing U.S. economy of the early 20th century, they were able to use these skills to find work.

Other Jewish immigrants joined the urban working class and took manual labor and unskilled jobs in the industrial sector (Morawska, 1990). The garment industry in particular became the lifeblood of the Jewish community and provided jobs to about one-third of all Eastern European Jews residing in the major cities (Goren, 1980, p. 582). Women as well as men were involved in the garment industry. Jewish women, like the women of more recent immigrant laborer groups, found ways to combine their jobs and their domestic responsibilities. As young girls, they worked in factories and sweatshops, and after marriage, they did the same work at home, sewing precut garments together or doing other piecework such as wrapping cigars or making artificial flowers, often assisted by their children (Amott & Matthaei, 1991).

Unlike most European immigrant groups, Jewish Americans became heavily involved in commerce and often found ways to start their own businesses and become self-employed. Drawing on their experience in the Old Country, many started businesses and small independent enterprises and developed an enclave economy. The Jewish neighborhoods were densely populated and provided a ready market for services of all kinds. Some Jewish immigrants became street peddlers or started bakeries, butcher or candy shops, or any number of other retail enterprises.

Capitalizing on their residential concentration and close proximity, Jewish immigrants created dense networks of commercial, financial, and social cooperation. The Jewish American enclave survived because of the cohesiveness of the group; the willingness of wives, children, and other relatives to work for little or no monetary compensation; and the commercial savvy of the early immigrants. Also, a large pool of cheap labor and sources of credit and other financial services were available within the community. The Jewish American enclave grew and provided a livelihood for many of the children and grandchildren of the immigrants (Portes & Manning, 1986). As has been the case with other enclave groups that we will discuss in future chapters, including Chinese Americans and Cuban Americans, economic advancement preceded extensive acculturation, and Jewish Americans made significant strides toward economic equality before they became fluent in English or were otherwise Americanized.

One obvious way in which an enclave immigrant group can improve its position is to develop an educated and acculturated second generation. The Americanized, English-speaking children of the Jewish immigrants used their greater familiarity with the dominant society and their language facility to help preserve and expand the family enterprise. Furthermore, as the second generation appeared, the American public school system was expanding, and education through the college level was free or inexpensive in New York City and other cities (Steinberg, 1981). There was also a strong push for the second and third generations to enter professions, but as Jewish Americans excelled in school, resistance to and discrimination against them increased. By the 1920s, many elite colleges and universities, such as Dartmouth, had established quotas that limited the number of Jewish students they would admit (Dinnerstein, 1977). These quotas were not abolished until after World War II.

The enclave economy and the Jewish neighborhoods established by the immigrants proved to be an effective base from which to integrate into American society. The descendants of the Eastern European Jewish immigrants gradually moved out of the ethnic neighborhoods, and their positions in the economy—their pushcarts, stores, and jobs in the garment industry—were taken over by more recent immigrants. When they left the enclave economy, many second- and third-generation Eastern European Jews did not enter the mainstream occupational structure at the bottom, as the immigrant laborer groups tended to do. They used the resources generated by the entrepreneurship of the early generations to gain access to prestigious and advantaged social class positions (Portes & Manning, 1986). As a group, studies show that Jewish Americans today surpass national averages in income, levels of education, and occupational prestige (Sklare, 1971; see also S. Cohen, 1985; Massarik & Chenkin, 1973). The relatively higher status of Russian Americans shown in Exhibits 2.6 and 2.7 is due in part to the fact that many Jewish Americans are of Russian descent.

Chains of Immigration

All of the immigrant groups tended to follow "chains" established and maintained by the members of their groups. Some versions of the traditional assimilation perspective (especially human capital theory) treat immigration and status attainment as purely individual (psychological) matters. To the contrary, scholars have demonstrated that immigration to the United States was in large measure a group (sociological) phenomenon. Immigrant chains stretched across the oceans and were held together by the ties of kinship, language, religion, culture, and a sense of common peoplehood (Bodnar, 1985; Tilly, 1990). The networks supplied information, money for passage, family news, and job offers.

Here is how chain immigration worked (and continues to work today): Someone from a village in, say, Poland, would make it to the United States. The successful immigrant would send word to the home village, perhaps by hiring a letter writer. Along with news and stories of his adventures, he would send his address. Within months, another immigrant from the village, perhaps a brother or other relative, would show up at the address of the original immigrant. After his months of experience in the new society, the original immigrant could lend assistance, provide a place to sleep, help with job hunting, and orient the newcomer to the area.

Before long, others would arrive from the village in need of the same sort of introduction to the mysteries of America. The compatriots would tend to settle close to one another, in the same building or on the same block. Soon, entire neighborhoods were filled with people from a certain village, province, or region. In these ethnic enclaves, the old language was spoken and the old ways observed. Businesses were started, churches or synagogues were founded, families were begun, and mutual aid societies and other organizations were formed. There was safety in numbers and comfort and security in a familiar, if transplanted, set of traditions and customs.

Immigrants often responded to U.S. society by attempting to recreate as much of their old world as possible. Partly to avoid the harsher forms of rejection and discrimination and partly to band together for solidarity and mutual support, immigrants created their own miniature social worlds within the bustling metropolises of the industrializing Northeast and the West Coast. These Little Italys, Little Warsaws, Little Irelands, Greektowns, Chinatowns, and Little Tokyos were safe havens that insulated the immigrants from the larger society and allowed them to establish bonds with one another, organize a group life, pursue their own group interests, and have some control over the pace of their adjustment to American culture. For some groups and in some areas, the ethnic subcommunity was a short-lived phenomenon. For others (the Jewish enclave discussed earlier, for example), the neighborhood became the dominant structure of their lives, and the networks continued to function long after their arrival in the United States.

The Campaign Against Immigration: Prejudice, Racism, and Discrimination

Today, it may be hard to conceive of the bitterness and intensity of the prejudice that greeted the Irish, Italians, Poles, Jews, and other new immigrant groups. Even as they were becoming an indispensable segment of the American workforce, they were castigated, ridiculed, attacked, and disparaged. The Irish were the first immigrant laborers to arrive and thus the first to feel this intense prejudice and discrimination. Campaigns against immigrants were waged, Irish neighborhoods were attacked by mobs, and Roman Catholic churches and convents were burned. Some employers blatantly refused to hire the Irish, often advertising their ethnic preferences with signs that read "No Irish Need Apply." Until later arriving groups pushed them up, the Irish were mired at the bottom of the job market. Indeed, at one time they were referred to as the "niggers of Boston" (Blessing, 1980; Potter, 1973; Shannon, 1964).

Other groups felt the same sting of rejection as they arrived. Italian immigrants were particularly likely to be the victims of violent attacks, one of the most vicious of which took place in New Orleans in 1891. The city's police chief had been assassinated, and rumors of Italian involvement in the murder were rampant. Hundreds of Italians were arrested, and nine were brought to trial. All were acquitted. However, anti-Italian sentiment was running so high that a mob lynched 11 Italians while police and city officials did nothing to stop it (Higham, 1963).

Anti-Catholicism

Much of the prejudice against the Irish and the new immigrants was expressed as anti-Catholicism. Prior to the mid-19th century, Anglo-American society had been almost exclusively Protestant. Catholicism, with its celibate clergy, Latin masses, and cloistered nuns, seemed alien, exotic, and threatening. The growth of Catholicism, especially because it was associated with non-Anglo immigrants, raised fears that the Protestant religions would lose status. There were even rumors that the Pope was planning to move the Vatican to America and organize a takeover of the U.S. government.

Although Catholics were often stereotyped as a single group, they varied along a number of dimensions. For example, the Catholic faith as practiced in Ireland differed significantly from that practiced in Italy, Poland, and other countries. Catholic immigrant groups often established their own parishes, with priests who could speak the old language. These cultural and national differences often separated Catholic groups, despite their common faith (Herberg, 1960).

Anti-Semitism

Jews from Russia and other countries of Eastern Europe faced intense prejudice and racism (or **anti-Semitism**) as they began arriving in large numbers in the 1880s. Biased sentiments and negative stereotypes of Jews have been a part of Western culture for centuries and, in fact, have been stronger and more vicious in Europe than in the United States. For nearly two millennia, European Jews have been chastised and persecuted as the "killers of Christ" and stereotyped as materialistic moneylenders and crafty businessmen. The stereotype that links Jews and moneylending has its origins in the fact that in premodern Europe, Catholics were forbidden by the church to engage in usury (charging interest for loans). Jews were under no such restriction, and they filled the gap thus created in the economy. The ultimate episode in the long history of European anti-Semitism was, of course, the Nazi Holocaust, in which 6 million Jews died. European anti-Semitism did not end with the demise of the Nazi regime, however, and it remains a concern throughout Europe and Russia.

Before the mass immigration of Eastern European Jews began in the late 19th century, anti-Semitism in the United States was relatively mild, perhaps because the number of Jews was so small. As the immigration continued, anti-Jewish prejudice increased in intensity and viciousness, fostering the view of Jews as cunning but dishonest merchants. In the late 19th century, Jews started to be banned from social clubs and the boardrooms of businesses and other organizations. Summer resorts began posting notices saying, "We prefer not to entertain Hebrews" (Goren, 1980).

By the 1920s and 1930s, anti-Semitism had become quite prominent among American prejudices and was being preached by the Ku Klux Klan and other extreme racist groups. Also, because many of the political radicals and labor leaders of the time were Jewish immigrants, anti-Semitism became fused with a fear of communism and other anti-capitalist doctrines. Some prominent Americans espoused anti-Semitic views, among them Henry Ford, the founder of Ford Motor Company; Charles Lindbergh, the aviator who was the first to fly solo across the Atlantic; and Father Charles Coughlin, a Catholic priest with a popular radio show (Selzer, 1972).

Anti-Semitism in the United States reached a peak before World War II and tapered off in the decades following the war, but it remains part of U.S. society (Anti-Defamation League, 2000). Anti-Semitism also has a prominent place in the ideologies of a variety of extremist groups that have emerged in recent years, including "skinheads" and various contemporary incarnations of the Ku Klux Klan. Some of this targeting of Jews seems to increase during economic recessions and may be related to the stereotypical view of Jewish Americans as extremely prosperous and materialistic.

A Successful Exclusion

The prejudice and racism directed against the immigrants also found expression in organized, widespread efforts to stop the flow of immigration. A variety of anti-immigrant organizations appeared almost as soon as the mass European immigration started in the 1820s. The strength of these campaigns waxed and waned, largely in harmony with the strength of the economy and the size of the job supply. Anti-immigrant sentiment increased in intensity, and the strength of its organized expressions grew during hard times and depressions and tended to soften when the economy improved. The campaign ultimately triumphed with the passage of the National Origins Act in 1924. This act drastically reduced the overall number of immigrants that would be admitted into the United States each year. The effectiveness of the numerical restrictions is clearly apparent in Exhibit 2.3.

The National Origins Act established a quota system that limited the number of immigrants that would be accepted each year from each sending nation, a system that was openly racist. For example, the size of the quota for European nations was based on the proportional representation of each nationality in the United States as of 1890. This year was chosen because it predated the bulk of the New Immigration and gave the most generous quotas to Northern and Western European nations. Immigration from Western Hemisphere nations was not directly affected by this legislation, but immigration from Asian nations was banned altogether. At this time, almost all of Africa was still a colonial possession of various European nations and received no separate quotas. In other words, the quota for immigrants from Africa was zero.

The result was that the quota system allocated nearly 70% of the available immigration slots to the nations of Northern and Western Europe, despite the fact that immigration to the United States from those areas had largely ended by the 1920s. The National Origins Act was very effective, and by the time the Great Depression took hold of the American economy, immigration had dropped to the lowest level in a century (see Exhibit 2.3). The National Origins Act remained in effect until 1965.

Patterns of Assimilation

In this subsection, we will explore some of the common patterns in the process of assimilation followed by European immigrants and their descendants. These patterns have been well established by research conducted in the traditional perspective and are consistent with the model of assimilation developed by Gordon. They include assimilation by generation, ethnic succession, and structural mobility. Each of these will be discussed separately.

The Importance of Generations

People today—social scientists, politicians, and ordinary citizens—often fail to recognize the time and effort it takes for a group to become completely Americanized. For most European immigrant groups, the process took generations, and it was the grandchildren or the great-grandchildren (or even great-great-grandchildren) of the immigrants who finally completed acculturation and integration. Mass immigration from Europe ended in the 1920s, but the assimilation of some European ethnic groups was not completed until late in the 20th century.

Here is a rough summary of how assimilation proceeded for these European immigrants: The first generation, the actual immigrants, settled in ethnic neighborhoods, such as "Little Italy" in New York City, and made only limited movement toward acculturation and integration. They focused their energies on the network of family and social relationships encompassed within their own groups. Of course, many of them—most often the men—had to leave their neighborhoods for work and other reasons, and these excursions required some familiarity with the larger society. Some English had to be learned, and taking a job outside the neighborhood is, almost by definition, a form of integration. Nonetheless, the first generation lived and died largely within the context of the Old Country, which had been recreated within the new.

The second generation, or the children of the immigrants, found themselves in a position of psychological or social marginality: They were partly ethnic and partly American but full members of neither group. They were born in America but in households and neighborhoods that were ethnic, not American. They learned the old language first and were socialized in the old ways. As they began their childhood, however, they entered the public schools, where they were socialized into the Anglo-American culture.

Very often, the world the second generation learned about at school conflicted with the world they inhabited at home. For example, the Old Country family values often dictated that children subordinate their self-interests to the interests of their elders and of the family as a whole. Marriages were arranged by parents, or at least were heavily influenced by and subject to their approval. Needless to say, these expectations conflicted sharply with American ideas about individualism and romantic love. Differences of this sort often caused painful conflict between the ethnic first generation and their Americanized children.

As the second generation progressed toward adulthood, they tended to move out of the old neighborhoods. Their geographic mobility was often motivated by social mobility. They were much more acculturated than their parents, spoke English fluently, and enjoyed a wider range of occupational choices and opportunities. Discriminatory policies in education, housing, and the job market sometimes limited them, but they were upwardly mobile, and in their pursuit of jobs and careers, they left behind the ethnic subcommunity and many of the customs of their parents.

The members of the third generation, or the grandchildren of the immigrants, were typically born and raised in non-ethnic settings. English was their first (and often their only) language, and their values and perceptions were thoroughly American. Although family and kinship ties with grandparents and the old neighborhood often remained strong, ethnicity for this generation was a relatively minor part of their daily realities and their self-images. Visits on weekends and holidays and family rituals revolving around the cycles of birth, marriage, and death—these activities might have connected the third generation to the world of their ancestors, but in terms of their everyday lives, they were American, not ethnic.

To summarize, the pattern of assimilation by generation progressed as follows:

- The first generation began the process and was at least slightly acculturated and integrated.
- The second generation was very acculturated and highly integrated (at least into the secondary sectors of the society).
- The third generation finished the acculturation process and enjoyed high levels of integration at both the secondary and the primary levels.

Exhibit 2.4 illustrates these patterns in terms of the structural assimilation of Italian Americans. The educational and occupational characteristics of this group converge with those of white Anglo-Saxon Protestants as the generations change. For example, the percentage of Italian Americans with some college shows a gap of more than 20 points between the first and second generations and WASPs. Italians of the third and fourth generations, though, are virtually identical to WASPs on this measure of integration in the secondary sector. The other differences between Italians and WASPs shrink in a similar fashion from generation to generation.

Exhibit 2.4 Some Comparisons Between Italians and WASPs

		Generation		
	WASPs*	First	Second	Third and Fourth
Percentage with some college	42.4%	19.0%	19.4%	41.7%
Average years of education	12.6	9.0	11.1	13.4
Percentage white collar	34.7	20.0	22.5	28.8
Percentage blue collar	37.9	65.0	53.9	39.0
Average occupational prestige	42.5	34.3	36.8	42.5
Percentage of "unmixed" Italian males marrying non-Italian females		21.9	51.4	67.3

SOURCE: Adapted from Alba (1985, Tables 5.3, 5.4, and 6.2). Data are originally from the NORC General Social Surveys, 1975–1980, and the Current Population Survey, 1979. Copyright © 1985 Richard D. Alba. Reprinted by permission.

*White Anglo-Saxon Protestants (WASPs) were not separated by generation, and some of the differences between groups may be the result of factors such as age. That is, older WASPs may have levels of education more comparable to first-generation Italian Americans than WASPs as a whole.

The first five measures of educational and occupational attainment in Exhibit 2.4 illustrate the generational pattern of integration (structural assimilation). The last comparison measures marital assimilation, or intermarriage. It displays the percentage of males of "unmixed," or 100%, Italian heritage who married females outside the Italian community. Note once more the tendency for integration, now at the primary level, to increase across the generations. The huge majority of first-generation males married within their group (only 21.9% married non-Italians). By the third generation, 67.3% of the males were marrying non-Italians.

Of course, this model of step-by-step, linear assimilation by generation fits some groups better than others. For example, immigrants from Northern and Western Europe (except for the Irish) were generally more similar, racially and culturally, to the dominant group and tended to be more educated and skilled. They experienced relatively easier acceptance and tended to complete the assimilation process in three generations or less. In contrast, immigrants from Ireland and from Southern and Eastern Europe were mostly uneducated, unskilled peasants who were more likely to join the huge army of industrial labor that manned the factories, mines, and mills. These groups were more likely to remain at the bottom of the American class structure for generations and to have risen to middle-class prosperity only in the recent past. As mentioned earlier, Eastern European Jews formed an enclave and followed a distinctly different pathway of assimilation, using the enclave as a springboard to launch the second and third generations into the larger society (although their movements were circumscribed by widespread anti-Semitic sentiments and policies).

It is important to keep this generational pattern in mind when examining immigration to the United States today. It is common for contemporary newcomers (especially Hispanics) to be criticized for their "slow" pace of assimilation, but their "progress" takes on a new aspect when viewed in the light of the generational time frame for assimilation followed by European immigrants. Especially with modern forms of transportation, immigration can be very fast. Assimilation, on the other hand, is by nature slow.

Ethnic Succession

A second factor that shaped the assimilation experience is captured in the concept of **ethnic succession,** or the myriad ways in which European ethnic groups unintentionally affected each other's position in the social class structure of the larger society. The overall pattern was that each European immigrant group tended to be pushed to higher social class levels and more favorable economic situations by the groups that arrived after them. As more experienced groups became upwardly mobile and began to move out of the neighborhoods that served as their "ports of entry," they were often replaced by a new group of immigrants who would begin the process all over again. Some neighborhoods in the cities of the Northeast served as the ethnic neighborhood—the first safe haven in the new society—for a variety of successive groups. Some of them continue to fill this role today.

This process can be understood in terms of the second stage of Gordon's model: integration at the secondary level (see Exhibit 2.1), or entry into the public institution and organizations of the larger society. Three pathways of integration tended to be most important for European immigrants: politics, labor unions, and the church. We will cover each in turn, illustrating with the Irish, the first immigrant laborers to arrive in large numbers, but the general patterns apply to all white ethnic groups.

Politics. The Irish tended to follow the Northern and Western Europeans in the job market and social class structure and were, in turn, followed by the wave of new immigrants. In many urban areas of the Northeast, the Irish moved into the neighborhoods and took jobs left behind by German laborers. After a period of acculturation and adjustment, the Irish began to create their own connections with the mainstream society and improve their economic and social position. They were replaced in their neighborhoods and at the bottom of the occupational structure by Italians, Poles, and other immigrant groups arriving after them.

As the years passed and the Irish gained more experience, they began to forge more links to the larger society, and, in particular, the Irish allied themselves with the Democratic Party and helped to construct the political machines that came to dominate many city governments in the 19th and 20th centuries. *Machine politicians* were often corrupt and even criminal, regularly subverting the election process, bribing city and state officials, using city budgets to fill the pockets of the political bosses and their cronies, and passing out public jobs as payoffs for favors and faithful service. Although not exactly models of good government, the political machines performed a number of valuable social services for their constituents and loyal followers. Machine politicians, such as Boss Tweed of Tammany Hall in New York City, could find people jobs, provide food and clothing for the destitute, aid victims of fires and other calamities, and intervene in the criminal and civil courts.

Much of the power of the urban political machines derived from their control of the city payroll. The leaders of the machines used municipal jobs and the city budget as part of a "spoils" system (as in "to the winner go the spoils") and as rewards for their supporters and allies. The faithful Irish party worker might be rewarded for service to the machine with a job in the police department (thus the stereotypical Irish cop) or some other agency. Private businessmen might be rewarded with lucrative contracts to supply services or perform other city business.

The political machines served as engines of economic opportunity and linked Irish Americans to a central and important institution of the dominant society. Using the resources controlled by local government as a power base, the Irish (and other immigrant groups after them) began to integrate themselves into the larger society and carve out a place in the mainstream structures of American society.

Labor unions. The labor movement provided a second link between the Irish, as well as other European immigrant groups, and the larger society. Although virtually all white ethnic groups had a hand in the creation and eventual success of the movement, many of the founders and early leaders were Irish. For example, Terence Powderly, an Irish Catholic, founded one of the first U.S. labor unions, and in the early years of the 20th century, about one-third of union leaders were Irish, and more than 50 national unions had Irish presidents (Bodnar, 1985, p. 111; Brody, 1980, p. 615).

As the labor movement grew in strength and gradually acquired legitimacy, the leaders of the movement also gained status, power, and other resources, while the rank-and-file membership gained job security, increased wages, and better fringe benefits. The labor movement provided another channel through which resources, power, status, and jobs flowed to the white ethnic groups.

Because of the way in which jobs were organized in industrializing America, union work typically required communication and cooperation across ethnic lines. The American workforce at the turn of the 20th century was multiethnic and multilingual, and union leaders had to coordinate and mobilize the efforts of many different language and cultural groups to represent the interests of the workers as a social class. Thus, labor union leaders became important intermediaries between the larger society and European immigrant groups.

Women were also heavily involved in the labor movement. Immigrant women were among the most exploited segments of the labor force, and they were involved in some of the most significant events in American labor history. For example, one of the first victories of the union movement occurred in New York City in 1909. The "Uprising of the 20,000" was a massive strike of mostly Jewish and Italian women (many in their teens) against the garment industry. The strike lasted 4 months despite attacks by thugs hired by the bosses and abuses by the police and the courts.

The strikers eventually won recognition of the union from many employers, a reversal of a wage decrease, and a reduction in the 56- to 59-hour week they were expected to work (Goren, 1980).

One of the great tragedies in the history of labor relations in the United States also involved European immigrant women. In 1911, a fire swept through the Triangle Shirtwaist Company, a garment industry shop located on the 10th floor of a building in New York City. The fire spread rapidly, and the few escape routes were quickly cut off. About 140 young immigrant girls died, and many chose to leap to their deaths rather than be consumed by the flames. The disaster outraged the public, and the funerals of the victims were attended by more than a quarter of a million people. The incident fueled a drive for reform and improvement of work conditions and safety regulations (Amott & Matthaei, 1991; see also Schoener, 1967).

European immigrant women also filled leadership roles in the labor movement serving as presidents and in other offices, although usually in female-dominated unions. One of the most colorful union activists was Mother Jones, an Irish immigrant who worked tirelessly to organize miners:

> Until she was nearly one hundred years old, Mother Jones was where the danger was greatest—crossing militia lines, spending weeks in damp prisons, incurring the wrath of governors, presidents, and coal operators—she helped to organize the United Mine Workers with the only tools she felt she needed: "convictions and a voice." (Forner, 1980, p. 281)

Women workers often faced opposition from men as well as from employers. The major unions were not only racially discriminatory but also hostile to organizing women. For example, women laundry workers in San Francisco at the start of the 20th century were required to live in dormitories and work from 6 a.m. until midnight. When they applied to the international laundry workers union for a charter, they were blocked by the male members. They eventually went on strike and won the right to an 8-hour workday in 1912 (Amott & Matthaei, 1991, p. 117).

Religion. A third avenue of mobility for the Irish and other white ethnic groups was provided by the religious institution. The Irish were the first large group of Catholic immigrants and were thus in a favorable position to eventually dominate the Church's administrative structure. The Catholic priesthood became largely Irish, and as they were promoted through the hierarchy, these priests became bishops and cardinals. The Catholic faith was practiced in different ways in different nations. As other Catholic immigrant groups began to arrive, conflict within the Irish-dominated Church increased. Both Italian and Polish Catholic immigrants demanded their own parishes in which they could speak their own languages and celebrate their own customs and festivals. Dissatisfaction was so intense that some Polish Catholics broke with Rome and formed a separate Polish National Catholic Church (Lopata, 1976).

The other Catholic immigrant groups eventually began to supply priests and other religious functionaries and to occupy leadership positions within the Church. Although the Church continued to be disproportionately influenced by the Irish, other white ethnic groups also used the Catholic Church as part of their power bases for gaining acceptance and integration into the larger society.

Other pathways. Besides party politics, the union movement, and religion, European immigrant groups forged other not-so-legitimate pathways of upward mobility. One alternative to legitimate success was offered by crime, a pathway that has been used by every ethnic group to some extent. Crime became particularly lucrative and attractive when *Prohibition,* the attempt to eliminate all alcohol use in the United States, went into effect in the 1920s. The criminalization of liquor failed to lower the demand, and Prohibition created a golden economic opportunity for those willing to take the risks involved in manufacturing and supplying alcohol to the American public.

Italian Americans headed many of the criminal organizations that took advantage of Prohibition. Criminal leaders and organizations with roots in Sicily, a region with a long history of secret anti-establishment societies, were especially important (Alba, 1985). The connections among organized crime, Prohibition, and Italian Americans are well-known, but it is not so widely recognized that ethnic succession operated in organized crime as it did in the legitimate opportunity structures. The Irish and Germans had been involved in organized crime for decades before the 1920s, and the Italians competed with these established gangsters and with Jewish crime syndicates for control of bootlegging and other criminal enterprises. The pattern of ethnic succession continued after the repeal of Prohibition, and members of groups newer to urban areas, including African Americans, Jamaicans, and Hispanic Americans, have recently challenged the Italian-dominated criminal "families."

Ethnic succession can also be observed in the institution of sports. Since the beginning of the 20th century, sports have offered a pathway to success and affluence that has attracted countless millions of young men and more recently, women. Success in many sports requires little in the way of formal credentials, education, or English fluency, and sports have been particularly appealing to the young members of minority groups that have few resources or opportunities.

For example, at the turn of the century, the Irish dominated the sport of boxing, but boxers from the Italian American community and other new immigrant groups eventually replaced them. Each successive wave of boxers reflected the concentration of a particular ethnic group at the bottom of the class structure. The succession of minority groups continues to this day, with boxing now dominated by African American and Latino fighters (Rader, 1983). A similar progression, or "layering," of ethnic and racial groups can be observed in other sports and in the entertainment industry.

The institutions of American society, both legitimate and illegal, reflect the relative positions of minority groups at a particular moment in time. Just a few generations ago, European immigrant groups dominated both crime and sports because they were blocked from legitimate opportunities. Now, the racial minority groups still excluded from the mainstream job market and mired in the urban underclass are supplying disproportionate numbers of young people to these alternative opportunity structures.

Continuing Industrialization and Structural Mobility

I have already mentioned that dominant–minority relations tend to change along with changes in subsistence technology, and we can find an example of this process in the history of European immigrant groups across the 20th century. Industrialization is a continuous process, and as it proceeded, the nature of work in America evolved and changed and created opportunities for upward mobility for the white ethnic groups. One important form of upward mobility throughout the 20th century, called **structural mobility,** resulted more from changes in the structure of the economy and the labor market than from any individual effort or desire to "get ahead."

Structural mobility is the result of the continuing mechanization and automation of the workplace. As machines replaced people in the workforce, the supply of manual, blue-collar jobs that had provided employment for so many first- and second-generation European immigrant laborers dwindled. At the same time, the supply of white-collar jobs increased, but access to the better jobs depended heavily on educational credentials. For white ethnic groups, a high school education became much more available in the 1930s, and college and university programs began to expand rapidly in the late 1940s, spurred in large part by the educational benefits made available to World War II veterans. Each generation of white ethnics, especially those born after 1925, was significantly more educated than its parents, and many were able to translate that increased human capital into upward mobility in the mainstream job market (Morawska, 1990).

The descendants of European immigrants became upwardly mobile not only because of their ambitions and efforts, but also because of the changing location of jobs and the progressively greater opportunities for education available to them. Of course, the pace and timing of this upward movement was highly variable from group to group and place to place. Ethnic succession continued to operate, and the descendants of the most recent immigrants from Europe (Italians and Poles, for example) tended to be the last to benefit from the general upgrading in education and the job market. Still, structural mobility is one of the keys to the eventual successful integration of all white ethnic groups shown in Exhibits 2.6 and 2.7. During these same years, the racial minority groups, particularly African Americans, were excluded from the dominant group's educational system and from the opportunity to compete for better jobs.

Variations in Assimilation

In the previous subsection, we discussed patterns that were common to European immigrants and their descendants. Now we address some of the sources of variation and diversity in assimilation, a complex process that is never exactly the same for any two groups. Sociologists have paid particular attention to the way that degree of similarity, religion, social class, and gender shaped the overall assimilation of the descendants of the mass European immigration. They have also investigated the way in which immigrants' reasons for coming to this country have affected the experiences of different groups.

Degree of Similarity

Since the dominant group consisted largely of Protestants with ethnic origins in Northern and Western Europe and especially in England, it is not surprising to learn that the degree of resistance, prejudice, and discrimination encountered by the different European immigrant groups varied in part by the degree to which they differed from these dominant group characteristics. The most significant differences related to religion, language, cultural values, and—for some groups—physical characteristics. Thus, Protestant immigrants from Northern and Western Europe experienced less resistance than the English-speaking Catholic Irish, who in turn were accepted more readily than the new immigrants, who were both non-English speaking and overwhelmingly non-Protestant.

The preferences of the dominant group correspond roughly to the arrival times of the immigrants. The most similar groups immigrated earliest, and the least similar tended to be the last to arrive. Because of this coincidence, resistance to any one group of immigrants tended to fade as new groups arrived. For example, anti-German prejudice and discrimination never became particularly vicious or widespread (except during the heat of the World Wars), because the Irish began arriving in large numbers at about the same time. Concerns about the German immigrants were swamped by the fear that the Catholic Irish could never be assimilated. Then, as the 19th century drew to a close, immigrants from Southern and Eastern Europe—even more different from the dominant group—began to arrive and made concerns about the Irish seem trivial.

In addition, the New Immigration was far more voluminous than the Old Immigration (see Exhibit 2.3). Southern and Eastern Europeans arrived in record numbers in the early 20th century, and the sheer volume of the immigration raised fears that American cities and institutions would be swamped by hordes of what were seen as racially inferior, unassimilable immigrants (a fear with strong echoes in the present).

Thus, a preference hierarchy was formed in American culture that privileged Northern and Western Europeans over Southern and Eastern Europeans and Protestants over Catholics and Jews. These rankings reflect the ease with which the groups have been assimilated and made their way into the larger society. This hierarchy of ethnic preference is still a part of American prejudice and white racial identity, as we saw in social distance scale results in Exhibit 1.7, although it is much more muted today than in the heyday of immigration.

Religion

A major differentiating factor in the experiences of the European immigrant groups, recognized by Gordon and other students of American assimilation, was religion. Protestant, Catholic, and Jewish immigrants lived in different neighborhoods, occupied different niches in the workforce, formed separate networks of affiliation and groups, and chose their marriage partners from different pools of people.

One important study that documented the importance of religion for European immigrants and their descendants (and also reinforced the importance of generations) was conducted by sociologist Ruby Jo Kennedy (1944). She studied intermarriage patterns in New Haven, Connecticut, over a 70-year period ending in the 1940s and found that the immigrant generation chose marriage partners from a pool whose boundaries were marked by ethnicity and religion. For example, Irish Catholics married other Irish Catholics, Italian Catholics married Italian Catholics, Irish Protestants married Irish Protestants, and so forth across all the ethnic and religious divisions she studied.

The pool of marriage partners for the children and grandchildren of the immigrants continued to be bounded by religion but not so much by ethnicity. Thus, later generations of Irish Catholics continued to marry other Catholics but were less likely to marry other Irish. As assimilation proceeded, ethnic group boundaries faded (or "melted"), but religious boundaries did not. Kennedy described this phenomenon as a **triple melting pot:** a pattern of structural assimilation within each of the three religious denominations (Kennedy, 1944, 1952).

Will Herberg (1960), another important student of American assimilation, also explored the connection between religion and ethnicity. Writing in the 1950s, he noted that the pressures of acculturation did not affect all aspects of ethnicity equally. European immigrants and their descendants were strongly encouraged to learn English, but they were not so pressured to change their religious beliefs. Very often, their religious faith was the strongest connection between later generations and their immigrant ancestors. The American tradition of religious tolerance allowed the descendants of the European immigrants to preserve this tie to their roots without being seen as "un-American." As a result, the Protestant, Catholic, and Jewish faiths eventually came to occupy roughly equal degrees of legitimacy in American society.

Thus, for the descendants of the European immigrants, religion became a vehicle through which their ethnicity could be expressed. For many members of this group, religion and ethnicity were fused, and ethnic traditions and identities came to have a religious expression.

Social Class

Social class is a central feature of social structure, and it is not surprising that it affected the European immigrant groups in a number of ways. First, social class combined with religion to shape the social world of their descendants. In fact, Gordon (1964) concluded that U.S. society in the 1960s actually incorporated not three, but four melting pots (one for each of the major ethnic/religious groups and one for black Americans), each of which was internally subdivided by social class. In his view, the most significant structural unit within American society was the **ethclass,** defined by the intersection of the religious, ethnic, and social class boundaries (e.g., working-class Irish Catholic, upper-class German Protestant, etc.). Thus, people were not "simply American," but tended to identify with, associate with, and choose their spouses from within their ethclass.

Second, social class affected structural integration. The huge majority of the post-1880s European immigrants were working class, and because they "entered U.S. society at the bottom of the economic ladder, and . . . stayed close to that level for the next half century, ethnic history has been essentially working class history" (Morawska, 1990, p. 215; see also Bodnar, 1985). For generations, many groups of Eastern and Southern European immigrants did not acculturate to middle-class American culture, but to an urban working-class, blue-collar set of lifestyles and values. Even today, ethnicity for many groups remains interconnected with social class factors—a familiar stereotype of white ethnicity is the hard-hat construction worker.

Gender

Anyone who wants to learn about the experience of immigration will find a huge body of literature incorporating every imaginable discipline and genre. The great bulk of this material, however, concerns the immigrant experience in general or focuses specifically on male immigrants. The experiences of female immigrants have been much less recorded and hence far less accessible. Many immigrant women came from cultures with strong patriarchal traditions, and they had far less access to leadership roles; education; and prestigious, high-paying occupations. As is the case with women of virtually all minority groups, the voices of immigrant women have been muted. The research that has been done, however, documents that immigrant women played multiple roles both during immigration and during the assimilation process. As would be expected in patriarchal societies, the roles of wife and mother were central, but immigrant women were involved in myriad other activities as well.

In general, male immigrants tended to precede women, and it was common for the males to send for the women only after they had secured lodging, jobs, and a certain level of stability. However, female immigrants' experiences were quite varied, often depending on the economic situation and cultural traditions of their home society. In some cases, women were not only prominent among the "first wave" of immigrants but also began the process of acculturation and integration. During the 19th century, for example, a high percentage of Irish immigrants were young single women. They came to America seeking jobs and often wound up employed in domestic work, a role that permitted them to live "respectably" in a family setting. In 1850, about 75% of all employed Irish immigrant women in New York City worked as servants, and the rest were employed in textile mills and factories. As late as 1920, an estimated 81% of employed Irish-born women in the United States worked as domestics. Factory work was the second most prevalent form of employment (Blessing, 1980; see also Steinberg, 1981).

Because the economic situation of immigrant families was typically precarious, it was common for women to be involved in wage labor. The type and location of the work varied from group to group. Whereas Irish women were concentrated in domestic work and factories and mills, this was rare for Italian women. Italian culture had strong norms of patriarchy, and "one of the culture's strongest prohibitions was directed against contact between women and male strangers" (Alba, 1985, p. 53). Thus, acceptable work situations for Italian women were likely to involve tasks that could be done at home: doing laundry, taking in boarders, and doing piecework for the garment industry. Italian women who worked outside the home were likely to find themselves in single-sex settings among other immigrant women. Thus, female immigrants from Italy tended to be far less acculturated and integrated than those from Ireland.

Eastern European Jewish women represent a third pattern of assimilation. They were refugees from religious persecution, and most came with their husbands and children in intact family units. According to Steinberg (1981), "Few were independent bread-winners, and when they did work, they usually found employment in the . . . garment industry. Often they worked in small shops as family members" (p. 161).

Generally, immigrant women, like working-class women in general, were expected to work until they married, after which time it was expected that their husbands would support them and their children. In many cases, however, immigrant men could not earn enough to support their families, and their wives and children were required by necessity to contribute to the family budget. Immigrant wives sometimes worked outside the home, or they found other ways to make money. They took in boarders, did laundry or sewing, tended gardens, and were involved in myriad other activities that permitted them to contribute to the family budget and still stay home and attend to family and child-rearing responsibilities. A 1911 report on Southern and Eastern European immigrant households found that about half kept lodgers and that the income from this activity amounted to about 25% of the husbands' wages. Children also contributed to the family income by taking after-school and summertime jobs. Compared with the men, immigrant women were more closely connected to home and family, less likely to learn to read or speak English or otherwise acculturate, and significantly more influential in preserving the heritage of their groups (Morawska, 1990, pp. 211–212).

When they sought employment outside the home, they found opportunities in the industrial sector and in clerical and sales work, occupations that were quickly stereotyped as "women's work." Women were seen as working only to supplement the family treasury, and this assumption was used to justify a lower wage scale. Sara Evans (1989) reports that in the late 1800s, "Whether in factories, offices, or private homes . . . women's wages were about half those of men" (p. 135).

Sojourners

Some versions of the traditional perspective and the "taken for granted" views of many Americans assume that assimilation is desirable and therefore desired. However, immigrant groups from Europe were highly variable in their interest in Americanization, a factor that greatly shaped their experiences.

Some groups were very committed to Americanization. Eastern European Jews, for example, came to America because of religious persecution and planned to make America their home from the beginning. They left their homeland in fear for their lives and had no plans and no possibility of returning. They intended to stay, for they had nowhere else to go. (The nation of Israel was not founded until 1948.) These immigrants committed themselves to learning English, becoming citizens, and familiarizing themselves with their new society as quickly as possible.

Other immigrants had no intention of becoming American citizens and therefore had little interest in Americanization. These **sojourners,** or "birds of passage," were oriented to the Old Country and intended to return once they had accumulated enough capital to be successful in their home villages or provinces. Because immigration records are not very detailed, it is difficult to assess the exact numbers of immigrants who returned to the Old Country (see Wyman, 1993). We do know, for example, that a large percentage of Italian immigrants were sojourners. It is estimated that although 3.8 million Italians landed in the United States between 1899 and 1924, around 2.1 million departed during the same interval (Nelli, 1980, p. 547).

The Descendants of European Immigrants Today

Geographical Distribution

Exhibit 2.5 shows the geographical distribution of 8 racial and ethnic groups across the United States. The map displays the single largest group in each state.

Exhibit 2.5 Largest Ancestry, 2000

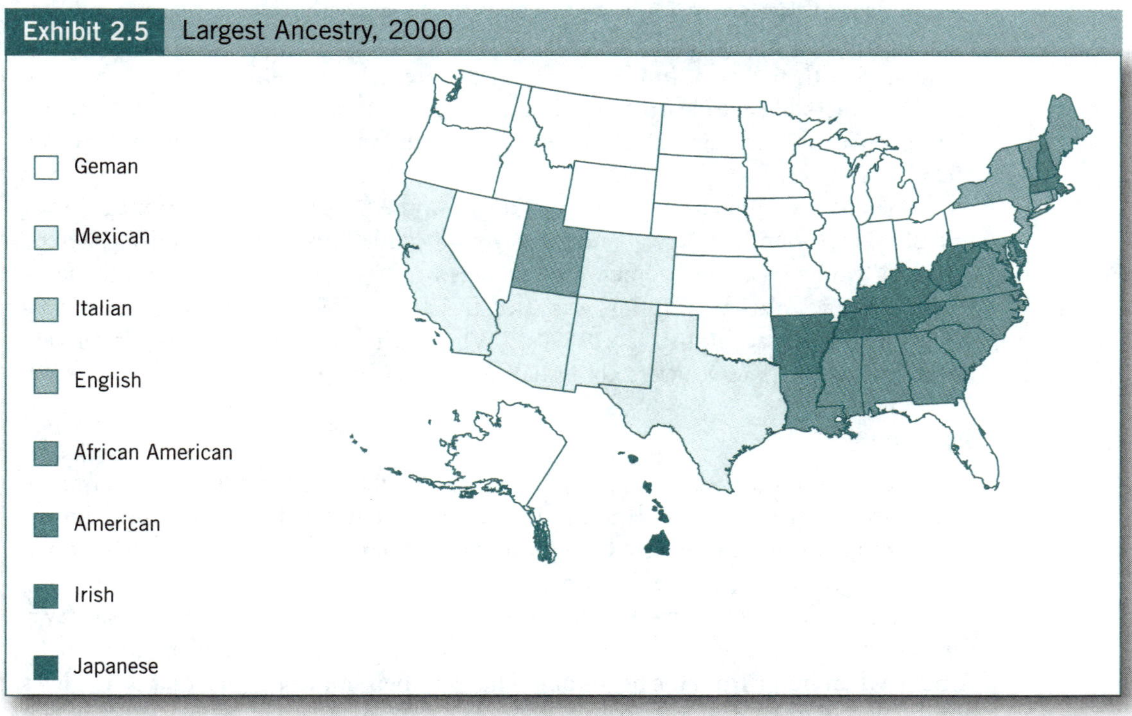

SOURCE: U.S. Bureau of the Census (2004a).

NOTE: People who choose "American" are a mixture of Scots-Irish and many other Caucasian groups.

First of all, the single largest ancestry group in the United States is German American, and this is reflected on the map by the predominance of white from Pennsylvania to the west coast. This pattern reflects their original settlement in the Midwest and east Texas, among other places. Although the map does not show it, Norwegian and Swedish Americans are also predominant in some areas of the upper Midwest, particularly in Minnesota and the Dakotas. Irish Americans and Italian Americans are also concentrated in their original areas of settlement with the Irish in Massachusetts, and Italians more concentrated in New York, New Jersey, and Connecticut.

Thus, almost a century after the end of mass immigration from Europe, the descendants of the immigrants have not wandered far from their ancestral locales. Of course, the map shows that the same point could be made for other groups, including African Americans (concentrated in the "black belt" across the states of the old Confederacy), Mexican Americans (concentrated along the southern border from Texas to California), and Native Americans. (Although too small to appear on the map, Native American concentration in the upper Midwest, eastern Oklahoma, and the Southwest reflects the locations of the reservations into which they were forced after the end of the Indian wars.)

Given all that has changed in American society over the past century—industrialization, population growth, urbanization, and massive mobility—the stable location of white ethnics (and other ethnic and racial groups) seems remarkable. Why aren't people distributed more randomly across the nation's landscape?

The stability is somewhat easier to explain for some groups. African Americans, Mexican Americans, and American Indians have been limited in their geographic as well as their social mobility by institutionalized discrimination, racism, and limited resources. We will examine the power of these constraints in detail in later chapters.

For white ethnics, on the other hand, the power of exclusion and rejection waned as the generations passed and the descendants of the immigrants assimilated and integrated. Their current locations are perhaps more a reflection of the idea (introduced in Chapter 1) that the United States is a nation of groups as well as individuals. Our group memberships, especially family and kin, exert a powerful influence on our decisions about where to live and work and, despite the transience and mobility of modern American life, can keep people connected to their relatives, the old neighborhood, their ethnic roots, and the sites of their ancestors' struggles.

Integration and Equality

Perhaps the most important point, for our purposes, about white ethnic groups (the descendants of the European immigrants) is that they are today on the verge of being completely assimilated. Even the groups that were the most despised and rejected in earlier years are acculturated, integrated, and thoroughly intermarried.

To illustrate this point, consider Exhibits 2.6 and 2.7, which illustrate the degree of integration and equality of a variety of white ethnic groups as long ago as 1990. The exhibits display data for 9 of the more than 60 white ethnic groups that people mentioned when asked to define their ancestries. The groups include the two largest white ethnic groups (German and Irish Americans) and seven more chosen to represent a range of geographic regions of origin and times of immigration.

The graphs show that, by 1990, all nine of the groups selected were at or above national norms ("all persons") for all measures of equality. There is some variation among the groups, of course, but all exceeded the national averages for both high school and college education and for median income. Also, Exhibit 2.7 shows that all nine groups had dramatically lower poverty rates (see the line in the graph and refer to the right-hand axis for values), usually less than half the national average. The bars in Exhibit 2.7 show median household income (refer to the left-hand axis for values). All nine groups exceed the national average, some—Russians, for example (many of whom are Jewish)—by a considerable margin (see Appendix [www.pineforge.com/healeyds3e] for information on the relative standing of some white ethnic groups).

Exhibit 2.6 Educational Attainment for Selected White Ethnic Groups, 1990

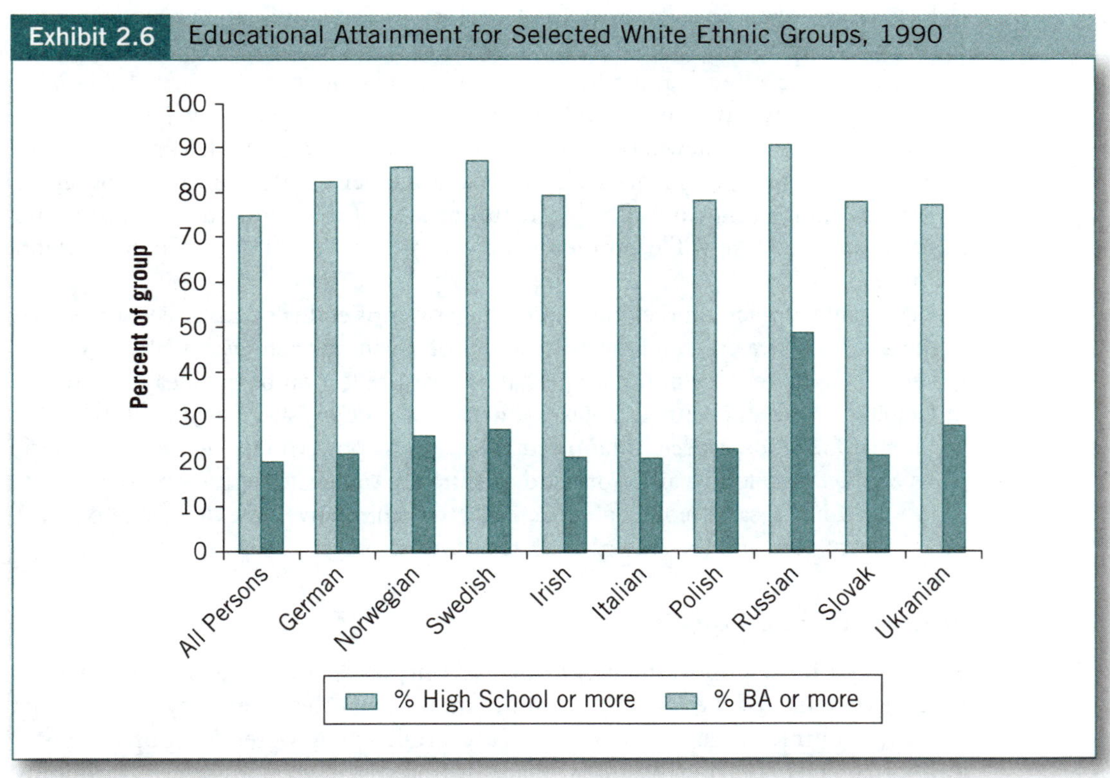

SOURCE: U.S. Bureau of the Census (1990a).

Exhibit 2.7 Median Household Income and Percent of Families Living in Poverty for Selected White Ethnic Groups, 1990

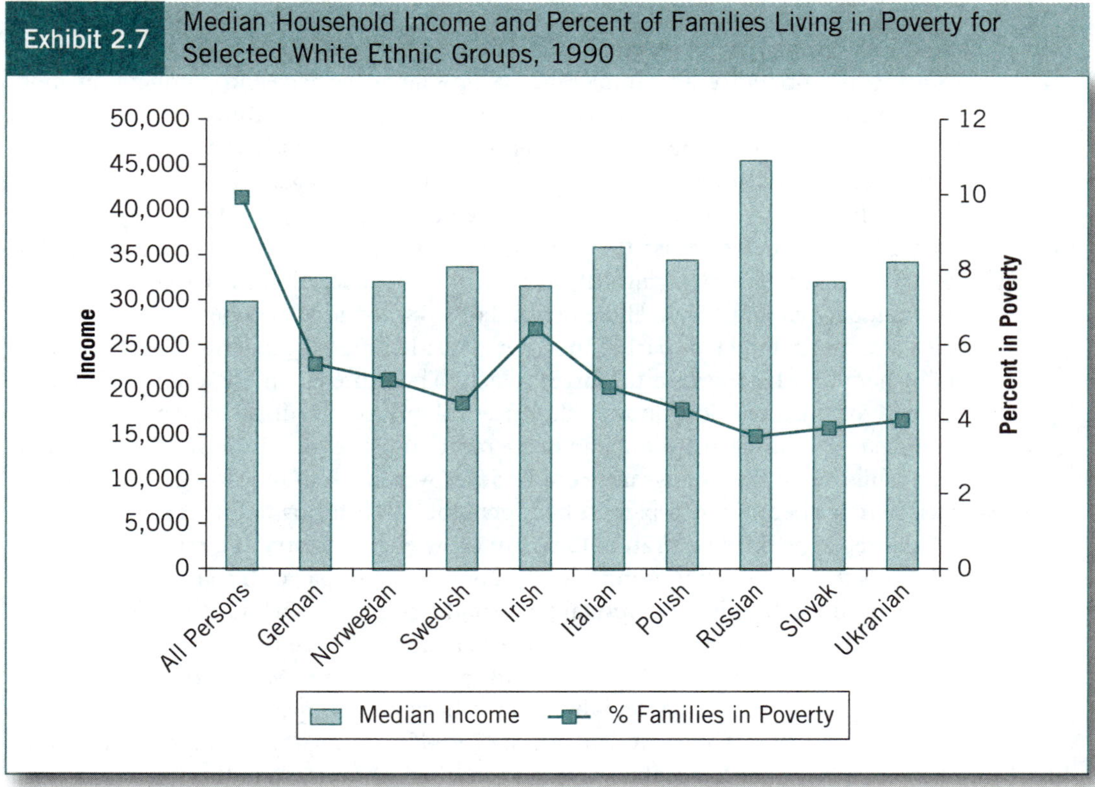

SOURCE: U.S. Bureau of the Census (1990a).

In other areas, the evidence for assimilation and equality is also persuasive. For example, the distinct ethnic neighborhoods that these groups created in American cities (Little Italy, Greektown, Little Warsaw, etc.) have faded away or been taken over by other groups, and the rate of intermarriage between members of different white ethnic groups is quite high. For example, based on data from the 1990 census, about 56% of all married whites have spouses whose ethnic backgrounds do not match their own (Alba, 1995, pp. 13–14).

The Twilight of White Ethnicity?[3]

Absorption into the American mainstream was neither linear nor continuous for the descendants of European immigrants. Over the generations, white ethnic identity sporadically reasserted itself in many ways, two of which are especially notable. First, there was a tendency for later generations to be more interested in their ancestry and ethnicity than were earlier generations. Marcus Hansen (1952) captured this phenomenon in his **principle of third-generation interest:** "What the second generation tries to forget, the third generation tries to remember" (p. 495). Hansen observed that the children of immigrants tended to minimize or deemphasize ("forget") their ethnicity to avoid the prejudice and intolerance of the larger society and compete on more favorable terms for jobs and other opportunities. As they became adults and started families of their own, the second generation tended to raise their children in nonethnic settings, with English as their first and only language.

By the time the third generation reached adulthood, especially the "new" immigrant groups that arrived last, the larger society had become more tolerant of white ethnicity and diversity, and having little to risk, the third generation tried to reconnect with its grandparents and roots. These descendants wanted to remember their ethnic heritage and understand it as part of their personal identities, their sense of who they were and where they belonged in the larger society. Thus, interest in the "old ways" and the strength of the identification with the ancestral group was often stronger in the more Americanized third generation than in the more ethnic second. Ironically, of course, the grandchildren of the immigrants could not recover much of the richness and detail of their heritage because their parents had spent their lives trying to forget it. Nonetheless, the desire of the third generation to reconnect with its ancestry and recover its ethnicity shows that assimilation is not a simple, one-dimensional, or linear process.

In addition to this generational pattern, the strength of white ethnic identity also responded to the changing context of American society and the activities of other groups. For example, in the late 1960s and early 1970s, there was a notable increase in the visibility of and interest in white ethnic heritage, an upsurge often referred to as the **ethnic revival.** The revival manifested itself in a variety of ways. Some people became more interested in their family's genealogical roots, and others increased their participation in ethnic festivals, traditions, and organizations. The "white ethnic vote" became a factor in local, state, and national politics, and appearances at the churches, meeting halls, and neighborhoods associated with white ethnic groups became almost mandatory for candidates for office. Demonstrations and festivals celebrating white ethnic heritages were organized, and buttons and bumper stickers proclaiming the ancestry of everyone from Irish to Italians were widely displayed. The revival was also endorsed by politicians, editorialists, and intellectuals (e.g., see Novak, 1973), reinforcing the movement and giving it additional legitimacy.

The ethnic revival may have been partly fueled, à la Hansen's principle, by the desire to reconnect with ancestral roots, even though most groups were well beyond their third generations by the 1960s. More likely, the revival was a reaction to the increase in pluralistic sentiment in the society in general and by the pluralistic, even separatist assertions of other groups that marked the decade. Virtually every minority group generated a protest movement (Black Power, Red Power, Chicanismo, etc.) and proclaimed a recommitment to its own heritage and to the authenticity of its own culture and experience. The visibility of these movements for cultural pluralism among racial minority groups helped make it more acceptable for European Americans to express their ethnicity and heritage.

Besides the general tenor of the times, the resurgence of white ethnicity had some political and economic dimensions that bring us back to issues of inequality and competition for resources. In the 1960s, a white ethnic urban working class made up largely of Irish and Southern and Eastern European groups still remained in the neighborhoods of the industrial Northeast and Midwest and continued to breathe life into the old networks and traditions (see Glazer & Moynihan, 1970; Greeley, 1974). At the same time that cultural pluralism was coming to be seen as more legitimate, this ethnic working class was feeling increasingly threatened by minority groups of color. In the industrial cities, it was not unusual for white ethnic neighborhoods to adjoin black and Hispanic neighborhoods, putting these groups in direct competition for housing, jobs, and other resources.

Many members of the white ethnic working class saw racial minority groups as inferior and perceived the advances being made by these groups as unfair, unjust, and threatening. They also reacted to what they saw as special treatment and attention being accorded on the basis of race, such as school busing and affirmative action. They had problems of their own (the declining number of good, unionized jobs; inadequate schooling; and deteriorating city services) and felt that their problems were being given lower priority and less legitimacy because they were white. The revived sense of ethnicity in the urban working-class neighborhoods was in large part a way of resisting racial reform and expressing resentment for the racial minority groups. Thus, among its many other causes and forms, the revival of white ethnicity that began in the 1960s was fueled by competition for resources and opportunities. As we will see throughout this text, such competition commonly leads to increased prejudice and a heightened sense of cohesion among group members.

White Ethnicity in the 21st Century

As the conflicts of the 1960s and 1970s faded, and white ethnic groups continued to leave the old neighborhoods and rise in the class structure, the strength of white ethnic identity resumed its slow demise. Today, several generations removed from the tumultuous 1960s, white ethnic identity has become increasingly nebulous and largely voluntary. It is often described as **symbolic ethnicity,** or as an aspect of self-identity that symbolizes one's roots in the Old Country but otherwise is minor. The descendants of the European immigrants, many of whom are now in at least their fifth or sixth generation, might feel vaguely connected to their ancestors, but this part of their identity does not affect their lifestyles, circles of friends and neighbors, job prospects, eating habits, or other everyday routines (Gans, 1979; Lieberson & Waters, 1988). For the descendants of the European immigrants today, ethnicity is an increasingly minor part of their identities that is expressed only occasionally or sporadically, if that. For example, they might participate in ethnic or religious festivals (e.g., St. Patrick's Day for Irish Americans, Columbus Day for Italian Americans), but these activities are seasonal or otherwise peripheral to their lives and self-images. The descendants of the European immigrants have choices, in stark contrast with their ancestors, members of racial minority groups, and many recent immigrants: They can stress their ethnicity, ignore it completely, or maintain any degree of ethnic identity they choose. Many people have ancestors in more than one ethnic group and may change their sense of affiliation over time, sometimes emphasizing one group's traditions, sometimes another's, and sometimes none at all (Waters, 1990).

In fact, white ethnic identity has become so ephemeral that it may be on the verge of disappearing altogether. For example, based on a series of in-depth interviews with white Americans from various regions of the nation, Gallagher (2001) found a sense of ethnicity so weak that it did not even rise to the level of "symbolic." In terms of Gordon's model, Gallagher's subjects were at the end of the process of assimilation. They were the products of ancestral lines so thoroughly intermixed and intermarried that any trace of a unique heritage from a particular group was completely lost. They had virtually no knowledge of the experiences of their immigrant ancestors or of the life and cultures of the ethnic communities they had inhabited, and for many, their ethnic ancestry was no more meaningful to them than their state of birth or their astrological sign. Their lack of interest in and information about their ethnic heritage was so complete that it led Gallagher to propose an addendum to Hansen's principle: "What the grandson wished to remember, the great-granddaughter has never been told."

At the same time that more specific white ethnic identities are disappearing, they are also evolving into new shapes and forms. In the view of many analysts, a new identity is developing that merges the various *hyphenated* ethnic identities (German-American, Polish-American, etc.) into a single, generalized *European American* identity based on race and a common history of immigration and assimilation. This new identity reinforces the racial lines of separation that run through contemporary society, but it does more than simply mark group boundaries. Embedded in this emerging identity is an understanding, often deeply flawed, of how the white immigrant groups succeeded and assimilated in the past, and a view, often deeply ideological, of how the racial minority groups and new immigrants should behave in the present. These understandings are encapsulated in "immigrant tales": legends that stress heroic individual effort and grim determination as key ingredients leading to success in the old days. These tales have become myth-like and feature impoverished, victimized immigrant ancestors who survived and made a place for themselves and their children by working hard, saving their money, and otherwise exemplifying the virtues of the Protestant ethic and American individualism. A central element of these tales is the idea that past generations became successful despite the brutal hostility of the dominant group and in the face of conditions that rival the worst faced by racial minority groups (slavery, segregation, attempted genocide, etc.). These immigrant tales and family legends strongly imply—and sometimes blatantly assert—that racial minorities and more recent immigrant groups could succeed in America by simply following the example set by European immigrants and their descendents (Alba, 1990; Gallagher, 2001).

To illustrate this near-mythic understanding of America's immigrant past, consider the thoughts of Shannon, a 21-year-old white female, when she was asked why she believed that blacks see racial inequality in situations in which she does not:

> I think that the black people have a very hard time accepting that they are not succeeding because they don't want to work, when they could work and they could succeed just like—I mean look at all the black people who have succeeded in this world—even in this

> country—how can they say that we're, like, suppressing them in any way. I mean look at all the ways you can succeed. I think that they are blaming the wrong people and I think that the Korean and the Chinese, I don't think they do that. . . . I mean when we came to this country no one had anything—I mean they [Asians] had less than the blacks when they came over to this country, way less. And look at where this country has come. They [blacks] can work just as hard and succeed way above their expectations if they just stopped and looked at themselves. (Gallagher, 2001, n.p.)

Shannon mixes negative stereotypes (e.g., she sees blacks as lazy and solely responsible for their own poverty) with selective misinformation (e.g., her assertion that Asians had less than blacks when they came to this country) as a way of distancing and denigrating blacks while simultaneously elevating whites (and other "good" minority groups).

These immigrant tales blend versions of human capital theory and traditional views of assimilation with prejudice and racism. Without denying or trivializing the resolve and fortitude of European immigrants, equating their experiences and levels of disadvantage with those of African Americans, American Indians, and Mexican Americans is widely off the mark, as we shall see in the remainder of this text. These views support an attitude of disdain and lack of sympathy for the multiple dilemmas faced today by the racial minority groups and by many contemporary immigrants. They permit more subtle expressions of prejudice and racism—forms of "modern racism" discussed in Chapter 1—and allow whites to use these highly distorted views of their immigrant ancestors as a rhetorical device to express a host of race-based grievances without appearing racist (Gallagher, 2001). Alba (1990) concludes as follows:

> The thrust of the [emerging] European American identity is to defend the individualistic view of the American system, because it portrays the system as open to those who are willing to work hard and pull themselves out of poverty and discrimination. Recent research suggests that it is precisely this individualism that prevents many whites from sympathizing with the need for African Americans and other minorities to receive affirmative action in order to overcome institutional barriers to their advancement. (p. 317)

The generations-long journey from immigrant to white ethnic seems to be drawing to a close. The separate white ethnic identities are merging into a larger sense of "whiteness" that unites descendants of the immigrants with the dominant group and provides a rhetorical device for expressing disdain for other groups, especially African Americans.

Gordon's stages of acculturation, integration, and intermarriage have largely been completed, and the descendents of the immigrants are now merging with the dominant group on the levels of identity and self-image. They increasingly share the white racial identity we discussed in Chapter 1, along with its sense of place and privilege. In their long sociological journey, immigrants from Europe became white ethnics and are now becoming simply white, differentiated from the dominant group only by a faint, diminishing echo of their ancestors' origins.

Contemporary Immigrants: Does the Traditional Perspective Apply?

How relevant is the traditional perspective on assimilation—created as it was to analyze the experiences of European immigrants—for understanding more recent immigrants? This is a key issue facing social scientists, government policy makers, and the general public today. Will contemporary immigrants duplicate the experiences of earlier groups? Will they acculturate before they integrate? Will religion, social class, and race be important forces in their lives? Will they take as many as three (or more) generations to assimilate? What will their patterns of intermarriage look like? Will they achieve socioeconomic parity with the dominant group? Will they eventually merge into the dominant group? When? How?

There is disagreement among sociologists (and among the general public and policy makers) about the answers to these questions. Some social scientists believe that the traditional perspective on assimilation does not apply and that the experiences of contemporary immigrant groups will differ greatly from those of European immigrants. They believe that assimilation today is fragmented, or **segmented,** and will have a number of different outcomes. Although some contemporary immigrant groups may integrate into the middle-class mainstream, others will find themselves permanently mired in the impoverished, alienated, and marginalized segments of racial minority groups. Still others may form close-knit enclaves based on their traditional cultures and become successful in the United States by resisting the forces of acculturation (Portes & Rumbaut, 2001a; Telles & Ortiz, 2008).

In contrast, other theorists believe that the traditional perspective on assimilation is still relevant and that contemporary immigrant groups will follow the established pathways of mobility and assimilation. For example, researchers studying the second generation of contemporary immigrant groups living in and around New York City found that they are, in general, rising in the social class structure of the larger society relative to their parents (Kasnitz, Mollenkopf, Waters, & Holloway, 2008). Of course, the process will be variable from group to group and place to place, but these theorists believe that even the groups that are today the most impoverished and marginalized will, in time, move into mainstream society.

How will the debate be resolved? We cannot say at the moment, particularly because many of the newest immigrant groups are still in the second generation. We can point out, however, that this debate is reminiscent of the critique of Park's theory of assimilation. In both cases, the argument is partly about time: Even the most impoverished and segmented groups may find their way into the economic mainstream eventually, at some unspecified time in the future. There are also other levels of meaning in the debate, however, related to one's perception of the nature of modern U.S. society. Is U.S. society today growing more tolerant of diversity, more open and equal? If so, this would seem to favor the traditionalist perspective. If not, this trend would clearly favor those who argue for the segmented assimilation hypothesis. Although we will not resolve this argument in this text, we will use the debate between the traditional and segmented views on assimilation as a useful framework as we consider the experiences of these groups (see Chapters 8, 9, and 10).

FOCUS ON CONTEMPORARY ISSUES: Language and Assimilation

A bumper sticker expresses a common sentiment: "Welcome to America. Now Speak English." Many Americans are concerned about the increase in the number of non-English speakers in their communities and the bumper sticker succinctly—if crudely—expresses the opinion that newcomers should learn English as a condition for admission to the United States and acceptance by the larger society. In Gordon's terms, the slogan expresses support for Anglo-conformity, the model that guided the assimilation of immigrants in the past.

The bumper sticker also states a common concern: How can we manage a multilingual society? Americans from all walks of life and political persuasions wonder about the difficulties of everyday communication and the problems of doing business and satisfying needs in communities where people speak multiple languages. Also, people wonder if increasing language diversity will weaken social solidarity and the sense of unity that every society requires in order to continue to function. According to the 2000 census, there are well over 300 different languages being spoken in the United States. Is this a threat to unity or efficiency? What does sociological research reveal about language acculturation for today's immigrants?

First of all, to put some perspective on the issue, recall the experiences of the first mass wave of immigrants to the United States (1820s–1920s) and the conclusions of the "traditional" perspective on assimilation that grew out of the attempts to understand those experiences. For the European immigrants and their descendents, learning English—along with Anglo values and customs—laid the groundwork for all other stages of assimilation. Acculturation was a prerequisite for integration, a precondition for the pursuit of education, better jobs, political power, and other resources.

Secondly, and perhaps more importantly, language acculturation happened by generation in the past. The first generation—especially the less-educated immigrant laborers who arrived between the 1880s and the 1920s—lived and died speaking their native language. Their children learned English in school, often served as bilingual go-betweens for their parents and the larger society, and largely failed to pass on the language of their parents to their children. The third generation tended to grow up in non-ethnic settings, and they overwhelmingly spoke English as their first and only language. Thus, by the third (or fourth) generation, English had replaced the old language, especially after mass immigration from Europe ended in the 1920s and 1930s and few newcomers arrived to keep the old ways alive.

Today, 80 years after the first wave of immigration ended, language continues to operate as a gatekeeper and opportunities in the mainstream society remain closed to those not fluent in "standard" (white middle class) English. The importance of language is not lost on contemporary immigrants, and language acculturation seems to be following, more or less, the generational pattern described in Gordon's model. Exhibit 2.8 displays the generational switch to English for all Hispanic and all Asian immigrants and for some of the largest contemporary immigrant groups. The data come from the 2000 U.S. census (Alba, 2004).

(Continued)

(Continued)

Although there is quite a bit of variation from group to group, the pattern in the graph is clear: The third generation of recent immigrant groups are overwhelmingly monolingual in English, just as European immigrant groups were. Although comparisons are necessarily inexact because of the lack of detailed information about language acculturation in the past, contemporary Asian immigrant groups are quite close to the levels of language acculturation of the European groups. Hispanic groups are less linguistically acculturated, but virtually all bilingual Hispanics also speak English "very well." As in the past, "the immigrant generation makes some progress but remains dominant in their native tongue, the second generation is bilingual, and the third generation speaks English only" (Waters & Jimenez, 2005, p. 110).

Exhibit 2.8 Percent of Each Generation Speaking English Only

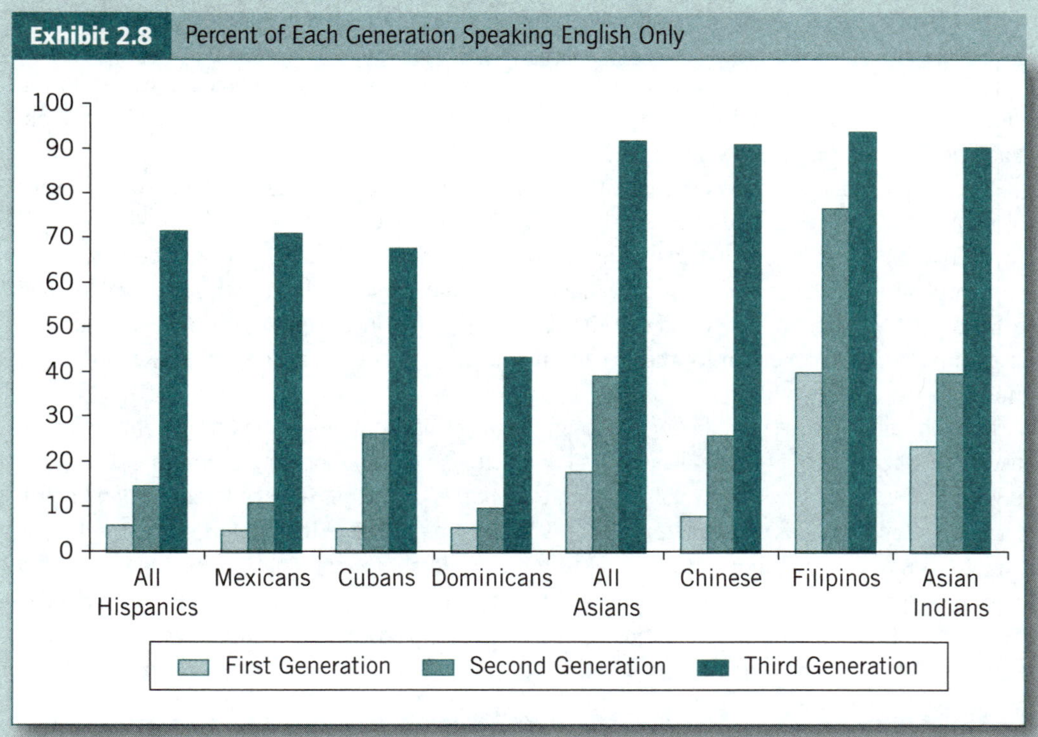

SOURCE: Alba (2004, Table 1). Copyright ©2004 Richard Alba. Reprinted by permission.

For many Americans, the finding that language acculturation is occurring now much as it did in the past will seem counterintuitive. Their everyday experience in their communities tells them that the strength of non-English languages (particularly Spanish) is *not* waning over the years but is growing more common and, for many, becoming more of a problem. How can we reconcile this impression with the information presented in Exhibit 2.8?

The persistence (or increase) of the "old" language that many observe daily is not the result of immigrant groups refusing to learn English, as is sometimes alleged (for example, see Huntington, 2004), but rather reflects the continuing high rate of immigration. Even as the children and grandchildren of immigrants learn English, the old language is replenished and sustained by the large number of newcomers. In other words, assimilation and pluralism are occurring simultaneously in the United States today: The movement of the second and third generations toward English is counterbalanced by continuing immigration. The assimilation of European immigrant groups was sharply reinforced by the slowing of immigration after the 1920s (see Exhibit 2.3). The pluralism and diversity of the United States today is sustained and reinforced by the continuing flow of new, post-1965 immigrants. This is an important difference in the assimilation experience of the two waves and we will explore it more in chapters to come. For now, we can say that immigration today will continue, newcomers will keep the "old" language alive, and language diversity will continue to be perceived as a problem and—for some—as a threat.

Given these trends, it seems likely that language will continue to be a matter of concern and an important political issue in the years ahead. A variety of positions addressing the issues of language diversity have been advanced. Some people would like to see more support for Spanish as a second language and the expansion of bilingual education in the schools. Others believe that the best course of action would be to make English the official language of the United States and, in a variety of ways, reinforce the primacy of the English language across the board (much as suggested by the bumper sticker slogan quoted at the start of this section). While we cannot assess all of these ideas, we will take a brief look at the latter proposal.

Generally, laws that would establish English as the nation's official language—or "English Only" laws—require that the official business of the society (including election ballots, court proceedings, public school assemblies, and street signs) be conducted *only* in English. Perhaps the leading voice in support of this policy is U.S.English, Inc., a well-known national organization that argues that having a single official language would unite "Americans . . . by providing a common means of communication; it encourages immigrants to learn English in order to use government services and participate in the democratic process; and it defines a much-needed common sense language policy" (U.S.English, n.d.).

Some questions come to mind about English Only laws. First, if immigrant groups are learning English by generation today, much as in the past, are these laws necessary? Would such laws speed up the acquisition of English in the first generation? This seems unlikely since a large percentage of immigrants—including those from Mexico—arrive with little formal education and low levels of literacy in their native language, as we will see in chapters to come. Furthermore, the laws would have little impact on the second and third generation, since they are already learning English at the "normal" pace.

Secondly, is there something behind the support for these laws besides concern for language diversity? Is support for English Only an expression of prejudice and rejection of immigrants in general and non-English, non-Anglo immigrants (the vast majority of the present wave) in particular? Recall the concept of modern racism (disguised or indirect ways of expressing disdain for and rejection of other

(Continued)

(Continued)

groups without appearing to be racist) from Chapter 1. Movements such as English Only provide a perfect cover for "non-racist racism." They permit people to express their fears and negative emotions and act on their stereotypes in language that is neutral and that even seems patriotic. Does the English Only movement hide a deeper, more exclusionist agenda? Is it a way of sustaining the dominance of Anglo culture, a manifestation of the ideological racism we discussed in Chapter 1? (see Golash-Boza, 2005; Gounari, 2006; and Hartman, 2005, for examples of the argument that "English only" is an expression of racism. See Mujica, 2003, for the counterargument).

This is not to say that all supporters of English Only laws are racist or prejudiced. These are difficult issues to deal with, in large part because they commonly evoke a multitude of strong emotions and sentiments. The point here is that some (many?) of those feelings and ideas are prejudicial and stereotypical and we must be careful to sort out the real challenges created by language diversity from the more hysterical and racist concerns. There are many good reasons to be concerned about immigration and assimilation and many issues that need to be addressed, but language acculturation doesn't seem to justify the degree of worry that is common across U.S. society.

Implications for Examining Dominant–Minority Relations

Chapters 1 and 2 have introduced many of the terms, concepts, and themes that form the core of the rest of this text. Although the connections between the concepts are not simple, some key points can be made to summarize these chapters and anticipate the material to come.

First, minority group status has much more to do with power and the distribution of resources than with simple numbers or the percentage of the population in any particular category. We saw this notion expressed in Chapter 1 in the definition of minority group and in our exploration of inequality. The themes of inequality and differentials in status were also covered in our discussion of prejudice, racism, and discrimination. To understand minority relations, we must examine some very basic realities of human society: inequalities in wealth, prestige, and the distribution of power. To discuss changes in minority-group status, we must be prepared to discuss changes in the way society does business; makes decisions; and distributes income, jobs, health care, and opportunity.

A second area of focus in the rest of the book is the question of how our society should develop. Assimilation and pluralism, with all their variations, define two broad directions. Each has been extensively examined and discussed by social scientists, by leaders and decision makers in American society, and by ordinary people from all groups and walks of life. The analysis and evaluation of these two broad directions is a thread running throughout this book.

COMPARATIVE FOCUS: Immigration, Emigration, and Ireland

Immigrating and adjusting to a new society are among the most wrenching, exciting, disconcerting, exhilarating, and heartbreaking of human experiences. Immigrants have recorded these feelings, along with the adventures and experiences that sparked them, in every possible medium, including letters, memoirs, poems, photos, stories, movies, jokes, and music. These immigrant tales recount the traumas of leaving home, dealing with a new language and customs, coping with rejection and discrimination, and thousands of other experiences. The most poignant of these stories express the sadness of parting from family and friends, perhaps forever.

Peter Jones captured some of these feelings in his song *Kilkelly,* based on letters written nearly 150 years earlier by an Irish father to his immigrant son—Jones's great-grandfather—in the United States. Each verse of the song paraphrases a letter and includes news of the family and community left behind and also expresses, in simple but powerful language, the deep sadness of separation and the longing for reunion:

> Kilkelly, Ireland, 18 and 90, my dear and loving son John
> I guess that I must be close on to eighty,
> Its thirty years since you're gone.
> Because of all of the money you send me,
> I'm still living out on my own.
> Michael has built himself a fine house
> and Brigid's daughters have grown.
> Thank you for sending your family picture,
> They're lovely young women and men.
> You say that you might even come for a visit,
> What joy to see you again.[4]

It is particularly appropriate to use an Irish song to illustrate the sorrows of immigration. Just as the United States has been a major receiver of immigrants for the last 200 years, Ireland has been a major supplier. Mass immigration from Ireland began with the potato famines of the 1840s and continued through the end of the 20th century, motivated by continuing hard times, political unrest, and unemployment. The sadness of Peter Jones's ancestors was repeated over and over as the youth of Ireland left for jobs in Great Britain, the United States, and hundreds of other places, never expecting to return. This mass immigration (combined with deaths from the potato famines) cut the 1840 Irish population of 7 million in half, and today, the population is still only about 4 million.

(Continued)

(Continued)

History rarely runs in straight lines, however. Today, after nearly 200 years of supplying immigrants, Ireland (along with other nations of Northern and Western Europe) has become a consumer. As illustrated in Exhibit 2.9, the number of newcomers entering Ireland increased more than 4 times over between 1987 and 2008, to almost 90,000, and the number of people leaving decreased dramatically, to less than 20,000. These numbers are miniscule compared to the volume of immigrants received by the United States each year, but the percentage of Ireland's population that consists of immigrants (13.8%) is actually greater than the comparable percentage in the United States (12.8%) (www.nationmaster.com).

Exhibit 2.9 Immigration and Emigration, Ireland, 1987 to 2008

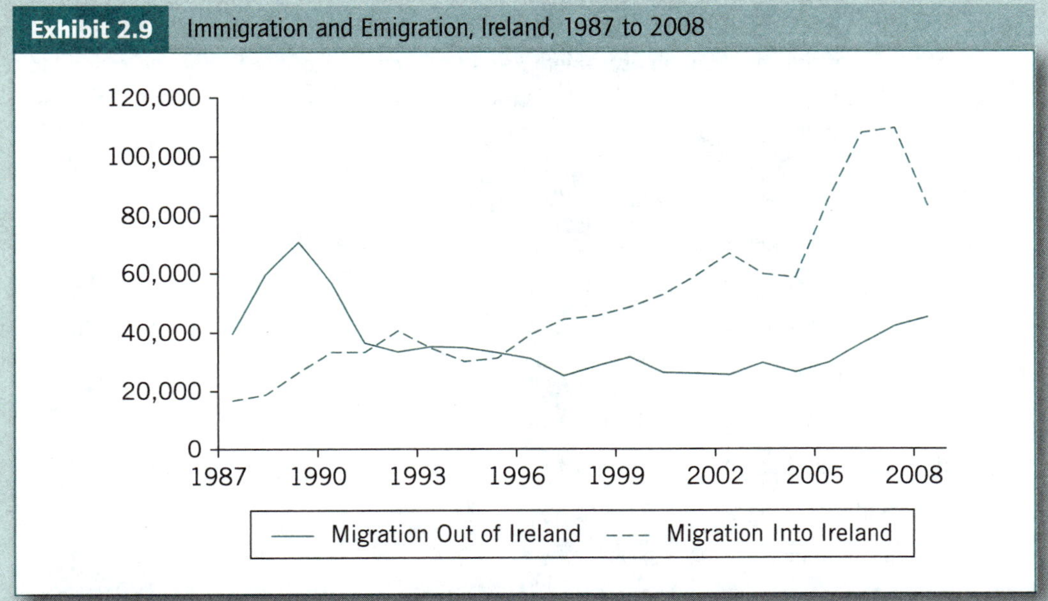

SOURCE: From Population and Migration Estimates, April 2008. Central Statistics Office, Ireland. 2008. Copyright © Central Statistics Office.

What explains the switch from immigration to emigration? The answers are not hard to find. After decades of unemployment and depression, the Irish economy entered a boom phase in the early 1990s. Spurred by investments from multinational corporations and the benefits of joining the European Economic Union (EEU), the Irish economy and the job supply have grown rapidly. The unemployment rate was less than 5% in 2007, and Ireland ranks 139th lowest out of almost 200 nations on this statistic (www.nationmaster.com).

Irish nationals who left Ireland to find work are now returning in large numbers, and people from Europe and other parts of the globe are also arriving. In addition, Ireland is receiving refugees and people seeking asylum. In 2007, for example, about 18% of immigrants were of Irish origin, 63%

were from the United Kingdom or other nations of the European Union, and 16% were from "the rest of the world," a category that includes the Middle East, Nigeria, and various "trouble spots" around the globe (Central Statistics Office, Ireland, 2008).

The immigration is changing the racial composition of Irish society. Although still a small minority of the total population, the number of Irish residents of African descent has increased by a factor of 8 between 1996 and 2006, from less than 5,000 to over 40,000. In the same time period, the number of Irish of Asian descent increased by a factor of 6, from about 8,000 to over 50,000. Each group is about 1% of the total population.

What awaits these newcomers when they arrive on the Emerald Isle? Will they be subjected to the Irish version of Anglo-conformity? Will Irish society become a melting pot? Will Gordon's ideas about assimilation be applicable to their experiences? Will their assimilation be segmented? Will the Irish, such immigrants themselves, be especially understanding and sympathetic to the traumas faced by the newcomers?

Although many Irish are very sympathetic to the immigrants and refugees, others have responded with racist sentiments and demands for exclusion, reactions that ironically echo the rejection Irish immigrants to the United States experienced in the 19th century. Irish radio and TV talk shows commonly discuss issues of immigration and assimilation and frequently evoke prejudiced statements from the audience, and there are also reports of racism and discrimination from across the society.

The rejection of non-Irish newcomers was manifested in the passage of the "Citizenship Amendment" to the Irish constitution, which was overwhelmingly supported (80% in favor) by the Irish electorate in June 2004. Prior to the passage of the amendment, any baby born in Ireland had the right to claim Irish citizenship. The amendment denied the right of citizenship to any baby that did not have at least one Irish parent and was widely interpreted as a hostile rejection of immigrants (see Fanning, 2003). One poll suggested that people supported the amendment because they believed that there were simply too many immigrants in Ireland (Neissen, Schibel, & Thompson, 2005).

Like the United States, Ireland finds itself dealing with diversity and debating what kind of society it should become. It is too early to tell whether the Irish experience will parallel the American experience or whether the sociological concepts presented in this chapter will prove useful in analyzing the Irish immigrant experience. We can be sure, however, that the experience of the immigrants in Ireland will be laced with plentiful doses of the loneliness and longing experienced by Peter Jones's ancestors. Times have changed, but today's immigrants will yearn for Abuja, Riga, or Baku with the same melancholy experienced by previous waves of immigrants yearning for Kilkelly, Dublin, or Galway. Who knows what songs and poems will come from this?

MAIN POINTS

- Assimilation and pluralism are two broad pathways of development for intergroup relations. The two are in some ways contrary processes but may appear together in a variety of combinations.
- Two types of assimilation are the melting pot and Anglo-conformity. The latter has historically been the dominant value in the United States.

- Gordon theorized that assimilation occurs through a series of stages, with integration being the crucial stage. In his view, it is common for American minority groups, especially racial minority groups, to be acculturated but not integrated. Once a group has begun to integrate, all other stages will follow in order.
- In the past few decades, there has been increased interest in pluralism. There are three types of pluralistic situations: cultural, or full, pluralism; structural pluralism; and enclave, or middleman, minority groups.
- According to many scholars, white ethnic groups survived decades of assimilation, albeit in altered forms. New ethnic (and racial) minority groups continue to appear, and old ones change form and function as society changes. As the 21st century unfolds, however, white ethnicity may well be fading in salience for most people, except perhaps as a context for criticizing other groups.
- In the United States today, assimilation may be segmented and have outcomes other than equality with and acceptance into the middle class.

STUDY SITE ON THE WEB

Don't forget the interactive quizzes and other resources and learning aids at **www.pineforge.com/healeyds3e**

FOR FURTHER READING

The following are two classic and widely influential works of scholarship on assimilation, religion, and white ethnic groups:

Gordon, Milton. 1964. *Assimilation in American Life.* New York: Oxford University Press.

Herberg, Will. 1960. *Protestant-Catholic-Jew: An Essay in American Religious Sociology.* New York: Anchor.

Here is a useful analysis of the changing meanings of ethnic identity for the descendants of European immigrants:

Alba, Richard. 1990. *Ethnic Identity: The Transformation of White America.* New Haven, CT: Yale University Press.

These three recent works argue that the "traditional" model of assimilation remains viable and is useful for analyzing the experiences of contemporary immigrants:

Alba, Richard, & Nee, Victor. 2003. *Remaking the American Mainstream: Assimilation and Contemporary Immigration.* Cambridge, MA: Harvard University Press.

Bean, Frank, & Stevens, Gillian. 2003. *America's Newcomers and the Dynamics of Diversity* New York: Russell Sage Foundation.

Kasnitz, Phillip, Mollenkopf, John, Waters, Mary, & Holloway, Jennifer. 2008. *Inheriting the City: The Children of Immigrants Come of Age.* New York: Russell Sage Foundation.

The following are three outstanding works analyzing contemporary immigrants and presenting the segmented assimilation hypothesis:

Telles, Edward E., & Ortiz, Vilma. 2008. *Generations of Exclusion: Mexican Americans, Assimilation, and Race.* New York: Russell Sage Foundation.

Portes, Alejandro, & Rumbaut, Richard. 2001a. *Ethnicities: Children of Immigrants in America.* New York: Russell Sage Foundation.

Portes, Alejandro, & Rumbaut, Richard. 2001b. *Legacies: The Story of the Immigrant Second Generation.* Berkeley: University of California Press.

QUESTIONS FOR REVIEW AND STUDY

1. Summarize Gordon's model of assimilation. Identify and explain each stage and how the stages are linked together. Explain Exhibits 2.2 and 2.4 in terms of Gordon's model.
2. "Human capital theory is not so much wrong as it is incomplete." Explain this statement. What does the theory leave out? What questionable assumptions does it make?
3. What are the major dimensions along which the experience of assimilation varies? Explain how and why the experience of assimilation can vary.
4. Define pluralism and explain the ways in which it differs from assimilation. Why has interest in pluralism increased? Explain the difference between and cite examples of structural and cultural pluralism. Describe enclave minority groups in terms of pluralism and in terms of Gordon's model of assimilation. How have contemporary theorists added to the concept of pluralism?
5. Define and explain segmented assimilation and explain how it differs from Gordon's model. What evidence is there that assimilation for recent immigrants is not segmented? What is the significance of this debate for the future of U.S. society? For other minority groups (e.g., African Americans)? For the immigrants themselves?
6. What patterns have been observed in the language acculturation of contemporary immigrant groups? Do these patterns tend to support the "traditional" or "segmented" models of assimilation? What role do prejudice and modern racism play in this debate?
7. Do American theories and understandings of assimilation apply to the case of Ireland?

INTERNET RESEARCH PROJECT

Update and expand the discussion of language and assimilation and the "English Only" movement presented in this chapter. Search the Internet to (a) find the status of pertinent legislation, (b) research the positions for and against making English the official language, and (c) find additional data or information on the patterns of language acculturation today. As you analyze and examine the information gathered, apply the concepts of pluralism, the melting pot, Anglo-conformity, structural integration, and human capital theory.

Notes

1. Puzo, Mario. 1972. *The Godfather Papers and Other Confessions.* New York: Putnam. Reprinted by permission of Donadio & Olson, Inc. Copyright © 1972 Mario Puzo.
2. Rodriguez, Luis. 1993. *Always Running: La Vida Loca,* pp. 83–84. Reprinted with permission of Curbstone Press. Distributed by Consortium.
3. This phrase comes from Alba (1990).
4. Copyright © Steve and Peter Jones, 1981. Used with permission.

Part II

The Evolution of Dominant–Minority Relations in the United States

The chapters in Part II explore several key questions: Why do some groups become minorities? How and why do dominant–minority relations change over time? These questions are more than casual or merely academic. Understanding the dynamics that created and sustained prejudice, racism, discrimination, and inequality in the past will build understanding about group relations in the present and future, and such understanding is crucial if we are ever to deal effectively with these problems.

Both chapters in Part II use African Americans as the primary case study. Chapter 3 focuses on the pre-industrial United States and the creation of slavery but also considers the fate of American Indians and Mexican Americans during the same time period. Chapter 4 analyzes the changes in group relations that were caused by the industrial revolution and focuses on the shift from slavery to segregation for African Americans and their migration out of the South. Throughout the 20th century, industrial technology continued to evolve and shape American society and group relationships. We begin to explore the consequences of these changes in Chapter 4, and we continue the investigation in the case studies of contemporary minority groups in Part III.

The concepts introduced in Part I are used throughout Chapters 3 and 4, and some very important new concepts and theories are introduced as well. By the end of Part II, you will be familiar with virtually the entire conceptual framework that will guide us through the remainder of this text.

A Note on the Morality and the History of Minority Relations in America: Guilt, Blame, Understanding, and Communication

Very often, when people confront the kind of material presented in the next few chapters, they react on a personal level. Some might feel a sense of guilt for America's less-than-wholesome history of group relations. Others might respond with anger about the injustice and unfairness that remains in American society. Still others might respond with denial or indifference and might argue that the events discussed in Chapters 3 and 4 are so distant in time that they have no importance or meaning today.

These reactions—guilt, anger, denial, and indifference—are common, and I ask you to consider them for a number of reasons. First, the awful things I will discuss did happen, and they were carried out largely by members of a particular racial and ethnic group: white Europeans and their descendants in America. No amount of denial, distancing, or disassociation can make these facts go away. African Americans, American Indians, Mexican Americans, and other groups were victims, and they paid a terrible price for the early growth and success of white American society.

Second, the successful domination and exploitation of these groups were made easier by the cooperation of certain members of each of the minority groups. The slave trade relied on agents and slavers who were black Africans, some American Indians aided and abetted the cause of white society, and some Mexicans helped to cheat other Mexicans. There is plenty of guilt to go around, and Euro Americans do not have a monopoly on greed, bigotry, or viciousness. Indeed, some white Southerners opposed slavery and fought for the abolition of the "peculiar institution." Many of the ideas and values on which the United States was founded (justice, equality, liberty) had their origins in European intellectual traditions, and minority group protest has often involved little more than insisting that the nation live up to these ideals. Segments of the white community were appalled at the treatment of American Indians and Mexicans. Some members of the dominant group devoted (and sometimes gave) their lives to end oppression, bigotry, and racial stratification.

My point here is to urge you to avoid, as far as possible, a "good-guy/bad-guy" approach to this subject matter. Guilt, anger, denial, and indifference are common reactions to this material, but these emotions do little to advance understanding, and often they impede communication between members of different groups. An understanding of America's racial past is vitally important for understanding the present.

Historical background provides a perspective for viewing the present and allows us to identify important concepts and principles that we can use to disentangle the intergroup complexities surrounding us.

The goal of the chapters to come is not to make you feel any particular emotion. I will try to present the often ugly facts as neutrally as possible and without extraneous editorializing. As scholars, your goal should be to absorb the material, understand the principles, and apply them to your own life and the society around you—not to indulge yourself in elaborate moral denunciations of American society, develop apologies for the past, or deny the realities of what happened. By dealing objectively with this material, we can begin to liberate our perspectives and build an understanding of the realities of American society and American minority groups.

The Development of Dominant–Minority Group Relations in Preindustrial America

The Origins of Slavery

I was born May 1815, of a slave mother, in Shelby County, Kentucky, and was claimed as the property of David White. I was brought up . . . or, more correctly speaking, I was flogged up; for where I should have received moral, mental, and religious instruction, I received stripes without number, the object of which was to degrade and keep me in subordination. . . . The first time I was separated from my mother, I was young and small . . . I was . . . hired out to labor for various persons and all my wages were expended for the education of [my master's daughter].

(Continued)

(Continued)

It was then I first commenced seeing and feeling that I was a wretched slave, compelled to work under the lash without wages, and often without clothes to hide my nakedness. . . .

All that I heard about liberty and freedom . . . I never forgot. Among other good trades I learned the art of running away to perfection. I made a regular business of it, and never gave it up, until I had broken the bands of slavery, and landed myself safely in Canada, where I was regarded as a man, and not a thing.

[Bibb describes his childhood and adolescence, his early attempts to escape to the North, and his marriage to Malinda.] Not many months [later,] Malinda made me a father. The dear little daughter was called Mary Frances. She was nurtured and caressed by her mother and father. . . .

Malinda's business was to labor out in the field the greater part of her time, and there was no one to take care of poor little Frances. . . . She was left at the house to creep under the feet of an unmerciful old mistress, Mrs. Gatewood (the owner's wife). I recollect that [we] came in from the field one day and poor little Frances came creeping to her mother smiling, but with large tear drops standing in her dear little eyes. . . . Her little face was bruised black with the whole print of Mrs. Gatewood's hand. . . . Who can imagine the feelings of a mother and father, when looking upon their infant child whipped and tortured with impunity, and they placed in a situation where they could afford it no protection? But we were all claimed and held as property; the father and mother were slaves!

On this same plantation, I was compelled to stand and see my wife shamefully scourged and abused by her master; and the manner in which this was done was so violent and inhuman that I despair in finding decent language to describe the bloody act of cruelty. My happiness or pleasure was all blasted; for it was sometimes a pleasure to be with my little family even in slavery. I loved them as my wife and child. Little Frances was a pretty child; she was quiet, playful, bright, and interesting. . . . But I could never look upon the dear child without being filled with sorrow and fearful apprehensions, of being separated by slaveholders, because she was a slave, regarded as property. . . . But Oh! When I remember that my daughter, my only child, is still there . . . it is too much to bear. If ever there was any one act of my life as a slave, that I have to lament over, it is that of being a father and a husband to slaves. I have the satisfaction of knowing that I am the father of only one slave. She is bone of my bone, and flesh of my flesh; poor unfortunate child. She was the first and shall be the last slave that ever I will father, for chains and slavery on this earth.

—Henry Bibb[1]

During the first years of my service in Dr. Flint's family, I was accustomed to share some indulgences with the children of my mistress. Though this seemed to me no more than right, I was grateful for it, and tried to merit the kindness by the faithful discharge of my duties. But I now entered on my fifteenth year—a sad epoch in the life of a slave girl. My master began to whisper foul words in my ear. Young as I was, I could not remain ignorant of their import. I tried to treat them with indifference or contempt. The master's age, my extreme youth, and the fear that misconduct would be reported to my grandmother made me bear this treatment for many months.

He was a crafty man, and resorted to many means to accomplish his purposes. Sometimes he had stormy, terrific ways that made his victims tremble; sometimes he assumed a gentleness that he thought must surely subdue. Of the two, I preferred his stormy moods, although they left me trembling. He tried his utmost to corrupt the pure principles my grandmother had instilled. He peopled my young mind with unclean images, such as only a vile monster could think of. I turned from him with disgust and hatred. But he was my master. I was compelled to live under the same roof with him, where I saw a man forty years my senior daily violating the most sacred commandments of nature. He told me I was his property; that I must be subject to his will in all things. My soul revolted against the mean tyranny. But where could I turn for protection? No matter whether the slave girl be as black as ebony or as fair as her mistress. In either case, there is no shadow of law to protect her from insult, from violence, or even from death; all these are inflicted by fiends who bear the shape of men. The mistress, who ought to protect the helpless victim, has no other feelings towards her but those of jealousy and rage. The degradation, the wrongs, the vices that grow out of slavery, are more than I can describe. They are greater than you would willingly believe. Surely, if you credited on half the truths that are told you concerning the helpless millions suffering in this cruel bondage, you at the north would not help tighten the yoke. You surely would refuse to do for the master, on your own soil, the mean and cruel work which trained bloodhounds and the lowest class of whites do for him at the south.

—Harriet Jacobs[2]

These memoirs of two escaped slaves, Henry Bibb and Harriet Jacobs, illustrate some of the features of Southern slavery. Bibb was married and had a child when he escaped to the North, where he spent the rest of his life working for the abolition of slavery. The passage printed here gives an overview of his early life and expresses his commitment to freedom and his family. He also describes some of the abuses he and his family suffered under the reign of a particularly cruel master. Bibb was unable to rescue his daughter from slavery and agonizes over leaving her in bondage.

Harriet Jacobs grew up as a slave in Edenton, North Carolina, and in this excerpt she recounts some of her experiences, especially the sexual abuse she suffered at the hand of her master. Her narrative illustrates the dynamics of power and sexual violence in the "peculiar institution" of slavery, and the very limited options she had for defending herself from the advances of her master. She eventually escaped from slavery by hiding in her grandmother's house for nearly 17 years and then making her way to the North.

Introduction

In this chapter, we examine the creation of minority-group status for three groups: American Indians, Mexican Americans, and especially African Americans. We will examine the creation of institutionalized inequality for each group and the development of cultural belief systems that attempted to justify and rationalize white privilege. To understand the dynamics of these processes, we must begin at the inception of the British colonial society that eventually became the United States.

Colonial America

From the first settlements in the 1600s until the 19th century, most people living in what was to become the United States relied directly on farming for food, shelter, and other necessities of life. In an agricultural society, land and labor are central concerns, and the struggle to control these resources led directly to the creation of minority-group status for three groups: African Americans, American Indians, and Mexican Americans. Why did the colonists create slavery? Why were Africans enslaved but not American Indians or Europeans? Why did American Indians lose their land and most of their population by the 1890s? How did the Mexican population in the Southwest become "Mexican Americans"? How did the experience of becoming a subordinated minority group vary by gender?

We will use many of the concepts introduced in Part I to answer these questions. Some new ideas and theories will also be introduced, and by the end of the chapter, we will have developed a theoretical model of the process that leads to the creation of a minority group. The creation of black slavery in colonial America—arguably the single most significant event in the early years of this nation—will be used to illustrate the process of minority-group creation. We will also consider the subordination of American Indians and Mexican Americans—two more historical events of great significance—as additional case studies. We will follow the experiences of African Americans through the days of segregation (Chapter 4) and into the contemporary era (Chapter 5). The story of the development of minority-group status for American Indians and Mexican Americans will be picked up again in Chapters 6 and 7, respectively.

Two broad themes underlie this chapter and, indeed, the remainder of the text:

1. The nature of dominant–minority group relations at any point in time is largely a function of the characteristics of the society as a whole. The situation of a minority group will reflect the realities of everyday social life and particularly the subsistence technology (the means by which the society satisfies basic needs such as food and shelter). As explained by Gerhard Lenski (see Chapter 1), the subsistence technology of a society acts as a foundation, shaping and affecting every other aspect of the social structure, including minority-group relations.

2. The *contact situation*—the conditions under which groups first come together—is the single most significant factor in the creation of minority-group status. The nature of the contact situation has long-lasting consequences for the minority group and the extent of racial or ethnic stratification, the levels of racism and prejudice, the possibilities for assimilation and pluralism, and virtually every other aspect of the dominant–minority relationship.

The Origins of Slavery in the British Colonies

By the beginning of the 1600s, Spanish explorers had conquered much of Central and South America, and the influx of gold, silver, and other riches from the New World had made Spain a powerful nation. Following Spain's lead, England proceeded to establish its presence in the Western Hemisphere, but its efforts at colonization were more modest than those of Spain. By the early 1600s, only two small colonies had been established: Plymouth, settled by pious Protestant families, and Jamestown, populated primarily by males seeking their fortunes.

By 1619, the British colony at Jamestown, Virginia, had survived for more than a decade. The residents of the settlement had fought with the local natives and struggled continuously to eke out a living from the land. Starvation, disease, and death were frequent visitors, and the future of the enterprise continued to be in doubt.

In August of that year, a Dutch ship arrived. The master of the ship needed provisions and offered to trade his only cargo: about 20 black Africans. Many of the details of this transaction have been lost, and we probably will never know exactly how these people came to be chained in the hold of a ship. Regardless, this brief episode was a landmark event in the formation of what would become the United States. In combination with the strained relations between the English settlers and American Indians, the presence of these first few Africans raised an issue that has never been fully resolved: How should different groups in this society relate to each other?

The colonists at Jamestown had no ready answer. In 1619, England and its colonies did not practice slavery, so these first Africans were probably incorporated into colonial society as **indentured servants,** contract laborers who are obligated to serve a master for a specific number of years. At the end of the indenture, or contract, the servant became a free citizen. The colonies depended heavily on indentured servants from the British Isles for labor, and this status apparently provided a convenient way of defining the newcomers from Africa, who were, after all, treated as commodities and exchanged for food and water.

The position of African indentured servants in the colonies remained ambiguous for several decades. American slavery evolved gradually and in small steps; in fact, there was little demand for African labor during the years following 1619. By 1625, there still were only 23 blacks in Virginia, and that number had increased to perhaps 300 by mid-century (Franklin & Moss, 1994, p. 57). In the decades before the dawn of slavery, we know that some African indentured servants did become free citizens. Some became successful farmers and landowners and, like their white neighbors, purchased African and white indentured servants themselves (Smedley, 1999). By the 1650s, however, many African Americans (and their offspring) were being treated as the property of others, or in other words, as slaves (Morgan, 1975).

It was not until the 1660s that the first laws defining slavery were enacted. In the century that followed, hundreds of additional laws were passed to clarify and formalize the status of Africans in colonial America. By the 1750s, slavery had been clearly defined in law and in custom, and the idea that a person could own another person—not just the labor or the energy or the work of a person, but the actual person—had been thoroughly institutionalized.

What caused slavery? The gradual evolution of the institution and the low demand for indentured servants from Africa suggest that slavery was not somehow inevitable or preordained. Why did the colonists deliberately create this repressive system? Why did they reach out all the way to Africa for their slaves? If they wanted to create a slave system, why didn't they enslave the American Indians nearby or the white indentured servants already present in the colonies?

Exhibit 3.1 The African Diaspora

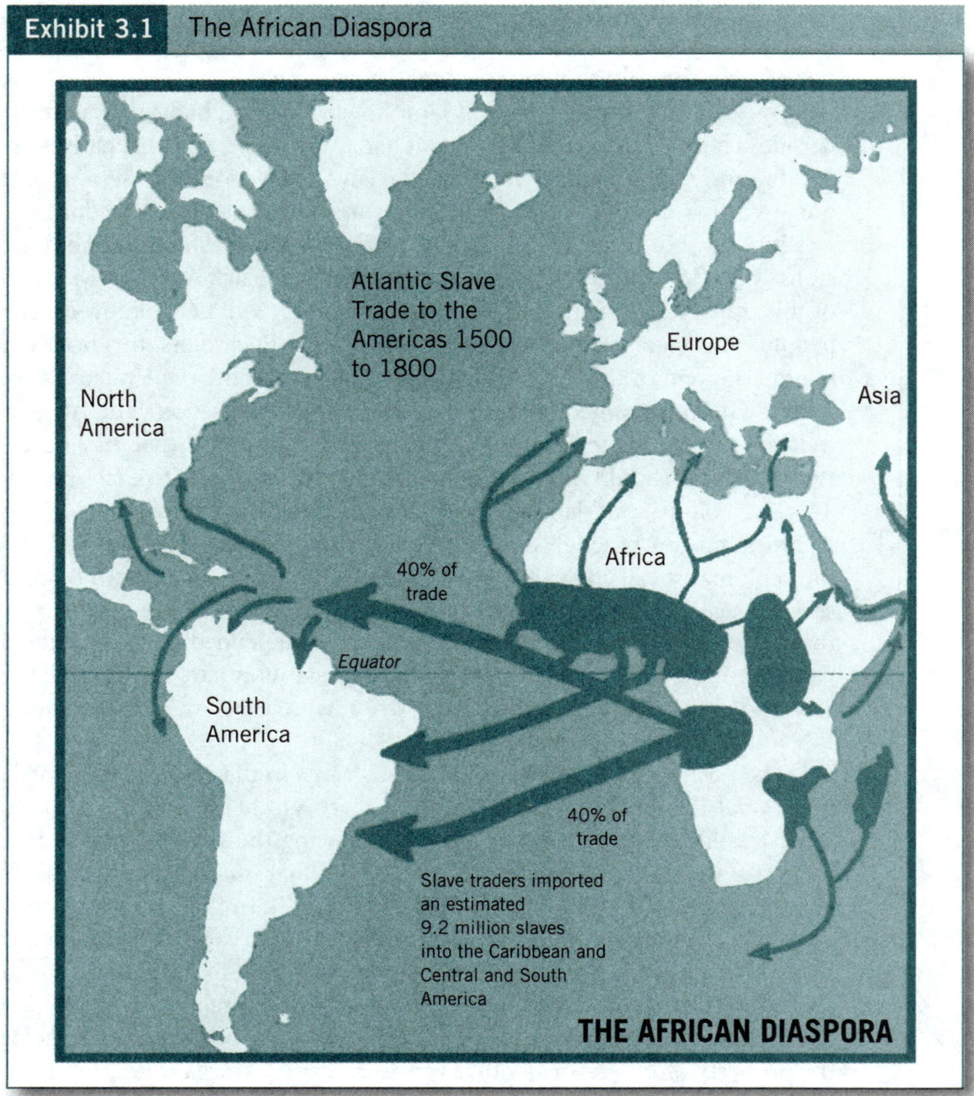

SOURCE: *Slave Trade and African American Ancestry* (n.d.). Original source of this map is *MacMillan Encyclopedia of World Slavery: 1st edition.* Copyright ©1998 Gale, a part of Cengage Learning, Inc. Reproduced by permission. www.cengage.com/permissions.

NOTE: The size of the arrows is proportional to the number of slaves. Note that the bulk went to South America and that there were also flows to Europe and Asia.

The Labor Supply Problem

American colonists of the 1600s saw slavery as a solution to several problems they faced. The business of the colonies was agriculture, and farmwork at this time was labor-intensive, performed almost entirely by hand. The industrial revolution was two centuries in the future, and there were few machines or labor-saving devices available to ease the everyday burden of work. A successful harvest depended largely on human effort.

As colonial society grew and developed, a specific form of agricultural production began to emerge. The **plantation system** was based on cultivating and exporting crops such as sugar, tobacco, and rice on large tracts of land using a large, cheap labor force. Profit margins tended to be small, so planters sought to stabilize their incomes by farming in volume and keeping the costs of production as low as possible. Profits in the labor-intensive plantation system could be maximized if a large, disciplined, and cheap workforce could be maintained by the landowners (Curtin, 1990; Morgan, 1975).

At about the same time the plantation system began to emerge, the supply of white indentured servants from the British Isles began to dwindle. Furthermore, the white indentured servants who did come to the colonies had to be released from their indenture every few years. Land was available, and these newly freed citizens tended to strike out on their own. Thus, landowners who relied on white indentured servants had to deal with high turnover rates in their workforces and faced a continually uncertain supply of labor.

Attempts to solve the labor supply problem by using American Indians failed. The tribes closest to the colonies were sometimes exploited for manpower. However, by the time the plantation system had evolved, the local tribes had dwindled in numbers as a result of warfare and disease. Other Indian nations across the continent retained enough power to resist enslavement, and it was relatively easy for American Indians to escape back to their kinfolk.

This left black Africans as a potential source of manpower. The slave trade from Africa to the Spanish and Portuguese colonies of South America was firmly established by the mid-1600s and could be expanded to fill the needs of the British colonies as well. The colonists came to see slaves imported from Africa as the most logical, cost-effective way to solve their vexing shortage of labor. The colonists created slavery to cultivate their lands and generate profits, status, and success. The paradox at the core of U.S. society had been established: The construction of a social system devoted to freedom and individual liberty "in the New World was made possible only by the revival of an institution of naked tyranny foresworn for centuries in the Old" (Lacy, 1972, p. 22).

The Contact Situation

The conditions under which groups first come into contact determine the immediate fate of the minority group and shape intergroup relations for years to come. We discussed the role of group competition in creating prejudice in Chapter 1. Here I expand on some these ideas by introducing two theories that will serve as analytical guides in understanding the contact situation.

The Noel Hypothesis

Sociologist Donald Noel (1968) identifies three features of the contact situation that in combination lead to some form of inequality between groups. The **Noel hypothesis** states, "If two or more groups come together in a contact situation characterized by ethnocentrism, competition, and a differential in power, then some form of racial or ethnic stratification will result" (p. 163). If the contact situation has all three characteristics, a dominant–minority group structure will be created.

Noel's first characteristic, **ethnocentrism,** is the tendency to judge other groups, societies, or lifestyles by the standards of one's own culture. Ethnocentrism is probably a universal component of human society, and some degree of ethnocentrism is essential to the maintenance of social solidarity and cohesion. Without some minimal level of pride in and loyalty to one's own society and cultural traditions, there would be no particular reason to observe the norms and laws, honor the sacred symbols, or cooperate with others in doing the daily work of society.

Regardless of its level of importance, ethnocentrism can have negative consequences. At its worst, it can lead to the view that other cultures and peoples are not just different, but inferior. At the very least, ethnocentrism creates a social boundary line that members of the groups involved will recognize and observe. When ethnocentrism exists in any degree, people will tend to sort themselves out along group lines and identify characteristics that differentiate "us" from "them."

Competition is a struggle over a scarce commodity. Competition between groups often leads to harsh negative feelings (prejudice) and hostile actions (discrimination). In competitive contact situations, the victorious group becomes the dominant group, and the losers become the minority group. The competition may center on land, labor, jobs, housing, educational opportunities, political office, or anything else that is mutually desired by both groups or that one group has and the other group wants. Competition provides the eventual dominant group with the motivation to establish superiority. The dominant group serves its own interests by ending the competition and exploiting, controlling, eliminating, or otherwise dominating the minority group.

The third feature of the contact situation is a **differential in power** between the groups. Power, as you may recall from Chapter 1, is the ability of a group to achieve its goals even in the face of opposition from other groups. The amount of power commanded by a group is a function of three factors. First, the size of the group can make a difference, and all other things being equal, larger groups are more powerful. Second, in addition to raw numbers, the degree of organization, discipline, and the quality of group leadership can make a difference in the ability of a group to pursue its goals. A third component of power is resources: anything that can be used to help the group achieve its goals. Depending on the context, resources might include anything from land to information to money. The greater the number and variety of resources at the disposal of a group, the greater that group's potential ability to dominate other groups. Thus, a larger, better-organized group with more resources at its disposal will generally be able to impose its will on smaller, less well-organized groups with fewer resources. The Noel hypothesis is diagrammed in Exhibit 3.2.

Exhibit 3.2 A Model of the Establishment of Minority Group Status

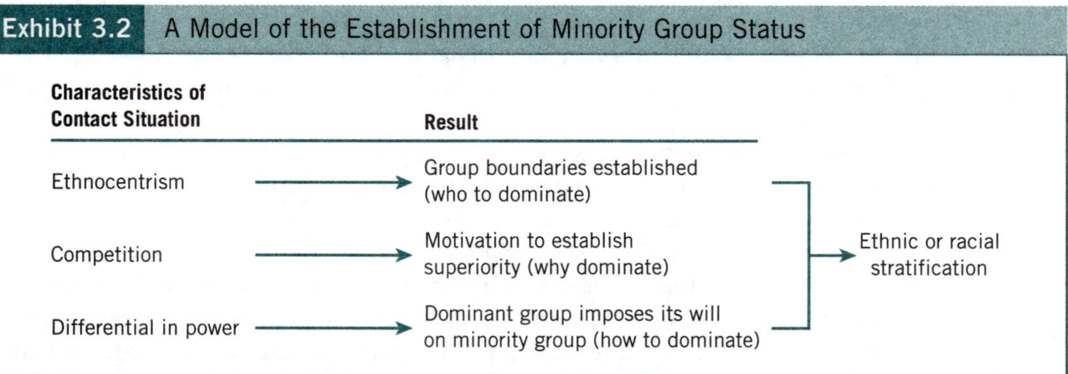

Note the respective functions of each of the three factors in shaping the contact situation and the emergence of inequality. If ethnocentrism is present, the groups will recognize their differences and maintain their boundaries. If competition is also present, the group that eventually dominates will attempt to maximize its share of scarce commodities by controlling or subordinating the group that eventually becomes the "minority" group. The differential in power allows the dominant group to succeed in establishing a superior position. Ethnocentrism tells the dominant group who to dominate, competition tells the dominant group why it should establish a structure of dominance, and power is how the dominant group's will is imposed on the minority group.

The Noel hypothesis can be applied to the creation of minority groups in a variety of situations. We will also use the model to analyze changes in dominant–minority structures over time.

The Blauner Hypothesis

The contact situation has also been analyzed by sociologist Robert Blauner, in his book *Racial Oppression in America* (1972). Blauner identifies two different initial relationships—colonization and immigration—and hypothesizes that:

> minority groups created by colonization will experience more intense prejudice, racism, and discrimination than those created by immigration. Furthermore, the disadvantaged status of colonized groups will persist longer and be more difficult to overcome than the disadvantaged status faced by groups created by immigration. (p. 52)

Colonized minority groups, such as African Americans, are forced into minority status by the superior military and political power of the dominant group. At the time of contact with the dominant group, colonized groups are subjected to massive inequalities and attacks on their cultures. They are assigned to positions, such as slave status, from which any form of assimilation is extremely difficult and perhaps even forbidden by the dominant group. Frequently, members of the minority group are identified by highly visible racial or physical characteristics that maintain and reinforce the oppressive system. Thus, minority groups created by colonization experience harsher and more persistent rejection and oppression than groups created by immigration.

Immigrant minority groups are at least in part voluntary participants in the host society. That is, although the decision to immigrate may be motivated by extreme pressures, such as famine or political persecution, immigrant groups have at least some control over their destination and their position in the host society. As a result, they do not occupy positions that are as markedly inferior as those of colonized groups. They retain enough internal organization and resources to pursue their own self-interests, and they commonly experience more rapid acceptance and easier movement to equality. The boundaries between groups are not so rigidly maintained, especially when the groups are racially similar. In discussing European immigrant groups, for example, Blauner (1972) states that entering into American society

> involved a degree of choice and self-direction that was for the most part denied to people of color. Voluntary immigration made it more likely that . . . European . . . ethnic groups would identify with America and see the host culture as a positive opportunity. (p. 56)

Acculturation and particularly integration were significantly more possible for European immigrant groups than for the groups formed under conquest or colonization.

Blauner (1972) stresses that the initial differences between colonized and immigrant minority groups have consequences that persist long after the original contact. For example, based on measures of equality—or integration into the secondary sector, the second step in Gordon's model of assimilation (see Chapter 2)—such as average income, years of education, and unemployment rate, the descendants of the European immigrants are equal with national norms today (see Chapter 2 for specific data). In contrast, the descendants of colonized and conquered groups (e.g., African Americans) are, on the average, below the national norms on virtually all measures of equality and integration (see Chapters 5–7 for specific data).

Blauner's two types of minority groups lie at opposite ends of a continuum, but there are intermediate positions between the extremes. Enclave and middleman minorities (see Chapter 2) often originate as immigrant groups who bring some resources and thus have more opportunities than colonized minority groups to carve out places for themselves in the host society. Unlike European groups, however, many of these minorities are also racially distinguishable, and certain kinds of opportunities may be closed to them. For instance, U.S. citizenship was expressly forbidden to immigrants from China until World War II. Federal laws restricted the entrance of Chinese immigrants, and state and local laws restricted their opportunities for education, jobs, and housing. For this and other reasons, the Asian immigrant experience cannot be equated with European immigrant patterns (Blauner, 1972). Because they combine characteristics of both the colonized and the immigrant minority group experience, we can predict that in terms of equality, enclave and middleman minority groups will occupy an intermediate status between the more assimilated white ethnic groups and the colonized racial minorities.

Blauner's typology has proven to be an extremely useful conceptual tool for the analysis of U.S. dominant–minority relations, and it is used extensively throughout this text. In fact, the case studies that comprise Part III of this text are arranged in approximate order, from groups created by colonization to those created by immigration. Of course, it is difficult to measure such things as the extent of colonization objectively or precisely, and the exact order of the groups is somewhat arbitrary.

The Creation of Slavery in the United States

The Noel hypothesis helps explain why colonists enslaved black Africans instead of white indentured servants or American Indians. First, all three groups were the objects of ethnocentric feelings on the part of the elite groups that dominated colonial society. Black Africans and American Indians were perceived as being different on religious as well as racial grounds. Many white indentured servants were Irish Catholics, criminals, or paupers. They not only occupied a lowly status in society, they were also perceived as different from the British Protestants who dominated colonial society.

Second, competition of some sort existed between the colonists and all three groups. The competition with American Indians was direct and focused on control of land. Competition with indentured servants, white and black, was more indirect; these groups were the labor force that the landowners needed to work their plantations and become successful in the New World.

Noel's third variable, differential in power, is the key variable that explains why Africans were enslaved instead of the other groups. During the first several decades of colonial history, the balance of power between the colonists and American Indians was relatively even, and in fact, often favored American Indians (Lurie, 1982). The colonists were outnumbered, and their muskets and cannons were only marginally more effective than bows and spears. The American Indian tribes were well-organized social units capable of sustaining resistance to and mounting reprisals against the colonists, and it took centuries for the nascent United States to finally defeat American Indians militarily.

White indentured servants, on the one hand, had the advantage of being preferred over black indentured servants (Noel, 1968). Their greater desirability gave them bargaining power and the ability to negotiate better treatment and more lenient terms than black indentured servants. If the planters had attempted to enslave white indentured servants, this source of labor would have dwindled even more rapidly.

Africans, on the other hand, had become indentured servants by force and coercion. In Blauner's terms, they were a colonized group that did not freely choose to enter the British colonies. Thus, they had no bargaining power. Unlike American Indians, they had no nearby relatives, no knowledge of the countryside, and no safe havens to which to escape. Exhibit 3.3 summarizes the impact of these three factors on the three potential sources of labor in colonial America.

Exhibit 3.3 The Noel Hypothesis Applied to the Origins of Slavery

	Three Causal Factors		
Potential Sources of Labor	**Ethnocentrism**	**Competition**	**Differential in Power**
White Indentured Servants	Yes	Yes	No
American Indians	Yes	Yes	No
Black Indentured Servants	Yes	Yes	Yes

SOURCE: From Noel (1968). Copyright ©1968. Reprinted by permission of The University of California Press via the Copyright Clearance Center.

Paternalistic Relations

Recall the first theme stated at the beginning of this chapter: The nature of intergroup relationships will reflect the characteristics of the larger society. The most important and profitable unit of economic production in the colonial South was the plantation, and the region was dominated by a small group of wealthy landowners. A society with a small elite class and a plantation-based economy will often develop a form of minority relations called **paternalism** (van den Berghe, 1967; Wilson, 1973). The key features of paternalism are vast power differentials and huge inequalities between dominant and minority groups, elaborate and repressive systems of control over the minority group, caste-like barriers between groups, elaborate and highly stylized codes of behavior and communication between groups, and low rates of overt conflict. Each of these characteristics will be considered in turn.

As slavery evolved in the colonies, the dominant group shaped the system to fit its needs. To solidify control of the labor of their slaves, the plantation elite designed and enacted an elaborate system of laws and customs that gave masters nearly total legal power over slaves. In these laws, slaves were defined as **chattel,** or personal property, rather than as persons, and they were accorded no civil or political rights. Slaves could not own property, sign contracts, bring lawsuits, or even testify in court (except against another slave). The masters were given the legal authority to determine almost every aspect of a slave's life, including work schedules, living arrangements, diets, and even names (Elkins, 1959; Franklin & Moss, 1994; Genovese, 1974; Jordan, 1968; Stampp, 1956).

The law permitted the master to determine the type and severity of punishment for misbehavior. Slaves were forbidden by law to read or write, and marriages between slaves were not legally recognized. Masters could separate husbands from wives and parents from children if it suited them. Slaves had little formal decision-making ability or control over their lives or the lives of their loved ones.

In colonial America, slavery became synonymous with race. Race, slavery, inferiority, and powerlessness became intertwined in ways that, according to many analysts, still affect the ways black and white Americans think about one another (Hacker, 1992). Slavery was a **caste system,** or closed stratification system. In a caste system, there is no mobility between social positions, and the social class you are born into (your ascribed status) is permanent. Slave status was for life and was passed on to any children a slave might have. Whites, no matter what they did, could not be made slaves.

Interaction between members of the dominant and minority groups in a paternalistic system is governed by a rigid, strictly enforced code of etiquette. Slaves were expected to show deference and humility and visibly display their lower status when interacting with whites. These rigid behavioral codes made it possible for blacks and whites to work together—sometimes intimately, sometimes for their entire lives—without threatening the power and status differentials inherent in the system. Plantation and farmwork required close and frequent contact between blacks and whites, and status differentials were maintained socially rather than by physically separating the groups (as was done during segregation).

The frequent but unequal interactions allowed the elites to maintain a *pseudotolerance,* an attitude of benevolent despotism, toward their slaves. Their prejudice and racism were often expressed as positive emotions of affection for their black slaves. The attitude of the planters toward their slaves was often paternalistic and even genteel (Wilson, 1973).

For their part, black slaves often could not hate their owners as much as they hated the system that constrained them. The system defined slaves as pieces of property owned by their masters—yet they were, undeniably, human beings. Thus, slavery was founded, at its heart, on a contradiction.

> The master learned to treat his slaves both as property and as men and women, the slaves learned to express and affirm their humanity even while they were constrained in much of their lives to accept their status as chattel. (Parish, 1989, p. 1)

The powerlessness of slaves made it difficult for them to openly reject or resist the system. Slaves had few ways in which they could directly challenge the institution of slavery or their position in it. Open defiance was ineffective and could result in punishment or even death. In general, masters would not be prosecuted for physically abusing their slaves.

One of the few slave revolts that occurred in the United States illustrates both the futility of overt challenge and the degree of repression built into the system. In 1831, in Southampton County, Virginia, a slave named Nat Turner led an uprising during which 57 whites were killed. The revolt was starting to spread when the state militia met and routed the growing slave army. More than 100 slaves died in the armed encounter, and Nat Turner and 13 others were later executed. Slave owners and white Southerners in general were greatly alarmed by the uprising and consequently tightened the system of control over slaves, making it even more repressive (Franklin & Moss, 1994). Ironically, the result of Nat Turner's attempt to lead slaves to freedom was greater oppression and control by the dominant group.

Others were more successful in resisting the system. Runaway slaves were a constant problem for slave owners, especially in the states bordering the free states of the North. The difficulty of escape and the low likelihood of successfully reaching the North did not deter thousands from attempting the feat, some of them repeatedly.

Many runaway slaves received help from the Underground Railroad, an informal network of safe houses supported by African Americans and whites involved in **abolitionism,** the movement to abolish slavery. These escapes created colorful legends and heroic figures, including Frederick Douglass, Sojourner Truth, and Harriet Tubman.

Besides running away and open rebellion, slaves used the forms of resistance most readily available to them: sabotage, intentional carelessness, dragging their feet, and work slowdowns. As historian Peter Parish (1989) points out, it is difficult to separate "a natural desire to avoid hard work [from a] conscious decision to protest or resist" (p. 73), and much of this behavior may fall more into the category of noncooperation than deliberate political rebellion. Nonetheless, these behaviors were widespread and document the rejection of the system by its victims.

On an everyday basis, the slaves managed their lives and families as best they could. Most slaves were neither docile victims nor unyielding rebels. As the institution of slavery developed, a distinct African American experience accumulated, and traditions of resistance and accommodation developed side-by-side. Most slaves worked to create a world for themselves within the confines and restraints of the plantation system, avoiding the more vicious repression as much as possible while attending to their own needs and those of their families. An African American culture was forged in response to the realities of slavery and was manifested in folklore, music, religion, family and kinship structures, and other aspects of everyday life (Blassingame, 1972; Genovese, 1974; Gutman, 1976).

The Dimensions of Minority Group Status

The situation of African Americans under slavery can be more completely described by applying some of the concepts developed in Part I.

Power, Inequality, and Institutional Discrimination

The key concepts for understanding the creation of slavery are power, inequality, and institutional discrimination. The plantation elite used its greater power resources to consign black Africans to an inferior status. The system of racial inequality was implemented and reinforced by institutionalized discrimination and became a central aspect of everyday life in the antebellum (pre–Civil War) South. The legal and political institutions of colonial society were shaped to benefit the landowners and give them almost total control over their slaves.

Prejudice and Racism

What about the attitudes and feelings of the people involved? What was the role of personal prejudice? How and why did the ideology of antiblack racism start? As we discussed in Chapter 1, individual prejudice and ideological racism are not so important as *causes* of the creation of minority group status but are more the *results* of systems of racial inequality (Jordan, 1968; Smedley, 1999). The colonists did not enslave black indentured servants because they were prejudiced or because they disliked blacks or thought them inferior. The decision to enslave black Africans was an attempt to resolve a labor supply problem. The primary roles of prejudice and racism in the creation of minority-group status are to rationalize and "explain" the emerging system of racial and ethnic advantage (Wilson, 1973).

Prejudice and racism help to mobilize support for the creation of minority-group status and to stabilize the system as it emerges. They can provide convenient and convincing justifications for exploitation. They can also help insulate a system like slavery from questioning and criticism and make it appear reasonable and even desirable. Thus, the intensity, strength, and popularity of antiblack Southern racism actually reached its height almost 200 years after slavery began to emerge. During the early 1800s, the American abolitionist movement brought slavery under heavy attack, and in response, the ideology of antiblack racism was strengthened (Wilson, 1973). The greater the opposition to a system of racial stratification or the greater the magnitude of the exploitation, the greater the need of the beneficiaries and their apologists to justify, rationalize, and explain.

Once created, dominant group prejudice and racism become widespread and common ways of thinking about the minority group. In the case of colonial slavery, antiblack beliefs and feelings became part of the standard package of knowledge, understanding, and truths shared by members of the dominant group. As the decades wore on and the institution of slavery solidified, prejudice and racism were passed on from generation to generation. For succeeding generations, antiblack prejudice became just another piece of information and perspective on the world learned during socialization. Antiblack prejudice and racism began as part of an attempt to control the labor of black indentured servants, became embedded in early American culture, and were established as integral parts of the socialization process for succeeding generations (see Myrdahl's "vicious cycle" in Chapter 1).

These conceptual relationships are presented in Exhibit 3.4. Racial inequality arises from the contact situation, as specified in the Noel hypothesis. As the dominant–minority relationship begins to take shape, prejudice and racism develop as rationalizations. Over time, a vicious cycle develops as prejudice and racism reinforce the pattern of inequality between groups, which was the cause of prejudice and racism in the first place. Thus, as the Blauner hypothesis states, the subordination of colonized minority groups is perpetuated through time.

Exhibit 3.4 A Model for the Creation of Prejudice and Racism

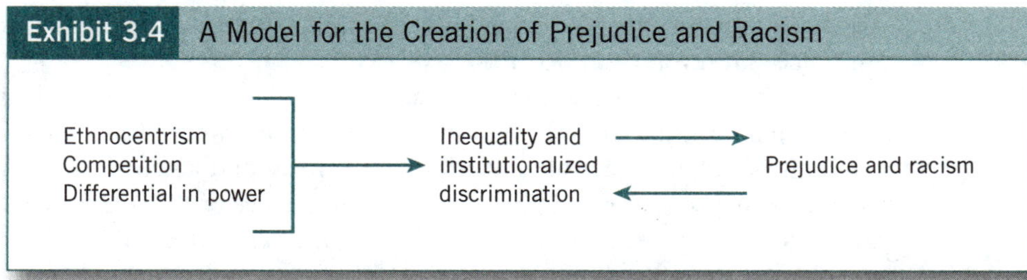

Assimilation

There is an enormous amount of literature on American slavery, and research on the nature and meaning of the system continues to this day. Many issues remain unsettled, however, and one of the more controversial, consequential, and interesting of these concerns the effect of slavery on the slaves.

Apologists for the system of slavery and some historians of the South writing early in the 20th century accepted the rationalizations inherent in antiblack prejudice and argued that slavery was actually beneficial for black Africans. According to this view, British-American slavery operated as a "school for civilization" (Phillips, 1918) that rescued savages from the jungles of Africa and exposed them to Christianity and Western civilization. Some argued that slavery was benevolent because it protected slaves from the evils and exploitation of the factory system of the industrial North. These racist views were most popular a century ago, early in the development of the social sciences. Since that time, scholars have established a number of facts (e.g., Western Africa, the area from which most slaves came, had been the site of a number of powerful, advanced civilizations) that make this view untenable by anyone but the most dedicated racist thinkers.

At the opposite extreme, slavery has been compared with Nazi concentration camps and likened to a "perverted patriarchy" that brainwashed, emasculated, and dehumanized slaves, stripping them of their heritage and culture. Historian Stanley Elkins provocatively argued this interpretation, now widely regarded as overstated, in his book *Slavery: A Problem in American Institutional and Intellectual Life* (1959). Although his conclusions might be overdrawn, Elkins' argument and evidence are important for any exploration of the nature of American slavery. In fact, much of the scholarship on slavery since the publication of Elkins' book has been an attempt to refute or at least modify the points he made.

Still a third view of the impact of slavery maintains that through all the horror and abuse of enslavement, slaves retained a sense of self and a firm anchor in their African traditions. This point of view stresses the importance of kinship, religion, and culture in helping African Americans cope and has been presented most poignantly in Alex Haley's semi-fictional family history *Roots* (1976), but it is also represented in the scholarly literature on slavery since Elkins (see Blassingame, 1972; Genovese, 1974).

The debate over the impact of slavery continues, and we cannot hope to resolve the issues here. However, it is clear that African Americans, in Blauner's terms, were a "colonized" minority group who were extensively—and coercively—acculturated. Language acculturation began on the slave ships, where different tribal and language groups were mixed together to inhibit communication and lower the potential for resistance and revolt (Mannix, 1962).

The plantation elite and their agents needed to communicate with their workforce and insisted on using English. Within a generation or two, African language use died out. Some scholars argue that certain African words and language patterns persist to the present day, but even if this is true, the significance of this survival is trivial compared with the coerced adoption of English. To the extent that culture depends on language, Africans under slavery experienced massive acculturation.

Acculturation through slavery was clearly a process that was forced on African Americans. Because they were a colonized minority group and unwilling participants in the system, they had little choice but to adjust to the conditions established by the plantation elite as best they could. Their traditional culture was suppressed, and their choices for adjustment to the system were sharply constrained. Black slaves developed new cultural forms and social relationships, but they did so in a situation with few options or choices (Blauner, 1972). The extent to which any African cultural elements survived the institution of slavery is a matter of some controversy, but given the power differentials inherent in the system, African Americans had few choices regarding their manner of adjustment.

Gender Relations

Southern agrarian society developed into a complex social system stratified by race and gender as well as by class. The plantation elite, small in number but wealthy and politically powerful, was at the top of the structure. Most whites in the South were small farmers, and relatively few of them owned slaves. In 1860, for example, only 25% of all Southern whites owned slaves (Franklin & Moss, 1994, p. 123).

The principal line of differentiation in the antebellum South was, of course, race, which was largely synonymous with slave versus non-slave status. Each of the racial groups was in turn stratified by gender. White women were subordinate to the males of the plantation elite, and the slave community echoed the patriarchal pattern of Southern society, except that the degree of gender inequality among blacks was sharply truncated by the fact that slaves had little autonomy and few resources. At the bottom of the system were African American female slaves. Minority women are generally in double jeopardy, oppressed through their gender as well as their race. For black female slaves, the constraints were triple: "Black in a white society, slave in a free society, women in a society ruled by men, female slaves had the least formal power and were perhaps the most vulnerable group of antebellum America" (White, 1985, p. 15).

The race and gender roles of the day idealized Southern white women and placed them on a pedestal. A romanticized conception of femininity was quite inconsistent with the roles women slaves were required to play. Besides domestic roles, female slaves also worked in the fields and did their share of the hardest, most physically demanding, least "feminine" farmwork. Southern ideas about feminine fragility and daintiness were quickly abandoned when they interfered with work and the profit to be made from slave labor (Amott & Matthaei, 1991).

Reflecting their vulnerability and powerlessness, women slaves were sometimes used to breed more slaves to sell. They were raped and otherwise abused by the males of the dominant group. John Blassingame (1972) expresses their vulnerability to sexual victimization:

> Many white men considered every slave cabin a house of ill-fame. Often through "gifts" but usually by force, white overseers and planters obtained the sexual favors of black women. Generally speaking, the women were literally forced to offer themselves "willingly" and receive a trinket for their compliance rather than a flogging for their refusal. (p. 83)

Note the power relationships implicit in this passage: Female slaves had little choice but to feign willing submission to their white owners.

The routines of work and everyday life differed for male and female slaves. Although they sometimes worked with the men, especially during harvest time, women more often worked in sex-segregated groups organized around domestic as well as farm chores. In addition to working in the fields, they attended the births and cared for the children of both races, cooked and cleaned, wove cloth and sewed clothes, and did the laundry. The women often worked longer hours than the men, doing housework and other chores long after the men retired (Robertson, 1996; White, 1985).

The group-oriented nature of their tasks gave female slaves an opportunity to develop same-sex bonds and relationships. Women cooperated in their chores, in caring for their children, in the maintenance of their quarters, and in myriad other domestic and family chores. These networks and interpersonal bonds could be used to resist the system. For example, slave women sometimes induced abortions rather than bring more children into bondage. Since they filled the role of midwife, they were able to effectively deceive slave owners and disguise the abortions as miscarriages (White, 1985). The networks of relationships among the female slaves provided mutual aid and support for everyday problems, solace and companionship during the travails of a vulnerable and exploited existence, and some ability to buffer and resist the influence and power of the slave owners (Andersen, 1993).

Slaves in the American system were brutally repressed and exploited, but females were even more subordinated than males. Also, their oppression sharply differentiated slave females from white females. The white "Southern belle," enshrined by Southern culture as chaste, untouchable, and unremittingly virtuous, had little in common with African American women under slavery.

FOCUS ON CONTEMPORARY ISSUES: Slavery and Indentured Servitude Today

As important as it was in the formation of the United States, you might see slavery as a distant piece of history, remote and bizarre. The idea that a person could be owned by another person, defined as a piece of property and bought and sold like livestock, might seem hopelessly alien in a culture so devoted to the cultivation of individual happiness and personal well-being. Yet, this ancient institution is not as remote as it might seem and, in fact, can be found today around the world, in advanced industrial nations, and in the United States.

The system of slavery we have considered in this chapter was linked to a certain level of development—the preindustrial, agrarian subsistence technology in which the control of a large, powerless workforce was a key to success. There are other systems of slavery, however, and many persist in the present. All feature similar dynamics to those noted in the Noel hypothesis: The motivation is supplied by a desire for profits, and the populations from which slaves are taken are relatively powerless and lack the resources to defend themselves. Furthermore, ethnocentrism is often a factor, as slaves and masters are frequently from different language, culture, racial, or religious groups. These differences may serve as the basis for the rationalization that the slaves deserve their fate, if the masters feel the need for an "explanation."

One major difference between the enslavement of blacks in the American South and contemporary versions of slavery is that the former was legal and above board. Modern slavery is criminal and underground, illegal (at least formally) around the globe. Thus, it is much harder to establish the numbers of people involved—although observers agree that the problem is substantial—and we have only approximations and estimates of the volume of the trade. One widely quoted estimate is that there are currently at least 12 million people living in some form of forced labor. Other estimates place the number anywhere from 4 million to 27 million (U.S. Department of State, 2008). Also, there are perhaps as many as 1 million slaves living in the United States (Epstein, 2006, p. 104).

Most modern-day slaves are laborers living within their country of birth. They are forced into bondage by various means, including through debt bondage. In this system, an individual is not owned outright as a slave. Rather, the person is required to work for little or no wages until some debt is paid off and his or her unfree status is maintained through time by usuriously high interest rates. For example, Skinner (2008) reports the case of a man in India working to pay off a debt of 62 cents incurred by his grandfather in 1958. With interest rates of 100% per year, he is forced to work in a quarry for no wage, three generations after the debt was originally incurred. It is thought that most forced labor slaves are in Southeast Asia, especially India and China.

Other slaves are part of an international system of trafficking in people, aided by globalization; instantaneous communication; and rapid, cheap travel. A large part of this trafficking is connected to commercial sexual operations such as prostitution, escort services, clubs featuring "adult" entertainment, and pornography. Sex trafficking involves children as well as women: The U.S. Department of State (2008) estimates that about 80% of transnational victims are women and girls and up to 50% are minors.

Sex traffickers find their victims in less-developed nations in which many women (and children) have been displaced from their traditional communities and villages and are no longer protected by those institutions. They are often duped into believing that they are being hired for legitimate jobs (domestic work or child care) in a more developed nation. When they arrive at their destination, their travel documents are taken and they are forced into sex work. They are isolated and kept powerless by their lack of documents, their illegal status, and their inability to speak the language of their new country. The huge power differentials between "slaves and masters" are reminiscent of American slavery, as is the masters' ability to treat their slaves any way they please.

Slaves and indentured servants are used to staff other businesses besides the sex trade. For example, Stein (2003) reports the case of "Mary," a Filipina who paid a labor broker $2,400 to connect her to a job in Taiwan working for a subcontractor of Motorola. When she landed in Taiwan, she discovered that she had to pay another broker an additional fee of $3,900 before she could begin work. Mary had to borrow virtually all of the money to cover these fees and was charged an interest rate of 10% a month. She was originally quite pleased with her Taiwanese wage, but now she finds that most of it will go to service her debts. She is bound to her job until she has paid off these loans.

(Continued)

(Continued)

In the United States, slavery and indentured servitude continue nearly 140 years after the Civil War (Bales & Soodalter, 2009). The United States is one of the prime destinations for victims of sex trafficking and for a variety of other workers who are bound by various forms of debt bondage. Some of these modern slaves provide the unskilled labor that keeps enclaves like Chinatowns functioning, while others work in agriculture, the seafood industry, landscaping, construction, and other areas. Many of these workers enter the United States legally as "guest workers" under a program run by the U.S. government. Once they are in the country, however, there is little federal or state oversight of their situation and, according to one report, these workers are often abused, forced to live and work in horrible conditions, and cheated of their wages by the brokers that bring them into the country. (Bauer, 2008). They lack the most fundamental of workers' rights and, should they protest their treatment, they can be swiftly deported.

Some of these modern forms of involuntary servitude are quite different from the system of American slavery. Instead of a journey from Africa that could last months, modern slaves can be shipped around the globe in hours or days. Instead of cotton plantations, slaves today work in factories or brothels. Like all forms of slavery, however, the modern versions are involuntary, coercive, and maintained by violence and force.

The Creation of Minority Status for American Indians and Mexican Americans

Two other groups became minorities during the preindustrial period. In this section, we will review the dynamics of these processes and make some comparisons with the enslavement of African Americans. As you will see, both the Noel and Blauner hypotheses provide some extremely useful insights into these experiences.

American Indians

As Europeans began to penetrate the New World, they encountered hundreds of societies that had lived on this land for thousands of years. American Indian societies were highly variable in culture, language, size, and subsistence technology. Some were small, nomadic, hunter-gatherer bands, whereas others were more developed societies in which people lived in settled villages and tended large gardens. Regardless of their exact nature, the inexorable advance of white society eventually devastated them all. Contact began in the East and established a pattern of conflict and defeat for American Indians that continued until the last of the tribes was finally defeated in the late 1800s. The continual expansion of white society into the West allowed many settlers to fulfill their dreams of economic self-sufficiency, but American Indians, who lost not only their lives and their land but also much of their traditional way of life, paid an incalculable price.

An important and widely unrecognized point about American Indians is that there is no such thing as *the* American Indian. Rather, there were—and are—hundreds of different tribes or nations, each with its own language, culture, home territory, and unique history. There are, of course, similarities from tribe to tribe, but there are also vast differences between, for example, the forest-dwelling tribes of Virginia, who lived in longhouses and cultivated gardens, and the nomadic Plains tribes, who relied on hunting to satisfy their needs. Each tribe had a unique blend of language, values, and social structure. Because of space constraints, we will not be able to take all these differences into account here. Nonetheless, it is important to be aware of the diversity and to be sensitive to the variety of peoples and histories subsumed within the general category of American Indian.

A second important point is that many American Indian tribes no longer exist or are vastly diminished in size. When Jamestown was established in 1607, it is estimated that there were anywhere from 1 million to more than 10 million American Indians living in what became the United States. By 1890, when the Indian Wars finally ended, the number of American Indians had fallen to fewer than 250,000. By the end of the nearly 300-year-long "contact situation," American Indian populations had declined by 75% or more (Wax, 1971, p. 17; see also McNickle, 1973).

Very little of this population loss was due directly to warfare and battle casualties. The greatest part was caused by European diseases brought over by the colonists and by the destruction of the food supplies on which American Indian societies relied. American Indians died by the thousands from measles, influenza, smallpox, cholera, tuberculosis, and a variety of other infectious diseases (Wax, 1971, p. 17; see also Oswalt & Neely, 1996; Snipp, 1989). Traditional hunting grounds and garden plots were taken over by the expanding American society, and game such as the buffalo was slaughtered to the point of extinction. The result of the contact situation for American Indians very nearly approached genocide.

American Indians and the Noel and Blauner Hypotheses

We have already used the Noel hypothesis to analyze why American Indians were not enslaved during the colonial era. Their competition with whites centered on land, not labor, and the Indian nations were often successful in resisting domination (at least temporarily). As American society spread to the West, competition over land continued, and the growing power, superior technology, and a greater resource base of the dominant group gradually pushed American Indians to near extinction.

Various attempts were made to control the persistent warfare, the most important of which occurred before the colonies' independence from Great Britain. In 1763, the British Crown ruled that the various tribes were to be considered "sovereign nations with inalienable rights to their land" (see Lurie, 1982; McNickle, 1973; Wax, 1971). In other words, each tribe was to be treated as a nation-state, like France or Russia, and the colonists could not simply expropriate tribal lands. Rather, negotiations had to take place, and treaties of agreement had to be signed by all affected parties. The tribes had to be compensated for any loss of land.

This policy was often ignored but was continued by the newborn federal government after the American Revolution. The principle of sovereignty is important because it established a unique relationship between the federal government and American Indians. The fact that white society ignored the policy and regularly broke the treaties gives American Indians legal claims against the federal government that are also unique.

East of the Mississippi River, the period of open conflict was brought to a close by the Indian Removal Act of 1830, which dictated a policy of forced emigration for the tribes. The law required all eastern tribes to move to new lands west of the Mississippi. Some of the affected tribes went without resistance, others fought, and still others fled to Canada rather than move to the new territory. Regardless, the Indian Removal Act "solved" the Indian problem in the East. The relative scarcity of American Indians in the eastern United States continues to the present, and the majority of American Indians live in the western two-thirds of the nation.

In the West, the grim story of competition for land accompanied by rising hostility and aggression repeated itself. Wars were fought, buffalo were killed, territory was expropriated, atrocities were committed on both sides, and the fate of the tribes became more and more certain. By 1890, the greater power and resources of white society had defeated the Indian nations. All of the great warrior chiefs were dead or in prison, and almost all American Indians were living on reservations controlled by agencies of the federal government. The reservations consisted of land set aside for the tribes by the government during treaty negotiations. Often, these lands were not the traditional homelands and were hundreds or even thousands of miles away from what the tribe considered to be "home." It is not surprising that the reservations were usually on undesirable, often worthless land.

The 1890s mark a low point in American Indian history, a time of great demoralization and sadness. The tribes had to find a way to adapt to reservation life and new forms of subordination to the federal government. Although elements of the tribal way of life survived, the tribes were impoverished and without resources and had little ability to pursue their own interests.

American Indians, in Blauner's terms, were a colonized minority group that faced high levels of prejudice, racism, and discrimination. Like African Americans, they were controlled by paternalistic systems (the reservations) and in a variety of ways were coercively acculturated. Furthermore, according to Blauner (1972), the negative consequences of colonized minority-group status will persist long after the contact situation has been resolved. As we will see in Chapter 6, there is a great deal of evidence to support this prediction.

Gender Relations

In the centuries before contact with Europeans, American Indian societies distributed resources and power in a wide variety of ways. At one extreme, some American

Indian societies were highly stratified, and many practiced various forms of slavery. Others stressed equality; sharing of resources; and respect for the autonomy and dignity of each individual, including women and children (Amott & Matthaei, 1991). American Indian societies were generally patriarchal and followed a strict gender-based division of labor, but this did not necessarily mean that women were subordinate. In many tribes, women held positions of great responsibility and controlled the wealth. For example, among the Iroquois (a large and powerful federation of tribes located in the Northeast), women controlled the land and the harvest, arranged marriages, supervised the children, and were responsible for the appointment of tribal leaders and decisions about peace and war (Oswalt & Neely, 1996). It was not unusual for women in many tribes to play key roles in religion, politics, warfare, and the economy. Some women even became highly respected warriors and chiefs (Amott & Matthaei, 1991).

Gender relations were affected in a variety of ways during the prolonged contact period, from the early 1600s to 1890. In some cases, the relative status and power of women rose. For example, the women of the Navajo tribe (located mainly in what is now Arizona and New Mexico) were traditionally responsible for the care of herd animals and livestock. When the Spanish introduced sheep and goats into the region, the importance of this sector of the subsistence economy increased, and the power and status of women grew along with it.

In other cases, women were affected adversely. The women of the tribes of the Great Plains, for example, suffered a dramatic loss as a result of contact. The sexual division of labor in these tribes was such that women were responsible for gardening, whereas men handled the hunting. When horses were introduced from Europe, the productivity of the male hunters was greatly increased. As their economic importance grew, males became more dominant, and women lost status and power. Women in the Cherokee Nation—a large tribe whose original homelands were in the Southeast—similarly lost considerable status and power under the pressure to assimilate. Traditionally, Cherokee land was cultivated, controlled, and passed down from generation to generation by the women. This matrilineal pattern was abandoned in favor of the European pattern of male ownership when the Cherokee attempted (futilely, as it turned out) to acculturate and avoid relocation under the Indian Relocation Act of 1830 (Evans, 1989).

Summary

By the end of the contact period, the surviving American Indian tribes were impoverished, powerless, and clearly subordinate to white society and the federal government. Like African Americans, they were sharply differentiated from the dominant group by race and, in many cases, internally stratified by gender. As was the case with African American slaves, the degree of gender inequality within the tribes was limited by their overall lack of autonomy and resources.

COMPARATIVE FOCUS: Hawaii

In 1788, while American Indians and whites continued their centuries-long struggle, white Europeans first made contact with the indigenous people of Hawaii (see map in Exhibit 3.5). The contact situation and the system of group relations that evolved on the island nation provide an interesting and instructive contrast with the history of American Indians.

In Hawaii, contact was not immediately followed by conquest and colonization. Early relations between Europeans and Hawaiians were organized around trade and commerce, not competition over the control of land or labor. Also, Hawaiian society was large, highly developed, and had sufficient military strength to protect itself from the relatively few Europeans who came to the islands in the early days. Thus, two of the three conditions stated in the Noel hypothesis for the emergence of a dominant–minority situation were not present in the early days of European–Hawaiian contact, and, consistent with the hypothesis, overt structures of conquest or dominance did not emerge until decades after first contact.

Exhibit 3.5 Map of the Hawaiian Islands

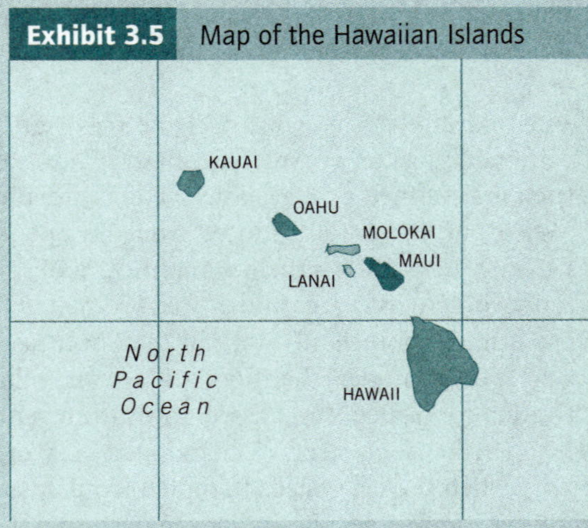

Contact with Europeans did bring other consequences, of course, including smallpox and other diseases to which native Hawaiians had no immunity. Death rates began to rise, and the population of native Hawaiians, which numbered about 300,000 in 1788, fell to less than 60,000 a century later (Kitano & Daniels, 1995, p. 137). White Europeans gradually turned the land to commercial agriculture and by the mid-1800s, white planters had established large sugar plantations, an enterprise that is extremely labor-intensive and that has often been associated with systems of enforced labor and slavery (Curtin, 1990). By that time, however, there were not enough native Hawaiians to fill the demand for labor, and the planters began to recruit abroad, mostly in China, Portugal, Japan, Korea, Puerto Rico, and the Philippines. Native Hawaiians continued to shrink in numbers and were gradually pushed off their land and to the margins of the emerging society.

The white plantation owners came to dominate the island economy and political structure. Other groups, however, were not excluded from secondary structural assimilation. Laws banning entire groups from public institutions and practices such as school segregation are unknown in Hawaiian history. Americans of Japanese ancestry, for example, are very powerful in Hawaiian politics. Most other groups have taken advantage of the relative openness of Hawaiian society and have carved out niches for themselves in the institutional structure.

In the area of primary structural assimilation, rates of intermarriage among the various groups are much higher than on the mainland, reflecting an openness to intimate relationships across group lines that has characterized Hawaii since first contact with Europeans. In particular, Native Hawaiians have intermarried freely with other groups (Kitano & Daniels, 1995).

Unlike the mainland society, Hawaii has no history of the most blatant and oppressive forms of group domination, racism, and legalized discrimination. Still, all is not perfect in this reputed racial paradise, and there is evidence of continuing ethnic and racial stratification, as well as prejudice and discrimination. In particular, Native Hawaiians today retain their minority-group status. The group is quite small and numbers about 150,000, an increase from the historic lows of the 19th century but still only about 12% of the state's population and a tiny minority of the U.S. population (U.S. Bureau of the Census, 2009a).

On the other hand, Native Hawaiians compare favorably with both American Indians and African Americans in terms of education, income, and poverty (see Exhibit 3.6). This relatively higher status today is consistent with both the Noel and Blauner hypotheses: They were not subjected to the harsh conditions (slavery, segregation, near genocide, and massive institutional discrimination) of the other two groups. Although they compare favorably to the two colonized and conquered groups, Native Hawaiians tend to be the poorest of the various ethnic and racial groups on the islands, and a protest movement of Native Hawaiians that stresses self-determination and the return of illegally taken land has been in existence since at least the 1960s.

Exhibit 3.6 Native Hawaiians Compared With Total Population, African Americans, and American Indians, 2007

	Group			
Indicator	**Total U.S. Population**	**Native Hawaiians**	**African Americans**	**American Indians**
% High School Graduate	84.0%	89.0%	79.4%	79.6%
% College Graduate	27.0%	17.7%	17.0%	15.7%
Median Household Income	$50,007	$55,682	$33,546	$37,168
% of Families in Poverty	9.8%	11.7%	21.7%	19.0%

SOURCE: U.S. Bureau of the Census (2009a).

Mexican Americans

As the population of the United States increased and spread across the continent, contact with Mexicans inevitably occurred. Spanish explorers and settlers had lived in what is now the Southwestern United States long before the wave of American settlers broke across this region. For example, Santa Fe, New Mexico, was founded in 1598, nearly a decade before Jamestown. As late as the 1820s, Mexicans and American Indians were almost the sole residents of the region.

In the early 1800s, four areas of Mexican settlement had developed, roughly corresponding to what was to become Texas, California, New Mexico, and Arizona. These areas were sparsely settled, and most Mexicans lived in what was later New Mexico (Cortes, 1980, p. 701). The economy of the regions was based on farming and herding. Most people lived in villages and small towns or on ranches and farms. Social and political life was organized around family and the Catholic Church and tended to be dominated by an elite class of wealthy landowners.

Texas

Some of the first effects of U.S. expansion to the West were felt in Texas early in the 1800s. Mexico was no military match for its neighbor to the north, and the farmland of East Texas was a tempting resource for the cotton-growing interests in the American South. Anglo Americans began to immigrate to Texas in sizable numbers in the 1820s, and by 1835, they outnumbered Mexicans 6 to 1. The attempts by the Mexican government to control these immigrants were clumsy and ineffective and eventually precipitated a successful revolution by the Anglo Americans, with some Mexicans joining the rebels. At this point in time, competition between Anglos and Texans of Mexican descent (called *Tejanos*) was muted by the abundance of land and opportunity in the area. Population density was low, fertile land was readily available for all, and the "general tone of the time was that of inter-cultural cooperation" (Alvarez, 1973, p. 922).

Competition between Anglo Texans and Tejanos became increasingly intense. When the United States annexed Texas in the 1840s, full-scale war broke out, and Mexico was defeated. Under the Treaty of Guadalupe Hidalgo in 1848, Mexico ceded much of the Southwest to the United States. In the Gadsden Purchase of 1853, the United States acquired the remainder of the territory that now composes the southwestern United States. As a result of these treaties, the Mexican population of this region had become, without moving an inch from their traditional villages and farms, both a conquered people and a minority group.

Following the war, intergroup relations continued to sour, and the political and legal rights of the Tejano community were often ignored in the hunger for land. Increasingly impoverished and powerless, the Tejanos had few resources with which to resist the growth of Anglo-American domination. They were badly outnumbered and stigmatized by the recent Mexican military defeat. Land that had once been Mexican increasingly came under Anglo control, and widespread violence and lynching reinforced the growth of Anglo dominance (Moquin & Van Doren, 1971).

California

In California, the Gold Rush of 1849 spurred a massive population movement from the East. Early relations between Anglos and *Californios* (native Mexicans in the state) had been relatively cordial, forming the basis for a multiethnic, bilingual state. The rapid growth of an Anglo majority after statehood in 1850 doomed these efforts, however, and the Californios, like the Tejanos, lost their land and political power.

Laws were passed encouraging Anglos to settle on land traditionally held by Californios. In such situations, the burden was placed on the Mexican American landowners to show that their deeds were valid. The Californios protested the seizure of their land but found it difficult to argue their cases in the English-speaking, Anglo-controlled court system. By the mid-1850s, a massive transfer of land to Anglo-American hands had taken place in California (Mirandé, 1985; see also Pitt, 1970).

Other laws passed in the 1850s made it increasingly difficult for Californios to retain their property and power as Anglo Americans became the dominant group as well as the majority of the population. The Mexican heritage was suppressed and eliminated from public life and institutions such as schools and local government. For example, in 1855, California repealed a requirement in the state constitution that all laws be published in Spanish as well as English (Cortes, 1980). Anglo Americans used violence, biased laws, discrimination, and other means to exploit and repress Californios, and the new wealth generated by gold mining flowed into Anglo hands.

Arizona and New Mexico

The Anglo immigration into Arizona and New Mexico was less voluminous than that into Texas and California, and both states retained Mexican numerical majorities for a number of decades. In Arizona, most of the Mexican population were immigrants themselves, seeking work on farms, ranches, in the mines, and on the railroads. The economic and political structures of the state quickly came under the control of the Anglo population.

Only in New Mexico did Mexican Americans retain some political power and economic clout, mostly because of the relatively large size of the group and their skill in mobilizing for political activity. New Mexico did not become a state until 1912, and Mexican Americans continued to play a prominent role in governmental affairs even after statehood (Cortes, 1980).

Thus, the contact situation for Mexican Americans was highly variable by region. Although some areas were affected more rapidly and more completely than others, the ultimate result was the creation of minority-group status for Mexican Americans (Acuna, 1999; Alvarez, 1973; McLemore, 1973; McWilliams, 1961; Moore, 1970; Stoddard, 1973).

Mexican Americans and the Noel and Blauner Hypotheses

The causal model we have applied to the origins of slavery and the domination of American Indians also provides a way of explaining the development of minority-group status for Mexican Americans. Ethnocentrism was clearly present from the very first contact between Anglo immigrants and Mexicans. Many American migrants to the Southwest brought with them the prejudices and racism they had acquired with regard to African Americans and American Indians. In fact, many of the settlers who moved into Texas came directly from the South in search of new lands for the cultivation of cotton. They readily transferred their prejudiced views to at least the poorer Mexicans, who were stereotyped as lazy and shiftless (McLemore, 1973). The visibility of group boundaries was heightened and reinforced by physical and religious differences. Mexicans were racially a mixture of Spanish and American Indian, and the differences in skin color and other physical characteristics provided a convenient marker of group membership. In addition, the vast majority of Mexicans were Roman Catholic, whereas the vast majority of Anglo Americans were Protestant.

Competition for land began with the first contact between the groups. However, for many years, population density was low in the Southwest, and the competition did not immediately or always erupt into violent domination and expropriation. Nonetheless, the loss of land and power for Mexican Americans was inexorable, although variable in speed.

The size of the power differential between the groups was variable and partly explains why domination was established faster in some places than in others. In both Texas and California, the subordination of the Mexican American population followed quickly after a rapid influx of Anglos and the military defeat of Mexico. Anglo Americans used their superior numbers and military power to acquire control of the political and economic structures and expropriate the resources of the Mexican American community. In New Mexico, the groups were more evenly matched in size, and Mexican Americans were able to retain a measure of power for decades.

Unlike the case of American Indians, however, the labor as well as the land of the Mexicans were coveted. On cotton plantations, ranches, farms, and in mining and railroad construction, Mexican Americans became a vital source of inexpensive labor. During times of high demand, this labor force was supplemented by workers who were encouraged to emigrate from Mexico. When demand for workers decreased, these laborers were forced back to Mexico. Thus began a pattern of labor flow that continues to the present.

As in the case of African Americans and American Indians, the contact period clearly established a colonized status for Mexican Americans in all areas of the Southwest. Their culture and language were suppressed even as their property rights were abrogated and their status lowered. In countless ways, they, too, were subjected to coercive acculturation. For example, California banned the use of Spanish in public schools, and bullfighting and other Mexican sports and recreational activities were severely restricted (Moore, 1970; Pitt, 1970). In contrast to African Americans, however, Mexican Americans were in close proximity to their homeland and maintained close ties with villages and families. Constant movement across the border with Mexico kept the Spanish language and much of the Mexican heritage alive in the Southwest. Nonetheless, 19th-century Mexican Americans fit Blauner's category of a colonized minority group, and the suppression of their culture was part of the process by which the dominant culture was established.

Anglo American economic interests benefited enormously from the conquest of the Southwest and the colonization of the Mexican people. Growers and other businessmen came to rely on the cheap labor of Mexican Americans and immigrant and day laborers from Mexico. The region grew in affluence and productivity, but Mexican Americans were now outsiders in their own land and did not share in the prosperity. In the land grab of the 1800s and the conquest of the indigenous Mexican population lies one of the roots of Mexican American relations with the dominant U.S. society today.

Gender Relations

Prior to the arrival of Anglo Americans, Mexican society in the Southwest was patriarchal and maintained a clear, gender-based division of labor. These characteristics tended to persist after the conquest and the creation of minority-group status.

Most Mexican Americans lived in small villages or on large ranches or farms. The women devoted their energies to the family, child rearing, and household tasks. As Mexican Americans were reduced to a landless labor force, women along with men suffered the economic devastation that accompanied military conquest by a foreign power. The kinds of jobs available to the men (mining, seasonal farmwork, railroad construction) often required them to be away from home for extended periods of time, and women, by default, began to take over the economic and other tasks traditionally performed by males.

Poverty and economic insecurity placed the family structures under considerable strain. Traditional cultural understandings about male dominance and patriarchy became moot when the men were absent for long periods of time and the decision-making power of Mexican American women increased. Also, women were often forced to work outside the household for the family to survive economically. The economics of conquest led to increased matriarchy and more working mothers (Becerra, 1988).

For Mexican American women, the consequences of contact were variable, even though the ultimate result was a loss of status within the context of the conquest and colonization of the group as a whole. Like black female slaves, Mexican American women became the most vulnerable part of the social system.

Comparing Minority Groups

American Indians and black slaves were the victims of the explosive growth of European power in the Western Hemisphere that began with Columbus's voyage in 1492. Europeans needed labor to fuel the plantations of the mid–17th-century American colonies and settled on slaves from Africa as the most logical, cost-effective means of resolving their labor-supply problems. Black Africans had a commodity the colonists coveted (labor), and the colonists subsequently constructed a system to control and exploit this commodity.

To satisfy the demand for land created by the stream of European immigrants to North America, the threat represented by American Indians had to be eliminated. Once their land was expropriated, American Indians ceased to be of much concern. The only valuable resource they possessed—their land—was under the control of white society by 1890, and American Indians were thought to be unsuitable as a source of labor.

Mexico, like the United States, had been colonized by a European power—in this case, Spain. In the early 1800s, the Mexican communities in the Southwest were a series of outpost settlements, remote and difficult to defend. Through warfare and a variety of other aggressive means, Mexican citizens living in this area were conquered and became an exploited minority group.

African Americans, American Indians, and Mexican Americans, in their separate ways, became involuntary players in the growth and development of European and, later, American economic and political power. None of these groups had much choice in its respective fate; all three were overpowered and relegated to an inferior, subordinate status. Many views of assimilation (such as the "melting pot" metaphor discussed in Chapter 2) have little relevance to these situations. These minority groups had little control over their destinies, their degree of acculturation, or even their survival as groups. These three groups were coercively acculturated in the context of paternalistic relations in an agrarian economy. Meaningful integration (structural assimilation) was not a real possibility, especially for African Americans and American Indians. In Milton Gordon's (1964) terms (see Chapter 2), we might characterize these situations as "acculturation without integration," or structural pluralism. Given the grim realities described in this chapter, Gordon's terms seem a little antiseptic, and Blauner's concept of colonized minority groups seems far more descriptive.

COMPARATIVE FOCUS: Mexico, Canada, and the United States

In this chapter, we argued that dominant–minority relations are profoundly shaped by the contact situation and by the characteristics of the groups involved, especially their subsistence technologies. We saw how these factors shaped relations with Native Americans and Mexican Americans and how they led British colonists to create a system of slavery to control the labor of African Americans. How do the experiences of the Spanish and the French in the Western Hemisphere compare with those of the British in what became the United States? What roles did the contact situation and subsistence technology play in the development of group relations in these two neighbors of the United States?[3]

The Spanish were the first of the three European nations to arrive in the Western Hemisphere, and they conquered much of what is now Central and South America about a century before Jamestown was founded. Their first encounter with a large American Indian society occurred in 1521, when they defeated the Aztec Empire, located in what is now central Mexico. The Aztec Empire was large, highly organized, and complex. It was ruled by an emperor and included scores of different societies, each with its own language and identity, which had been conquered by the fiercely warlike Aztecs. The bulk of the population of the empire consisted of peasants or agricultural laborers who farmed small plots of land owned by members of the elite classes, to whom they paid rent. Peasants are a fundamental part of any labor-intensive, preindustrial agrarian society and were just as common in Spain as they were in Aztec society.

When the Spanish defeated the Aztecs, they destroyed their cities, their temples, and their leadership (the emperor, the nobility, priests, etc.). They did not destroy the Aztec social structure; rather, they absorbed it and used it for their own benefit. For example, the Aztec Empire had financed its central government by collecting taxes and rent from citizens and tribute from conquered tribes. The Spanish simply grafted their own tax collection system onto this structure and diverted the flow from the Aztec elite classes (which they had, at any rate, destroyed) to themselves (Russell, 2009).

The Spanish tendency to absorb rather than destroy operated at many levels. For example, Aztec peasants became Spanish (and then Mexican) peasants, occupying roughly the same role in the new society that they had in the old, save for paying their rent to different landlords. There was also extensive interbreeding between the Spanish and the conquered tribes of Mexico, but again, unlike the situation in the English colonies, the Spanish recognized the resultant racial diversity and developed an elaborate system for classifying people by race. They recognized as many as 56 racial groups, including whites, **mestizos** (mixed European-Indian), and **mulattos** (mixed European-African) (Russell, 2009). The society that emerged was highly race conscious, and race was highly correlated with social class: The elite classes were white, and the lower classes were nonwhite. However, the large-scale intermarriage and the official recognition of mixed-race peoples did establish the foundation for a racially mixed society. Today, the huge majority of the Mexican population is mestizo, although there remains a very strong correlation between race and class, and the elite positions in the society tend to be monopolized by people of "purer" European ancestry.

The French began to colonize Canada at about the same time the English established their colonies further south. The dominant economic enterprise in the early days was not farming, but trapping and the fur trade. The French developed a lucrative trade in this area by allying themselves with some American Indian tribes. The Indians produced the furs and traded them to the French, who then sold them on the world market. Like the Spanish in Mexico, the French in Canada tended to link to and absorb Native American social structures. There was also a significant amount of intermarriage between the French and Native Americans, resulting in a mixed-race group, called *Métis,* who had their own identities and, indeed, their own settlements along the Canadian frontier (Russell, 2009).

Note the profound differences in these three contact situations between Europeans and Native Americans. The Spanish confronted a large, well-organized social system and found it expeditious to adapt Aztec practices to their own benefit. The French developed an economy that required cooperation with at least some of the Native American tribes they encountered, and they, too, found benefits in adaptation. In contrast, the tribes encountered by the English were much smaller and much less developed than the Aztecs, and there was no particular reason for the English to adapt to or absorb these social structures. Furthermore, because the business of the British colonies was agriculture (not trapping), the competition at the heart of the contact situation was for land, and American Indians were seen as rivals for control of that most valuable resource. Thus, the English tended to confront and exclude American Indians, keeping them on the outside of their emerging society and building strong boundaries between their own "civilized" world and the "savages" that surrounded them. The Spanish and French colonists had to adapt their societies to fit with American Indians, but the English faced no such restraints. They could create their institutions and design their social structure to suit themselves (Russell, 2009).

(Continued)

(Continued)

As we have seen, one of the institutions created in the British colonies was slavery based on African labor. Slavery was also practiced in New Spain (Mexico) and New France (Canada), but the institution evolved in very different ways in those colonies and never assumed the importance that it did in the United States. Why? As you might suspect, the answer has a lot to do with the nature of the contact situation. Like the British colonists, both the Spanish and French attempted large-scale agricultural enterprises that might have created a demand for imported slave labor. In the case of New Spain, however, there was a large population of Native American peasants available to fill the role played by blacks in the British colonies. Although Africans became a part of the admixture that shaped modern Mexico racially and socially, demand for black slaves never matched that of the British colonies. Similarly, in Canada, slaves from Africa were sometimes used, but farmers there tended to rely on the flow of labor from France to fill their agricultural needs. The British opted for slave labor from Africa over indentured labor from Europe, and the French made the opposite decision.

Another difference among the three European nations that helps to explain the divergent development of group relations is their relative level of modernization. Compared with England, Spain and France were more traditional and feudalistic in their cultures and social structures. Among other things, this meant that they had to shape their agricultural enterprises in the New World around the ancient social relations between peasants and landlords they brought from the Old World. Thus, the Spanish and French colonists were limited in their actions by these ancient customs, traditions, and understandings. Such old-fashioned institutions were much weaker in England, and thus the British colonists were much freer to design their social structure to suit their own needs. Whereas the Spanish and French had to shape their colonial societies to fit both American Indian social patterns and European traditions, the English could improvise and attend only to their own needs and desires. The closed, complex, and repressive institution of American slavery—designed and crafted from scratch in the New World—was one result.

Finally, we should note that many of the modern racial characteristics of these three neighboring societies were foreshadowed in their colonial origins (for example, the greater concentration of African Americans in the United States and the more racially intermixed population of Mexico). The differences run much deeper than race alone, of course, and include differences in class structure and relative levels of industrialization and affluence. For our purposes, however, this brief comparison of the origins of dominant–minority relations underscores the importance of the contact situation in shaping group relations for centuries to come.

MAIN POINTS

- Dominant–minority relations are shaped by the characteristics of society as a whole, particularly by subsistence technology. The contact situation is the single most important factor in the development of dominant–minority relations.
- The Noel hypothesis states that when a contact situation is characterized by ethnocentrism, competition, and a differential in power, ethnic or racial stratification will result. In

colonial America, Africans were enslaved instead of white indentured servants or American Indians because only they fit all three conditions. American slavery was a paternalistic system.

- Prejudice and racism are more the results of systems of racial and ethnic inequality than they are the causes. They serve to rationalize, "explain," and stabilize these systems.
- Slavery and indentured servitude persist in the modern world. Systems of involuntary servitude can be found today around the globe, including in the United States.
- The competition with American Indians centered on control of the land. American Indian tribes were conquered and pressed into a paternalistic relationship with white society. American Indians became a colonized minority group and were subjected to forced acculturation.
- Mexican Americans were the third minority group created during the preindustrial era. Mexican Americans competed with white settlers over both land and labor. Like Africans and American Indians, Mexican Americans were a colonized minority group subjected to forced acculturation.
- Conquest and colonization affected men and women differently. Women's roles changed, and they sometimes were less constrained by patriarchal traditions. These changes were always in the context of increasing powerlessness and poverty for the group as a whole, however, and minority women have been doubly oppressed by their gender roles as well as their minority-group status.

STUDY SITE ON THE WEB

Don't forget the interactive quizzes and other resources and learning aids at **www.pineforge.com/healeyds3e**

FOR FURTHER READING

Here are five vital sources on the origins and psychological and cultural impact of slavery in America:

Genovese, Eugene D. 1974. *Roll, Jordan, Roll.* New York: Pantheon.

Gutman, Herbert G. 1976. *The Black Family in Slavery and Freedom.* New York: Vintage.

Levine, Lawrence. 1977. *Black Culture and Black Consciousness.* New York: Oxford University Press.

Rawick, George P. 1972. *From Sundown to Sunup: The Making of the Black Community.* Westport, CT: Greenwood Press.

Stuckey, Sterling. 1987. *Slave Culture: Nationalist Theory and the Foundations of Black America.* New York: Harper & Row.

The following is an eloquent and moving account of the conquest of American Indians:

Brown, Dee. 1970. *Bury My Heart at Wounded Knee.* New York: Holt, Rinehart & Winston.

Here is a collection of valuable and insightful American Indian accounts of the last 500 years.

Nabakov, Peter. (Ed.). 1999. *Native American Testimony* (Rev. ed.). New York: Penguin.

Three classic overviews of the historical development of Mexican Americans follow:

Acuna, Rodolfo. 1999. *Occupied America* (4th ed.). New York: Harper & Row.

McWilliams, Carey. 1961. *North From Mexico: The Spanish-Speaking People of the United States.* New York: Monthly Review Press.

Mirandé, Alfredo. 1985. *The Chicano Experience: An Alternative Perspective.* Notre Dame, IN: University of Notre Dame Press.

QUESTIONS FOR REVIEW AND STUDY

1. State and explain the two themes presented at the beginning of the chapter. Apply each to the contact situations between white European colonists and African Americans, American Indians, and Mexican Americans. Identify and explain the key differences and similarities among the three situations.
2. Explain what a plantation system is and why this system of production is important for understanding the origins of slavery in colonial America. Why are plantation systems usually characterized by (a) paternalism, (b) huge inequalities between groups, (c) repressive systems of control, (d) rigid codes of behavior, and (e) low rates of overt conflict?
3. Explain the Noel and Blauner hypotheses and how they apply to the contact situations covered in this chapter. Explain each of the following key terms: ethnocentrism, competition, power, colonized minority group, immigrant minority group. How did group conflict vary when competition was over land versus when it was over labor?
4. Explain the roles of prejudice and racism in the creation of minority-group status. Do prejudice and racism help cause minority-group status, or are they caused by minority-group status? Explain.
5. Compare and contrast gender relations in regard to each of the contact situations discussed in this chapter. Why do the relationships vary?
6. Compare and contrast modern systems of slavery to antebellum U.S. slavery. Does the Noel hypothesis apply to the modern forms?
7. What does it mean to say that, under slavery, acculturation for African Americans was coerced? What are the implications of this forced acculturation for assimilation, inequality, and African American culture?
8. Compare and contrast the contact situations of Native Hawaiians with American Indians. What were the key differences in the contact situation, and how are these differences reflected in the current situations of the groups?
9. Compare and contrast the contact situations in colonial America, Canada, and Mexico. What groups were involved in each situation? What was the nature of the competition, and what were the consequences?

INTERNET RESEARCH PROJECT

The *slave narratives* are one interesting source of information about the nature of everyday life under slavery. The narratives were compiled during the 1930s in interviews with ex-slaves, and although they are limited in many ways, the interviews do provide a close-up, personal view of the system of slavery from the perspective of its victims. To use this resource, go to http://newdeal.feri.org/asn/index.htm and read the home page carefully, especially the cautions. Select several of the narratives and analyze them in terms of the concepts introduced in this chapter (e.g., paternalism, labor-intensive systems of work, the Noel and Blauner hypotheses).

Extend the information on modern slavery and indentured servitude presented in this chapter. Do an Internet search and gather information about the scope and dynamics of the modern slave trade. Where is it practiced? How? Who are the victims? Who are the beneficiaries? Does the Noel hypothesis apply to modern slavery? If so, how?

Notes

1. Quoted in *Puttin' on Ole Massa: The Slave Narratives of Henry Bibb, William Wells Brown, and Solomon Northup* by Gilbert Osofsky. Copyright © 1969. Reprinted with permission of Marcia Osofsky, PhD.

2. Reprinted by permission of the publisher from *Incidents in the Life of a Slave Girl, Written by Herself* by Harriet A. Jacobs, edited and with an introduction by Jean Fagan Yellin, pp. 27–28, Cambridge, MA: Harvard University Press. Copyright © 1987, 2000 by the President and Fellows of Harvard College.

3. This section is largely based on Russell (2009).

4

Industrialization and Dominant–Minority Relations

From Slavery to Segregation and the Coming of Postindustrial Society

A war sets up in our emotions: one part of our feelings tells us it is good to be in the city, that we have a chance at life here, that we need but turn a corner to become a stranger, that we need no longer bow and dodge at the sight of the Lords of the Land. Another part of our feelings tells us that, in terms of worry and strain, the cost of living in the kitchenettes is too high, that the city heaps too much responsibility on us and gives too little security in return. . . .

The kitchenette, with its filth and foul air, with its one toilet for thirty or more tenants, kills our black babies so fast that in many cities twice as many of them die as white babies. . . .

The kitchenette scatters death so widely among us that our death rate exceeds our birth rate, and if it were not for the trains and autos bringing us daily into the city from the plantations, we black folk who dwell in northern cities would die out entirely over the course of a few years. . . .

(Continued)

(Continued)

The kitchenette throws desperate and unhappy people into an unbearable closeness of association, thereby increasing latent friction, giving birth to never-ending quarrels of recrimination, accusation, and vindictiveness, producing warped personalities.

The kitchenette injects pressure and tension into our individual personalities, making many of us give up the struggle, walk off and leave wives, husbands, and even children behind to shift as best they can. . . .

The kitchenette reaches out with fingers of golden bribes to the officials of the city, persuading them to allow old firetraps to remain standing and occupied long after they should have been torn down.

The kitchenette is the funnel through which our pulverized lives flow to ruin and death on the city pavement, at a profit.

—Richard Wright[1]

Richard Wright (1908–1960), one of the most powerful writers of the 20th century, lived through and wrote about many of the social changes discussed in this chapter. He grew up in the South during the height of the Jim Crow system, and his passionate hatred for segregation and bigotry is expressed in his major works, *Native Son* (1940) and the autobiographical *Black Boy* (1945). In 1941, Wright helped to produce *Twelve Million Black Voices,* a folk history of African Americans. A combination of photos and brief essays, the work is a powerful commentary on three centuries of oppression.

The selection above is adapted from "Death on the City Pavement," which expresses Wright's view of the African American migration out of the South that began in the early 1900s as a reaction to Jim Crow segregation. Wright himself moved from the South to the North, a bittersweet journey that often traded harsh, rural repression for overcrowded, anonymous ghettos. Housing discrimination, both overt and covert, confined African American migrants to the least desirable, most overcrowded areas of the city—in many cases, the neighborhoods that had first housed immigrants from Europe. Unscrupulous landlords subdivided buildings into the tiniest possible apartments ("kitchenettes"), and as impoverished newcomers who could afford no better, African American migrants were forced to cope with overpriced, substandard housing as best they could.

Introduction

One theme stated at the beginning of Chapter 3 was that a society's subsistence technology shapes dominant–minority group relations. A corollary of this theme, explored in this chapter, is that *dominant–minority group relations change as the subsistence technology changes.* As we saw in Chapter 3, dominant–minority relations in the formative years of the United States were profoundly shaped by agrarian technology and the desire to control land and labor. The agrarian era ended in the 1800s, and since that time, the United States has experienced two major transformations in subsistence technology, each of which has, in turn, transformed dominant–minority relations.

The first transformation began in the early 1800s as American society began to experience the effects of the industrial revolution, or the shift from agrarian technology to machine-based, manufacturing technology. In the agrarian era, as we saw in Chapter 3, work was labor intensive, done by hand or with the aid of draft animals. As industrialization proceeded, work became **capital intensive** as machines replaced people and animals.

The new industrial technology rapidly increased the productivity and efficiency of the U.S. economy and quickly began to change all other aspects of society, including the nature of work; politics; communication; transportation; family life; birth and death rates; the system of education; and, of course, dominant–minority relations. The groups that had become minorities during the agrarian era (African Americans, American Indians, and Mexican Americans) faced new possibilities and new dangers, but industrialization also created new minority groups, new forms of exploitation and oppression, and—for some—new opportunities to rise in the social structure and succeed in America. In this chapter, we will explore this transformation and illustrate its effects on the status of African Americans. The impact of industrialization on other minority groups will be considered in the case studies presented in Part III.

The second transformation in subsistence technology brings us to more recent times. Industrialization is a continuous process, and beginning in the mid-20th century, the United States entered the postindustrial era, also called **deindustrialization.** This shift in subsistence technology was marked by a decline in the manufacturing sector of the economy and a decrease in the supply of secure, well-paying, blue-collar, manual labor jobs. At the same time, there was an expansion in the service- and information-based sectors of the economy and an increase in the proportion of white-collar and "high tech" jobs. Like the 19th-century industrial revolution, these 20th-century changes have had profound implications not just for dominant–minority relations, but for every aspect of modern society. Work, family, politics, popular culture, and thousands of other characteristics of American society are being transformed as the subsistence technology continues to develop and modernize. In the latter part of this chapter, we examine this latest transformation in general terms and point out some of its implications for minority groups. Some new concepts are also presented, laying the groundwork for the case studies in Part III, in which the effects of late industrialization on America's minority groups will be considered in detail.

Industrialization and the Shift From Paternalistic to Rigid Competitive Group Relations

As I mentioned in Chapter 2, the industrial revolution began in England in the mid-1700s and spread from there to the rest of Europe, to the United States, and eventually to the rest of the world. The key innovations associated with this change in subsistence technology were the application of machine power to production and the harnessing of inanimate sources of energy, such as steam and coal, to fuel the machines. As machines replaced humans and animals, work became many times more productive, the economy grew, and the volume and variety of goods produced increased dramatically.

In an industrial economy, the close, paternalistic control of minority groups found in agrarian societies becomes irrelevant. Paternalistic relationships such as slavery are found in societies with labor-intensive technologies and are designed to organize and control a large, involuntary, geographically immobile labor force. An industrial economy, in contrast, requires a workforce that is geographically and socially mobile, skilled, and literate. Furthermore, with industrialization comes urbanization, and close, paternalistic controls are difficult to maintain in a city.

Thus, as industrialization progresses, agrarian paternalism tends to give way to **rigid competitive group relations.** Under this system, minority-group members are freer to compete for jobs and other valued commodities with dominant group members, especially the lower-class segments of the dominant group. As competition increases, the threatened members of the dominant group become more hostile, and attacks on the minority groups tend to increase. Whereas paternalistic systems seek to directly dominate and control the minority group (and its labor), rigid competitive systems are more defensive in nature. The threatened segments of the dominant group seek to minimize or eliminate minority-group encroachment on jobs, housing, or other valuable goods or services (van den Berghe, 1967; Wilson, 1973).

Paternalistic systems such as slavery required members of the minority group to be active, if involuntary, participants. In contrast, in rigid competitive systems, the dominant group seeks to eliminate competition from the minority group or, at the least, handicap its ability to compete effectively.

We have already considered a situation in which a dominant group attempted to protect itself from a perceived threat. As you will recall, the National Origins Act was passed in the 1920s to stop the flow of cheaper labor from Europe and protect jobs and wages (see Chapter 2). In this chapter, we consider dominant-group attempts to keep African Americans powerless and impoverished as U.S. society shifted from an agricultural to an industrial base.

The Impact of Industrialization on African Americans: From Slavery to Segregation

Industrial technology began to transform American society in the early 1800s, but its effects were not felt equally in all regions. The northern states industrialized first, while the South remained primarily agrarian. This economic diversity was one of the underlying causes of the regional conflict that led to the Civil War. Because of its more productive technology, the North had more resources and defeated the Confederacy in a bloody war of attrition. Slavery was abolished, and black–white relations in the South entered a new era when the Civil War ended in April 1865.

The Southern system of race relations that ultimately emerged after the Civil War was designed in part to continue the control of African American labor institutionalized under slavery. It was also intended to eliminate any political or economic threat from the

African American community. This rigid competitive system grew to be highly elaborate and inflexible, partly because of the high racial visibility and long history of inferior status and powerlessness of African Americans in the South, and partly because of the particular needs of Southern agriculture. In this section, we look at black–white relations from the end of the Civil War through the ascendance of segregation in the South and the mass migration of African Americans to the cities of the industrializing North.

Reconstruction

The period of **Reconstruction,** from 1865 to the 1880s, was a brief respite in the long history of oppression and exploitation of African Americans. The Union Army and other agencies of the federal government, such as the Freedman's Bureau, were used to enforce racial freedom in the defeated Confederacy. Black Southerners took advantage of the Fifteenth Amendment to the Constitution, passed in 1870, which states that the right to vote cannot be denied on the grounds of "race, color, or previous condition of servitude." They registered to vote in large numbers and turned out on Election Day, and some were elected to high political office. Schools for the former slaves were opened, and African Americans purchased land and houses and founded businesses.

The era of freedom was short, however, and Reconstruction began to end when the federal government demobilized its armies of occupation and turned its attention to other matters. By the 1880s, the federal government had withdrawn from the South, Reconstruction was over, and black Southerners began to fall rapidly into a new system of exploitation and inequality.

Reconstruction was too brief to change two of the most important legacies of slavery. First, the centuries of bondage left black Southerners impoverished, largely illiterate and uneducated, and with few power resources. When new threats of racial oppression appeared, African Americans found it difficult to defend their group interests. These developments are consistent with the Blauner hypothesis (see Chapter 3): Colonized minority groups face greater difficulties in improving their disadvantaged status because they confront greater inequalities and have fewer resources at their disposal.

Second, slavery left a strong tradition of racism in the white community. Antiblack prejudice and racism originated as rationalizations for slavery but had taken on lives of their own over the generations. After two centuries of slavery, the heritage of prejudice and racism was thoroughly ingrained in Southern culture. White Southerners were predisposed by this cultural legacy to see racial inequality and exploitation of African Americans as normal and desirable. They were able to construct a social system based on the assumption of racial inferiority after Reconstruction ended and the federal government withdrew.

De Jure Segregation

The system of race relations that replaced slavery in the South was **de jure segregation,** sometimes referred to as the **Jim Crow system**. Under segregation, the minority group is physically and socially separated from the dominant group and consigned to an inferior position in virtually every area of social life. The phrase *de jure* ("by law") means that the system is sanctioned and reinforced by the legal code; the inferior status of African Americans was actually mandated, or required, by state and local laws. For example, Southern cities during this era had laws requiring African Americans to ride at the back of the bus. If an African American refused to comply with this seating arrangement, he or she could be arrested.

De jure segregation came to encompass all aspects of Southern life. Neighborhoods, jobs, stores, restaurants, and parks were segregated. When new social forms such as movie theaters, sports stadiums, and interstate buses appeared in the South, they, too, were quickly segregated.

The logic of segregation created a vicious cycle (see Exhibit 1.6, in Chapter 1): The more African Americans were excluded from the mainstream of society, the greater their objective poverty and powerlessness became. The more inferior their status and the greater their powerlessness, the easier it was to mandate more inequality. High levels of inequality reinforced racial prejudice and made it easy to use racism to justify further separation. The system kept turning on itself, finding new social niches to segregate and reinforcing the inequality that was its starting point. For example, at the height of the Jim Crow era, the system had evolved to the point that some courtrooms maintained separate Bibles for African American witnesses to swear on. Also, in Birmingham, Alabama, it was against the law for blacks and whites to play checkers or dominoes together (Woodward, 1974).

What were the causes of this massive separation of the races? Once again, the concepts of the Noel hypothesis prove useful. Because strong antiblack prejudice was already in existence when segregation began, we do not need to account for ethnocentrism. The post-Reconstruction competition between the racial groups was reminiscent of the origins of slavery in that black Southerners had something that white Southerners wanted: labor. In addition, a free black electorate threatened the political and economic dominance of the elite segments of the white community. Finally, after the withdrawal of federal troops and the end of Reconstruction, white Southerners had sufficient power resources to end the competition on their own terms and construct repressive systems of control for black Southerners.

The Origins of De Jure Segregation

Although the South lost the Civil War, its basic class structure and agrarian economy remained intact. The plantation elite, with their huge tracts of land, remained the dominant class, and cotton remained the primary cash crop. As was the case before the Civil War, the landowners needed a workforce to farm the land. Because of the depredations and economic disruptions of the war, the old plantation elite was short on cash and liquid capital. Hiring workers on a wage system was not feasible for them. In fact, almost as soon as the war ended, Southern legislatures attempted to force African Americans back into involuntary servitude by passing a series of laws known as the "Black Codes." Only the beginning of Reconstruction and the active intervention of the federal government halted the implementation of this legislation (Geschwender, 1978; W. Wilson, 1973).

The plantation elite solved their need for a workforce this time by developing a system of **sharecropping,** or tenant farming. The sharecroppers worked the land, which was actually owned by the planters, in return for payment in shares of the profit when the crop was taken to market. The landowner would supply a place to live, and food and clothing on credit. After the harvest, tenant and landowner would split the profits (sometimes very unequally), and the tenant's debts would be deducted from his or her share. The accounts were kept by the landowner. Black sharecroppers lacked political and civil rights and found it difficult to keep unscrupulous white landowners honest. Landowners could inflate the indebtedness of the sharecropper and claim that they were still owed money even after profits had been split. Under this system, sharecroppers had few opportunities to improve their situations and could be bound to the land until their "debts" were paid off (Geschwender, 1978).

By 1910, more than half of all employed African Americans worked in agriculture, and more than half of the remainder (25% of the total) worked in domestic occupations, such as maid or janitor (Geschwender, 1978, p. 169). The labor shortage in Southern agriculture was solved, and the African American community once again found itself in a subservient status. At the same time, the white Southern working class was protected from direct job competition with African Americans. As the South began to industrialize, white workers were able to monopolize the better-paying jobs. With a combination of direct discrimination by whites-only labor unions and strong antiblack laws and customs, white workers erected barriers that excluded black workers and reserved the better industrial jobs in cities and mill towns for themselves. White workers took advantage of the new jobs brought by industrialization, while black Southerners remained a rural peasantry, excluded from participation in this process of modernization.

In some sectors of the changing Southern economy, the status of African Americans actually fell lower than it had been during slavery. For example, in 1865, 83% of the artisans in the South were African Americans; by 1900, this percentage had fallen to 5% (Geschwender, 1978, p. 170). The Jim Crow system confined African Americans to the agrarian and domestic sectors of the labor force, denied them the opportunity for a decent education, and excluded them from politics. The system was reinforced by still more laws and customs that drastically limited the options and life opportunities available to black Southerners.

A final force behind the creation of de jure segregation was more political than economic. As the 19th century drew to a close, a wave of agrarian radicalism known as *populism* spread across the country. This anti-elitist movement was a reaction to changes in agriculture caused by industrialization. The movement attempted to unite poor whites and blacks in the rural South against the traditional elite classes. The economic elite was frightened by the possibility of a loss of power and split the incipient coalition between whites and blacks by fanning the flames of racial hatred. The strategy of "divide and conquer" proved to be effective (as it often has both before and since this time), and the white elite classes in states throughout the South eliminated the possibility of future threats by depriving African Americans of the right to vote (Woodward, 1974).

The disenfranchisement of the black community was accomplished by measures such as literacy tests, poll taxes, and property requirements. The literacy tests were officially justified as promoting a better-informed electorate but were shamelessly rigged to favor white voters. The requirement that voters pay a tax or prove ownership of a certain amount of property could also disenfranchise poor whites, but again, the implementation of these policies was racially biased.

The policies were extremely effective, and by the early 20th century, the political power of the Southern black community was virtually nonexistent. For example, as late as 1896 in Louisiana, there had been more than 100,000 registered African American voters, and African American voters were a majority in 26 parishes (counties). In 1898, the state adopted a new constitution containing stiff educational and property requirements for voting unless the voter's father or grandfather had been eligible to vote as of January 1, 1867. At that time, the Fourteenth and Fifteenth Amendments, which guaranteed suffrage for black males, had not yet been passed. Such "grandfather clauses" made it easy for white males to register while disenfranchising blacks. By 1900, only about 5,000 African Americans were registered to vote in Louisiana, and African American voters were not a majority in any parish. A similar decline occurred in Alabama, where an electorate of more than 180,000 African American males was reduced to 3,000 by provision of a new state constitution. This story repeated itself throughout the South, and African American political powerlessness had become a reality by 1905 (Franklin & Moss, 1994, p. 261).

This system of legally mandated racial privilege was approved by the U.S. Supreme Court, which ruled in the case of *Plessy v. Ferguson* (1896) that it was constitutional for states to require separate facilities (schools, parks, etc.) for African Americans as long as the separate facilities were fully equal. The Southern states paid close attention to "separate" but ignored "equal."

Reinforcing the System

Under de jure segregation, as under slavery, the subordination of the African American community was reinforced and supplemented by an elaborate system of racial etiquette. Everyday interactions between blacks and whites proceeded according to highly stylized and rigidly followed codes of conduct intended to underscore the inferior status of the African American community. Whites were addressed as "Mister" or "Ma'am," whereas African Americans were called by their first names or perhaps by an honorific title such as "Aunt," "Uncle," or "Professor." These titles were sometimes intended as compliments, but were always framed in the context of the mutually recognized lower status of blacks. Blacks were expected to assume a humble and deferential manner, remove their hats, cast their eyes downward, and enact the role of the subordinate in all interactions with whites. If an African American had reason to call on anyone in the white community, he or she was expected to go to the back door.

These expectations and "good manners" for black Southerners were systematically enforced. Anyone who ignored them ran the risk of reprisal, physical attacks, and even death by lynching. During the decades in which the Jim Crow system was being imposed, there were thousands of lynchings in the South. From 1884 until the end of the century, lynchings averaged almost one every other day (Franklin & Moss, 1994, p. 312). The bulk of this violent terrorism was racial and intended to reinforce the system of racial advantage or punish real or imagined transgressors. Also, various secret organizations, such as the Ku Klux Klan, engaged in terrorist attacks against the African American community and anyone else who failed to conform to the dictates of the system.

Increases in Prejudice and Racism

As the system of racial advantage formed and solidified, levels of prejudice and racism increased (Wilson, 1973). The new system needed justification and rationalization, just as slavery did, and antiblack sentiment, stereotypes, and ideologies of racial inferiority grew stronger. At the start of the 20th century, the United States in general—not just the South—was a very racist and intolerant society. This spirit of rejection and scorn for all out-groups coalesced with the need for justification of the Jim Crow system and created an especially negative brand of racism in the South.

The "Great Migration"

Although African Americans lacked the power resources to resist the resurrection of Southern racism and oppression, they did have one option that had not been available under slavery: freedom of movement. African Americans were no longer legally tied to a specific master or to a certain plot of land. In the early 20th century, a massive population movement out of the South began. Slowly at first, African Americans began to move to other regions of the nation and from the countryside to the city. The movement increased when hard times hit Southern agriculture and slowed down during better times. It has been said that African Americans voted against Southern segregation with their feet.

As Exhibits 4.1 and 4.2 show, an urban black population living outside the South is a 20th-century phenomenon. About half of African Americans continue to live in the South, but the group is more evenly distributed across the nation and more urbanized than the population as a whole than a century ago.

Exhibit 4.1 Regional Distribution of African American Population, 1890–2007

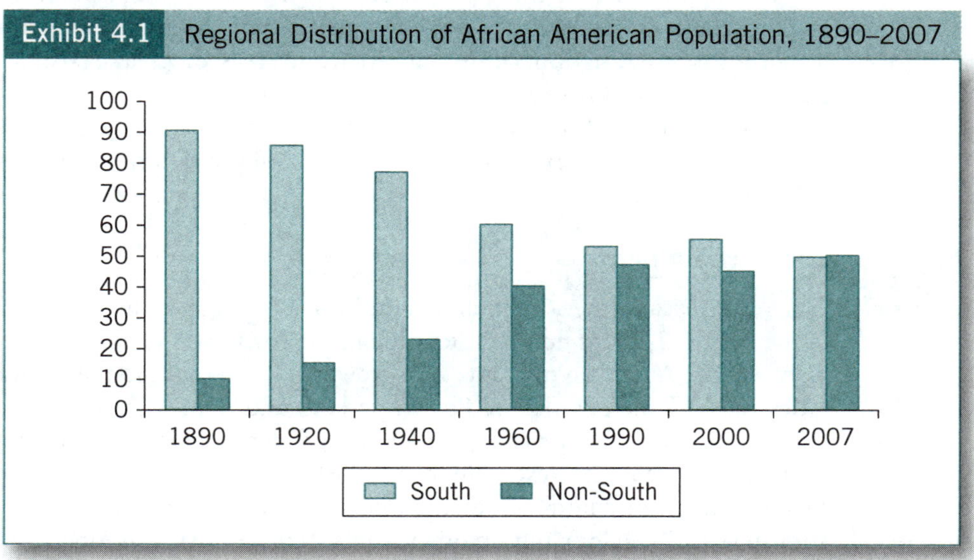

SOURCES: 1890–1960, Geschwender (1978); 1990, Heaton, Chadwick, & Jacobson (2000); 2000, U.S. Bureau of the Census (2004d); 2007, computed from U.S. Bureau of the Census (2009b, p. 23).

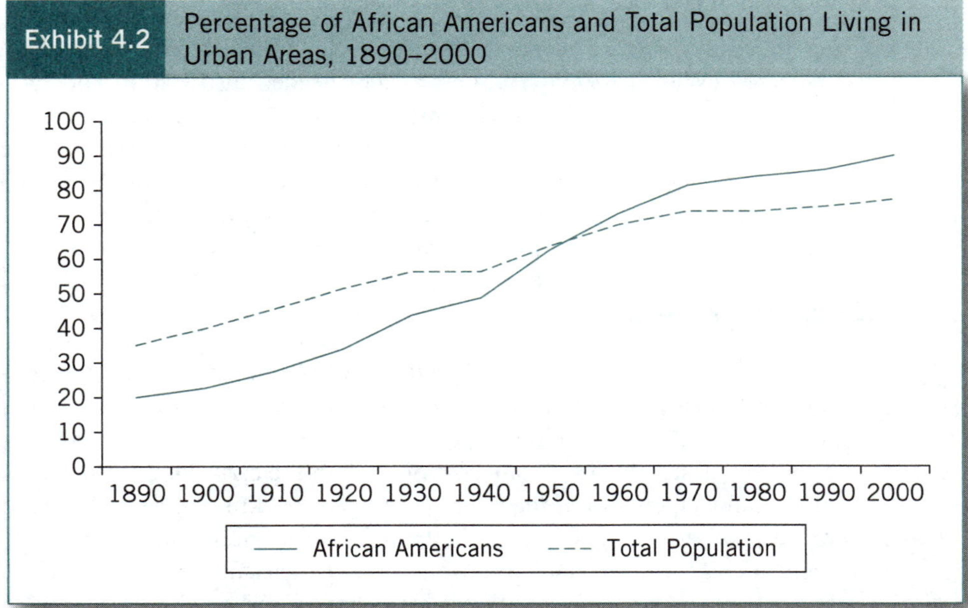

Exhibit 4.2 Percentage of African Americans and Total Population Living in Urban Areas, 1890–2000

SOURCES: 1890–1960, Geschwender (1978); 1990, Pollard & O'Hare (1999, p. 27); 2000, U.S. Bureau of the Census (2000i).

NOTE: Definitions of *urban* vary over the years, and these percentages should be regarded as approximations.

The significance of this population redistribution is manifold. Most important, perhaps, was the fact that by moving out of the South and from rural to urban areas, African Americans moved from areas of great resistance to racial change to areas of lower resistance. In the Northern cities, for example, it was far easier to register and to vote. Black political power began to grow and eventually provided many of the crucial resources that fueled the civil rights movement of the 1950s and 1960s.

Life in the North

What did African American migrants find when they got to the industrializing cities of the North? There is no doubt that life in the North was better for the vast majority of African American migrants. The growing Northern African American communities relished the absence of Jim Crow laws and oppressive racial etiquette, the relative freedom to pursue jobs, and the greater opportunities to educate their children. Inevitably, however, life in the North fell short of utopia. Many aspects of African American culture—literature, poetry, music—flourished in the heady new atmosphere of freedom, but on other fronts, Northern African American communities faced discrimination in housing, schools, and the job market. Along with freedom and such cultural flowerings as the Harlem Renaissance came black ghettos and new forms of oppression and exploitation.

Competition With White Ethnic Groups

It is useful to see the movement of African Americans out of the South in terms of the resultant relationship with other groups. Southern blacks began to move to the North at about the same as the "New Immigration" from Europe (see Chapter 2) began to end. By the time substantial numbers of black Southerners began arriving in the North, European immigrants and their descendants had had years, decades, and even generations to establish themselves in the job markets, political systems, labor unions, and neighborhoods of the North. Many of the European ethnic groups had also been the victims of discrimination and rejection, and, as we discussed in Chapter 2, their hold on economic security and status was tenuous for much of the 20th century. They saw the newly arriving black migrants as a threat to their status, a perception that was reinforced by the fact that industrialists and factory owners often used African Americans as strikebreakers and scabs. The white ethnic groups responded by developing defensive strategies to limit the dangers presented by these migrants from the South. They tried to exclude African Americans from their labor unions and other associations and limit their impact on the political system. They also attempted, often successfully, to maintain segregated neighborhoods and schools (although the legal system outside the South did not sanction overt de jure segregation).

This competition led to hostile relations between black Southern migrants and white ethnic groups, especially the lower- and working-class segments of those groups. Ironically, however, in another phase of the ethnic succession discussed in Chapter 2, the newly arriving African Americans actually helped white ethnic groups become upwardly mobile. Dominant-group middle- and upper-class whites became less contemptuous of white ethnic groups as their alarm over the presence of African Americans increased. The greater antipathy of the white community toward African Americans made the European immigrant groups less undesirable and thus hastened their admittance to the institutions of the larger society. For many white ethnic groups, the increased tolerance of the larger society coincided happily with the coming of age of the more educated and skilled descendants of the original immigrants, further abetting the rise of these groups in the U.S. social class structure (Lieberson, 1980).

For more than a century, each new European immigrant group had helped to push previous groups up the ladder of socioeconomic success and out of the old, ghettoized neighborhoods. Black Southerners got to the cities after immigration from Europe had been curtailed, and no newly arrived immigrants appeared to continue the pattern of succession for African Americans in the North. Instead, American cities developed concentrations of low-income blacks who were economically vulnerable and politically weak and whose position was further solidified by antiblack prejudice and discrimination (Wilson, 1987).

The Origins of Black Protest

As I pointed out in Chapter 3, African Americans have always resisted their oppression and protested their situation. Under slavery, however, the inequalities they faced were so great and their resources so meager that the protest was ineffective. With the increased freedom that followed slavery, a national African American leadership developed and spoke out against oppression, and founded organizations that eventually helped to lead the fight for freedom and equality. Even at its birth, the black protest movement was diverse and incorporated a variety of viewpoints and leaders.

Booker T. Washington was the most prominent African American leader prior to World War I. Washington had been born in slavery and was the founder and president of Tuskegee Institute, a college in Alabama dedicated to educating African Americans. His public advice to African Americans in the South was to be patient, to accommodate to the Jim Crow system for now, to raise their levels of education and job skills, and to take full advantage of whatever opportunities became available. This nonconfrontational stance earned Washington praise and support from the white community and widespread popularity in the nation. Privately, he worked behind the scenes to end discrimination and implement full racial integration and equality (Franklin & Moss, 1994; Hawkins, 1962; Washington, 1965).

Washington's most vocal opponent was W. E. B. Du Bois, an intellectual and activist who was born in the North and educated at some of the leading universities of the day. Among his many other accomplishments, Du Bois was part of a coalition of blacks and white liberals who founded the National Association for the Advancement of Colored People (NAACP) in 1909. Du Bois rejected Washington's accommodationist stance and advocated immediate pursuit of racial equality and a direct assault on de jure segregation. Almost from the beginning of its existence, the NAACP filed lawsuits that challenged the legal foundations of Jim Crow segregation (Du Bois, 1961). As we shall see in Chapter 5, this legal strategy was eventually successful and led to the demise of the Jim Crow system.

Washington and Du Bois may have differed on matters of strategy and tactics, but they agreed that the only acceptable goal for African Americans was an integrated, racially equal United States. A third leader who emerged early in the 20th century called for a very different approach to the problems of U.S. race relations. Marcus Garvey was born in Jamaica and immigrated to the United States during World War I. He argued that the white-dominated U.S. society was hopelessly racist and would never truly support integration and racial equality. He advocated separatist goals, including a return to Africa. Garvey founded the Universal Negro Improvement Association in 1914 in his native Jamaica and founded the first U.S. branch in 1916. Garvey's organization was very popular for a time in African American communities outside the South, and he helped to establish some of the themes and ideas of black nationalism and pride in African heritage that would become prominent again in the pluralistic 1960s (Essien-Udom, 1962; Garvey, 1969, 1977; Vincent, 1976).

These early leaders and organizations established some of the foundation for later protest movements, but prior to the mid-20th century, they made few actual improvements in the situation of African Americans in the North or South. Jim Crow was a formidable opponent, and the African American community lacked the resources to successfully challenge the status quo until the century was well along and some basic structural features of American society had changed.

Applying Concepts

Acculturation and Integration

During this era of Southern segregation and migration to the North, assimilation was not a major factor in the African American experience. Rather, the black–white relations of the time are better described as a system of structural pluralism combined with great inequality. Excluded from the mainstream but freed from the limitations of slavery, African Americans constructed a separate subsociety and subculture. In all regions of the nation, African Americans developed their own institutions and organizations, including separate neighborhoods, churches, businesses, and schools. Like immigrants from Europe in the same era, they organized their communities to cater to their own needs and problems and pursue their agenda as a group.

During the era of segregation, a small, African American middle class emerged based on leadership roles in the church, education, and business. A network of black colleges and universities was constructed to educate the children of the growing middle class, as well as other classes. Through this infrastructure, African Americans began to develop the resources and leadership that in the decades ahead would attack, head-on, the structures of racial inequality.

Gender and Race

For African American men and women, the changes wrought by industrialization and the population movement to the North created new possibilities and new roles. However, as African Americans continued to be the victims of exploitation and exclusion in both the North and the South, African American women continued to be among the most vulnerable groups in society.

Following emancipation, there was a flurry of marriages and weddings among African Americans, as they were finally able to legitimate their family relationships (Staples, 1988). African American women continued to have primary responsibility for home and children. Historian Herbert Gutman (1976) reported that it was common for married women to drop out of the labor force and attend solely to household and family duties, because a working wife was too reminiscent of a slave role. This pattern became so widespread that it created serious labor shortages in many areas (Gutman, 1976; see also Staples, 1988).

The former slaves were hardly affluent, however, and as sharecropping and segregation began to shape race relations in the South, women often had to return to the fields or to domestic work for the family to survive. One former slave woman noted that women "do double duty, a man's share in the field and a woman's part at home" (Evans, 1989, p. 121). During the bleak decades following the end of Reconstruction, Southern black families and black women in particular lived "close to the bone" (Evans, 1989, p. 121).

In the cities and in the growing African American neighborhoods in the North, African American women played a role that in some ways paralleled the role of immigrant women from Europe. The men often moved north first and sent for the women after they had attained some level of financial stability or after the pain of separation became too great (Almquist, 1979). In other cases, African American women by the thousands left the South to work as domestic servants; they often replaced European immigrant women, who had moved up in the job structure (Amott & Matthaei, 1991).

In the North, discrimination and racism created constant problems of unemployment for the men, and families often relied on the income supplied by the women to make ends meet. It was comparatively easy for women to find employment, but only in the low-paying, less desirable areas, such as domestic work. In both the South and the North, African American women worked outside the home in larger proportions than did white women. For example, in 1900, 41% of African American women were employed, compared with only 16% of white women (Staples, 1988, p. 307).

In 1890, more than a generation after the end of slavery, 85% of all African American men and 96% of African American women were employed in just two occupational categories: agriculture and domestic or personal service. By 1930, 90% of employed African American women were still in these same two categories, whereas the corresponding percentage for employed African American males had dropped to 54% (although nearly all of the remaining 46% were unskilled workers) (Steinberg, 1981, pp. 206–207). Since the inception of segregation, African American women have had consistently higher unemployment rates and lower incomes than African American men and white women (Almquist, 1979). These gaps, as we shall see in Chapter 5, persist to the present day.

During the years following Emancipation, some issues did split men and women, within both the African American community and the larger society. Prominent among these was *suffrage,* or the right to vote, which was still limited to men only. The abolitionist movement, which had been so instrumental in ending slavery, also supported universal suffrage. Efforts to enfranchise women, though, were abandoned by the Republican Party and large parts of the abolitionist movement to concentrate on efforts to secure the vote for African American males in the South. Ratification of the Fifteenth Amendment in 1870 extended the vote, in principle, to African American men, but the Nineteenth Amendment enfranchising women would not be passed for another 50 years (Almquist, 1979; Evans, 1989).

COMPARATIVE FOCUS: South African Apartheid

Exhibit 4.3 Map of Africa Showing South Africa

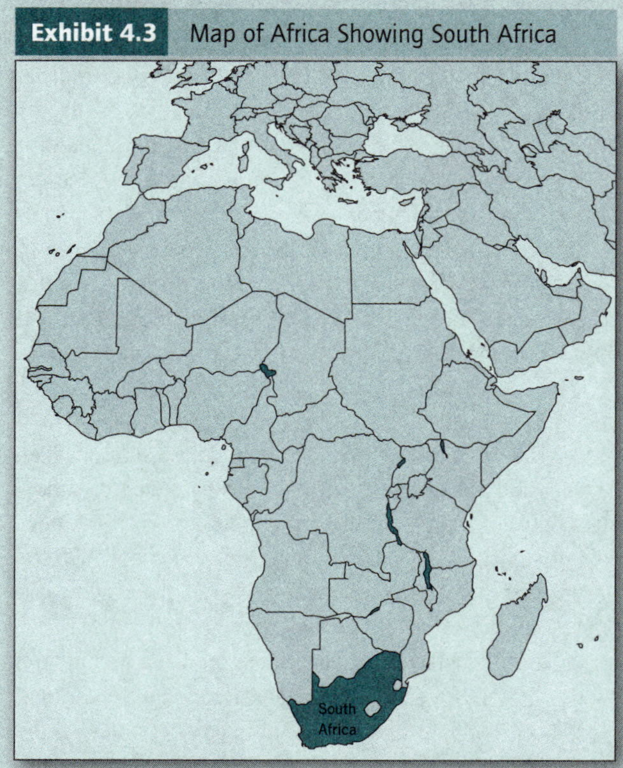

Systems of legally sanctioned racial segregation can be found in other nations and historical eras, but perhaps the most infamous system—called **apartheid**—was constructed in South Africa (see Exhibit 4.3). As in the United States, South African segregation was intended to control the labor of the black population and eliminate all political and economic threats from the group. A small minority of whites (about 10%) dominated the black African population and enjoyed a level of race-based privilege rarely equaled in the history of the world. Today, although enormous problems of inequality and racism remain, South Africa has officially dismantled the machinery of racial oppression, has enfranchised nonwhites, and has elected three black presidents.

Some background will illuminate the dynamics of the system. Europeans first came into contact with Southern Africa in the 1600s, at about the time the British were establishing colonies in North America. First to arrive were the Dutch, who established ports on the coast to resupply merchant ships for the journey between Asia and Europe. Some of the Dutch moved into the interior to establish farms and sheep and cattle ranches. The "trekkers," as they were called, regularly fought with indigenous black Africans and with tribes moving into the area from the north. These interracial conflicts were extremely bloody and resulted in enslavement for some black Africans, death for others, and a gradual push of the remaining black Africans into the interior. In some ways, this contact period resembled that between European Americans and Native Americans, and in other ways, it resembled the early days of the establishment of black slavery in North America.

In the 1800s, South Africa became a British colony, and the new governing group attempted to grant more privileges to blacks. These efforts stopped far short of equality, however, and South Africa continued to evolve as a racially divided, white-dominated society into the 20th century. The white

(Continued)

(Continued)

community continued to be split between people of Dutch (Boers) and English descent, and hostilities erupted into violence on a number of occasions. In 1899, British and Dutch factions fought each other in the Boer War, a bitter, intense struggle that widened and solidified the divisions between the two white communities. Generally, the descendants of the Dutch have been more opposed to racial change than have the descendants of the British.

In 1948, the National Party, the primary political vehicle of the Afrikaans, or Dutch, segment of the white community, came into control of the state. As the society modernized and industrialized, there was growing concern about controlling the majority black population. Under the leadership of the National Party, the system of apartheid was constructed to firmly establish white superiority. In Afrikaans, *apartheid* means "separate" or "apart"; the basic logic of the system was to separate whites and blacks in every area of life: schools, neighborhoods, jobs, buses, churches, and so forth. Apartheid resembled the Jim Crow system of segregation in the United States except it was even more repressive, elaborate, and unequal.

Although the official government propaganda claimed that apartheid would permit blacks and whites to develop separately and equally, the system was clearly intended to solidify white privilege and black powerlessness. By keeping blacks poor and powerless, white South Africans created a pool of workers who were both cheap and docile. Whites of even modest means could afford the luxuries of personal servants, and employers could minimize their payrolls and their overhead. Of the dominant–minority situations considered in this text, perhaps only American slavery rivals apartheid for its naked, unabashed subjugation of one group for the benefit of the other.

Note that the coming of apartheid reverses the relationship between modernization and control of minority groups in the United States. As the United States industrialized and modernized, group relations evolved from paternalistic (slavery) to rigid competitive forms (de jure segregation), with the latter representing a looser form of control over the minority group. In South Africa after 1948, group relations became more rigid, and the structures of control became stronger and more oppressive. Why the difference?

Just as U.S. Southerners attempted to defend their privileged status and resist the end of de jure segregation in the 1950s and 1960s, white South Africans were committed to retaining their status and the benefits it created. Although South Africans of British descent tended to be more liberal in matters of race than those of Dutch descent, both groups were firmly committed to white supremacy. Thus, unlike the United States, in which there was almost constant opposition to racial oppression in any form—slavery or segregation—there was little internal opposition among South African whites to the creation of apartheid.

Furthermore, South African blacks in the late 1940s were comparatively more powerless than blacks in the United States at the same time. Although South African black protest organizations existed, they were illegal and had to operate underground or from exile and under conditions of extreme repression. In the United States, in contrast, blacks living outside the South were able to organize and pool their resources to assist in the campaign against Jim Crow, and these activities were protected (more or less) by the national commitment to civil liberties and political freedom.

A final difference between the two situations has to do with numbers. Whereas in the United States, blacks are a numerical minority, they are the great majority of the population in South Africa. Part of the impetus for establishing the rigid system of apartheid was the fear among whites that they would be "swamped" by the numerical majority unless black powerlessness was perpetuated. The difference in group size helped to contribute to what has been described as a "fortress" mentality among some white South Africans: the feeling that they were defending a small (but luxurious) outpost, surrounded and besieged by savage hordes who threatened their immediate and total destruction. This strong sense of threat among whites and the need to be vigilant and constantly resist the least hint of racial change made the system seem impregnable and perpetual to many observers.

Apartheid lasted about 40 years. Through the 1970s and 1980s, changes within South Africa and in the world in general built up pressure against the system. Internally, protests against apartheid by blacks began in the 1960s and continued to build in intensity. The South African government responded to these protests with violent repression, and thousands died in the confrontations with police and the army. Nonetheless, anti-apartheid activism continued to attack the system from below.

Apartheid also suffered from internal weaknesses and contradictions. For example, jobs were strictly segregated, along with all other aspects of South African society. In a modern, industrial economy, however, new types of jobs are continually being created, and old jobs are continually lost to mechanization and automation, making it difficult to maintain simple, caste-like rules about who can do what kinds of work. Also, many of the newer jobs required higher levels of education and special skills, and the number of white South Africans was too small to fill the demand. Thus, some black South Africans were slowly rising to positions of greater affluence and personal freedom even as the system attempted to coerce and repress the group as a whole.

Internationally, pressure on South Africa to end apartheid was significant. Other nations established trade embargoes and organized boycotts of South African goods. South Africa was officially banned from the Olympics and other international competitions. Although many of these efforts were more symbolic than real and had only minor impact on everyday social life, they sustained an outcast status for South Africa and helped create an atmosphere of uncertainty among its economic and political elite.

In the late 1980s, these various pressures made it impossible to ignore the need for reform any longer. In 1990, F. W. de Klerk, the leader of the National Party and the prime minister of the nation, began a series of changes that eventually ended apartheid. He lifted the ban on many outlawed black African protest organizations, and perhaps most significantly, he released Nelson Mandela from prison. Mandela was the leader of the African National Congress (ANC), one of the oldest and most important black organizations, and he had served a 27-year prison term for actively protesting apartheid. Together, de Klerk and Mandela helped to ease South Africa through a period of rapid racial change that saw voting rights being extended to blacks; the first open election in South African history; and in 1994, Mandela's election to a 5-year term as president. In 1999, Mandela was replaced by Thabo M. Mbeki, another black South African. Mbeki was reelected in 2004 but was ousted in September 2008 after a bitter struggle with ANC rival Jacob Zuma. Though a charismatic figure with strong support among the rank-and-file of the party, Zuma's standing has been compromised by allegations of corruption, charges of rape, and other scandals. Nevertheless, Zuma was elected the third black president of South Africa in the spring of 2009.

(Continued)

(Continued)

The future of South Africa remains unclear. Although the majority black population now has political power, deep racial divisions remain. In many urban and white areas, South Africa maintains a first-world infrastructure but the black population continues to live in third-world poverty. For example, South Africa will host the 2010 soccer World Cup and is expanding airports, improving roads, and building hotels and stadiums to provide first-class facilities for the hordes of fans that will arrive to witness the matches. At the same time, much of the black population continues to live in apartheid-era townships—pockets of third-world poverty with no running water or sewage systems, poor or nonexistent medical care, and grossly overcrowded and understaffed schools.

The problems of racial and class inequality facing South Africa are enormous, and this experiment in racial reform might still fail. Should it succeed in meeting these challenges, on the other hand, this dramatic transition away from massive racism and institutionalized discrimination could still provide a model of change for other racially divided societies.

Industrialization, the Shift to Postindustrial Society, and Dominant–Minority Group Relations: General Trends

The process of industrialization that began in the 19th century continued to shape the larger society and dominant–minority relations throughout the 20th century. At the start of the 21st century, the United States bears little resemblance to the society it was a century ago. The population has more than tripled in size and has urbanized even more rapidly than it has grown. New organizational forms (bureaucracies, corporations, multinational businesses) and new technologies (nuclear power, computers) dominate everyday life. Levels of education have risen, and the public schools have produced one of the most literate populations and best-trained workforces in the history of the world.

Minority groups have also grown in size during this period, and most have become even more urbanized than the general population (see Exhibit 4.2). Minority-group members have come to participate in an increasing array of occupations, and their average levels of education have also risen. Despite these real improvements, however, virtually all U.S. minority groups continue to face racism, poverty, discrimination, and exclusion. This section outlines the ways in which industrialization has changed American society, and we will examine some of its implications for minority groups in general. We will also note some of the ways in which industrialization has aided minority groups and address some of the barriers to full participation in the larger society that continue to operate in the present era. The impact of industrialization and the coming of postindustrial society will be considered in detail in the case studies that make up Part III of this text.

Urbanization

We have already noted that urbanization made close, paternalistic controls of minority groups irrelevant. For example, the racial etiquette required by Southern de jure segregation, such as African Americans deferring to whites on crowded sidewalks, tended to disappear in the chaos of an urban rush hour.

Besides weakening dominant-group controls, urbanization also created the potential for minority groups to mobilize and organize large numbers of people. As stated in Chapter 1, the sheer size of a group is a source of power. Without the freedom to organize, however, size means little, and urbanization increased both the concentration of populations and the freedom to organize.

Occupational Specialization

One of the first and most important results of industrialization, even in its earliest days, was an increase in occupational specialization and the variety of jobs available to the workforce. The growing needs of an urbanizing population increased the number of jobs available in the production, transport, and sale of goods and services. Occupational specialization was also stimulated by the very nature of industrial production. Complex manufacturing processes could be performed more efficiently if they were broken down into the narrower component tasks. It was easier and more efficient to train the workforce in the simpler, specialized jobs. Assembly lines were invented, the work was subdivided, the division of labor became increasingly complex, and the number of different occupations continued to grow.

The sheer complexity of the industrial job structure made it difficult to maintain rigid, caste-like divisions of labor between dominant and minority groups. Rigid competitive forms of group relations, such as Jim Crow segregation, became less viable as the job market became more diversified and changeable. Simple, clear rules about which groups could do which jobs disappeared. As the more repressive systems of control weakened, job opportunities for minority-group members sometimes increased. However, as the relationships between group memberships and positions in the job market became more blurred, conflict between groups also increased. For example, as we have noted, African Americans moving from the South often found themselves in competition for jobs with members of white ethnic groups, labor unions, and other elements of the dominant group.

Bureaucracy and Rationality

As industrialization continued, privately owned corporations and businesses came to have workforces numbering in the hundreds of thousands. Gigantic factories employing thousands of workers became common. To coordinate the efforts of these huge workforces, bureaucracy became the dominant form of organization in the economy and, indeed, throughout U.S. society.

Bureaucracies are large-scale, impersonal, formal organizations that run "by the book." They are governed by rules and regulations (i.e., "red tape") and are "rational" in that they attempt to find the most efficient ways to accomplish their tasks. Although they typically fail to attain the ideal of fully rational efficiency, bureaucracies tend to recruit, reward, and promote employees on the basis of competence and performance (Gerth & Mills, 1946).

The stress on rationality and objectivity can counteract the more blatant forms of racism and increase the array of opportunities available to members of minority groups. Although they are often nullified by other forces (see Blumer, 1965), these anti-prejudicial tendencies do not exist at all or are much weaker in preindustrial economies.

The history of the concept of race illustrates the effect of rationality and scientific ways of thinking. Today, virtually the entire scientific community regards race as a biological triviality, a conclusion based on decades of research. This scientific finding undermined and contributed to the destruction of the formal systems of privilege based solely on race (e.g., segregated school systems) and individual perceptual systems (e.g., traditional prejudice) based on the assumption that race is a crucial personal characteristic.

Growth of White-Collar Jobs and the Service Sector

Industrialization changed the composition of the labor force. As work became more complex and specialized, the need to coordinate and regulate the production process increased, and as a result, bureaucracies and other organizations grew larger still. Within these organizations, white-collar occupations—those that coordinate, manage, and deal with the flow of paperwork—continued to expand. As industrialization progressed, mechanization and automation reduced the number of manual or blue-collar workers, and white-collar occupations became the dominant sector of the job market in the United States.

The changing nature of the workforce can be illustrated by looking at the proportional representation of three different types of jobs:

1. **Extractive (or primary) occupations** are those that produce raw materials, such as food and agricultural products, minerals, and lumber. The jobs in this sector often involve unskilled manual labor, require little formal education, and are generally low paying.
2. **Manufacturing (or secondary) occupations** transform raw materials into finished products ready for sale in the marketplace. Like jobs in the extractive sector, these blue-collar jobs involve manual labor, but they tend to require higher levels of skill and are more highly rewarded. Examples of occupations in this sector include the assembly-line jobs that transform steel, rubber, plastic, and other materials into finished automobiles.
3. **Service (or tertiary) occupations** are those in which the workers do not produce "things"; rather, they provide services. As urbanization increased and self-sufficiency decreased, opportunities for work in this sector grew. Examples of tertiary occupations include police officer, clerk, waiter, teacher, nurse, doctor, and cab driver.

The course of industrialization is traced in the changing structure of the labor market depicted in Exhibit 4.4. In 1840, when industrialization was just beginning in the United States, most of the workforce (70%) was in the extractive sector, with agriculture being the dominant occupation. As industrialization progressed, the manufacturing or secondary sector grew, reaching a peak after World War II. Today, the large majority of U.S. jobs (over 80%) are in the service, or tertiary, sector.

Exhibit 4.4 The Changing Workforce in the United States: The Distribution of Jobs, 1840–2007

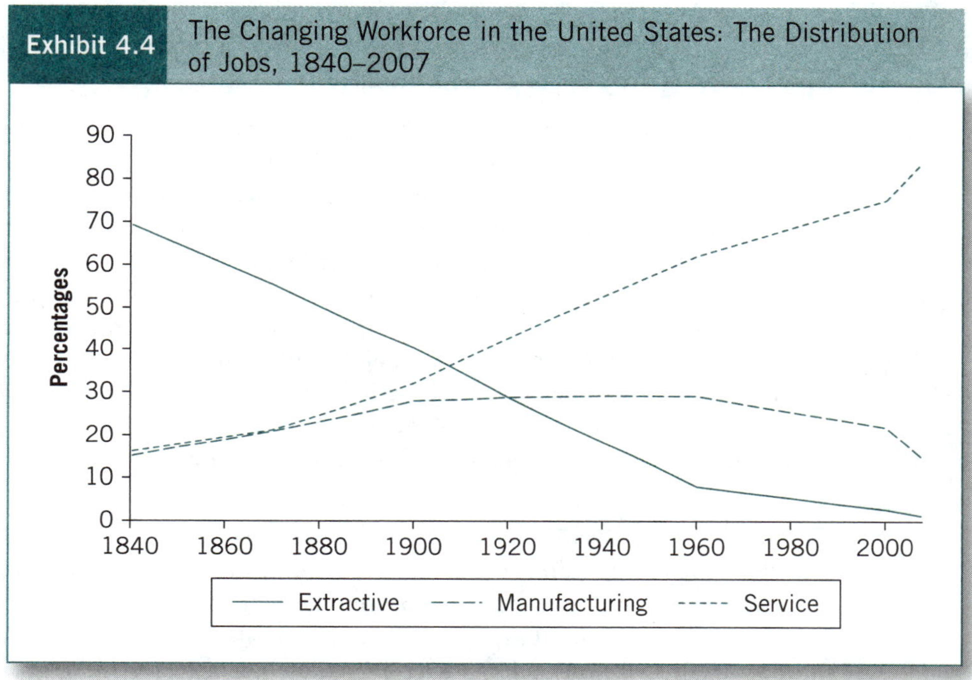

SOURCE: 1840–1990, adapted from Lenski, Nolan, & Lenski (1995); 2000, calculated from U.S. Bureau of the Census (2005); 2007, calculated from U.S. Bureau of the Census (2009b).

This shift away from blue-collar jobs and manufacturing since the 1960s is sometimes referred to as *deindustrialization*, or discussed in terms of the emergence of a *postindustrial society*. The U.S. economy has lost millions of unionized, high-paying factory jobs over the past several decades, and the downward trend will continue. The industrial jobs that sustained so many generations of American workers have been moved to other nations where wages are considerably lower than in the United States or have been eliminated by robots or other automated manufacturing processes (see Rifkin, 1996).

The changing structure of the job market helps to clarify the nature of intergroup competition and the sources of wealth and power in society. Job growth in the United States today is largely in the service sector, and these occupations are highly variable. At one end are low-paying jobs with few, if any, benefits or chances for advancement (e.g., washing dishes in a restaurant). At the upper end are high-prestige, lucrative positions, such as Supreme Court justice, scientist, and financial analyst. The new service sector jobs are either highly desirable technical, professional, or administrative jobs with demanding entry requirements (e.g., physician or nurse) or low-paying, low-skilled jobs with few benefits and little security (e.g., receptionist, nurse's aide). For the last half-century, job growth in the United States has been either in areas in which educationally deprived minority-group members find it difficult to compete or in areas that offer little compensation, upward mobility, or security. As we will see in Part III, the economic situation of contemporary minority groups reflects these fundamental trends.

The Growing Importance of Education

Education has been an increasingly important prerequisite for employability in the United States and in other advanced industrial societies. A high school or, increasingly, a college degree has become the minimum entry-level requirement for employment. However, opportunities for high-quality education are not distributed equally across the population. Some minority groups, especially those created by colonization, have been systematically excluded from the schools of the dominant society, and today, they are less likely to have the educational backgrounds needed to compete for better jobs.

Access to education is a key issue for all U.S. minority groups, and the average educational levels of these groups have been rising since World War II. Still, minority children continue to be much more likely to attend segregated, underfunded, deteriorated schools and to receive inferior educations (see Orfield, 2001).

A Dual Labor Market

The changing composition of the labor force and increasing importance of educational credentials has split the U.S. labor market into two segments or types of jobs. The **primary labor market** includes jobs usually located in large, bureaucratic organizations. These positions offer higher pay, more security, better opportunities for advancement, health and retirement benefits, and other amenities. Entry requirements include college degrees, even when people with fewer years of schooling could competently perform the work.

The **secondary labor market,** sometimes called the competitive market, includes low-paying, low-skilled, insecure jobs. Many of these jobs are in the service sector. They do not represent a career and offer little opportunity for promotion or upward mobility. Very often, they do not offer health or retirement benefits; have high rates of turnover; and are part-time, seasonal, or temporary.

Many American minority groups are concentrated in the secondary job market. Their exclusion from better jobs is perpetuated not so much by direct or overt discrimination as by educational and other credentials required to enter the primary sector. The differential distribution of educational opportunities, in the past as well as in the present, effectively protects workers in the primary sector from competition from minority groups.

Globalization

Over the past century, the United States became an economic, political, and military world power with interests around the globe. These worldwide ties have created new minority groups through population movement and have changed the status of others. Immigration to this country has been considerable for the past three decades. The American economy is one of the most productive in the world, and jobs, even those in the low-paying secondary sector, are the primary goal for millions of newcomers. For other immigrants, the United States continues to play its historic role as a refuge from political and religious persecution.

Many of the wars, conflicts, and other disputes in which the United States has been involved have had consequences for American minority groups. For example, both Puerto Ricans and Cuban Americans became U.S. minority groups as the result of processes set in motion during the Spanish-American War of 1898. Both World War I and World War II created new job opportunities for many minority groups, including African Americans and Mexican Americans. After the Korean War, international ties were forged between the United States and South Korea, and this led to an increase in immigration to the U.S. from that nation. In the 1960s and 1970s, the military involvement of the United States in Southeast Asia led to the arrival of Vietnamese, Cambodians, and other immigrant groups from Southeast Asia.

Dominant–minority relations in the United States have been increasingly played out on an international stage as the world has effectively "shrunk" in size and become more interconnected by international organizations, such as the United Nations; by ties of trade and commerce; and by modern means of transportation and communication. In a world in which two-thirds of the population is nonwhite and many important nations (such as China, India, and Nigeria) represent peoples of color, the treatment of racial minorities by the U.S. dominant group has come under increased scrutiny. It is difficult to preach principles of fairness, equality, and justice—which the United States claims as its own—when domestic realities suggest an embarrassing failure to fully implement these standards. Part of the pressure for the United States to end blatant systems of discrimination such as de jure segregation came from the desire to maintain a leading position in the world.

The Shift From Rigid to Fluid Competitive Relationships

The recent changes in the structure of American society are so fundamental and profound that they are often described in terms of a revolution in subsistence technology: from an industrial society, based on manufacturing, to a postindustrial society, based on information processing and computer-related or other new technologies.

As the subsistence technology has evolved and changed, so have American dominant–minority relations. The rigid competitive systems (such as Jim Crow) associated with earlier phases of industrialization have given way to **fluid competitive systems** of group relations. In fluid competitive relations, the formal or legal barriers to competition such as Jim Crow laws or apartheid no longer exist. Both geographic and social mobility are greater, and the limitations imposed by minority-group status are less restrictive and burdensome. Rigid caste systems of stratification, in which group membership determines opportunities, adult statuses, and jobs, are replaced by more open class systems, in which there are weaker relationships between group membership and wealth, prestige, and power. Because fluid competitive systems are more open and the position of the minority group is less fixed, the fear of competition from minority groups becomes more widespread for the dominant group, and intergroup conflict increases. Exhibit 4.5 compares the characteristics of the three systems of group relations.

Exhibit 4.5 Characteristics of Three Systems of Group Relationships

	Systems of Group Relationships		
		Competitive	
	Paternalistic	Rigid	Fluid
Subsistence Technology:	**Agrarian**	**Early Industrial**	**Advanced Industrial**
Stratification	**Caste.** Group determines status.	**Mixed.** Elements of caste and class. Status largely determined by group.	**Variable.** Status strongly affected by group. Inequality varies within groups.
Division of labor	**Simple.** Determined by group.	**More complex.** Job largely determined by group, but some sharing of jobs by different groups.	**Most complex.** Group and job less related. Complex specialization and great variation within groups.
Contact between groups	**Common,** but statuses unequal.	**Less common,** and mostly unequal.	**More common.** Highest rates of equal-status contact.
Overt intergroup conflict	**Rare**	**More common**	**Common**
Power differential	**Maximum.** Minority groups have little ability to pursue self-interests.	**Less.** Minority groups have some ability to pursue self-interests.	**Least.** Minority groups have more ability to pursue self-interests.

SOURCE: Based on J. Farley (2000, p. 109). Reprinted by permission of Pearson Education, Inc., Upper Saddle River, NJ.

Compared with previous systems, the fluid competitive system is closer to the American ideal of an open, fair system of stratification in which effort and competence are rewarded and race, ethnicity, gender, religion, and other "birthmarks" are irrelevant.

However, as we will see in chapters to come, race and ethnicity continue to affect life chances and limit opportunities for minority-group members even in fluid competitive systems. As suggested by the Noel hypothesis (Chapter 3), people continue to identify themselves with particular groups (ethnocentrism), and competition for resources continues to play out along group lines. Consistent with the Blauner hypothesis (Chapter 3), the minority groups that were formed by colonization remain at a disadvantage in the pursuit of opportunities, education, prestige, and other resources.

Gender Inequality in a Globalizing, Postindustrial World

Deindustrialization and globalization are transforming gender relations along with dominant–minority relations. Everywhere, even in the most traditional and sexist societies, women are moving away from their traditional wife and mother roles, taking on new responsibilities, and facing new challenges. Some women are also encountering new dangers and new forms of exploitation that perpetuate their lower status and extend it into new areas.

In the United States, the transition to a postindustrial society has changed gender relations and the status of women on a number of levels. Women and men are now equal in terms of levels of education (U.S. Bureau of the Census, 2009b), and the shift to fluid competitive group relations has weakened the barriers to gender equality along with the barriers to racial equality. The changing role of women is also shaped by other characteristics of a modern society: smaller families, high divorce rates, and rising numbers of single mothers who must work to support their children as well as themselves.

Many of these trends have coalesced to motivate women to enter the paid labor force in unprecedented numbers over the past half-century. Women are now employed at almost the same levels as men. In the year 2007, for example, 65% of single women (vs. about 70% of single men) and about 61% of married women (vs. about 77% of married men) had jobs outside the home. Furthermore, between 1970 and 2007, the participation in the workforce of married women with children increased from a little less than 40% to almost 70% (U.S. Bureau of the Census, 2009b, p. 376).

Many women workers enter the paid labor force to compensate for the declining earning power of men. Before deindustrialization began to transform U.S. society, men monopolized the more desirable, higher-paid, unionized jobs in the manufacturing sector. For much of the 20th century, these blue-collar jobs paid well enough to subsidize a comfortable lifestyle, a house in the suburbs, and vacations, with enough money left over to save for a rainy day or for college for the kids. However, when deindustrialization began, many of these desirable jobs were lost to automation and to cheaper labor forces outside the United States and were replaced, if at all, by low-paying jobs in the service sector. Thus, deindustrialization tended to drive men's wages down, and many women were forced to take jobs to supplement the family income. In contrast, women have taken jobs in sectors of the economy that tended to be relatively unaffected by the shift to an information society (such as elementary school teacher) or in areas that actually benefitted from this shift (finance, insurance, and real estate—the "FIRE" sector).

These trends are reflected in Exhibit 4.6, which shows median income for male and female full-time, year-round workers. Note that the comparison is limited to full-time workers. This eliminates any difference in income that is caused by the fact that women tend to be less involved in the paid labor force. Also, income is expressed in 2007 dollars, and this eliminates the effects of inflation on wages.

The chart shows that average wages for men have been stagnant or actually declining since the early 1970s. Women's wages, in contrast, have been steadily rising. In 1955, women's income was less than two-thirds of men's income. By 2007, the percentage had risen to 78%.

Exhibit 4.6 Median Income per Year for Full-Time Year-Round Workers by Gender, 1955–2007 (In 2007 Dollars)

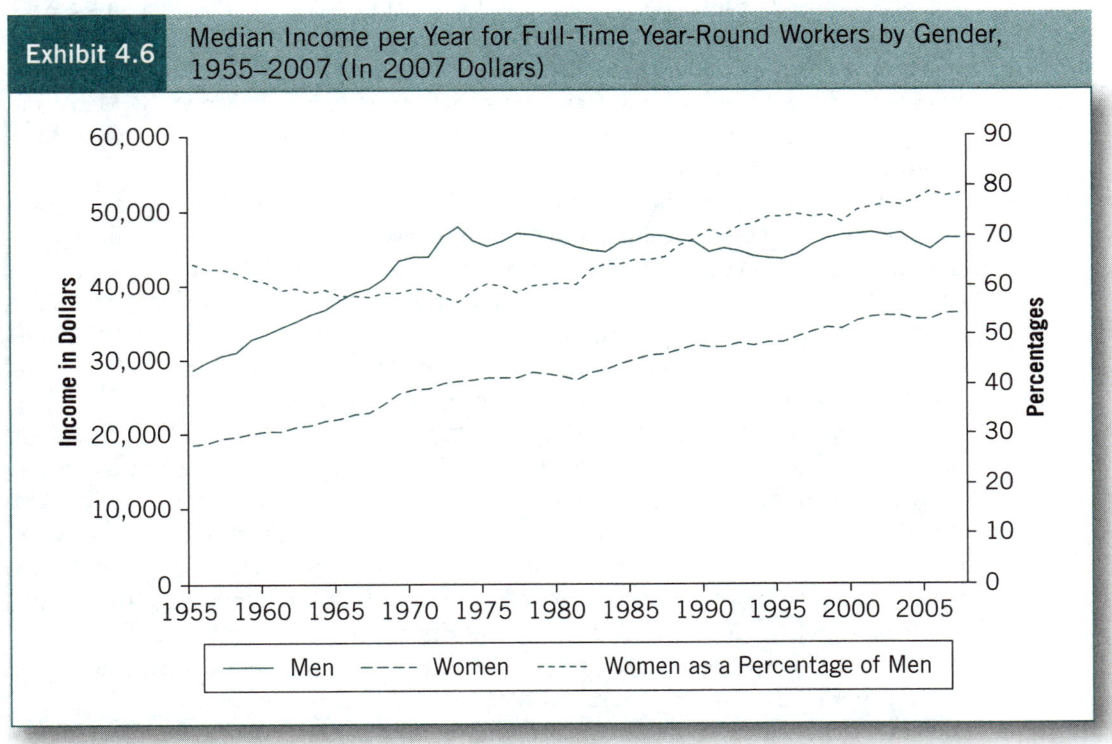

SOURCE: U.S. Bureau of the Census (2008b), *Historical Income Tables*, Table p. 36.

NOTE: Read incomes on left-hand axis and women's income as a percentage of men's income on right-hand axis.

A large number of the "new" women workers have taken jobs in a limited number of female-dominated occupations, most of which are in the less-well-paid service sector, and this pattern of occupational segregation is one important reason for the continuing gender gap in income. For example, Exhibit 4.7 lists some of the occupations that were dominated by females in 1988 and 2007, along with the percentages of females in comparable but higher-status occupations. In 2007, 92% of nurses and nearly 100% of dental hygienists were female. The comparable figures for physicians and dentists were 30% and 28%, respectively.

Exhibit 4.7 Percentage of Females in Selected Occupations, 1988 and 2007

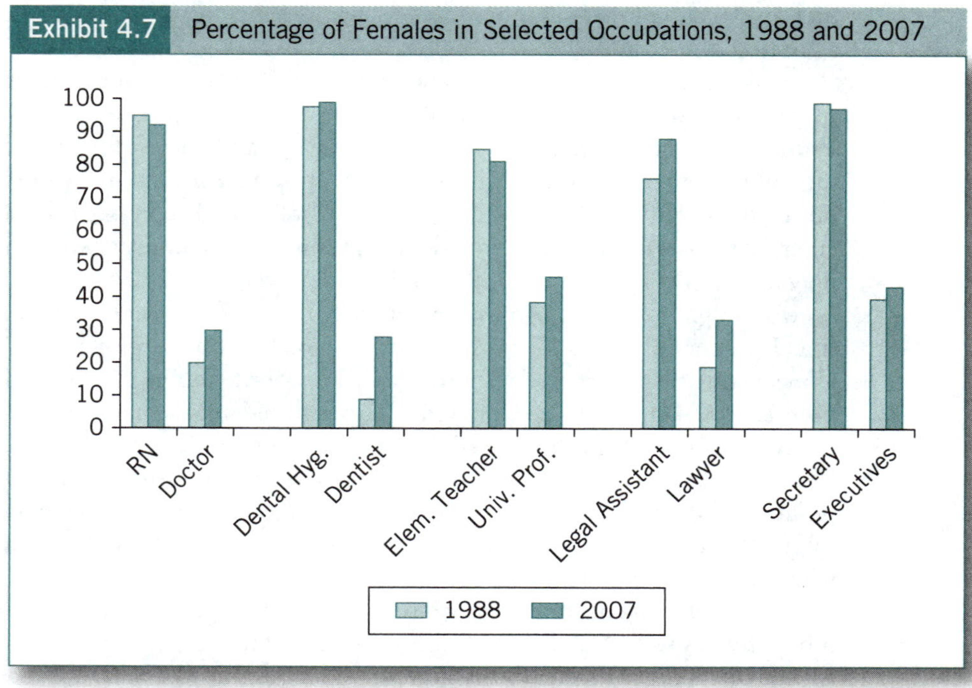

SOURCE: 1988, U.S. Bureau of the Census (1990b, pp. 389–390); 2007, U.S. Bureau of the Census (2009b, pp. 384–385).

In part, this occupational segregation is a result of the choices women make to balance the demands of their jobs with their family obligations. Whereas men are expected to make a total commitment to their jobs and careers, women have been expected to find ways to continue to fulfill their domestic roles even while working full time, and many "female jobs" offer some flexibility in this area (Shelton & John, 1996). For example, many women become elementary educators despite the lower salaries because the job offers predictable hours and long summer breaks, both of which can help women meet their child care and other family responsibilities. This pattern of gender occupational segregation testifies to the lingering effects of minority status for women and the choices they make to reconcile the demands of career and family.

Exhibit 4.7 also shows that gender segregation in the world of work is declining, at least in some areas. Women are moving into traditionally male (and higher-paid) occupations, as reflected by the rising percentages of female physicians, dentists, college professors, and lawyers. Also, some of the occupational areas that have traditionally had high concentrations of women—for example, finance, insurance, and real estate—actually benefited from deindustrialization and the shift to a service economy. Job opportunities in the finance, insurance, and real estate sector have expanded rapidly since the 1960s and have provided opportunities for women to rise in the social structure, and this has, in turn, tended to elevate average salaries for women in general (Farley, 1996). The movement of females into these more lucrative occupations is another reason why the gender gap in income is decreasing, as reflected in Exhibit 4.6.

How have deindustrialization and globalization affected women internationally? In part, the trends worldwide parallel those in the United States. According to the United Nations (2006), indicators such as rising education levels for women and lower rates of early marriage and childbirth show that women around the world are moving out of their traditional (and often highly controlled and repressed) status. They are entering the labor force in unprecedented numbers virtually everywhere, and women now make up at least a third of the paid global workforce.

Although the status of women is generally rising, the movement away from traditional gender roles also brings exposure to new forms of exploitation. Around the globe, women have become a source of cheap labor, often in jobs that have recently been exported from the U.S. economy. For example, many manufacturing jobs formerly held by men in the United States have migrated just south of the border to Mexico, where they are held by women. *Maquiladoras* are assembly plants built by corporations (often headquartered in the United States) to take advantage of the plentiful supply of working-class females who will work for low wages and in conditions that would not be tolerated in the United States.

The weakening of traditional gender roles has increased women's vulnerability in other areas as well. A global sex trade in prostitution and pornography is flourishing and accounts for a significant portion of the economies of Thailand, the Philippines, and other nations. This international industry depends on impoverished women (and children) pushed out of the subsistence rural economy by industrialization and globalization and made vulnerable for exploitation by their lack of resources and power (Poulan, 2003).

Across all these changes and around the globe, women commonly face the challenge of reconciling their new work demands with their traditional family responsibilities. Also, women face challenges and issues, such as sexual harassment and domestic violence, that clearly differentiate their status from that of men. In this context, minority-group women face compounded disadvantages because the issues they deal with as women are complicated by the barriers created by racial and ethnic prejudice and discrimination. As we shall see in Part III, minority-group and immigrant women are often the poorest, most vulnerable and exploited groups in U.S. society and around the globe.

Modern Institutional Discrimination

Virtually all American minority groups continue to lag behind national averages in income, employment, and other measures of equality (see the Appendix [www.pineforge.com/healeyds3e] for examples), despite the greater fluidity of group relations; the greater openness in the U.S. stratification system; the dramatic declines in overt prejudice (see Chapter 5); and the introduction of numerous laws designed to ensure that all people are treated equally, without regard to race, gender, or ethnicity. After all this change, shouldn't there be less minority-group inequality?

As we will discuss in Chapter 5, many Americans attribute the persisting patterns of inequality to the minority groups' lack of willpower or motivation to get ahead. In the remaining chapters of this text, however, I argue that the major barrier facing minority groups in late-industrial, post–Jim Crow America is a more subtle but still powerful form of discrimination: **modern institutional discrimination.**

As you may recall from Chapter 1, institutional discrimination is built into the everyday operation of the social structure of society. The routine procedures and policies of institutions and organizations are arranged so that minority-group members are automatically put at a disadvantage. In the Jim Crow era in the South, for example, African Americans were deprived of the right to vote by overt institutional discrimination and could acquire little in the way of political power.

The forms of institutional discrimination that persist in the present are more subtle and less overt than those that defined the Jim Crow system. In fact, they are often unintentional or unconscious and are manifested more in the results for minority groups than in the intentions or prejudices of dominant-group members. Modern institutional discrimination is not necessarily linked to prejudice, and the decision makers who implement it may sincerely think of themselves as behaving rationally and in the best interests of their organizations.

When employers make hiring decisions based solely on educational criteria, they may be putting minority-group members at a disadvantage. When banks use strictly economic criteria to deny money for home mortgages or home improvement loans in certain rundown neighborhoods, they may be handicapping the efforts of minority groups to cope with the results of the blatant, legal housing segregation of the past. When businesspeople decide to lower their overhead by moving their operations away from center cities, they may be reducing the ability of America's highly urbanized minority groups to earn a living and educate their children. When educators rely solely on standardized tests of ability that have been developed from white, middle-class experiences to decide who will be placed in college preparatory courses, they may be limiting the ability of minority-group children to compete for jobs in the primary sector.

Any and all of these decisions can and do have devastating consequences for minority individuals, even though decision makers may be entirely unaware of the discriminatory effects. Employers, bankers, and educators do not have to be personally prejudiced for their actions to have negative consequences for minority groups. Modern institutional discrimination helps to perpetuate systems of inequality that can be just as pervasive and stifling as those of the past.

To illustrate, consider the effects of **past-in-present institutional discrimination,** which involves practices in the present that have discriminatory consequences because of some pattern of discrimination or exclusion in the past (Feagin & Feagin, 1986). One form of this discrimination is found in workforces organized around the principle of seniority. In these systems, which are quite common, workers who have been on the job longer have higher incomes; more privileges; and other benefits, such as longer vacations. The "old-timers" often have more job security and are designated in official, written policy as the last to be fired or laid off in the event of hard times. Workers and employers alike may think of the privileges of seniority as just rewards for long years of service, familiarity with the job, and so forth.

Personnel policies based on seniority may seem perfectly reasonable, neutral, and fair. However, they can have discriminatory results in the present because, in the past, members of minority groups and women were excluded from specific occupations by racist or sexist labor unions, discriminatory employers, or both. As a result, minority-group workers and women may have fewer years of experience than dominant-group workers and may be the first to go when layoffs are necessary. The adage "last hired, first fired" describes the situation of minority-group and female employees who are more vulnerable, not because of some overtly racist or sexist policy, but because of the routine operation of the seemingly neutral principle of seniority.

To illustrate further, the U.S. economy entered a severe downturn in 2008, but the burden was not felt equally across all segments of the population. Minority groups, because of their exclusion from educational, occupational, and other opportunities in the past, are more vulnerable to hard times in the present. The unemployment rate for college-educated whites at the end of 2008 was 2.3%. In contrast, the unemployment rate for African Americans and Hispanic Americans was 13.3% and 11.4%, respectively (Karabell, 2009). The greater vulnerability of minority groups to economic and social disasters parallels their greater likelihood of victimization during natural disasters, as we discussed in the section on Hurricane Katrina in Chapter 1.

Affirmative Action

Since it is more subtle and indirect, institutional discrimination is more difficult to identify, measure, and eliminate. Some of the most heated disputes in recent group relations have concerned public policy and law in this area. Among the most controversial issues are affirmative action programs that attempt to reduce the effects of past discrimination or increase diversity in the workplace or in schools. In the 1970s and 1980s, the Supreme Court found that programs designed to favor minority employees as a strategy for overcoming past discrimination are constitutional (e.g., *Firefighters Local Union No. 1784 v. Stotts,* 1984; *Sheet Metal Workers v. EEOC,* 1986; *United Steelworkers of America, AFL-CIO-CLC v. Weber,* 1979). Virtually all these early decisions concerned blatant policies of discrimination, which are becoming increasingly rare as we move further away from the days of Jim Crow. Even so, the decisions were based on narrow margins (votes of 5 to 4) and featured acrimonious and bitter debates. More recently, the Supreme Court narrowed the grounds on which such past grievances could be redressed, and dealt serious blows to affirmative action programs (e.g., *Adarand Constructors Inc. v. Pena,* 1995).

The most recent case involving affirmative action programs in the workplace is *Ricci v. DeStefano* (2009), which involved firefighters in New Haven, Connecticut. In 2003, the city administered a test for promotion in the city's fire department. Over 100 people took the test, but no African American scored high enough to qualify for promotion. The city decided to throw out the test results on the grounds that its dramatically unequal racial results strongly suggested that it was biased against African

Americans. This decision is consistent with the concept of *disparate impact*: If a practice has unequal results, federal policy and court precedents tend to assume that the policy is racially biased. The city feared that using these possibly "tainted" test scores might result in lawsuits by black and other minority firefighters. Instead, a lawsuit was filed by several white and Hispanic firefighters who *had* qualified for promotion, claiming that invalidating the test results amounted to reverse racial discrimination. In yet another 5–4 ruling, the Supreme Court ruled in favor of the white plaintiffs in the spring of 2009.

The issue in *Ricci v. DeStefano* is not overt Jim Crow discrimination, but a test that might be discriminatory in its results, although not in its intent. New Haven was attempting to avoid racial discrimination. This case illustrates some of the difficult issues that accompany attempts to address modern institutional discrimination: How far do employers need to go to ensure racial fairness? Should policies and procedures be judged by the outcomes or their intents? What do "fairness" and "equal treatment" mean in a society in which minority groups have only recently won formal equality and still have lower access to quality schooling and jobs in the mainstream economy? Did the city of New Haven go too far in its attempt to avoid discrimination (five of the Supreme Court Justices thought so)? Can there be a truly fair, race-neutral policy for employment and promotion in the present when opportunities and resources have been allocated on the basis of race for so long in the past? If the problem is color-coded, can the solution be color-neutral?

Another prominent battleground for affirmative action programs has been in higher education. Since the 1960s, many colleges and universities have implemented programs to increase the number of minority students on campus at both the undergraduate and graduate levels, sometimes admitting minority students who had lower grade point averages (GPAs) or test scores than dominant-group students who were turned away. In general, advocates of these programs have justified them in terms of redressing the discriminatory practices of the past or increasing diversity on campus and making the student body a more accurate representation of the surrounding society. To say the least, these programs have been highly controversial and the targets of frequent lawsuits, some of which have found their way to the highest courts in the land.

Recent decisions by the Supreme Court have limited the application of affirmative action in education. In two lawsuits involving the University of Michigan in 2003 (*Grutter v. Bollinger* and *Gratz v. Bollinger*), the Supreme Court held that the university's law school *could* use race as one criterion in deciding admissions, but that undergraduate admissions *could not* award an automatic advantage to minority applicants. In other words, universities could take account of an applicant's race, but only in a limited way, as one factor among many.

In the spring of 2007, the court further narrowed the scope of affirmative action in a ruling that involved two public school systems (*Parents Involved in Community Schools v. Seattle School District No. 1*, 2006; *Meredith v. Jefferson County Board of Education*, 2005). At issue were the plans in Seattle and Louisville to further racial integration and diversity in their schools despite the extensive residential segregation in their areas. Students were assigned to schools partly on the basis of race, and the Supreme Court ruled that these plans violated the equal protection clause of the U.S. Constitution (Barnes, 2007).

What lies ahead for affirmative action? On one hand, there seems to be a clear trend in court decisions to narrow the scope and applicability of these programs. Also, there is very little public support for affirmative action, especially for programs that are perceived as providing specific numerical quotas in jobs or university admissions for minority groups. For example, a representative sample of Americans was asked in a 2006 survey if they supported "preferences in hiring and promotion" for blacks. Only 12% of white respondents expressed support and, more surprising perhaps, preferences were supported by less than a majority of black respondents (43%) and only 19% of female respondents (National Opinion Research Center, 1972–2007).

On the other hand, opposition to affirmative action is not unanimous, and there is considerable support for some types of programs. Although white (and many minority-group) Americans object to fixed quotas or preferences, there is support for programs that expand the opportunities available to minority groups, including enhanced job training, education, and recruitment in minority communities (Wilson, 2009). Programs of this sort are more consistent with traditional ideologies and value systems that stress individual initiative, personal responsibility, and equality of opportunity. Also, many businesses and universities are committed to the broad principles of affirmative action—the need to address past injustices and the importance of providing diversity in the workplace and classroom—and they are likely to sustain their programs (to the extent allowed by court decisions and legislation) into the future. By and large, it seems that affirmative action programs, especially those that stress equality of opportunity, will continue in some form, perhaps quite limited, into the foreseeable future.

Social Change and Minority Group Activism

This chapter has focused on the continuing industrial revolution and its impact on minority groups in general and black–white relations in particular. For the most part, changes in group relations have been presented as the results of the fundamental transformation of the U.S. economic institution from agrarian to industrial to late industrial (or postindustrial). However, the changes in the situation of African Americans and other minority groups did not "just happen" as society modernized. Although the opportunity to pursue favorable change was the result of broad structural changes in American society, the realization of these opportunities came from the efforts of the many who gave their time, their voices, their resources, and sometimes their lives in pursuit of racial justice in America. Since World War II, African Americans have often been in the vanguard of protest activity, and we focus on the contemporary situation of this group in the next chapter.

FOCUS ON CONTEMPORARY ISSUES: Hate Crimes

Hate crimes are violent attacks or other acts of intimidation motivated by the group membership of the victim or victims. Victims can be chosen randomly and are often strangers to their assailants: They are chosen as representatives of a group, not because of who they are as individuals. These crimes are expressions of hatred or disdain, strong prejudice, and blatant racism, and are not committed for profit or gain. Two of the most publicized and disturbing hate crimes occurred in 1998. In Texas, James Byrd, a black man, was beaten and dragged behind a pickup truck by three white men until he died. In Wyoming, college student Matthew Shepard was robbed, beaten, and tied to a fence post and left to die. He was in a coma when found and died in a hospital a few days later. His assailants allegedly selected him as a victim because he was gay. Other hate crimes across the nation include assaults, arson against black churches, vandalism of Jewish synagogues, cross burnings, nooses prominently tied to office doors of black university professors, and other acts of intimidation and harassment. Furthermore, a number of violent, openly racist extremist groups—skinheads, the Ku Klux Klan (KKK), White Aryan Resistance (WAR), and Aryan Nations—have achieved widespread notoriety and have a prominent presence in some communities as well as on the Internet.

In Chapter 1, I made the point that prejudice in the United States has changed from overt and blatant forms to more subtle and indirect expressions. Do hate crimes and hate groups contradict this point? Do they balance the shift to modern racism with an opposite shift to blatant, violent racism? What causes these attacks? What are the implications?

As we will see in chapters to come, racial violence, hate crimes, and extremist racist groups are hardly new to the United States. Violence between whites and nonwhites began in the earliest days of this society (e.g., conflicts with Native Americans, the kidnapping and enslavement of Africans) and has continued, in one form or another, to the present. Contemporary racist attacks and hate crimes, in all their manifestations, have deep roots in the American past.

Also, racist and extremist groups are no strangers to American history. The Klan, for example, was founded almost 150 years ago, shortly after the Civil War, and has since played a significant role in local and state politics and in everyday life at various times and places—and not just in the South. During the turbulent 1920s, the Klan reached what was probably the height of its popularity. It had a membership in the millions and was said to openly control many U.S. senators, governors, and local politicians.

Are hate crimes increasing or decreasing? It's difficult to answer this question even though the FBI has been collecting and compiling information on hate crimes for over a decade. Not all localities report these incidents or classify them in the same way and, perhaps more important, not all hate crimes are reported. Thus, the actual volume of hate crimes may be many times greater than the "official" rate compiled by the FBI (for a recent analysis, see Fears, 2007).

Keeping these limitations in mind, here is some of what is known. Exhibit 4.8 reports the breakdown of hate crimes in 2007 and shows that in most incidents, victims were selected because of

(Continued)

(Continued)

Exhibit 4.8 Hate Crimes by Target Groups, 2007

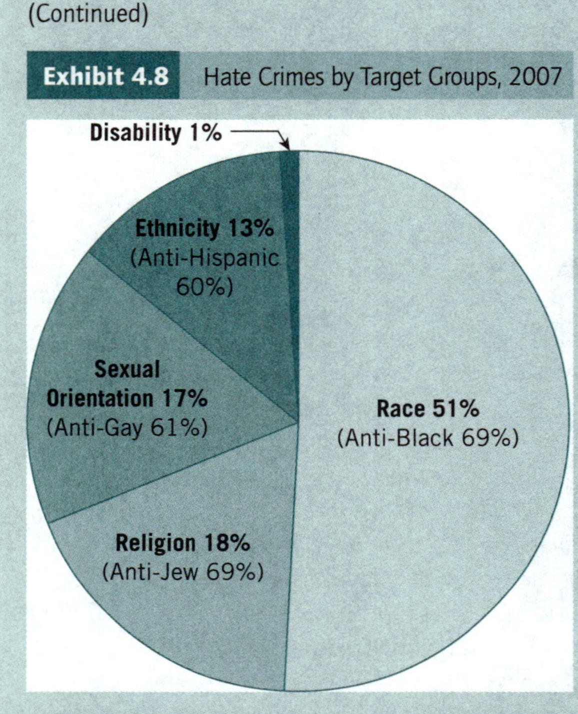

SOURCE: FBI (2009).

their race. In the great majority (69%) of the racial cases, blacks were the target group. Most of the incidents involving religion (69%) targeted Jewish victims, and most of the anti-ethnic attacks were against Hispanics (60%). The majority (61%) of the attacks motivated by the sexual orientation of the victims were directed against male homosexuals (Federal Bureau of Investigation [FBI], 2009).

Exhibit 4.9 shows the total number of hate crimes in the United States that were reported to the police from 1996 to 2007. The volume of hate crime is also presented for the four main target groups. In all cases, the number of hate crimes seems to be holding steady in the last several years covered in the graph.

The FBI currently provides information about hate crimes only through 2007. What has been happening since? The Southern Poverty Law Center (SPLC) reports that the rate has been

Exhibit 4.9 Total Number of Hate Crimes per Year and Number of Incidents by Target Group, 1996–2007

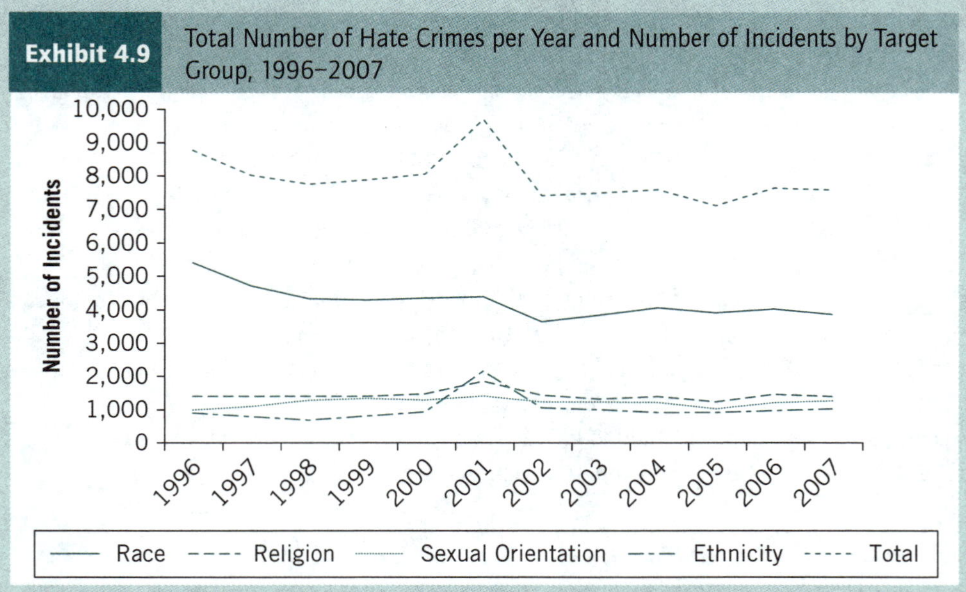

SOURCE: FBI (2009).

increasing, spurred by the frustrations generated by a weak economy and high rates of immigration, and the election of an African American to the highest office in the land (Holthouse, 2009). The SPLC estimates that there were 926 hate groups (defined as groups that "have beliefs or practices that attack or malign an entire class of people, typically for their immutable characteristics") active in the United States in 2008. According to their count, this is an increase of 4% over the previous year and an increase of 50% since 2000 (Holthouse, 2009). These groups include the KKK, various skinhead and white power groups, and black groups such as the Nation of Islam. The SPLC maintains a map showing the location of the known hate groups at its Web site. The map in Exhibit 4.10 shows that the greatest concentration is in the Southeast, Texas, and California.

Exhibit 4.10 Distribution of Hate Groups, 2007

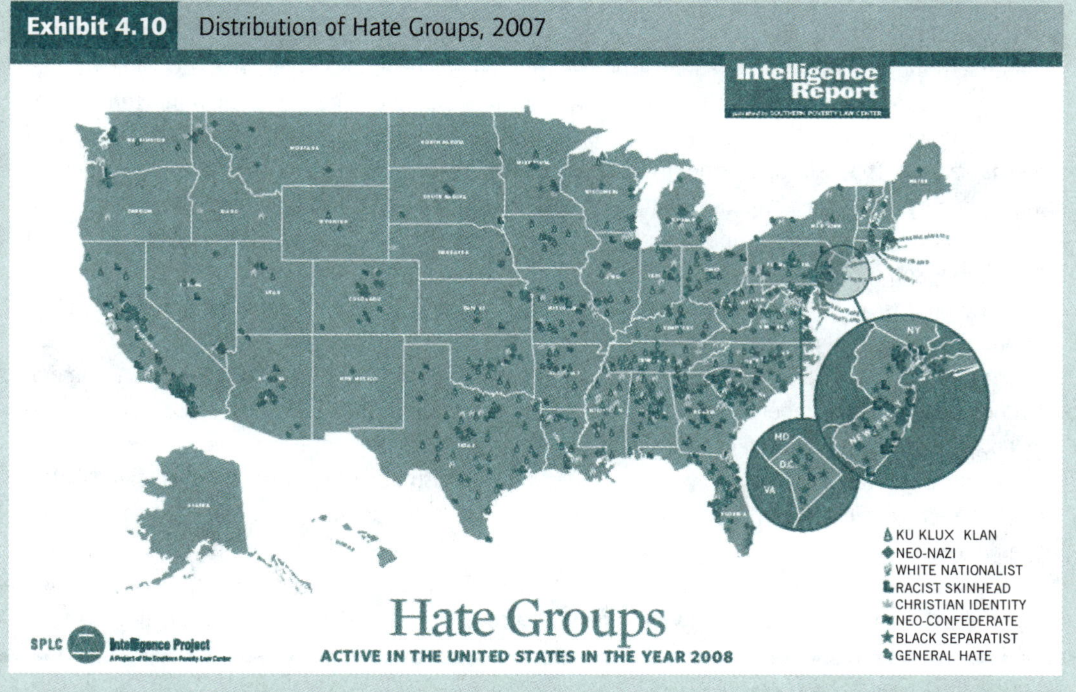

SOURCE: Southern Poverty Law Center, http://www.splcenter.org/intel/map/images/splc_hategroups.pdf. Reprinted by permission of the Southern Intelligence Law Center, Intelligence Project.

What motivates hate groups and the perpetrators of hate crimes? According to some analysts, there are two main types of hate crimes. Many hate crimes are motivated by *thrill seeking*, or the quest for excitement. These offenses are often committed by groups that search out random victims in gay bars, in synagogues, or in minority neighborhoods. The second common type of hate crime is *defensive*: The perpetrators feel that their territory has been invaded or that members of the other group are threatening their resources or status. They strike to punish or expel the invaders, recover their rightful share of resources, or restore their prestige (Gerstenfeld, 2004).

(Continued)

(Continued)

Who are the perpetrators? The overwhelming majority are young males, the same group most likely to be involved in other violent crimes. They also tend to have lower levels of education and few job skills and are the same group that seems to be most likely to join extremist racist groups like the KKK (Schafer & Navarro, 2004). These working- and lower-class males are most likely to feel threatened by what they see as the unjust rise in status of racial minority groups and recent immigrants. They attack other groups to claim or preserve the higher status associated with being white in this society. Thus, hate crimes and hate groups may be the extreme, bitter edge of the struggle to preserve white privilege.

The connection between social class and hate crimes also reflects some broad structural changes in the economy. As we have noted in this chapter, the United States has shifted from an industrial, manufacturing economy to a postindustrial, information-processing economy. This economic change has meant a decline in the supply of secure, well-paying, blue-collar jobs. Many manufacturing jobs have been lost to other nations with cheaper workforces; others have been lost to automation and mechanization. The resultant tensions have been further exacerbated by industry downsizing, increasing inequality in the class structure, and rising costs of living. These economic forces squeeze the middle and lower ranges of the dominant group's class system, creating considerable pressure and frustration, some of which may be manifested in furious but random attacks on immigrants and minority groups. These ideas are also supported by the spontaneous, unplanned, and highly emotional nature of many of these crimes.

If these points are valid, they may shed some light on the assertion of the SPLC that the volume of hate crimes and the number of hate groups have been increasing since 2007. The sense of threat and anxiety and the desire to protect status may increase as the economy contracts and the rate of unemployment rises. Even if the economy recovers fully, a postindustrial job structure provides relatively few desirable employment opportunities for people with lower levels of education. This is a "social class" dilemma that cuts across lines of race and ethnicity and affects all people with modest educational credentials. However, the effects of deindustrialization may be experienced differently by white males, especially those whose racial identity presumes a sense of superiority and a place of privilege.

MAIN POINTS

- Group relations change as the subsistence technology and the level of development of the larger society change. As nations industrialize and urbanize, dominant–minority relations change from paternalistic to rigid competitive forms.
- In the South, slavery was replaced by de jure segregation, a system that combined racial separation with great inequality. The Jim Crow system was motivated by a need to control labor and was reinforced by coercion and intense racism and prejudice.
- Black Southerners responded to segregation in part by moving to northern urban areas. The Northern African American population enjoyed greater freedom and developed some

political and economic resources, but a large concentration of low-income, relatively powerless African Americans developed in the ghetto neighborhoods.
- In response to segregation, the African American community developed a separate institutional life centered on family, church, and community. An African American middle class emerged, as well as a protest movement.
- African American women remain one of the most exploited groups. Combining work with family roles, African American females were employed mostly in agriculture and domestic service during the era of segregation.
- Industrialization continued throughout the 20th century and profoundly affected dominant–minority relations. Urbanization, specialization, bureaucratization, and other trends have changed the shape of race relations, as have the changing structure of the occupational sector and the growing importance of education. Group relations have shifted from rigid to fluid competitive. Modern institutional discrimination is one of the major challenges facing minority groups.

STUDY SITE ON THE WEB

Don't forget the interactive quizzes and other resources and learning aids at **www.pineforge.com/healeyds3e**

FOR FURTHER READING

The following is a classic analysis of the shift from a manufacturing to a service-based, information society:

Bluestone, Barry, & Harrison, Bennet. 1982. *The Deindustrialization of America.* New York: Basic Books.

Here are three outstanding analyses of black–white relations in the United States, with a major focus on the historical periods covered in this chapter:

Geschwender, James A. 1978. *Racial Stratification in America.* Dubuque, IA: William C. Brown.

Wilson, William J. 1973. *Power, Racism, and Privilege: Race Relations in Theoretical and Sociohistorical Perspectives.* New York: Free Press.

Woodward, C. Vann. 1974. *The Strange Career of Jim Crow* (3rd rev. ed.). New York: Oxford University Press.

This work is a comprehensive and provocative look at modern institutional discrimination:

Feagin, Joe R. 2001. *Racist America.* New York: Routledge.

Here is a compact, masterful review of the myths and realities surrounding affirmative action:

Pincus, Fred. 2003. *Reverse Discrimination: Dismantling the Myth.* Boulder, CO: Lynne Rienner.

QUESTIONS FOR REVIEW AND STUDY

1. A corollary to two themes presented at the beginning of Chapter 3 is offered at the start of Chapter 4. How exactly does the material in the chapter illustrate the usefulness of this corollary?
2. Explain paternalistic and rigid competitive relations and link them to industrialization. How does the shift from slavery to de jure segregation illustrate the dynamics of these two systems?
3. What was the Great Migration to the North? How did it change American race relations?
4. Explain the transition from rigid competitive to fluid competitive relations, and explain how this transition is related to the coming of postindustrial society. Explain the roles of urbanization, bureaucracy, the service sector of the job market, and education in this transition.
5. What is modern institutional discrimination? How does it differ from "traditional" institutional discrimination? Explain the role of affirmative action in combating each.
6. Explain the impact of industrialization and globalization on gender relations. Compare and contrast these changes with the changes that occurred for racial and ethnic minority groups.

INTERNET RESEARCH PROJECT

A. Everyday Life Under Jim Crow

The daily workings of the Jim Crow system of segregation are analyzed and described in a collection of interviews, photos, and memories archived at www.americanradioworks.publicradio.org/features/remembering. Explore the site, look at the photos, listen to the clips, and analyze them in terms of the concepts introduced in this chapter.

B. The Debate Over Affirmative Action

Update and supplement the debate on affirmative action presented at the end of the chapter. Start with the newspaper home pages listed in the Appendix (www.pineforge.com/healeyds3e) and search for recent news items or opinion pieces on the issue. Search the Internet for other viewpoints and perspectives from other groups and positions on the political spectrum. One place you might start is http://aad.english.ucsb.edu, a Web site that presents diverse opinions on the topic and brings many different voices to the debates. Analyze events and opinions in terms of the concepts introduced in this chapter, especially modern institutional discrimination.

Notes

1. From *Twelve Million Black Voices* by Richard Wright. Copyright ©1941 by Richard Wright. Published by Thunder's Mouth Press, an imprint of Avalon Publishing Group Incorporated.

Part III

Understanding Dominant-Minority Relations in the United States Today

In Part III, we turn to contemporary intergroup relations. The emphasis is on the present situation of American minority groups, but the recent past is also investigated to see how present situations developed. We explore the ways minority and dominant groups respond to a changing American society and to each other, and how minority groups define and pursue their own self-interests in interaction with other groups, American culture and values, and the institutions of the larger society.

The themes and ideas developed in the first two parts of this text will continue to be central to the analysis. For example, the case studies are presented in an order that roughly follows the Blauner hypothesis: Colonized groups are presented first, and we end with groups created by immigration. Also, we will continue to rely on the concepts of the Noel hypothesis to analyze and explain contemporary dominant–minority patterns (see Chapter 3 for a review of these concepts).

The history and present conditions of each minority group are unique, and no two groups have had the same experiences. To help identify and understand these differences, the concepts developed in the first two parts of this text and a common comparative frame of reference are used throughout Part III. The focus is on assimilation and pluralism; inequality and power; and prejudice, racism, and discrimination. For ease of comparison, the final sections of Chapters 5 through 8 use many of the same titles and subtitles and the information is presented in the same order.

Much of the conceptual frame of reference employed in these case studies can be summarized in six themes. The first five themes are based on material from previous chapters; the last is covered in the forthcoming chapters.

1. Consistent with the Noel hypothesis, the present conditions of America's minority groups reflect their contact situations, especially the nature of their competition with the dominant group (e.g., competition over land versus competition over labor) and the size of the power differential between groups at the time of contact.

2. Consistent with the Blauner hypothesis, minority groups created by colonization experience economic and political inequalities that have lasted longer and been more severe than those experienced by minority groups created by immigration.

3. Power and economic differentials and barriers to upward mobility are especially pronounced for groups identified by racial or physical characteristics, as opposed to cultural or linguistic traits.

4. Consistent with the themes stated in Chapters 3 and 4, dominant–minority relations reflect the economic and political characteristics of the larger society and change as those characteristics change. Changes in the subsistence technology of the larger society are particularly consequential for dominant–minority relations. The shift from a manufacturing to a service economy (deindustrialization) is one of the key factors shaping dominant–minority relations in the United States today.

5. The development of group relations, both in the past and for the future, can be analyzed in terms of assimilation (more unity) and pluralism (more diversity). Group relations in the past (e.g., the degree of assimilation permitted or required of the minority group) reflected mainly dominant-group needs and wishes. Although the pressure for Americanization remains considerable, there is more flexibility and variety in group relations today.

6. Since World War II, minority groups have gained significantly more control over the direction of group relationships. This trend reflects the decline of traditional prejudice in the larger society and the successful efforts of minority groups to protest, resist, and change patterns of exclusion and domination. These successes have been possible, in large part, because American minority groups have increased their share of political and economic resources.

5 African Americans

From Segregation to Modern Institutional Discrimination and Modern Racism

The children called home "Hornets" or, more frequently, "the projects" or simply, the "jects" (pronounced "jets"). Pharoah [a nine-year-old resident] called it "The graveyard." But they never referred to it by its full name: the Governor Henry Horner Homes. . . . Nothing here, the children would tell you, was as it should be. . . .

If [Pharoah and his brother] had one guidepost in their young lives . . . it was their mother, LaJoe. They depended on her; she depended on them. The boys would do anything for their mother. A shy, soft-spoken woman, LaJoe was known for her warmth and generosity, not only to her own children but to her children's friends . . . . LaJoe had often mothered children who needed advice or comforting. Many young men and women still called her "Mom." She let so many people through her apartment, sometimes just to use the bathroom, that she hid the toilet paper in the kitchen because it had often been stolen.

But the neighborhood, which hungrily devoured its children, had taken its toll of LaJoe as well. In recent years, she had become more tired as she questioned her ability to raise her children here. . . . LaJoe had watched and held on as the neighborhood slowly decayed. . . . First, the middle-class whites fled to the suburbs. Then, the middle-class blacks left for safer neighborhoods. Then, the businesses moved, some to the suburbs, others to the South. Over the past 10 years, the city had lost a third of its manufacturing jobs. And there were few jobs left for those who lived in Henry Horner.

(Continued)

(Continued)

To LaJoe, the neighborhood had become a black hole. She could more easily recite what wasn't there than what was. There were no banks, only currency exchanges, which charged customers up to $8.00 for every welfare check cashed. There were no public libraries, movie theaters, skating rinks, or bowling alleys to entertain the neighborhood's children. For the infirm, there were two neighborhood clinics, both of which teetered on the edge of bankruptcy. . . . The death rate of newborn babies exceeded infant mortality rates in a number of Third World countries, including Chile, Costa Rica, Cuba, and Turkey. And there was no rehabilitation center, though drug abuse was rampant.

According to a 1980 profile of the [area], 60,110 people lived there, 88% of them black, 46% of them below the poverty level. It was an area so impoverished that, when Mother Teresa visited in 1982, she assigned nuns from her Missionaries of Charity to work there.

—Alex Kotlowitz[1]

The high-rises of the Henry Horner project in Chicago have been demolished and replaced with low-rise buildings and townhouse units. However, the grim realities of "concentrated poverty" illustrated in this passage live on in low-income, black and minority neighborhoods across the nation. The story of the Horner projects presented in Kotlowitz's classic, *There Are No Children Here* (1991) shows the bitter consequences of combining class and race, of compounding poverty with segregation, joblessness, inadequate schooling, and strong traditions of racism and rejection. In a nation that today is led by a black man, a nation with many wealthy and powerful African Americans, there is another America: bleak, violent, rife with hopelessness, separate, marginal, and unequal.

Introduction

At the dawn of the 20th century, African Americans were primarily a Southern rural peasantry, victimized by de jure segregation, exploited by the sharecropping system of agriculture, and blocked from the better-paying industrial and manufacturing jobs in urban areas. Segregation had disenfranchised them and stripped them of the legal and civil rights they had briefly enjoyed during Reconstruction. As we saw in Chapter 4, the huge majority of African Americans had very limited access to quality education; few political rights; few occupational choices; and very few means of expressing their views, grievances, and concerns to the larger society or to the world.

Today, a century later, African Americans are highly urbanized, dispersed throughout the United States, and represented in virtually every occupational grouping. The most significant change, without question, is the election of Barack Obama to the presidency of the United States, but African Americans are also visible across the board at the highest levels of American society: from the Supreme Court to corporate boardrooms to the most prestigious universities. Some of the best-known, most successful, and most respected (and wealthiest) people in the world in recent years have been

African Americans: Martin Luther King Jr., Malcolm X, Michael Jordan, Shirley Chisholm, Jesse Jackson, Bill Cosby, Toni Morrison, Maya Angelou, Muhammad Ali, Oprah Winfrey, Colin Powell, and Condoleezza Rice, to name just a few. Furthermore, some of the most important and prestigious American corporations (including Merrill Lynch, American Express, and Time Warner) have been led by African Americans.

How did these changes come about, and what do they signify? What problems are obscured by these glittering success stories? Do racism, prejudice, and discrimination continue to be significant problems? Is it true that barriers to racial equality have been eliminated? How do the Noel and Blauner hypotheses (see Chapter 3) and the other concepts developed earlier in this text help us understand contemporary black–white relations?

To understand the trajectories of change that have led to the present, we must deal with the watershed events in black–white relations: the end of de jure segregation, the triumph (and the limitations) of the **civil rights movement** of the 1950s and 1960s, the urban riots and **Black Power movement** of the 1960s, and the continuing racial divisions within U.S. society since the 1970s. Behind these events lie the powerful pressures of industrialization and modernization, the shift from rigid to fluid competitive group relations, changing distributions of power and forms of intergroup competition, declining levels of traditional prejudice, and new ideas about assimilation and pluralism. In less abstract terms, black–white relations changed as a direct result of protest; resistance; and the concerted actions of thousands of individuals, both blacks and whites.

The End of de Jure Segregation

As a colonized minority group, African Americans entered the 20th century facing extreme inequality, relative powerlessness, and sharp limitations on their freedom. Their most visible enemy was the system of de jure segregation in the South (see Chapter 4), the rigid competitive system of group relations that controlled the lives of most African Americans.

Why and how did de jure segregation come to an end? Recall from Chapter 4 that dominant–minority relationships change as the larger society and its subsistence technology change. As the United States industrialized and urbanized during the 20th century, a series of social, political, economic, and legal processes were set in motion that ultimately destroyed Jim Crow segregation.

The mechanization and modernization of agriculture in the South had a powerful effect on race relations. Farmwork became less labor intensive and machines replaced people, so the need to maintain a large, powerless workforce declined (Geschwender, 1978). Thus, one of the primary motivations for maintaining Jim Crow segregation and the sharecropping system of farming lost force.

In addition, the modernization of Southern agriculture helped to spur the migration northward and to urban areas, as discussed in Chapter 4. Outside the rural South, African Americans found it easier to register to vote and pursue other avenues for improving their situations. The weight of the growing African American vote was first felt in the 1930s and was large enough to make a difference in local, state, and even national elections by the 1940s. In 1948, for example, President Harry Truman recognized that he could not be reelected without the support of African American voters. As a result, the Democratic Party adopted a civil rights plank in the party platform, the first time since Reconstruction that a national political party had taken a stand on race relations (Wilson, 1973).

The weight of these changes accumulated slowly, and no single date or specific event marks the end of de jure segregation. The system ended as it had begun: gradually and in a series of discrete episodes and incidents. By the mid-20th century, resistance to racial change was weakening, and the power resources of African Americans were increasing. This enhanced freedom and strength fueled a variety of efforts that sped the demise of Jim Crow segregation. Although a complete historical autopsy is not necessary here, a general understanding of the reasons for the death of Jim Crow segregation is essential for an understanding of modern black–white relations.

Wartime Developments

One of the first successful applications of the growing stock of black power resources occurred in 1941, as the United States was mobilizing for war against Germany and Japan. Despite the crisis atmosphere, racial discrimination was common, even in the defense industry. A group of African Americans, led by labor leader A. Philip Randolph, head of the Brotherhood of Sleeping Car Porters, threatened to march on Washington to protest the discriminatory treatment.

To forestall the march, President Franklin D. Roosevelt signed Executive Order No. 8802, banning discrimination in defense-related industries, and created a watchdog federal agency, the Fair Employment Practices Commission, to oversee compliance with the new antidiscriminatory policy (Franklin & Moss, 1994; Geschwender, 1978). President Roosevelt's actions were significant in two ways. First, a group of African Americans not only had their grievances heard at the highest level of society but also succeeded in getting what they wanted. Underlying the effectiveness of the planned march was the rising political and economic power of the Northern African American community and the need to mobilize all segments of the population for a world war. Second, the federal government made an unprecedented commitment to fair employment rights for African Americans. This alliance between the federal government and African Americans was tentative, but it foreshadowed some of the dynamics of racial change in the 1950s and 1960s.

The Civil Rights Movement

The civil rights movement was a multifaceted campaign to end legalized segregation and ameliorate the massive inequalities faced by African Americans. The campaign lasted for decades and included lawsuits and courtroom battles as well as protest marches and demonstrations. We begin our examination with a look at the movement's successful challenge to the laws of racial segregation.

Brown v. Board of Education of Topeka

Undoubtedly, the single most powerful blow to de jure segregation was delivered by the U.S. Supreme Court in *Brown v. Board of Education of Topeka* in 1954. The Supreme Court reversed the *Plessy v. Ferguson* decision of 1896 (see Chapter 4) and ruled that racially separate facilities are inherently unequal and therefore unconstitutional. Segregated school systems—and all other forms of legalized racial segregation—would have to end. The landmark *Brown* decision was the culmination of decades of planning and effort by the National Association for the Advancement of Colored People (NAACP), and individuals such as Thurgood Marshall, the NAACP's chief counsel (who was appointed to the Supreme Court in 1967).

The strategy of the NAACP was to attack Jim Crow by finding instances in which the civil rights of an African American had been violated and then bringing suit against the relevant governmental agency. These lawsuits were intended to extend far beyond the specific case being argued. The goal was to persuade the courts to declare segregation unconstitutional not only in the specific instance being tried but in all similar cases. The *Brown* decision was the ultimate triumph of this strategy. The significance of the Supreme Court's decision was not that Linda Brown—the child in whose name the case was argued—would attend a different school or even that the school system of Topeka, Kansas, would be integrated. Instead, the significance lay in the rejection of the principle of de jure segregation in the South and, by implication, throughout the nation. The *Brown* decision changed the law and dealt a crippling blow to Jim Crow segregation.

The blow was not fatal, however. Southern states responded to the *Brown* decision by stalling and mounting campaigns of massive resistance. Jim Crow laws remained on the books for years. White Southerners actively defended the system of racial privilege and attempted to forestall change through a variety of means, including violence and intimidation. The Ku Klux Klan, largely dormant since the 1920s, reappeared along with other racist and terrorist groups, such as the White Citizens' Councils. White politicians and other leaders competed with each other to express the most adamant statements of racist resistance (Wilson, 1973). One locality, Prince Edward County in central Virginia, chose to close its public schools rather than integrate. The schools remained closed for 5 years. During that time, the white children attended private, segregated academies, and the county provided no education at all for African American children (Franklin, 1967).

Nonviolent Direct Action Protest

The principle established by *Brown* (1954) was assimilationist: It ordered the educational institutions of the dominant group to be opened up freely and equally to all. Southern states and communities overwhelmingly rejected the principle of equal access and shared facilities. Centuries of racist tradition and privilege were at stake, and considerable effort would be required to overcome Southern defiance and resistance. The central force in this struggle was a protest movement, the beginning of which is often traced to Montgomery, Alabama, where on December 1, 1955, Rosa Parks, a seamstress and NAACP member, rode the city bus home from work, as she usually did. As the bus filled, she was ordered to surrender her seat to a white male passenger. When she refused, the police were called, and Rosa Parks was jailed for violating a local segregation ordinance.

Although Mrs. Parks was hardly the first African American to be subjected to such indignities, her case stimulated a protest movement in the African American community, and a boycott of the city buses was organized. Participants in the boycott set up carpools, shared taxis, and walked (in some cases, for miles) to and from work. They stayed off the buses for more than a year, until victory was achieved and the city was ordered to desegregate its buses. The Montgomery bus boycott was led by the Reverend Martin Luther King Jr., the new minister of a local Baptist church.

From these beginnings sprang the protest movement that eventually defeated de jure segregation. The central strategy of the movement involved **nonviolent direct action,** a method by which the system of de jure segregation was confronted head-on, not in the courtroom or in the state legislature, but in the streets. The movement's principles of nonviolence were adopted from the tenets of Christianity and from the teachings of Mohandas Gandhi, Henry David Thoreau, and others. Dr. King (1958, 1963, 1968) expressed the philosophy in a number of books and speeches. Nonviolent protest was intended to confront the forces of evil rather than the people who happened to be doing evil, and it attempted to win the friendship and support of its enemies rather than to defeat or humiliate them. Above all, nonviolent protest required courage and discipline; it was not a method for cowards (King, 1958).

The movement used different tactics for different situations, including sit-ins at segregated restaurants, protest marches and demonstrations, prayer meetings, and voter registration drives. The police and terrorist groups such as the KKK often responded to these protests with brutal repression and violence, and protesters were routinely imprisoned, beaten, and attacked by police dogs. The violent resistance sometimes escalated to acts of murder, including the 1963 bombing of a black church in Birmingham, Alabama, which took the lives of four little girls, and the 1968 assassination of Dr. King. Resistance to racial change in the South was intense. It would take more than protests and marches to finally extirpate de jure segregation, and the U.S. Congress finally provided the necessary tools (see D'Angelo, 2001; Killian, 1975; King, 1958, 1963, 1968; Morris, 1984).

Landmark Legislation

The successes of the protest movement, combined with changing public opinion and the legal principles established by the Supreme Court, coalesced in the mid-1960s to stimulate the passage of two laws that, together, ended Jim Crow segregation. In 1964, at the urging of President Lyndon B. Johnson, the U.S. Congress passed the Civil Rights Act of 1964, banning discrimination on the grounds of race, color, religion, national origin, or gender. The law applied to publicly owned facilities such as parks and municipal swimming pools, businesses and other facilities open to the public, and any programs that received federal aid. Congress followed this up with the Voting

Rights Act in 1965, initiated by President Johnson, which required that the same standards be used to register all citizens in federal, state, and local elections. The act banned literacy tests, whites-only primaries, and other practices that had been used to prevent African Americans from registering to vote. This law gave the franchise back to black Southerners and laid the groundwork for increasing black political power. This landmark federal legislation, in combination with court decisions and the protest movement, finally succeeded in crushing Jim Crow.

The Success and Limitations of the Civil Rights Movement

Why did the civil rights movement succeed? A comprehensive list of reasons would be legion, but we can cite some of the most important causes of its success, especially those consistent with the general points about dominant–minority relations that have been made in previous chapters.

First, as noted above, the continuing industrialization and urbanization of the society as a whole—and the South in particular—weakened the Jim Crow, rigid competitive system of minority-group control and segregation. There was less need to maintain a large, powerless workforce as agricultural production was mechanized and the movement of blacks out of the South and into cities gave them more access to power resources to defend their interests and advance their goals.

Second, following World War II, the United States enjoyed a period of prosperity that lasted into the 1960s. Consistent with the Noel hypothesis (see Chapter 3), this was important, because it reduced the intensity of intergroup competition, at least outside the South. During prosperous times, resistance to change tends to weaken. If the economic "pie" is expanding, the "slices" claimed by minority groups can increase without threatening the size of anyone else's portions, and the prejudice generated during intergroup competition (à la Robber's Cave, Chapter 1) may be held in check. Thus, these "good times" muted the sense of threat experienced in the dominant group from the demands for equality made by the civil rights movement.

Third, some of this economic prosperity found its way into African American communities and increased their pool of economic and political resources. Networks of independent, African American–controlled organizations and institutions, such as churches and colleges, were created or grew in size and power. The increasingly elaborate infrastructure of the black community included protest organizations, such as the NAACP (see Chapter 4), and provided material resources, leadership, and "people power" to lead the fight against segregation and discrimination.

Fourth, the goals of the civil rights movement were assimilationist; the movement embraced the traditional American values of liberty, equality, freedom, and fair treatment. It demanded civil, legal, and political rights for African Americans, rights available to whites automatically. Thus, many whites did not feel threatened by the movement because they saw it as consistent with mainstream American values, especially in contrast with the intense, often violent resistance of many Southern whites.

Fifth, the perceived legitimacy of the goals of the movement also opened up the possibility of alliances with other groups (white liberals, Jews, college students). The support of others was crucial because black Southerners had few resources of their own other than their numbers and their courage. By mobilizing the resources of other, more powerful groups, black Southerners forged alliances and created sympathetic support that was brought to bear on their opposition.

Finally, widespread and sympathetic coverage from the mass media, particularly television, was crucial to the success of the movement. The oft-repeated scenario of African Americans being brutally attacked while demonstrating for their rights outraged many Americans and reinforced the moral consensus that eventually rejected "old-fashioned" racial prejudice along with Jim Crow segregation.

The civil rights movement ended de jure segregation in the South but found it difficult to survive the demise of its primary enemy. The confrontational tactics that had been so effective against the Jim Crow system proved less useful when attention turned to the actual distribution of jobs, wealth, political power, and other valued goods and services. Outside the South, the allocation of opportunity and resources had always been the central concern of the African American community. Let's take a look at these concerns.

Developments Outside the South

De Facto Segregation

Chapter 4 discussed some of the difficulties encountered by African Americans as they left the rural South. Discrimination by labor unions, employers, industrialists, and white ethnic groups was common. Racial discrimination outside the South was less blatant but was still pervasive, especially in housing, education, and employment.

The pattern of racial separation and inequality outside the South is often called **de facto segregation:** segregation resulting from the apparently voluntary choices of dominant and minority groups alike. Theoretically, no person, law, or specific group is responsible for de facto segregation; it "just happens" as people and groups make decisions about where to live and work.

The distinction between de facto and de jure segregation can be misleading, however, and the de facto variety is often the de jure variety in thin disguise. Although cities and states outside the South may not have had actual Jim Crow laws, de facto segregation was often the direct result of intentionally racist decisions made by governmental and quasi-governmental agencies such as real estate boards, school boards, and zoning boards (see Massey & Denton, 1993). For example, shortly after World War I, the real estate board in the city of Chicago adopted a policy that required its members, on penalty of "immediate expulsion," to follow a policy of racial residential segregation (A. Cohen & Taylor, 2000).

Regardless of who or what was responsible for these patterns, African Americans living outside the South faced more poverty, higher unemployment, and lower-quality housing and schools than did whites, but there was no clear equivalent of Jim Crow to attack or to blame for these patterns of inequality. In the 1960s, the African American community outside the South expressed its frustration over the slow pace of change in two ways: urban unrest and a movement for change that rose to prominence as the civil rights movement faded.

Urban Unrest

In the mid-1960s, the frustration and anger of urban African American communities erupted into a series of violent uprisings. The riots began in the summer of 1965 in Watts, a neighborhood in Los Angeles, and over the next 4 years, virtually every large black urban community experienced similar outbursts. Racial violence was hardly a new phenomenon in America. Race riots occurred as early as the Civil War, and various time periods had seen racial violence of considerable magnitude. The riots of the 1960s were different, however. Most race riots in the past had involved attacks by whites against blacks, often including the invasion and destruction of African American neighborhoods (see, e.g., D'Orso, 1996; Ellsworth, 1982). The urban unrest of the 1960s, in contrast, consisted largely of attacks by blacks against the symbols of their oppression and frustration. The most obvious targets were white-owned businesses operating in black neighborhoods and the police, who were seen as an army of occupation and whose excessive use of force was often the immediate precipitator of riots (Conot, 1967; National Advisory Commission, 1968).

The Black Power Movement

The urban riots of the 1960s were an unmistakable sign that the problems of race relations had not been resolved with the end of Jim Crow segregation. Outside the South, the problems were different and called for different solutions. Even as the civil rights movement was celebrating its victory in the South, a new protest movement rose to prominence. The Black Power movement was a loose coalition of organizations and spokespersons that encompassed a variety of ideas and views, many of which differed sharply from those of the civil rights movement. Some of the central ideas included racial pride ("Black is beautiful" was a key slogan of the day), interest in African heritage, and black nationalism. In contrast to the assimilationist goals of the civil rights movement, Black Power groups worked to increase African American control over schools, police, welfare programs, and other public services operating in black neighborhoods.

Most adherents of the Black Power movement felt that white racism and institutional discrimination, forces buried deep in the core of American culture and society, were the primary causes of racial inequality in America. Thus, if African Americans were ever to be truly empowered, they would have to liberate themselves and do it on their own terms. Some Black Power advocates specifically rejected the goal of assimilation into white society, arguing that integration would require blacks to become part of the very system that had for centuries oppressed, denigrated, and devalued them and other peoples of color.

The Nation of Islam

The themes of Black Power voiced so loudly in the 1960s were decades or even centuries old. Marcus Garvey had popularized many of these ideas in the 1920s, and they were espoused and further developed by the Nation of Islam, popularly known as the Black Muslims, in the 1960s.

One of the best-known organizations within the Black Power movement, the Black Muslims were angry, impatient, and outspoken. They denounced the hypocrisy, greed, and racism of American society and advocated staunch resistance and racial separation. The Black Muslims did more than talk, however. Pursuing the goals of autonomy and self-determination, they worked hard to create a separate, independent, African American economy within the United States. They opened businesses and stores in African American neighborhoods and tried to deal only with other Muslim-owned firms. Their goal was to develop the African American community economically and supply jobs and capital for expansion solely by using their own resources (Essien-Udom, 1962; Lincoln, 1961; Malcolm X, 1964; Wolfenstein, 1993).

The Nation of Islam and other Black Power groups distinguished between racial *separation* and racial *segregation*. The former is a process of empowerment whereby a group becomes stronger as it becomes more autonomous and self-controlled. The latter is a system of inequality in which the African American community is powerless and is controlled by the dominant group. Thus, the Black Power groups were working to find ways in which African Americans could develop their own resources and deal with the dominant group from a more powerful position, a strategy similar to that followed by minority groups that form ethnic enclaves (see Chapter 2).

The best-known spokesperson for the Nation of Islam was Malcolm X, one of the most charismatic figures of the 1960s. Malcolm X forcefully articulated the themes of the Black Power movement. Born Malcolm Little, he converted to Islam and joined the Nation of Islam while serving a prison term as a young man. He became the chief spokesperson for the Black Muslims and a well-known but threatening figure to the white community. After a dispute with Elijah Muhammad, the leader of the Nation of Islam, Malcolm X founded his own organization in which he continued to express and develop the ideas of black nationalism. Like so many other protest leaders of the era, Malcolm X was assassinated, in 1965.

Black Power leaders such as Malcolm X advocated autonomy, independence, and a pluralistic direction for the African American protest movement. They saw the African American community as a colonized, exploited population in need of liberation from the unyielding racial oppression of white America rather than integration into the system that was the source of its oppression.

Protest, Power, and Pluralism

The Black Power Movement in Perspective

By the end of the 1960s, the riots had ended, and the most militant and dramatic manifestations of the Black Power movement had faded. In many cases, the passion of Black Power activists had been countered by the violence of the police and other agencies, and many of the most powerful spokespersons of the movement were dead; others were in jail or in exile. The nation's commitment to racial change wavered and weakened as other concerns, such as the Vietnam War, competed for attention. Richard M. Nixon was elected president in 1968 and made it clear that his administration would not ally itself with the black protest movement. Pressure from the federal government for racial equality was reduced. The boiling turmoil of the mid-1960s faded, but the idea of Black Power had become thoroughly entrenched in the African American community.

In some part, the pluralistic themes of Black Power were a reaction to the failure of assimilation and integration in the 1950s and 1960s. Laws had been passed; court decisions had been widely publicized; and promises and pledges had been made by presidents, members of Congress, ministers, and other leaders. For many African Americans, though, little had changed. The problems of their parents and grandparents continued to constrain and limit their lives and, as far into the future as they could see, the lives of their children. The pluralistic Black Power ideology was a response to the failure to go beyond the repeal of Jim Crow laws and fully implement the promises of integration and equality.

However, black nationalism was and remains more than simply a reaction to a failed dream. It was also a different way of defining what it means to be black in America. In the context of black–white relations in the 1960s, the Black Power movement served a variety of purposes. First, along with the civil rights movement, it helped carve out a new identity for African Americans. The traditional cultural stereotypes of black Americans stressed laziness, irresponsibility, and inferiority. This image needed to be refuted, rejected, and buried. The **black protest movements** supplied a view of African Americans that emphasized power, assertiveness, seriousness of purpose, intelligence, and courage.

Second, Black Power served as a new rallying cry for solidarity and unified action. Following the success of the civil rights movement, these new themes and ideas helped to focus attention on "unfinished business": the black–white inequalities that remained in U.S. society.

Finally, the ideology provided an analysis of the problems of American race relations in the 1960s. The civil rights movement had, of course, analyzed race relations in terms of integration, equality of opportunity, and an end to exclusion. After the demise of Jim Crow, that analysis became less relevant. A new language was needed to describe and analyze the continuation of racial inequality. Black Power argued that the continuing problems of U.S. race relations were structural and institutional, not individual or legal. To take the next steps toward actualizing racial equality and justice would require a fundamental and far-reaching restructuring of the society. Ultimately, white Americans, as the beneficiaries of the system, would not support such restructuring. The necessary energy and commitment had to come from African Americans pursuing their own self-interests.

The nationalistic and pluralistic demands of the Black Power movement evoked defensiveness and a sense of threat in white society. By questioning the value of assimilation and celebrating a separate African heritage equal in legitimacy with white European heritage, the Black Power movement questioned the legitimacy and worth of Anglo-American values. In fact, many Black Power spokespersons condemned those values fiercely and openly and implicated them in the creation and maintenance of a centuries-long system of racial repression. Today, over 40 years after the success of the civil rights movement, assertive and critical demands by the African American community continue to be perceived as threatening.

Gender and Black Protest

Both the civil rights movement and the Black Power movement tended to be male dominated. African American women were often viewed as supporters of men rather than as equal partners in liberation. Although African American women were heavily involved in the struggle, they were often denied leadership roles or decision-making positions in favor of men. In fact, the women in one organization, the Student Nonviolent Coordinating Committee (SNCC), wrote position papers to protest their relegation to lowly clerical positions and the frequent references to them as "girls" (Andersen, 1993, p. 284). The Nation of Islam emphasized female subservience, imposing a strict code of behavior and dress for women and separating the sexes in many temple and community activities. Thus, the battle against racism and the battle against sexism were separate struggles with separate and often contradictory agendas, as the black protest movement continued to subordinate women (Amott & Matthaei, 1991).

When the protest movements began, however, African American women were already heavily involved in community and church work, and they often used their organizational skills and energy to further the cause of black liberation. In the view of many, African American women were the backbone of the movement, even if they were often relegated to less glamorous but vital organizational work (S. Evans, 1979).

Fannie Lou Hamer of Mississippi, an African American who became a prominent leader in the black liberation movement, illustrates the importance of the role played by women. Born in 1917 to sharecropper parents, Hamer's life was so circumscribed that until she attended her first rally at the beginning of the civil rights movement, she was unaware that blacks could—even theoretically—register to vote. The day after the rally, she quickly volunteered to register:

> I guess if I'd had any sense I'd a-been a little scared, but what was the point of being scared? The only thing they could do to me was kill me and it seemed like they'd been trying to do that a little bit at a time ever since I could remember. (Hamer, quoted in Evans, 1989, p. 271)

As a result of her activism, Hamer lost her job, was evicted from her house, and was jailed and beaten on a number of occasions. She devoted herself entirely to the civil rights movement and founded the Freedom Party, which successfully challenged the racially segregated Democratic Party and the all-white political structure of the State of Mississippi (Evans, 1979; Hamer, 1967).

Much of the energy that motivated black protest was forged in the depths of segregation and exclusion, a system of oppression that affected all African Americans. Not all segments of the community had the same experience; the realities faced by the black community were, as always, differentiated by class as well as gender.

COMPARATIVE FOCUS: Race in Another America[2]

Traditional antiblack prejudice in the United States has included feelings of contempt and dislike along with an array of stereotypes alleging biological inferiority and laziness. These ideas and emotions reflect the particular history of black–white relations in the United States, especially the centuries of slavery and decades of legally sanctioned, state-sponsored racial inequality under segregation. Other nations, even close neighbors to the United States, have different experiences, different histories, different cultures, and different sets of stereotypes and emotions.

One of the key characteristics of traditional U.S. antiblack prejudice is a simple "two race" view: Everyone belongs to one and only one race, and a person is either black or white. This perception is a legacy of the assumption of black inferiority that was at the heart of both U.S. slavery and Jim Crow segregation. The Southern states formalized the racial dichotomy in law as well as custom with the "one-drop rule": Any trace of black ancestry, even "one drop" of African blood, meant that a person was legally black and subject to all the limitations of extreme racial inequality.

This two-race model persists in the present, and many Americans continue to insist on a single racial category for everyone, regardless of actual racial inheritance. This rigid perception may be challenged by the increases in racial intermarriage and the number of mixed-race individuals in the society, but, in fact, "race mixing" has always been a part of the U.S. experience, and there have always been people of mixed-race heritage. In the past, especially under slavery, interracial unions were generally coercive, and, following the one-drop rule, the offspring were classified, socially and legally, as black. The United States has a very long history of ignoring the reality that people can be *both* black and white.

The U.S. perception of race contrasts sharply with the racial sensibilities in many other nations. Throughout Central and South America, for example, race is perceived as a continuum of possibilities and combinations, not as a simple split between white and black. This does not mean that these societies are egalitarian, racially open utopias. To the contrary, they incorporate a strong sense of status and position and clear notions of who is higher and who is lower. However, other factors such as social class are considered more important than race as criteria for judging and ranking other people. In fact, social class can affect perceptions of skin color to the extent that people of higher status can be seen as "whiter" than those of lower status, regardless of actual skin color (For example, see Schwartzman, 2007).

One interesting comparison is between the United States and Brazil, the largest nation in South America. The racial histories of Brazil and the United States run parallel in many ways, and prejudice, discrimination, and racial inequality are very much a part of Brazilian society, past and present. Like other Central and South Americans, however, Brazilians recognize many gradations of skin color and the different blends that are possible in people of mixed-race heritage. Commonly used terms in Brazil include *branco* (white), *moreno* (brown), *moreno claro* (light brown), *claro* (light), *pardo* (mixed race), and *negro* and *preto* (black). Some reports count scores of Brazilian racial categories, but Telles (2004) reports that less than 10 are in common use. Still, this system is vastly more

(Continued)

(Continued)

complex than the traditional dichotomous U.S. perception of race (although Brazil may be moving toward a simpler, more twofold system even as racial classification in the United States becomes more complex. See Daniel [2006] for an analysis.).

Why the differences in racial perception? Why does Brazil have a more open-ended, less rigid system than the United States? This issue cannot be fully explored in these few paragraphs, but the point can be made that the foundation for these perceptions was laid in the distant past. The Portuguese, the colonial conquerors of Brazil, were mostly single males who married into other racial groups. These intermarriages produced a large class of mixed-race people who, unlike in the U.S. experience, were recognized as such. Also, slavery was not so thoroughly equated with race in Brazil as it was in North America. Although slave status was certainly regarded as undesirable and unfortunate, it did not carry the same presumption of racial inferiority as in North America, where slavery, blackness, and inferiority were tightly linked in the dominant ideology—an equation with powerful echoes in the present. After slavery ended, Brazil did not go through a period of legalized racial segregation like the Jim Crow system in the U.S. South or apartheid in South Africa. Thus, there was less need politically, socially, or economically to divide people into rigid groups in Brazil.

I should stress that Brazil is not a racial utopia, as is sometimes claimed. Prejudice is an everyday reality, the legacy of slavery is strong, and there is a very high correlation between skin color and social status. Black Brazilians have much higher illiteracy, unemployment, and poverty rates than whites and are much less likely to have access to a university education. Whites dominate the more prestigious and lucrative occupations and the leadership positions in the economy and in politics, whereas blacks are concentrated at the bottom of the class system, with mixed-race people in between (Kuperman, 2001). It would be difficult to argue that race prejudice in Brazil is less intense than in the United States. On the other hand, given the vastly different perceptions of race in the two societies, we can conclude that Brazilian prejudice has a different content and emotional texture and reflects a different contact situation and national history.

Black–White Relations Since the 1960s: Issues and Trends

While black–white relations have changed in the United States—at least in some ways—over the past four decades, the basic outlines of black inequality and white dominance have persisted. To be sure, as I mentioned at the start of this chapter, some progress has been made in integrating the society and eliminating racial inequality. The election of Barack Obama—unimaginable just a few decades ago (and maybe even a few years ago)—stands as one unmistakable symbol of racial progress, a breakthrough so stunning that it has led many to the conclusion that America is now "post-racial" and that people's fates are no longer connected to the color of their skin. We will assess the significance of the 2008 presidential election toward the end of this chapter.

Without denying the signs of progress, the situation of the African American community today has stagnated on many dimensions, and the problems that remain are deep-rooted and inextricably mixed with the structure and functioning of modern American society. As was the case in earlier eras, racism and racial inequality today cannot be addressed apart from the trends of change in the larger society, especially changes in subsistence technology. This section examines the racial separation that continues to characterize so many areas of U.S. society and applies many of the concepts from previous chapters to present-day black–white relations.

Continuing Separation, Continuing Violence

More than 40 years ago, a presidential commission charged with investigating black urban unrest warned that the United States was "moving toward two societies, one black, one white, separate and unequal" (National Advisory Commission, 1968). We could object to the commission's use of the phrase "moving toward," with its suggestion that U.S. society was at one time racially unified, but the warning still seems prophetic. Without denying the progress toward integration that has been made, African Americans and white Americans continue to live in worlds that are indeed separate and unequal, especially when the racial differences are confounded by social class.

Each group has committed violence and hate crimes against the other, but the power differentials and the patterns of inequality that are the legacy of America's racist past guarantee that African Americans will more often be seen as "invaders," pushing into areas where they do not belong and are not wanted (see the section on hate crime in Chapter 4). Sometimes the reactions to these perceived intrusions are immediate and bloody, but other, subtler attempts to maintain the exclusion of African Americans continue to be part of everyday life, even at the highest levels of society. For example, in a lawsuit reminiscent of Jim Crow days, a national restaurant chain was accused of discriminating against African American customers by systematically providing poor service to them. In 2004, the company agreed to pay $8.7 million to settle the lawsuit (McDowell, 2004). In another example, Texaco, in 1996, was sued for discrimination by several of its minority employees. The case was settled out of court after a tape recording of company executives plotting to destroy incriminating documents and making racist remarks was made public (Eichenwald, 1996).

Many African Americans mirror the hostility of whites, and frustration and anger at the remaining barriers to full racial equality and justice can be intense. While Obama's election and inauguration stirred strong optimism and positive attitudes toward the future in the black community (see "Most Blacks Say MLK's Vision Fulfilled," 2009), the more typical mood is pessimistic (recall our discussion of public opinion poll results and the differences in black and white perceptions of U.S. race relations from Chapter 1).

The discontent and frustration have been manifested in violence and riots over the past several decades. The most widely publicized instance was the racial violence that began with the 1991 arrest and beating of Rodney King by police officers in Los Angeles. The attack on King was videotaped and shown repeatedly on national and international news, and contrary to the expectations of most that saw the videotape, the police officers were acquitted of almost all charges in April 1992. On hearing word of the acquittals, African American communities in several cities erupted in violence. The worst disturbance occurred in the Watts section of Los Angeles, where 58 people lost their lives and the rioting resulted in millions of dollars in property damage (Wilkiens, 1992).

In some ways, the riots following the 1992 King verdict were different from the riots of the 1960s. The more recent event was multiracial and involved Hispanics as well as African Americans. In fact, most of the 58 fatalities were from these two groups. Also, many of the businesses looted and burned were owned by Korean Americans, and many of the attacks were against whites directly, as in the beating of truck driver Reginald Denny (also, ironically, captured on videotape).

In other ways, the events were similar. Both were spontaneous and expressed diffuse but bitter discontent with the racial status quo. Both signaled the continuing racial inequality; urban poverty and despair; and the reality of separate nations, unequal and hostile (for more on these urban uprisings, see Gooding-Williams, 1993).

The Criminal Justice System and African Americans

No area of race relations is more volatile and controversial than the relationship between the black community and the criminal justice system. There is considerable mistrust and resentment of the police among African Americans, and the perception that the entire criminal justice system is stacked against them is widespread. These perceptions are not without justification: the police and other elements of the criminal justice system have a long tradition of abuse, harassment, and mistreatment of black citizens. The perception of the police as the enemy and the entire criminal justice system as an occupying force remains common. For example, a 2005 poll found that only 32% of blacks were "confident in the ability of police to protect them from violent crime" as compared to 57% of whites (Jones, 2005).

The great majority of social science research in this area has documented the continuing bias of the criminal justice system, at all levels, against African Americans (and other minorities). In a comprehensive summary of this research, Rosich (2007) concludes that, while blatant and overt discrimination has diminished over the past few decades, the biases that remain have powerful consequences for the black community, even though they often are more subtle and harder to tease out. Even slight acts of discrimination against blacks can accumulate over the stages of processing in the criminal justice system and result in large differences in racial outcomes. The magnitude of these racial differences is documented by a report that found that, while African Americans constitute 16% of all young people in the United States, they make up 28% of juvenile arrests, 34% of those formally processed by the courts, and 58% of those sent to adult prison (National Council on Crime and Delinquency, 2007, p. 37). Civil rights advocates and other spokespersons for the black community charge that there is a dual justice system in the United States and that black adults as well as juveniles are more likely to receive harsher treatment than whites charged with similar crimes.

Perhaps the most important manifestation of these biases is that black males are much more likely than white males to be involved in the criminal justice system, and in many communities, a third or more of young African American men are under the supervision of the system: in jail or prison or on probation or parole (Mauer & Huling, 2000, p. 417). This phenomenal level of imprisonment is largely the result of a national "get tough" policy on drugs and especially on crack cocaine that began in the 1980s. Crack cocaine is a cheap form of the drug, and the street-level dealers who have felt the brunt of the national antidrug campaign have been disproportionately young African American males from less affluent areas. Some see this crackdown as a not-so-subtle form of racial discrimination. For example, federal laws require a mandatory prison term of 5 years for possession of 5 grams of crack cocaine, a drug much more likely to be dealt by poor blacks. In contrast, comparable levels of sentencing for dealing powder cocaine—the more expensive form of the drug—are not reached until the accused possesses a minimum of *500* grams (Rosich, 2007, p. 6). Exhibit 5.1 shows the differential arrest rates for black and white juveniles and demonstrates that the African American community has suffered a double victimization from crack cocaine: first from the drug itself and then from the attempt to police the drug.

Exhibit 5.1 Drug Abuse Arrest Rates for Juveniles Age 10–17 per 100,000 Population by Race, 1980–2003

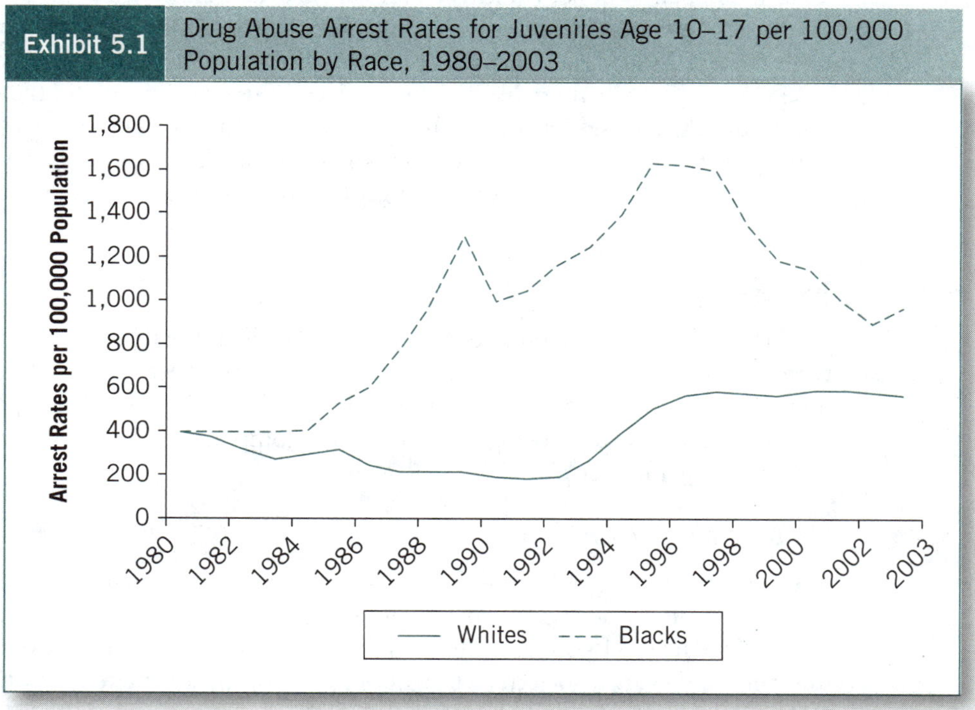

SOURCE: Snyder & Sickmund (2006, p. 144).

The scope of the relationship between the African American community and the criminal justice system is further documented in two recent studies. The first (Pettit & Western, 2004) focused on men born between 1965 and 1969 and found that 3% of whites, compared with 20% of blacks, had been imprisoned by the time they were

30 years old. Also, the study found that education was a key variable affecting the probability of imprisonment: Nearly 60% of African American men in this cohort who had not completed high school went to prison. The second study (Pew Charitable Trust, 2008) found that black men were imprisoned at far higher rates than white men: While less than 1% of all white men are in prison, the rate for black men is 7%. Furthermore, 11% of black men aged 20–34 are imprisoned.

On another level, more pervasive if less dramatic, is the issue of racial profiling: the police use of race as an indicator when calculating whether a person is suspicious or dangerous (Randall Kennedy, 2001). The tendency to focus more on blacks and to disproportionately stop, question, and follow them is a form of discrimination that generates resentment and increases the distrust (and fear) many African Americans feel toward their local police forces. According to some, humiliating encounters with police (for example, being stopped and questioned for "driving while black") are virtually a rite of passage for black men (Randall Kennedy, 2001, p. 7). According to one national survey, more than half of all black men and 25% of black females feel that they have been unfairly stopped by police (Morin & Cottman, 2001; see also Weitzer & Tuch, 2005).

The charges of racial profiling and discrimination in the war against drugs can be controversial. Many argue that racial profiling is at some level based on the fact that blacks are statistically more likely to be involved in street crime and in the illegal drug trade (for example, see Taylor & Whitney, 2002). At another level, these patterns sustain the ancient perceptions of African Americans as dangerous outsiders, and they feed the tradition of resentment and anger toward the police in the African American community.

Increasing Class Inequality

As black Americans moved out of the rural South and as the repressive force of de jure segregation receded, social class inequality within the African American population increased. Since the 1960s, the black middle class has grown, but black poverty continues to be a serious problem, especially when compounded by segregation and joblessness in the inner city.

The Black Middle Class

A small, African American middle class, based largely on occupations and businesses serving only the African American community, had been in existence since before the Civil War (Frazier, 1957). Has this more affluent segment benefited from increasing tolerance in the larger society, civil rights legislation, and affirmative action programs? Is the African American middle class growing in size and affluence?

The answers to these questions are not entirely clear, but research strongly suggests that the size and affluence of the African American middle class is less than is often assumed. For example, one study (Kochhar, 2004) found that, between 1996 and 2002, the percentage of blacks that could be considered middle and upper class never exceeded 25% of the black population. The comparable figure for whites was almost 60%. Thus, by this definition, the black middle and upper class was less than half the size of the white middle and upper class.

Another study (Oliver & Shapiro, 2006) indicates that the African American middle class is not only smaller but also much less affluent. The researchers studied racial differences in wealth, which includes income as well as all other financial assets: the value of houses, cars, savings, other property, and so forth. Exhibit 5.2 compares the wealth of blacks and whites, using two different definitions of middle class and two different measures of wealth. *Middle-class* status is defined, first, in terms of level of education, with a college education indicating middle-class status and, second, in terms of occupation, with a white-collar occupation indicating middle-class status. *Wealth* is defined first in terms of *net worth,* which includes all assets (houses, cars, and so forth) minus debt. The second measure, *net financial assets,* is the same as net worth but excludes the value of a person's investments in a home and cars. This second measure is a better indicator of the resources that are available to invest in educating the next generation or financing new businesses.

Exhibit 5.2 Wealth by Definition of Middle Class by Race (in Dollars)

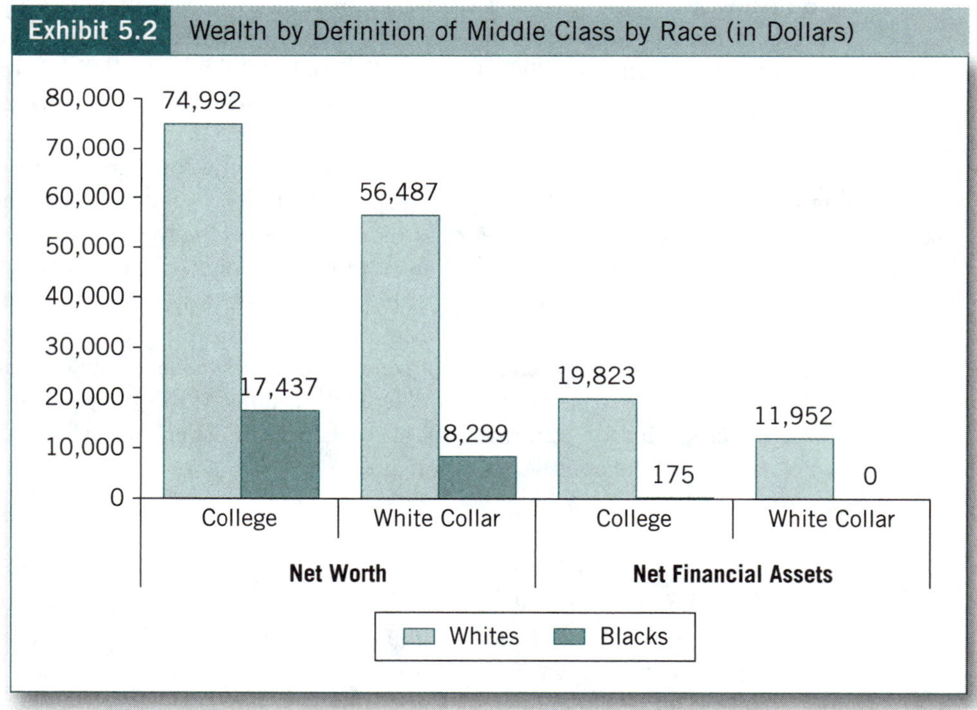

SOURCE: Oliver & Shapiro (2006, p. 96). Copyright ©1995 by Routledge. Reprinted by permission of Routledge/Taylor & Francis.

By either definition, the black middle class is at a distinct disadvantage. There are huge differentials in net worth between blacks and whites and even greater differences in net financial assets. Note, in fact, that the net financial assets of blacks in white-collar occupations are exactly zero. Once their equity in houses and cars is subtracted out, they are left with no wealth at all, a statistic that strongly underscores the greater precariousness of middle-class standing for blacks. (For other studies that document the lower size and affluence of the black middle class, see Avery & Rendall, 2002; Pollard & O'Hare, 1999; Shapiro, 2004.)

These economic differences are due partly to discrimination in the present and partly to the racial gaps in income, wealth, and economic opportunity inherited from past generations. As suggested by the concept of *net financial assets* in Exhibit 5.2, economically advantaged white families have passed along a larger store of resources, wealth, and property to the present generation. Thus, the greater economic marginality of the African American middle class today is a form of *past-in-present institutional discrimination* (see Chapter 4). It reflects the greater ability of white parents (and grandparents) to finance higher education and to subsidize business ventures and home mortgages (Oliver & Shapiro, 2006).

Not only is their economic position more marginal, middle-class African Americans commonly report that they are also unable to escape the narrow straitjacket of race. No matter what their level of success, occupation, or professional accomplishments, race continues to be seen as their primary defining characteristic in the eyes of the larger society (Benjamin, 2005; Cose, 1993; Hughes & Thomas, 1998). Without denying the advances of some, many analysts argue that the stigma of race continues to set sharp limits on the life chances of African Americans.

There is also a concern that greater class differentiation may decrease solidarity and cohesion within the African American community. Today, there is greater income inequality among African Americans than ever before, with the urban poor at one extreme and some of the wealthiest, most recognized figures in the world at the other: millionaires, celebrities, business moguls, politicians, and sports and movie stars. Will the more affluent segment of the African American community disassociate itself from the plight of the less fortunate and move away from the urban neighborhoods, taking with it its affluence, articulateness, and leadership skills? If this happens, it would reinforce the class division and further seal the fate of impoverished African Americans, who are largely concentrated in urban areas.

Urban Poverty

African Americans have become an urban minority group, and the fate of the group is inextricably bound to the fate of America's cities. The issues of black–white relations cannot be successfully addressed without dealing with urban issues, and vice versa.

As we saw in Chapter 4, automation and mechanization in the workplace have eliminated many of the manual labor jobs that sustained city dwellers in earlier decades (Kasarda, 1989). The manufacturing, or secondary, segment of the labor force has declined in size, and the service sector has continued to expand (see Exhibit 4.4). The more desirable jobs in the service sector have more and more demanding educational prerequisites. The service sector jobs available to people with lower educational credentials pay low wages, often less than the minimum necessary for the basics, including food and shelter, and offer little in the way of benefits, security, and links to more rewarding occupations. This form of past-in-present institutional discrimination constitutes a powerful handicap for colonized groups such as African Americans, who have been excluded from educational opportunities.

Furthermore, many of the blue-collar jobs that have escaped automation have migrated away from the cities. Industrialists have been moving their businesses to areas where labor is cheaper, unions have less power, and taxes are lower. This movement to the suburbs, to the "sunbelt," and "offshore" has been devastating for the inner city. Poor transportation systems, the absence of affordable housing outside the center city, inability to afford automobiles, and outright housing discrimination have combined to keep urban poor people of color confined to center-city neighborhoods, distant from opportunities for jobs and economic improvement (Feagin, 2001; Massey & Denton, 1993; Wilson, 2009).

Sociologist Rogelio Saenz (2005) recently analyzed the situation of blacks in the 15 largest metropolitan areas in the nation and found that they are much more likely than whites to be living in highly impoverished neighborhoods, cut off from the "economic opportunities, services, and institutions that families need to succeed" (p. 1). We referred to this pattern in Chapter 1 when we discussed the vulnerability of African Americans to natural disasters such as Hurricane Katrina, and again in Chapter 4 when we noted the greater impact of the recent economic downturn on minority communities. Saenz found that the greater vulnerability and social and geographical isolation of blacks is pervasive and includes not only higher rates of poverty and unemployment but also large differences in access to cars and even phones for poor blacks—amenities taken for granted in the rest of society. In the areas studied by Saenz, blacks were as much as 3 times more likely to not have a car (and thus a means to get to jobs outside center-city areas) and as much as 8 times more likely to not have a telephone.

Some of these industrial and economic forces affect all poor urbanites, not just minority groups or African Americans in particular. The dilemma facing many African Americans is in some part not only racism or discrimination; the impersonal forces of evolving industrialization and social class structures contribute as well. However, when racial stigma and centuries of prejudice (even disguised as modern racism) are compounded with economic marginalization, the forces limiting and constraining African Americans with lower levels of education and few job skills become extremely formidable.

For the past 60 years, the African American poor have been increasingly concentrated in narrowly delimited urban areas ("the ghetto") in which the scourge of poverty has been compounded and reinforced by a host of other problems, including joblessness, high dropout rates from school, crime, drug use, teenage pregnancy, and welfare dependency. These increasingly isolated neighborhoods are fertile grounds for the development of oppositional cultures, which reject or invert the values of the larger society. The black urban counterculture may be most visible in music, fashion, speech, and other forms of popular culture, but it is also manifest in widespread lack of trust in the larger society and whites in particular. An **urban underclass,** barred from the mainstream economy and the primary labor force and consisting largely of poor African Americans and other minority groups of color, is quickly becoming a permanent feature of the American landscape (Kasarda, 1989; Massey & Denton, 1993; Wilson, 1987, 1996, 2009).

Consider the parallels and contrasts between the plight of the present urban underclass and black Southerners under de jure segregation: In both eras, a large segment of the African American population was cut off from opportunities for success and growth. In the earlier era, African Americans were isolated in rural areas; now they are isolated in urban areas, especially center cities. In the past, escape from segregation was limited primarily by political and legal restrictions and blatant racial prejudice; escape from poverty in the present is limited by economic and educational deficits and a more subtle and amorphous prejudice. The result is the same: "The overwhelming number of blacks started the twentieth century clustered in America's poorest spaces—southern farms; they ended it also concentrated disproportionately in the nation's most disadvantaged locations—central cities" (Katz & Stern, 2006. p. 88). Many African Americans remain a colonized minority group, isolated, marginalized, and burdened with a legacy of powerlessness and poverty.

Closed Networks and Racial Exclusion

The continuing importance of race as a primary factor in the perpetuation of class inequality is dramatically illustrated in a recent research project. Royster (2003) interviewed black and white graduates of a trade school in Baltimore. Her respondents had completed the same curricula and earned similar grades. In other words, they were nearly identical in terms of the credentials they brought to the world of work. Nonetheless, the black graduates were employed less often in the trades for which they had been educated, had lower wages, got fewer promotions, and experienced longer periods of unemployment. Virtually every white graduate found secure and reasonably lucrative employment. The black graduates, in stark contrast, usually were unable to stay in the trades and became, instead, low-skilled, low-paid workers in the service sector.

What accounts for these differences? Based on extensive interviews with the subjects, Royster (2003) concluded that the differences could not be explained by training or by personality characteristics. Instead, she found that what really mattered was not "what you know" but "who you know." The white graduates had access to networks of referrals and recruitment that linked them to the job market in ways that simply were not available to black graduates. In their search for jobs, whites were assisted more fully by their instructors and were able to use intraracial networks of family and friends, connections so powerful that they "assured even the worst [white] troublemaker a solid place in the blue collar fold" (p. 78).

Needless to say, these results run contrary to some deeply held American values, most notably the widespread, strong support for the idea that success in life is due to individual effort, self-discipline, and the other attributes enshrined in the Protestant ethic. The strength of this faith is documented in a recent survey that was administered to a representative sample of adult Americans. The respondents were asked whether they thought that people got ahead by hard work, luck, or a combination of the two. Fully 69% of the sample chose "hard work," and another 20% chose "hard work and luck equally" (National Opinion Research Center, 1972–2007). This overwhelming support for the importance of individual effort is echoed in human capital theory and many "traditional" sociological perspectives on assimilation (see Chapter 2).

Royster's (2003) results demonstrate that the American belief that hard work alone will get people ahead is simply wrong. To the contrary, access to jobs is controlled by nepotism, cronyism, personal relationships, and networks of social relations that are decidedly not open to everyone. These subtle patterns of exclusion and closed intraracial networks are more difficult to document than the blatant discrimination that was at the core of Jim Crow segregation, but they can be just as devastating in their effects and just as powerful as mechanisms for perpetuating racial gaps in income and employment.

The Family Institution and the Culture of Poverty

The nature of the African American family institution has been a continuing source of concern and controversy. On one hand, some analysts see the African American family as structurally weak, a cause of continuing poverty and a variety of other problems. No doubt the most famous study in this tradition was the Moynihan (1965) report, which focused on the higher rates of divorce, separation, desertion, and illegitimacy among African American families and the fact that black families were far more likely to be female headed than were white families. Moynihan concluded that the fundamental barrier facing African Americans was a family structure that he saw as crumbling, a condition that would perpetuate the cycle of poverty entrapping African Americans (p. iii). Today, most of the differences between black and white family institutions identified by Moynihan are even more pronounced. Exhibit 5.3, for example, compares the percentage of households headed by females (black and white) with the percentage of households headed by married couples. Over 40% of black households are female headed, which is nearly 3 times the rate of white households, although the trends seem to have stabilized since the mid-1990s.

Exhibit 5.3 Percentage of Family Households With Married Couples and Headed by Females, 1970–2007

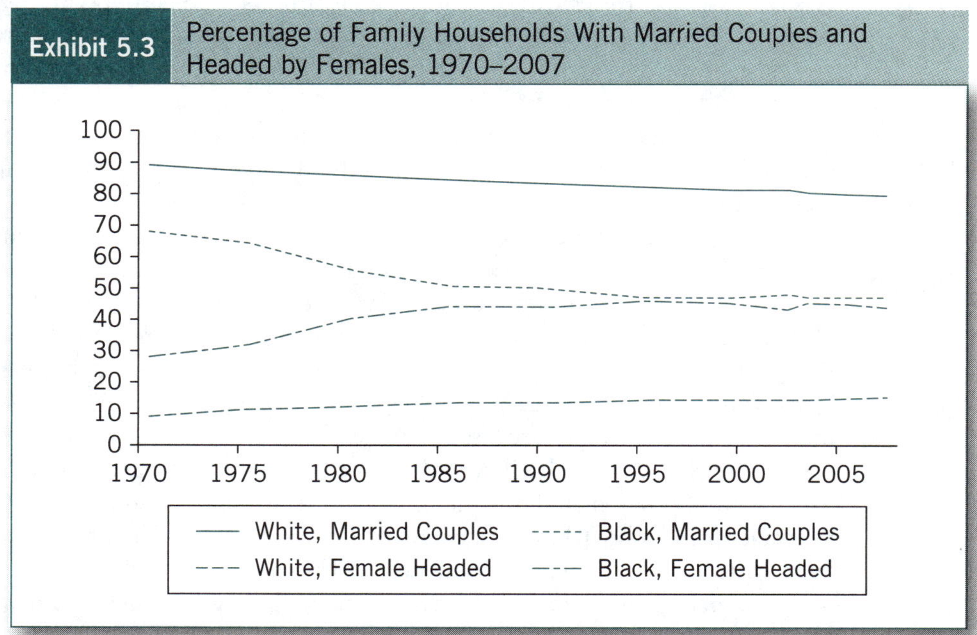

SOURCE: U.S. Bureau of the Census (1977, 2009b, p. 54).

The line of analysis implicit in the Moynihan (1965) report locates the problem of urban poverty in the characteristics of the African American community, particularly in the African American family. These structures are seen as "broken" in important ways and in need of being "fixed." This argument is consistent with the **culture of poverty theory,** which argues that poverty is perpetuated by the particular characteristics of the poor. Specifically, poverty is said to encourage **fatalism** (the sense that one's destiny is beyond one's control) and an orientation to the present rather than the future. The desire for instant gratification is a central trait of the culture of poverty, as opposed to the ability to defer gratification, which is thought to be essential for middle-class success. Other characteristics include violence, authoritarianism, and high rates of alcoholism and family desertion by males (Lewis, 1959, 1965, 1966).

The culture of poverty theory leads to the conclusion that the problem of urban poverty would be resolved if female-headed family structures and other cultural characteristics correlated with poverty could be changed. Note that this approach is consistent with the traditional assimilationist perspective and human capital theory: The poor have "bad" or inappropriate values. If they could be equipped with "good" (i.e., white, middle-class) values, the problem would be resolved.

An opposing perspective, more consistent with the concepts and theories that underlie this text, sees the matriarchal structure of the African American family as the *result* of urban poverty—rather than a cause—and a reflection of racial discrimination and the scarcity of jobs for urban African American males. In impoverished African American urban neighborhoods, the supply of men able to support a family is reduced by high rates of unemployment, incarceration, and violence, and these conditions are in turn created by the concentration of urban poverty and the growth of the "underclass" (Massey & Denton, 1993; Wilson, 1996, 2009). Thus, the burden of child rearing tends to fall on females, and female-headed households are more common in these neighborhood than in more advantaged areas.

Female-headed African American families tend to be poor, not because they are weak in some sense but because of the lower wages accorded to women in general and to African American women in particular, as documented in Exhibit 5.4. Note that black female workers have the lowest wages throughout the time period. Also note that the gap between black women and white men has narrowed over the years. In 1955, black women earned about 33% of what white men earned. By 2007, the number had increased to 67%, largely because the wages for males (blacks as well as whites) have been relatively flat since the 1970s, while women's wages (again for whites and blacks) have risen. This pattern reflects the impact of deindustrialization: the shift away from manufacturing, which has eliminated many good blue-collar jobs, and the rise of employment sectors in which women tend to be more concentrated. A similar pattern was documented in Exhibit 4.6, which compared the wages of all full-time, year-round workers by gender.

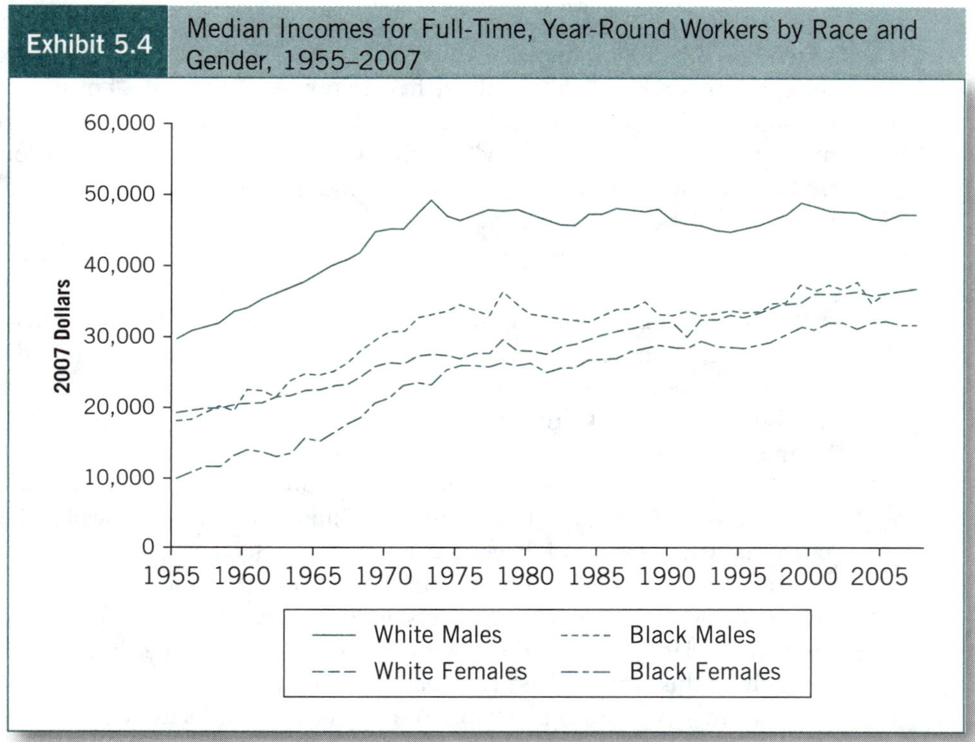

Exhibit 5.4 Median Incomes for Full-Time, Year-Round Workers by Race and Gender, 1955–2007

SOURCE: Compiled from U.S. Bureau of the Census (2009d).

The poverty associated with black female–headed households reflects the interactive effects of sexism and racism on black women, not some weakness in the black family. African American urban poverty is the result of the complex forces of past and present institutional discrimination, American racism and prejudice, the precarious position of African American women in the labor force, and continuing urbanization and industrialization. The African American family is not in need of "fixing," and the attitudes and values of the urban underclass are more the results of impoverishment than they are the causes. The solution to African American urban poverty lies in fundamental changes in the urban-industrial economy and sweeping alterations in the distribution of resources and opportunities.

Mixed Race and New Racial Identities

As we have discussed, Americans traditionally see race as a simple dichotomy: People are either black or white, with no intermediate categories. In the past, the social convention of the one-drop rule meant that people of mixed racial descent were classified as black. To illustrate, consider the story of Gregory Williams (1995), known then as

Billy, a white boy growing up in the segregated South in the late 1940s and early 1950s. When Billy was 10, his father revealed that he was "half-colored." Under the one-drop rule, that made Billy black. Billy at first refused to believe it: "I'm not colored, I'm white! I look white! I've always been white! I go to the 'whites only' school, 'whites only' movie theaters, and 'whites only' swimming pool" (p. 34). Gradually, he comes to realize that his life—not just his life chances and his relations with others, but his very identity—has been transformed by the revelation of his father's race.

In the past, mixed-race people like Gregory Williams had few choices: Others classified him as black, and the rigid social conventions of the day forced him to accept that identity, with all its implications. Today, four decades after the formal end of Jim Crow segregation, Americans are confronting the limitations of this dichotomous racial convention. People of mixed-race descent are increasing in number and, in fact, are some of the most prominent and well-known people in U.S. society. President Obama is the obvious example of a highly visible mixed-race person, but others include Tiger Woods, the professional golfer (who defines himself—tongue in cheek—as Cablanasian: Caucasian, black, American Indian, and Asian); vocalist Mariah Carey; Yankee baseball star Derek Jeter; and actress Halle Berry.

How do people of multiracial descent define themselves today? How are they defined by others? Have the old understandings of race become irrelevant? Is there still pressure to place people in one and only one group? There has been a fair amount of research on this issue, and we can begin to formulate some answers.

One important study illustrates some of the possible identities for mixed-race individuals. Rockquemore and Brunsma (2008) interviewed a sample of several hundred mixed-race college students, confining their attention to people who had one white and one black parent. They found that today, unlike the situation faced by Gregory Williams, the meaning of mixed-race identity is conceptually complex and highly variable (see also Brunsma, 2005). They identified four main categories that their respondents used to understand their biracialism, and these are presented here in order from most to least common. However, the sample they assembled was not representative, and there is no reason to assume that these same percentages would characterize all biracial Americans.

1. The most common racial identity in the sample was the *border identity.* These respondents (58% of the sample) don't consider themselves to be either black or white. They define themselves as belonging to a third, separate category that is linked to both groups but is unique. One respondent declared, "I'm not black, I'm biracial" (Rockquemore & Brunsma, 2008, p. 43). The authors make a further distinction:

   a. Some border identities are "validated," or recognized and acknowledged, by others. These respondents see themselves as biracial, and they are also seen that way by family, friends, and the community.

   b. Other border identities are "unvalidated" by others. These individuals see themselves as biracial but are classified by others as black. For example, one respondent said, "I consider myself biracial but I experience the world as a black person" (Rockquemore & Brunsma, 2008, p. 45). This disconnect may be the result of the persistence of traditional dichotomous racial thinking and the fact that some people lack the

> category of "biracial" in their thinking. According to the authors, people in this category are of special interest because of the tensions created by the conflict between their self-image and the way they are defined by others.

2. The second most common identity in the sample was the *singular identity.* These individuals saw themselves not as biracial but as exclusively black (13%) or exclusively white (3%). As the case of Gregory Williams illustrated, the singular black identity is most consistent with American traditional thinking about race. The authors argue that the fact that this identity was *not* the most common in their sample illustrates the complexity of racial identity for biracial people today.

3. A third identity was the *transcendent identity.* The respondents in this category (15%) reject the whole notion of race, along with the traditional categories of black and white, and insist that they should be seen as unique individuals and not placed in a category, especially since those categories carry multiple assumptions about character, personality, intelligence, attitudes, and a host of other characteristics. Respondents with the transcendent identity were in a constant battle to avoid classification in our highly race-conscious society. One respondent's remarks are illustrative:

> I'm just John, you know? . . . I'm a good guy, just like me for that. . . . When I came here [to college], it was like I was almost forced to look at other people as being white, black, Asian, or Hispanic. And so now, I'm still trying to go, "I'm just John," but uh, you gotta be something. (p. 49)

4. The final racial identity is the least common (4%) but perhaps the most interesting. The authors describe the racial identity of these individuals as *protean,* or changing as the individual moves from group to group and through the various social contexts of everyday life. There are different "ways of being" in groups of blacks versus groups of whites, and the individuals with the protean racial identity slip effortlessly from one mode to the next and are accepted by both groups as insiders. The authors point out that most people adjust their *behavior* to different situations (e.g., a fraternity party versus a family Thanksgiving dinner), but these individuals also change their *identity* and adjust who they are to different circumstances. Respondents with the protean identity feel empowered by their ability to fit in with different groups and feel that they are endowed with a high degree of "cultural savvy" (p. 47). In our increasingly diverse, multicultural and multiracial society, the ability to belong easily to multiple groups may prove to be a unique strength.

What can we conclude? Racial identity, like so many other aspects of our society, is evolving and becoming more complex. Traditional definitions such as the one-drop rule live on but in an attenuated, weakened form. Also, racial identity, like other aspects of the self-concept, can be situational or contingent on social context rather than permanent or fixed. Given the world in which he lived, Gregory Williams had no choice but to accept a black racial identity. Today, in a more tolerant and pluralistic social environment, biracial people have choices and some space in which to carve out their own unique identity. According to Rockquemore and Brunsma (2008), these identity choices are contingent on a number of factors, including personal appearance, but they are always made in the context of a highly race-conscious society with long and strong traditions of racism and prejudice.

Prejudice and Discrimination

Traditional Prejudice and Modern Racism

Public opinion polls and other sources of evidence document a dramatic decline in traditional, overt, antiblack prejudice since the mid-20th century. Exhibit 5.5 displays this trend using a number of survey items administered to representative samples of U.S. citizens. In 1942, the huge majority—a little more than 70%—of white Americans thought that black and white children should attend different schools. Forty years later, in 1982, support for separate schools had dropped to less than 10%. Similarly, support for the right of white people to maintain separate neighborhoods declined from 65% in 1942 to 18% in the early 1990s. In more recent decades, the percentage of white respondents who support laws against interracial marriage decreased from almost 40% in the early 1970s to about 10% in 2002, and the percentage that believe that blacks are inferior fell from 26% to 8% between the early 1970s and 2006.

Exhibit 5.5 Declining Traditional Prejudice in the United States, 1942–2006 (White Americans Only)

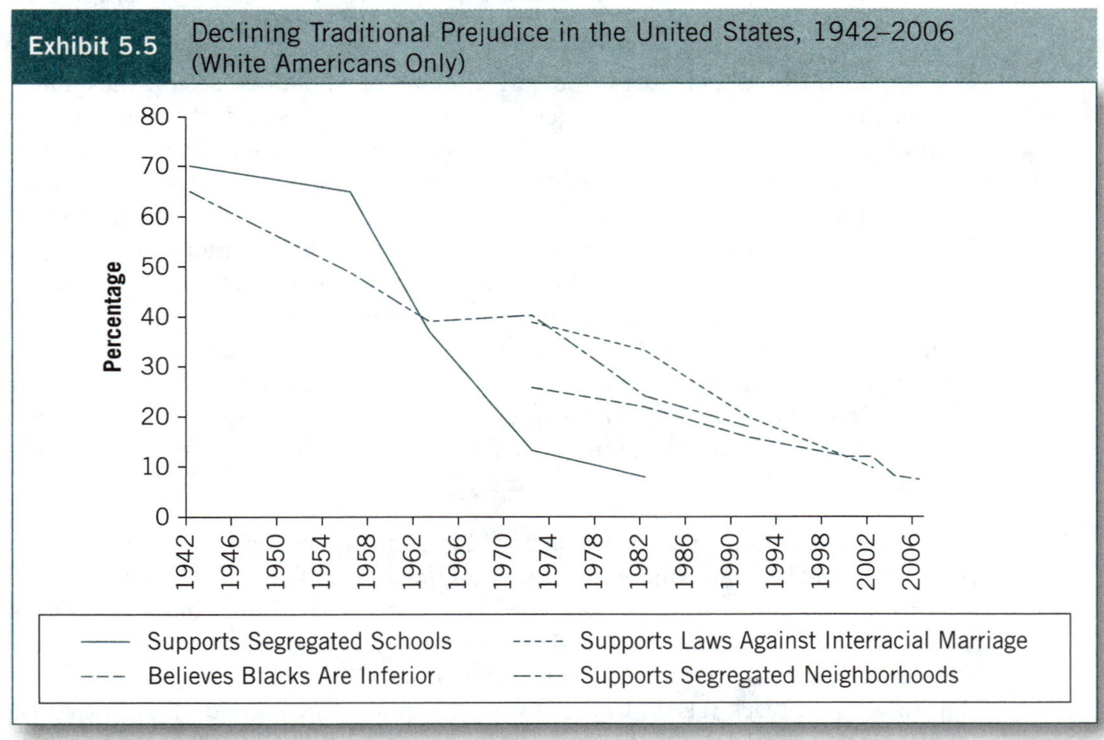

SOURCE: 1942, 1956, 1962, Hyman & Sheatsley (1964); 1972–2006, National Opinion Research Center (1972–2007).

NOTE: Results are accurate to within ±3%.

The overall trend is unmistakable: There has been a dramatic decline in support for prejudiced statements since World War II. In the early 1940s, most white Americans supported prejudiced views. In recent years, only a small minority has expressed such views.

These trends document a genuine decline in levels of prejudice in the United States. However, we should not accept these changes at face value and take them as proof that racial prejudice is no longer a problem in society. First of all, these survey items also show that prejudice has not vanished. A percentage of the white population continues to endorse highly prejudicial sentiments and opinions. Second, the polls show only what people *say* they feel and think, and this can be different from what they truly believe. Exhibit 5.5 may document a decline in people's willingness to admit their prejudice as much as a genuine improvement in intergroup attitudes and feelings.

An additional possibility is that the exhibit is misleading and that prejudice remains substantial but has taken on new forms and modes of expression. I raised this possibility in Chapter 1 when I introduced the concept of modern or color-blind racism. A number of researchers have been pursuing this more subtle, complex, and indirect way to express negative feelings toward minority groups and opposition to change in dominant–minority relations (see Bobo, 1988, 2001; Bonilla-Silva, 2001, 2006; Kinder & Sears, 1981; Kluegel & Smith, 1982; McConahy, 1986; Sears, 1988).

People affected by modern racism have negative feelings (the affective aspect of prejudice) toward minority groups but reject the idea of genetic or biological inferiority and do not think in terms of the traditional stereotypes. Instead, their prejudicial feelings are expressed indirectly and subtly. The attitudes that define modern racism tend to be consistent with some tenets of the traditional assimilation perspective discussed in Chapter 2, especially human capital theory, and the Protestant ethic: the traditional American value system that stresses individual responsibility and the importance of hard work. Specifically, modern racism assumes that:

- There is no longer any serious or important racial, ethnic, or religious discrimination in American society;
- Any remaining racial or ethnic inequality is the fault of members of the minority group;
- Demands for preferential treatment or affirmative action for minorities are therefore unjustified; and
- Minority groups (especially African Americans) have already gotten more than they deserve (Sears & Henry, 2003).

Modern racism tends to "blame the victim" and place the responsibility for change and improvements on minority groups, not on society.

To illustrate the difference between traditional prejudice and modern racism, consider the results of a recent public opinion survey administered to a representative sample of Americans (National Opinion Research Center, 1972–2007). Respondents were asked to choose from among four explanations of why black people, on the average, have "worse jobs, income, and housing than white people." Respondents could choose as many explanations as they wanted.

One explanation, consistent with traditional antiblack prejudice, attributed racial inequality to the genetic or biological inferiority of African Americans ("The differences are mainly because blacks have less in-born ability to learn."). Only 8% of the white respondents chose this explanation. A second explanation attributed continuing racial inequality to discrimination and a third to the lack of opportunity for an education. Of white respondents, 31% chose the former and 44% chose the latter.

A fourth explanation, consistent with modern racism, attributes racial inequality to a lack of effort by African Americans ("The differences are because most blacks just don't have the motivation or willpower to pull themselves up out of poverty."). Of the white respondents, 50% chose this explanation, the most popular of the four. Thus, modern racism—the view that the root of the problem of continuing racial inequality lies in the black community, not the society as a whole—has a great deal of support among white Americans.

What makes this view an expression of prejudice? Besides blaming the victim, it deflects attention away from centuries of oppression and continuing inequality and discrimination in modern society. It stereotypes African Americans and encourages the expression of negative feelings against them (but without invoking the traditional image of innate inferiority).

Researchers consistently have found that modern racism is correlated with opposition to policies and programs intended to reduce racial inequality (Bobo, 2001). In the survey summarized earlier, for example, respondents who blamed continuing racial inequality on the lack of motivation or willpower of blacks—the "modern racists"—were the least likely to support government help for African Americans and affirmative action programs. In fact, as Exhibit 5.6 shows, the modern racists were less supportive of these programs than the traditional racists (those who chose the "less in-born ability" explanation).

Exhibit 5.6 Support for Affirmative Action and Government Help for Blacks by Explanation of Racial Inequality, 2006 (White Americans Only)

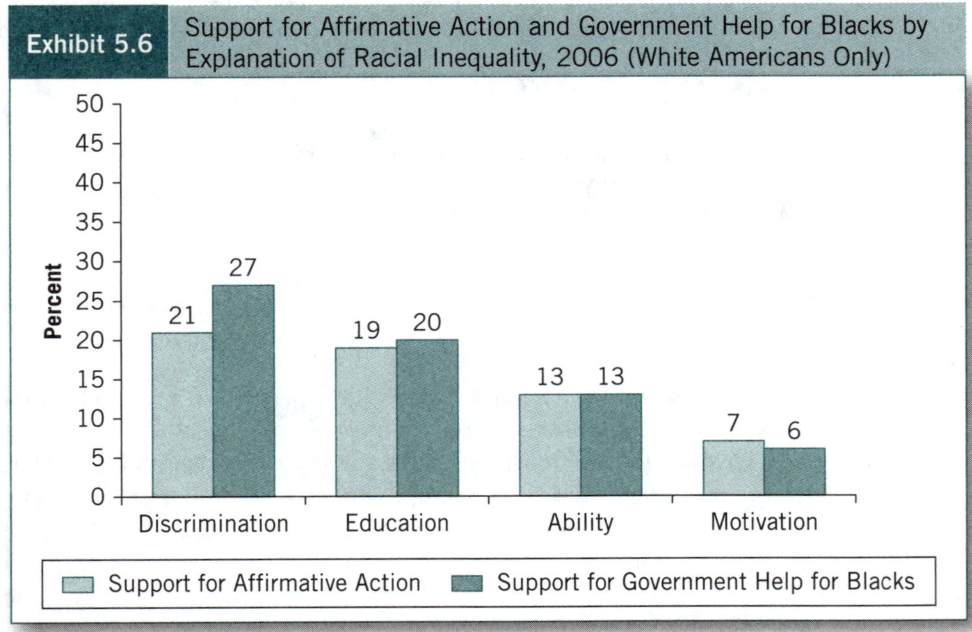

SOURCE: National Opinion Research Center (1972–2007). Reprinted by permission of National Opinion Research Council.

In the view of many researchers, modern racism has taken the place of traditional or overt prejudice. If this view is correct, the "report card" on progress in the reduction of racial hostility in the United States must be rather mixed. On one hand, we should not understate the importance of the fading of blatant, overt prejudice. On the other hand, we cannot ignore the evidence that antiblack prejudice has changed in form rather than declined in degree. Subtle and diffuse prejudice is probably preferable to the blunt and vicious variety, but it should not be mistaken for its demise.

Modern Institutional Discrimination

Paralleling the softening of traditional prejudice are changes in discrimination from blunt and overt to subtle and covert. The clarity of Jim Crow has yielded to the ambiguity of modern institutional discrimination (see Chapter 4) and the continuing legacy of past discrimination in the present. The dilemmas of the black urban underclass provide a clear, if massive, example of modern institutional discrimination. As long as American businesses and financial and political institutions continue to operate as they do, jobs will continue to migrate, cities will continue to lack the resources to meet the needs of their poorer citizens, and urban poverty will continue to sustain itself, decade after decade. The individual politicians, bankers, industrialists, and others who perpetuate and benefit from this system are not necessarily prejudiced and may not even be aware of these minority group issues, yet their decisions can and do have profound effects on the perpetuation of racial inequality in America.

The effects of past discrimination on the present can be illustrated by the relatively low level of black business ownership. From the beginning of slavery through the end of Jim Crow segregation four decades ago, the opportunities for black Americans to start their own businesses were severely restricted (even forbidden) by law. The black-owned businesses that did exist were confined to the relatively less-affluent market provided by the black community—a market they had to share with firms owned by dominant-group members. At the same time, customs and laws prevented the black-owned businesses from competing for more-affluent white customers. The lack of opportunity to develop and maintain a strong business base in the past—and the consequent inability to accumulate wealth, experience, and other resources—limits the ability of African Americans to compete successfully for economic opportunities in the present (Oliver & Shapiro, 2001).

How can the pervasive problems of racial inequality be addressed in the present atmosphere of modern racism, low levels of sympathy for the urban poor, and subtle but powerful institutional discrimination? Many people advocate a "color-blind" approach to the problems of racial inequality: The legal and political systems should simply ignore skin color and treat everyone the same. This approach seems sensible to many people because, after all, the legal and overt barriers of Jim Crow discrimination are long gone, and, at least at first glance, there are no obvious limits to the life chances of blacks.

In the eyes of others, a color-blind approach is doomed to failure: In order to end racial inequality and deal with the legacy of racism, the society must follow race-conscious programs that explicitly address the problems of race and racism. Color-blind strategies amount to inaction, and all that is needed to perpetuate (or widen) the present racial gap is to do nothing.

Assimilation and Pluralism

Acculturation

The Blauner hypothesis (see Chapter 3) states that the culture of groups created by colonization will be attacked, denigrated, and—if possible—eliminated, and this assertion seems well validated by the experiences of African Americans. African cultures and languages were largely eradicated under slavery. As a powerless, colonized minority group, slaves had few opportunities to preserve their heritage, even though traces of African homelands have been found in black language patterns, kinship systems, music, folk tales, and family legends (see Levine, 1977; Stuckey, 1987).

Cultural domination continued under the Jim Crow system, albeit through a different structural arrangement. Under slavery, slaves and their owners worked together, and interracial contact was common. Under de jure segregation, intergroup contact diminished, and blacks and whites generally became more separate. After slavery ended, the African American community had somewhat more autonomy (although still few resources) to define itself and develop a distinct culture.

The centuries of cultural domination and separate development have created a unique black experience in America. African Americans share language, religion, values, beliefs, and norms with the dominant society but have developed distinct variations on the general themes.

The acculturation process may have been slowed (or even reversed) by the Black Power movement. Beginning in the 1960s, on one hand, there has been an increased interest in African culture, language, clothing, and history, and a more visible celebration of unique African American experiences (e.g., Kwanzaa) and the innumerable contributions of African Americans to the larger society. On the other hand, many of those traditions and contributions have been in existence all along. Perhaps all that really changed was the degree of public recognition.

Secondary structural assimilation. Structural assimilation, or integration, involves two different phases. Secondary structural assimilation refers to integration in more public areas, such as the job market, schools, and political institutions. We can assess integration in this area by comparing residential patterns, income distributions, job profiles, political power, and levels of education of the different groups. Each of these areas is addressed in the next section. (See the Appendix [www.pineforge.com/healeyds3e] for additional information on how African Americans compare to other U.S. groups.) We then discuss the primary structural assimilation (integration in intimate associations, such as friendship), which, according to Gordon, follows secondary structural assimilation. Finally, we will examine patterns of intermarriage.

Residential patterns. After a century of movement out of the rural South, African Americans today are highly urbanized and much more spread out across the nation. About 90% of African Americans are urban (see Exhibit 4.2), and over 80% reside in larger cities. About half of all African Americans reside in the South (see Exhibit 4.1), and about 37% now live in the Northeast and Midwest (overwhelmingly in urban areas). Exhibit 5.7 clearly shows the concentration of African Americans in the states of the old Confederacy; the urbanized East Coast corridor from Washington, DC, to Boston; the old industrial centers of the Midwest; and to a lesser extent, California.

Exhibit 5.7 Geographical Distribution of African American Population, 2000

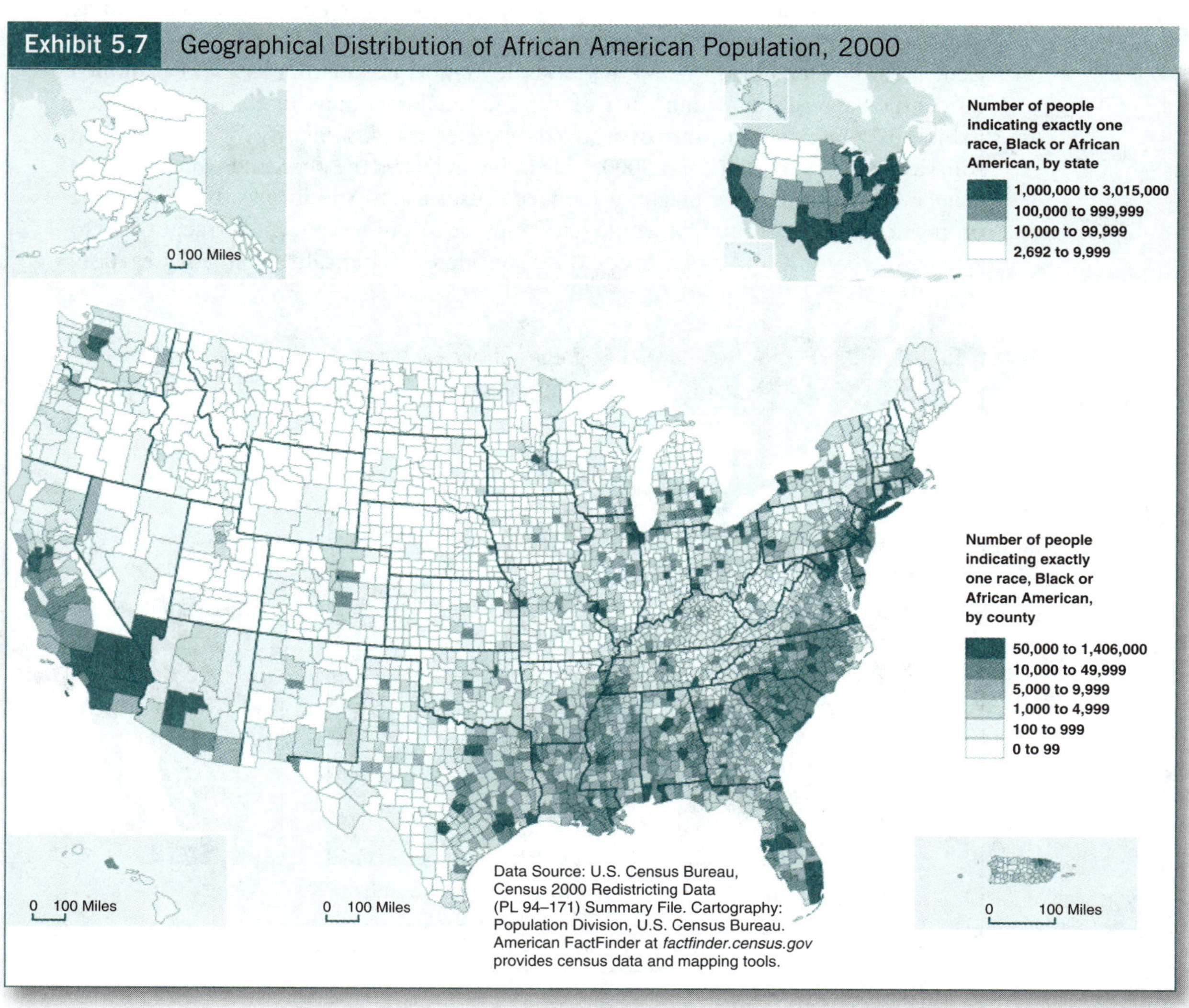

SOURCE: U.S. Bureau of the Census (2000b).

In the decades since Jim Crow segregation ended in the 1960s, residential integration has advanced slowly, if at all. Black and white Americans continue to live in separate areas, and racial residential segregation has been the norm. This pattern is reinforced by the fact that African Americans are more urbanized than whites and especially concentrated in densely populated center-city areas. Today, the extent of residential segregation varies around the nation, but African Americans continue to be residentially isolated, especially in the older industrial cities of the Northeast and Midwest and in the South.

Is racial residential segregation increasing or decreasing? Looking at the United States as a whole, the answer to this question is somewhat unclear because the studies that have been done use different methodologies, definitions, and databases and come to different conclusions (for example, see Glaeser & Vigdor, 2001; Lewis Mumford Center, 2001). One illustrative study (Iceland, Weinberg & Steinmetz, 2002) examined residential segregation within each of the four major regions of the United States. Exhibit 5.8 presents a measure of segregation called the *dissimilarity index* for African Americans for 1980, 1990, and 2000. This index indicates the degree to which a group is *not* evenly spread across neighborhoods or census tracts. Specifically, the index is the proportion of each group that would have to move to a different census tract or area to achieve integration, and scores over 0.6 are considered to indicate extreme segregation.

Exhibit 5.8 Racial Residential Segregation in 220 Metropolitan Areas, 1980–2000

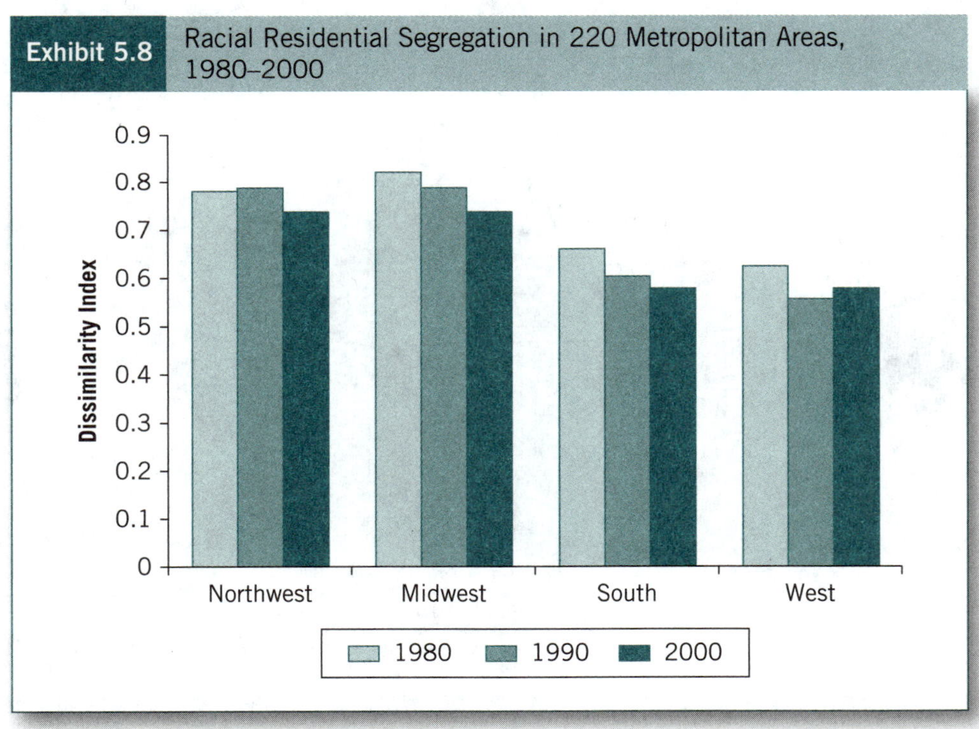

SOURCE: Iceland, Weinberg, & Steinmetz (2002, p. 640).

In 1980, all regions scored at or above the 0.6 mark, with the highest levels of segregation found in the Midwest. By 2000, there were declines in all regions, and two (the South and West) had fallen slightly below the 0.60 mark. Thus, according to this study, racial residential segregation is declining but remains quite high across the nation.

The continuing patterns of residential segregation are reinforced by a variety of practices, including *racial steering* (guiding clients to same-race housing areas) by realtors and barely disguised discrimination. For example, in an investigation of housing discrimination in the rental apartment market conducted over the telephone, Massey (2000) demonstrated that compared with speakers of "white English," speakers of "black English" were less likely to be told that an advertised unit was available, more likely to be required to pay an application fee, and more likely to have credit mentioned as an issue (p. 4). Also, banks and other financial institutions are more likely to refuse home mortgages to black applicants than to white applicants and are more likely to "redline," or deny, home improvement loans for houses in minority group neighborhoods (Feagin, 2001, pp. 155–159). "White flight" away from integrated areas also contributes to the pattern of racial separation, as whites flee from even minimal neighborhood integration. These practices are sometimes supplemented with harassment and even violence against African Americans who move into white-majority neighborhoods.

Contrary to popular belief among whites, African American preference for living in same-race neighborhoods plays a small role in perpetuating these patterns. For example, one study of representative samples of African Americans from four major American cities (Atlanta, Boston, Detroit, and Los Angeles) found that African Americans overwhelmingly preferred to live in areas split 50-50 between blacks and whites (Krysan & Farley, 2002, p. 949). Finally, the social class and income differences between blacks and whites are also relatively minor factors in perpetuating residential segregation, as the African American middle class is just as likely to be segregated as the African American poor (Stoll, 2004, p. 26).

School integration. In 1954, the year of the landmark *Brown v. Board of Education* desegregation decision, the great majority of African Americans lived in states operating segregated school systems. Compared with white schools, Jim Crow schools were severely underfunded and had fewer qualified teachers, shorter school years, and inadequate physical facilities. School integration was one of the most important goals of the civil rights movement in the 1950s and 1960s, and, aided by pressure from the courts and the federal government, considerable strides were made toward this goal for several decades. More recently, the pressure from the federal government has eased, and one recent report found that schools are being resegregated today at the fastest rate since the 1950s. For example, as displayed in Exhibit 5.9, schools in the Southern states actually reached their highest levels of racial integration in the late 1980s, over 20 years ago, when 44% of black students attended white-majority schools. Since that time, this percentage has drifted downward and reached a low of less than 30% in 2005 (Orfield & Lee, 2006).

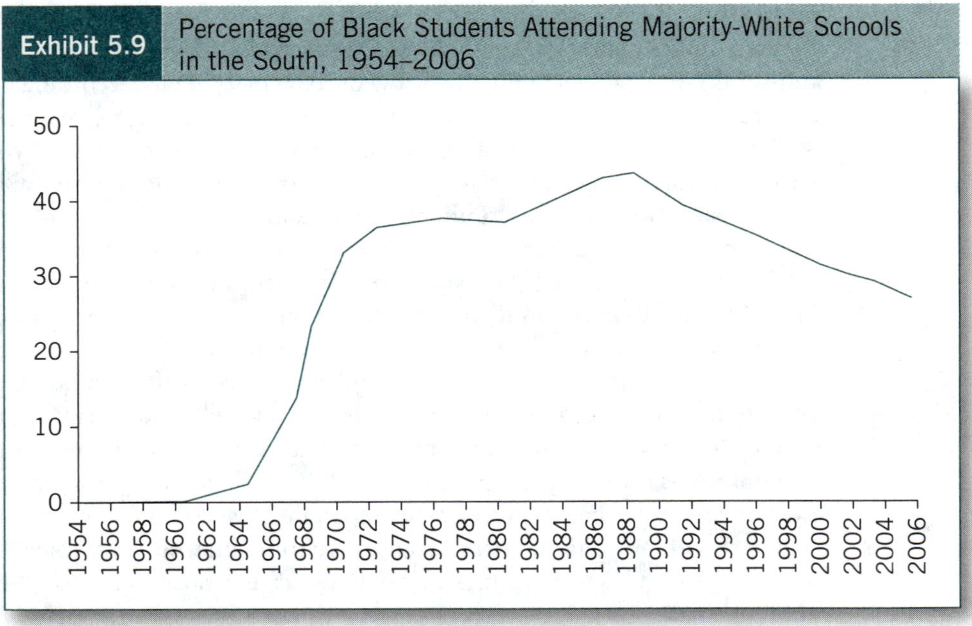

Exhibit 5.9 Percentage of Black Students Attending Majority-White Schools in the South, 1954–2006

SOURCE: Orfield & Lee (2007).

Exhibit 5.10 shows the extent of school segregation for the United States as a whole in the 1993–1994 and 2005–2006 school years. Three indicators of school segregation are used. The first is the percentage of white and black students in majority-white schools, and the second is the percentage of each in "majority-minority" schools, or schools in which at least 51% of the student body is nonwhite. The third indicator is the percentage attending schools that are extremely segregated, where minorities make up over 90% of the student body.

Exhibit 5.10 clearly shows that the goal of racial integration in the public schools has not been achieved. In both school years, the overwhelming majority of white students attended predominantly white schools, while the great majority of black students attended schools that were predominantly minority. The percentage of black students in "majority-minority" schools was higher in the 2005–2006 school year than in the 1993–1994 year, as was the percentage of black students in extremely segregated schools. The degree of racial isolation declined slightly between the two time periods, as the percentage of white students in majority-white schools dropped from 91% to 87%. According to analyst Richard Fry (2007), this was due to a massive increase (55%) in Hispanic students in the schools, not an increase in black–white contacts (p. 1).

Underlying and complicating the difficulty of school integration is the widespread residential segregation mentioned previously. The challenges for school integration are especially evident in those metropolitan areas, such as Washington, DC, that consist

Exhibit 5.10 School Integration, 1993–1994 and 2005–2006

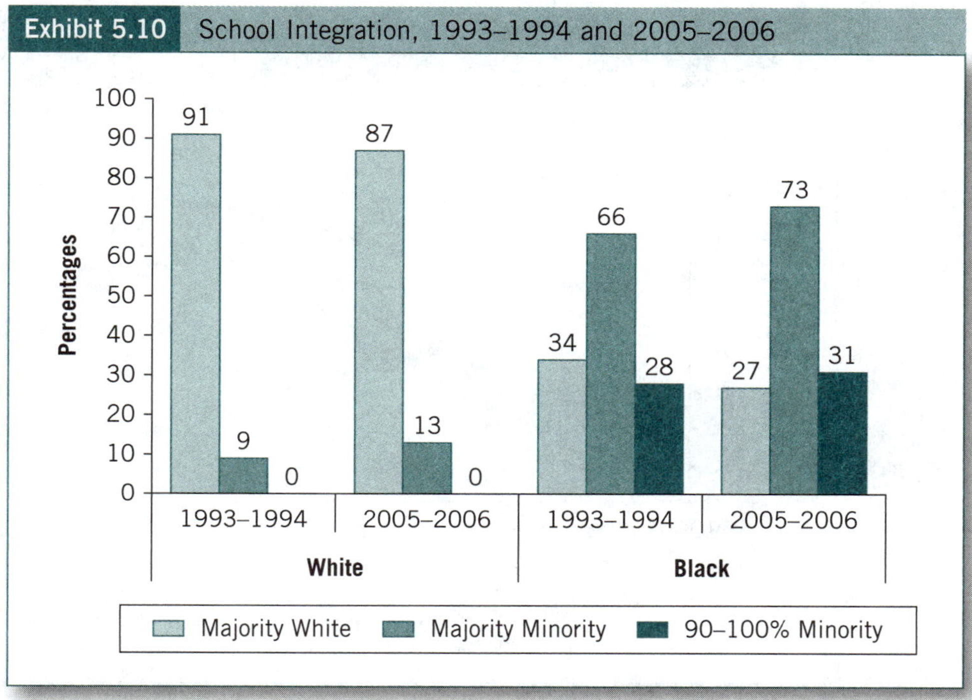

SOURCE: Fry (2007).

of a largely black-populated inner city surrounded by largely white-populated rings of suburbs. Even with busing, political boundaries would have to be crossed before the school systems could be substantially integrated. Without a renewed commitment to integration, American schools will continue to resegregate. This is a particularly ominous trend, because it directly affects the quality of education. For example, years of research demonstrate that the integration of schools—by social class as well as by race—is related to improved test scores (Orfield & Lee, 2006).

In terms of the quantity of education, the gap between whites and blacks has generally decreased over the past several decades. Exhibit 5.11 displays the percentage of the population over 25 years old, by race and sex, who have high school diplomas. The racial gap has shrunk dramatically at the high school level, though it has not disappeared. Part of the remaining difference in educational attainment is due to social class factors. For example, African American students are more likely to drop out of high school. Research has shown that "students are more likely to drop out . . . when they get poor grades, are older than their classmates, come from a single-parent family, have parents who dropped out . . . or live in a central city" (O'Hare, Pollard, Mann, & Kent, 1991, p. 21). On the average, African American students are more exposed to these risk factors than are white students. When the effects of social class background are taken into account, differences in dropout rates nearly disappear (O'Hare et al., 1991, p. 21).

Exhibit 5.11 Percentage of Persons Age 25 and Older Completing High School by Sex and Race, 1960–2007

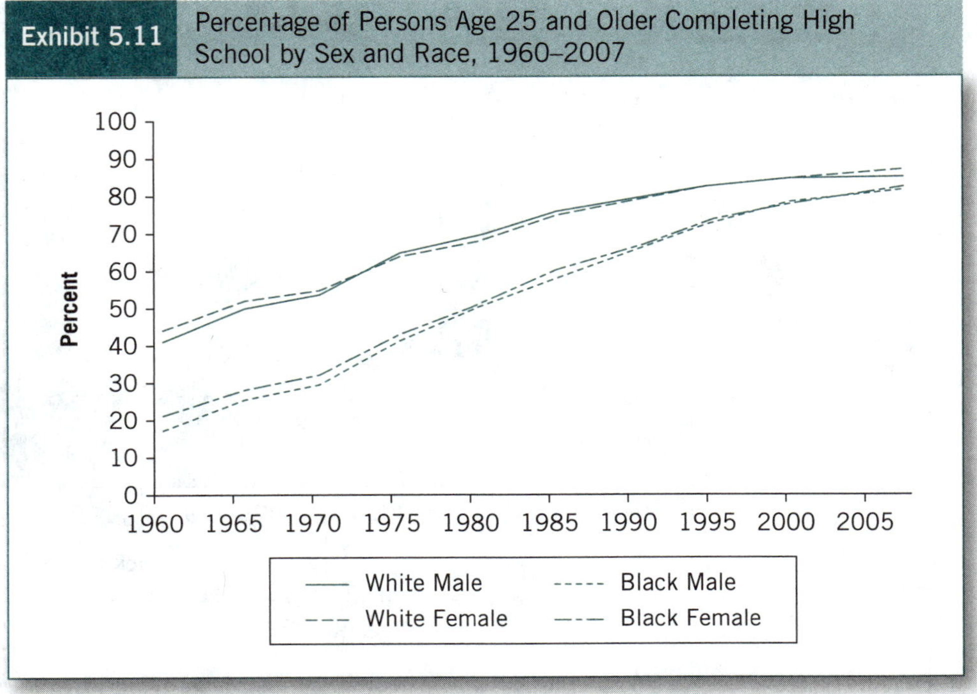

SOURCE: U.S. Bureau of the Census (2009b, p. 145).

At the college level, the trends somewhat parallel the narrowing gap in levels of high school education, as shown in Exhibit 5.12. In 1960, white males held a distinct advantage over all other race/gender groups: They were about 3.5 times more likely than African American males to have a college degree. By 2007, the advantage of white males had shrunk, but they were still almost twice as likely as black males to have a college degree. These racial differences are larger with more advanced degrees, however, and differences such as these will be increasingly serious in an economy in which jobs more often require an education beyond high school.

Political power. The 2008 election of President Barack Obama to the presidency of the United States—certainly the most significant event in the political history of African Americans—was the culmination of the gradual accumulation of black political power over the past 100 years. We will consider the meaning of this election in a separate section; in this current section, we will consider the growth of black political power more generally.

Two trends have increased the political power of African Americans since World War II. One is the movement out of the rural South, a process that concentrated African Americans in areas in which it was easier to get people registered to vote. African American communities are virtually guaranteed some political representation

Exhibit 5.12 Percentage of Persons 25 Years of Age and Older with College Degrees, 1960–2007

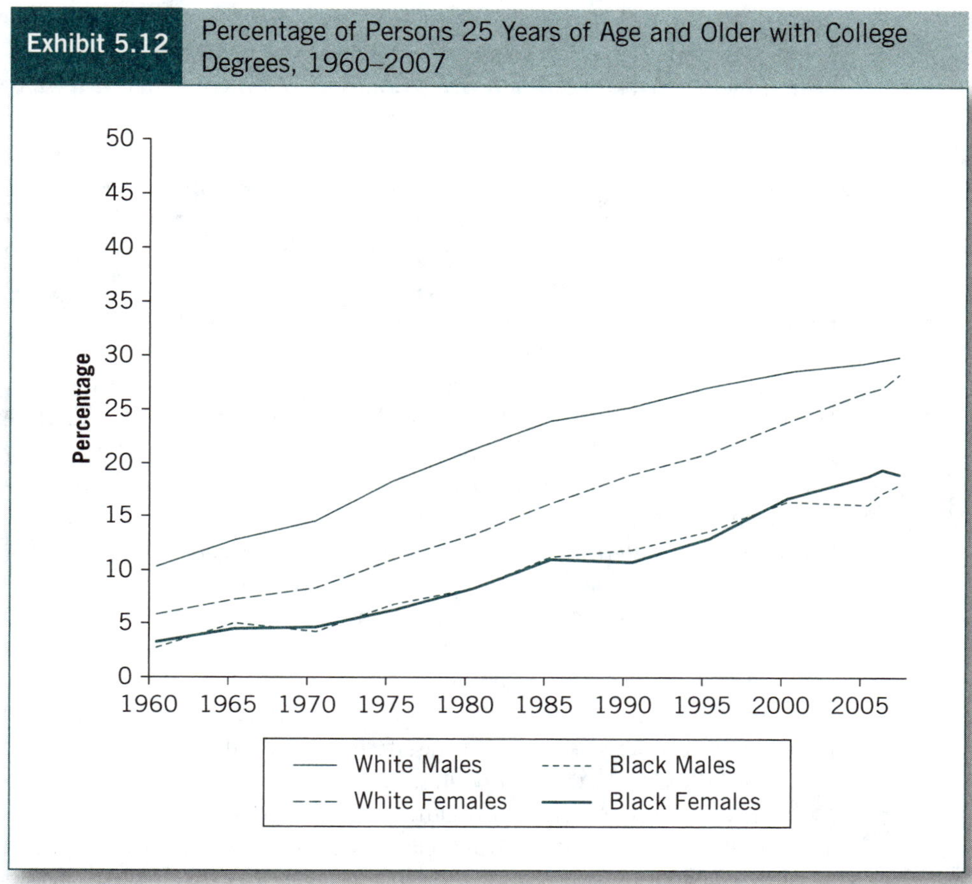

SOURCE: U.S. Bureau of the Census (2009b, p. 145).

by their high degree of geographical concentration at the local level, especially in the cities of the South, Northeast, and Midwest. Most large cities in those areas—including New York City, Atlanta, Cleveland, Chicago, and Detroit—have had at least one black mayor. The number of African American elected officials at all levels of government increased from virtually zero at the turn of the 20th century to more than 9,000 in 2002 (U.S. Bureau of the Census, 2009b, p. 251).

On the national level, the concentration of the black population in urban areas has resulted in greater representation in the House of Representatives (where elections are by smaller districts) than in the Senate (where elections are statewide). The first African American representative to the U.S. Congress (other than those elected during Reconstruction) was elected in 1928. By 1954, there were still only three African American Representatives (Franklin, 1967, p. 614), and currently there are 42, about 9% of the total (U.S. Bureau of the Census, 2009b, p. 247).

In 2004, Barack Obama became only the third African American senator since Reconstruction. The other two were Edward Brooke, R-Mass, who served two terms beginning in 1967, and Carol Moseley Braun, D-Ill, who served one term beginning in 1993. In the spring of 2009, Roland Burns became the fourth (and, at present, the only) African American senator when he was appointed to fill the remainder of Obama's term. In other branches of the federal government, both Colin Powell and Condoleezza Rice have served as secretary of state, and Clarence Thomas serves as the second African American justice to serve on the Supreme Court, the other being Thurgood Marshall. With the notable exception of President Obama, these are the highest governmental offices ever held by African Americans.

The other trend that has increased African Americans' political power is the dismantling of the institutions and practices that disenfranchised Southern blacks during Jim Crow segregation (see Chapter 4). In particular, the Voting Rights Act of 1965 specifically prohibited many of the practices (poll taxes, literacy tests, and whites-only primaries) traditionally used to keep African Americans politically powerless. The effectiveness of these repressive policies can be seen in the fact that as late as 1962, only 5% of the African American population of Mississippi and 13% of the African American population of Alabama were registered to vote (O'Hare et al., 1991, p. 33).

Since the 1960s, the number of African Americans in the nation's voting-age population has increased from slightly less than 10% to about 13%. The black vote figured prominently in several presidential elections in the past (President Kennedy in 1960, President Carter in 1976, and President Clinton in 1992 and 1996), but the potential for political power was generally not fully mobilized and actual turnout has been much lower for blacks than for whites. In the hotly contested presidential races of 2000 and 2004, however, a variety of organizations (such as the NAACP) made a concerted and largely successful effort to increase turnout for African Americans and, in both years, black turnout was comparable to that of whites. In the 2008 presidential election, the turnout for blacks was the highest in history. Slightly more than 65% of African Americans voted, an increase of a whopping 5% from 2004 and virtually equal to the turnout of whites (66.1%) (Lopez & Taylor, 2009).

Jobs and income. Integration in the job market and racial equality in income follow the trends established in many other areas of social life: The situation of African Americans has improved since the end of de jure segregation but has stopped well short of equality. Among males, whites are much more likely to be employed in the highest-rated and most lucrative occupational area, whereas blacks are overrepresented in the service sector and in unskilled labor.

Although huge gaps remain, we should also note that the present occupational distribution represents a rapid and significant upgrading, given the fact that as recently as the 1930s, the majority of African American males were unskilled agricultural laborers. A similar improvement has occurred for African American females. In the 1930s, about 90% of employed African American women worked in agriculture or in domestic service (Steinberg, 1981, pp. 206–207). The percentage of African American women in these categories has dropped dramatically, and the majority of African

American females are employed in the two highest occupational categories, although typically at the lower levels of these categories. For example, in the top-rated "managerial and professional" category, women are more likely to be concentrated in less-well-paid occupations, such as nurse or elementary school teacher (see Exhibit 4.7), whereas men are more likely to be physicians and lawyers.

Unemployment rates vary by sex and by age, and African American males frequently have higher unemployment rates than do African American females. Among white Americans, females have always had a higher unemployment rate. The reasons for greater unemployment among African Americans are various and complex. As we have seen, lower levels of education and concentration in the job-poor center cities play a part. So, too, does lower seniority and the concentration of African Americans in positions more likely to become obsolete in a developing economy. At the core of these patterns of unemployment and disadvantage, however, are discrimination, both individual and institutional, and the continuing presence of prejudice and racism (Feagin, 2001).

The racial differences in education and jobs are reflected in a persistent racial income gap, as shown in Exhibit 5.13. In the late 1960s, black median household income was about 58% of white median household income. The gap remained relatively steady through the 1980s, closed during the boom years of the 1990s, and then widened again during the first years of the new century as the economy soured.

Exhibit 5.13 Median Household Income by Race, 1967–2008

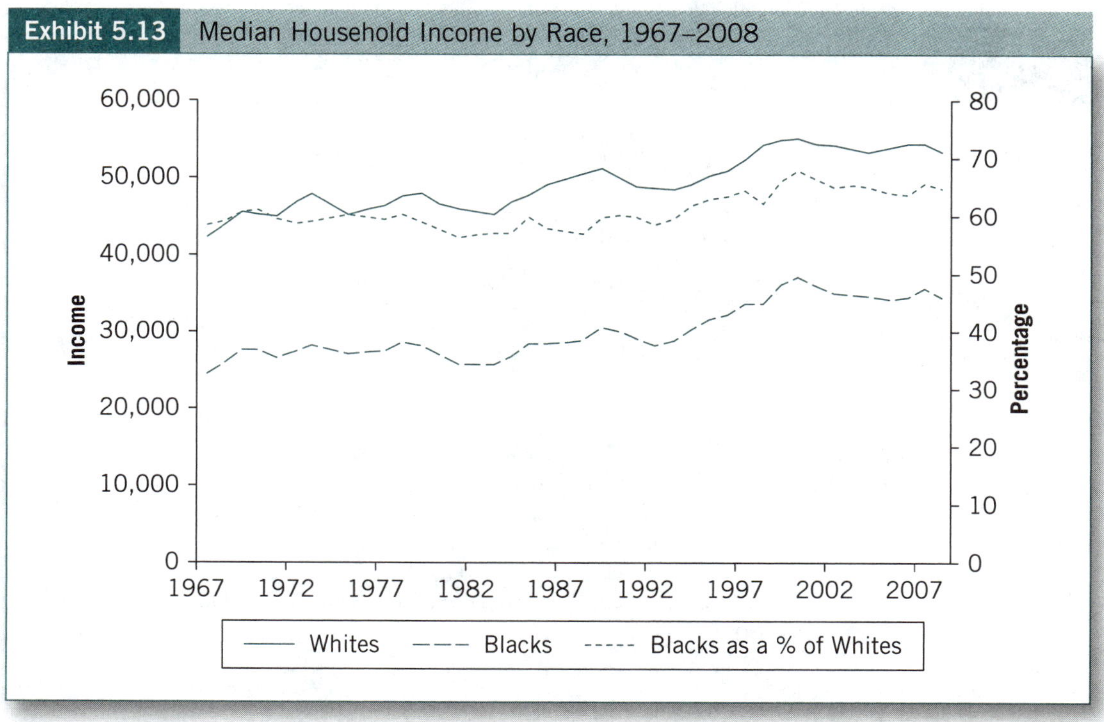

SOURCE: U.S. Bureau of the Census (2009c).

Exhibit 5.13 depicts the racial income gap in terms of the median, an average that shows the difference between "typical" white and black families. Exhibit 5.14 supplements this information by comparing the distribution of income within each racial group and highlights the differences in the percentage of each group in low-, middle-, and upper-income categories. The data are averages collected from three surveys conducted between 2005 and 2007 by the U.S. Bureau of the Census.

To read this graph, note that income categories are arrayed from top to bottom and that the horizontal axis has a zero point in the middle of the graph. The percentage of white households in each income category is represented by the bars to the left of the zero point, and the same information is presented for black households by the bars to the right of the zero point.

Starting at the bottom, note that the bars representing black households are considerably wider than those for white households. This reflects the fact that black Americans are more concentrated in the lower income brackets. For example, 15.7% of black households had incomes of $10,000 or less versus only 6% of white households.

Moving up the figure, we can see that black households continue to be overrepresented in the income categories at the bottom and middle. As we continue

Exhibit 5.14 Distribution of Household Income for Non-Hispanic Whites and Blacks, 2007 (in Dollars)

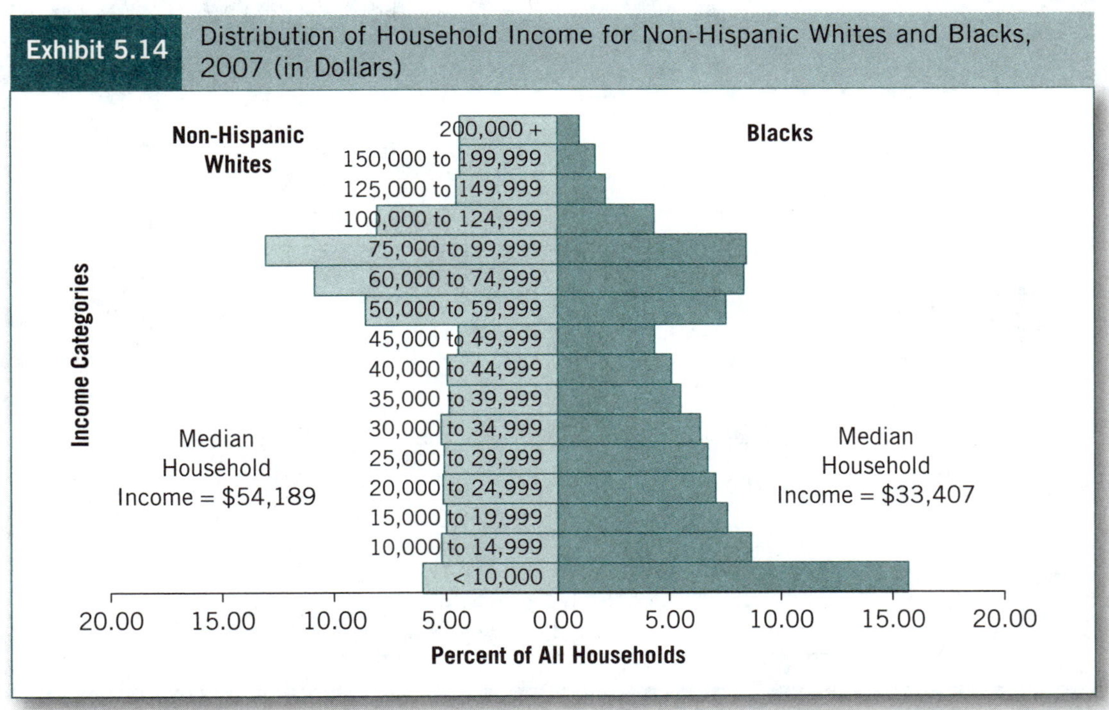

SOURCE: U.S. Bureau of the Census (2009a).

upward, note that there is a noticeable clustering for both black and white households in the $50,000 to $124,000 categories, income ranges that would be associated with a middle- to upper–middle-class lifestyle. In this income range, however, it is the white households that are overrepresented: 40% of white households versus only 29% of black households had incomes in this range. The racial differences are even more dramatic in the two very highest income ranges: Almost 9% of white households had incomes greater than $150,000 versus only 2.6% of black households. Graphs such as this convincingly refute the notion, common among "modern racists" and many other Americans, that there are no important racial inequalities in the United States today.

Finally, poverty affects African Americans at much higher rates than it does white Americans. Exhibit 5.15 shows the percentage of white and black Americans living below the federally established "official" poverty level from 1966 through 2007. The poverty rate for African American families runs about 3 times greater than the rate for whites, even though the rate for both groups trends down. For example, in 1970, African American poverty was more than 3.3 times the rate of white poverty (33% versus 10%). By 2007, fewer families of both races were living in poverty (about 24% for blacks and 9% for whites), but the racial differential was still 2.5 times greater for African American families. Tragically, the highest rates of

Exhibit 5.15 Percentage of Families and Children Under 18 in Poverty, 1966–2007

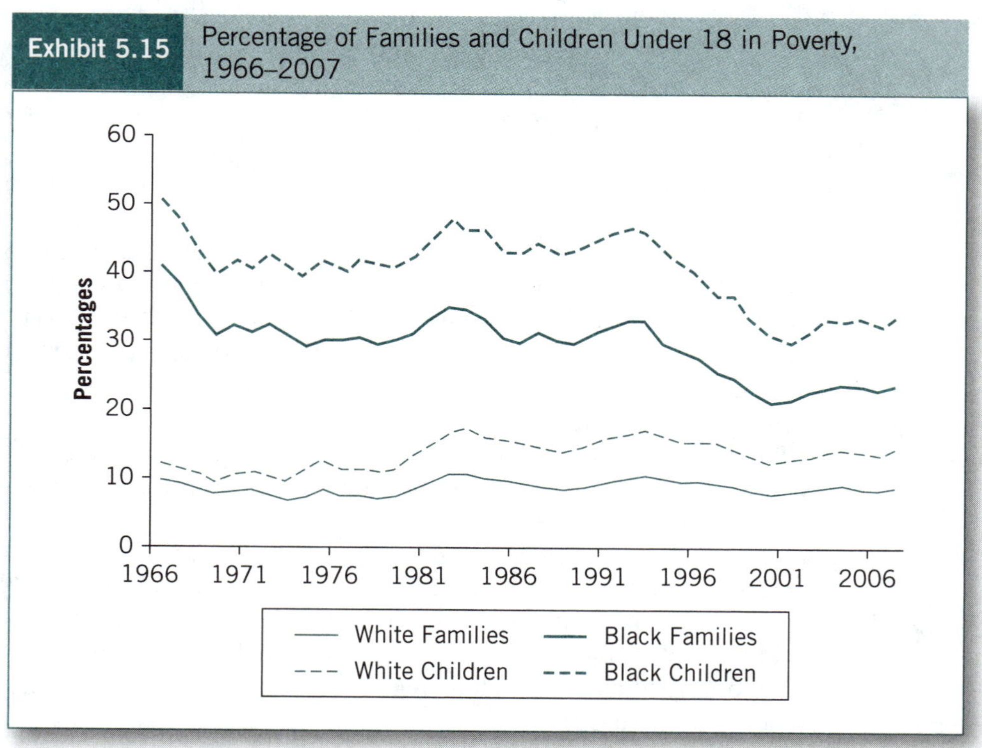

SOURCE: U.S. Bureau of the Census (2009e).

poverty continue to be found among children, especially African American children. Note the increase in poverty rates for black families and black and white children in the early years of the 21st century, after falling for nearly a decade. Again, graphs like this convincingly refute the notion that serious racial inequality is a thing of the past for U.S. society.

Primary Structural Assimilation

Interracial contact in the more public areas of society, such as schools or the workplace, is certainly more common today, and as Gordon's model (see Chapter 2) of assimilation predicts, this has led to increases in more intimate contacts across racial lines. For example, the percentage of African Americans who say they have "good friends" who are white increased from 21% in 1975 to 78% in 1994. Comparable increases have occurred for whites: In 1975, only 9% said they had "good friends" who were black, and that percentage rose to 73% in 1995 (Thernstrom & Thernstrom, 1997, p. 521).

One study looked at changing intimate relationships among Americans by asking a nationally representative sample about the people with whom they discuss "important matters." Although the study did not focus on black–white relations per se, the researchers did find that the percentage of whites who included African Americans as intimate contacts increased from 9% to over 15% between 1984 and 2004 (McPherson, Miller, Smith-Lovin, & Brashears, 2006). While this increase would be heartening to those committed to a more integrated, racially unified society, these low percentages could also be seen as discouraging as they suggest that about 85% of white Americans maintain racially exclusive interpersonal networks of friends and acquaintances.

Consistent with the decline in traditional, overt prejudice, Americans are much less opposed to interracial dating and marriage today. The Gallup poll, for example, reports that 75% of white Americans express approval of black–white marriage, up from just 20% approval in 1968. The comparable percentage of blacks was 85%, up from 56% in 1968 (Gallup Organization, 2007). Approval of interracial dating and marriage appears to be especially high among younger people: In a 2007 poll, 86% of Americans in the 18 to 29 age range approved of interracial marriage, as opposed to 30% of those aged 65 and older (Wellner, 2007).

Behavior appears to be following attitudes, as the rates of interracial dating and marriage are increasing. A number of studies find that interracial dating is increasingly common (see Wellner, 2007), and marriages between blacks and whites are also increasing in number, although still a tiny percentage of all marriages. According to the U.S. Bureau of the Census (2009b), there were 65,000 black–white married couples in 1970 (including persons of Hispanic origin), about 0.10% of all married couples. By 2007, the number of black–white married couples had increased more than sevenfold, to 464,000, but this is still only about 0.80% of all married couples (p. 52).

FOCUS ON CONTEMPORARY ISSUES: The Election of Barack Obama and Post-Racial America

In spite of the bitter cold, more than a million people filled the mall at the nation's capital. They came to celebrate, to participate, and to witness a turning point in history. Millions more around the country and around the globe watched on television and on the Internet as Barack Hussein Obama took the oath of office and became the 44th president of the United States. To many, the ceremony marked the end of an era and a final, decisive rejection of American racism, injustice, and unfairness. Hope and optimism surged: If it was possible for a person of color to rise to the highest office in the United States, arguably the most powerful position in the world, what else was possible? What *couldn't* be achieved? Barriers and limitations melted away, obstacles and impediments crumbled and, at least for a time, people everywhere felt their horizons stretch and their goals expand. Had the United States finally fulfilled its promise and become what it had often proclaimed itself to be: the last, best hope for the world, a bastion of decency and fairness in a world filled with injustice, oppression, and despair?

People will be discussing and debating this inauguration for generations and, of course, only time will permit final judgments and assessments. Was this truly the dawning of a new day? Or was the significance of the day being overblown? What did the triumph of President Obama mean for the day-to-day lives of black Americans and other colonized minority groups? Did it truly alter their life chances and the prospects for their children? Racism and the structures that perpetuate inequality have been powerful and resilient features of American life since colonial days. Were we mistaking the triumph of one man for the dissolution of the systems of white privilege and minority group disadvantage?

What can we learn by focusing the concepts and perspectives developed in this text on the election of President Barack Obama? Should we stress the progress marked by this historic election and rejoice in the ability of U.S. society to grow and remake itself? Or should we stress the challenges that remain for African Americans and other minority groups, especially those that are afflicted by urban poverty and systematically excluded from the mainstream? Is this truly a breakthrough or merely a distraction from the grim realities of everyday racism and disenfranchisement? Can it be both?

A Post-Racial Society?

What could the term *post-racial* mean in the context of Obama's victory? Different people attach different meanings to the term, so let's begin by sorting out some common interpretations.

The strongest positive interpretation of post-racial would be that antiblack prejudice, racism, and discrimination have lost their force. We can describe a post-racial society in the words of Dr. Martin Luther King's famous 1963 "I Have a Dream" speech: In such a society, all would be judged by the content of their character, not by the color of their skin. In this interpretation, President Obama's election signified the end of prejudgment (or prejudice) based on skin color or ethnicity (and religion and gender?) and presaged the disappearance (or at least the drastic reduction) of the gaps between

(Continued)

(Continued)

dominant and minority groups in income, education, occupational profiles, political power, and other dimensions of secondary structural assimilation.

A second interpretation of post-racial—weaker but still positive—stresses the diminishing power of racial identity in American society: In a post-racial United States, people's lives and perceptions would be much less constricted or determined by their race. While racial inequality may continue, multiculturalism and tolerance rule the day, and race is no more important in everyday life than a multitude of other lifestyle and cultural differences between people, including religion, political ideology, education, occupation, or musical preferences. In this view, the all-embracing color line established during slavery and perpetuated during segregation is now blurred and negotiable. Americans are freer than ever to manufacture their own identities and lifestyles and to change them as they see fit or, indeed, to completely abandon them for other identities if they so choose. The argument that racial identity has become an individual choice—not unilaterally imposed by the larger society—is reminiscent of the concepts of *symbolic ethnicity* for white ethnic groups (see Chapter 2) and the protean identity described by Rockquemore and Brunsma (2008) in their sample of biracial people earlier in this chapter. This view is also compatible with many of the trends we have discussed throughout this text: the growing diversity of our society, the decline of the white numerical majority, and the increasing number of mixed-race individuals. Can people of color now choose to be as racial or nonracial as they want to be?

A third view sees the term post-racial as empty rhetoric, a mistaken and greatly exaggerated interpretation of the significance of Obama's victory. This view stresses the continuing racial gaps and the continuing power of antiblack prejudice, even if disguised as modern racism. From this perspective, the United States remains a racist society and a bastion of white privilege and supremacy, and the success of one man means little or nothing for the millions trapped by poverty and institutionalized discrimination and marginalized from mainstream society. At first glance, at least, this view seems most consistent with the hypotheses and concepts stressed throughout this text. In particular, the Blauner hypothesis (see Chapter 3), with its stress on the continuing power of a colonized origin, would seem to urge that claims of the demise of racism and racial inequality be treated with a strong dose of skepticism.

Of course, there are many other ways to view Obama's election, and the truth—always complex and subtle—may well lie in some mixture of these three views. Nevertheless, let's take a look at the election and changing U.S. society and see which of the three interpretations, if any, is most supported by the evidence.

Was Race a Factor in Obama's Election?

If the strongest positive interpretation of post-racial is accurate and Obama's election signaled the demise of race issues in U. S. society, his campaign and his support base should have been nonracial. Was it?

Practical Politics and an Early Victory

Any politician seeking office in a pluralistic, diverse society must rely on coalitions of blocs of voters for victory. This is especially true for minority candidates. To have a chance at the polls, Obama had to reach people everywhere, not just in the black community or in minority neighborhoods. From the start, he sought to construct a winning coalition by stressing the issues about which Americans were most concerned: the economy, the war in Iraq, health care, and the national policy on energy and the environment, among others. He did not focus on "black" issues (e.g., civil rights, or racism in the criminal justice system), and his plan was to discuss issues of race "only in the context of other issues" (Ifill, 2009, p. 53). The campaign strategy was to present Obama as a viable, competent candidate that happened to be black, not as "the black candidate."

The power of this strategy and Obama's ability to attract the support of large numbers of white voters was demonstrated in Iowa, the first state test in the race for the Democratic nomination for president. Iowa is only 7% black, but Obama attracted nearly 40% of the voters in the statewide caucuses, a huge boost to the campaign and a clear demonstration of his appeal to a broad coalition of voters. While he had to fight for literally every vote following his victory in Iowa and lost several primaries to chief rival Hillary Clinton, this early triumph sent a clear signal of his broad appeal and his ability to attract support from across the electorate—a fact that seems consistent with the idea that his campaign signaled the coming of a post-racial era.

A New Generation

Obama's campaign heralded the rise of a new generation of black politicians. The older generation—men and women now in their 70s and 80s or long deceased—had cleared the way with the civil rights movement, voter registration drives, campaigns to raise U.S. awareness about racial inequality, and continuing efforts to keep the issues of racial justice at the forefront of the public consciousness. The older generation—including Jesse Jackson and Al Sharpton, both of whom had run for the Democratic presidential nomination in campaigns past—had forced the larger society to dismantle the Jim Crow system, make at least a formal commitment to racial equality, and enfranchise the black community. They campaigned as black Americans first and foremost and kept up the pressure to make racial equality a reality, not just a formal commitment. They succeeded in erasing many racial barriers, and their efforts created the opportunity for the next generation of African American politicians to enter the mainstream.

Barack Obama is the most prominent member of this younger generation of black leadership. Others include Governor Deval Patrick of Massachusetts and Mayor Cory Booker of Newark, New Jersey. These younger African American leaders are not "race men"—candidates who stress racial issues and their racial identity. Rather, they are pragmatic, flexible, less ideological in their positions, and are even willing to challenge their elders when they see fit. For example, several (including Obama) have espoused support for charter schools as one strategy for dealing with the woeful state of inner-city education, a position that is anathema to the older generation that sees the charter school movement as a strategy to avoid racial integration (Ifill, 2009).

Consistent with the idea of an emerging post-racial America, Obama was born in 1961 and grew up in Hawaii and Indonesia, far removed from the realities of Jim Crow segregation and the legacy of systemic, state-sponsored racial inequality. Obama was not the first choice of the "old line" black leadership (who tended to favor Hillary Clinton) and, in fact, was the target of some decidedly negative remarks from

(Continued)

(Continued)

Jesse Jackson (Weisman, 2008). What Obama presented to the American public was not the passion and fire of racial rhetoric but an image of competence, articulate integrity, and the promise of change. While he is of course aware of the debt his generation owes to the civil rights pioneers, his message to the electorate in 2008 urged the need to move forward on issues that affected *all* Americans.

Race and the Campaign

What role did race play in the campaign? In recent decades, consistent with the rise of the more muted and subtle modern racism, racial issues and racism in political campaigns have been presented in code words, not blatant attacks. A classic example of the way the race card has been played is the infamous Willie Horton ads run in the 1988 presidential campaign between George H. W. Bush and Michael Dukakis, then governor of Massachusetts. Willie Horton was a black man who had been convicted of murder but was released from a Massachusetts prison on a weekend furlough program that had been established during Dukakis's term as governor. During his furlough, Horton embarked on a crime spree and committed several felonies, including assault and rape, before being apprehended again. The ads were used to paint the liberal Dukakis as soft on crime and punishment, not tough enough to be entrusted with the leadership of the nation. The not-so-subtle subtext of the ads, however, stressed the traditional stereotype of the menacing black male–violent, out of control, and a threat to white women.

Attempts were made to brand Obama as a soft-hearted liberal who was weak on crime, law and order, and national defense–all common political code words for race and racism. The most notable of these episodes stemmed from Obama's link to the flamboyant, outspoken Pastor Jeremiah Wright, who had been the minister of Obama's Chicago church. In the spring of 2008, a video of Reverend Wright surfaced and was replayed endlessly on cable news channels and the Internet (see YouTube at http://www.youtube.com/watch?v=9hPR5jnjtLo). In the video, Pastor Wright condemns U.S. society for its treatment of black Americans and urges his followers not to sing "God Bless America" but "God Damn America" for its killing of innocents and its repression and mistreatment of blacks. Wright argued that the 9/11 terrorist attacks were provoked by American attacks on innocents–including the World War II bombings of Nagasaki and Hiroshima–and condemned the U.S. support of "state terrorism" against Palestinians and black South Africans (Ross & El-Buri, 2008).

Wright's remarks derailed the Obama campaign for weeks as they sought a way to defuse the issue. Their concern was that the Wright video would be used to drive a wedge between the candidate and his white supporters by emphasizing his racial identity and activating the antiblack prejudice that lay beneath the surface of American society. Just as Willie Horton was used to brand Governor Dukakis as a soft-headed liberal, Jeremiah Wright was used in an attempt to brand Obama and raise those ancient American cultural connections between race and incompetence.

After considerable confusion and mixed messages from the campaign, Obama finally dissociated himself from Wright and, in an elegant, carefully crafted speech on race and America, addressed the underlying issues. Obama acknowledged both America's racist past and the continuing importance of racism in the present (in terms reminiscent of the concept of past-in-present discrimination introduced in Chapter 4). He argued that Wright's view of America was distorted and that Wright's error was that he "elevated what is wrong with America above all that we know is right with America" (Obama, 2008).

Contrary to those who argue for the diminishing importance of race, Obama stated that the society has been "stuck in a racial stalemate for years" and that he did not "believe that we can get beyond our racial divisions in a single election cycle, or with a single candidacy." But, he argued, "we can move beyond our old racial wounds, and . . . in fact we have no choice if we are to continue on the path to a more perfect union." Finally, he argued that Wright's mistake was that he spoke as if the United States was static and incapable of change: "What we know—what we have seen—is that this America can change. This is the true genius of this nation" (Obama, 2008).

The speech put the campaign back on track and put the furor over Pastor Wright in the past. It also made clear that Obama himself—the supposed harbinger of a new racial age—had no illusions about the waning strength of racism or the sudden emergence of a new age of racial justice and fairness.

The issue of race continued to lurk in the near background of the campaign. Indeed, as many have remarked, it would be naïve to think that a person of color could run for the highest office in the land without raising racial concerns in the minds of Americans. Although there were persistent tendencies to see Obama as something other than a "true American"—including rumors that he was Muslim, or that a "fist bump" he exchanged with his wife was a signal to terrorists, or that he consorted with political radicals and revolutionaries—the campaign managed to stay on track and defuse or deflect the rumors. Ultimately, the image that Obama was a worthy candidate who happened to be black (rather than a black candidate who might be worthy) triumphed at the polls on Election Day.

Race and Support for Obama

How did Obama supporters break out along racial lines? In many ways, the election reflected the increasing diversity of U.S. society. For the first time in history, white voters were less than 75% of the electorate—a dramatic decline since 1976, when 90% of voters were white, and a clear reflection of the changing composition of the U.S. population (see Exhibit 5.16). Black Americans comprised 13% of all voters, up from 11% in 2004, and, unlike in the past, this turnout was proportional to the share of black Americans in the total population. The Hispanic vote also increased, but only by 1 point to 9% of the electorate, still far below their relative share of population (ABC News, 2008).

Obama supporters reflected the emerging, more diverse America and were 61% white, 23% black, and 11% Hispanic. In contrast, John McCain's supporters were 90% white (ABC News, 2008). Obama's support was broad-based, and he pulled a larger percentage of voters from every category and sub-category of the electorate (except those age 65+) than John Kerry (the Democratic candidate for president) had in 2004 (see Exhibit 5.16).

(Continued)

(Continued)

Exhibit 5.16 Support for Obama in 2008 and Changes in Support for the Democratic Candidate Since 2004

	Obama %	McCain %	Democrat Gains/ Losses, 2004–2008
Total	52	46	+ 4
Race/Ethnic Group			
White	43	55	+ 2
Black	95	4	+ 7
Hispanic	66	32	+ 13
Age Group			
18–29	66	32	+ 12
30–44	52	46	+ 6
45–64	49	49	+ 2
65+	45	53	– 2
Income Group			
Less than $50,000	60	38	+ 5
$50,000–$99,999	49	49	+ 5
$100,000+	49	50	+ 8
Party Affiliation			
Republican	9	89	+ 3
Democrat	89	10	0
Independent	52	44	+ 3
Political Ideology			
Conservative	20	78	+ 5
Moderate	60	39	+ 6
Liberal	88	10	+ 3
Residence			
Urban	63	35	+ 9
Suburban	50	48	+ 3
Rural	45	53	+ 3

SOURCE: Pew Research Center (2008). Based on exit polls.

There are clearly racial dimensions to Obama's support, but his backers came from every faction in society, including conservatives and Republicans. His campaign was perhaps especially notable for its ability to mobilize younger voters: His support among this group was up a whopping 12 percentage points compared to the Democratic candidate in 2004.

Was the Election Post-Racial?

What can we conclude? The term post-racial might apply to some aspects of the election, including the fact that Obama drew support from a broad cross-section of Americans. On the other hand, the continuing power of race in the United States lurked just beneath the surface and manifested itself in such episodes as the furor over Rev. Wright's remarks and the persistent tendency to see Obama as an "other," not quite a "true American." Race was not the paramount issue (as it might have been in years past), but the campaign was waged in a society that had not (yet?) outgrown the traditions of race, racial inequality, and racism (see Feagin & Wingfield, 2009; Wise, 2009).

A New Racial Order or Same Old Racial Perceptions?

Barack Obama has been consistently identified as "African American" and "black" throughout the campaign, during the inauguration, and still today. In the context of American traditions of race and racism, what do these labels signify?

The racial labeling of President Obama as black or African American is quite consistent with the long, deep traditions of American racism, including the one-drop rule. This is especially the case since the label African American does not apply to him literally, at least as the term is usually understood. He is not descended from African American slaves, nor did he have relatives in the United States prior to the immigration of his father in 1959 from Kenya. To be sure, President Obama is both African and American, but he is not "African American." His father was black, but his mother was white, and, like many Americans, his European roots can be traced to a variety of locales, including Ireland.

In one way, consistent with the second view of a post-racial United States, President Obama—along with other prominent mixed-race individuals—may well serve as an icon for an emerging era of changed consciousness about race: His mixed-race background and the fact that he does not fit into the traditional rigid categories challenges—in a very prominent way—the usefulness and validity of those categories. Recall that, although only 2% of the population in the 2000 census chose to identify themselves with more than one race, it has been projected that as much as 20% of the population will identify as "mixed" by 2050.

On the other hand, the very persistence of the labels applied to President Obama suggests that we have not yet made the transition to a new racial consciousness and have not completely rejected the racist simplicities of past generations. Seeing and labeling Obama as black or African American—as a member of a clearly defined and delimited group—allows people to avoid the ambiguities of mixed race or thinking in new ways about the color line that has been at the core of our society for so long. This labeling sustains the place of race in American life as a fundamental characteristic by

(Continued)

(Continued)

which to differentiate and identify people. It also continues the perception that only "others" (nonwhites) have race (see Chapter 1)—other prominent politicians and Obama's opponents in the election are not routinely labeled "white."

Have Racial Gaps Decreased?

Perhaps the crucial test of the power of race in American society lies in the size of the racial gaps documented in this chapter. In a truly post-racial society, these gaps would be nonexistent or, at least, diminishing over time. A review of the facts shows a closing of the racial gap in some areas. For example, Exhibits 5.11 and 5.12 show a dramatic narrowing of the racial gap in high school education and some narrowing in college education. On other dimensions, the picture is more mixed, even though a determined optimist could perhaps argue that the racial gap is narrowing in some ways. For example, Exhibits 5.5, 5.13 and 5.15 may be seen as indicating some narrowing of the income and poverty gaps, at least over the long run.

In other areas of social life—residential and school segregation, and the imprisonization of young black males—the differences between blacks and whites continue to verify the power of the Blauner hypothesis (see Chapter 3): Minority groups created by colonization and conquest will face stronger, more persistent racism and resistance than groups created by immigration; the degree of inequality will be greater and the struggle for liberation and equality will be lengthier.

Conclusions

Which of the three versions of the interpretation of post-racial seems most viable in the light of the information presented here? The strongest, most positive view—the vision of a society in which racial equality has been achieved—is clearly exaggerated. The truth perhaps lies in some mixture of the two other views: While race may be losing some of its historic power to shape our perception and control our lives—and may be becoming a more "voluntary" identity—U.S. society continues to be deeply divided by race.

What does Obama's victory mean in terms of the issues raised in this text? Although a truly post-racial society remains a distant dream, this momentous event does show that, in 2008—in circumstances dominated by severe economic woes, an unpopular war, and the failed presidency of George W. Bush—the United States was ready to turn for leadership to an exceptionally articulate and charismatic man who happened to be black. For a person of color to become the president of the United States is an extraordinary event, the significance of which will shape American society (and the world) for decades to come. It is a great thing, momentous and earth-shaking. But it is not everything.

Is the Glass Half Empty or Half Full?

The contemporary situation for African Americans is perhaps what might be expected for a group so recently "released" from exclusion and subordination. The average situation for African Americans improved vastly during the latter half of the 20th century in virtually every area of social life. As demonstrated by the data presented in this chapter, however, racial progress stopped well short of equality. In assessing the present situation, one might stress the improved situation of the group (the glass is half full) or the challenges that remain before full racial equality and justice are achieved (the glass is half empty). Perhaps the most reasonable approach is to recognize that in many ways, the overall picture of racial progress is "different" rather than "better," and that over the past century of change, a large percentage of the African American population has traded rural peasantry for urban poverty and now faces an array of formidable and deep-rooted problems.

The situation for African Americans is intimately intermixed with the plight of our cities and the changing nature of the labor force. It is the consequence of nearly 400 years of prejudice, racism, and discrimination, but it also reflects broader social forces, such as urbanization and industrialization. Consistent with their origin as a colonized minority group, the relative poverty and powerlessness of African Americans persists long after other groups (e.g., the descendents of the European immigrants who arrived between the 1820s and 1920s) have achieved equality and acceptance. African Americans were enslaved to meet the labor demands of an agrarian economy, became a rural peasantry under Jim Crow segregation, were excluded from the opportunities created by early industrialization, and remain largely excluded from the better jobs in the emerging postindustrial economy.

Progress toward racial equality may have slowed since the heady days of the 1960s, and in many areas, earlier advances seem hopelessly stagnated, at least for the less-educated and -skilled blacks in the ghettos. Public opinion polls indicate that there is little support or sympathy in the white community for the cause of African Americans. Traditional prejudice has declined, only to be replaced by modern racism. In the court of public opinion, African Americans are often held responsible for their own plight. Biological racism has been replaced by indifference to racial issues or blaming the victims.

Of course, in acknowledging the challenges that remain, we should not downplay the real improvements that have been made in the lives of African Americans. Compared with the days of Jim Crow, African Americans are on the average more prosperous and more politically powerful, and some are among the most revered of current popular heroes (the glass is half full). However, the increases in average income and education and the glittering success of the few obscure a tangle of problems for the many—problems that may well grow worse as America moves further into the postindustrial era. Poverty, unemployment, a failing educational system, residential segregation, subtle racism, and continuing discrimination continue to be inescapable realities for millions of African Americans. In many African American neighborhoods, crime, drugs, violence, poor health care, malnutrition, and a host of other factors compound these problems (the glass is half empty).

Given this gloomy situation, it should not be surprising to find significant strength in pluralistic, nationalistic thinking, as well as resentment and anger in the African American community. Black nationalism and Black Power remain powerful ideas, but their goals of development and autonomy for the African American community remain largely rhetorical sloganeering without the resources to bring them to actualization.

The situation of the African American community in the early days of the 21st century might be characterized as structural pluralism combined with inequality. The former characterization testifies to the failure of assimilation and the latter to the continuing effects, in the present, of a colonized origin. The problems that remain are less visible (or perhaps just better hidden from the average white, middle-class American) than those of previous eras. Responsibility is more diffused, the moral certainties of opposition to slavery or to Jim Crow laws are long gone, and contemporary racial issues must be articulated and debated in an environment of subtle prejudice and low levels of sympathy for the grievances of African Americans. Urban poverty, modern institutional discrimination, and modern racism are less dramatic and more difficult to measure than an overseer's whip, a lynch mob, or a sign that says "Whites Only," but they can be just as real and just as deadly in their consequences.

MAIN POINTS

- At the beginning of the 20th century, the racial oppression of African Americans took the form of a rigid competitive system of group relations, de jure segregation. This system ended because of changing economic and political conditions, changing legal precedents, and a mass movement of protest initiated by African Americans.
- The U.S. Supreme Court decision in *Brown v. Board of Education of Topeka* (1954) was the single most powerful blow struck against legalized segregation. A nonviolent direct-action campaign was launched in the South to challenge and defeat segregation. The U.S. Congress delivered the final blows to de jure segregation with the 1964 Civil Rights Act and the 1965 Voting Rights Act.
- Outside the South, the concerns of the African American community had centered on access to schooling, jobs, housing, health care, and other opportunities. African Americans' frustration and anger were expressed in the urban riots in the 1960s. The Black Power movement addressed the massive problems of racial inequality remaining after the victories of the civil rights movement.
- Black–white relations since the 1960s have been characterized by continuing inequality, separation, and hostility, along with substantial improvements in status for some African Americans. Class differentiation within the African American community is greater than ever before.
- The African American family has been perceived as weak, unstable, and a cause of continuing poverty. The culture of poverty theory attributes poverty to certain characteristics of the poor. An alternative view sees problems such as high rates of family desertion by men as the *result* of poverty rather than the cause.
- Antiblack prejudice and discrimination are manifested in more subtle, covert forms (modern racism and institutional discrimination) in contemporary society.
- Black-white biracial people are developing a variety of racial identities in addition to the traditional black-only identity based on the one-drop rule.

- African Americans are largely acculturated, but centuries of separate development have created a unique black experience in American society.
- Despite real improvements in their status, the overall secondary structural assimilation of African Americans remains low. Evidence of racial inequalities in residence, schooling, politics, jobs, income, unemployment, and poverty is massive and underlines the realities of the urban underclass.
- In the area of primary structural assimilation, interracial interaction and friendships appear to be rising. Interracial marriages are increasing, although they remain a tiny percentage of all marriages.
- Compared with their situation at the start of the 20th century, African Americans have made considerable improvements in their quality of life. However, the distance to true racial equality remains enormous.

STUDY SITE ON THE WEB

Don't forget the interactive quizzes and other resources and learning aids at **www.pineforge.com/healeyds3e**

FOR FURTHER READING

Two very readable overviews of contemporary black–white relations are the following:

Feagin, Joe. 2001. *Racist America: Roots, Current Realities, and Future Reparations.* New York: Routledge.

Hacker, Andrew. 1992. *Two Nations: Black and White, Separate, Hostile, and Unequal.* New York: Scribner's.

In this work, Massey and Denton argue powerfully that residential segregation is the key to understanding urban black poverty:

Massey, Douglas, & Denton, Nancy. 1993. *American Apartheid: Segregation and the Making of the Underclass.* Cambridge, MA: Harvard University Press.

Here are two excellent sources about the Southern civil rights movement:

Morris, Aldon D. 1984. *The Origins of the Civil Rights Movement.* New York: Free Press.

Williams, Juan. 1987. *Eyes on the Prize: America's Civil Rights Years 1954–1965.* New York: Penguin.

This is a two-volume collection of articles by leading scholars that presents a comprehensive analysis of black–white relations in America:

Smelser, Neil J., Wilson, William J., & Mitchell, Faith. (Eds.). 2001. *America Becoming: Racial Trends and Their Consequences.* Washington, DC: National Academies Press.

The following is the latest in a long list of powerful analyses of black urban poverty by a master scholar and policy analyst:

Wilson, William J. 2009. *More Than Just Race.* New York: Norton.

QUESTIONS FOR REVIEW AND STUDY

1. What forces led to the end of de jure segregation? To what extent was this change a result of broad social forces (e.g., industrialization), and to what extent was it the result of the actions of African Americans acting against the system (e.g., the Southern civil rights movement)? By the 1960s and 1970s, how had the movement for racial change succeeded, and what issues were left unresolved? What issues remain unresolved today?
2. What are the differences between de jure segregation and de facto segregation? What are the implications of these differences for movements to change these systems? That is, how must movements against de facto segregation differ from movements against de jure segregation in terms of tactics and strategies?
3. Describe the differences between the Southern civil rights movement and the Black Power movement. Why did these differences exist? Do these movements remain relevant today? If so, how?
4. How does gender affect contemporary black–white relations? Is it true that African American women are a "minority group within a minority group"? If so, how?
5. What are the implications of increasing class differentials among African Americans? Does the greater affluence of middle-class blacks mean that they are no longer a part of a minority group? Will future protests by African Americans be confined only to working-class and lower-class blacks?
6. Regarding contemporary black–white relations, is the glass half empty or half full? Considering the totality of evidence presented in this chapter, which of the following statements would you agree with and why? (1) American race relations are the best they've ever been, and racial equality has been essentially achieved (even though some problems remain). (2) American race relations have a long way to go before society achieves true racial equality.
7. What do you think the term *post-racial* means? Has the United States become post-racial? Cite evidence from this chapter both for and against the idea that we are now post-racial. What evidence seems the most important or powerful? Why?

INTERNET RESEARCH PROJECT

In the year 2000, a team of reporters from the *New York Times* conducted a year-long investigation of how black–white relations are being lived out by ordinary people in churches, schools, neighborhoods, and other venues. A series of 15 articles detailing and analyzing these experiences was published, and all are available online at www.nytimes.com/library/national/race. Read at least three or four of these stories and analyze them in terms of the concepts and conclusions presented in this chapter. What do these stories imply about black–white inequality, prejudice, discrimination, assimilation, pluralism, and racial separation? Is the glass half empty or half full?

Notes

1. From *There Are No Children Here* by Alex Kotlowitz. Copyright © 1991 by Alex Kotlowitz. Used by permission of Doubleday, a division of Random House, Inc., and the David Black Agency as agent for the author.

2. This is the title of Telles's (2004) masterful, comparative analysis of race relations in Brazil and the United States.

American Indians

From Conquest to Tribal Survival in a Postindustrial Society

Like most Indian people, I have several names. In Indian Way, names come to you in the course of your life, not just when you're born. Some come during childhood ceremonies; others are given on special occasions throughout your life. Each name gives you a new sense of yourself and your own possibilities. And each name gives you something to live up to. It points out the direction you're supposed to take in this life. One of my names is Tate Wikuwa, which means "Wind Chases the Sun" in the Dakota language. That name was my great grandfather's. Another name, bestowed on me by my Native Canadian brethren, is Gwarth-ee-lass, meaning "He Leads the People."

I find special inspiration in both of those names. The first, to me, represents total freedom—a goal even most of those outside prison walls never achieve. When I think that name to myself . . . I feel free in my heart, able to melt through stone walls and steel bars and ride the wind through pure sunlight to the Sky World. No walls or bars or rolls of razor wire can stop me from doing that. And the second name . . . to me, represents total commitment, a goal I strive for even within these walls.

Maybe it seems presumptuous, even absurd—a man like me, in prison for two lifetimes, speaking of leading his people. But, like Nelson Mandela, you never know when you will suddenly and unexpectedly be called upon. He, too, knows what it's like to sit here in prison, year after year, decade after decade. I try to keep myself ready if ever I'm needed. I work at it within these walls, with my fellow inmates, with my supporters around the world, with people of good will everywhere.

(Continued)

(Continued)

A strong leader shows mercy. He compromises for the good of all. He listens to every side and never makes hasty decisions that could hurt the people. I'm trying very hard to be the kind of leader I myself could respect.

So, in our way, my names tell me and others who I am. Each of my names should be an inspiration to me. Here at Leavenworth—in fact anywhere in the U.S. prison system—my official name is #89637-132. Not much imagination, or inspiration, there.

My Christian name, though I don't consider myself to be a Christian, is Leonard Peltier. The last name's French, from the French fur hunters and voyageurs who came through our country more than a century ago, and I take genuine pride in that holy blood; too. . . . My first name was given to me by my grandmother, who said I cried so hard as a baby that I sounded like a "little lion": She named me Leonard, she said, because it sounded like "lion-hearted."

Though my bloodline is predominantly Ojibway and Dakota Sioux, I have also married into, and been adopted in the traditional way by, the Lakota Sioux people. All Lakota/Dakota/Nakota people—also known as Sioux—are one great nation of nations. Indians are many nations, but one People. I myself was brought up on both Sioux and Ojibway (Chippewa) reservations in the land known to you as America.

I would like to say with all sincerity—and with no disrespect—that I don't consider myself an American citizen. I am a native of Great Turtle Island. I am of the Ikce Wicasa, the Common People, the Original People. Our sacred land is under occupation, and we are now all prisoners, not just me.

Even so, I love being an Indian, for all of its burdens and all of its responsibilities. Being an Indian is my greatest pride. I thank Wakan Tanka, the Great Mystery, for making Indian. I love my people. If you must accuse of something, accuse me of that—being Indian. To that crime—and to that crime alone—I plead guilty.

My crime's being an Indian. What's yours?

—Leonard Peltier (1999, pp. 61–64)[1]

Leonard Peltier has been in federal prison since 1977. He is serving two consecutive life terms for the murder of two federal agents during a shoot-out on a Sioux reservation. Many believe that his conviction was unfair or even rigged and was based more on his leadership role in the American Indian Movement (AIM), a protest group he helped to organize, than on his actions during the shoot-out.

In this excerpt from his biographical *Prison Writings* (1999), Peltier reflects on what being an Indian means to him and, in his musings, we can hear an authentic Indian voice, reflective of a culture that has survived, even after centuries of attempts to suppress and undermine it. Whatever the merit of his case, voices like Peltier's demonstrate the persistence of a group that is often assumed to have perished in the days of the Wild West. For many people, perhaps the most surprising fact about American Indians is that they are still here.

Introduction

We discussed the contact period for American Indians in Chapter 3. As you recall, the contact period began in the earliest colonial days and lasted nearly 300 years, ending only with the final battles of the Indian wars in the late 1800s. The Indian nations fought for their land and to preserve their cultures and ways of life. The tribes had enough power to win many battles, but they eventually lost all the wars. The superior resources of the burgeoning white society made the eventual defeat of American Indians inevitable, and by 1890, the last of the tribes had been conquered, their leaders had been killed or were in custody, and their people were living on government-controlled reservations.

Early in the 20th century, 100 years ago, American Indians were, in Blauner's (1972) terms, a conquered and colonized minority group. Like the slave plantations, the reservations were paternalistic systems that controlled American Indians with federally mandated regulations and government-appointed Indian agents. For most of the 20th century, as Jim Crow segregation, Supreme Court decisions, industrialization, and urbanization shaped the status of other minority groups, American Indians subsisted on the fringes of development and change, marginalized, relatively powerless, and isolated. Their links to the larger society were weaker and, compared with other minority groups, they were less affected by the forces of social and political evolution.

The last years of the 20th century witnessed some improvement in the status of American Indians in general and some tribes, especially those with casinos and other gaming establishments, made notable progress toward parity with national standards. Also, the tribes are now more in control of their own affairs, and many have used their increased autonomy and independence to effectively address problems in education, health, joblessness, and other areas. Despite this progress, however, large gaps remain between American Indians and the dominant group in virtually every areas of social and economic life.

In this chapter, we will bring the history of American Indians up to the present and explore both recent progress and persisting problems. Some of the questions we address include the following: What accounts for the lowly position of this group for much of the last 100 years? How can we explain the improvements in the most recent decade? Now, early in the 21st century, what problems remain, and how does the situation of American Indians compare with other colonized and conquered minority groups? What are the most promising strategies for closing the remaining gaps between American Indians and the larger society?

Please note that this chapter presents information about American Indians in a variety of formats. The main focus is on American Indians residing in the "lower" 48 states (i.e., excluding Hawaii and Alaska). As I did with African Americans, I will rely primarily on information from the U.S. Census to characterize the situation of this group and make comparisons to the larger society and to other minority groups.

Size of the Group

How many Indians are there? There are several different answers to this question, partly because of the way census information is collected and partly because of the social and subjective nature of race and group membership. The most current answers come from the American Community Survey (ACS), conducted every year by the U.S. Bureau of the Census since the last full census in 2000. This survey provides estimates for the number of American Indians and Alaska Natives (AIAN) and figures for each group separately and for some of the larger American Indian tribes.

The task of determining the size of the group also is complicated by the way the census collects information on race. As you recall, beginning with the 2000 census, people were allowed to claim membership in more than one racial category. If we define "American Indians" as consisting of people who identify themselves only as American Indian, we will get one estimate of the size of the group. If we use a broader definition and include people who claim mixed racial ancestry, our estimate of group size will be much larger.

At any rate, Exhibit 6.1 shows that there were about 4.3 million people who claimed at least some American Indian or Alaska Native ancestry but only about 2.4 million if we confine the group to people who select one race only. By either count, the group is a tiny minority (about 1%) of the total population of the United States. Exhibit 6.1 also presents information for American Indians and Alaska Natives separately and for the 10 largest tribal groupings.

Exhibit 6.1 American Indians and Alaska Natives (AIAN), 2007

	Alone (one race)	Alone or in Combination (two or more races)
TOTAL AIAN	2,374,222	4,333,179
American Indian	1,951,772	3,390,281
Ten Largest Tribal Groupings:		
Cherokee	298,510	965,593
Navajo	288,682	333,397
Choctaw	85,871	189,902
Sioux	116,634	181,745
Chippewa	108,880	166,854
Apache	65,940	125,779
Pueblo	72,275	88,313
Iroquois	45,088	87,909
Creek	38,781	77,532
Lumbee	62,421	71,462
Alaska Native	109,050	148,799

	Alone (one race)	Alone or in Combination (two or more races)
Tribal Groupings (based on 2000 census only):		
Eskimo	47,239	56,824
Tlingit-Haida	15,212	22,786
Alaska Athabascan	14,700	18,874
Aleut	12,069	17,551

SOURCES: U.S. Bureau of the Census (2007); Ogunwole, 2006, p. 2.

American Indians have been growing rapidly over the past several decades, but this fact needs to be seen in the full context of American Indian history. As I mentioned in Chapter 3, in 1492, there were at least 1 million American Indians, perhaps many more, living in what is now the continental ("lower 48") United States (Snipp, 1992, p. 354). Losses suffered during the contact period reduced the population to fewer than 250,000 by 1900, a loss of at least 75%. Recent population growth perhaps has restored the group to its pre-Columbian size.

As displayed in Exhibit 6.2, growth was slow in the early decades of the 20th century but much more rapid in recent decades. The more recent growth is a result of, in part, higher birthrates. Mainly, however, the growth is a result of changing

Exhibit 6.2 Population of American Indians, 1900–2007

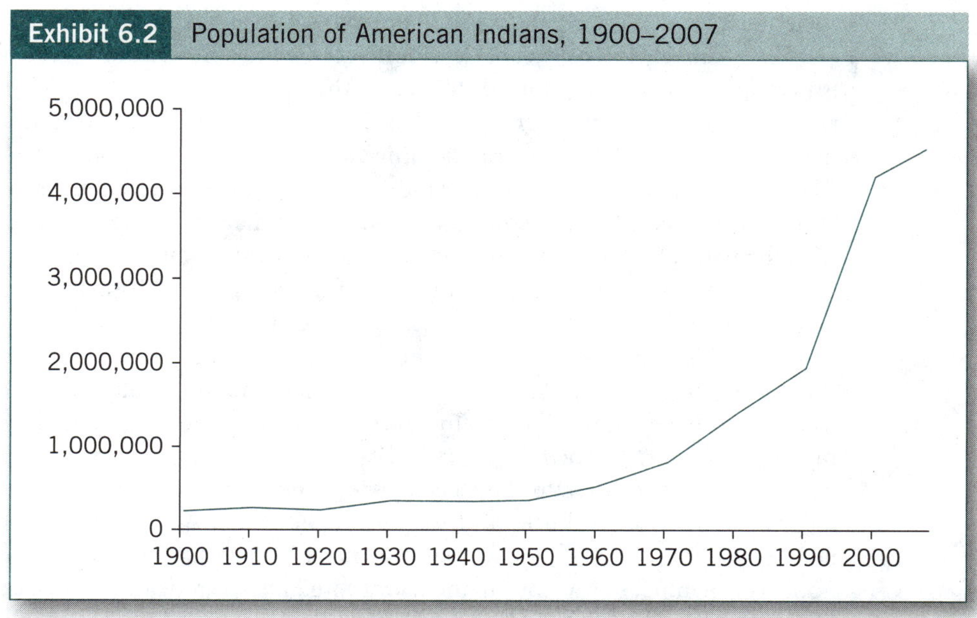

SOURCES: 1900–1990, Thornton (2001, p. 142). 2000–2007, U.S. Bureau of the Census (2009b, p. 9).

definitions of race in the larger society and a much greater willingness of people to claim Indian ancestry, a pattern that again underscores the basically social nature of race (Thornton, 2001).

American Indian Cultures

The dynamics of American Indian and Anglo-American relationships have been shaped by the vast differences in culture, values, and norms between the two groups. These differences have hampered communication in the past and continue to do so in the present. A comprehensive analysis of American Indian cultures is well beyond the scope of this text, but the past experiences and present goals of the group can be appreciated only with some understanding of their views of the world.

We must note here, as we did in Chapter 3, that there were (and are) hundreds of different tribes in what is now the United States, each with its own language and heritage, and that a complete analysis of American Indian culture would have to take this diversity into account. However, some patterns and cultural characteristics are widely shared across the tribes, and we will concentrate on these similarities.

Before exploring the content of their culture, we should note that most Native American tribes that existed in what is now the United States relied on hunting and gathering to satisfy their basic needs, although some cultivated gardens as well. This is important because, as noted by Lenski (2005; see Chapter 1), societies are profoundly shaped by their subsistence technology.

Hunting-and-gathering societies often live on the thin edge of hunger and want. They survive by stressing cultural values such as sharing and cooperation and by maintaining strong bonds of cohesion and solidarity. As you will see, American Indian societies are no exception to this fundamental survival strategy.

The relatively lower level of development of Native Americans is reflected in what is perhaps their most obvious difference with Western cultures: their ideas about the relationship between human beings and the natural world. In the traditional view of many American Indian cultures, the universe is a unity. Humans are simply a part of a larger reality, no different from or more important than other animals, plants, trees, and the earth itself. The goal of many American Indian tribes was to live in harmony with the natural world, not "improve" it or use it for their own selfish purposes, views that differ sharply from Western concepts of development, commercial farming, and bending the natural world to the service of humans. The gap between the two worldviews is evident in the reaction of one American Indian to the idea that his people should become farmers: "You ask me to plow the ground. . . . Shall I take a knife and tear my mother's bosom? You ask me to cut grass and make hay . . . but how dare I cut my mother's hair?" (Brown, 1970, p. 273).

The concept of private property, or the ownership of things, was not prominent in American Indian cultures and was, from the Anglo-American perspective, most notably absent in conceptions of land ownership. The land simply existed, and the notion of owning, selling, or buying it was foreign to American Indians. In the words of Tecumseh, a chief of the Shawnee, a man could no more sell the land than the "sea or the air he breathed" (Josephy, 1968, p. 283).

As is typical at the hunting-and-gathering level of development, American Indian cultures and societies also tended to be more oriented toward groups (e.g., the extended family, clan, or tribe) than toward individuals. The interests of the self were subordinated to those of the group, and child-rearing practices strongly encouraged group loyalty (Parke & Buriel, 2002). Cooperative, group activities were stressed over those of a competitive, individualistic nature. The bond to the group was (and is) so strong that "students go hungry rather than ask their parents for lunch money, for in asking they would be putting their needs in front of the group's needs" (Locust, 1990, p. 231).

Many American Indian tribes were organized around egalitarian values that stressed the dignity and worth of every man, woman, and child. Virtually all tribes had a division of labor based on gender, but women's work was valued, and they often occupied far more important positions in tribal society than was typical for women in Anglo-American society. In many of the American Indian societies that practiced gardening, women controlled the land. In other tribes, women wielded considerable power and held the most important political and religious offices. Among the Iroquois, for example, a council of older women appointed the chief of the tribe and made decisions about when to wage war (Amott & Matthaei, 1991).

These differences in values, compounded by the power differentials that emerged, often placed American Indians at a disadvantage when dealing with the dominant group. The American Indian conception of land ownership and their lack of experience with deeds, titles, contracts, and other Western legal concepts often made it difficult for them to defend their resources from Anglo-Americans. At other times, cultural differences led to disruptions of traditional practices, further weakening American Indian societies. For example, Christian missionaries and government representatives tried to reverse the traditional American Indian division of labor, in which women were responsible for the gardening. In the Western view, only males did farmwork. Also, the military and political representatives of the dominant society usually ignored female tribal leaders and imposed Western notions of patriarchy and male leadership on the tribes (Amott & Matthaei, 1991).

Relations With the Federal Government After the 1890s

By the end of the Indian Wars in 1890, Americans Indians had few resources with which to defend their self-interests. In addition to being confined to the reservations, the group was scattered throughout the western two thirds of the United States and split by cultural and linguistic differences. Politically, the power of the group was further limited by the facts that the huge majority of American Indians were not U.S. citizens and that most tribes lacked a cultural basis for understanding representative democracy as practiced in the larger society.

Economically, American Indians were among the most impoverished groups in the society. Reservation lands were generally of poor quality, traditional food sources such as buffalo and other game had been destroyed, and traditional hunting grounds and gardening plots had been lost to white farmers and ranchers. The tribes had few means of satisfying even their most basic needs. Many became totally dependent on the federal government for food, shelter, clothing, and other necessities.

Prospects for improvement seemed slim. Most reservations were in remote areas, far from sites of industrialization and modernization, and American Indians had few of the skills (knowledge of English, familiarity with Western work habits and routines) that would have enabled them to compete for a place in the increasingly urban and industrial American society of the early 20th century. Off the reservations, racial prejudice and strong intolerance limited them. On the reservations, they were subjected to policies designed either to maintain their powerlessness and poverty or to force them to Americanize. Either way, the future of American Indians was in serious jeopardy, and their destructive relations with white society continued in peace as they had in war.

Reservation Life

As would be expected for a conquered and still hostile group, the reservations were intended to closely supervise American Indians and maintain their powerlessness. Relationships with the federal government were paternalistic and featured a variety of policies designed to coercively acculturate the tribes.

Paternalism and the Bureau of Indian Affairs

The reservations were run not by the tribes but by an agency of the federal government: the U.S. **Bureau of Indian Affairs (BIA)** of the U.S. Department of the Interior. The BIA and its local superintendent controlled virtually all aspects of everyday life, including the reservation budget, the criminal justice system, and the schools. The BIA (again, not the tribes) even determined tribal membership.

The traditional leadership structures and political institutions of the tribes were ignored as the BIA executed its duties with little regard for, and virtually no input from, the people it supervised. The BIA superintendent of the reservations "ordinarily became the most powerful influence on local Indian affairs, even though he was a government employee, not responsible to the Indians but to his superiors in Washington" (Spicer, 1980, p. 117). The superintendent controlled the food supply and communications to the world outside the reservation. This control was used to reward tribal members who cooperated and to punish those who did not.

Coercive Acculturation: The Dawes Act and Boarding Schools

Consistent with the Blauner hypothesis, American Indians on the reservations were subjected to coercive acculturation or forced Americanization. Their culture was attacked, their languages and religions were forbidden, and their institutions were circumvented and undermined. The centerpiece of U.S. Indian policy was the Dawes Allotment Act of 1887, a deeply flawed attempt to impose white definitions of land ownership and to transform American Indians into independent farmers by dividing their land among the families of each tribe. The intention of the act was to give each Indian family the means to survive like their white neighbors.

Although the law might seem benevolent in intent (certainly thousands of immigrant families would have been thrilled to own land), it was flawed by a gross lack of understanding of American Indian cultures and needs, and in many ways, it was a direct attack on those cultures. Most American Indian tribes did not have a strong agrarian tradition, and little or nothing was done to prepare the tribes for their transition to peasant yeomanry. More important, American Indians had little or no concept of land as private property, and it was relatively easy for settlers, land speculators, and others to separate Indian families from the land allocated to them by this legislation. By allotting land to families and individuals, the legislation sought to destroy the broader kinship, clan, and tribal social structures and replace them with Western systems that featured individualism and the profit motive (Cornell, 1988).

About 140 million acres were allocated to the tribes in 1887. By the 1930s, nearly 90 million of those acres—almost 65%—had been lost. Most of the remaining land was desert or otherwise nonproductive (Wax, 1971, p. 55). From the standpoint of the Indian Nations, the Dawes Allotment Act was a disaster and a further erosion of their already paltry store of resources (for more details, see Josephy, 1968; Lurie, 1982; McNickle, 1973; Wax, 1971).

Coercive acculturation also operated through a variety of other avenues. Whenever possible, the BIA sent American Indian children to boarding schools, sometimes hundreds of miles away from parents and kin, where they were required to speak English, convert to Christianity, and become educated in the ways of Western civilization. Consistent with the Blauner (1972) hypothesis, tribal languages, dress, and religion were forbidden, and to the extent that native cultures were mentioned at all, they were attacked and ridiculed. Children of different tribes were mixed together as roommates to speed the acquisition of English. When school was not in session, children were often boarded with local white families, usually as unpaid domestic helpers or farmhands, and prevented from visiting their families and revitalizing their tribal ties (Hoxie, 1984; Spicer, 1980; Wax, 1971).

American Indians were virtually powerless to change the reservation system or avoid the campaign of acculturation. Nonetheless, they resented and resisted coerced Americanization, and many languages and cultural elements survived the early reservation period, although often in altered form. For example, the traditional tribal religions remained vital through the period despite the fact that by the 1930s, the great majority of Indians had affiliated with one Christian faith or another. Furthermore, many new religions were founded, some combining Christian and traditional elements (Spicer, 1980).

The Indian Reorganization Act

By the 1930s, the failure of the reservation system and the policy of forced assimilation had become obvious to all who cared to observe. The quality of life for American Indians had not improved, and there was little economic development and fewer job opportunities on the reservations. Health care was woefully inadequate, and education levels lagged far behind national standards.

The plight of American Indians eventually found a sympathetic ear in the administration of Franklin D. Roosevelt, who was elected president in 1932, and John Collier, the man he appointed to run the BIA. Collier was knowledgeable about American Indian issues and concerns and was instrumental in securing the passage of the **Indian Reorganization Act (IRA)** in 1934.

This landmark legislation contained a number of significant provisions for American Indians and broke sharply with the federal policies of the past. In particular, the IRA rescinded the Dawes Act of 1887 and the policy of individualizing tribal lands. It also provided means by which the tribes could expand their landholdings. Many of the mechanisms of coercive Americanization in the school system and elsewhere were dismantled. Financial aid in various forms and expertise were made available for the economic development of the reservations. In perhaps the most significant departure from earlier policy, the IRA proposed an increase in American Indian self-governance and a reduction of the paternalistic role of the BIA and other federal agencies.

Although sympathetic to American Indians, the IRA had its limits and shortcomings. Many of its intentions were never realized, and the empowerment of the tribes was not unqualified. The move to self-governance generally took place on the dominant group's terms and in conformity with the values and practices of white society. For example, the proposed increase in the decision-making power of the tribes was contingent on their adoption of Anglo-American political forms, including secret ballots, majority rule, and written constitutions. These were alien concepts to those tribes that selected leaders by procedures other than popular election (e.g., leaders might be chosen by councils of elders) or that made decisions by open discussion and consensus building (i.e., decisions required the agreement of everyone with a voice in the process, not a simple majority). The incorporation of these Western forms illustrates the basically assimilationist intent of the IRA.

The IRA had variable effects on American Indian women. In tribes that were male dominated, the IRA gave women new rights to participate in elections, run for office, and hold leadership roles. In other cases, new political structures replaced traditional forms, some of which, as in the Iroquois culture, had accorded women considerable power. Although the political effects were variable, the programs funded by the IRA provided opportunities for women on many reservations to receive education and training for the first time. Many of these opportunities were oriented toward domestic tasks and other traditionally Western female roles, but some prepared American Indian women for jobs outside the family and off the reservation, such as clerical work and nursing (Evans, 1989).

In summary, the Indian Reorganization Act of 1934 was a significant improvement over prior federal Indian policy but was bolder and more sympathetic to American Indians in intent than in execution. On the one hand, not all tribes were capable of taking advantage of the opportunities provided by the legislation, and some ended up being further victimized. For example, in the Hopi tribe, located in the Southwest, the act allowed a Westernized faction of the tribe to be elected to leadership roles, with the result that dominant-group firms were allowed to have access to the mineral resources, farmland, and water rights controlled by the tribe. The resultant development generated wealth for the white firms and their Hopi allies, but most of the tribe continued to languish in poverty (Churchill, 1985). On the other hand, some tribes prospered (at least comparatively speaking) under the IRA. One impoverished, landless group of Cherokee in Oklahoma acquired land, equipment, and expert advice through the IRA, and between 1937 and 1949, they developed a prosperous, largely debt-free farming community (Debo, 1970, pp. 294–300). Many tribes remained suspicious of the IRA, and by 1948, fewer than 100 tribes had voted to accept its provisions.

Termination and Relocation

The IRA's stress on the legitimacy of tribal identity seemed "un-American" to many. There was constant pressure on the federal government to return to an individualistic policy that encouraged (or required) Americanization. Some viewed the tribal structures and communal-property-holding patterns as relics of an earlier era and as impediments to modernization and development. Not so incidentally, some elements of dominant society still coveted the remaining Indian lands and resources, which could be more easily exploited if property ownership were individualized.

In 1953, the assimilationist forces won a victory when Congress passed a resolution calling for an end to the reservation system and to the special relationships between the tribes and the federal government. The proposed policy, called termination, was intended to get the federal government "out of the Indian business." It rejected the IRA and proposed a return to the system of private land ownership imposed on the tribes by the Dawes Act. Horrified at the notion of termination, the tribes opposed the policy strongly and vociferously. Under this policy, all special relationships—including treaty obligations—between the federal government and the tribes would end. Tribes would no longer exist as legally recognized entities, and tribal lands and other resources would be placed in private hands (Josephy, 1968).

About 100 tribes, most of them small, were terminated. In virtually all cases, the termination process was administered hastily, and fraud, misuse of funds, and other injustices were common. The Menominee of Wisconsin and the Klamath on the West Coast were the two largest tribes to be terminated. Both suffered devastating economic losses and precipitous declines in quality of life. Neither tribe had the business or tax base needed to finance the services (e.g., health care and schooling) formerly provided by the federal government, and both were forced to sell land, timber, and other scarce resources to maintain minimal standards of living. Many poor American Indian families were forced to turn to local and state agencies, which placed severe strain on welfare budgets. The experience of the Menominee was so disastrous that at the concerted request of the tribe, reservation status was restored in 1973 (Deloria, 1969; McNickle, 1973; Raymer, 1974). The Klamath reservation was restored in 1986 (Snipp, 1996).

At about the same time that the termination policy came into being, various programs were established to encourage American Indians to move to urban areas. The movement to the city had already begun in the 1940s, spurred by the availability of factory jobs during World War II. In the 1950s, the movement was further encouraged with programs of assistance and by the declining government support for economic development on the reservation, the most dramatic example of which was the policy of termination (Green, 1999). Centers for American Indians were established in many cities, and various services (e.g., job training, housing assistance, English instruction) were offered to assist in the adjustment to urban life. The urbanization of the American Indian population is displayed in Exhibit 6.3. Note the rapid increase in the movement to the city that began in the 1950s. Almost 60% of all American Indians are now urbanized, and since 1950, Indians have urbanized faster than the general population. Nevertheless, American Indians are still the least urbanized minority group. The population as a whole is about 80% urbanized; in contrast, African Americans (see Exhibit 4.2) are about 90% urbanized.

Exhibit 6.3 Urbanization of American Indians 1900–2000

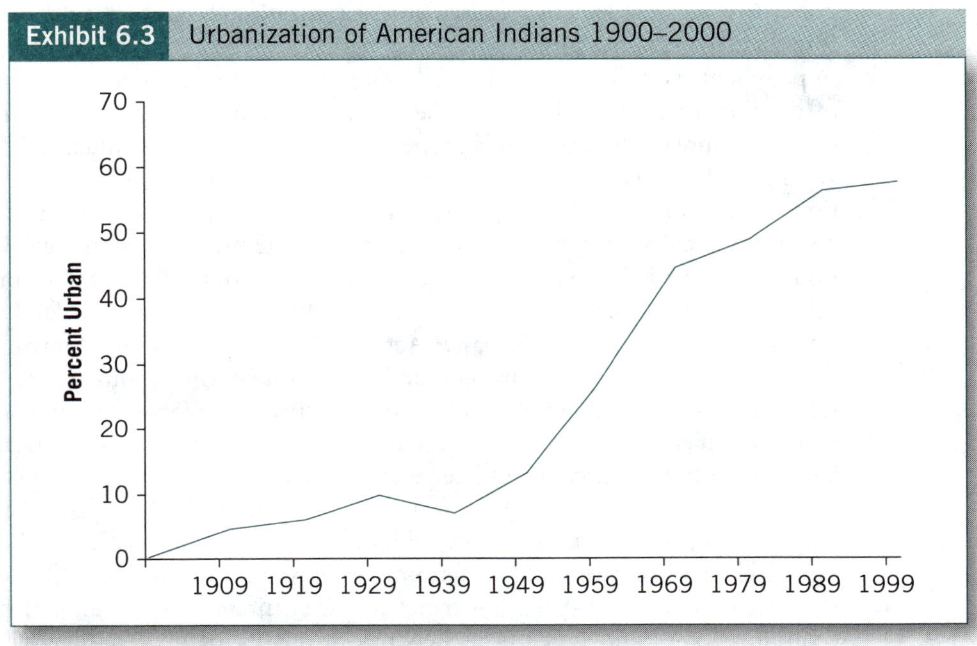

SOURCES: 1900–1990: Thornton (2001, p. 142). 2000: U.S. Bureau of the Census (2000a).

As with African Americans, American Indians arrived in the cities after the mainstream economy had begun to de-emphasize blue-collar or manufacturing jobs. Because of their relatively low average levels of educational attainment and their racial and cultural differences, American Indians in the city tended to encounter the same problems experienced by African Americans and other minority groups of color: high rates of unemployment, inadequate housing, and all of the other travails of the urban underclass.

American Indian women also migrated to the city in considerable numbers. The discrimination, unemployment, and poverty of the urban environment often made it difficult for the men of the group to fulfill the role of breadwinner; thus, the burden of supporting the family tended to fall on the women. The difficulties inherent in combining child rearing and a job outside the home are compounded by isolation from the support networks provided by extended family and clan back on the reservations. Nevertheless, one study found that American Indian women in the city continue to practice their traditional cultures and maintain the tribal identity of their children (Joe & Miller, 1994).

American Indians living in the city are, on the average, better off than those living on reservations, where unemployment can reach 80% or even 90%. The improvement is relative, however. Although many individual Indians prosper in the urban environment, income figures for urban Indians as a whole are comparable with those for African Americans and well below those for whites. American Indian unemployment rates run about twice the national average (Cornell, 1988). Thus, a move to the city often means trading rural poverty for the urban variety, with little net improvement in life chances.

American Indians will probably remain more rural than other minority groups for years to come. Despite the poverty and lack of opportunities for schooling and jobs, the reservation offers some advantages in services and lifestyle. On the reservation, there may be opportunities for political participation and leadership roles that are not available in the cities, where American Indians are a tiny minority. Reservations also offer kinfolk, friends, religious services, and tribal celebrations (Snipp, 1989). Lower levels of education, work experience, and financial resources combine with the prejudice, discrimination, and racism of the larger society to lower the chances of success in the city and will probably sustain a continuing return to the reservations.

Although the economic benefits of urbanization have been slim for the group as whole, other advantages have accrued from life in the city. It was much easier to establish networks of friendship and affiliation across tribal lines in the cities, and urban Indians have been one of the sources of strength and personnel for a movement of protest that began early in the 20th century. Virtually all of the organizational vehicles of American Indian protest have had urban roots.

Self-Determination

The termination policy aroused so much opposition from American Indians and was such an obvious disaster that the pressure to push tribes to termination faded in the late 1950s, although the act itself was not repealed until 1975. Since the 1960s, federal Indian policy has generally returned to the tradition set by the IRA. Termination and forced assimilation continue to be officially rejected, and within limits, the tribes have been granted more freedom to find their own way, at their own pace, of relating to the larger society.

Several federal programs and laws have benefited the tribes during the past few decades, including the antipoverty and "Great Society" campaigns launched in the 1960s. In 1970, President Richard Nixon affirmed the government's commitment to fulfilling treaty obligations and the right of the tribes to self-governance. The Indian Self-Determination and Education Assistance Act was passed in 1975. This legislation increased aid to reservation schools and American Indian students and increased tribal control over the administration of the reservations, from police forces to schools to road maintenance.

The Self-Determination Act primarily benefited the larger tribes and those that had well-established administrative and governing structures. Smaller and less well-organized tribes have continued to rely heavily on the federal government (Snipp, 1996). Nonetheless, in many cases, this new phase of federal policy has allowed

American Indian tribes to plot their own courses free of paternalistic regulation, and just as important, it gave them the tools and resources to address their problems and improve their situations. Decision making was returned to local authorities, who were "held more accountable to local needs, conditions, and cultures than outsiders" (Taylor & Kalt, 2006, p. xi).

In the view of many, self-determination is a key reason for the recent improvements in the status of American Indians, and we will look at some of these developments after examining the American Indian protest movement.

Protest and Resistance

Early Efforts

As BIA-administered reservations and coercive Americanization came to dominate tribal life in the 20th century, new forms of Indian activism appeared. The modern protest movement was tiny at first and, with few exceptions, achieved a measure of success only in recent decades. In fact, the American Indian protest movement in the past was not so much unsuccessful as simply ignored. The movement has focused on several complementary goals: protecting American Indian resources and treaty rights, striking a balance between assimilation and pluralism, and finding a relationship with the dominant group that would permit a broader array of life chances without sacrificing tribal identity and heritage.

Formally organized, American Indian protest organizations have existed since the 1910s, but the modern phase of the protest movement began during World War II. Many American Indians served in the military or moved to the city to take jobs in aid of the war effort and were thereby exposed to the world beyond the reservation. Also, political activism on the reservation, which had been stimulated by the IRA, continued through the war years, and the recognition that many problems were shared across tribal lines grew.

These trends helped to stimulate the founding of the National Congress of American Indians (NCAI) in 1944. This organization was pantribal (i.e., included members from many different tribes); its first convention was attended by representatives of 50 different tribes and reservations (Cornell, 1988). The leadership consisted largely of American Indians educated and experienced in the white world. However, the NCAI's program stressed the importance of preserving the old ways and tribal institutions as well as protecting Indian welfare. An early victory for the NCAI and its allies came in 1946 when an Indian Claims Commission was created by the federal government. This body was authorized to hear claims brought by the tribes with regard to treaty violations. The commission has settled hundreds of claims, resulting in awards of millions of dollars to the tribes, and it continues its work today (Weeks, 1988).

In the 1950s and 1960s, the protest movement was further stimulated by the threat of termination and by the increasing number of American Indians living in the cities who developed friendships across tribal lines. Awareness of common problems, rising levels of education, and the examples set by the successful protests of other minority groups also increased readiness for collective action.

Red Power

By the 1960s and 1970s, American Indian protest groups were finding ways to express their grievances and problems to the nation. The Red Power movement, like the Black Power movement (see Chapter 5), encompassed a coalition of groups, many considerably more assertive than the NCAI, and a varied collection of ideas, most of which stressed self-determination and pride in race and cultural heritage. Red Power protests included a "fish-in" in the state of Washington in 1965, an episode that also illustrates the nature of American Indian demands. Washington had tried to limit the fishing rights of several different tribes on the grounds that the supply of fish was diminishing and needed to be protected. The tribes depended on fishing for subsistence and survival and argued that their right to fish had been guaranteed by treaties signed in the 1850s and that it was the pollution and commercial fishing of the dominant society that had depleted the supply of fish. They organized a "fish-in" in violation of the state's policy and were met by a contingent of police officers and other law officials. Violent confrontations and mass arrests ensued. Three years later, after a lengthy and expensive court battle, the tribes were vindicated, and the U.S. Supreme Court confirmed their treaty rights to fish the rivers of Washington State (Nabakov, 1999).

Another widely publicized episode took place in 1969, when American Indians from various tribes occupied Alcatraz Island in San Francisco Bay, the site of a closed federal prison. The protesters were acting on an old law that granted American Indians the right to reclaim abandoned federal land. The occupation of Alcatraz was organized in part by the American Indian Movement (AIM), founded in 1968. More militant and radical than the previously established protest groups, AIM aggressively confronted the BIA, the police, and other forces that were seen as repressive. With the backing of AIM and other groups, Alcatraz was occupied for nearly four years and generated a great deal of publicity for the Red Power movement and the plight of American Indians.

In 1972, AIM helped to organize a march on Washington, D.C., called the "Trail of Broken Treaties." Marchers came from many tribes and represented both urban and reservation Indians. The intent of the marchers was to dramatize the problems of the tribes. The leaders demanded the abolition of the BIA, the return of illegally taken land, and increased self-governance for the tribes, among other things. When they reached Washington, some of the marchers forcibly occupied the BIA offices. Property was damaged (by which side is disputed), and records and papers were destroyed. The marchers eventually surrendered, but none of their demands were met. The following year, AIM occupied the village of Wounded Knee in South Dakota to protest the violation of treaty rights. Wounded Knee was the site of the last armed confrontation between Indians and whites in 1890 and was selected by AIM for its deep symbolic significance. The occupation lasted more than two months and involved several armed confrontations with federal authorities, one of which resulted in the arrest of Leonard Peltier whose memoir opened this chapter. Again, the protest ended without achieving any of the demands made by the Indian leadership (Olson & Wilson, 1984). Since the early 1970s, the level of protest activity has declined, just as it has for the African American protest movement. Lawsuits and court cases have predominated over dramatic, direct confrontations.

Ironically, the struggle for Red Power encouraged assimilation as well as pluralism. The movement linked members of different tribes and forced Indians of diverse heritages to find common ground, often in the form of a "generic" American Indian culture. Inevitably, the protests were conducted in English, and the grievances were expressed in ways that were understandable to white society, thus increasing the pressure to acculturate even while arguing for the survival of the tribes. Furthermore, successful protest required that American Indians be fluent in English, trained in the law and other professions, skilled in dealing with bureaucracies, and knowledgeable about the formulation and execution of public policy. American Indians who became proficient in these areas thereby took on the characteristics of their adversaries (Hraba, 1979).

As the pantribal protest movement forged ties between members of diverse tribes, the successes of the movement and changing federal policy and public opinion encouraged a rebirth of commitment to tribalism and "Indianness." American Indians were simultaneously stimulated to assimilate (by stressing their common characteristics and creating organizational forms that united the tribes) and to retain a pluralistic relationship with the larger society (by working for self-determination and enhanced tribal power and authority). Thus, part of the significance of the Red Power movement was that it encouraged both pantribal unity and a continuation of tribal diversity (Olson & Wilson, 1984). Today, American Indians continue to seek a way of existing in the larger society that merges assimilation with pluralism.

Exhibit 6.4 summarizes this discussion of federal policy and Indian protest. The four major policy phases since the end of overt hostilities in 1890 are listed on the left. The thrust of the government's economic and political policies are listed in the next two columns, followed by a brief characterization of tribal response. The last column shows the changing bases for federal policy, sometimes aimed at weakening tribal tribes and individualizing American Indians and sometimes (including most recently) aimed at working with and preserving tribal structures.

Exhibit 6.4 Federal Indian Policy and Indian Response

Period	Economic Impact	Political Impact	Indian Response	Government Approach
Reservation. Late 1800s–1930s	Land loss (Dawes Act) & Welfare Dependency	Government control of reservation and coerced acculturation	Some resistance, growth of religious movements	Individualistic, creation of self-sufficient farmers
Reorganization (IRA). 1930s and 1940s	Stabilize land base and support some development of reservation	Establish federally sponsored tribal governments	Increased political participation in many tribes. Some pantribal activity	Incorporate tribes as groups, creation of self-sufficient "Americanized" communities

Period	Economic Impact	Political Impact	Indian Response	Government Approach
Termination and Relocation. Late 1940s–early 1960s	Withdrawal of government support for reservations, promotion of urbanization	New assault on tribes, new forms of coercive acculturation	Increased pantribalism, widespread and intense opposition to termination	Individualistic, dissolve tribal ties and promote incorporation into the modern, urban labor market
Self-determination 1960s–present	Develop reservation economies, increased integration of Indian labor force	Support for tribal governments	Greatly increased political activity	Incorporate tribes as self-sufficient communities with access to federal programs of support and welfare

SOURCE: Based on Cornell, Kalt, Krepps, & Taylor (1998, p. 5). Copyright © July 31, 1998. Reprinted with permission.

FOCUS ON CONTEMPORARY ISSUES: Were American Indians the Victims of Genocide?

I pointed out at the start of this chapter that, by 1900, American Indians had lost at least 75% of their population base and numbered fewer than 250,000 people. Behind these sterile numbers lie devastating losses of land and lives and untold agony for millions of people. No one seriously questions the extent of the suffering experienced by American Indians (or that they inflicted suffering against whites as well) and graphic, detailed accounts of death by starvation, disease, and military action are widely available in popular culture as well as in scholarly works. There also can be no question that atrocities and massacres were committed by both sides and that the 300-year contact period between whites and Indians was relentlessly bloody and horribly cruel.

A question that is still debated, however, is whether these events should be considered genocide: a deliberate attempt to destroy American Indians and their culture. Did the dominant group and the U.S. government pursue an intentional policy of extermination or was the population loss simply a sad, unavoidable result of a clash of civilizations?

(Continued)

(Continued)

Issues like genocide—quite rightly—can evoke intense emotion, and the term "genocide" is often used somewhat metaphorically to stress the enormity of the losses suffered by American Indians and the racist policies of the dominant group. Thus, we should begin our consideration of the issue by defining what is meant by the term that is our focus. Genocide is an internationally recognized crime which consists of acts "committed with the intent to destroy, in whole or in part, a national, ethnic, racial, or religious group" (Office of the United Nations High Commissioner for Human Rights, n.d.).

Genocide includes actions other than outright killing: inflicting serious bodily or mental harm or creating conditions of life designed to cause the destruction of the group are also included within the definition of the crime.

Some of our core concepts are applicable to this discussion. Genocide almost always involves a dominant-minority group situation, and the victimized group is regarded with contempt, racism, and extreme prejudice. The prejudice is so intense, in fact, that the victimized group is seen as subhuman, and killing them is not regarded as "murder." Also, power, one of the concepts in the Noel Hypothesis, is a key element in genocide; the dominant group must have sufficient power resources to attempt the mass extermination of the minority group.

Before addressing American Indians, let's briefly consider some well-known historical examples of genocide to provide some comparison and context. Unfortunately, there are many instances to draw from, including attacks against Armenians by Turks a century ago, "ethnic cleansing" in the former Yugoslavia in the 1980s and 1990s, and ongoing conflicts in the Darfur region of Sudan.

The most infamous example of genocide was the effort of German Nazis to exterminate Jews, Slavs, Gypsies, and other "inferior" groups. The Nazi mass murders began in the 1930s and ended only at the conclusion of World War II. Millions of people, including 6 million Jews, were systematically slaughtered in the Nazi death camps, and the Jewish population of Europe was very nearly wiped out. This massive, highly bureaucratized and rationally organized genocide was motivated and "justified" by deep racism and anti-Semitism. Nazi ideology demonized Jews and pictured them as a separate, lower, contemptible race that had to be destroyed for the good of all "proper" Germans and for the health for the Third Reich.

A more recent episode of genocide occurred in the tiny African nation of Rwanda in the early 1990s. The two main Rwandan ethnic groups, Hutus and Tutsis, have a long history of mutual enmity that had been exacerbated by their German and Belgian colonial ruler's policy of "divide and conquer." The Hutus were allocated a privileged status in the colonial era and their greater power continued after Rwanda became independent in 1962. The sporadic clashes between the tribal groups blossomed into full-blown genocide in 1994, occasioned by a Tutsi-led rebellion and the death of the Hutu president of Rwanda in a plane crash that was thought to have been the result of sabotage and Tutsi treachery. Hutu factions had been preparing for an attack, and the plane crash became the precipitating event for the genocide. The slaughter that ensued resulted in the deaths of perhaps 800,000 Tutsis, perhaps many more. No one was spared—pregnant women, children, and old people—and much of the killing was done by neighbors and acquaintances with bare hands or machete. The killing was encouraged by Hutu-controlled radio, which characterized the Tutsi as "cockroaches" and hurled a variety of other epithets against them (see Gourevitch, 1999). Insults such as these express the prejudice and contempt of the dominant group but they also abet the slaughter by minimizing the humanity of the victimized group and maximizing their perceived lower status and "otherness."

How does the history of American Indians compare? First, note that international law specifies that acts of genocide must be intentional. The Nazis clearly and openly intended to carry out their "Final Solution" and exterminate the Jewish people and the Hutus that lead the Rwandan genocide meant to annihilate their Tutsi neighbors. What was the intent of whites with regard to Indians? To be classified as genocide, there must be an intention to exterminate the group as a whole (as opposed to killing enemy combatants in battle).

It is not difficult to find statements showing that some whites clearly wanted to eliminate American Indians. One famous incident can be used to illustrate. In 1864, troops under the command of Colonel John Chivington attacked a Cheyenne village near Sand Creek, Colorado, and killed several hundred Indians, most of them women, children, and old men. The incident is sometimes called the Battle of Sand Creek and sometimes the Massacre at Sand Creek, but what makes it a candidate for genocide is Chivington's motivation as revealed in the following quotations: "My intention is kill all Indians I come across," including babies and infants because "nits make lice" (Churchill, 1985, p. 229).

At the same time, however, it is not hard to find white expressions of sympathy for the plight of the Indians and outrage over incidents such as Sand Creek (Lewy, 2004). As many have noted, sympathy for American Indians in the 19th century tended to be most intense in the areas furthest removed from actual battle. Nevertheless, there is no reason to suspect their sincerity (although, as in the case of the Dawes Act, sympathy unalloyed by understanding of Indian culture could have harmful consequences). Although it is abundantly clear that some—perhaps many, perhaps most—whites wanted to exterminate all Indians, the sentiment was not universal or unanimous.

We also must take account of the reasons for the population loss. As I mentioned in Chapter 3, much of the population decline was caused by the diseases imported by European colonists, not by deliberate attacks like Hutus killing Tutsis or like the assembly lines of death created by the Nazis. Although there were a few instances of "biological warfare" in which Indians were deliberately infected with smallpox, the diseases simply took their toll unguided by intention or deliberate plan (Lewy, 2004, p. 56).

On the other hand, it can be argued that the intent to exterminate was implicit in the coercive, one-sided assimilation that was the centerpiece of policies such as the Dawes Act and institutions

(Continued)

(Continued)

such as the Indian schools. If these policies had succeeded, the American Indian way of life would have been destroyed, even though individual descendents of the tribes might have survived. Also, the deliberate attempts to destroy the Indian food base (e.g., by slaughtering buffalo herds on the Great Plains), to move Indian tribes from their homelands, and the poor support for reservations could be seen as attempts to create living conditions so desperate and impoverished that they would result in massive loss of life and the disappearance of the group. The intention to exterminate does not have to be overtly stated to be effective or to have that result.

We want to be careful in applying a term like genocide and not dilute its power. We also want to be clear about what actually happened to Indians and not minimize the horror or loss. Was this genocide? Certainly, it looks like genocide and various authors, scholars, and activists have made that case (see, for example, Churchill, 1997 and Stannard, 1992).

Others acknowledge the enormous suffering but argue that the case for genocide is weakened by the fact that most of the population loss was caused by the impersonal spread of disease, not direct violence or physical assaults (Lewy, 2004).

What would a jury decide? Did American Indians nearly disappear as a group? Yes. Was there intent to exterminate this group? Yes, at least many members of the dominant group. Did the U.S. government create conditions for the conquered tribes that were so desperate that they resulted—directly or indirectly—in widespread loss of life? Yes, in many instances and for many years. However, the story of American Indians doesn't feature the legal clarity of the state-sponsored, systematic slaughter of the Nazis or the bloody neighbor-to-neighbor violence of Hutus killing Tutsis. We may never know what an impartial jury would decide and we may have to leave the matter unresolved and the question unanswered. Most importantly, perhaps, we must recognize the strength of the arguments of both sides and clearly recognize that this sorrowful chapter of U.S. history does, at least in some ways, rise to the definition of genocide set by international law.

The Continuing Struggle for Development in Contemporary American Indian–White Relations

Conflicts between American Indians and the larger society are far from over. Although the days of deadly battle are (with occasional exceptions) long gone, the issues that remain are serious, difficult to resolve, and, in their way, just as much matters of life and death. American Indians face enormous challenges in their struggle to improve their status, but largely as a result of their greater freedom from stifling federal control since the 1970s, they also have some resources, some opportunities, and a leadership that is both talented and resourceful (Bordewich, 1996).

Natural Resources

Ironically, land allotted to American Indian tribes in the 19th century sometimes turned out to be rich in resources that became valuable in the 20th century. These resources include oil, natural gas, coal, and uranium, basic sources of energy in the larger society. In addition (and despite the devastation wreaked by the Dawes Act of 1887), some tribes hold title to water rights, fishing rights, woodlands that could sustain a lumbering industry, and wilderness areas that could be developed for camping, hunting, and other forms of recreation. These resources are likely to become more valuable as the earth's natural resources and undeveloped areas are further depleted in the future.

The challenge faced by American Indians is to retain control of these resources and to develop them for their own benefit. Threats to the remaining tribal lands and assets are common. Mining and energy companies continue to cast envious eyes on American Indian land, and other tribal assets are coveted by real estate developers, fishermen (recreational as well as commercial), backpackers and campers, and cities facing water shortages (Harjo, 1996).

Some tribes have succeeded in developing their resources for their own benefit, in part because of their increased autonomy and independence since the passage of the 1975 Indian Self-Determination Act. For example, the White Mountain Apaches of Arizona operate nine tribally owned enterprises, including a major ski resort, a logging operation and sawmill, and a small casino. These businesses are the primary economic engines of the local area, and unemployment on the White Mountain reservation is only a quarter of the national reservation average (Cornell & Kalt, 1998). On many other reservations, however, even rich stores of resources lie dormant, awaiting the right combination of tribal leadership, expertise, and development capital. The Crow tribe of Montana, for example, controls a huge supply of coal and has extensive timber, water, mineral, and other resources. Yet unemployment on the reservation runs 60%, and the tribe gets very little return on their wealth. "All those resources have not produced wealth. Nor have they produced a viable, working economy" (Cornell & Kalt, 1998, p. 5).

On a broader level, tribes are banding together to share expertise and negotiate more effectively with the larger society. For example, 25 tribes founded the Council of Energy Resource Tribes in 1975 to coordinate and control the development of the mineral resources on reservation lands. Since its founding, the council has successfully negotiated a number of agreements with dominant group firms, increasing the flow of income to the tribes and raising their quality of life (Cornell, 1988; Snipp, 1989).

Attracting Industry to the Reservation

Many efforts to develop the reservations have focused on creating jobs by attracting industry through such incentives as low taxes, low rents, and a low-wage pool of labor—not unlike the package of benefits offered to employers by less developed nations in Asia, South America, and Africa. With some notable exceptions, these efforts have not been particularly successful (for a review, see Cornell, 2006; Vinje, 1996). Reservations are often so geographically isolated that transportation costs become prohibitive. The jobs that have materialized are typically low wage and have few benefits; usually, non-Indians fill the more lucrative managerial positions. Thus, the opportunities for building economic power or improving the standard of living from these jobs are sharply limited. These new jobs may transform "the welfare poor into the working poor" (Snipp, 1996, p. 398), but their potential for raising economic vitality is low.

To illustrate the problems of developing reservations by attracting industry, consider the Navajo, the second-largest American Indian tribe. The Navajo reservation spreads across Arizona, New Mexico, and Utah and encompasses about 20 million acres, an area a little smaller than either Indiana or Maine. Although the reservation seems huge on a map, much of the land is desert not suitable for farming or other uses. As they have for the past several centuries, the Navajo today rely heavily on the cultivation of corn and sheepherding for sustenance.

Most wage-earning jobs on the reservation are with the agencies of the federal government (e.g., the BIA) or with the tribal government. Tourism is large and growing, but the jobs available in that sector are typically low wage and seasonal. There are reserves of coal, uranium, and oil on the reservation, but these resources have not generated many jobs. In some cases, the Navajo have resisted the damage to the environment that would be caused by mines and oil wells because of their traditional values and respect for the land. When exploitation of these resources has been permitted, the companies involved often use highly automated technologies that generate few jobs (Oswalt & Neely, 1996).

Exhibits 6.5 and 6.6 contrast Navajo income, poverty, and education with non-Hispanic whites and all American Indians. Median income for Navajo men is a third lower than income for non-Hispanic whites, and Navajo women earn almost $5,500 less than the men of their tribe and $9,000 less than non-Hispanic women. Thus, there is a sizable gender gap alongside the racial gap in incomes. The poverty rate for the Navajo is about 4.5 times greater than the rate for non-Hispanic whites, and the tribe is far below national standards in terms of education.

However, some tribes have managed to achieve relative prosperity by bringing jobs to their people. The Choctaw Nation of Mississippi, for example, has become one of the largest employers in the state. Tribal leaders have been able to attract companies such as Xerox and Harley-Davidson by promising (and delivering) high-quality labor for relatively low wages. Incomes have risen, unemployment is relatively low, and the tribe has built schools, hospitals, and a television station and administers numerous other services for its members (Bordewich, 1996). The median income for Choctaw men, although still only about 80% of the figure for non-Hispanic whites, is $7,000 greater than that of Navajo men, and Choctaw women also earn more, on the average, than Navajo women. The Choctaw poverty rate is about half that of the Navajo, and Choctaws almost match non-Hispanic whites in high school education.

Exhibit 6.5 Poverty and Education for Non-Hispanic Whites (NHW), All American Indians (AI), Navajo, and Choctaw

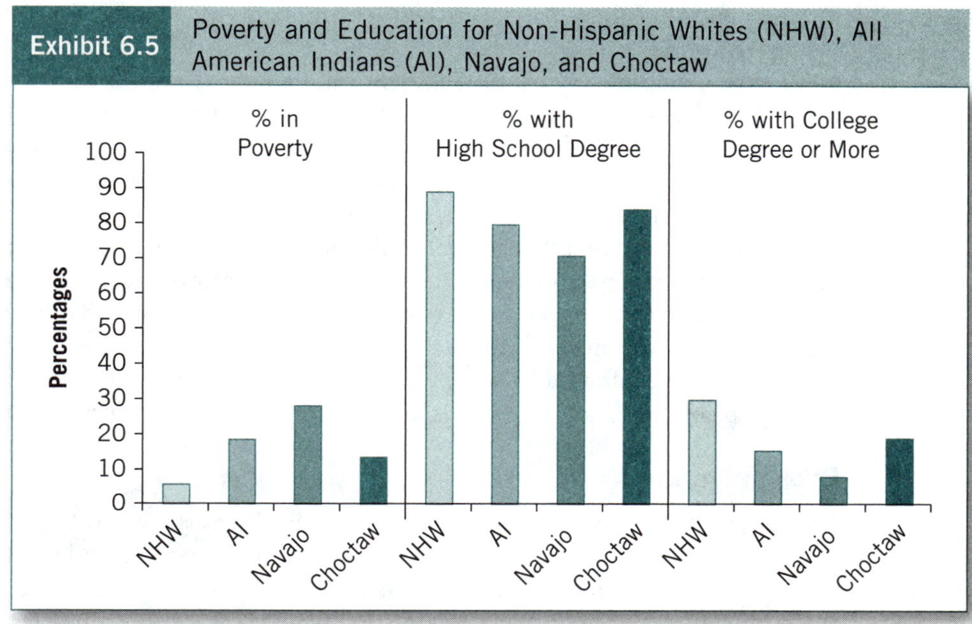

SOURCE: U.S. Bureau of the Census, 2005–2007 (2007).

Exhibit 6.6 Median Income from Full-Time, Year-Round Workers, Males and Females, 2007

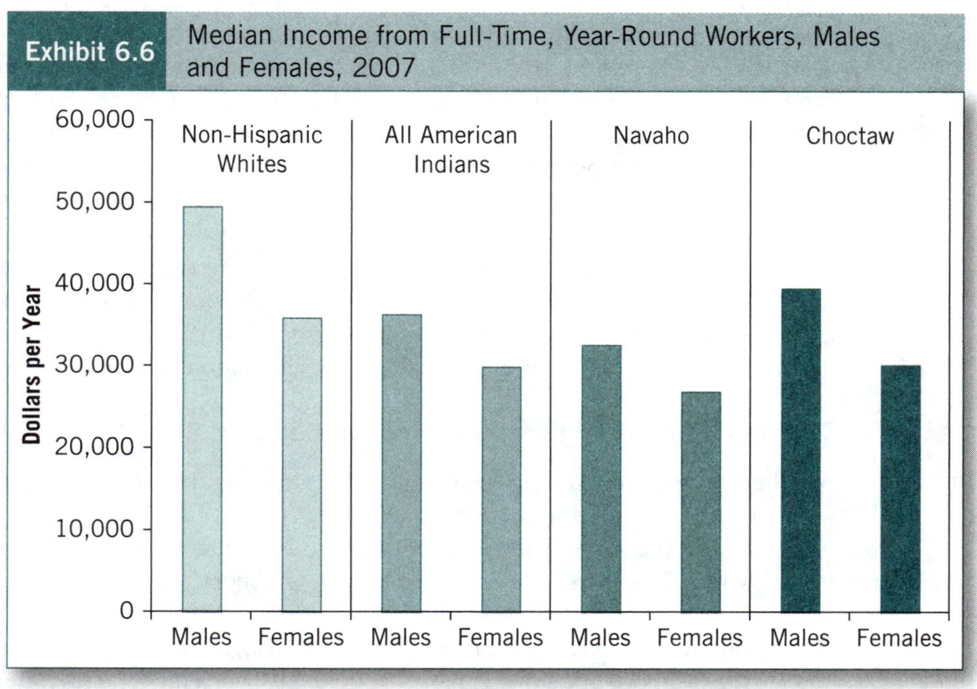

SOURCE: U.S. Bureau of the Census, 2005–2007 (2007).

Twenty percent of the Choctaw are college educated, more than twice the comparable figure for the Navajo.

The Choctaw are not the most affluent tribe, and the Navajo are not the most destitute. They illustrate the mixture of partial successes and failures that typify efforts to bring prosperity to the reservations; together, these two cases suggest that attracting industry and jobs to the reservations is a possible—but difficult and uncertain—strategy for economic development.

It is worth repeating that self-determination, the ability of tribes to control development on the reservation, seems to be one of the important keys to success. Tribes like the Choctaw are, in a sense, developing ethnic enclaves (see Chapter 2) in which they can capitalize on local networks of interpersonal relationships. As with other groups that have followed this strategy, success in the enclave depends on solidarity and group cohesion, not Americanization and integration (see Cornell, 2006).

Broken Treaties

For many tribes, the treaties signed with the federal government in the 19th century offer another potential resource. These treaties were often violated by white settlers, the military, state and local governments, the BIA, and other elements and agencies of the dominant group, and many tribes are pursuing this trail of broken treaties and seeking compensation for the wrongs of the past. For example, in 1972, the Passamaquoddy and Penobscot tribes filed a lawsuit demanding the return of 12.5 million acres of land—more than half the state of Maine—and $25 billion in damages. The tribes argued that this land had been illegally taken from them more than 150 years earlier. After eight years of litigation, the tribes settled for a $25 million trust fund and 300,000 acres of land. Although far less than their original demand, the award gave the tribes control over resources that could be used for economic development, job creation, upgrading educational programs, and developing other programs that would enhance human and financial capital (Worsnop, 1992).

Virtually every tribe has similar grievances, and if pursued successfully, the long-dead treaty relationship between the Indian nations and the government could be a significant fount of economic and political resources. Of course, lawsuits require considerable (and expensive) legal expertise and years of effort to bring to fruition. Because there are no guarantees of success, this avenue has some sharp limitations and risks.

Gaming and Other Development Possibilities

Another resource for American Indians is the gambling industry, the development of which was made possible by federal legislation passed in 1988. There are currently more than 400 gaming establishments on reservations (National Indian Gaming Commission, 2008) and the industry has grown more than 100 times over, from $212 million in revenues in 1988 (Spilde, 2001) to almost $27 billion in 2008. Exhibit 6.7 charts the growth of revenues from gaming on American Indian reservations from 1995 to 2008. To provide some context for these numbers, the total revenue from gambling in the entire state of Nevada—not just Las Vegas—in 2008 was about 12 billion (Stutz, 2009).

Exhibit 6.7 Revenues From Gaming at American Indian Casinos, 1995–2008

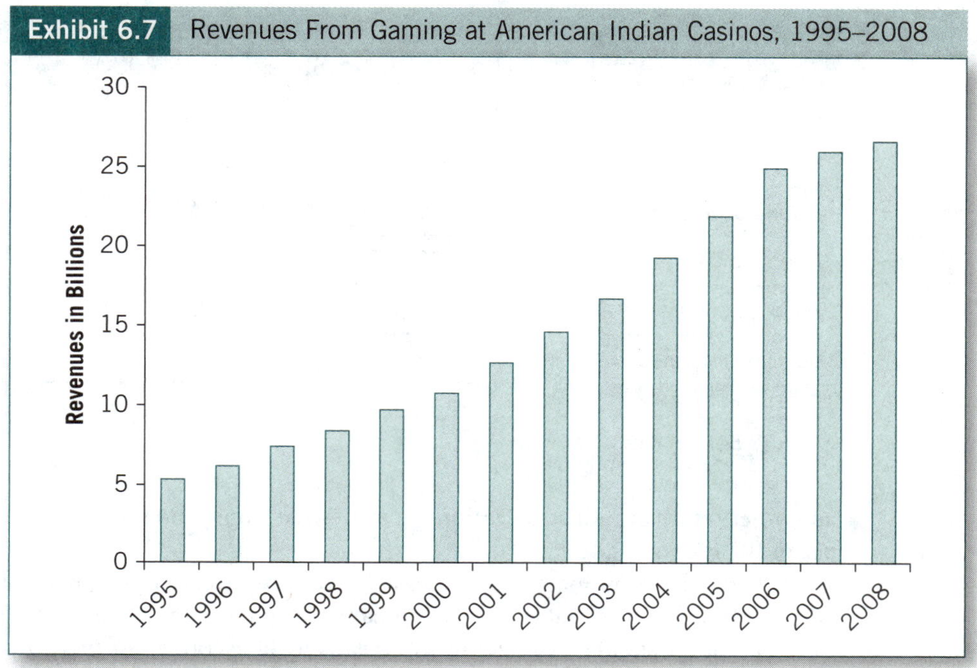

SOURCE: National Indian Gaming Commission (2009).

The single most profitable Indian gambling operation is the Foxwoods Casino in Connecticut, operated by the Pequot tribe. The casino is said to be the largest in the world and to generate more revenue than the casinos of Atlantic City. The profits from the casino are used to benefit tribal members in a variety of ways, including the repurchase of tribal lands, housing assistance, medical benefits, educational scholarships, and public services, such as a tribal police force (Bordewich, 1996). Other tribes have used gambling profits to purchase restaurants and marinas and to finance the development of outlet malls, manufacturing plants, and a wide variety of other businesses and enterprises (Spilde, 2001).

The power of gaming to benefit the tribes is suggested by the information displayed in Exhibit 6.8. The table shows that on a number of indicators, both gaming and nongaming reservations enjoyed significant improvements in their quality of life in the last decade of the 20th century, but that gaming reservations improved more rapidly. For example, all reservations increased their per capita income faster than the nation as a whole (+11%), but gaming reservations improved faster (+36%) than nongaming reservations (+21%).

Various tribes have sought other ways to capitalize on their freedom from state regulation and taxes. Some have established small but profitable businesses selling cigarettes tax-free. Also, because they are not subject to state and federal environmental regulations, some reservations are exploring the possibility of housing nuclear waste

Exhibit 6.8 Various Indicators of Improvement on Gaming vs. Nongaming Reservations and the United States, 1990–2000

Indicator	Nongaming	Gaming	U.S.
Per capita income	+21%	+36%	+11%
Family poverty	–7%	–12%	–1%
Unemployment	–2%	–5%	–1%
High school graduates	–1%	+2%	–1%
College graduates	+2%	+3%	+4%

SOURCE: Taylor & Kalt (2006, p. xi).

and other refuse of industrialization—a somewhat ironic and not altogether attractive use of the remaining Indian lands.

Clearly, the combination of increased autonomy, treaty rights, natural resources, and gambling means that American Indians today have an opportunity to dramatically raise their standards of living and creatively take control of their own destinies. Some tribes have enjoyed enormous benefits, but, for others, these assets remain a potential waiting to be actualized. Without denying the success stories or the improvements in recent years, the lives of many American Indians continue to be limited by poverty and powerlessness, prejudice, and discrimination. We document these patterns in the next section.

Contemporary American Indian–White Relations

This section uses many of the terms and concepts we have developed over the first five chapters to analyze the contemporary situation of American Indians. Compared with other groups, information about American Indians is scant. Nonetheless, a relatively clear picture emerges. The portrait stresses a mixed picture for this group: improvements for some tribes combined with continued colonization, marginalization, and impoverishment for others. American Indians as a group face continuing discrimination and exclusion and continue the search for a meaningful course between assimilation and pluralism.

Prejudice and Discrimination

Anti-Indian prejudice has been a part of American society from the beginning. Historically, negative feelings such as hatred and contempt have been widespread and strong, particularly during the heat of war, and various stereotypes of Indians have been common. One stereotype, especially strong during periods of conflict, depicts Indians as bloodthirsty, ferocious, cruel savages capable of any atrocity. The other image of American Indians is that of "the noble Red Man" who lives in complete harmony with nature and symbolizes goodwill and pristine simplicity (Bordewich, 1996, p. 34).

Although the first stereotype tended to fade away as hostilities drew to a close, the latter image retains a good deal of strength in modern views of Indians found in popular culture and among some environmentalist and "new age" spiritual organizations.

A variety of studies have documented continued stereotyping of Native Americans in the popular press, textbooks, the media, cartoons, and various other places (for example, see Aleiss, 2005; Bird, 1999; Rouse & Hanson, 1991).

In the tradition of "the noble Red Man," American Indians are often portrayed as bucks and squaws, complete with headdresses, bows, tepees, and other such "generic" Indian artifacts. These portrayals obliterate the diversity of American Indian culture and lifestyles. American Indians are often referred to in the past tense, as if their present situation were of no importance or, worse, as if they no longer existed. Many history books continue to begin the study of American history in Europe or with the "discovery" of America, omitting the millennia of civilization prior to the arrival of European explorers and colonizers. Contemporary portrayals of American Indians, such as in the movie *Dances With Wolves* (1990), are more sympathetic but still treat the tribes as part of a bucolic past forever lost, not as peoples with real problems in the present.

The persistence of stereotypes and the extent to which they have become enmeshed in modern culture is illustrated by continuing controversies surrounding nicknames for athletic teams (the Washington Redskins, the Cleveland Indians, and the Atlanta Braves) and the use of American Indian mascots, tomahawk "chops," and other practices offensive to many American Indians. Protests have been staged at some athletic events to increase awareness of these derogatory depictions, but as was the case so often in the past, the protests have been attacked, ridiculed, or simply ignored.

There are relatively few studies of anti-Indian prejudices in the social science literature, and it is therefore difficult to characterize changes over the past several decades. We do not know whether there has been a shift to more symbolic or "modern" forms of anti-Indian racism, as there has been for antiblack prejudice, or whether the stereotypes of American Indians have declined in strength or changed in content.

One of the few records of national anti-Indian prejudice over time is that of social distance scale results (see Exhibit 1.7). When the scales were first administered in 1926, American Indians were ranked in the middle third of all groups (18th out of 28), at about the same level as Southern and Eastern Europeans and slightly above Mexicans, another colonized group. The ranking of American Indians remained stable until 1977, when there was a noticeable rise in their position relative to other groups. In the most recent polls, the social distance scores of American Indians fell (indicating less prejudice), but the relative ranking still placed them with other racial minority groups. These shifts may reflect a decline in levels of prejudice, a change from more overt forms to more subtle modern racism, or both. Remember, however, that the samples for the social distance research were college students for the most part and do not necessarily reflect trends in the general population (see also Hanson & Rouse, 1987; Smith & Dempsey, 1983).

Research also is unclear about the severity or extent of discrimination against American Indians. Certainly, the group's lower average levels of education limit their opportunities for upward mobility, choice of occupations, and range of income. This is a form of institutional discrimination in the sense that the opportunities to develop human capital are much less available to American Indians than to much of the rest of the population. In terms of individual discrimination or more overt forms of exclusion, there is simply too little evidence to sustain clear conclusions (Snipp, 1992). The situation of American Indian women is also underresearched, but Snipp reports that, like their counterparts in other minority groups and the dominant group, they "are systematically paid less than their male counterparts in similar circumstances" (p. 363).

The very limited evidence available from social distance scales suggests that overt anti-Indian prejudice has declined, perhaps in parallel with antiblack prejudice. A great deal of stereotyping remains, however, and demeaning, condescending, or negative portrayals of American Indians are common throughout the dominant culture. Institutional discrimination is a major barrier for American Indians, who have not had access to opportunities for education and employment.

Assimilation and Pluralism

Acculturation

Despite more than a century of coercive Americanization, many tribes have been able to preserve much of their traditional cultures. For example, many tribal languages continue to be spoken on a daily basis. About 20% of all American Indians in the continental United States speak a language other than English at home, about the same percentage as the total population. Exhibit 6.9 suggests the extent of language acculturation. For 6 of the 10 largest tribes, less than 10% speak the tribal language at home. In some tribes, however, the picture is dramatically different. For example, most Navajo and Pueblo Indians speak the tribal language at home, and about 25% of Navajo and 18% of Pueblo speak English less than "very well" (Ogunwole, 2006, p. 7).

Exhibit 6.9 Percent of Total Population, All American Indians, and 10 Largest Tribes That Speak a Language Other Than English at Home, 2007

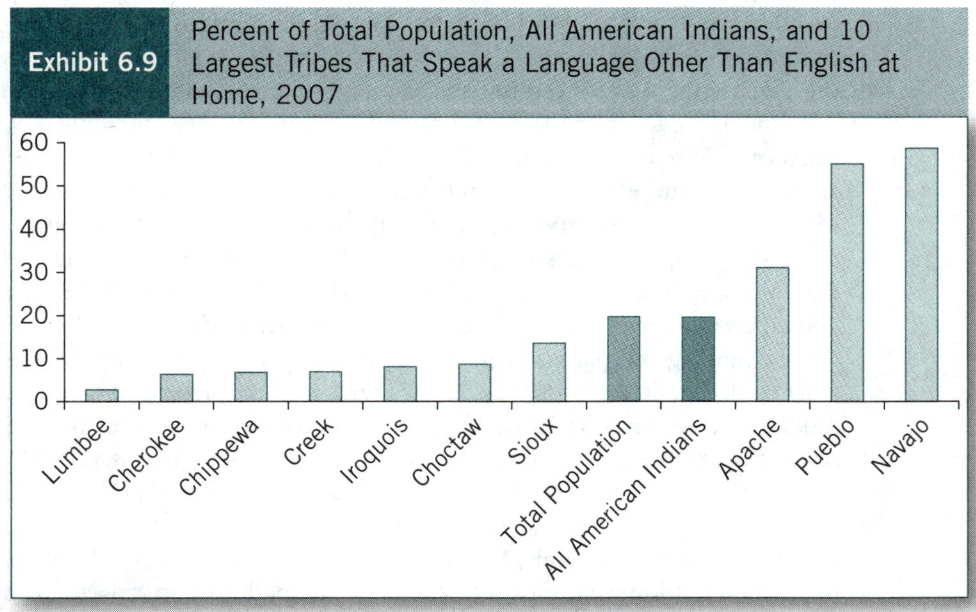

SOURCE: U.S. Bureau of the Census (2007).

Traditional culture is retained in other forms besides language. Religions and value systems, political and economic structures, cuisine, and recreational patterns have all survived the military conquest and the depredations of reservation life; each pattern has been altered, however, by contact with the dominant group. Cornell (1987), for example, argues that although American Indians have been affected by the "American dream" of material success through hard, honest work, their individual values continue to reflect their greater orientation to the group rather than to the individual.

The tendency to filter the impact of the larger society through continuing, vital American Indian culture also is illustrated by the Native American Church. The Native American Church is an important American Indian religion, with more than 100 congregations across the nation. This religion combines elements from both cultures, and church services freely mix Christian imagery and the Bible with attempts to seek personal visions by using peyote, a hallucinogenic drug. The latter practice is consistent with the spiritual and religious traditions of many tribes but clashes sharply with the laws and norms of the larger society. The difference in traditions has generated many skirmishes with the courts and, as recently as 2004, the right of the Native American Church to use peyote was upheld by the Supreme Court of Utah ("Utah Supreme Court," 2004).

American Indians have been considerably more successful than African Americans in preserving their traditional cultures. The differences in the relationship between each minority group and the dominant group help explain this pattern. African Americans were exploited for labor, whereas the competition with American Indians involved land. African cultures could not easily survive, because the social structures that transmitted the cultures and gave them meaning were destroyed by slavery and sacrificed to the exigencies of the plantation economy.

In contrast, American Indians confronted the dominant group as tribal units, intact and whole. The tribes maintained integrity throughout the wars and throughout the reservation period. Tribal culture was indeed attacked and denigrated during the reservation era, but the basic social unit that sustained the culture survived, albeit in altered form. The fact that American Indians were placed on separate reservations, isolated from one another and the "contaminating" effects of everyday contact with the larger society, also abetted the preservation of traditional languages and culture (Cornell, 1990).

Indian cultures seem healthy and robust in the current atmosphere of greater tolerance and support for pluralism in the larger society combined with increased autonomy and lower governmental regulation on the reservations. However, a number of social forces are working against pluralism and the survival of tribal cultures. Pantribalism may threaten the integrity of individual tribal cultures as it represents American Indian grievances and concerns to the larger society. Opportunities for jobs, education, and higher incomes draw American Indians to more developed urban areas and will continue to do so as long as the reservations are underdeveloped.

Many aspects of the tribal cultures can be fully expressed and practiced only with other tribal members on the reservations. Thus, many American Indians must choose between "Indianness" on the reservations and "success" in the city. The younger, more educated American Indians will be most likely to confront this choice, and the future vitality of traditional American Indian cultures and languages will hinge on which option is chosen.

Secondary Structural Assimilation

This section assesses the degree of integration of American Indians into the various institutions of public life, following the general outlines of the parallel section in Chapter 5.

Residential Patterns. Since the Indian Removal Act of 1830 (see Chapter 3), American Indians have been concentrated in the western two thirds of the nation, as illustrated in Exhibit 6.10, although some pockets of population still can be found in the East. The states with the largest concentrations of American Indians—California, New Mexico, and Arizona—together include about one third of all American Indians, and another 10% live in Oklahoma. American Indians belong to hundreds of different tribes, the 10 largest of which were listed in Exhibit 6.1.

Exhibit 6.10 Percentage of County Populations Choosing AIAN, Alone and in Combination, 2000

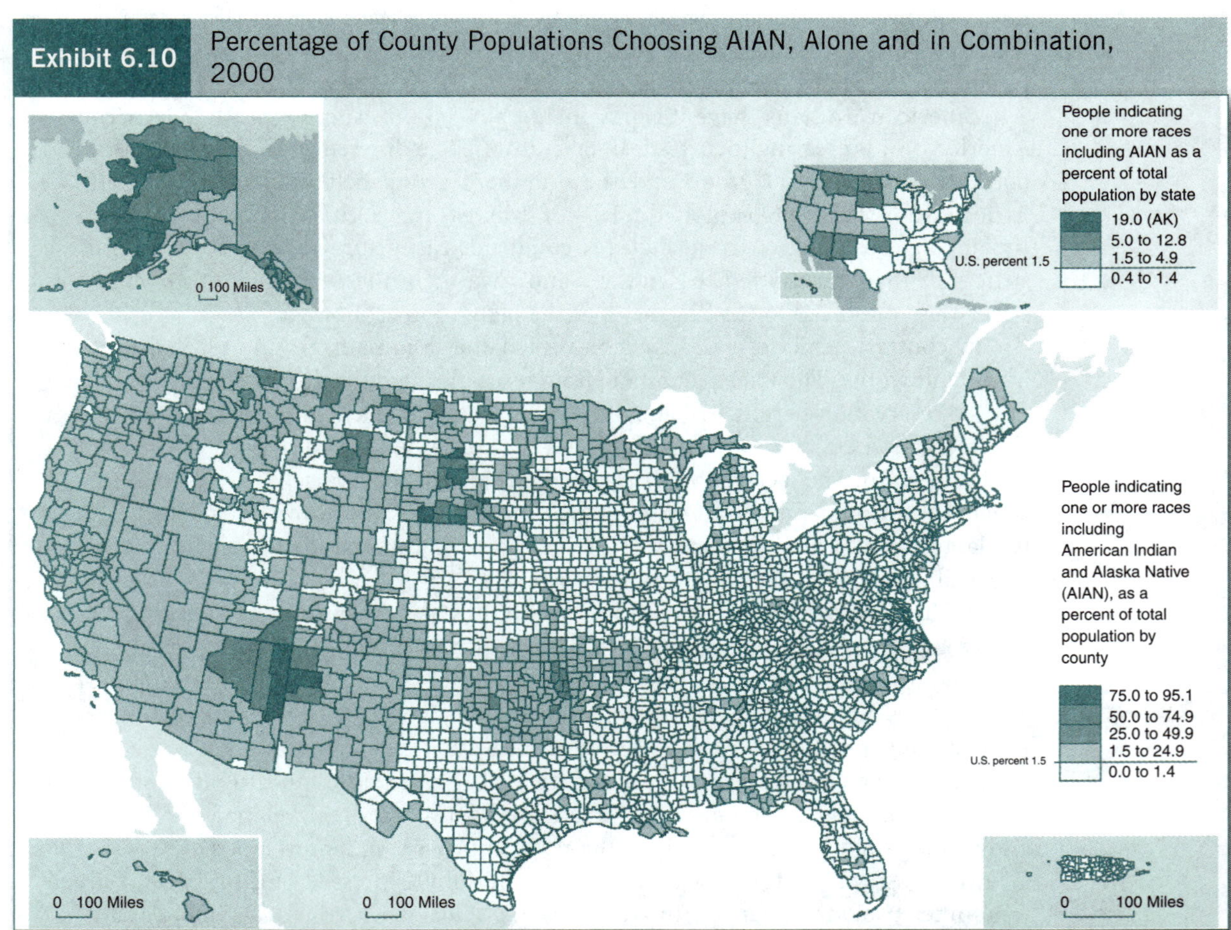

SOURCE: Ogunwole (2002).

Exhibit 6.11 provides some information about the levels of residential segregation of American Indians. The data in the exhibit are limited to metropolitan areas only. Because American Indians are such a small, rural group, the exhibit is limited to only 13 metropolitan areas, most in the West. The Northeast is not included because of the small numbers of American Indians living in the metropolitan areas of that region. Residential segregation is measured using the dissimilarity index, the same statistic used in Exhibit 5.7 for African Americans.

Although based on small numbers, the exhibit shows that residential segregation is much lower for American Indians than for African Americans (see Exhibit 5.7) and approaches the "high" range (0.6) only in the western region. The level of residential segregation declined slightly between 1980 and 2000, but remember that more than a third of American Indians live on rural reservations where the levels of residential segregation are quite high.

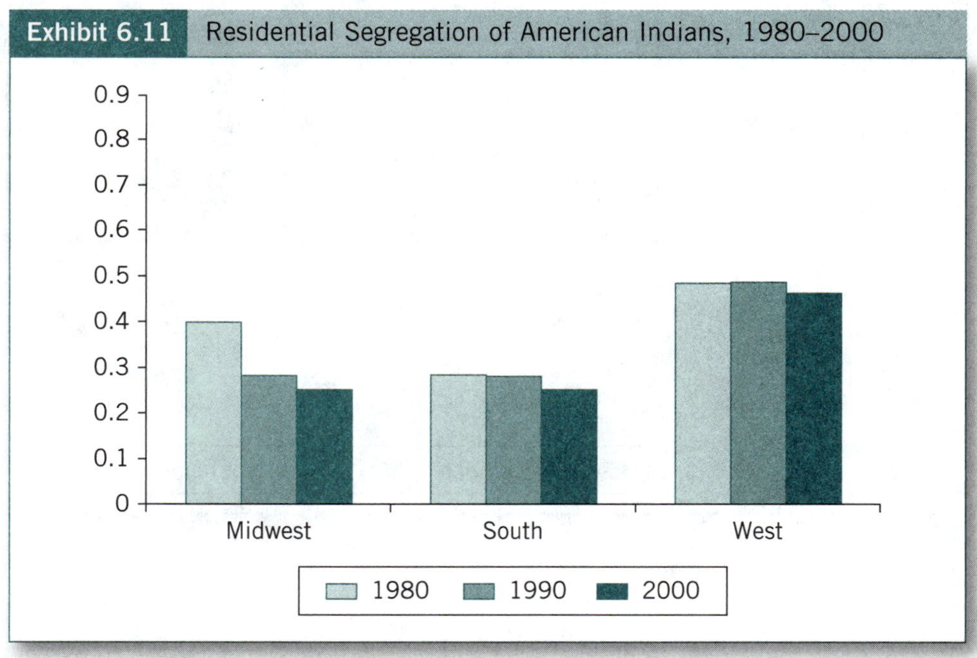

Exhibit 6.11 Residential Segregation of American Indians, 1980–2000

SOURCE: Iceland, Weinberg, & Steinmetz (2002, p. 23).

School Integration and Educational Attainment. As a result of the combined efforts of missionaries and federal agencies, American Indians have had a long but not necessarily productive acquaintance with Western education. Until the last few decades, schools for American Indians were primarily focused on Americanizing children, not on educating them. For many tribes, the percentage of high school graduates has increased in the recent past, but American Indians as a whole are still below national levels. However, several tribes—including 4 of the 10 largest tribes—now exceed the national percentage of high school graduates. The gap in college education is closing as well but remains large. None of the 10 largest tribes approaches the national norm on this variable. The Iroquois have the highest percentage of college graduates (a little more than 20%) but they are still about seven percentage points below the national figure. The differences in schooling are especially important because the lower levels of educational attainment limit mobility and job opportunities in the postindustrial job market. The educational levels of American Indians are displayed in Exhibit 6.12.

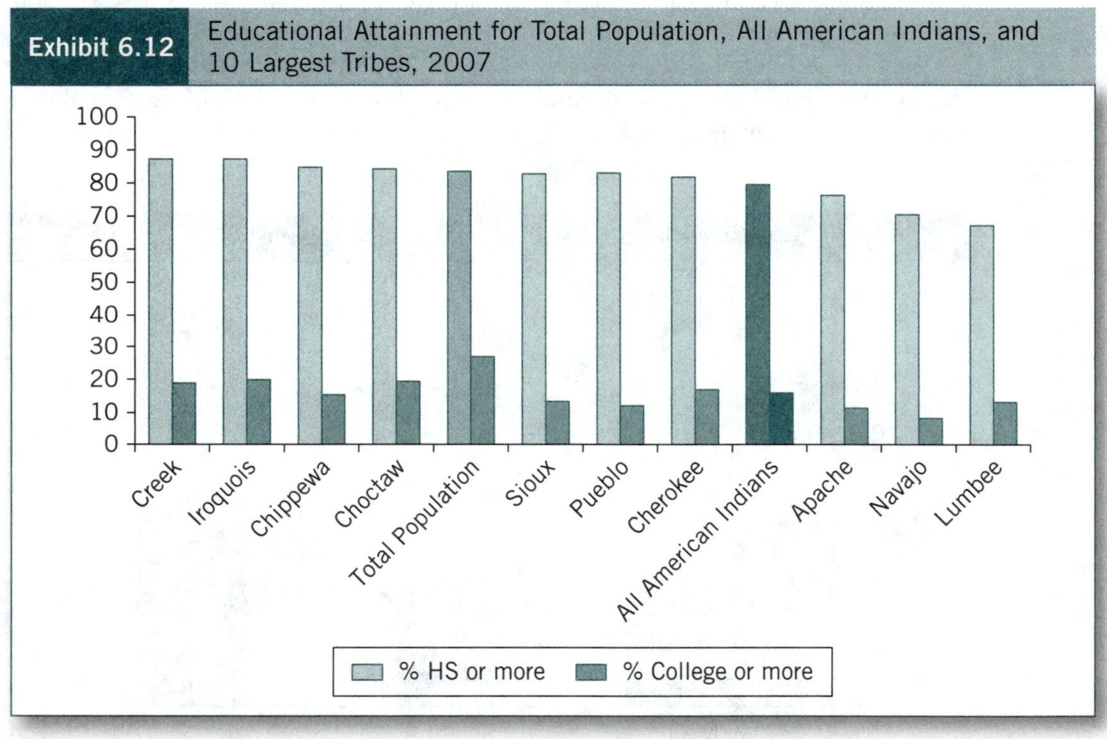

Exhibit 6.12 Educational Attainment for Total Population, All American Indians, and 10 Largest Tribes, 2007

SOURCE: U.S. Bureau of the Census (2007).

One positive development for the education of American Indians is the rapid increase in tribally controlled colleges, more than 30 of which have been built since the 1960s. These institutions are mostly two-year community colleges located on or near reservations, and some have been constructed with funds generated in the gaming industry. They are designed to be more sensitive to the educational and cultural needs of the group, and tribal college graduates who transfer to four-year colleges are more likely to graduate than other American Indian students (Pego, 1998; see also American Indian Higher Education Consortium, 2008).

Exhibit 6.13 displays the extent of school segregation for American Indians in the 1993–1994 and 2005–2006 school years, using the same measures as in Exhibit 5.9.

American Indian school children are less segregated than African Americans, but the degree of racial isolation is still substantial and is actually increasing. The percentage of American Indian children attending "majority-minority" schools increased from 44% to 49% between the two school years. The percentage in extremely segregated schools, however, held steady at 21%, about 10 percentage points lower than African American children.

Exhibit 6.13 School Integration, 1993–1994 and 2005–2006

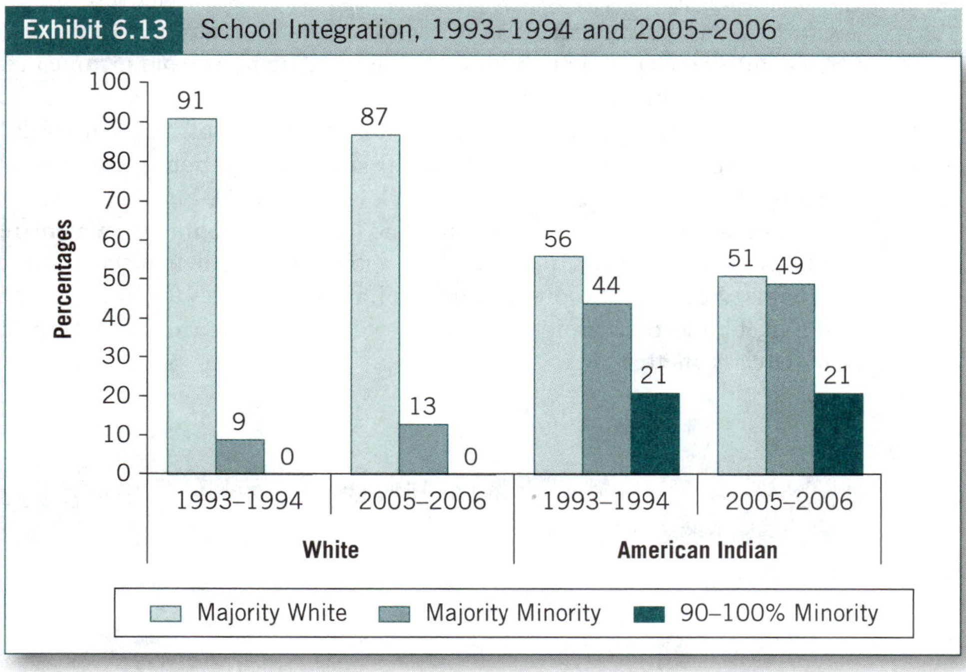

SOURCE: Fry (2007).

Political Power. The ability of American Indians to exert power as a voting bloc or to otherwise directly affect the political structure is very limited by group size; they are a tiny percentage of the electorate. Furthermore, their political power is limited by their lower average levels of education, language differences, lack of economic resources, and fractional differences within and between tribes and reservations. The number of American Indians holding elected office is minuscule, far less than 1% (Pollard & O'Hare, 1999, p. 41). In 1992, however, Ben Nighthorse Campbell of Colorado, a member of the Northern Cheyenne tribe, was elected to the U.S. Senate, where he served until 2005.

Jobs and Income. Some of the most severe challenges facing American Indians relate to work and income. The problems are especially evident on the reservations, where jobs have traditionally been scarce and affluence rare. As in the case of African Americans, the overall unemployment rate for all American Indians is about double the rate for whites. For Indians living on or near reservations, however, the rate is much higher, almost 50%. The rate sometimes rises to 70% to 80% on the smaller, more isolated reservations (Bureau of Indian Affairs, 2005).

Nationally, American Indians are underrepresented in the higher status, more lucrative professions and overrepresented in unskilled labor and service jobs (Ogunwole, 2006). As is the case for African Americans, American Indians who hold white-collar jobs are more likely than whites to work in relatively low-level occupations such as typist or retail salesperson (Pollard & O'Hare, 1999).

The income data in Exhibit 6.14 show median household income in 2007 for the total U.S. population, all American Indians, and the 10 largest tribes. Overall, American Indian per capita income was about 75% of national levels. There is a good deal of variability among the 10 largest tribes but, again, none approaches national norms. These incomes reflect lower levels of education as well as the interlocking forces of past discrimination and lack of development on many reservations. The rural isolation of much of the population and their distance from the more urbanized centers of economic growth limit possibilities for improvement and raise the likelihood that many reservations will remain the rural counterparts to urban underclass ghettos.

Exhibit 6.14 Median Household Income for Total Population, All American Indians, and 10 Largest Tribes

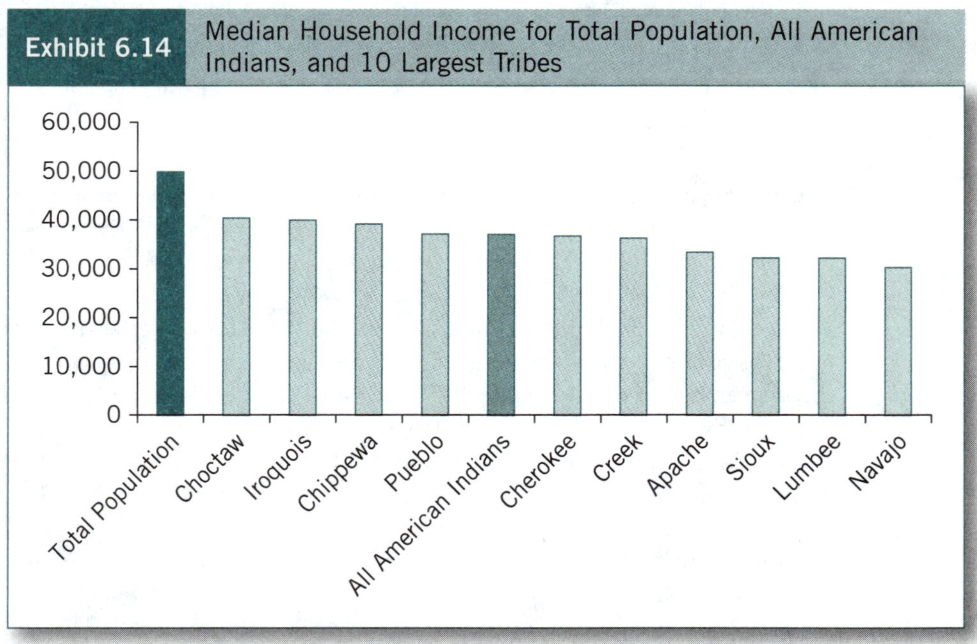

SOURCE: U.S. Bureau of the Census (2007, 2009b).

Exhibit 6.15 supplements the information in Exhibit 6.14 by displaying the distribution of income for AIAN compared with non-Hispanic whites. This type of graph was introduced in the chapter on African Americans and follows the same format as Exhibit 5.13. In both graphs, the pattern of income inequality is immediately obvious. Starting at the bottom, we see that, like African Americans, the AIAN group is overrepresented in the lowest income categories. For example, almost 15% of AIAN have incomes less than $10,000, more than double the percentage of non-Hispanic whites (7%) in this range.

Moving up the figure through the lower- and middle-income brackets, we see that AIAN households continue to be overrepresented. As was the case with Exhibit 5.13, there is a notable clustering of both groups in the $50,000 to $100,000 categories, but it is whites who are overrepresented at these higher income levels: Almost a third of white households compared with only 25% of AIAN households are in these categories. The income differences between the groups are especially obvious at the top of the figure. About 13% of white households versus 5% of AIAN households are in the top three income categories. Exhibit 6.15 also shows the median household income for both groups in 2007, and the difference of almost $20,000 further illustrates the lower socioeconomic level of American Indians.

Exhibit 6.15 Distribution of Household Income for Non-Hispanic Whites and American Indians and Alaska Natives, 2007 (in Dollars)

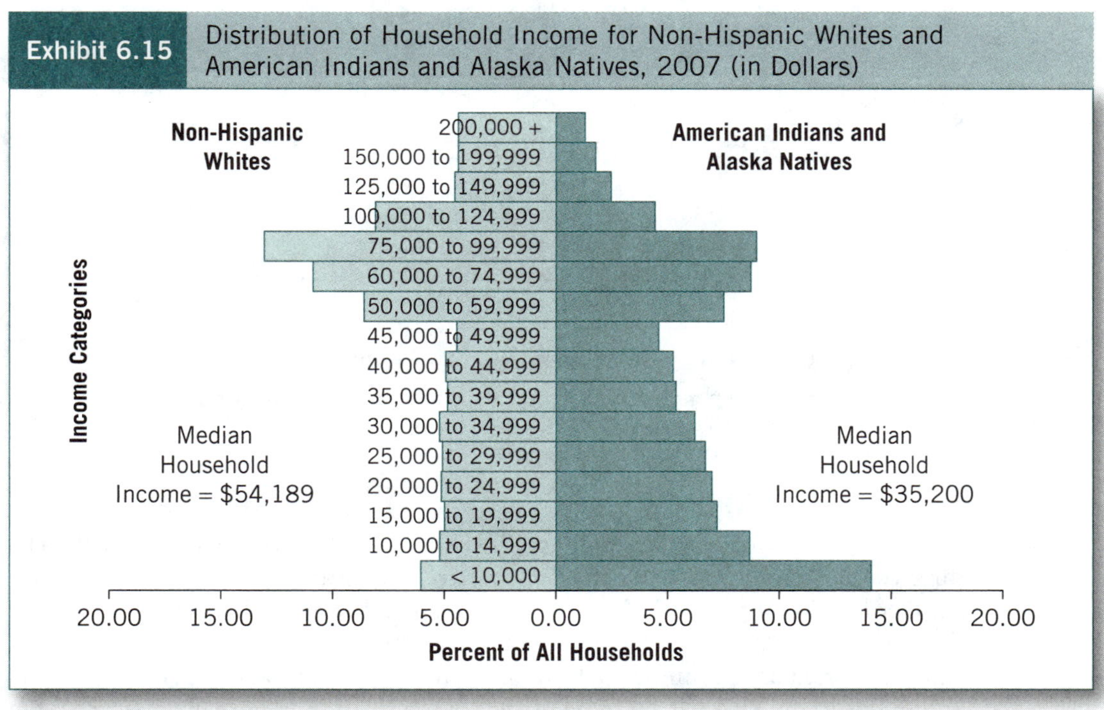

SOURCE: U.S. Bureau of the Census (2007).

Finally, Exhibit 6.16 shows the poverty levels for the total population, all American Indians, and the 10 largest tribes. The poverty rate for all American Indian families is almost double the national rate, and 4 of the 10 largest tribes have an even higher percentage of families living in poverty. The poverty rates for children show a similar pattern, with very high rates for the Navajo and Sioux.

Taken together, this information on income and poverty shows that, despite the progress that American Indians have made over the past several decades, a very sizeable socioeconomic gap persists.

Exhibit 6.16 Poverty Rates for Families and Children for Total Population, All American Indians, and 10 Largest Tribes

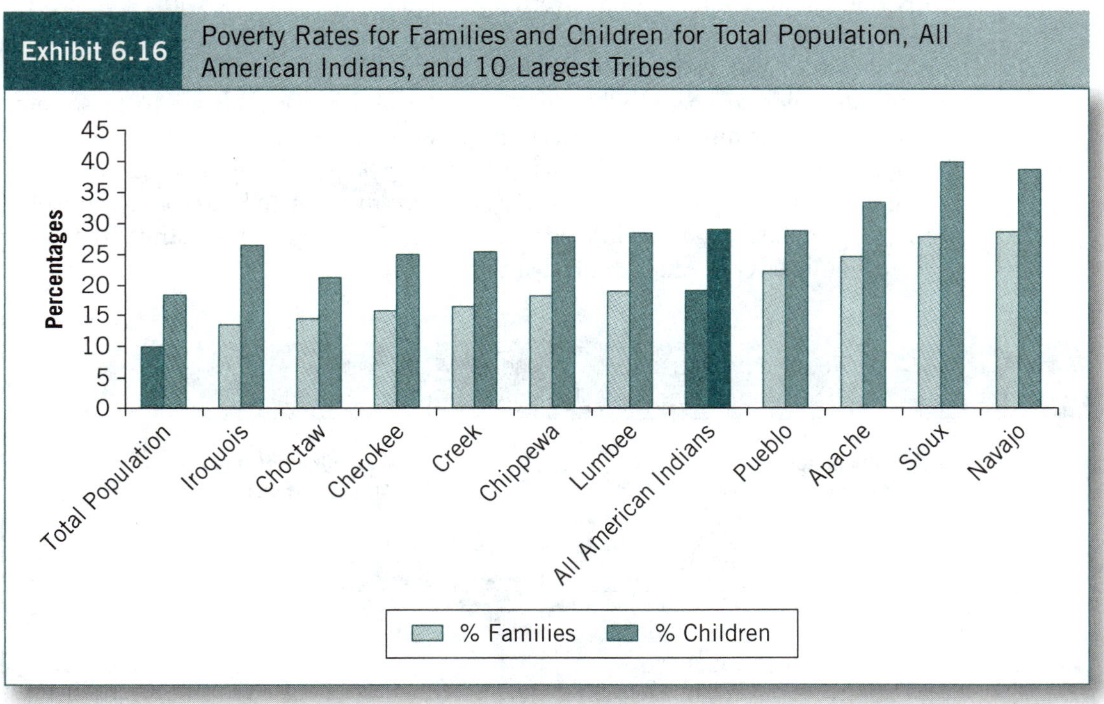

SOURCE: U.S. Bureau of the Census (2007).

Primary Structural Assimilation. Rates of out-marriage for American Indians are quite high compared with other groups, as displayed in Exhibit 6.17. For each of the last three census years, more than half of all married American Indians had spouses from another racial group, a much higher rate than any other group. This pattern is partly the result of the small size of the group. As less than 1% of the total population, American Indians are numerically unlikely to find dating and marriage partners within the group, especially in some regions of the country and urban areas where the group is especially small in size. For example, an earlier study found that in New England, which has the lowest relative percentage of American Indians in any region, more than 90% of Indian marriages are outside the group. In the mountain states, which have a greater number of American Indians who are also highly concentrated on reservations, only about 40% of Indian marriages were outside the group (Snipp, 1989, pp. 156–159). Also, the social and legal barriers to Indian-white intermarriages have been comparatively weak (Qian, Zhenchao, & Lichter, 2007).

Exhibit 6.17 Interracial Marriage by Group: Percent of Married People With Spouse of Another Race

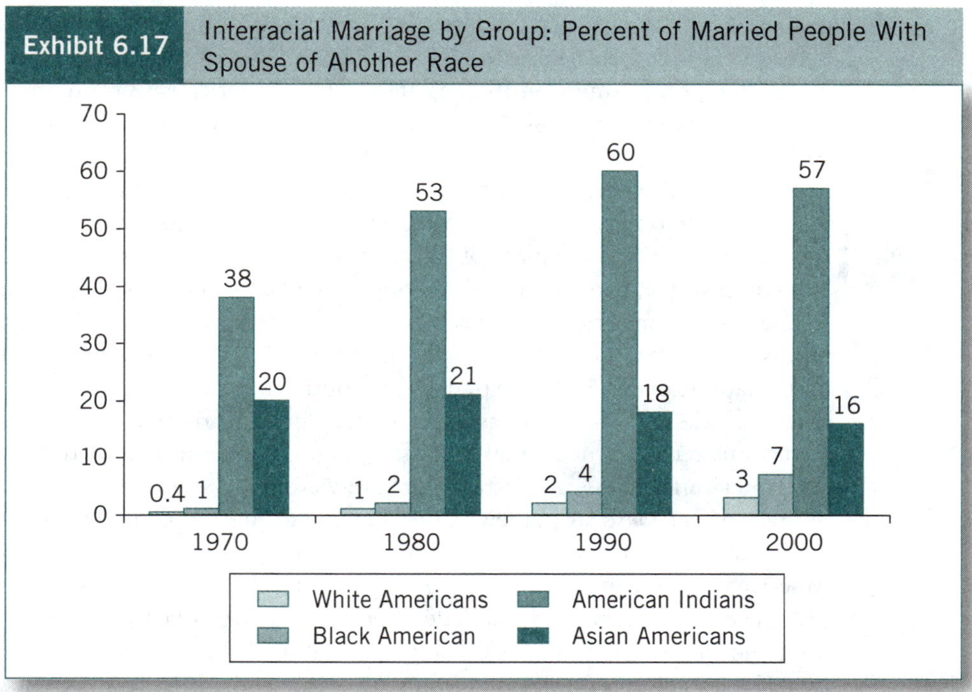

SOURCE: U.S. Bureau of the Census (2007).

The high rate of out-marriage is also an indication of the extent of acculturation and integration for some American Indians. Marriages with non-Indians are associated with higher levels of education, greater participation in the labor force, higher income levels, and lower rates of poverty (Snipp, 1989). Thus, out-marriage is more characteristic of American Indians who have left the reservation to pursue opportunities for education and careers in the cities.

Comparing Minority Groups

Comparing the experiences of American Indians with other groups will further our understanding of the complexities of dominant-minority relationships and permit us to test the explanatory power of the concepts and theories that are central to this text. No two minority groups have had the same experiences, and our concepts and theories should help us understand the differences and the similarities. We will make it a point to compare groups in each of the chapters in this part of the text. We begin by comparing American Indians with African Americans.

First, note the differences in the stereotypes attached to the two groups during the early years of European colonization. While Indians were seen as cruel savages, African Americans under slavery were seen as lazy, irresponsible, and in constant need of supervision. The two stereotypes are consistent with the outcomes of the contact period. The supposed irresponsibility of blacks under slavery helped justify their subordinate, highly controlled status, and the alleged savagery of American Indians helped to justify their near extermination by white society.

Second, both American Indians and African Americans were colonized minority groups, but their contact situations were governed by very different dynamics (competition for labor vs. land) and a very different dominant-group agenda (the capture and control of a large, powerless work force versus the elimination of a military threat). These differing contact situations shaped subsequent relationships with the dominant group and the place of the groups in the larger society.

For example, consider the situations of the two groups a century ago. The most visible enemy for African Americans was de jure segregation, the elaborate system of repression in the South that controlled them politically, economically, and socially (see Chapters 4 and 5). In particular, the southern system of agriculture needed the black population—but only as a powerless, cheap workforce. The goals of African Americans centered on dismantling this oppressive system, assimilation, and equality.

American Indians, in contrast, were not viewed as a source of labor and, after their military defeat, were far too few in number and dispersed geographically to constitute a political threat. Thus, there was little need to control them in the same way African Americans were controlled. The primary enemies of the tribes were the reservation system, various agencies of the federal government (especially the BIA), rural isolation, and the continuing attacks on their traditional cultures and lifestyles, which are typical for a colonized minority group. American Indians had a different set of problems, different resources at their disposal, and different goals in mind. They have always been more oriented toward a pluralistic relationship with the larger society and preserving what they could of their autonomy, their institutions, and their heritage. Although African Americans spent much of the 20th century struggling for inclusion and equality, American Indians were fighting to maintain or recover their traditional cultures and social structures. This difference in goals reflects the different histories of the two groups and the different circumstances surrounding their colonization.

Progress and Challenges

What does the future hold for American Indians? Their situation has certainly changed over the past 100 years, but is it "better" or just "different," as is the case for large segments of the African American community? The answer seems to be a little of both, as the group grows in size and improves its status. To reach some conclusions, we will look at several aspects of the situation of American Indians and assess the usefulness of our theoretical models and concepts.

Since the 1960s, the decline of intolerance in the society at large, the growth of pride in ancestry in many groups (e.g., Black Power), and the shift in federal government policy to encourage self-determination have all helped to spark a reaffirmation of commitment to tribal cultures and traditions. As was the case with African Americans and the Black Power movement, the Red Power movement asserted a distinct and positive Indian identity, a claim for the equal validity of American Indian cultures within the broad framework of the larger society. During the same time period, the favorable settlements of treaty claims, the growth in job opportunities, and the gambling industry have enhanced the flow of resources and benefits to the reservations. In popular culture, American Indians have enjoyed a strong upsurge of popularity and sympathetic depictions. This enhanced popularity accounts for much of the growth in population size as people of mixed ancestry resurrect and reconstruct their Indian ancestors and their own ethnic identities.

Linear or simplistic views of assimilation do not fit the current situation or the past experiences of American Indians very well. Some American Indians are intermarrying with whites and integrating into the larger society; others strive to retain a tribal culture in the midst of an urbanized, industrialized society; and still others labor to use the profits from gaming and other enterprises for the benefit of the tribe as a whole. Members of the group can be found at every degree of acculturation and integration, and the group seems to be moving toward assimilation in some ways and away from it in others.

From the standpoint of the Noel and Blauner hypotheses, we can see that American Indians have struggled with conquest and colonization, experiences made more difficult by the loss of so much of their land and other resources and by the concerted, unrelenting attacks on their culture and language. The legacy of conquest and colonization was poor health and housing, an inadequate and misdirected education system, and slow (or nonexistent) economic development. For most of the 20th century, American Indians were left to survive as best they could on the margins of the larger society, too powerless to establish meaningful pluralism and too colonized to pursue equality.

Today, the key to further progress for many, if not all, members of this group is economic development on reservation lands and the further strengthening of the tribes as functioning social units. Some tribes do have assets—natural resources, treaty rights, and the gambling industry—that could fuel development. However, they often do not have the expertise or the capital to finance the exploitation of these resources. They must rely, in whole or in part, on non-Indian expertise and white-owned companies and businesses. Thus, non-Indians, rather than the tribes, may be the primary beneficiaries of some forms of development (this would, of course, be quite consistent with American history). For those reservations for which gambling is not an option and for those without natural resources, investments in human capital (education) may offer the most compelling direction for future development.

Urban Indians confront the same patterns of discrimination and racism that confront other minority groups of color. Members of the group with lower levels of education and job skills face the prospects of becoming a part of a permanent urban underclass. More educated and skilled American Indians share with African Americans the prospect of a middle-class lifestyle that is more partial and tenuous than that of comparable segments of the dominant group.

The situation of American Indians today is vastly superior to the status of the group a century ago, and this chapter has documented the notable improvements that have occurred for many tribes since 1990. Given the depressed and desperate conditions of the reservations in the early 20th century, however, it would not take much to show an improvement. American Indians are growing rapidly in numbers and are increasingly diversified by residence, education, and degree of assimilation. Some tribes have made dramatic progress over the past several decades, but enormous problems remain both on and off the reservations. The challenge for the future, as it was in the past, is to find a course between pluralism and assimilation, pantribalism and traditional lifestyles that will balance the issues of quality of life against the importance of retaining an Indian identity.

COMPARATIVE FOCUS: Australian Aborigines and American Indians

The history of American Indians—their conquest and domination by a larger, more powerful society—has many parallels from around the globe, a reflection of the rise of European societies to power and their frequent conquest of indigenous societies in Africa, North and South America, and Asia. A comparative analysis of these episodes suggests that similar dynamics came into play, even though each episode has its own unique history. To illustrate, we will use some of the concepts developed in this text to compare the impact of European domination on Australian Aborigines and the indigenous peoples of North America.

Australia came under European domination in the late 1700s, nearly two centuries after the establishment of Jamestown and the beginning of Anglo-Indian relations. In other ways, however, the two contact situations shared many features. In both cases, the colonial power was Great Britain, and first contacts occurred in the preindustrial era (although Britain had begun to industrialize by the late 1700s). Also, the indigenous peoples of both North America and Australia were thinly spread across vast areas and were greatly inferior to the British in their technological development.

The Aboriginal peoples had lived in Australia for 50,000 years by the time the British arrived. Estimates of their population size vary, but there may have been as many as a million Aborigines at the time of contact with the British ("A Sorry Tale," 2000). They were organized into small, nomadic, hunting-and-gathering bands and were generally much less developed than the tribes of North America and lacked the population base, social organization, and resources that would have permitted sustained resistance to the invasion of their land. There was plenty of violence in the contact situation, but unlike the situation in North America, no sustained military campaigns pitting large armies against each other.

The initial thrust of colonization was motivated by Great Britain's need for a place to send its convicts after losing the Revolutionary War to the fledgling United States. The European population in Australia grew slowly at first and consisted mostly of prisoners. The early economic enterprises centered on subsistence farming and sheepherding, not large-scale enterprises that required forced labor (at least not on the same scale as in North America).

Early relations between the English and the Aborigines were hostile and centered on competition for land. In their ethnocentrism, the invaders denied that the Aborigines had any claims to the land and simply pushed them aside or killed them if they resisted. As in the Americas, European diseases took their toll, and the indigenous population declined rapidly. Because they were not desired as laborers (although many became semi-unfree servants), they were pushed away from the areas of white settlement into the fringes of development, where they and their grievances could be ignored. As in North America, they were seen as "savages"—a culture that would (and in the view of the emerging dominant group, should) wither away and disappear.

To the extent that there was contact between the Aborigines and the larger society, it was often in the form of coercive acculturation. For example, throughout much of the 20th century, the Australian government, aided by various church organizations, actually removed children of mixed parentage from their Aboriginal mothers and placed them in orphanages. The idea behind this program was to give these children a chance to leave their Aboriginal culture behind, marry whites, and enter the larger society. This policy, abandoned only in the 1960s, resulted in the state-sponsored orphaning of thousands of Aboriginal children. Some of the angriest and most militant members of the current generation of Aborigines belong to this "stolen generation" (for a report on this program, see Australian Human Rights and Equal Opportunity Commission, 1997).

The contemporary situation of Australian Aborigines has many parallels with American Indians, as does their past. The group is largely rural and continues to live on land that is less desirable. After the initial—and dramatic—declines, their numbers have been increasing of late, partly because of higher birth rates and partly because of changing perceptions, growing sympathy for their plight, and increased willingness of people to claim their aboriginal heritage. The population fell to a low of less than 100,000 at the start of the 20th century but is now put at 517,000, or about 2.5% of the total population (Australian Bureau of Statistics, 2009).

Just as in North America, there is a huge gap between the indigenous population and the rest of society on every statistic that measures quality of life, equality, and access to resources. Life expectancy for Aborigines is as much as 20 years lower than the general population, and their infant mortality rate is two to three times higher. They have much less access to health care, and Aboriginal communities are much more afflicted with alcoholism, suicide, and malnutrition than the general population. Unemployment rates are double the rate in the general population, average income is about 65% of the national average, and only about half as many Aboriginal peoples as non-Aboriginal in the 18–24 age group have completed high school (all statistics are from the Australian Bureau of Statistics at http://www.abs.gov.au).

The issues animating Aboriginal affairs have a familiar ring for anyone familiar with American Indians. They include concerns for the preservation of Aboriginal culture, language, and identity; self-determination and autonomy; the return of lands illegally taken by the Anglo invaders; and an end to discrimination and unequal treatment.

(Continued)

(Continued)

As in North America, Aboriginal relations are in flux, and the overall picture is mixed. For example, in 1998, the federal government of Australia was condemned by the United Nations Committee on the Elimination of Racial Discrimination for its handling of Aboriginal land claims. Australia is the only developed nation to have ever received this censure (Pilger, 2000). However, in 2008, the Australian Government formally apologized to the Aboriginal people for their mistreatment over the years and for programs such as the one that created the "stolen generation" (BBC, 2008).

The Aboriginal peoples of Australia, like American Indians, face many, often overwhelming challenges to secure a better future for themselves and for their children. Their history and their present situation clearly validate both the Blauner and Noel hypotheses: They are a colonized minority group, victims of European domination, with all that that status implies.

MAIN POINTS

- American Indian and Anglo-American cultures are vastly different, and these differences have hampered communication and understanding, usually in ways that harmed American Indians or weakened the integrity of their tribal structures.
- At the beginning of the 20th century, American Indians faced the paternalistic reservation system, poverty and powerlessness, rural isolation and marginalization, and the BIA. American Indians continued to lose land and other resources.
- The Indian Reorganization Act (IRA) of 1934 attempted to increase tribal autonomy and to provide mechanisms for improving the quality of life on the reservations. The policy of termination was proposed in the 1950s. The policy was a disaster, and the tribes that were terminated suffered devastating economic losses and drastic declines in quality of life.
- American Indians began to urbanize rapidly in the 1950s but are still less urbanized than the population as a whole. They are the least urbanized American minority group.
- The Red Power movement rose to prominence in the 1960s and had some successes but was often simply ignored. The Red Power movement was partly assimilationist even though it pursued pluralistic goals and greater autonomy for the tribes.
- Current conflicts between American Indians and the dominant group center on control of natural resources, preservation of treaty rights, and treaties that have been broken in the past. Another possible source of development and conflict is in the potentially lucrative gambling industry.
- There is some indication that anti-Indian prejudice has shifted to more "modern" forms. Institutional discrimination and access to education and employment remain major problems confronting American Indians.
- American Indians have preserved much of their traditional culture, although in altered form. The secondary structural assimilation of American Indians remains relatively low, despite recent improvements in quality of life for many tribes. Primary structural assimilation is comparatively high.

- Over the course of the last 100 years, American Indians have struggled from a position of powerlessness and isolation. Today, the group faces an array of problems similar to those faced by all American colonized minority groups of color as they try to find ways to raise their quality of life and continue their commitment to their tribes and to an Indian identity.

STUDY SITE ON THE WEB

Don't forget the interactive quizzes and other resources and learning aids at **www.pineforge.com/healeyds3e**

FOR FURTHER READING

This work is a good overview of the history and present situation of American Indian women.

Amott, Teresa, & Matthaei, Julie. 1991. "I Am the Fire of Time: American Indian Women." In T. Amott & J. Matthaei (Eds.), *Race, Gender, and Work: A Multicultural History of Women in the United States* (pp. 31–62). Boston: South End Press.

This work provides a comprehensive, dispassionate analysis of current problems and future possibilities.

Bordewich, Fergus. 1996. *Killing the White Man's Indian.* New York: Doubleday.

This book is a passionately written, highly readable account of the military defeat and the establishment of dominance over American Indians.

Brown, Dee. 1970. *Bury My Heart at Wounded Knee.* New York: Holt, Rinehart & Winston.

Following are the three major works of the well-known American Indian activist, writer, and professor of Indian studies.

Deloria, Vine. 1995. *Red Earth, White Lies.* New York: Scribners.

Deloria, Vine. 1970. *We Talk, You Listen.* New York: Macmillan.

Deloria, Vine. 1969. *Custer Died for Your Sins.* New York: Macmillan.

This work takes a comprehensive look at economic development and other issues on reservations across the nation.

The Harvard Project on American Indian Economic Development. 2008. *The State of the Native Nations.* New York: Oxford University Press.

This work is a fascinating collection of personal accounts by American Indians from pre-Colombian times to the present day.

Nabakov, Peter (Ed.). 1999. *Native American Testimony.* New York: Penguin.

This work is a valuable scholarly study covering a variety of aspects of the American Indian condition.

Snipp, C. Matthew. 1989. *American Indians: The First of This Land.* New York: Russell Sage Foundation.

QUESTIONS FOR REVIEW AND STUDY

1. What were the most important cultural differences between American Indian tribes and the dominant society? How did these affect relations between the two groups?
2. Compare and contrast the effects of paternalism and coercive acculturation on American Indians after the end of the contact period with those of African Americans under slavery. What similarities and differences existed in the two situations? Which system was more oppressive and controlling? How? How did these different situations shape the futures of the groups?
3. How did federal Indian policy change over the course of the 20th century? What effects did these changes have on the tribes? Which were more beneficial? Why? What was the role of the Indian protest movement in shaping these policies?
4. What options do American Indians have for improving their position in the larger society and developing their reservations? Which strategies seem to have the most promise? Which seem less effective? Why?
5. Compare and contrast the contact situations of American Indians, African Americans, and Australian Aborigines. What are the most crucial differences in the situations? What implications did these differences have for the development of each group's situation after the initial contact situation?
6. Characterize the present situation of American Indians in terms of acculturation and integration. How do they compare to African Americans? What factors in the experiences of the two groups might help explain contemporary differences?
7. What gender differences can you identify in the experiences of American Indians? How do these compare with the gender differences in the experiences of African Americans?
8. Given the information and ideas presented in this chapter, speculate about the future of American Indians. How likely are American Indian cultures and languages to survive? What are the prospects for achieving equality?

INTERNET RESEARCH PROJECTS

Use the Internet to develop a profile of American Indians by answering the questions asked here. Some addresses are provided as starting points, but you will have to use your own initiative to cruise the Internet and answer all questions fully.

A. Size of Population (U.S. Bureau of the Census: http://www.census.gov; Bureau of Indian Affairs: http://www.doi.gov/bureau-indian-affairs.html)

   1. Counting people who select only one racial category, how many American Indians are there?

2. How does the number change when people who selected more than one category are counted as members of the group?
3. Which of these two totals (if either) should be regarded as the "true" number of American Indians? Why?
4. How many separate tribes are recognized by the federal government?
5. How many federal reservations are there? In what regions of the nation are they concentrated? Which is the largest? Which is the smallest?

B. Gambling (National Indian Gaming Association: http://www.indiangaming.org)

1. How many reservations are involved in gaming or gambling?
2. What is the approximate annual revenue from these enterprises?
3. How is that revenue used?

C. Health (Indian Health Services: http://www.ihs.gov)

1. What are the birth rates and death rates for Native Americans?
2. Are these higher or lower than national norms or the rates for white Americans?
3. What are the mortality rates for various age groups compared with national norms?

Death Rates (deaths per 1,000 population)		
Age Groups:	**American Indians**	**Total Population**
Infants (ages 0–1)		
Young adults (18–25)		
Senior citizens (65+)		

4a. Select two age groups, and find the five most common causes of death for the group:

Causes of Death	**Age Group: ________**		**Age Group: ________**	
	American Indian	**Total Population**	**American Indian**	**Total Population**
1st most common				
2nd				
3rd				
4th				
5th				

4b. Describe how these patterns vary from national norms.

D. Issues (National Congress of American Indians: http://www.ncai.org. Also, search for American Indian newspapers or periodicals that are online. For example, *Indian Country Today*, "America's Leading Indian News Source," is available at http://www.indiancountry.com)

1. Cite and briefly explain three current issues in *Indian Country Today* or whatever newspaper or periodical you've found.
2. Analyze each issue in terms of the concepts used in the text (especially assimilation, pluralism, self-determination, or development of the reservation, institutional discrimination, protest and resistance, and inequality).
3. How would members of other groups (e.g., white or black Americans) view each issue?

Note

1. From *Prison Writings: My Life Is My Sun Dance* by Leonard Peltier. Copyright © 1999 by Leonard Peltier. Reprinted by permission of St. Martin's Press, LLC, and the Leonard Peltier Defense Offense Committee.

7

Hispanic Americans

Colonization, Immigration, and Ethnic Enclaves

By the spring of 2005, Lucresia was desperate to reunite her family. Her husband Jesus had crossed the border to the United States illegally six years earlier, driven by the lack of jobs in Mexico. He had found work in Texas and had sent enough money home to not only support his family but to build them a new house. But he had not been home in two years, afraid that he would not be able to return to the United States once he crossed the border.

Against the objections of her family, Lucresia arranged to cross the border at Pima County, Arizona, a desolate desert of unending scrub, heat, and sand. She paid the coyotes (smugglers) more than $3,000 to deliver her and her two children toTucson, a walk of many days through the unforgiving desert from the border. Three days into the trek, Lucresia collapsed. The smugglers decided to keep the party of 18 migrants moving and they left her in the desert. Her 15-year-old son stayed by her side as she, dehydrated and incoherent, slowly died. Her son survived and eventually was sent back to Mexico.

Upon hearing of her death, Lucresia's father vowed to recover her remains and provide her with a decent burial. He traveled to the United States on a tourist visa and searched the vast desert for his daughter for weeks. He was guided by the memories of his grandson and took pictures of likely landmarks—a particularly shaped tree or a sandy creek bed—and sent them to Lucresia's son in hopes that he would recognize something. He found the remains of several other

(Continued)

(Continued)

immigrants who had died in the desert before he found Lucresia. He was able to identify her skeletal remains by the shoes she wore, her dentures, and three rings still attached to the flesh-less fingers of her left hand.

—Based on Marosi (2005) and private communication
with members of the Green Valley Samaritans, who regularly patrol
the desert of Southern Arizona to try to prevent other deaths like Lucresia's

Since the early 1990s, globalization has disrupted the Mexican economy and pushed thousands out of work. Desperate to support their families, they take the only course available to them and cross the border to the United States. They find work in the low-wage, unskilled sector of the economy, live as frugally as they can, and send billions of dollars back to their home villages.

As the volume of emigration from Mexico has increased over the past several decades, U.S. citizens became increasingly concerned, especially after the 9/11 attacks. The Border Patrol was expanded, particularly at the most commonly used border crossings, and large walls were built to try to limit the flow of people. In response, the smugglers and coyotes found new crossing points, seeking out the least patrolled areas, including the Sonoran desert that straddles the border between Mexico and Arizona. One result of this cat-and-mouse game was a sharp increase in deaths along the border: Lucresia is one of thousands who have died trying to find a better life for themselves and their families.

The problems associated with the population movement along the Southern border have attracted the attention of a number of groups. Some, like the Green Valley Samaritans, seek to limit the number of deaths and the amount of suffering by providing humanitarian aid, water, and medicine to those trying to cross the desert. Their actions are completely legal and they coordinate with the Border Patrol and other law enforcement agencies. Others, organized groups and individuals, seek to discourage immigration. Although some groups fill water tanks along the most likely migration routes, others vandalize and sabotage these efforts and seek to intimidate the migrants. One member of the Green Valley Samaritans reports finding a noose hanging in a tree next to one of the water tanks her group maintains. The furor over Mexican immigration, like virtually every group conflict in our history, brings out the best and worst of the American spirit: selfless humanitarianism and raw racism.

Introduction

The United States is home to many different Spanish-origin groups. Before the Declaration of Independence was signed, before slavery began, even before Jamestown was founded, the ancestors of some of these groups were already in North America. Other Hispanic groups are recent immigrants and new members of U.S. society. The label *Hispanic American* includes a number of groups that are diverse and distinct from each other. These groups connect themselves to a variety of traditions; like the larger society, they are dynamic and changeable, unfinished and evolving. Hispanic Americans share a language and some cultural traits but do not generally think of themselves as a single social entity. Many identify with their national-origin groups (e.g., Mexican American) rather than broader, more encompassing labels.

In this chapter, we look at the development of Hispanic American groups over the past century, examine their contemporary relations with the larger society, and assess their current status. We focus on the three largest Hispanic groups: Mexican Americans, Puerto Ricans, and Cuban Americans but include several smaller groups as well: Exhibit 7.1 shows the size of the largest Hispanic groups and some information on growth since 1990. Mexican Americans, the largest single group, are 9.7% of the total U.S. population (and about two thirds of all Hispanic Americans), but the other groups are small in size. Considered as a single group, however, Hispanic Americans are more than 15.1% of the total population, and they became the largest U.S. minority group, surpassing African Americans, in the spring of 2004. The relative sizes of the major subgroups of Latino Americans are displayed in Exhibit 7.2, and Exhibit 7.3 shows the countries of origin of the largest Hispanic American groups.

Exhibit 7.1 Size and Growth of Hispanic Groups by Nation or Territory of Origin, 1990–2007

Country of Origin	1990	2000	2007	Growth (number of times larger, 1990–2007)	Percent of Total Population, 2007
Mexico	13,496,000	20,641,000	29,166,981	2.2	9.7%
Puerto Rico[a]	2,728,000	3,406,000	4,120,205	1.5	1.4%
Cuba	1,044,000	1,242,000	1,611,478	1.5	0.5%
Dominican Republic	520,521	799,768	1,208,060	2.3	0.4%
El Salvador	565,081	708,741	1,474,342	2.6	0.5%
Colombia	378,726	496,748	798,639	2.1	0.3%
Other Hispanics[b]	3,621,672	4,794,763	7,047,732	2.0	2.3%
Total Hispanic	22,355,990	32,091,000	45,427,437	2.0	15.1%
Percentage of U.S. population	9.0%	11.4%	15.1%		
Total U.S. population	248,710,000	281,422,000	301,621,159	1.2	

SOURCES: 1990: U.S. Bureau of the Census (1990c). 2000: U.S. Bureau of the Census (2000h). 2007: U.S. Bureau of the Census (2007).

NOTES:

a. Living on mainland only.

b. Includes people from Peru, Ecuador, Argentina, Costa Rica, Guatemala, and many other nations.

Exhibit 7.2 Hispanic Americans by Nation or Territory of Origin, 2007

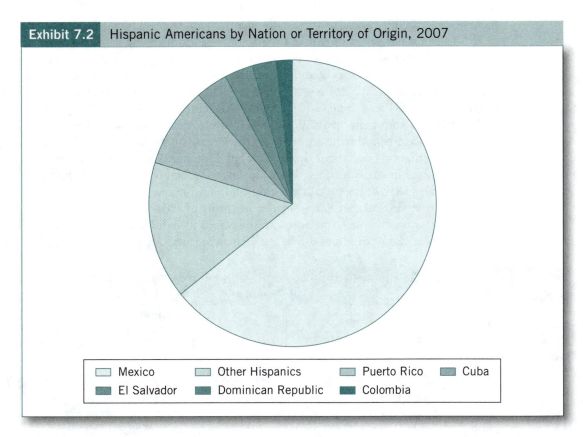

Mexico
Other Hispanics
Puerto Rico
Cuba
El Salvador
Dominican Republic
Colombia

Exhibit 7.3 Points of Origin for Largest Latino Groups

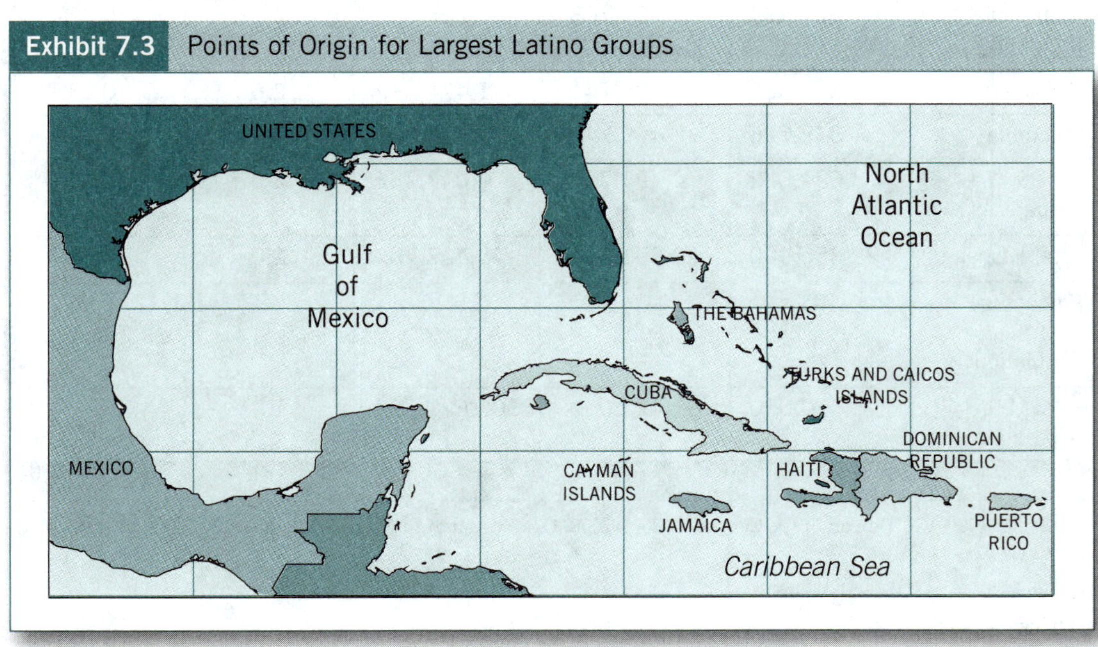

Latinos are growing rapidly, partly because of their relatively high birth rates, but mainly because of immigration. The number of Mexican Americans more than doubled between 1990 and 2007, and Latino groups in general are growing at rates above the national average. This growth is projected to continue well into the century, and Hispanic Americans will become an increasingly important part of life in the United States. The U.S. census in 2000 showed that one in ten Americans was Hispanic, but by 2050, this ratio will increase to one out of every four (see Exhibit 1.1). One result of these high rates of immigration is that the majority (in some cases, the great majority) of many Hispanic groups are first generations or foreign-born. The percentages are displayed in Exhibit 7.4.

Exhibit 7.4 Percent Foreign-Born by Country of Origin, 2007

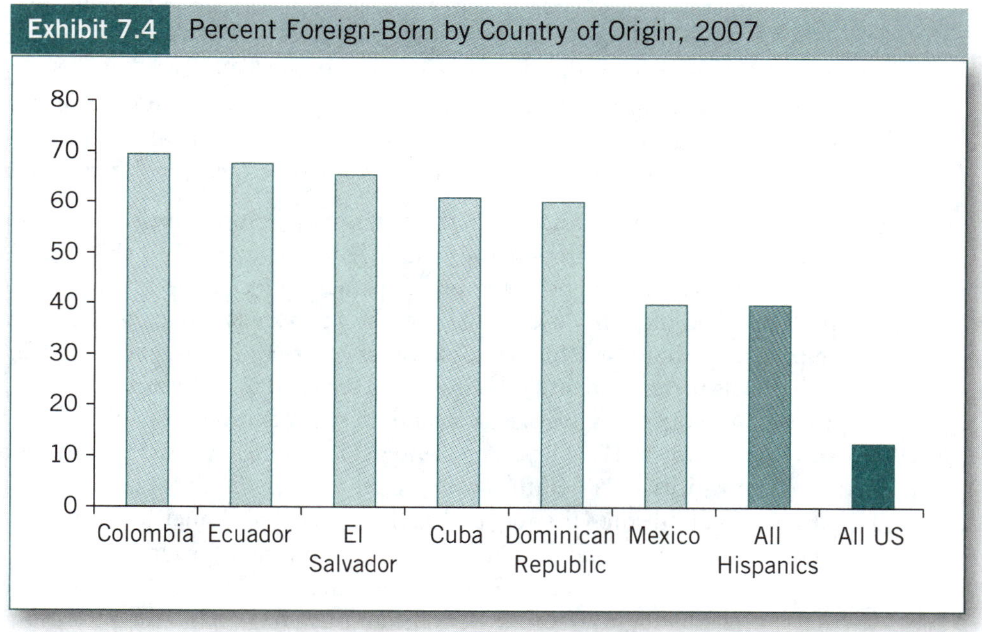

SOURCE: U.S. Bureau of the Census (2007).

It is appropriate to discuss Hispanic Americans at this point because they include both colonized and immigrant groups, and in that sense, they combine elements of the polar extremes of Blauner's typology of minority groups. We would expect that the Hispanic groups that were more colonized in the past would have much in common with African Americans and Native Americans today. Hispanic groups whose experiences more closely model those of immigrants would have different characteristics and follow different pathways of adaptation. We test these ideas by reviewing the histories of the groups and by analyzing their current status and degree of acculturation and integration.

Two additional introductory comments can be made about Hispanic Americans:

- Hispanic Americans are partly an ethnic minority group (i.e., identified by cultural characteristics such as language) and partly a racial minority group (identified by their physical appearance). Latinos bring a variety of racial backgrounds to U.S. society. For example, Mexican Americans combine European and Native American ancestries and are identifiable by their physical traits as well as by their culture and language. Puerto Ricans, in contrast, are a mixture of white and black ancestry. The original inhabitants of the island, the Arawak and Caribe tribes, were decimated by the Spanish conquest, and the proportion of Native American ancestry is much smaller in Puerto Rico than it is in Mexico. Africans were originally brought to the island as slaves, and there has been considerable intermarriage between whites and blacks. The Puerto Rican population today varies greatly in its racial characteristics, combining every conceivable combination of white and African ancestry. Hispanic Americans are often the victims of racial discrimination in the United States. Racial differences often (but not always) overlap with cultural distinctions and reinforce the separation of Hispanic Americans from Anglo-American society. Even members of the group who are completely acculturated may still experience discrimination based on their physical appearance.

- As is the case with all American minority groups, labels and group names are important. The term *Hispanic American* is widely applied to this group and might seem neutral and inoffensive to non-Hispanics. In fact, a recent survey shows that the preferred designation varies widely by the primary language and generation of the respondent. About two thirds of Spanish-speakers and first-generation (foreign-born) individuals prefer to identify themselves in terms of their countries of origin, although a slight majority of English speakers and third-generation Hispanics prefer to be called simply "American" (Pew Research Center, 2005, p. 19). An earlier study showed that a sizeable majority (67%) of the group prefer the *Hispanic* label to *Latino* (Jones, 2001). At any rate, both the Hispanic and Latino labels are similar to "American Indian" in that they were invented and applied by the dominant group and may reinforce the mistaken perception that all Spanish-speaking peoples are the same. Also, the term "Hispanic" highlights Spanish heritage and language but deemphasizes the roots of these groups in African American and Native American civilizations. Further, the Hispanic label is sometimes mistakenly applied to immigrant groups that bring French, Portuguese, or English traditions (e.g., Haitians, Brazilians, and Jamaicans, respectively). Conversely, the *Latino* label stresses the common origins of these groups in Latin America and the fact that each culture is a unique blend of diverse traditions. In this chapter, the terms *Latino* (or *Latina)* and *Hispanic* are used interchangeably.

Mexican Americans

We applied the Noel and Blauner hypotheses to this group in Chapter 3. Mexicans living in what is now the Southwestern United States were conquered and colonized in the 19th century and used as a cheap labor force in agriculture, ranching, mining, railroad construction, and other areas of the dominant-group economy in the Southwest. In the competition for control of land and labor, they became a minority group, and the contact situation left them with few power resources with which to pursue their self-interests.

By the dawn of the 20th century, the situation of Mexican Americans resembled that of American Indians in some ways. Both groups were small, numbering about one half of 1% of the total population (Cortes, 1980, p. 702). Both differed from the dominant group in culture and language, and both were impoverished, relatively powerless, and isolated in rural areas distant from the centers of industrialization and modernization. In other ways, Mexican Americans resembled African Americans in the South in that they also supplied much of the labor power for the agricultural economy of their region, and both were limited to low-paying occupations and subordinate status in the social structure. All three groups were colonized and, at least in the early decades of the 20th century, lacked the resources to end their exploitation and protect their cultural heritages from continual attack by the dominant society (Mirandé, 1985).

Some important differences also existed in the situation of Mexican Americans and the other two colonized minority groups. Perhaps the most crucial difference was the proximity of the sovereign nation of Mexico. Population movement across the border was constant, and Mexican culture and the Spanish language were continually rejuvenated, even as they were attacked and disparaged by Anglo-American society.

Cultural Patterns

Besides language differences, Mexican American and Anglo-American cultures differ in many ways. Whereas the dominant society is largely Protestant, the overwhelming majority of Mexican Americans are Catholic, and the church remains one of the most important institutions in any Mexican American community. Religious practices also vary; Mexican Americans (especially men) are relatively inactive in church attendance, preferring to express their spiritual concerns in more spontaneous, less routinized ways.

In the past, everyday life among Mexican Americans was often described in terms of the "culture of poverty" (see Chapter 5), an idea originally based on research in several different Hispanic communities (see Lewis, 1959, 1965, 1966). This perspective asserts that Mexican Americans suffer from an unhealthy value system that includes a weak work ethic, fatalism, and other negative attitudes. Today, this characterization is widely regarded as exaggerated or simply mistaken. More recent research shows that the traits associated with the culture of poverty tend to characterize people who are poor and uneducated, rather than any particular racial or ethnic group. In fact, a number of studies show that there is little difference between the value systems of Mexican Americans and other Americans of similar length of residence in the United States, social class, and educational backgrounds (e.g., see Buriel, 1993; Moore & Pinderhughes, 1993; Pew Research Center, 2005; Valentine & Mosley, 2000).

Another area of cultural difference involves **machismo**, a value system that stresses male dominance, honor, virility, and violence. The stereotypes of the dominant group exaggerate the negative aspects of machismo and often fail to recognize that machismo can also be expressed through being a good provider, a respected father, and in other nondestructive ways. In fact, the concern for male dignity is not unique to Hispanics and can be found in many cultures in varying strengths and expressions, including Anglo-American. Thus this difference is one of degree rather than kind (Moore & Pachon, 1985).

Compared with Anglo-Americans, Mexican Americans tend to place more value on family relations and obligations. Strong family values are the basis for support networks and cooperative efforts in the community and influence everyday life to a greater extent than in the Anglo community. For example, the decision to immigrate to the United States is frequently made to support the family and immigrants often live in Spartan conditions to maximize the amount of money they can send home. These values can conflict with the emphasis on individualism and individual success in the dominant culture and may inhibit geographical mobility and people's willingness to pursue educational and occupational opportunities distant from their home communities (Moore, 1970).

These cultural and language differences have inhibited communication with the dominant group and have served as the basis for excluding Mexican Americans from the larger society. However, they also have provided a basis for group cohesion and unity that has sustained common action and protest activity.

Immigration

Although Mexican Americans originated as a colonized minority group, their situation since the early 1900s (and especially since the 1960s) has been largely shaped by immigration. The numbers of documented Mexican immigrants to the United States are shown in Exhibit 7.5. The fluctuations in the rate of immigration can be explained

Exhibit 7.5 Legal Immigration From Mexico, 1900–2008

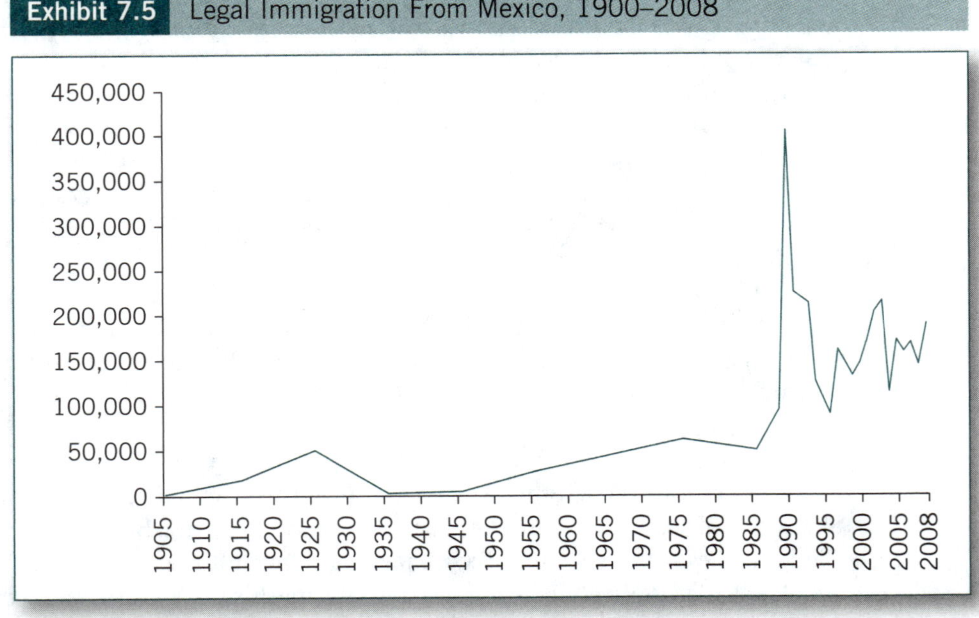

SOURCE: U.S. Department of Homeland Security (2008).

NOTE: The very high numbers of "immigrants" in the late 1980s and early 1990s were the result of people already in the United States legalizing their status under the provisions of the Immigration Reform and Control Act (IRCA) policy.

by conditions in Mexico, the varying demand for labor in the low-paying, unskilled sector of the U.S. economy, broad changes in North America and the world, and changing federal immigration policy. As you will see, competition, one of the key variables in Noel's hypothesis, has shaped the relationships between Mexican immigrants and the larger American society.

Push and Pull

Like the massive wave of immigrants from Europe that arrived between the 1820s and 1920s (see Chapter 2), Mexicans have been **pushed** from their homeland and **pulled** toward the United States by a variety of sweeping changes in their society and in the global system of societies. European immigration was propelled by the changes wrought by industrialization, urbanization, and rapid population growth. Mexican immigrants have been motivated by similarly broad forces, including continuing industrialization and globalization.

At the heart of the immigration lies a simple fact: The almost 2,000-mile-long border between Mexico and the United States is the longest continuous point of contact between a less developed and a more developed nation in the world. For the past century, the United States has developed faster than Mexico, moving from an industrial to a postindustrial society and sustaining a substantially higher standard of living. The continuing wage gap between the two nations has made even menial work in the North attractive to millions of Mexicans (and other Central and South Americans). The less-developed Mexican economy has been unable to supply full employment for its population, especially since the passage of the North American Free Trade Agreement (NAFTA) in 1994, which opened the Mexican border to U.S. and Canadian products and disrupted the rural economy, displacing millions of peasants who were forced to leave their home communities in search of work to support their families. Mexico has generally produced a large number of people who need work, and the United States has offered jobs that pay more—often much more—than the wages available south of the border. Just as the air flows from high to low pressure, people move from areas of lower to higher economic opportunities. The flow is not continuous, however, and has been affected by conditions in both the sending and receiving nations.

Conditions in Mexico, Fluctuating Demand for Labor, and Federal Immigration Policy

Generally, for the past 100 years, Mexico has served as a reserve pool of cheap labor for the benefit of U.S. businesses, agricultural interests, and other groups, and the volume of immigration largely reflects changing economic conditions in the United States. Immigration increased when times were good in the United States and decreased when times were bad, a pattern reinforced by the policies and actions of the federal government. The most important events in the complex history of Mexican immigration to the United States are presented in Exhibit 7.6, along with some comments regarding the nature of the event and its effects.

Exhibit 7.6 Significant Dates in Mexican Immigration

Dates	Event	Result	Effect on Immigration to the United States
1910	Mexican Revolution	Political turmoil and unrest in Mexico	Increased
Early 20th century	Mexican Industrialization	Many groups (especially rural peasants) displaced	Increased
1920s	National Origins Act of 1924	Decreased immigration to the U.S. from Europe	Increased
1930s	Great Depression	Decreased demand for labor and increased competition for jobs leads to repatriation campaign	Decreased, many return to Mexico, often by force
1940s	World War II	Increased demand for labor leads to Bracero Guest Worker Program	Increased
1950s	Concern over illegal immigrants	Operation Wetback	Decreased, many return to Mexico
1965	Repeal of National Origins Act	New immigration policy gives high priority to close family of citizens	Increased (see Exhibit 7.5)
1986	IRCA	Illegal immigrants given opportunity to legalize status	Many illegal immigrants gain legal status
1994	NAFTA	Borders more open, many groups in Mexico (especially rural peasants) displaced	Increased

Prior to the early 1900s, the volume of immigration was generally low and largely unregulated. People crossed the border—in both directions—as the need arose, informally and without restriction. The volume of immigration, and concern about controlling the border, began to rise with the increase of political and economic turmoil in Mexico in the early decades of the 20th century but still remained a comparative trickle.

Immigration increased in the 1920s when federal legislation curtailed the flow of cheap labor from Europe and then decreased in the 1930s when hard times came to the United States (and the world) during the Great Depression. Many Mexicans in the United States returned home during that decade, sometimes voluntarily, often by force. As competition for jobs increased, efforts began to expel Mexican laborers, just as the Noel hypothesis would predict. The federal government instituted a **repatriation** campaign aimed specifically at deporting undocumented Mexican immigrants. In many localities, repatriation was pursued with great zeal, and the campaign intimidated many legal immigrants and native-born Mexican Americans into moving to Mexico. The result was that the Mexican American population of the United States declined by an estimated 40% during the 1930s (Cortes, 1980, p. 711).

When the depression ended and U.S. society began to mobilize for World War II, federal policy toward immigrants from Mexico changed once more as employers again turned to Mexico for workers. In 1942, the *Bracero program* was initiated to permit contract laborers—usually employed in agriculture and other areas requiring unskilled labor—to work in the United States for a limited amount of time. When their contracts expired, the workers were required to return to Mexico.

The Bracero program continued for several decades after the end of the war and was a crucial source of labor for the American economy. In 1960 alone, braceros supplied 26% of the nation's seasonal farm labor (Cortes, 1980, p. 703). The program generated millions of dollars of profit for growers and other employers, because they were paying braceros much less than American workers would have received (Amott & Matthaei, 1991).

At the same time that the Bracero program permitted emigration from Mexico, other programs and agencies worked to deport undocumented (or illegal) immigrants, large numbers of whom entered the United States with the braceros. Government efforts reached a peak in the early 1950s with "**Operation Wetback**," a program under which federal authorities deported almost 4 million Mexicans (Grebler, Moore, & Guzman, 1970).

During Operation Wetback, raids on the homes and places of business of Mexican Americans were common, and authorities often ignored their civil and legal rights. In an untold number of cases, U.S. citizens of Mexican descent were deported along with illegal immigrants. These violations of civil and legal rights have been a continuing grievance of Mexican Americans (and other Latinos) for decades (Mirandé, 1985).

In 1965, the overtly racist national immigration policy incorporated in the 1924 National Origins Act (see Chapter 2) was replaced by a new policy that gave a high priority to immigrants who were family and kin of U.S. citizens. The immediate family (parents, spouses, and children) of U.S. citizens could enter without numerical restriction. Some numerical restrictions were placed on the number of immigrants from each sending country, but about 80% of these restricted visas were reserved for other close relatives of citizens. The remaining 20% of the visas went to people who had skills needed in the labor force (Bouvier & Gardner, 1986, pp. 13–15; Rumbaut, 1991, p. 215).

Immigrants have always tended to move along chains of kinship and other social relationships, and the new policy reinforced those tendencies. The social networks connecting Latin America with the United States expanded, and the rate of emigration from Mexico increased sharply after 1965 (see Exhibit 7.5) as immigrants became citizens and sent for other family members.

Most of the Mexican immigrants, legal as well as undocumented, who have arrived since 1965 continue the pattern of seeking work in the low-wage, unskilled sectors of the labor market in the cities and fields of the Southwest. For many, work is seasonal or temporary. When the work ends, they often return to Mexico, commuting across the border as has been done for decades

In 1986, Congress attempted to deal with illegal immigrants, most of whom were thought to be Mexican, by passing the Immigration Reform and Control Act (IRCA). This legislation allowed undocumented immigrants who had been in the country continuously since 1982 to legalize their status. According to the U.S. Immigration and Naturalization Service (1993, p. 17), about 3 million people, 75% of them Mexican, have taken advantage of this provision and these numbers account for the spike in the number of Mexican immigrants in the late 1980s (see Exhibit 7.5). IRCA has not slowed the volume of illegal immigration. In 1988, at the end of the amnesty application period, there were almost 3 million undocumented immigrants in the United States. In 2008, the number of undocumented immigrants was estimated at 11.6 million (Hoefer, Rytina, & Baker, 2008).

Immigration to the United States From Mexico Today

Mexican immigration to the U.S. continues to reflect the difference in level of development and standard of living between the two societies. Mexico remains a much more agricultural nation and continues to have a much lower standard of living, as measured by average wages, housing quality, health care, or any number of other criteria. To illustrate, according to United Nations data, the per capita income of the United States ($45,047) is more than five times greater than the per capita income of Mexico ($8,346) (United Nations, 2009). Many Mexicans live in poverty, and the population continues to grow. Many people are unable to find a place in their home economy and are drawn to the opportunities for work provided by their affluent northern neighbor. Because the average years of schooling in Mexico is only about seven years (Nationmaster.com, n.d.), they bring much lower levels of job skills and continue to compete for work in the lower levels of the U.S. job structure.

The impetus to immigrate has been reinforced by the recent globalization of the Mexican economy. In the past, the Mexican government insulated its economy from foreign competition with a variety of tariffs and barriers. These protections have been abandoned over the past several decades, and Mexico, like many less developed nations, has opened its doors to the world economy. The result has been a flood of foreign agricultural products (cheap corn in particular), manufactured goods, and capital, which, although helpful in some parts of the economy, has disrupted social life and forced many Mexicans, especially the poor and rural dwellers, out of their traditional way of life.

Probably the most significant changes to Mexican society have come from the North American Trade Agreement, or NAFTA. Starting in 1994, this policy united the three nations of North America in a single trading zone. U.S. companies began to move their manufacturing operations to Mexico, attracted by lower wages, less stringent environmental regulations, and weak labor unions. They built factories (called "*maquiladoras*") along the border and brought many new jobs to the Mexican economy. However, other jobs—no longer protected from global competition—were lost, more than offsetting these gains, and Mexican wages have actually declined since

NAFTA, increasing the already large number of Mexicans living in poverty. One analyst estimates that over 2.5 million families have been driven out of the rural economy because they cannot compete with U.S. and Canadian agribusinesses (Faux, 2004).

Thus, globalization in general and NAFTA in particular, have reinforced the long-term relationship between the two nations. Mexico, like other nations of the less developed "South," continues to produce a supply of unskilled, less-educated workers, while the United States, like other nations of the more developed and industrialized "North," provides a seemingly insatiable demand for cheap labor. Compared with what is available at home, the wages in *el Norte* are quite attractive, even when the jobs are at the margins of the mainstream economy or in the irregular, underground economy (e.g., day laborers paid off the books, illegal sweat-shop jobs in the garment industry, and sex work) and even when the journey requires Mexican immigrants to break American laws, pay large sums of money to "coyotes" to guide them across borders, and live in constant fear of raids by *La Migra.*

Finally, as is usually the case in sizable population movements, contemporary Mexican immigrants are motivated primarily by simple economics and the greater availability of work and higher wages of the North. Predictably, when the U.S. economy faltered recently and the supply of jobs shrunk, the number of immigrants declined dramatically. Exhibit 7.7 displays the recent decline based on data compiled

Exhibit 7.7 Migration In and Out of Mexico

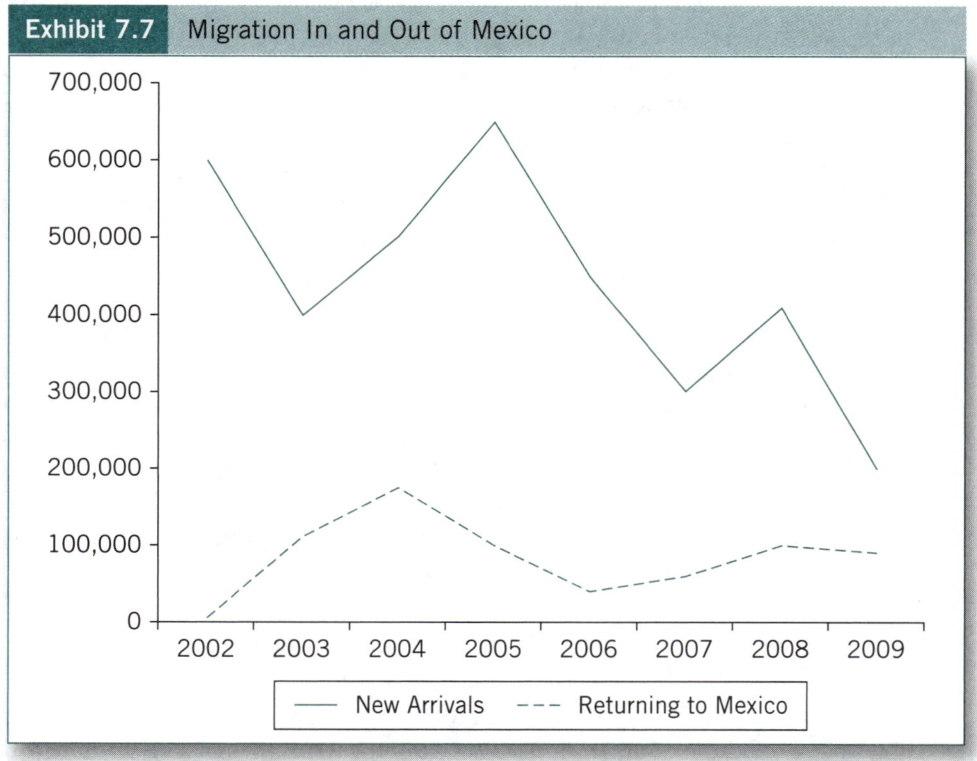

SOURCE: Passell & Cohn (2009). Copyright © 2009 Pew Hispanic Center, a Pew Research Center project, www.pewhispanic.org.

by the Pew Research Center. The pattern of Mexican immigration is tuned to the fluctuating forces of push and pull and, for the last century (and more), Mexicans have served as a reserve labor supply, swelling in good times and declining when the U.S. economy sours.

The Continuing Debate Over Immigration Policy

Immigration has once again become a hotly debated issue in the United States. How many immigrants should be admitted? From which nations? With what skills? Should the relatives of U.S. citizens continue to receive a high priority? And, perhaps the issue that generates the most passion, what should be done about illegal immigrants?

Virtually all of these questions, even those that are phrased in general, abstract terms, are mainly about the large volume of Mexican immigrants and the porous U.S. southern border.

The federal government is attempting to reduce the flow by building walls on its border with Mexico and beefing up the Border Patrol, both with increased personnel and more high-tech surveillance technology. These efforts have been largely futile and communities across the nation—not just in border states—are feeling the impact of Mexican immigration and wondering how to respond. Many citizens support extreme measures to close the borders—bigger, thicker walls and even the use of deadly force—while others ponder ways to absorb the newcomers without disrupting local school systems, medical facilities, or housing markets. The nation is divided on many of the issues related to immigration. For example, a May 2006 poll indicated that the public is nearly evenly split on whether immigration should be "kept at present levels" (39%) or "decreased" (34%). In the same poll, a healthy minority of respondents choose a third alternative: 22% felt that immigration should be increased (Pew Research Center, 2006).

Many different reforms for immigration policy have been proposed and continue to be debated. One key issue is the treatment of undocumented immigrants: Should they be deported, imprisoned, or should some provision be made for them to legalize their status, as was done in the IRCA legislation of 1986? If the latter, should the opportunity to attain legal status extend to all or only to immigrants who meet certain criteria (e.g., those with steady jobs and clean criminal records)? Many feel that amnesty is unjust because immigrants who entered illegally have, after all, broken the law. Others point to their economic contributions and the severe damage to the economy that would result from mass deportation. Still others worry about the negative impact illegal immigrants might be having on the job prospects for the less skilled members of the larger population, including the urban underclass that is disproportionately minority. We address some of these issues later in this chapter and in Chapters 8 and 9.

Immigration, Colonization, and Intergroup Competition

Three points can be made about Mexican immigration to the United States. First, the flow of population from Mexico was and is stimulated and sustained by powerful political and economic interests in the United States. Systems of recruitment and networks of communication and transportation have been established to routinize the flow of people and make it a predictable source of labor for the benefit of U.S. agriculture and other employers. The movement of people back and forth across the border was well established long before current efforts to regulate and control it. Depending on U.S. policy, this immigration is sometimes legal and encouraged and sometimes illegal and discouraged. Regardless of the label, the river of people has been steadily flowing for decades in response to opportunities for work in the North (Portes, 1990).

Second, Mexican immigrants enter a social system in which a colonized status for the group has already been established. The paternalistic traditions and racist systems that were established in the 19th century shaped the positions that were open to Mexican immigrants in the 20th century. Mexican Americans continued to be treated as a colonized group despite the streams of new arrivals, and the history of the group in the 20th century has many parallels with African Americans and American Indians. Thus Mexican Americans might be thought of as a colonized minority group that happens to have a large number of immigrants or, alternatively, as an immigrant group that incorporates a strong tradition of colonization.

Third, this brief review of the twisting history of U.S. policy on Mexican immigration should serve as a reminder that prejudice, racism, and discrimination increase as competition and the sense of threat between groups increases. The very qualities that make Mexican labor attractive to employers have caused bitter resentment among those segments of the Anglo population who feel that their own jobs and financial security are threatened. Often caught in the middle, Mexican immigrants and Mexican Americans have not had the resources to avoid exploitation by employers or rejection and discrimination by others. The ebb and flow of the efforts to regulate immigration (and sometimes even deport U.S. citizens of Mexican descent) can be understood in terms of competition, differentials in power, and prejudice.

Developments in the United States

As the flow of emigration from Mexico fluctuated with the need for labor, Mexican Americans struggled to improve their status. In the early decades of the 20th century, like other colonized minority groups, they faced a system of repression and control in which they were accorded few rights and had little political power.

Continuing Colonization

Throughout much of the 20th century, Mexican Americans have been limited to less desirable, low-wage jobs. Split labor markets, in which Mexican Americans are paid less than Anglos for the same jobs, have been common. The workforce has often been further split by gender, with Mexican American women assigned to the worst jobs and receiving the lowest wages in both urban and rural areas (Takaki, 1993).

Men's jobs often took them away from their families to work in the mines and fields. In 1930, 45% of all Mexican American men worked in agriculture, with another 28% in unskilled nonagricultural jobs (Cortes, 1980, p. 708). The women were often forced by economic necessity to enter the job market; in 1930, they were concentrated in farmwork (21%), unskilled manufacturing jobs (25%), and domestic and other service work (37%) (Amott & Matthaei, 1991, pp. 76–77). They were typically paid less than both Mexican American men and Anglo women. In addition to their job responsibilities, Mexican American women had to maintain their households and raise their children, often facing these tasks without a spouse (Zinn & Eitzen, 1990).

As the United States industrialized and urbanized during the century, employment patterns became more diversified. Mexican Americans found work in manufacturing, construction, transportation, and other sectors of the economy. Some Mexican Americans, especially those of the third generation or later, moved into middle- and upper-level occupations, and some began to move out of the Southwest. Still, Mexican Americans in all regions (especially recent immigrants) tended to be concentrated at the bottom of the occupational ladder. Women increasingly worked outside the home, but their employment was largely limited to agriculture, domestic service, and the garment industry (Amott & Matthaei, 1991; Cortes, 1980).

Like African Americans in the segregated South, Mexican Americans were excluded from the institutions of the larger society by law and by custom for much of the 20th century. There were separate (and unequal) school systems for Mexican American children, and in many communities, Mexican Americans were disenfranchised and accorded few legal or civil rights. There were "whites-only" primary elections modeled after the Jim Crow system, and residential segregation was widespread. The police and the court system generally abetted or ignored the rampant discrimination against the Mexican American community. Discrimination in the criminal justice system and civil rights violations have been continual grievances of Mexican Americans throughout the century.

Protest and Resistance

Like all minority groups, Mexican Americans have attempted to improve their collective position whenever possible. The beginnings of organized resistance and protest stretch back to the original contact period in the 19th century, when protest was usually organized on a local level. Regional and national organizations made their appearance in the 20th century (Cortes, 1980).

As with African Americans, Mexican Americans' early protest organizations were integrationist and reflected the assimilationist values of the larger society. For example, one of the earlier and more significant groups was the League of United Latin American Citizens (LULAC), founded in Texas in 1929. LULAC promoted Americanization and greater educational opportunities for Mexican Americans. The group also worked to expand civil and political rights and to increase equality for Mexican Americans. LULAC fought numerous court battles against discrimination and racial segregation (Moore, 1970).

The workplace has been a particularly conflictual arena for Mexican Americans. Split labor market situations increased anti-Mexican American prejudice; some labor unions tried to exclude Mexican immigrants from the United States, along with immigrants from Asia and Southern and Eastern Europe (Grebler, Moore, & Guzman, 1970).

At the same time, Mexican Americans played important leadership roles in the labor movement. Since early in the century, Mexican Americans have been involved in union organizing, particularly in agriculture and mining. When excluded by Anglo labor unions, they often formed their own unions to work for the improvement of working conditions. As the 20th century progressed, the number and variety of groups pursuing the Mexican American cause increased. During World War II, Mexican Americans served in the armed forces, and as with other minority groups, this experience increased their impatience with the constraints on their freedoms and opportunities. After the war ended, a number of new Mexican American organizations were founded, including the Community Service Organization in Los Angeles and the American GI Forum in Texas. Compared with older organizations such as LULAC, the new groups were less concerned with assimilation per se, addressed a broad range of community problems, and attempted to increase Mexican American political power (Grebler et al., 1970).

Chicanismo

The 1960s were a time of intense activism and militancy for Mexican Americans. A protest movement guided by an ideology called **Chicanismo** began at about the same time as the Black Power and Red Power movements. Chicanismo encompassed a variety of organizations and ideas, united by a heightened militancy and impatience with the racism of the larger society and strongly stated demands for justice, fairness, and equal rights. The movement questioned the value of assimilation and sought to increase awareness of the continuing exploitation of Mexican Americans; it adapted many of the tactics and strategies (marches, rallies, voter registration drives, and so on) of the civil rights movement of the 1960s.

Chicanismo is similar in some ways to the Black Power ideology (see Chapter 5). It is partly a reaction to the failure of U.S. society to implement the promises of integration and equality. It rejected traditional stereotypes of Mexican Americans, proclaimed a powerful and positive group image and heritage, and analyzed the group's past and present situation in American society in terms of victimization, continuing exploitation, and institutional discrimination. The inequalities that separated Mexican Americans and the larger society were seen as the result of deep-rooted, continuing racism and the cumulative effects of decades of exclusion. According to Chicanismo, the solution to these problems lay in group empowerment, increased militancy, and group pride, not in assimilation to a culture that had rationalized and abetted the exploitation of Mexican Americans (Acuna, 1988; Grebler et al., 1970; Moore, 1970).

Some of the central thrusts of the 1960s protest movement are captured in the widespread adoption of **Chicanos**, which had been a derogatory term, as a group name for Mexican Americans. Other minority groups underwent similar name changes at about the same time. For example, African Americans shifted from *Negro* to *black* as a group designation. These name changes were not merely cosmetic; they marked fundamental shifts in group goals and desired relationships with the larger society. The new names came from the minority groups themselves, not from the dominant group, and they expressed the pluralistic themes of group pride, self-determination, militancy, and increased resistance to exploitation and discrimination.

Organizations and Leaders

The Chicano movement saw the rise of many new groups and leaders, one of the most important of whom was Reies Lopez Tijerina, who formed the Alianza de Mercedes (Alliance of Land Grants) in 1963. The goal of this group was to correct what Tijerina saw as the unjust and illegal seizure of land from Mexicans during the 19th century. The Alianza was militant and confrontational, and to bring attention to their cause, members of the group seized and occupied federal lands. Tijerina spent several years in jail as a result of his activities, and the movement eventually lost its strength and faded from view in the 1970s.

Another prominent Chicano leader was Rodolfo Gonzalez, who founded the Crusade for Justice in 1965. The crusade focused on abuses of Mexican American civil and legal rights and worked against discrimination by police and the criminal courts. In a 1969 presentation at a symposium on Chicano liberation, Gonzalez expressed some of the nationalistic themes of Chicanismo and the importance of creating a power base within the group (as opposed to assimilating or integrating):

> Where [whites] have incorporated themselves to keep us from moving into their neighborhoods, we can also incorporate ourselves to keep them from controlling our neighborhoods. We . . . have to understand economic revolution. . . . We have to understand that liberation comes from self- determination, and to start to use the tools of nationalism to win over our barrio brothers. . . . We have to understand that we can take over the institutions within our community. We have to create the community of the Mexicano here in order to have any type of power. (Moquin & Van Doren, 1971, pp. 381–382)

A third important leader was José Angel Gutierrez, organizer of the La Raza Unida (People United) party. La Raza Unida offered alternative candidates and ideas to Democrats and Republicans. Its most notable success was in Crystal City, Texas, where in 1973 it succeeded in electing its entire slate of candidates to local office (Acuna, 1988).

Without a doubt, the best-known Chicano leader of the 1960s and 1970s was the late Cesar Chávez, who organized the United Farm Workers, the first union to successfully represent migrant workers. Chávez was as much a labor leader as a leader of the Mexican American community, and he also organized African Americans, Filipinos, and Anglo-Americans. Migrant farmworkers have few economic or political resources, and the migratory nature of their work isolates them in rural areas and makes them difficult to contact. In the 1960s (and still today), many were undocumented immigrants who spoke little or no English and who returned to the cities or to their country of origin at the end of the season. As a group, farmworkers were nearly invisible in the social landscape of the United States in the 1960s, and organizing this group was a demanding task. Chávez's success in this endeavor is one of the more remarkable studies in group protest.

Like Dr. Martin Luther King, Jr., Chávez was a disciple of Gandhi and a student of nonviolent direct protest (see Chapter 5). His best-known tactic was the boycott; in 1965, he organized a grape-pickers' strike and a national boycott of grapes. The boycott lasted five years and ended when the growers recognized the United Farm Workers as the legitimate representative of farmworkers. Chávez and his organization achieved a major victory, and the agreement provided for significant improvements in the situation of the workers (for a biography of Chávez, see Levy, 1975).

Gender and the Chicano Protest Movement

Mexican American women were heavily involved in the Chicano protest movement. Jessie Lopez and Dolores Huerta were central figures in the movement to organize farmworkers and worked closely with Cesar Chávez. However, as was the case for African American women, Chicano women encountered sexism and gender discrimination within the movement even as they worked for the benefit of the group as a whole. Their dilemmas are described by activist Sylvia Gonzales:

> Along with her male counterpart, she attended meetings, organized boycotts, did everything asked of her. . . . But, if she [tried to assume leadership roles], she was met with the same questioning of her femininity which the culture dictates when a woman is not self-sacrificing and seeks to fulfill her own needs. . . . The Chicano movement seemed to demand self-actualization for only the male members of the group. (Amott & Matthaei, 1991, p. 83)

Despite these difficulties, Chicano women contributed to the movement in a variety of areas. They helped to organize poor communities and worked for welfare reform. Continuing issues include domestic violence, child care, the criminal victimization of women, and the racial and gender oppression that limits women of all minority groups (Amott & Matthaei, 1991; see also Mirandé & Enriquez, 1979).

Mexican Americans and Other Minority Groups

Like the Black Power and Red Power movements, Chicanismo began to fade from public view in the 1970s and 1980s. The movement could claim some successes, but perhaps the clearest victory was in raising the awareness of the larger society about the grievances and problems of Mexican Americans. Today, many Chicanos continue to face poverty and powerlessness and continuing exploitation as a cheap agricultural labor force. The less educated, urbanized segments of the group share the prospect of becoming a permanent urban underclass with other minority groups of color.

Over the course of the 20th century, the ability of Chicanos to pursue their self-interests has been limited by both internal and external forces. Like African Americans, the group has been systematically excluded from the institutions of the larger society. Continuing emigration from Mexico has increased the size of the group, but these immigrants bring few resources with them that could be directly or immediately translated into economic or political power in the United States.

Unlike immigrants from Europe, who settled in the urban centers of the industrializing East Coast, Mexican Americans tended to work and live in rural areas distant from and marginal to urban centers of industrialization and opportunities for education, skill development, and upward mobility. They were a vitally important source of labor in agriculture and other segments of the economy but only to the extent that they were exploitable and powerless. As Chicanos moved to the cities, they continued to serve as a colonized, exploited labor force concentrated at the lower end of the stratification system. Thus, the handicaps created by discrimination in the past were reinforced by continuing discrimination and exploitation in the present, perpetuating the cycles of poverty and powerlessness.

At the same time, however, the flow of immigration and the constant movement of people back and forth across the border kept Mexican culture and the Spanish language alive. Unlike African Americans under slavery, Chicanos were not cut off from their homeland and native culture. Mexican American culture was attacked and disparaged, but, unlike African culture, it was not destroyed.

Clearly, the traditional model of assimilation does not describe the experiences of Mexican Americans very well. They have experienced less social mobility than European immigrant groups and have maintained their traditional culture and language more completely. Like African Americans, the group is split along lines of social class. Although many Mexican Americans (particularly of the third generation and later) have acculturated and integrated, a large segment of the group continues to fill the same economic role as their ancestors: an unskilled labor force for the development of the Southwest, augmented with new immigrants at the convenience of U.S. employers. For the less educated and for recent immigrants, cultural and racial differences combine to increase their social visibility, mark them for exploitation, and rationalize their continuing exclusion from the larger society.

Puerto Ricans

Puerto Rico became a territory of the United States after the defeat of Spain in the Spanish-American War of 1898. The island was small and impoverished, and it was difficult for Puerto Ricans to avoid domination by the United States. Thus, the initial contact between Puerto Ricans and U.S. society was made in an atmosphere of war and conquest. By the time Puerto Ricans began to migrate to the mainland in large numbers, their relationship to U.S. society was largely that of a colonized minority group, and they generally retained that status on the mainland.

Migration (Push and Pull) and Employment

At the time of initial contact, the population of Puerto Rico was overwhelmingly rural and supported itself by subsistence farming and by exporting coffee and sugar. As the century wore on, U.S. firms began to invest in and develop the island economy, especially the sugarcane industry. These agricultural endeavors took more and more of the land. Opportunities for economic survival in the rural areas declined, and many peasants were forced to move into the cities (Portes, 1990).

Movement to the mainland began gradually and increased slowly until the 1940s. In 1900, there were about 2,000 Puerto Ricans living on the mainland. By the eve of World War II, this number had grown to only 70,000, a tiny fraction of the total population. Then, during the 1940s, the number of Puerto Ricans on the mainland increased more than fourfold, to 300,000, and during the 1950s, it nearly tripled, to 887,000 (U.S. Commission on Civil Rights, 1976, p. 19).

This massive and sudden population growth was the result of a combination of circumstances. First, Puerto Ricans became citizens of the United States in 1917, so their movements were not impeded by international boundaries or immigration restrictions. Second, unemployment was a major problem on the island. The sugarcane industry continued to displace the rural population, urban unemployment was high, and the population continued to grow. By the 1940s, a considerable number of Puerto Ricans were available to seek work off the island and, like Chicanos, could serve as a cheap labor supply for U.S. employers.

Third, Puerto Ricans were "pulled" to the mainland by the same labor shortages that attracted Mexican immigrants during and after World War II. Whereas the latter responded to job opportunities in the West and Southwest, Puerto Ricans moved to the Northeast. The job profiles of these two groups were similar; both were concentrated in the low-wage, unskilled sector of the job market. However, the Puerto Rican migration began many decades after the Mexican migration, at a time when the United States was much more industrialized and urbanized. As a result, Puerto Ricans have been more concentrated then Mexican immigrants in urban labor markets (Portes, 1990).

Movement between the island and the mainland was facilitated by the commencement of affordable air travel between San Juan and New York City in the late 1940s. New York had been the major center of settlement for Puerto Ricans on the mainland even before annexation. A small Puerto Rican community had been established in the city, and as with many groups, organizations and networks were established to ease the transition and help newcomers with housing, jobs, and other issues. Although they eventually dispersed to other regions and cities, Puerto Ricans on the mainland remain centered in New York City. More than two thirds currently reside in the cities of the Northeast (U.S. Bureau of the Census, 2004b).

Economics and jobs were at the heart of the move to the mainland. The rate of Puerto Rican migration has followed the cycle of boom and bust, just as it has for Mexican immigrants. The 1950s, the peak decade for Puerto Rican migration, was a period of rapid U.S. economic growth. Migration was encouraged, and job recruiters traveled to the island to attract workers. By the 1960s, however, the supply of jobs on the island had expanded appreciably, and the average number of migrants declined from the peak of 41,000 per year in the 1950s to about 20,000 per year. In the 1970s, the U.S. economy faltered, unemployment grew, and the flow of Puerto Rican migration actually reversed itself, with the number of returnees exceeding the number of migrants in various years (U.S. Commission on Civil Rights, 1976, p. 25). The population movement continues, and about half of all Puerto Ricans live on the mainland today (U.S. Bureau of the Census, 2009b).

As the U.S. economy expanded and migration accelerated after World War II, Puerto Ricans moved into a broader range of jobs and locations in the society, and the group grew more economically diversified and more regionally dispersed. Still, the bulk of the group remains concentrated in lower-status jobs in the larger cities of the Northeast. Puerto Rican men have often found work as unskilled laborers or in service occupations, particularly in areas where English language facility was not necessary (e.g., janitorial work). The women have often been employed as domestics or seamstresses for the garment industry in New York City (Portes, 1990).

Transitions

Although Puerto Ricans are not "immigrants," the move to the mainland does involve a change in culture and language (Fitzpatrick, 1980, p. 858). Despite nearly a century of political affiliation, Puerto Rican and Anglo cultures differ along many dimensions. Puerto Ricans are overwhelmingly Catholic, but the religious practices and rituals on the mainland are quite different from those on the island. Mainland Catholic parishes often reflect the traditions and practices of other cultures and groups. On the island, "Religious observance reflects the spontaneous and expressive practices of the Spanish and the Italian and not the restrained and well-organized worship of the Irish and Germans" (Fitzpatrick, 1980, p. 865). Also, there are few Puerto Rican priests or even Spanish-speaking clergy on the mainland; thus, members of the group often feel estranged from and poorly served by the church (Fitzpatrick, 1987).

A particularly unsettling cultural difference between the island and the mainland involves skin color and perceptions of race. Puerto Rico has a long history of racial intermarriage. Slavery was less monolithic, and the island had no periods of systematic, race-based segregation like the Jim Crow system. Thus, although skin color prejudice still exists in Puerto Rico, it has never been as categorical as on the mainland. On the island, race is perceived as a continuum of possibilities and combinations, not as a simple dichotomous split between white and black.

Furthermore, in Puerto Rico, other factors, such as social class, are considered to be more important than race as criteria for judging and classifying others. In fact, as we have discussed, social class can affect perceptions of skin color and people of higher status might be seen as lighter skinned. Coming from this background, Puerto Ricans find the rigid racial thinking of U.S. culture disconcerting and even threatening.

The confusion and discomfort that can result was documented and illustrated by a study of Puerto Rican college students in New York City. Dramatic differences were found between the personal racial identification of the students and their perceptions of how Anglos viewed them. When asked for their racial identification, most of the students classified themselves as "tan," with one third labeling themselves "white" and only 7% considering themselves "black." When asked how they thought they were racially classified by Anglos, however, none of the students used the "tan" classification: 58% felt that they were seen as "white," and 41% felt that they were seen as "black" (Rodriguez, 1989, pp. 60–61; see also Rodriguez & Cordero-Guzman, 1992).

Another study documented dramatic differences in the terms used to express racial identity between women on the mainland and those in Puerto Rico. The latter identify their racial identity primarily in skin color terms: black, white, or *trigueña* (a "mixed-race" category with multiple skin tones), while mainland women identified themselves in nonracial terms, such as Hispanic, Latina, Hispanic American, or American. In the view of the researchers, these labels serve to deflect the stigma associated with black racial status in the United States (Landale & Oropesa, 2002).

In the racially dichotomized U.S. culture, many Puerto Ricans feel they have no clear place. They are genuinely puzzled when they first encounter prejudice and discrimination based on skin color and are uncertain about their own identity and self-image. The racial perceptions of the dominant culture can be threatening to Puerto Ricans to the extent that they are victimized by the same web of discrimination and disadvantage that affects African Americans. There are still clear disadvantages to being classified as black in U.S. society. Institutionalized racial barriers can be extremely formidable, and in the case of Puerto Ricans, they may combine with cultural and linguistic differences to sharply limit opportunities and mobility.

Puerto Ricans and Other Minority Groups

Puerto Ricans arrived in the cities of the Northeast long after the great wave of European immigrants and several decades after African Americans began migrating from the South. They have often competed with other minority groups for housing, jobs, and other resources. A pattern of ethnic succession can be seen in some neighborhoods and occupational areas in which Puerto Ricans have replaced other groups that have moved out (and sometimes up).

Because of their more recent arrival, Puerto Ricans on the mainland were not subjected to the more repressive paternalistic or rigid competitive systems of race relations like slavery or Jim Crow. Instead, the subordinate status of the group is manifested in their occupational, residential, and educational profiles and by the institutionalized barriers to upward mobility that they face. Puerto Ricans share many problems with other urban minority groups of color: poverty, failing educational systems, and crime. Like African Americans, their fate is dependent on the future of the American city, and a large segment of the group is in danger of becoming part of a permanent urban underclass.

Like Mexican Americans, Puerto Ricans on the mainland combine elements of both an immigrant and a colonized minority experience. The movement to the mainland is voluntary in some ways, but in others, it is strongly motivated by the transformations in the island economy that resulted from modernization and U.S. domination. Like Chicanos, Puerto Ricans tend to enter the labor force at the bottom of the occupational structure and face similar problems of inequality and marginalization. Also, Puerto Rican culture retains a strong vitality and is continually reinvigorated by the considerable movement back and forth between the island and the mainland.

Cuban Americans

The contact period for Cuban Americans, like Puerto Ricans, dates back to the Spanish-American War. At that time, Cuba was a Spanish colony but became an independent nation as a result of the war. Despite its nominal independence, the United States remained heavily involved in Cuban politics and economics for decades, and U.S. troops actually occupied the island on two different occasions.

The development of a Cuban American minority group bears little resemblance to the experience of either Chicanos or Puerto Ricans. As recently as the 1950s, there had not been much population movement from Cuba to the United States, even during times of labor shortages, and Cuban Americans were a very small group, numbering no more than 50,000 (Perez, 1980, p. 256).

Immigration (Push and Pull)

The conditions for a mass immigration were created in the late 1950s, when a Marxist revolution brought Fidel Castro to power in Cuba. Castro's government was decidedly anti-American and began to restructure Cuban society along socialist lines. The middle and upper classes lost political and economic power, and the revolution made it difficult, even impossible, for Cuban capitalists to remain in business. Thus, the first Cuban immigrants to the United States tended to come from the more elite classes and included affluent and powerful people who controlled many resources.

The United States was a logical destination for those displaced by the revolution. Cuba is only 90 miles from southern Florida, the climates are similar, and the U.S. government, which was as anti-Castro as Castro was anti-American, welcomed the new arrivals as political refugees fleeing from Communist tyranny. Prior social, cultural, and business ties also pulled the immigrants in the direction of the United States. Since gaining its independence in 1898, Cuba has been heavily influenced by its neighbor to the north, and U.S. companies helped to develop the Cuban economy. At the time of Castro's revolution, the Cuban political leadership and the more affluent classes were profoundly Americanized in their attitudes and lifestyles (Portes, 1990). Furthermore, many Cuban exiles viewed southern Florida as an ideal spot from which to launch a counterrevolution to oust Castro.

Immigration was considerable for several years. More than 215,000 Cubans arrived between the end of the revolution and 1962, when an escalation of hostile relations resulted in the cutoff of all direct contact between Cuba and the United States. In 1965, an air link was reestablished, and an additional 340,000 Cubans made the journey. When the air connection was terminated in 1973, immigration slowed to a trickle once more. In 1980, however, the Cuban government permitted another period of open immigration. Using boats of every shape, size, and degree of seaworthiness, about 124,000 Cubans crossed to Florida. These immigrants are often referred to as the **Marielitos**, after the port of Mariel from which many of them debarked. This wave of immigrants generated a great deal of controversy in the United States, because the Cuban government used the opportunity to rid itself of a variety of convicted criminals and outcasts. However, the Marielitos also included people from every segment of Cuban society, a fact that was lost in the clamor of concern about the "undesirables" (Portes & Manning, 1986, p. 58).

Regional Concentrations

The overwhelming majority of Cuban immigrants settled in southern Florida, especially in Miami and the surrounding Dade County. Today, Cuban Americans remain one of the most spatially concentrated minority groups in the United States, with 67% of all Cuban Americans residing in Florida, and 52% in the Miami area alone (U.S. Bureau of the Census, 2001).

This dense concentration has led to a number of disputes and conflicts between the Hispanic, Anglo, and African American communities in the area. Issues have centered on language, jobs, and discrimination by the police and other governmental agencies. The conflicts have often been intense, and on more than one occasion, they have erupted into violence and civil disorder.

Socioeconomic Characteristics

Compared with other streams of immigrants from Latin America, Cubans are, on the average, unusually affluent and well educated. Among the immigrants in the early 1960s were large numbers of professionals, landowners, and businesspeople. In later years, as Cuban society was transformed by the Castro regime, the stream included fewer elites, largely because there were fewer left in Cuba, and more political dissidents and working-class people. Today (as will be displayed in the exhibits presented later in this chapter), Cuban Americans rank higher than other Latino groups on a number of dimensions, a reflection of the educational and economic resources they brought with them from Cuba and the favorable reception they enjoyed from the United States (Portes, 1990).

These assets gave Cubans an advantage over Chicanos and Puerto Ricans, but the differences between the three Latino groups run deeper and are more complex than a simple accounting of initial resources would suggest. Cubans adapted to U.S. society in a way that is fundamentally different from the other two Latino groups.

The Ethnic Enclave

Most of the minority groups we have discussed to this point have been concentrated in the unskilled, low-wage segments of the economy in which jobs are not secure and not linked to opportunities for upward mobility. Many Cuban Americans have bypassed this sector of the economy and much of the discrimination and limitations associated with it. Like several other groups, such as Jewish Americans, Cuban Americans are an enclave minority (see Chapter 2). An ethnic enclave is a social, economic, and cultural subsociety controlled by the group itself. Located in a specific geographical area or neighborhood inhabited solely or largely by members of the group, the enclave encompasses sufficient economic enterprises and social institutions to permit the group to function as a self-contained entity, largely independent of the surrounding community.

The first wave of Cuban immigrants brought with them considerable resources and business expertise. Although much of their energy was focused on ousting Castro and returning to Cuba, they generated enough economic activity to sustain restaurants, shops, and other small businesses that catered to the exile community.

As the years passed and the hope of a return to Cuba dimmed, the enclave economy grew. Between 1967 and 1976, the number of Cuban-owned firms in Dade County increased ninefold, from 919 to about 8,000. Six years later, the number had reached 12,000. Most of these enterprises are small, but some factories employ hundreds of workers (Portes & Rumbaut, 1996). In addition to businesses serving their own community, Cuban-owned firms are involved in construction, manufacturing, finance, insurance, real estate, and an array of other activities. Over the decades, Cuban-owned firms have become increasingly integrated into the local economy and increasingly competitive with firms in the larger society. The growth of economic enterprises has been paralleled by a growth in the number of other types of groups and organizations and in the number and quality of services available (schools, law firms, medical care, funeral parlors, and so on). The enclave has become a largely autonomous community capable of providing for its members from cradle to grave (Logan, Alba, & McNulty, 1994; Peterson, 1995; Portes & Bach, 1985).

The fact that the enclave economy is controlled by the group itself is crucial; it separates the ethnic enclave from "the ghetto," or neighborhoods that are impoverished and segregated. In ghettos, members of other groups typically control the local economy; the profits, rents, and other resources flow out of the neighborhood. In the enclave, profits are reinvested and kept in the neighborhood. Group members can avoid the discrimination and limitations imposed by the larger society and can apply their skills, education, and talents in an atmosphere free from language barriers and prejudice. Those who might wish to venture into business for themselves can use the networks of cooperation and mutual aid for advice, credit, and other forms of assistance. Thus, the ethnic enclave provides a platform from which Cuban Americans can pursue economic success independent of their degree of acculturation or English language ability.

The effectiveness of the ethnic enclave as a pathway for adaptation is illustrated by a study of Cuban and Mexican immigrants, all of whom entered the United States in 1973. At the time of entry, the groups were comparable in levels of skills, education, and English language ability. The groups were interviewed on several different occasions, and although they remained comparable on many variables, there were dramatic differences between the groups that reflected their different positions in the labor market. The majority of the Mexican immigrants were employed in the low-wage job sector. Less than 20% were self-employed or employed by another person of Mexican descent. Conversely, 57% of the Cuban immigrants were self-employed or employed by another Cuban (i.e., they were involved in the enclave economy). Among the subjects in the study, self-employed Cubans reported the highest monthly incomes ($1,495), and Cubans otherwise employed in the enclave earned the second-highest incomes ($1,111). The lowest incomes ($880) were earned by Mexican immigrants employed in small, nonenclave firms; many of these people worked as unskilled laborers in seasonal, temporary, or otherwise insecure jobs (Portes, 1990; see also Portes & Bach, 1985).

The ability of the Mexican immigrants to rise in the class system and compete for place and position was severely constrained by the weight of past discrimination, the preferences of employers in the present, and their own lack of economic and political power. Cuban immigrants who found jobs in the enclave did not need to expose themselves to American prejudices or rely on the job market of the larger society. They entered an immigrant context that had networks of mutual assistance and support and linked them to opportunities more consistent with their ambitions and their qualifications.

The fact that success came faster to the group that was less acculturated reverses the prediction of many theories of assimilation. The pattern has long been recognized by some leaders of other groups, however, and is voiced in many of the themes of Black Power, Red Power, and Chicanismo that emphasize self-help, self-determination, nationalism, and separation. However, ethnic enclaves cannot be a panacea for all immigrant or other minority groups. They develop only under certain limited conditions, namely, when business and financial expertise and reliable sources of capital are combined with a disciplined labor force willing to work for low wages in exchange for on-the-job training, future assistance and loans, or other delayed benefits. Enclave enterprises usually start on a small scale and cater only to other ethnics. Thus, the early economic returns are small, and prosperity follows only after years of hard work, if at all. Most important, eventual success and expansion beyond the boundaries of the enclave depend on the persistence of strong ties of loyalty, kinship, and solidarity. The pressure to assimilate might easily weaken these networks and the group cohesion (Portes & Manning, 1986).

Cuban Americans and Other Minority Groups

The adaptation of Cuban Americans contrasts sharply with the experiences of colonized minority groups and with the common understanding of how immigrants are "supposed" to acculturate and integrate. Cuban Americans are neither the first nor the only group to develop an ethnic enclave, and their success has generated prejudice and resentment from the dominant group and from other minority groups. Whereas Puerto Ricans and Chicanos have been the victims of stereotypes labeling them "inferior," higher-status Cuban Americans have been stereotyped as "too successful," "too clannish," and "too ambitious." The former stereotype commonly emerges to rationalize exploitative relationships; the latter expresses disparagement and rejection of groups that are more successful in the struggle to acquire resources (see Chapter 3). Nonetheless, the stereotype of Cubans is an exaggeration and a misperception that obscures the fact that poverty and unemployment are major problems for many members of this group (see the exhibits at the end of this chapter).

New Hispanic Groups: Immigrants From the Dominican Republic, El Salvador, and Colombia

Immigration to the United States from Latin America, the Caribbean, and South America has been considerable, even excluding Mexico. As with other sending nations, the volume of immigration increased after 1965 and has averaged about 200,000 per year since the 1980s. Generally, Latino immigrants—not counting Mexico—have been 20% to 25% of all immigrants since the 1960s.

The sending nations for these immigrants are economically less developed, and most have long-standing relations with the United States. We have already discussed the roles that Mexico and Puerto Rico have historically played as sources of cheap labor and the ties that led Cubans to immigrate to the United States. Each of the other sending nations has been similarly linked to the United States, the dominant economic and political power in the region.

Although the majority of these immigrants bring educational and occupational qualifications that are modest by U.S. standards, they tend to be more educated, more urbanized, and more skilled than the average citizens of the nations from which they come. Contrary to widely held beliefs, these immigrants do not represent the poorest of the poor, the "wretched refuse" of their homelands. They tend to be rather ambitious, as evidenced by their willingness to attempt success in a society that has not been notably hospitable to Latinos or people of color in the past. These immigrants are not only fleeing poverty or joblessness, they are also attempting to pursue their ambitions and seek opportunities for advancement that are simply not available in their country of origin (Portes & Rumbaut, 1996).

This characterization applies to legal and unauthorized immigrants alike. In fact, the latter may illustrate the point more dramatically, because the cost of illegally entering the United States can be considerable, much higher than the cost of a legal entry. The venture may require years of saving money or the combined resources of a large kinship group. Forged papers and other costs of being smuggled into the country can easily amount to thousands of dollars, a considerable sum in nations in which the usual wage is a tiny fraction of the U.S. average (Orreniou, 2001). Also, the passage can be extremely dangerous and can require a level of courage (or desperation) not often associated with the undocumented and illegal. Many Mexican would-be immigrants have died along the border, and many other immigrants have been lost at sea (for example, see "Dominicans Saved From Sea," 2004).

Rather than attempting to cover all South and Central American groups, we will select the three largest to serve as "case studies" and consider immigrants from the Dominican Republic, El Salvador, and Colombia. Together, these groups comprise 7% to 8% of all immigrants in recent years and about 20% of the immigrants from Central and South America and the Caribbean. These groups had few members in the United States before the 1960s, and all have had high rates of immigration over the past four decades. However, the motivation of the immigrants and the immigration experience has varied from group to group, as we shall see later.

Exhibit 7.8 Map of Central and South America and the Caribbean Showing the Dominican Republic, El Salvador, and Colombia

Three Case Studies

Each of the groups selected for case studies has a high percentage of foreign-born members (see Exhibit 7.4), and, predictably with so many members in the first generation, proficiency in English is an important issue. Although Colombians approach national norms in education, the other two groups have relatively low levels of human capital (education), and all are well above national norms in terms of poverty.

Although these groups share some common characteristics, there are also important differences between them. They differ in their "racial" characteristics, with Dominicans being more African in appearance, Colombians more European, and Salvadorans more Indian. The groups tend to settle in different places. Dominicans and Colombians are clustered along the East Coast, particularly in New York, New Jersey, and Florida, but Salvadorans are more concentrated on the West Coast (U.S. Department of Homeland

Security, 2008). Finally, the groups differ in the conditions of their entry or their contact situation, a difference that, as we have seen, is quite consequential. Salvadorans are more likely to be political refugees fleeing a brutal civil war and political repression, while Dominicans and Colombians are more likely to be motivated by economics and the employment possibilities offered in the United States. We will consider each of these groups briefly and explore some of these differences further.

Dominicans. The Dominican Republic shares the Caribbean island of Hispaniola with Haiti. The island economy is still largely agricultural, although the tourist industry has grown in recent years. Unemployment and poverty are major problems, and Dominicans average less than five years of education (Nationmaster.com, n.d.).

Dominican immigrants, like those from Mexico, are motivated largely by economics, and they compete for jobs with Puerto Ricans, other immigrant groups, and native-born workers with lower levels of education and jobs skills. Although Dominicans are limited in their job options by the language barrier, they are somewhat advantaged by their willingness to work for lower wages, and they are especially concentrated in the service sector, as day laborers (men) or domestics (women). Dominicans maintain strong ties with home and are a major source of income and support for the families left behind.

In terms of acculturation and integration, Dominicans are roughly similar to Mexican Americans and Puerto Ricans, although some studies suggest that they are possibly the most impoverished immigrant group (see, for example, Camarota, 2002). A high percentage of Dominicans are undocumented, and many spend considerable money and take considerable risks to get to the United States. If these less visible members of the community were included in the official, government-generated statistics used in exhibits presented later in this chapter, it is very likely that the portrait of poverty and low levels of education and jobs skills would be even more dramatic.

Salvadorans. El Salvador, like the Dominican Republic, is a relatively poor nation, with a high percentage of the population relying on subsistence agriculture for survival. It is estimated that about 50% of the population is below poverty level, and there are major problems with unemployment and underemployment. About 80% of the population is literate, and the average number of years of school completed is a little more than five (Nationmaster.com, n.d.).

El Salvador, like many sending nations, has a difficult time providing sufficient employment opportunities for its population, and much of the pressure to immigrate is economic. However, El Salvador also suffered through a brutal civil war in the 1980s, and many of the Salvadorans in the United States today are actually political refugees. The United States, under the administration of then-President Reagan, refused to grant political refugee status to Salvadorans, and many were returned to El Salvador. This federal policy resulted in high numbers of undocumented immigrants and also stimulated a sanctuary movement, led by American clergy, which helped Salvadoran immigrants, both undocumented and legal, to stay in United States. As was the case with Dominicans, if the undocumented immigrants from El Salvador were included in official government statistics, the picture of poverty would become even more extreme.

Colombians. Colombia is somewhat more developed than most other Central and South American nations but has suffered from more than 40 years of internal turmoil, civil war, and government corruption. The nation is a major center for the production and distribution of drugs to the world in general and the United States in particular, and the drug industry and profits are complexly intertwined with domestic strife. Colombian Americans are closer to U.S. norms of education and income than other Latino groups, and recent immigrants are a mixture of less skilled laborers and well-educated professionals seeking to further their career. Colombians are residentially concentrated in urban areas, especially in Florida and the Northeast, and often settle in areas close to other Latino neighborhoods. Of course, the huge majority of Colombian Americans are law abiding and not connected with the drug trade, but still they must deal with the pervasive stereotype that pictures Colombians as gangsters and drug smugglers (not unlike the Mafia stereotype encountered by Italian Americans).

COMPARATIVE FOCUS: Immigration to Europe Versus Immigration to the United States

The volume of immigration in the world today is at record levels. Almost 200 million people, about 3% of the world's population, live outside their countries of birth, and there is hardly a nation or region that has not been affected (Population Reference Bureau, 2008b). The United States has by far the highest number of foreign-born citizens, and the flow of immigrants (including both undocumented and legal) from Mexico to the United States is the single largest population movement. However, the United States is only one of many destination nations, and the issues of immigration and assimilation that are being debated so fervently here are echoed in many other nations.

In particular, the nations of Western Europe—highly developed, advanced industrial economies—are prime destinations for immigrants. Like the United States, these nations have very high standards of living, and they offer myriad opportunities for economic survival, even though the price may be to live at the margins of the larger society or to take jobs scorned by the native-born. An additional powerful factor that "pulls" people to this region is that Western European nations have very low birthrates and, in some cases (e.g., Germany, Greece, and Spain), their populations are projected to actually decline in coming decades (Population Reference Bureau, 2008a). The labor force shortages thus created will continue to attract immigrants to Western Europe for decades to come.

The immigration to Western Europe is varied and includes people from all walks of life, from highly educated professionals to peasant laborers. The most prominent flows include movements from Turkey to Germany, Africa to Spain and Italy, and from many former British colonies (Jamaica, India, Nigeria, and so on) to the United Kingdom. This immigration is primarily an economic phenomenon motivated by the search for jobs and survival, but the stream also includes refugees and asylum-seekers spurred by civil war, genocide, and political unrest.

(Continued)

(Continued)

In terms of numbers, the volume of immigration to Western Europe is much smaller than the flow to the United States, but its proportional impact is comparable. About 13% of the U.S. population is foreign-born, and many Western European nations (including Belgium, Germany, and Sweden) have a similar profile (Organization for Economic Co-operation and Development, 2009).

Thus, it is not surprising that, in both cases, immigration has become a major concern and a significant political issue. A major difference, as we saw when discussing Ireland in Chapter 2, is that Western European nations have less experience in dealing with a large influx of newcomers or managing a pluralistic society. Furthermore, many Western European nations make it difficult or impossible for immigrants to achieve citizenship or full membership in the society.

To focus on one example, Germany has by far the largest immigrant community of any Western European nation and has been dealing with a large foreign-born population for decades. Germany began to allow large numbers of immigrants to enter as temporary workers or "guest workers" *(Gastarbeiter)* to help staff its expanding economy beginning in the 1960s. Most of these immigrants came from Turkey, and they were seen by Germans as temporary workers only, people who would return to their homeland when they were no longer needed. Thus, the host society saw no particular need to encourage immigrants to acculturate and integrate.

Contrary to this perception, many immigrants stayed and settled permanently, and their millions of descendents today speak only German and have no knowledge of or experience with their "homeland." Although acculturated, they are not integrated and, in fact—and in stark contrast with the United States—they were denied the opportunity to become citizens until recently. A German law passed nearly a century ago reserved citizenship for ethnic Germans, regardless of place of birth. Under this policy, recent immigrants from, say, Ukraine were eligible for citizenship if they could prove that they had German ancestors—even if they spoke no German and had no familiarity with German culture or traditions. In contrast, Turks living in Germany were not eligible for citizenship regardless of how long they or their family had been residents. This law was changed in 1999 to permit greater flexibility in qualifying for citizenship but, still more recently, Germany has passed new laws that make it harder for foreigners to enter the country. To gain admission, immigrants may have to pass a language test and have a guaranteed job or a place in school. The immigrant community sees these new laws as a form of rejection, and there have been bitter (and sometimes violent) demonstrations in response ("Europe: The Integration Dilemma," 2007).

Clashes of this sort have been common across Western Europe in recent years, especially with the growing Muslim communities. Many Europeans see Islamic immigrants as unassimilable, too foreign or exotic to ever fit into the mainstream of their society. These conflicts have been punctuated by violence and riots in France, Germany, the Netherlands, and other places.

Across Europe, just as in the United States (and Canada), nations are wrestling with issues of inclusion and diversity: What should it mean to be German, or French, or British, or Dutch? How much diversity can be tolerated before national cohesion is threatened? What are the limits of tolerance? What is the best balance between assimilation and pluralism? Struggles over the essential meaning of national identity are increasingly common throughout the developed world.

FOCUS ON CONTEMPORARY ISSUES: Will America Grow "Whiter" or "Browner"?

With Dr. Eileen O'Brien[1]

As we saw in Exhibit 7.1, Latino American groups are growing rapidly. What are the implications of this growth—especially when combined with the rapidly increasing size of Asian Americans—for the traditional American black-white racial order? Virtually since its birth, U.S. society has been organized into black and white communities, separate and vastly unequal. This structural, economic, and political reality has been reinforced by the traditional U.S. perception that there are only two races and that everyone is, unambiguously, either black or white. What will happen to this simple dichotomy as groups that are neither black nor white—Latinos, Asian Americans, and others—continue to grow in numbers and significance in the everyday life of U.S. society?

One possibility, called the whitening thesis, stresses the point that Latinos (and Asian Americans) are not black and hypothesizes that they eventually will be accepted as white. An opposing position, called the browning thesis, stresses that these groups are not white and predicts that they will ally with other "peoples of color" and threaten the dominance of whites. We consider each of these views below, as well as a third possible future for the racial order of the United States.

Whitening

In this model, Latinos and Asian Americans will become part of the white American racial group while blacks will remain disproportionately unequal, powerless, and marginalized. The racial identities of Latinos and Asians will become "thinner," declining in salience as they increasingly access the privileges of whiteness, much like Irish and Italian before them. As they assimilate, the "white" racial identity will take primacy over their ethnic connections, and their sense of ethnicity will become largely symbolic. This prediction is based on Gordon's assimilation model, which, as you recall, postulates that immigrants move through a series of stages and become more incorporated into various aspects of the life of the dominant society in a relatively linear fashion. Once a group has completed acculturation, integration, and intermarriage, they will begin to racially identify with the dominant group.

George Yancy (2003) has tested the whitening thesis on a nationally representative data set, and his analysis places Latinos and Asian Americans in the middle stages of assimilation, because their residential patterns, marital patterns, and several key political beliefs align more closely with white Americans than they do with black Americans. If Gordon's model holds true, these groups will come to identify as white over the next several generations.

Another research project (Murguia & Foreman, 2003) focused on Mexican Americans and found that they tend to prefer spouses, neighbors, coworkers, and friends who are either Puerto Rican or white, not black. The researchers also found that Mexican Americans tend to endorse modern racism (see Chapters 1 and 5): the ideas that racism is not much of a barrier to success and that people of color are largely responsible for their own hardships. This alignment with the ideology of the dominant-group positions Mexican Americans well on the path to whiteness.

(Continued)

(Continued)

Finally, note that an important part of the whitening process is to distance oneself from the perpetually stigmatized black group. To the extent that a whitening process occurs for Latino and Asian Americans, these groups will tend to use both traditional and modern antiblack racism to emphasize their differences and align themselves more with the attitudinal and cultural perspectives of the dominant group. We discussed this type of dynamic in our coverage of the racial identity of Puerto Ricans who come to the mainland.

Browning

The browning thesis argues that whites will gradually lose their dominant status as Latino and Asian American groups grow in numbers. The balance of power will tip toward the nonwhite groups, who will use their greater numbers to challenge whites for position in the society.

Some theorists see the loss of white dominance as very negative, a threat to the integrity of Anglo-American culture. This "doomsday" version of the browning thesis has most notably been presented by political scientist Samuel Huntington (2004) who argues that Latinos are "unassimilable" because of their alleged unwillingness to learn English and absorb other aspects of U.S. culture. This perspective is based largely on nativism, ethnocentrism, and prejudice and is not given much credence by most sociologists. Indeed, much of the evidence presented in this and previous chapters on the assimilation of Hispanic Americans shows that this view is simply wrong (e.g., see exhibits 7.9 and 7.10). Nevertheless, this version of the browning thesis has gained momentum in popular culture and in some talk radio and cable TV shows. It also manifests itself in the political arena in debates over immigration policy and in the movement to make English the "official" language of the nation (sees Chapter 2).

A different version of the browning thesis has taken hold among some sociologists. For example, Feagin and O'Brien (2004) put a positive spin on the idea of the declining white numerical majority. They believe that as "minority groups" grow in size, whites will be forced to share power in a more democratic, egalitarian, and inclusive fashion. This shift will be more likely to the extent that minority groups can forge alliances with each other against the dominant group. These combinations may be foreshadowed by studies of generational differences in the racial attitudes of immigrants, some of which show that native-born or second-generation Latinos and Asian Americans are more likely to express solidarity with African Americans than are the foreign-born and recently arrived members of their group (Murguia & Foreman, 2004).

In contrast to the whitening thesis, the browning thesis expects Latinos and Asian Americans to embrace a more color-conscious worldview and find ways to leverage their growing numbers, in alliance with African Americans, to improve their status in American society.

This version of the browning thesis also adopts a more global perspective. It recognizes that the world is occupied by many more "people of color" than by whites of European descent and that the growing numbers of nonwhites in the United States can be an important resource in the global marketplace. For example, people around the world commonly speak several languages on a daily basis, but Americans are almost entirely monolingual and this places them at a disadvantage in a global marketplace that values linguistic diversity. The United States might improve its position if it encourages the "fluent bilingualism" of its Latino and Asian American citizens rather than insist on "English only" (see Chapter 2).

Something Else?

Still another group of scholars challenges both the browning and the whitening theses and foresees a three-way racial dynamic. These scholars focus on the tremendous diversity within the Latino and Asian American communities in the United States in terms of relative wealth, skin color, and other "racial" characteristics, religion, and national origins. This diversity leads them to conclude that only some Latino and Asian Americans will "whiten." Eduardo Bonilla-Silva sketches out a future racial trichotomy: whites, honorary whites, and the collective black. In this schema, well-off and light-skinned Latinos and Asians would not "become white" but rather would occupy an intermediary "honorary whites" status. This status would afford them much of the privileges and esteem not widely accorded to people of color, but it would still be a conditional status, which potentially could be revoked in times of economic crisis or at any other time that those in power would find necessary. Bonilla-Silva predicts that groups like Chinese Americans and lighter-skinned Latinos would fit into the honorary white category, while darker-skinned Latinos and Asians would fit into the collective black category, along with, of course, American blacks.

Murguia and Foreman (2003) provide some findings from their study of Mexican Americans that can be used to illustrate this process. They point out that skin color and educational level make a difference in whether or not Latinos ally with blacks. Mexican Americans with darker skin, higher educational levels, and those born in the United States are less likely to buy into the antiblack stereotypes of the larger culture and more likely to recognize the significance of racism in their own lives. Attitudes such as these may form the basis of future alliances between some (but not all) Latinos, Asian Americans, and African Americans.

Conclusion

Will the United States grow browner or whiter? In the face of high levels of immigration and the growing importance of groups that are in the "racial middle"—groups that are neither black nor white—it seems certain that the traditional, dichotomous black-white racial order cannot persist. What will replace it? Whichever thesis proves correct, it seems certain that new understandings of race and new relationships between racial groups will emerge in the coming decades.

Contemporary Hispanic–White Relations

As in previous chapters, we will use the central concepts of this text to review the status of Latinos in the United States. Where relevant, comparisons are made between the major Latino groups and the minority groups discussed in previous chapters.

Prejudice and Discrimination

The American tradition of prejudice against Latinos was born in the 19th-century conflicts that created minority group status for Mexican Americans. The themes of the original anti-Mexican stereotypes and attitudes were consistent with the nature of the contact situation: As Mexicans were conquered and subordinated, they were characterized as inferior, lazy, irresponsible, low in intelligence, and dangerously criminal (McWilliams, 1961). The prejudice and racism, supplemented with the echoes of the racist ideas and beliefs brought to the Southwest by many Anglos, helped to justify and rationalize the colonized, exploited status of the Chicanos.

These prejudices were incorporated into the dominant culture and were transferred to Puerto Ricans when they began to arrive on the mainland. As we have already mentioned, this stereotype does not fit Cuban Americans. Instead, their affluence has been exaggerated and perceived as undeserved or achieved by unfair or "un-American" means, a characterization similar to the traditional stereotype of Jews but just as prejudiced as the perception of Latino inferiority.

There is some evidence that the level of Latino prejudice has been affected by the decline of explicit American racism. For example, social distance scale results show a decrease in the scores of Mexicans, although their group ranking tends to remain stable. Conversely, prejudice and racism against Latinos tend to increase during times of high immigration, as the Noel hypothesis would predict. At present, prejudice, discrimination, racism, and hate crimes and other attacks seem particularly concentrated along the Mexican border, where the volume of immigration has been particularly high in recent years.

Although discrimination of all kinds, institutional as well as individual, has been common against Latino groups, it has not been as rigid or as total as the systems that controlled African American labor under slavery and segregation. However, discrimination against Latinos has not dissipated to the same extent as it has against European immigrant groups and their descendants. Because of their longer tenure in the United States and their original status as a rural labor force, Mexican Americans have probably been more victimized by the institutionalized forms of discrimination than have other Latino groups.

Assimilation and Pluralism

Acculturation

Latinos are highly variable in their extent of acculturation but are often seen as "slow" to change, learn English, and adopt Anglo customs. Contrary to this perception, research shows that Hispanics are following many of the same patterns of assimilation as European groups. Their rates of acculturation increase with length of residence and are higher for the native-born (Espinosa & Massey, 1997; Goldstein & Suro, 2000; Valentine & Mosley, 2000).

The dominant trend for Hispanic groups, as for immigrants from Europe in the past (see Chapter 2) is that language acculturation increases over the generations, as the length of residence in the United States increases and as education increases. One study, which combines six different surveys conducted since 2000 and is based on more than 14,000 respondents, illustrates these points. Results are displayed in Exhibits 7.9 through 7.11.

Exhibit 7.9 Percentage of Hispanic Americans Who Speak English "Very Well" by Generation

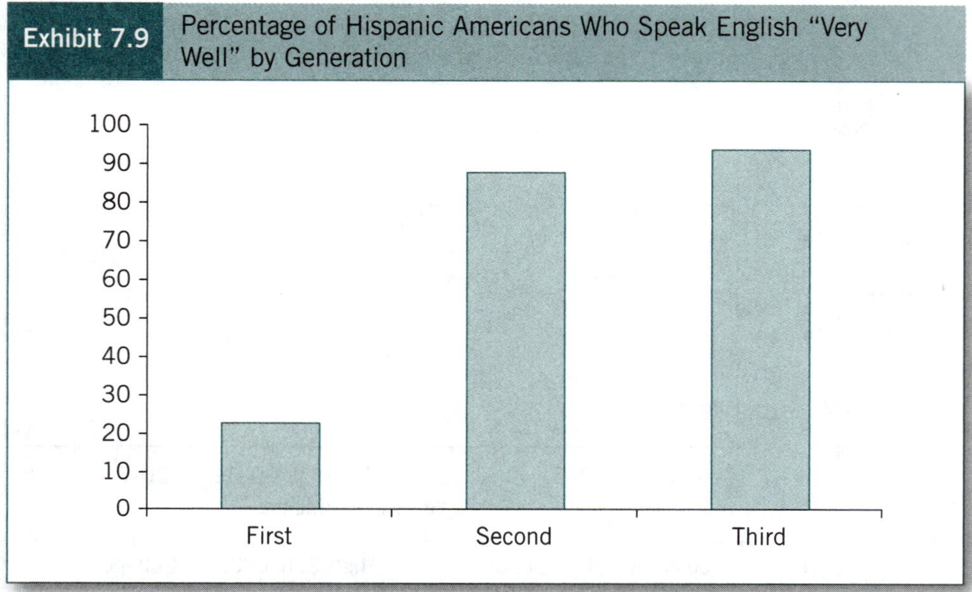

SOURCE: Hakimzadeh & Cohn (2007). Copyright © 2007 Pew Hispanic Center, a Pew Research Center project, www.pewhispanic.org.

Exhibit 7.10 Percentage of Foreign-Born Hispanic Americans Who Speak English "Very Well" by Years of Residence in the United States

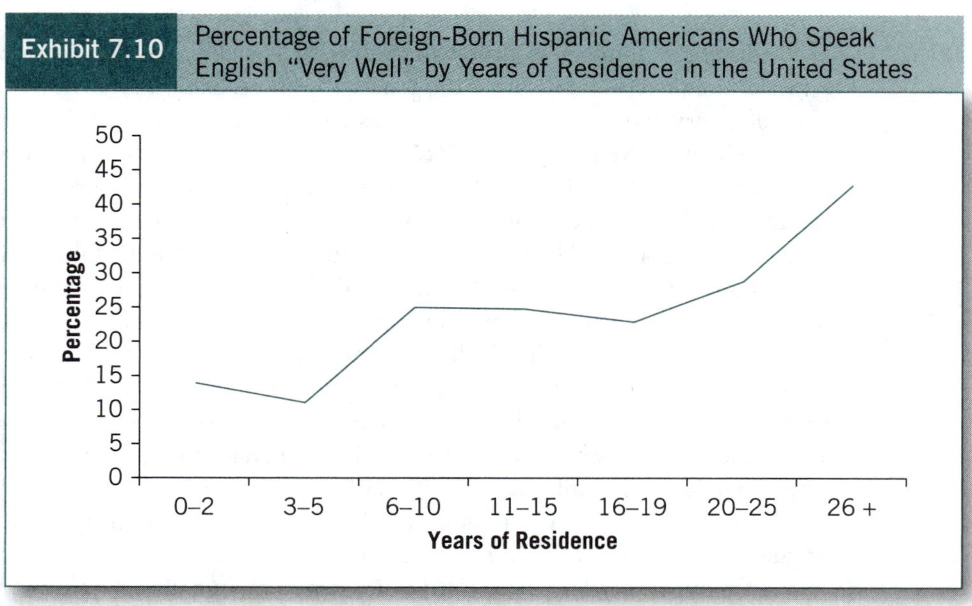

SOURCE: Hakimzadeh & Cohn (2007). Copyright © 2007 Pew Hispanic Center, a Pew Research Center project, www.pewhispanic.org.

Exhibit 7.11 Percentage of Hispanic Americans Who Speak English "Very Well" by Years of Residence and Levels of Education

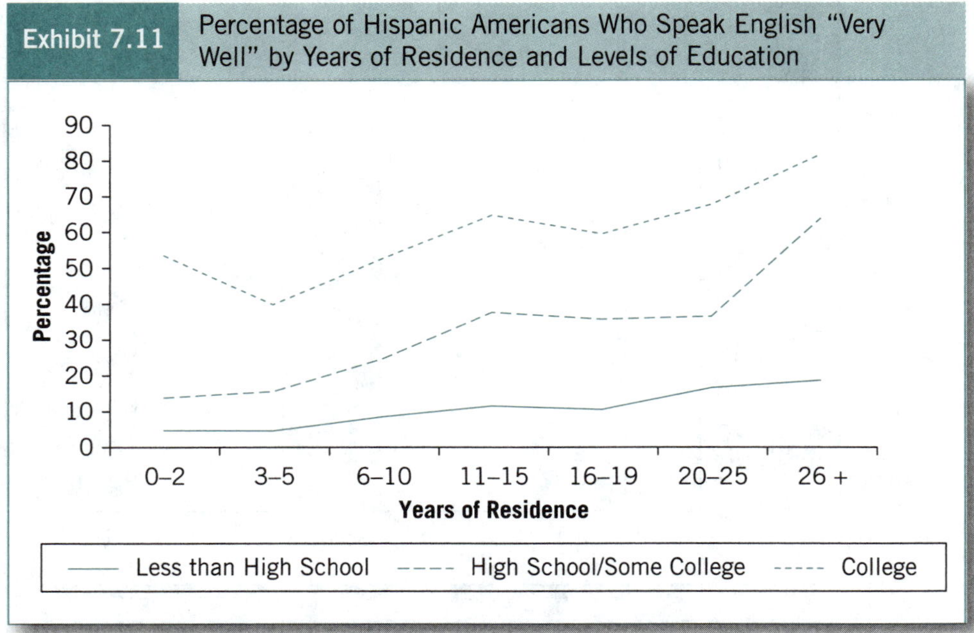

SOURCE: Hakimzadeh & Cohn (2007). Copyright © 2007 Pew Hispanic Center, a Pew Research Center project, www.pewhispanic.org.

A different study showed that the values of Hispanics come to approximate the values of the society as a whole as the generations pass. Exhibit 7.12 shows some results of a 2002 survey of Latinos and compares cultural values by English language proficiency, which, as we saw in Exhibits 7.9 and 7.10, is closely related to length of residence and generation. In this study, most Latinos (72%) who spoke predominantly Spanish were first generation while most (78%) who spoke predominantly English were third generation. The second generation is most likely to be bilingual.

Exhibit 7.12 shows the results for four different survey items that measure values and opinions. The values of predominantly Spanish-speakers are distinctly different from non-Latinos, especially on the item that measures support for the statement that "children should live with their parents until they are married." Virtually all of the Spanish-speakers supported the statement, but English-speaking Latinos approximated the more independent and individualistic values of Anglos. For each of the other three items, a similar acculturation of values occurred.

Even while acculturation continues, however, Hispanic culture and the Spanish language are revitalized by immigration. By its nature, assimilation is a slow process that can require decades or generations to complete. In contrast, immigration can be fast, often accomplished in less than a day. Thus, even as Hispanic Americans acculturate and integrate, Hispanic culture and language are sustained and strengthened. What is perceived to be slow acculturation for these groups is mostly the result of fast and continuous immigration.

Exhibit 7.12 Percent of Latinos Agreeing by Primary Language

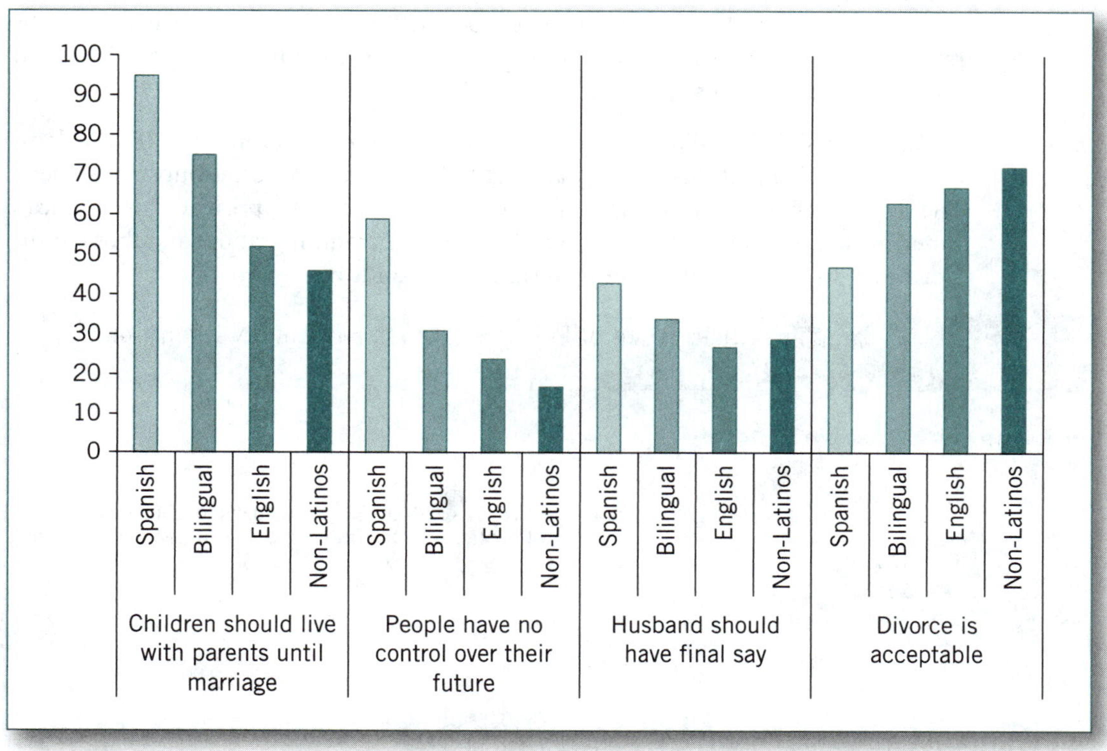

SOURCE: Pew Research Center (2004).

FULL TEXT OF SURVEY ITEMS:

"It is better for children to live in their parents' home until they are married."

"It doesn't do any good to plan for the future because you don't have any control over it."

"In general, the husband should have the final say in family matters."

"Divorce is acceptable."

Furthermore, colonized minority groups such as Chicanos and Puerto Ricans were not encouraged to assimilate in the past. Valued primarily for the cheap labor they supplied, they were seen as otherwise inferior or undesirable and unfit for integration. For much of the 20th century, Latinos were excluded from the institutions and experiences (e.g., school) that could have led to greater equality and higher rates of acculturation. Prejudice, racism, and discrimination combined to keep most Latino groups away from the centers of modernization and change and away from opportunities to improve their situation.

Finally, for Cubans, Dominicans and other groups, cultural differences reflect the fact that they are largely recent immigrants. Their first generations are alive and well, and as is typical for immigrant groups, they keep the language and traditions alive.

Secondary Structural Assimilation

In this section, we survey the situation of Latinos in the public areas and institutions of American society, beginning with where people live. Additional information on the relative standing of Hispanic American groups can be found in the Appendix (www.pineforge.com/healeyds3e).

Residence. Exhibit 7.13 shows the regional concentrations of Latinos in 2007. The legacies of the varied patterns of entry and settlement for the largest groups are evident. The higher concentrations in the Southwest reflect the presence of Mexican Americans; those in Florida are the result of the Cuban immigration, and those in the Northeast display the settlement patterns of Puerto Ricans.

Exhibit 7.13 Geographical Distribution of People of Hispanic or Latino Origin (All Races), 2007

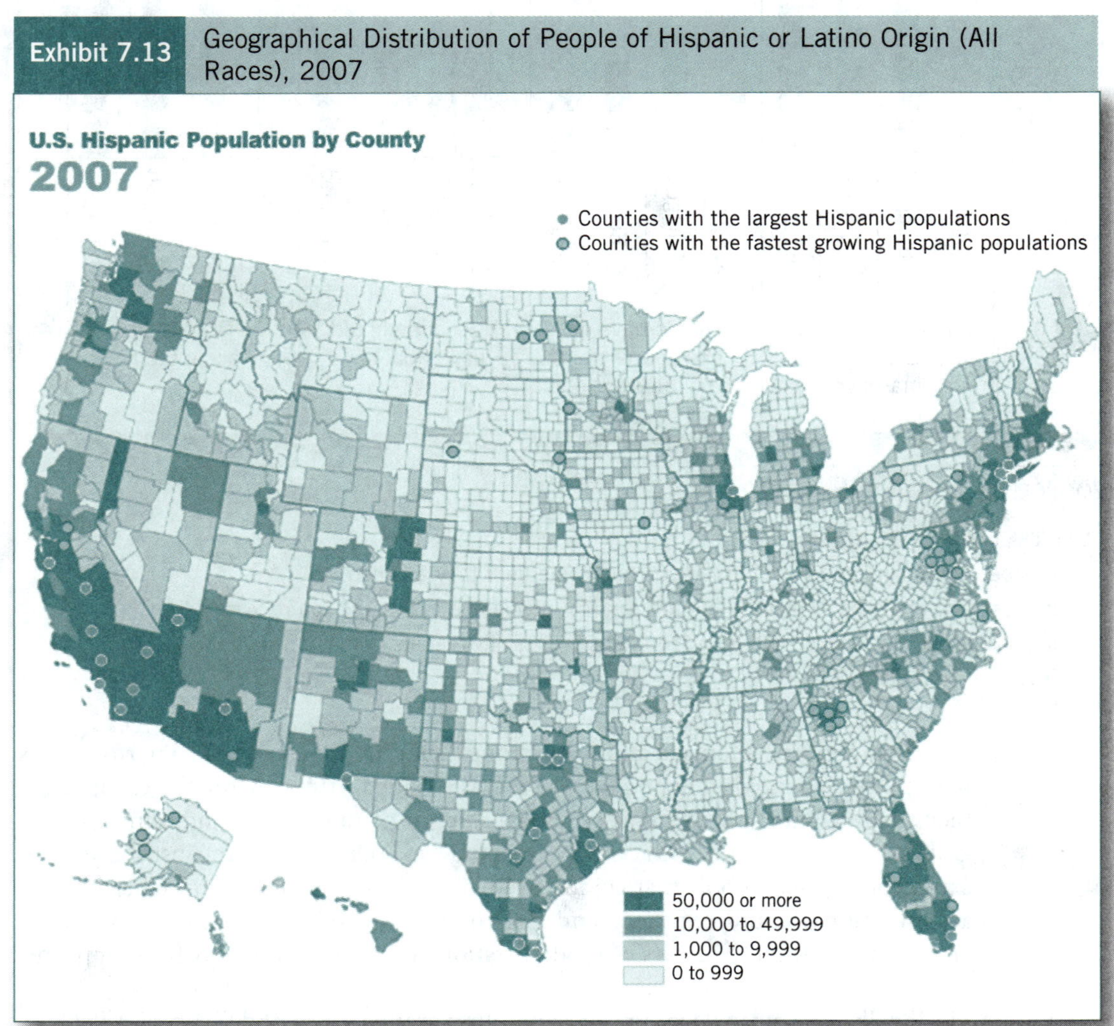

SOURCE: Pew Hispanic Center (http://pewhispanic.org/states/population/). Copyright © 2007 Pew Hispanic Center, a Pew Research Center project.

Exhibit 7.14 highlights the areas of the nation in which Latinos are growing fastest. A quick glance at the map will reveal that many of the high-growth areas are distant from the traditional points of entry for this group. In particular, the Hispanic American population is growing rapidly in coastal New England, the Deep South, the Midwest, the Northwest, and even Alaska. Among many other forces, this population movement is a response to the availability of jobs in factories, mills, chicken-processing plants and slaughter houses, farms, construction, and other low-skilled areas of the economy.

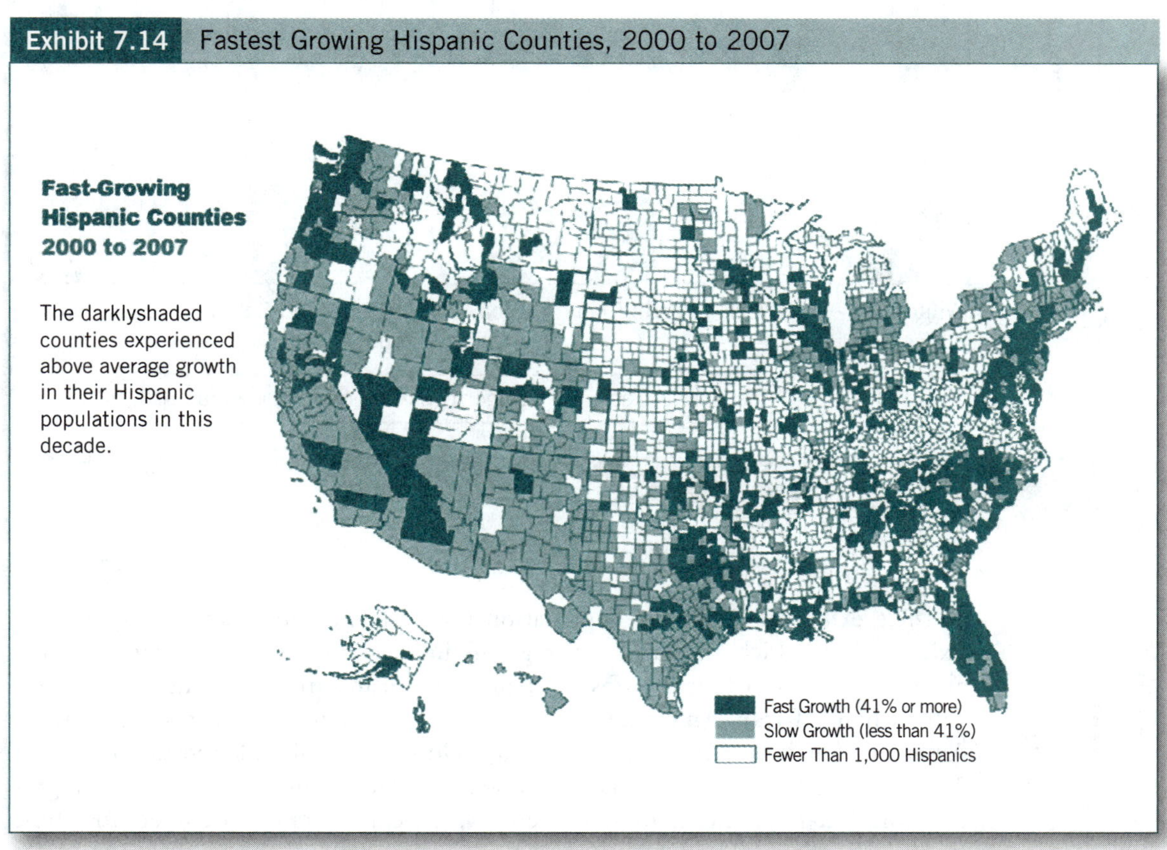

Exhibit 7.14 Fastest Growing Hispanic Counties, 2000 to 2007

SOURCE: Pew Hispanic Center (http://pewhispanic.org/states/population/).

Across the nation, Latino groups are highly urbanized, as shown in Exhibit 7.15. More than 90% of all groups live in cities, and this percentage rises to nearly 100% for some. Mexican Americans are more rural than the other groups, but, in sharp contrast to their historical role as an agrarian workforce, the percentage of the group living outside urban areas is tiny today.

Exhibit 7.15 Urbanization for Non-Hispanic Whites and Six Hispanic American Groups by Nation or Territory of Origin, 2000

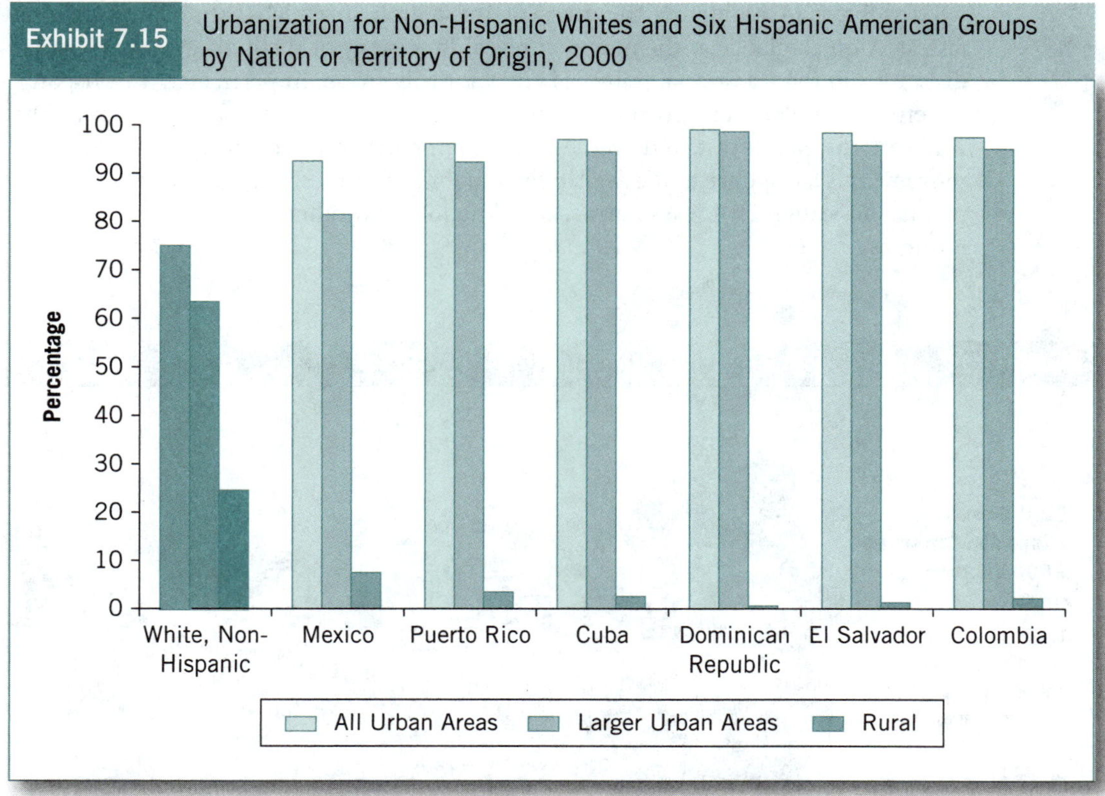

SOURCE: U.S. Bureau of the Census (2000h).

The extent of residential segregation for Hispanic Americans is displayed in Exhibit 7.16, which shows the average dissimilarity index for 220 metropolitan areas grouped into four regions. Hispanic Americans are less residentially segregated than African Americans (see Exhibit 5.7), but, in contrast to African Americans, their segregation has generally held steady or slightly increased over the 20-year period. Among other factors, this is a reflection of high rates of immigration and "chain" patterns of settlement, which concentrate newcomers in ethnic neighborhoods.

Education. Exhibit 7.17, like Exhibit 5.9 for African Americans, shows the extent of school segregation for Hispanic Americans for the 1993–1994 and the 2005–2006 school years. In both years, Hispanic American children were more segregated than African American children. Furthermore, the percentages of Hispanic children in both majority-minority and extremely segregated schools increased over the time period. These patterns reflect recent high rates of immigration and the tendency for newcomers to reside in the same neighborhoods as their coethnics (see the patterns of residential segregation in Exhibit 7.15).

Exhibit 7.16 Residential Segregation in 220 Metropolitan Areas, Hispanic Americans

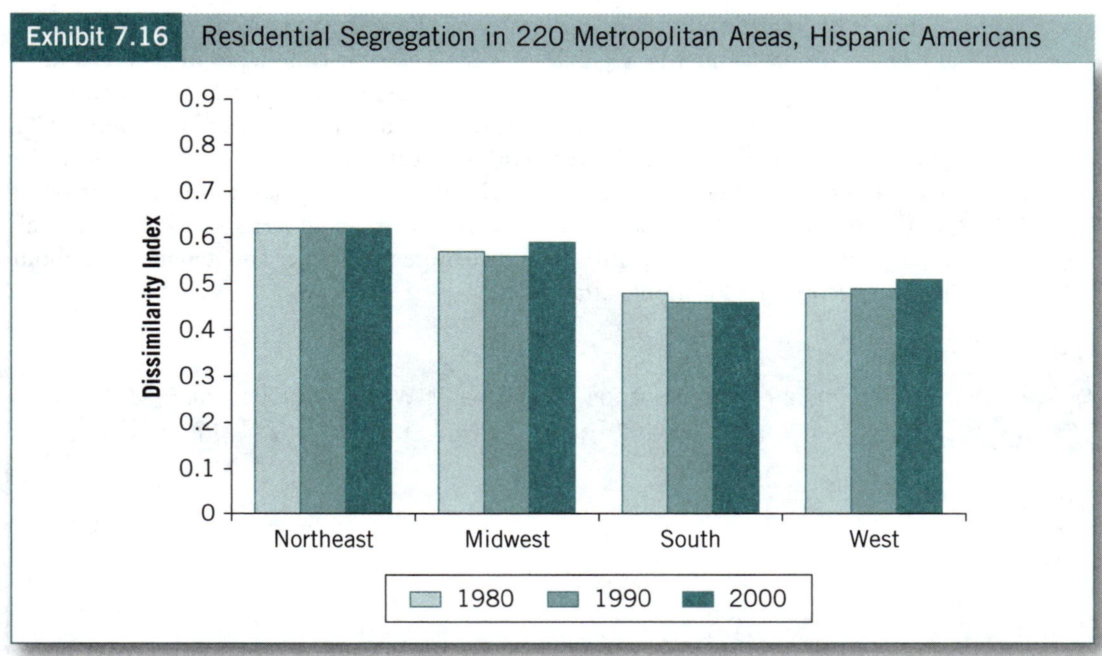

SOURCE: Iceland, Weinberg, & Steinmetz (2002, p. 84).

Exhibit 7.17 School Integration For Hispanic Americans, 1993–1994 and 2005–2006

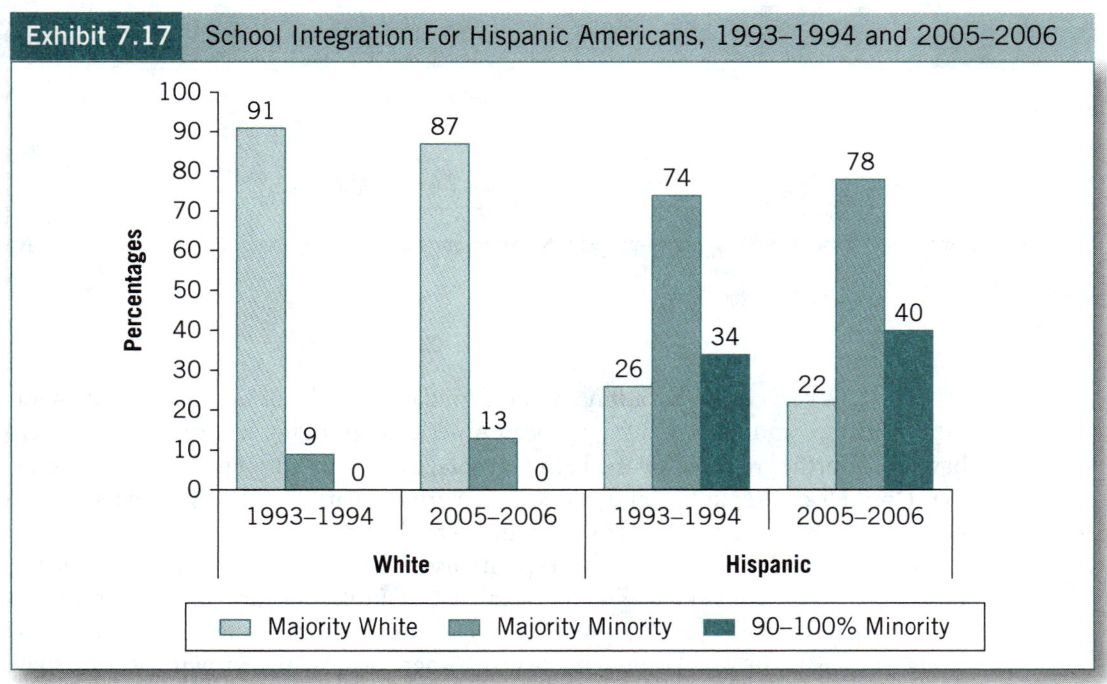

SOURCE: Fry (2007).

Levels of education for Hispanic Americans have risen in recent years but still are far below national standards (see Exhibit 7.18). Hispanic Americans in general and all subgroups, except Colombian Americans, fall well below non-Hispanic whites for high school education. In particular, about 54% of Mexican Americans and only about 45% of Salvadoran Americans and Guatemalan Americans have high school degrees. At the college level, Colombian and Cuban Americans match national norms, but the other groups and Hispanic Americans as a whole are far below non-Hispanic whites. For all Hispanic groups, there is very little difference by gender: males and females have about the same record of educational attainment.

Exhibit 7.18 Educational Attainment for Non-Hispanic Whites, All Hispanic Americans, and Selected Groups by Nation or Territory of Origin, 2007

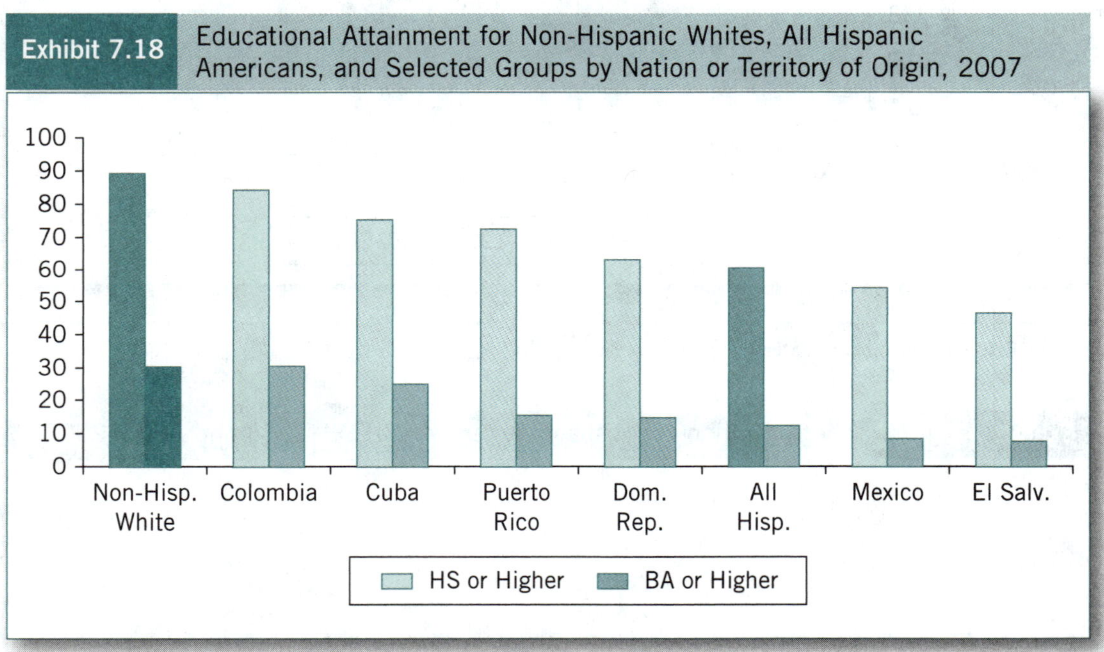

SOURCE: U.S. Bureau of the Census (2007).

The lower levels of education are the cumulative results of decades of systematic discrimination and exclusion for Mexican Americans and Puerto Ricans. These levels have been further reduced by the high percentage of recent immigrants from Mexico, the Dominican Republic, and Central American nations like El Salvador and Guatemala who have very modest educational backgrounds.

Given the role that educational credentials have come to play in the job market, these figures are consistent with the idea that assimilation may be segmented for some Hispanic groups (see Chapters 2 and 9), who may contribute in large numbers, along with African Americans and Native Americans, to the growth of an urban underclass.

Political Power. The political resources available to Hispanic Americans have increased over the years, but the group is still proportionally underrepresented. The number of Hispanics of voting age has doubled in the past two decades, and Hispanics today constitute more than 10% of the voting-age population. Yet, because registration rates and actual turnout have been low, the Hispanic community has not had an impact on the political structure proportionate to its size. For example, in the presidential elections between 1992 and 2004, actual voter turnout for Hispanic Americans was less than 30%, less than half of the comparable rate for non-Hispanic whites (U.S. Bureau of the Census, 2009b, p. 252). In the 2008 presidential election, turnout increased for Hispanic Americans (as well as African Americans and Asian Americans) and they accounted for about 9.5% of all voters, up from 8.2% in 2004 (Lopez & Taylor, 2009, p. 1). Clearly, the impact of the Hispanic American vote on national politics will increase as the group grows in size, but participation is likely to remain lower than other groups for some time because of the large percentage of recent, non-English-speaking immigrants and noncitizens in the group.

At the national level, there are now 23 Hispanic Americans in the House of Representatives, more than double the number in 1990 and about 6% of the total. In addition, the 110th Congress included three Hispanic American senators. Most of these representatives and senators are members of the Democratic Party, but, in a reflection of the diversity of the group, nearly 20% are Republicans. On the local and state level, the number of public officials identified as Hispanic increased by more than 50% between 1985 and 2007, from 3,147 to 4,954 (U.S. Bureau of the Census, 2009b, p. 251).

Although still underrepresented, these figures suggest that Hispanic Americans will become increasingly important in American political life as their numbers continue to grow and their rates of naturalization rise. A preview of their increasing power has been displayed in recent years as Hispanic communities across the nation have mobilized and engaged in massive demonstrations to express their opposition to restrictive immigration policies (for example, see Aizenman, 2006).

Jobs and Income. The economic situation of Hispanic Americans is mixed. Many members of these groups, especially those who have been in the United States for several generations, are doing " . . . just fine. They have, in ever increasing numbers, accessed opportunities in education and employment and have carved out a niche of American prosperity for themselves and their children" (Camarillo & Bonilla, 2001, pp. 130–131). For many others, however, the picture is not so promising. They face the possibility of becoming members of an impoverished, powerless, and economically marginalized urban underclass, like African Americans and other minority groups of color.

Occupationally, Hispanic American groups are concentrated in the less-desirable, lower-paid service and unskilled segments of the job market, although the groups with higher levels of human capital (e.g., education) compare more favorably with the dominant group. This is generally what would be expected for a group with such a high percentage of first-generation members who bring such modest levels of education and job skills.

Unemployment, low income, and poverty continue to be issues for all Hispanic groups. The official unemployment rates for Hispanic Americans run about twice the rate for non-Hispanic whites, and Exhibit 7.19 shows that Hispanics in general and most subgroups have dramatically lower median household incomes than non-Hispanic whites.

Exhibit 7.19 Median Household Income for Non-Hispanic Whites, All Hispanic Americans, and Selected Groups by Nation or Territory of Origin, 2007

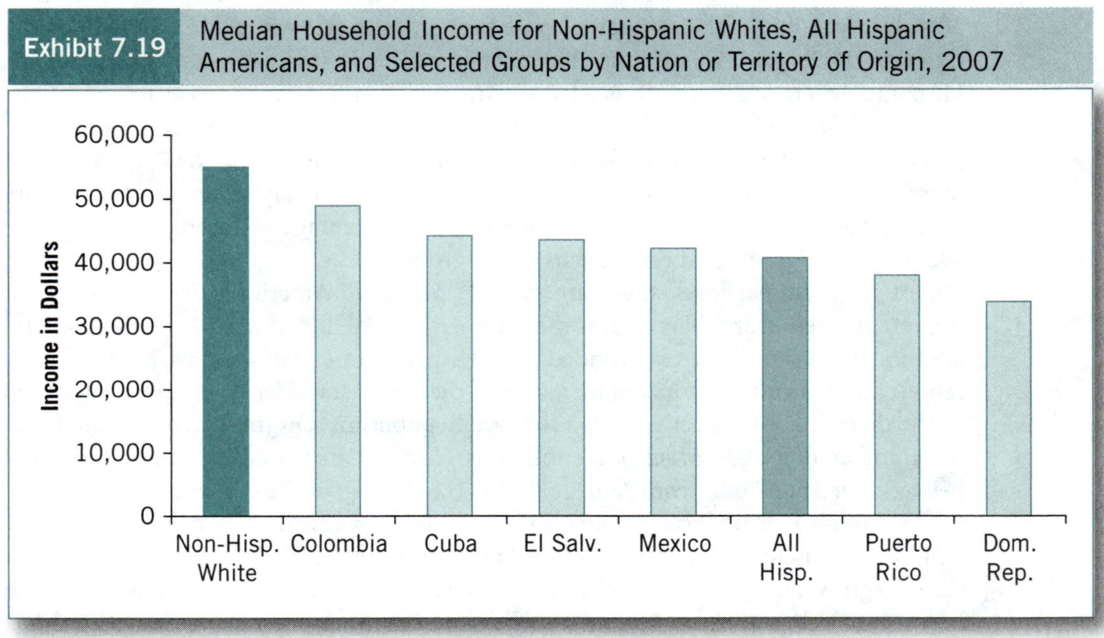

SOURCE: U.S. Bureau of the Census (2007).

Exhibit 7.20 supplements the information on median income by displaying the overall distribution of income for Hispanic Americans and non-Hispanic whites for 2007. The figure shows a greater concentration (wider bars) of Hispanics in the lower income categories and a lower concentration (narrower bars) in the income groups at the very top of the figure. There is a noticeable concentration of both groups in the $50,000 to $125, 000 categories, but whites outnumber Hispanics by about 40% to 33% in these income ranges. In the highest two income categories, whites outnumber Hispanic Americans by more than two to one: about 8.7% of whites are in these highest categories versus only 3.4% of Hispanics.

Recent information about how the Hispanic American subgroups are distributed across income categories is not available. Although all groups have members in all income categories, we can assume that Mexican Americans, Dominican Americans, and Puerto Ricans would be disproportionately represented in the lowest income categories and Cuban and Colombian Americans in the higher groups.

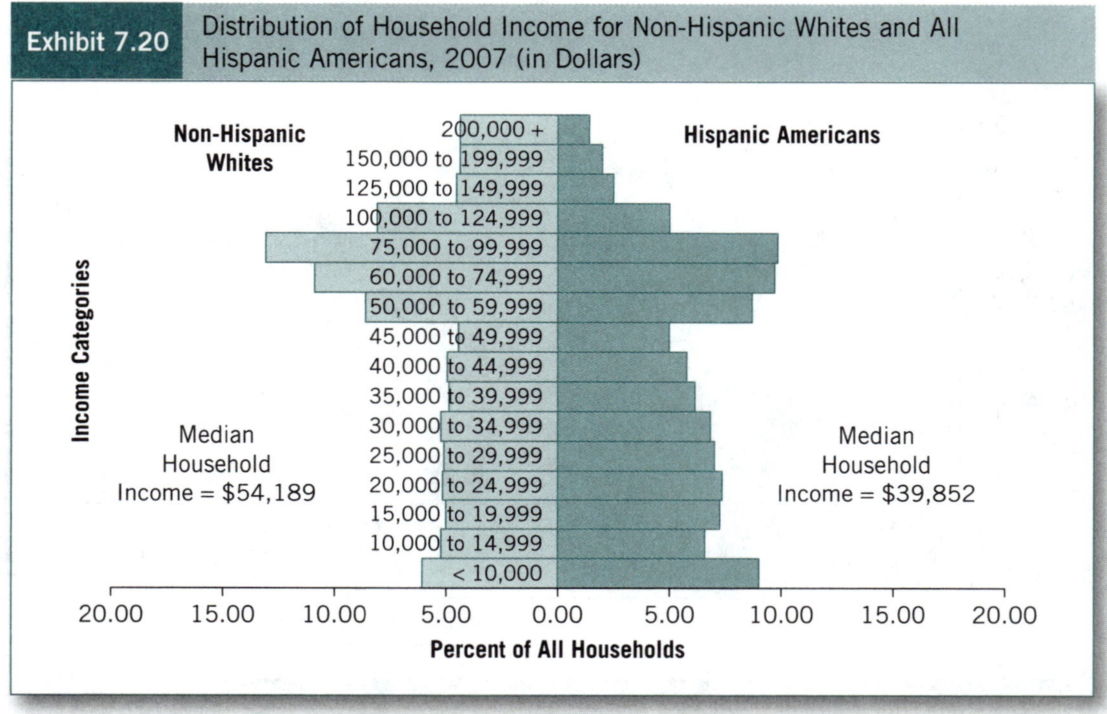

Exhibit 7.20 Distribution of Household Income for Non-Hispanic Whites and All Hispanic Americans, 2007 (in Dollars)

SOURCE: U.S. Bureau of the Census (2007).

Exhibit 7.21 finishes the socioeconomic profile by displaying levels of poverty for Hispanic Americans, a pattern that is consistent with previous information on income and education. The poverty rate for all Hispanic American families is three times the rate for Non-Hispanic whites but lower than the rate for African Americans (see Exhibit 5.14). However, there is considerable diversity across the subgroups, with Colombians and Cubans very close to national norms and Dominicans the most impoverished. For all groups, children have higher poverty rates than families.

These socioeconomic profiles reflect the concentration of many Hispanic groups in the low-wage sector of the economy, a long tradition of discrimination and exclusion for Mexican Americans and Puerto Ricans, high rates of recent immigration, and the lower amounts of human capital (education, job training) controlled by these groups. The higher rates of unemployment for these groups reflect not only discrimination but also the lack of security and seasonal nature of many of the jobs they hold. Cuban Americans, buoyed by a more privileged social class background and their enclave economy, rank higher on virtually all measures of wealth and prosperity.

There is a split labor market differentiated by gender, within the dual market differentiated by race and ethnicity. Hispanic women—like minority group women in general—are among the lowest-paid, most-exploitable, and least-protected segments

Exhibit 7.21 Poverty Levels for Non-Hispanic Whites, All Hispanic Americans, and Selected Groups by Nation or Territory of Origin, 2007

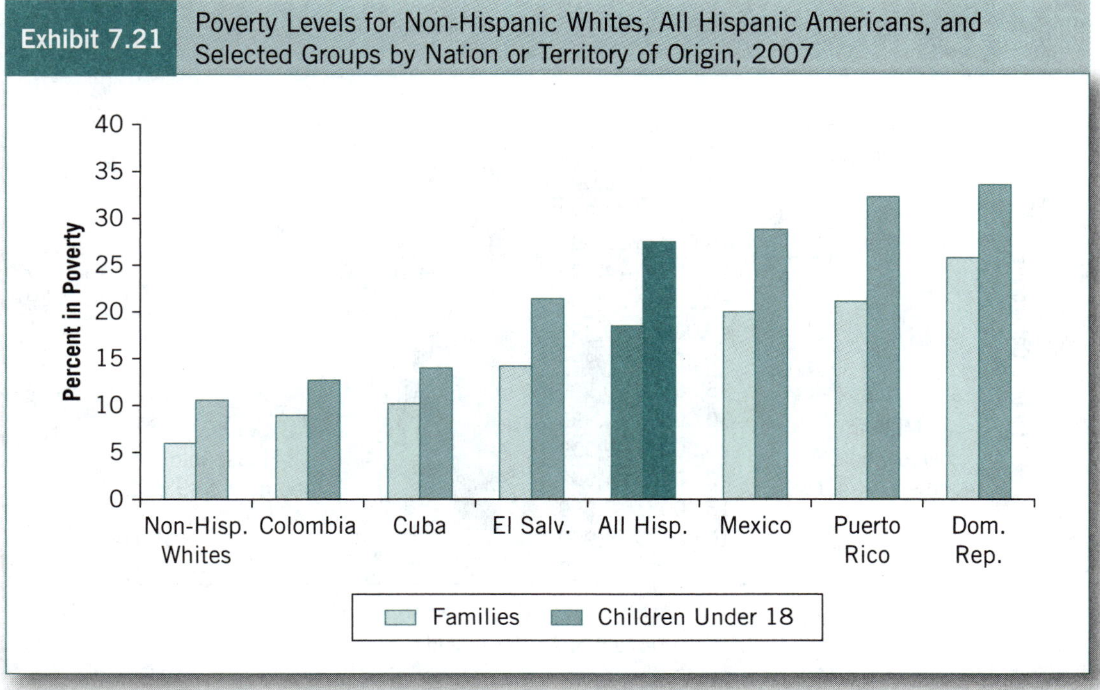

SOURCE: U.S. Bureau of the Census (2007).

of the U.S. labor force. The impact of poverty is especially severe for Latino women because they often find themselves with the responsibility of caring for their children alone. In 2007, 18.5% of all Hispanic American households were headed by females, and this percentage ranged from a low of 13% for Cuban American households to a high of 36.3% for Dominican American households (U.S. Bureau of the Census, 2007, 2009b). This pattern is the result of many factors, among them the status of Latino men in the labor force. The jobs available to Latino men often do not pay enough to support a family, and many jobs are seasonal, temporary, or otherwise insecure.

Female-headed Latino families are affected by a triple economic handicap: They have only one wage earner whose potential income is limited by discrimination against both women and Latinos. The result of these multiple disadvantages is an especially high rate of poverty. Whereas 22% of non-Hispanic, white, female-headed households fall below the poverty line, the percentage is 37.1% for Hispanic American households headed by females (U.S. Bureau of the Census, 2007, 2009b).

Summary. The socioeconomic situation of Latinos is complex and diversified. Although members of all groups have successfully entered the mainstream economy, poverty and exclusion continue to be major issues. Highly concentrated in deteriorated urban areas (barrios), segments of these groups, like other minority groups of color, face the possibility of permanent poverty and economic marginality.

Primary Structural Assimilation

Overall, the extent of intimate contact between Hispanic Americans and the dominant group probably has been higher than for either African Americans or American Indians (see, e.g., Quillian & Campbell, 2003; Rosenfield, 2002). This pattern may reflect the fact that Latinos are partly ethnic minority groups and partly racial minority groups. Some studies report that contact is greater for the more affluent social classes, in the cities, and for the younger generations (who are presumably more Americanized) (Fitzpatrick, 1976; Grebler et al., 1970; Rodriguez, 1989). Conversely, the rate of contact has probably been decreased by the rapid increase in immigration and the tendency of the first generation to socialize more with their co-ethnics.

Rates of intermarriage are higher for Latinos than for African Americans, but neither are a very high percentage of all marriages. Black-and-white interracial couples make up less than 1% of all marriages, and the comparable figure for Latinos was 3.7% of all marriages in 2007 (U.S. Bureau of the Census, 2009b, p. 51).

Assimilation and Hispanic Americans

As test cases for what we have called the traditional view of American assimilation, Latinos fare poorly. Mexican Americans continue to be concentrated in the low-wage sector of the labor market, a source of cheap labor for the dominant group's economy. Puerto Ricans, who are more recent arrivals, occupy a similar profile and position.

The fundamental reality faced by both groups, in their histories and in their present situations, is their colonized status in U.S. society. Many Mexican Americans and Puerto Ricans have risen in the social class and occupational structure of the larger society, but other members share many problems with other urban minority groups of color.

The traditional views of the nature of assimilation likewise fail to describe the experiences of Cuban Americans. They are more prosperous, on the average, than either Mexican Americans or Puerto Ricans, but they became successful by remaining separate. Because their immigration is so recent, it is too early to tell how Dominicans, Salvadorans, and Colombians will fare in the assimilation process. We can be sure, however, that their experiences will be as varied and volatile as the larger Hispanic American groups.

There is no single Hispanic American experience or pattern of adjustment to the larger society. We have focused mainly on three of the many Latino groups in the United States, and the diversity of their experiences suggests the variety and complexity of what it means to be a minority group in U.S. society. Their experiences also illustrate some of the fundamental forces that shape the experiences of minority groups: the split labor market and the U.S. appetite for cheap labor; the impact of industrialization; the dangers of a permanent urban underclass; the relationships between competition and levels of prejudice and rejection; and the persistence of race as a primary dividing line between people and groups.

MAIN POINTS

- Hispanic Americans are a diverse and growing part of U.S. society. Many distinct groups exist, but the three largest are Mexican Americans, Puerto Ricans, and Cuban Americans. The various Hispanic groups do not think of themselves as a single entity.
- Hispanic Americans have some characteristics of colonized groups and some of immigrant groups. Similarly, these groups are racial minorities in some ways and ethnic minorities in others.
- Since the beginning of the 20th century, Mexico has served as a reserve labor force for the development of the U.S. economy. Immigrants from Mexico entered a social system in which the colonized status of the group was already established. Mexican Americans remained a colonized minority group despite the large numbers of immigrants in the group and have been systematically excluded from opportunities for upward mobility by institutional discrimination and segregation.
- A Mexican American protest movement has been continuously seeking to improve the status of the group. In the 1960s, a more intense and militant movement emerged, guided by the ideology of Chicanismo.
- Puerto Ricans began to move to the mainland in large numbers only in recent decades. The group is concentrated in the urban Northeast, in the low-wage sector of the job market.
- Cubans began immigrating after Castro's revolution in the late 1950s. They settled primarily in southern Florida, where they created an ethnic enclave.
- Dominicans, Salvadorans, and Colombians are three of the many Hispanic groups that began immigrating to the U.S. in large numbers after the 1965 change in federal immigration policy.
- The overall levels of anti-Hispanic prejudice and discrimination may have declined, along with the general decline in explicit, overt racism in American society. Recent high levels of immigration, conversely, seem to have increased anti-Hispanic prejudice and discrimination, especially along the southern border and in areas with large numbers of immigrants.
- Levels of acculturation are variable from group to group and generation to generation. Acculturation increases with length of residence. The vitality of Latino cultures has been sustained by recent immigration.
- Secondary structural assimilation also varies from group to group. Poverty, unemployment, lower levels of educational attainment, and other forms of inequality continue to be major problems for Hispanic groups, even the relatively successful Cuban Americans.
- Primary structural assimilation with the dominant group is greater than for African Americans.

STUDY SITE ON THE WEB

Don't forget the interactive quizzes and other resources and learning aids at www.pineforge.com/healeyds3e

FOR FURTHER READING

This work provides a general overview of Mexican American history combined with an argument that the experiences of this group closely resemble those of colonized groups.

Acuna, Rodolfo. 1999. *Occupied America* (4th ed.). New York: Harper & Row.

This is a comprehensive overview of the Cuban Community in southern Florida.

Garcia, Maria Cristina. 1996. *Havana USA: Cuban Exiles and Cuban Americans in South Florida, 1959–1994.* Berkeley: University of California Press.

This is a good overview of the history and present situation of Puerto Ricans on the mainland.

Fitzpatrick, Joseph P. 1987. *Puerto Rican Americans: The Meaning of Migration to the Mainland* (2nd ed.). Englewood Cliffs, NJ: Prentice Hall.

This is a landmark analysis of Latino immigration, ethnic enclaves, and patterns of assimilation.

Portes, Alejandro, & Bach, Robert L. 1985. *Latin Journey: Cuban and Mexican Immigrants in the United States.* Berkeley: University of California Press.

This is a very important study of assimilation among Mexican Americans.

Telles, Edward, & Ortiz, Vilma. 2008. *Generations of Exclusion: Mexican Americans, Assimilation, and Race.* New York: Russell Sage.

QUESTIONS FOR REVIEW AND STUDY

1. At the beginning of this chapter, it is stated that Hispanic Americans "combine elements of the polar extremes [immigrant and colonized] of Blauner's typology of minority groups" and that they are "partly an ethnic minority group and partly a racial minority group." Explain these statements in terms of the rest of the material presented in the chapter.
2. What important cultural differences between Mexican Americans and the dominant society shaped the relationships between the two groups?
3. How does the history of Mexican immigration demonstrate the usefulness of Noel's concepts of differentials in power and competition?
4. Compare and contrast the protest movements of Mexican Americans, American Indians, and African Americans. What similarities and differences existed in Chicanismo, Red Power, and Black Power? How do the differences reflect the unique experiences of each group?

5. In what ways are the experiences of Puerto Ricans and Cuban Americans unique compared with those of other minority groups? How do these differences reflect other differences, such as differences in contact situation?

6. The Cuban American enclave has resulted in a variety of benefits for the group. Why don't other minority groups follow this strategy?

7. What images of Latinas are common in U.S. society? How do these images reflect the experiences of these groups?

8. Describe the situation of the major Hispanic American groups in terms of acculturation and integration. Which groups are closest to equality? What factors or experiences might account for the differences between groups? In what ways might the statement "Hispanic Americans are remaining pluralistic even while they assimilate" be true?

INTERNET RESEARCH PROJECTS

A. Mexican Migration Project

1. The Mexican Migration Project was created to learn more about the complex process of Mexican migration to the United States. The project is binational and has been gathering data since 1982. A number of individual stories of Mexican migrants are available online at http://mmp.opr.princeton.edu/expressions/stories-en.aspx. Read the introduction and then select several of the stories to read. Analyze each using the concepts developed in this chapter, especially the idea that Mexico serves as a reserve pool of cheap labor for the benefit of U.S. businesses.

B. Mapping Immigration

1. Go to http://projects.nytimes.com/immigration/ and select (click on) the interactive map on the right side of the screen. Under "Immigration Explorer" select Mexico and then start with the earliest year (1880) for which information is available. Where did Mexican Americans live in that year? Next, click each year on the time line and observe what happens to the Mexican American population. What happened in 1930? Why did the Mexican American population decline? What happened to cause the population to decline in 1950? How would you describe the geographic spread of the Mexican American population since 1950? Is this movement similar to the movement to the North of African Americans? How?

2. Repeat this exercise with the other groups covered in this chapter: Cuban Americans, Dominicans, and Salvadorans. Try to explain the changes you observe using the information and concepts presented in this chapter.

Note

1. This section is largely based on O'Brien, Eileen. 2008. *The Racial Middle: Latinos and Asian Americans Living Beyond the Racial Divide.* New York: New York University Press.

Asian Americans

"Model Minorities"?

Teachers and guidance counselors often treated Chinese [American] students as "model minorities." Counselors advised them to apply to selective high schools [and] teachers assumed they were good at math and science even when they weren't. These expectations caused some anxiety among students who were not academically inclined, but they also reinforced their academic performance. One Chinese man explained his ambivalent feelings about these expectations:

> Well I guess it could be a good and a bad. Being Chinese and being among all the different racial groups. I was always pointed out as "He's Chinese: He must be the smart one . . . ." And it is bad. We carry that as Chinese. "Hard working, comes from a very good family background and really, really smart." And, in a way, that has helped me. I have a standard to uphold. And also from my parents, you got to do better. You got to do better.
>
> —Kasnitz, Mollenkopf, Waters, &
> Holloway (2008, p. 159)

It starts out simply, with a crowd of Vietnamese youth standing in a parking lot. . . . But one can be seen kneeling, cradling his head within his arms. What follows shatters many conceptions held by Dorchester's (a neighborhood in Boston, Massachusetts) tight-knit Vietnamese community about their kids. Vietnamese students are among the highest achieving of any cultural group in the city in academics, but even those who . . . get straight A's are not immune to gang violence. . . .

(Continued)

(Continued)

The two-and-a-half minute video shows a brutal gang-beating of two teenagers, one boy and one girl, by over 20 others. . . . The youngest assailants are in their pre-teens, the oldest are in their early twenties, and it is clear . . . that some of the older men are calling the shots and there are multiple groups involved.

One man snaps his fingers and five teenage girls brutally attack another. Another slaps a young boy, signaling the beginning of a free-for-all with punches, kicks, and even a bicycle. By the end, both victims are immobile, possibly unconscious.

Police are investigating the incident . . . but are not revealing details at this time. Both victims . . . survived without serious permanent injuries

"It is not surprising to me that the incident happened," said Hiep Chu, . . . a leader in the Vietnamese community. "The Vietnamese family needs a lot more support. It's all coming from a lack of services. The cultural differences and the language are very tough."

"The kids don't necessarily speak Vietnamese anymore, but their parents aren't able to express themselves in English. Their parents don't understand where their kids evolved, on the streets," said Chu.

—Pete Stidman (2008)

These brief passages illustrate two fundamental truths about Asian Americans: First, they are widely seen as successful, smart, and hard-working and, second, there is sometimes a wide gap between this positive stereotype and the truth. How accurate is the "model minority" view? Does it apply to all Asian American groups? Have Asian Americans always been viewed this way? What hidden agendas are buried in the most positive views of these groups? What realities are obscured by this flattering image? In this chapter, we will review the history and present status of Asian Americans and attempt a balanced appraisal of the label of "model minority."

Introduction

A variety of groups from Asia are becoming increasingly prominent in the United States. Although they are often seen as the same and classified into a single category in government reports, these groups vary in their languages, in their cultural and physical characteristics, and in their experiences in the United States. Some of these groups are truly newcomers to America, but others have roots in this country stretching back for more than 150 years.

In this chapter, we begin with an overview of the largest Asian American groups and then briefly examine the traditions and customs that they bring with them to America. We will then focus on the two oldest Asian American groups, Chinese Americans and Japanese Americans, and cover some of the newer Asian groups more briefly. Throughout the chapter, we will be especially concerned with the perception that Asian Americans in general and Chinese and Japanese Americans in particular are "**model minorities**": successful, affluent, highly educated people who do not suffer from the problems usually associated with minority group status. How accurate is this view? Have Asian Americans forged a pathway to upward mobility that could be followed by other groups? Do the concepts and theories that have guided this text (particularly the Blauner and Noel hypotheses) apply? Does the success of these groups mean that the United States is truly an open, fair, and just society? We explore these questions throughout the chapter and in a special section toward the end of the chapter.

Exhibit 8.1 lists the largest Asian American groups and illustrates their diversity. As was the case with American Indians and Hispanic Americans, *Asian American* is a convenient label imposed by the larger society (and by government agencies such as the Census Bureau) that obscures the differences between the groups. These six largest groups are distinct from each other in culture and physical appearance, and each has had its own unique experience in America. A variety of smaller Asian American groups (Hmongs, Pakistanis, Cambodians, and Laotians, for example), not covered in this chapter, further add to this diversity.

Exhibit 8.1 Size and Growth of Asian American Groups, 1990–2007

Group	1990	2000	2007	Growth (number of times larger) 1990–2007	Percent of Total Population, 2007
Chinese	1,645,472	2,633,849	3,538,407	2.2	1.2
Filipino	1,406,770	2,089,701	3,053,179	2.2	1.0
Asian Indians	815,447	1,785,336	2,765,815	3.4	0.9
Vietnamese	614,547	1,171,776	1,642,950	2.6	0.6
Koreans	798,849	1,148,951	1,555,293	2.0	0.5
Japanese	847,562	958,945	1,220,922	1.4	0.4
All Asian American groups	6,908,638	11,070,913	14,940,775	2.2	5.0
Percent of U.S. population	2.8%	3.9%	5.0%		
Total U.S. population	248,710,000	281,422,000	301,621,159	1.2	

SOURCES: 1990: U.S. Bureau of the Census (1990); 2000: U.S. Bureau of the Census (2000f); 2007: U.S. Bureau of the Census (2007).

Several features of Exhibit 8.1 are worth noting. First, Asians Americans are a small fraction of the total U.S. population. Even when aggregated, they account for only 5% of all Americans. In contrast, African Americans and Hispanic Americans are each more than 12% of the total population (see Exhibit 1.1).

Second, most Asian American groups have grown dramatically in recent decades, largely because of high rates of immigration since the 1965 changes in U.S. immigration policy. All of the groups listed in Exhibit 8.1 grew faster than the total population between 1990 and 2007. The Japanese American population grew at the slowest rate (largely because immigration from Japan has been low in recent decades), but the number of Asian Indians more than tripled, and all of the other groups listed in the table more than doubled. This rapid growth is projected to continue for decades to come, and the impact of Asian Americans on everyday life and American culture will increase accordingly. Today, fewer than 5 out of every 100 Americans are in this group, but this ratio will grow to nearly 10 out of every 100 by the year 2050 (see Exhibit 1.1). The relative sizes of the largest Asian American groups are presented in Exhibit 8.2, and their nations of origin are displayed in Exhibit 8.3.

Like Hispanic Americans, most Asian American groups have a high percentage of foreign-born members. The great majority of four of the six groups listed in

Exhibit 8.2 Largest Asian American Groups, 2007

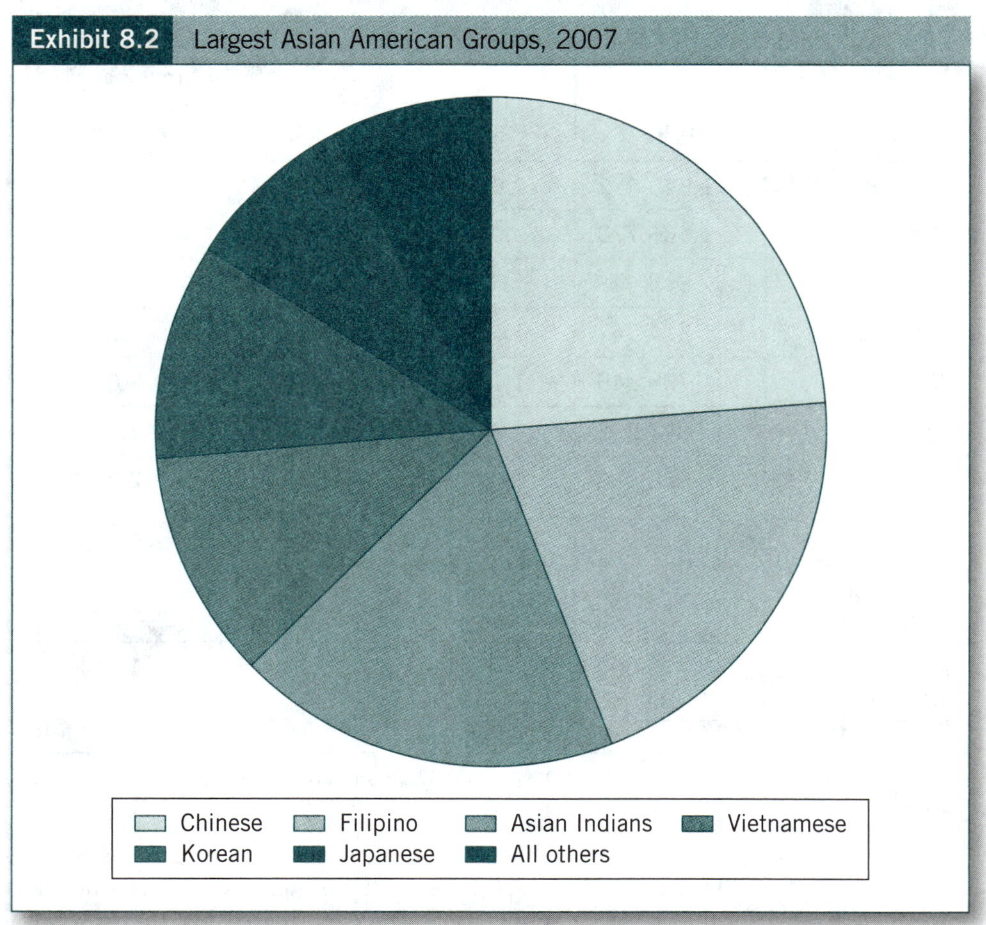

SOURCES: U.S. Bureau of the Census (2007, 2009b).

Exhibit 8.4 are first generation, and even Japanese Americans, the lowest ranked group, more than double the national norm for foreign-born members.

Exhibit 8.3 Map Showing China, the Philippines, India, South Korea, Vietnam, and Japan

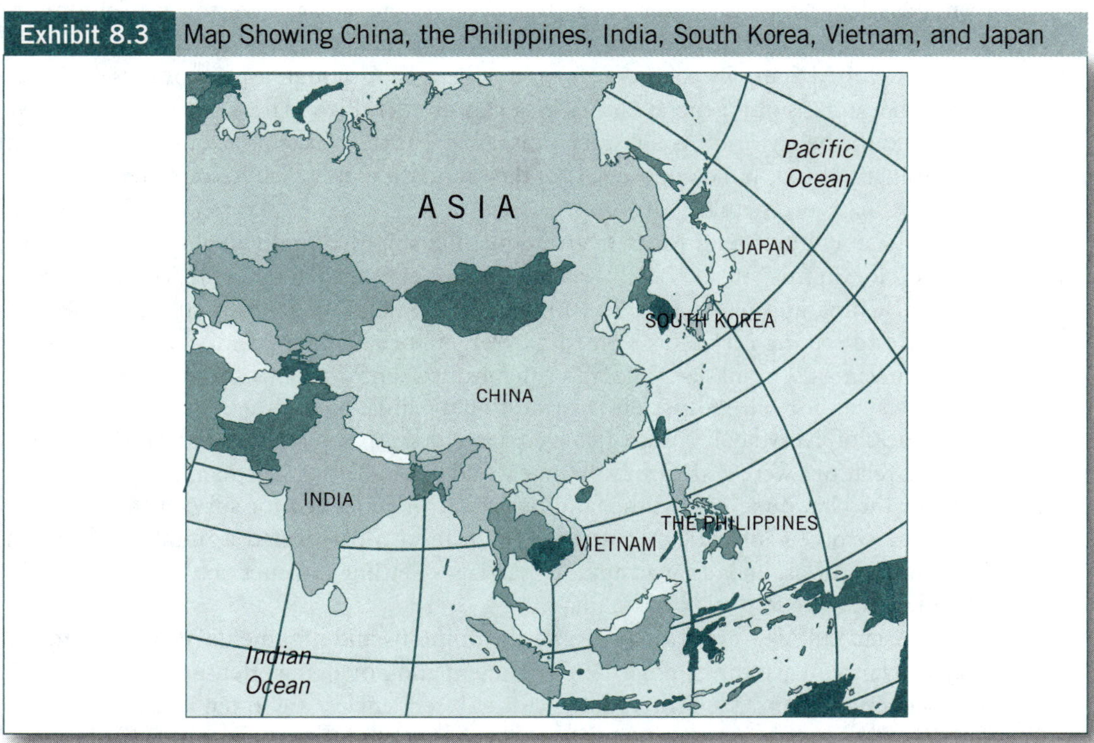

Exhibit 8.4 Percentage Foreign-Born by Country of Origin, 2007

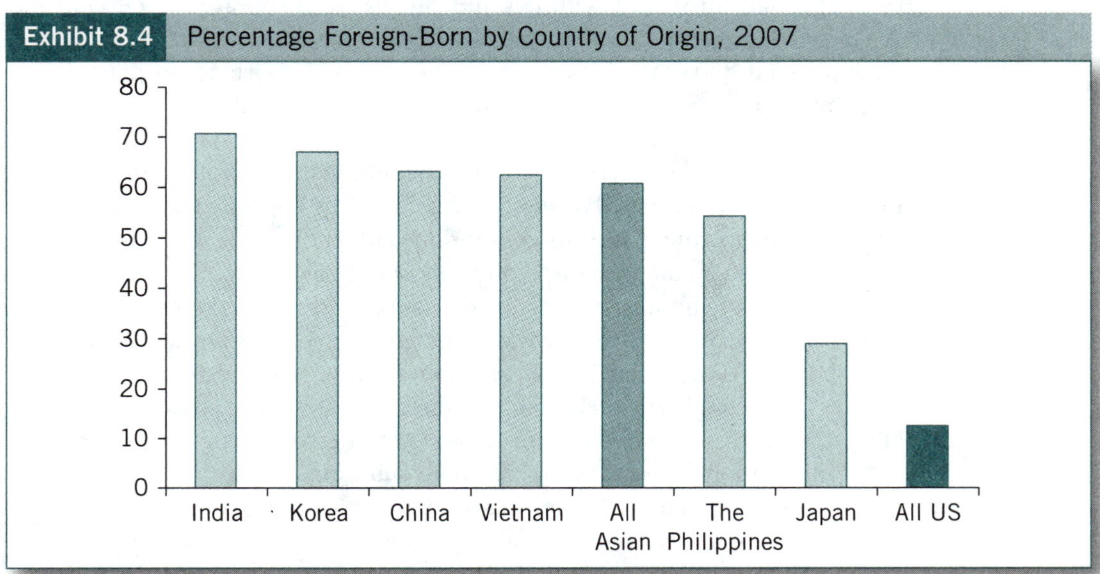

SOURCES: U.S. Bureau of the Census (2007, 2009b).

Origins and Cultures

Asian Americans have brought a wealth of traditions to the United States. They speak many different languages and practice religions as diverse as Buddhism, Confucianism, Islam, Hinduism, and Christianity. Asian cultures predate the founding of the United States by centuries or even millennia. Although no two of these cultures are the same, some general similarities can be identified. These cultural traits have shaped the behavior of Asian Americans, as well as the perceptions of members of the dominant group, and compose part of the foundation on which Asian American experiences have been built.

Asian cultures tend to stress group membership over individual self-interest. For example, Confucianism, which was the dominant ethical and moral system in traditional China and had a powerful influence on many other Asian cultures, counsels people to see themselves as elements in larger social systems and status hierarchies. Confucianism emphasizes loyalty to the group, conformity to societal expectations, and respect for one's superiors. In traditional China, as in other Asian societies, the business of everyday life was organized around kinship relations, and most interpersonal relations were with family members and other relatives (Lyman, 1974). The family or the clan often owned the land on which all depended for survival, and kinship ties determined inheritance patterns. The clan also performed a number of crucial social functions, including arranging marriages, settling disputes between individuals, and organizing festivals and holidays.

Asian cultures stress sensitivity to the opinions and judgments of others and the importance of avoiding public embarrassment and not giving offense. Especially when discussing Japanese culture, these cultural tendencies are often contrasted with Western practices in terms of "guilt versus shame" and the nature of personal morality (Benedict, 1946). In Western cultures, individuals are encouraged to develop and abide by a conscience, or an inner moral voice, and behavior is guided by one's personal sense of guilt. In contrast, Asian cultures stress the importance of maintaining the respect and good opinion of others and avoiding shame and public humiliation. Group harmony, or *wa* in Japanese, is a central concern, and displays of individualism are discouraged. These characteristics are reflected in the Japanese proverb: "The nail that sticks up must be hammered down" (Whiting, 1990, p. 70). Asian cultures emphasize proper behavior, conformity to convention and the judgments of others, and avoiding embarrassment and personal confrontations ("saving face").

Traditional Asian cultures were male dominated, and women were consigned to subordinate roles. A Chinese woman was expected to serve first her father, then her husband, and, if widowed, her eldest son. Confucianism also decreed that women should observe the Four Virtues: chastity and obedience, shyness, a pleasing demeanor, and skill in the performance of domestic duties (Amott & Matthaei, 1991). Women of high status in traditional China symbolized their subordination by binding their feet. This painful, crippling practice began early in life and required women to wrap their feet tightly to keep them artificially small. The bones in the arch were broken so that the toes could be bent under the foot, further decreasing the size of the foot. Bound feet were considered beautiful, but they also immobilized women and were intended to prevent them from "wandering away" from domestic and household duties (Jackson, 2000; Takaki, 1993, pp. 209–210).

The experiences of Asian Americans in the United States modified these patriarchal values and traditional traits. For the groups with longer histories in U.S. society, such as Chinese Americans and Japanese Americans, the effects of these values on individual personality may be slight, but for more recently arrived groups, the effects may be more powerful. The cultural and religious differences among the Asian American groups also reflect the recent histories of each of the sending nations. For example, Vietnam was a colony of China for 1,000 years, but for much of the past century, it was a colony of France. Although Vietnamese culture has been heavily influenced by China, many Vietnamese are Catholic, a result of the efforts of the French to convert them. The Philippines and India were also colonized by Western nations—the former by Spain and then by the United States and the latter by Great Britain. As a result, many Filipinos are Catholic, and many Indian immigrants are familiar with English and with Anglo culture.

These examples are, of course, the merest suggestion of the diversity of these groups. In fact, Asian Americans, who share little more than a slight physical resemblance and some broad cultural similarities, are much more diverse than Hispanic Americans, who are overwhelmingly Catholic and share a common language and a historical connection with Spain (Min, 1995).

Contact Situations and the Development of the Chinese American and Japanese American Communities

The earliest Asian groups to arrive in substantial numbers were from China and Japan. Their contact situations not only shaped their own histories but also affected the present situation of all Asian Americans in many ways. As we will see, the contact situations for both Chinese Americans and Japanese Americans featured massive rejection and discrimination. Both groups adapted to the racism of the larger society by forming enclaves, a strategy that eventually produced some major benefits for their descendants.

Chinese Americans

Early Immigration and the Anti-Chinese Campaign

Immigrants from China to the United States began to arrive in the early 1800s and were generally motivated by the same kinds of social and economic forces that have inspired immigration everywhere for the past two centuries. Chinese immigrants were "pushed" to leave their homeland by the disruption of traditional social relations, caused by the colonization of much of China by more industrialized European nations, and by rapid population growth (Chan, 1990; Lyman, 1974; Tsai, 1986). At the same time, these immigrants were "pulled" to the West Coast of the United States by the Gold Rush of 1849 and by other opportunities created by the development of the West.

The Noel hypothesis (see Chapter 3) provides a useful way to analyze the contact situation that developed between Chinese and Anglo-Americans in the mid-19th century. As you recall, Noel argues that racial or ethnic stratification will result when a contact situation is characterized by three conditions: ethnocentrism, competition, and a differential in power. Once all three conditions were met on the West Coast, a vigorous campaign against the Chinese began, and the group was pushed into a subordinate, disadvantaged position.

Ethnocentrism based on racial, cultural, and language differences was present from the beginning, but at first, competition for jobs between Chinese immigrants and native-born workers was muted by a robust, rapidly growing economy and an abundance of jobs. Initially, politicians, newspaper editorial writers, and business leaders praised the Chinese for their industriousness and tirelessness (Tsai, 1986). Before long, however, the economic boom slowed, and the supply of jobs began to dry up. The Gold Rush petered out, and the transcontinental railroad, which thousands of Chinese workers had helped to build, was completed in 1869. The migration of Anglo-Americans from the East continued, and competition for jobs and other resources increased. An anti-Chinese campaign of harassment, discrimination, and violent attacks began. In 1871, in Los Angeles, a mob of "several hundred whites shot, hanged, and stabbed 19 Chinese to death" (Tsai, 1986, p. 67). Other attacks against the Chinese occurred in Denver, Colorado; Seattle, Washington; Tacoma, Washington; and Rock Springs, Wyoming (Lyman, 1974).

As the West Coast economy changed, the Chinese came to be seen as a threat, and elements of the dominant group tried to limit competition. The Chinese were a small group—there were only about 100,000 in the entire country in 1870—and by law, they were not permitted to become citizens. Hence, they controlled few power resources with which to withstand these attacks. During the 1870s, Chinese workers were forced out of most sectors of the mainstream economy, and in 1882, the anti-Chinese campaign experienced its ultimate triumph when the U.S. Congress passed the Chinese Exclusion Act, banning virtually all immigration from China. The act was one of the first restrictive immigration laws and was aimed solely at the Chinese. It established a "rigid competitive" relationship between the groups (see Chapter 4) and eliminated the threat presented by Chinese labor by excluding Chinese from American society.

The primary antagonists of Chinese immigrants were native-born workers and organized labor. White owners of small businesses, feeling threatened by Chinese-owned businesses, also supported passage of the Chinese Exclusion Act (Boswell, 1986). Other social classes, such as the capitalists who owned larger factories, might actually have benefited from the continued supply of cheaper labor created by immigration from China. Conflicts such as the anti-Chinese campaign can be especially intense because they can confound racial and ethnic antagonisms with disputes between different social classes.

The ban on immigration from China remained in effect until World War II, when China was awarded a yearly quota of 105 immigrants in recognition of its wartime alliance with the United States. However, large-scale immigration from China did not resume until federal policy was revised in the 1960s.

Population Trends and the "Delayed" Second Generation

Following the Chinese Exclusion Act, the number of Chinese in the United States actually declined (see Exhibit 8.5), as some immigrants passed away or returned to China and were not replaced by newcomers. The huge majority of Chinese immigrants in the 19th century had been young adult male sojourners who intended to work hard, save money, and return to their homes in China (Chan, 1990). After 1882, it was difficult for anyone from China, male or female, to enter the United States, and the Chinese community in the United States remained overwhelmingly male for many decades. At the end of the 19th century, for example, males outnumbered females by more than 25 to 1, and the sex ratio did not approach parity for decades (Wong, 1995, p. 64; see also Ling, 2000). The scarcity of Chinese women in the United States delayed the second generation (the first born in the United States), and it wasn't until the 1920s, 80 years after immigration began, that as many as one third of all Chinese in the United States were native-born (Wong, 1995, p. 64).

Exhibit 8.5 Population Growth for Chinese and Japanese Americans, 1850–2007

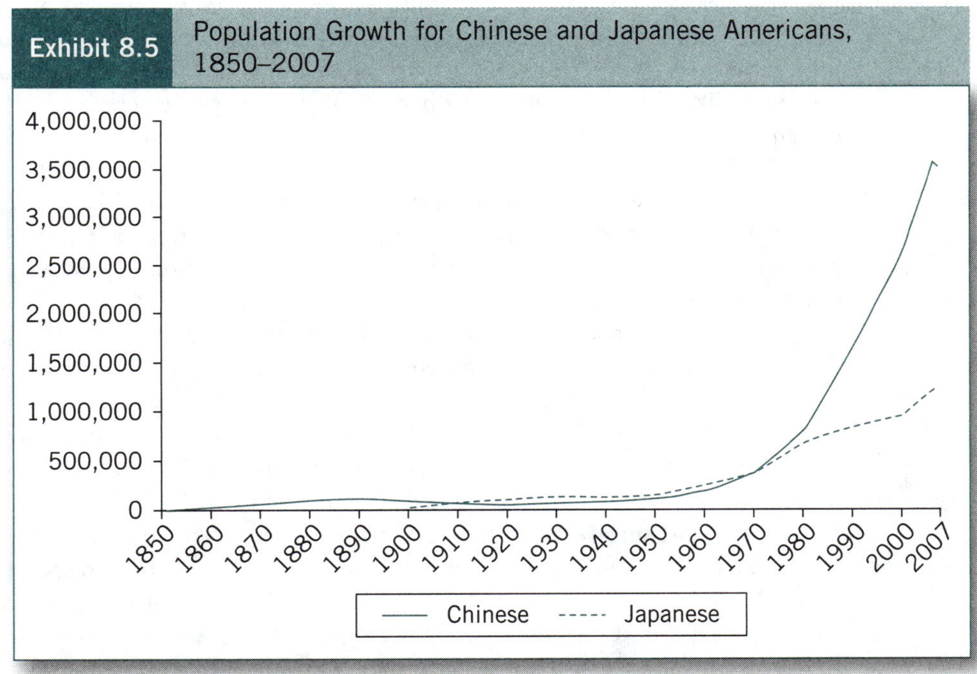

SOURCES: Kitano (1980, p. 562); Lee (1998, p. 15); U.S. Bureau of the Census (2007, 2009b); Xie & Goyette (2004).

The delayed second generation may have reinforced the exclusion of the Chinese American community, which began as a reaction to the overt discrimination of the dominant group (Chan, 1990). The children of immigrants are usually much more acculturated, and their language facility and greater familiarity with the larger society often permits them to represent the group and speak for it more effectively. In the case of Chinese Americans (and other Asian groups), members of the second generation were citizens of the United States by birth, a status from which the immigrants were barred, and they had legal and political rights not available to their parents. Thus, the decades-long absence of a more Americanized, English-speaking generation increased the isolation of Chinese Americans.

The Ethnic Enclave

The Chinese became increasingly urbanized as the anti-Chinese campaign and rising racism took their toll. Forced out of towns and smaller cities, they settled in larger urban areas, such as San Francisco, which offered the safety of urban anonymity and ethnic neighborhoods where the old ways could be practiced and contact with the hostile larger society minimized. Chinatowns had existed since the start of the immigration, and they now took on added significance as safe havens from the storm of anti-Chinese venom. The Chinese withdrew to these neighborhoods and became an "invisible minority" (Tsai, 1986, p. 67).

These early Chinatowns were ethnic enclaves like those founded by Jews on the East Coast and the more recently founded Cuban community in Miami, and a similar process formed them. The earliest urban Chinese included merchants and skilled artisans who, like the early wave of Cuban immigrants, were experienced in commerce (Chan, 1990). They established businesses and retail stores that were typically small in scope and modest in profits. As the number of urban Chinese increased, the market for these enterprises became larger and more spatially concentrated. New services were required, the size of the cheap labor pool available to Chinese merchants and entrepreneurs increased, and the Chinatowns became the economic, cultural, and social centers of the community.

Within the Chinatowns, elaborate social structures developed that mirrored traditional China in many ways. The enforced segregation of the Chinese in America helped preserve much of the traditional food, dress, language, values, and religions of their homeland from the pressures of Americanization. The social structure was based on a variety of types of organizations, including family and clan groups and **huiguan**, or associations based on the region or district in China from which the immigrant had come. These organizations performed various, often overlapping, social and welfare services, including settling disputes, aiding new arrivals from their regions, and facilitating the development of mutual aid networks (Lai, 1980; Lyman, 1974). Life was not always peaceful in Chinatown, and there were numerous disputes over control of resources and the organizational infrastructure. In particular, secret societies called **tongs** contested the control and leadership of the merchant-led huiguan and the clan associations. These sometimes bloody conflicts were sensationalized in the American press as "Tong Wars," and they contributed to the popular stereotypes of Asians as exotic, mysterious, and dangerous (Lai, 1980; Lyman, 1974).

Despite these internal conflicts, American Chinatowns evolved into highly organized, largely self-contained communities, complete with their own leadership and decision-making structures. The internal "city government" of Chinatown was the Chinese Consolidated Benevolent Association (CCBA). Dominated by the larger huiguan and clans, the CCBA coordinated and supplemented the activities of the various organizations and represented the interests of the community to the larger society.

The local CCBAs, along with other organizations, also attempted to combat the anti-Chinese campaign, speaking out against racial discrimination and filing numerous lawsuits to contest racist legislation (Lai, 1980). The effectiveness of the protest efforts was handicapped by the lack of resources in the Chinese community and by the fact that Chinese immigrants could not become citizens. Attempts were made to mobilize international pressure to protest the treatment of the Chinese in the United States. At the time, however, China was itself colonized and dominated by other nations (including the United States). China was further weakened by internal turmoil and could mount no effective assistance for its citizens in the United States (Chan, 1990).

Survival and Development

The Chinese American community survived despite the widespread poverty, discrimination, and pressures created by the unbalanced sex ratio. Members of the group began to seek opportunities in other regions, and Chinatowns appeared and grew in New York, Boston, Chicago, Philadelphia, and many other cities.

The patterns of exclusion and discrimination that began during the 19th-century anti-Chinese campaign were common throughout the nation and continued well into the 20th century. Chinese Americans responded by finding economic opportunity in areas where dominant-group competition for jobs was weak, continuing their tendency to be an "invisible" minority group. Very often, they started small businesses that served either other members of their own group (restaurants, for example) or that relied on the patronage of the general public (laundries, for example). The jobs provided by these small businesses were the economic lifeblood of the community but were limited in the amount of income and wealth they could generate. Until recent decades, for example, most restaurants served primarily other Chinese, especially single males. Because their primary clientele was poor, the profit potential of these businesses was sharply limited. Laundries served the more affluent dominant group, but the returns from this enterprise declined as washers and dryers became increasingly widespread in homes throughout the nation. The population of Chinatown was generally too small to sustain more than these two primary commercial enterprises (Zhou, 1992).

As the decades passed, the enclave economy and the complex subsociety of Chinatown evolved. However, discrimination, combined with defensive self-segregation, ensured the continuation of poverty, limited job opportunities, and substandard housing. Relatively hidden from general view, Chinatown became the world in which the second generation grew to adulthood.

The Second Generation

Whereas the immigrant generation generally retained its native language and customs, the second generation was much more influenced by the larger culture. The institutional and organizational structures of Chinatown were created to serve the older, mostly male immigrant generation, but younger Chinese Americans tended to look beyond the enclave to fill their needs. They came in contact with the larger society through schools, churches, and voluntary organizations such as the YMCA and YWCA. They abandoned many traditional customs and were less loyal to and interested in the clan and regional associations that the immigrant generation had constructed. They founded organizations of their own that were more compatible with their Americanized lifestyles (Lai, 1980).

As with other minority groups, World War II was an important watershed for Chinese Americans. During the war, job opportunities outside the enclave increased, and after the war, many of the 8,000 Chinese Americans who served in the armed forces were able to take advantage of the GI Bill to further their education (Lai, 1980, p. 226). In the 1940s and 1950s, many second-generation Chinese Americans moved out of the enclave, away from the traditional neighborhoods, and pursued careers in the larger society. This group was mobile and Americanized, and with educational credentials comparable with the general population, they were prepared to seek success outside Chinatown.

In another departure from tradition, the women of the second generation also pursued education, and as early as 1960, median years of schooling for Chinese American women were slightly higher than for Chinese American men (Kitano & Daniels, 1995). Chinese American women also became more diverse in their occupational profile as the century progressed. In 1900, three quarters of all employed Chinese American women worked in manufacturing (usually in garment industry sweatshops or in canning factories) or in domestic work. By 1960, less than 2% were in domestic work, 32% were in clerical occupations, and 18% held professional jobs, often as teachers (Amott & Matthaei, 1991, pp. 209–211).

An American Success Story?

The men and women of the second generation achieved considerable educational and occupational success and helped to establish the idea that Chinese Americans are a "model minority." A closer examination reveals, however, that the old traditions of anti-Chinese discrimination and prejudice continued to limit the life chances of even the best-educated members of this generation. Second-generation Chinese Americans earned less, on the average, and had less-favorable occupational profiles than comparably educated white Americans, a gap between qualifications and rewards that reflects persistent discrimination. Kitano and Daniels (1995) conclude, for example, that although well-educated Chinese Americans could find good jobs in the mainstream economy, the highest, most lucrative positions—and those that required direct supervision of whites—were still closed to them (see also Hirschman &Wong, 1984).

Furthermore, many Chinese Americans, including many of those who stayed in the Chinatowns to operate the enclave economy and the immigrants who began arriving after 1965, do not fit the image of success at all. A large percentage of these Chinese Americans face the same problems as other colonized, excluded, exploited minority groups of color. They rely for survival on low-wage jobs in the garment industry, the service sector, and the small businesses of the enclave economy and are beset by poverty and powerlessness, much like the urban underclass segments of other groups.

Thus, Chinese Americans can be found at both ends of the spectrum of success and affluence, and the group is often said to be "bipolar" in its occupational structure (see Barringer, Takeuchi, & Levin, 1995; Takaki, 1993; Wong, 1995; Zhou & Logan, 1989). Although a high percentage of Chinese Americans are found in more desirable occupations—sustaining the idea of Asian success—others, less visible, are concentrated at the lowest levels of the society. Later in this chapter, we will again consider the socioeconomic status of Chinese Americans and the accuracy of the image of success and affluence.

Japanese Americans

Immigration from Japan began to increase shortly after the Chinese Exclusion Act of 1882 took effect, in part to fill the gap in the labor supply created by the restrictive legislation (Kitano, 1980). The 1880 census counted only a few hundred Japanese in the United States, but the group increased rapidly over the next few decades. By 1910, the Japanese in the United States outnumbered the Chinese and remained the larger of the two groups until large-scale immigration resumed in the 1960s (see Exhibit 8.5).

The Anti-Japanese Campaign

The contact situation for Japanese immigrants resembled that of the Chinese. They immigrated to the same West Coast regions as the Chinese, entered the labor force in a similar position, and were a small group with few power resources. Predictably, the feelings and emotions generated by the anti-Chinese campaign transferred to them. By the early 1900s, an anti-Japanese campaign to limit competition was in full swing. Efforts were being made to establish a rigid competitive system of group relations and to exclude Japanese immigrants in the same way the Chinese had been barred (Kitano, 1980; Kitano & Daniels, 1995; Petersen, 1971).

Japanese immigration was partly curtailed in 1907 when a "gentlemen's agreement" was signed between Japan and the United States limiting the number of laborers Japan would allow to emigrate (Kitano & Daniels, 1995, p. 59). This policy remained in effect until the United States changed its immigration policy in the 1920s and barred immigration from Japan completely. The end of Japanese immigration is largely responsible for the slow growth of the Japanese American population displayed in Exhibit 8.5.

Most Japanese immigrants, like the Chinese, were young male laborers who planned to eventually return to their homeland or bring their wives after they were established in their new country (Duleep, 1988). The agreement of 1907 curtailed the immigration of men, but because of a loophole, females were able to continue to immigrate until the 1920s. Japanese Americans were thus able to maintain a relatively balanced sex ratio, marry, and begin families, and a second generation of Japanese Americans began to appear without much delay. Native-born Japanese numbered about half of the group by 1930 and were a majority of 63% on the eve of World War II (Kitano & Daniels, 1995, p. 59).

The anti-Japanese movement also attempted to dislodge the group from agriculture. Many Japanese immigrants were skilled agriculturists, and farming proved to be their most promising avenue for advancement (Kitano, 1980). In 1910, between 30% and 40% of all Japanese in California were engaged in agriculture; from 1900 to 1909, the number of independent Japanese farmers increased from fewer than 50 to about 6,000 (Jibou, 1988, p. 358).

Most of these immigrant farmers owned small plots of land, and they made up only a minuscule percentage of West Coast farmers (Jibou, 1988). Nonetheless, their presence and relative success did not go unnoticed and eventually stimulated discriminatory legislation, most notably the **Alien Land Act**, passed by the California legislature in 1913 (Kitano, 1980). This bill declared that aliens who were ineligible for citizenship (effectively meaning only immigrants from Asia) were also ineligible to own land. The act did not achieve its goal of dislodging the Japanese from the rural economy. They were able to dodge the discriminatory legislation by various devices, mostly by putting titles of land in the names of their American-born children, who were citizens by law (Jibou, 1988).

The Alien Land Act was one part of a sustained campaign against the Japanese in the United States. In the early decades of this century, the Japanese were politically disenfranchised and segregated from dominant-group institutions in schools and residential areas. They were discriminated against in movie houses, swimming pools, and other public facilities (Kitano & Daniels, 1988). The Japanese were excluded from the mainstream economy and confined to a limited range of poorly paid occupations (see Yamato, 1994). Thus, there were strong elements of systematic discrimination, exclusion, and colonization in their overall relationship with the larger society.

The Ethnic Enclave

Spurned and disparaged by the larger society, the Japanese, like the Chinese, constructed a separate subsociety. The immigrant generation, called **Issei** (from the Japanese word *ichi,* meaning "one"), established an enclave in agriculture and related enterprises, a rural counterpart of the urban enclaves constructed by other groups we have examined.

By World War II, the Issei had come to dominate a narrow but important segment of agriculture on the West Coast, especially in California. Although the Issei were never more than 2% of the total population of California, Japanese American-owned farms produced as much as 30% to 40% of various fruits and vegetables grown in that state. As late as 1940, more than 40% of the Japanese American population was involved directly in farming, and many more were dependent on the economic activity stimulated by agriculture, including the marketing of their produce (Jibou, 1988, pp. 359–360). Other Issei lived in urban areas, where they were concentrated in a narrow range of businesses and services, such as domestic service and gardening, some of which catered to other Issei and some of which served the dominant group (Jibou, 1988).

Japanese Americans in both the rural and urban sectors maximized their economic clout by doing business with other Japanese-owned firms as often as possible. Gardeners and farmers purchased supplies at Japanese-owned firms, farmers used other members of the group to haul their products to market, and businesspeople relied on one another and mutual credit associations, rather than dominant-group banks, for financial services. These networks helped the enclave economy to grow and also permitted the Japanese to avoid the hostility and racism of the larger society. However, these very same patterns helped sustain the stereotypes that depicted the Japanese as clannish and unassimilable. In the years before World War II, the Japanese American community was largely dependent for survival on their networks of cooperation and mutual assistance, not on Americanization and integration.

The Second Generation (Nisei)

In the 1920s and 1930s, anti-Asian feelings continued to run high, and Japanese Americans continued to be excluded and discriminated against despite (or perhaps because of) their relative success. Unable to find acceptance in Anglo society, the second generation, called **Nisei**, established clubs, athletic leagues, churches, and a multitude of other social and recreational organizations within their own communities (Kitano & Daniels, 1995). These organizations reflected the high levels of Americanization of the Nisei and expressed values and interests quite compatible with those of the dominant culture. For example, the most influential Nisei organization was the Japanese American Citizens League, whose creed expressed an ardent patriotism that was to be sorely tested: "I am proud that I am an American citizen. . . . I believe in [American] institutions, ideas and traditions; I glory in her heritage; I boast of her history, I trust in her future" (Kitano & Daniels, 1995, p. 64).

Although the Nisei enjoyed high levels of success in school, the intense discrimination and racism of the 1930s prevented most of them from translating their educational achievements into better jobs and higher salaries. Many occupations in the mainstream economy were closed to even the best-educated Japanese Americans, and anti-Asian prejudice and discrimination did not diminish during the hard times and high unemployment of the Great Depression in the 1930s. Many Nisei were forced to remain within the enclave, and in many cases, jobs in the produce stands and retail shops of their parents were all they could find. Their demoralization and anger over their exclusion were eventually swamped by the larger events of World War II.

The Relocation Camps

On December 7, 1941, Japan attacked Pearl Harbor, killing almost 2,500 Americans. President Franklin D. Roosevelt asked Congress for a declaration of war the next day. The preparations for war stirred up a wide range of fears and anxieties among the American public, including concerns about the loyalty of Japanese Americans. Decades of exclusion and anti-Japanese prejudice had conditioned the dominant society to see Japanese Americans as sinister, clannish, cruel, unalterably foreign, and racially inferior. Fueled by the ferocity of the war itself and fears about a Japanese invasion of the mainland, the tradition of anti-Japanese racism laid the groundwork for a massive violation of civil rights.

Two months after the attack on Pearl Harbor, President Roosevelt signed Executive Order 9066, which led to the relocation of Japanese Americans living on the West Coast. By the late summer of 1942, more than 110,000 Japanese Americans, young and old, male and female—virtually the entire West Coast population—had been transported to **relocation camps**, where they were imprisoned behind barbed-wire fences patrolled by armed guards. Many of these people were American citizens, yet no attempt was made to distinguish between citizen and alien. No trials were held, and no one was given the opportunity to refute the implicit charge of disloyalty.

The government gave families little notice to prepare for evacuation and secure their homes, businesses, and belongings. They were allowed to bring only what they could carry, and many possessions were simply abandoned. Businesspeople sold their establishments and farmers sold their land, at panic sale prices. Others locked up their stores and houses and walked away, hoping that the evacuation would be short-lived and their possessions undisturbed.

The internment lasted for nearly the entire war. At first, Japanese Americans were not permitted to serve in the armed forces, but eventually more than 25,000 escaped the camps by volunteering for military service. Nearly all of them served in segregated units or in intelligence work with combat units in the Pacific Ocean. Two all-Japanese combat units served in Europe and became the most decorated units in American military history (Kitano, 1980). Other Japanese Americans were able to get out of the camps by means other than the military. Some, for example, agreed to move to militarily nonsensitive areas far away from the West Coast (and their former homes). Still, when the camps closed at the end of the war, about half of the original internees remained (Kitano & Daniels, 1988).

The strain of living in the camps affected Japanese Americans in a variety of ways. Lack of activities and privacy, overcrowding, boredom, and monotony were all common complaints. The camps disrupted the traditional forms of family life, as people had to adapt to barracks living and mess hall dining. Conflicts flared between those who counseled caution and temperate reactions to the incarceration and those who wanted to protest in more vigorous ways. Many of those who advised moderation were Nisei intent on proving their loyalty and cooperating with the camp administration.

Despite the injustice and dislocations of the incarceration, the camps did reduce the extent to which women were relegated to a subordinate role. Like Chinese women, Japanese women were expected to devote themselves to the care of the males of their family. In Japan, for example, education for females was not intended to challenge their intellect so much as to make them better wives and mothers. In the camps, however, pay for the few jobs available was the same for both men and women, and the mess halls and small living quarters freed women from some of the burden of housework. Many took advantage of the free time to take classes to learn more English and other skills. The younger women were able to meet young men on their own, weakening the tradition of family-controlled, arranged marriages (Amott & Matthaei, 1991).

Some Japanese Americans protested the incarceration from the start and brought lawsuits to end the relocation program. Finally, in 1944, the Supreme Court ruled that detention was unconstitutional. As the camps closed, some Japanese American individuals and organizations began to seek compensation and redress for the economic losses the group had suffered. In 1948, Congress passed legislation to authorize compensation to Japanese Americans. About 26,500 people filed claims under this act. These claims were eventually settled for a total of about $38 million—less than one tenth the actual economic losses. Demand for meaningful redress and compensation continued, and in 1988, Congress passed a bill granting reparations of about $20,000 in cash to each of the 60,000 remaining survivors of the camps. The law also acknowledged that the relocation program had been a grave injustice to Japanese Americans (Biskupic, 1989).

The World War II relocation devastated the Japanese American community and left it with few material resources. The emotional and psychological damage inflicted by this experience is incalculable. The fact that today, only six decades later, Japanese Americans are equal or superior to national averages on measures of educational achievement, occupational prestige, and income is one of the more dramatic transformations in minority group history.

Japanese Americans After World War II

In 1945, Japanese Americans faced a world very different from the one they had left in 1942. To escape the camps, nearly half of the group had scattered throughout the country and lived everywhere but on the West Coast. As Japanese Americans attempted to move back to their former homes, they found their fields untended, their stores vandalized, their possessions lost or stolen, and their lives shattered. In some cases, there was simply no Japanese neighborhood to return to; the Little Tokyo area of San Francisco, for example, was now occupied by African Americans who had moved to the West Coast to take jobs in the defense industry (Amott & Matthaei, 1991).

Japanese Americans themselves had changed as well. In the camps, the Issei had lost power to the Nisei. The English-speaking second generation had dealt with the camp administrators and held the leadership positions. Many Nisei had left the camps to serve in the armed forces or to find work in other areas of the country. For virtually every American minority group, the war brought new experiences and a broader sense of themselves, the nation, and the world. A similar transformation occurred for the Nisei. When the war ended, they were unwilling to rebuild the Japanese community as it had been before.

Like second-generation Chinese Americans, the Nisei had a strong record of success in school, and they also took advantage of the GI Bill to further their education. When anti-Asian prejudice began to decline in the 1950s and the job market began to open, the Nisei were educationally prepared to take advantage of the resultant opportunities (Kitano, 1980).

The Issei-dominated enclave economy did not reappear after the war. One indicator of the shift away from an enclave economy was the fact that the percentage of Japanese American women in California who worked as unpaid family laborers (i.e., worked in family-run businesses for no salary) declined from 21% in 1940 to 7% in 1950 (Amott & Matthaei, 1991, p. 231). Also, between 1940 and 1990, the percentage of the group employed in agriculture declined from about 50% to 3%, and the percentage employed in personal services fell from 25% to 5% (Nishi, 1995, p. 116).

By 1960, Japanese Americans had an occupational profile very similar to that of whites except that they were actually overrepresented among professionals. Many were employed in the primary economy, not in the ethnic enclave, but there was a tendency to choose "safe" careers (e.g., in engineering, optometry, pharmacy, accounting) that did not require extensive contact with the public or supervision of whites (Kitano & Daniels, 1988, p. 70).

Within these limitations, the Nisei, their children (**Sansei**), and their grandchildren (**Yonsei**) have enjoyed relatively high status, and their upward mobility and prosperity have contributed to the perception that Asian Americans are a "model minority." An additional factor contributing to the high status of Japanese Americans (and to the disappearance of Little Tokyos) is that unlike Chinese Americans, the number of immigrants from Japan has been quite small, and the community has not had to devote many resources to newcomers. Furthermore, recent immigrants from Japan tend to be highly educated professional people whose socioeconomic characteristics add to the perception of success and affluence.

The Sansei and Yonsei are highly integrated into the occupational structure of the larger society. Compared with their parents, their connections with their ethnic past are more tenuous, and in their values, beliefs, and personal goals, they resemble dominant-group members of similar age and social class (Kitano & Daniels, 1995; see also Spickard, 1996).

Comparing Minority Groups

What factors account for the differences in the development of Chinese Americans and Japanese Americans and other racial minority groups? First, unlike the situation of African Americans in the 1600s and Mexican Americans in the 1800s, the dominant group had no desire to control the labor of these groups. The contact situation featured economic competition (e.g., for jobs) during an era of rigid competition between groups (see Exhibit 4.5), and Chinese Americans and Japanese Americans were seen as a threat to security that needed to be eliminated, not as a labor pool that needed to be controlled.

Second, unlike American Indians, Chinese Americans and Japanese Americans in the early 20th century presented no military danger to the larger society, so there was little concern with their activities once the economic threat had been eliminated. Third, Chinese Americans and Japanese Americans had the ingredients and experiences necessary to form enclaves. The groups were allowed to "disappear," but unlike other racial minority groups, the urban location of their enclaves left them with opportunities for schooling for later generations. As many scholars argue, the particular mode of incorporation developed by Chinese Americans and Japanese Americans is the key to understanding the present status of these groups.

Contemporary Immigration to the United States From Asia

Immigration from Asia has been considerable since the 1960s, averaging close to 300,000 per year and running about 30% to 35% of all immigrants. As was the case with Hispanic immigrants, the sending nations are considerably less developed than the United States, and the primary motivation for most of these immigrants is economic. However, the Asian immigrant stream also includes a large contingent of highly educated professionals seeking opportunities to practice their careers and expand their skills. Although these more elite immigrants contribute to the image of "Asian success," other Asian immigrants are low skilled, less educated, and undocumented. Thus, this stream of immigrants, like Chinese Americans, is "bipolar" and includes a healthy representation of people from both the top and the bottom of the occupational and educational hierarchies.

Of course, other factors besides mere economics attract these immigrants to the United States. The United States has maintained military bases throughout the region (including Japan, South Korea, and the Philippines) since the end of World War II, and many Asian immigrants are the spouses of American military personnel. Also, U.S. involvement in the war in Southeast Asia in the 1960s and 1970s created interpersonal ties and governmental programs that drew refugees from Vietnam, Cambodia, and Laos.

As in Chapter 7, rather than attempting to cover all the separate Asian American groups, we will concentrate on four case studies and consider immigration from India, Vietnam, Korea, and the Philippines. Together, these four groups make up about half of all immigrants from Asia.

Four Case Studies

These groups are small, and they all include a high percentage of foreign-born members (see Exhibit 8.4). The groups are quite variable in their backgrounds, their occupational profiles, their levels of education, and their incomes. In contrast with Hispanic immigrants, however, they tend to have higher percentages of members who are highly educated, fluent in English, and prepared to compete for good jobs in the American job market.

As we have done so often, we must note the diversity across these four groups. First, we can repeat the point that the category "Asian American" is an arbitrary designation imposed on peoples who actually have little in common and who come from nations that vary in language, culture, religion, "racial" characteristics, and scores of other ways. More specifically, these four groups are quite different from each other.

Perhaps the most striking contrast is between immigrants from India, many of who are highly educated and skilled, and those from Vietnam, who have a socioeconomic profile that, in some ways, resembles non-Asian racial minorities in the United States. Part of the difference between these two groups relates to their contact situations and can be illuminated by applying the Blauner hypothesis. Immigrants from India are at the "immigrant" end of Blauner's continuum. They bring high levels of human capital and strong educational credentials and are well equipped to compete for favorable positions in the occupational hierarchy. The Vietnamese, in contrast, began their American experience as a refugee group fleeing the turmoil of war. Although they do not fit Blauner's "conquered or colonized" category, most Vietnamese Americans had to adapt to American society with few resources and few contacts with an established immigrant community. The consequences of these vastly different contact situations are suggested by the data presented in the exhibits at the end of this chapter.

These groups also vary in their settlement patterns. Most are concentrated along the West Coast, but Indians are roughly equally distributed on both the East and West Coasts, and Vietnamese have a sizable presence in Texas, in part related to the fishing industry along the Gulf Coast.

Asian Indians. India is the second most populous nation in the world, and its huge population of more than a billion people incorporates a wide variety of different languages (India has 19 official languages, including English), religions, and ethnic groups. Overall, the level of education is fairly low: The population averages about five years of formal schooling and is about 60% literate (Nationmaster.com, n.d.). However, about 10% of the population does reach the postsecondary level of education, which means that there are about 100 million (10% of a billion) well-educated Indians looking for careers commensurate with their credentials. Because of the relative lack of development in the Indian economy, many members of this educated elite must search for career opportunities abroad, and not just in the United States. It is also important to note that, as a legacy of India's long colonization by the British, English is the language of the educated. Thus, Indian immigrants tend to be not only well educated but also English speaking.

Immigration from India to the United States was low until the mid-1960s, and the group was quite small at that time. The group more than quadrupled in size between 1980 and 2000, and Indians are now the third-largest Asian American group (behind Chinese and Filipinos).

Immigrants from India tend to be a select, highly educated and skilled group. According to the 2000 census, Indians are very overrepresented in some of the most prestigious occupations, including computer engineering, physicians, and college professors (U.S. Bureau of the Census, 2000h). Immigrants from India are part of a worldwide movement of educated peoples from less developed countries to more developed countries. One need not ponder the differences in career opportunities, technology, and compensation for long to get some insight into the reasons for this movement. Other immigrants from India are more oriented to commerce and small business, and there is a sizable Indian ethnic enclave in many cities (Kitano & Daniels, 1995; Sheth, 1995).

Koreans. Immigration from Korea to the United States began early in the 20th century, when laborers were recruited to help fill the void in the job market left by the 1882 Chinese Exclusion Act. This group was extremely small until the 1950s, when the rate of immigration rose because of refugees and "war brides" after the Korean War. Immigration did not become substantial, however, until the 1960s. The size of the group increased fivefold in the 1970s and tripled between 1980 and 2000 but is still only 0.5% of the total population.

Recent immigrants from Korea consist mostly of families and include many highly educated people. Although differences in culture, language, and race make Koreans visible targets of discrimination, the high percentage of Christians among them (almost half of South Koreans are Christian) may help them appear more "acceptable" to the dominant group. Certainly, Christian church parishes play a number of important roles for the Korean American community, offering assistance to newcomers and the less fortunate, serving as a focal point for networks of mutual assistance, and generally assisting in the completion of the myriad chores to which immigrant communities must attend (e.g., government paperwork, registering to vote, and so on) (Kitano & Daniels, 2001).

Korean American immigrants have formed an enclave, and the group is heavily involved in small businesses and retail stores, particularly fruit and vegetable retail stores, or greengroceries. According to one study, Koreans had the second highest percentage of self-employment among immigrant groups (Greeks were the highest), with about 24% of the group in this occupational category (Kritz & Gurak, 2004, p. 36). Another data source, also based on the 2000 census, shows that Koreans have the highest rate of business ownership among 11 different minority groups (U.S. Bureau of the Census, 2002), including other enclave minorities. Japanese Americans had the second-highest rate

(108 businesses per 1,000 population), Chinese Americans were third (104 per 1,000 population), and Cuban Americans were fourth (101 per 1,000 population). In contrast, racial minority groups with strong histories of colonization and exclusion were at the bottom of the rankings: African Americans (24 businesses per 1,000) and Puerto Ricans (21 per 1,000) (see also Pollard & O'Hare, 1999, p. 39; Kim, Hurh, & Fernandez, 1989; Logan, Alba, & McNulty, 1994).

As is the case for other groups that have pursued this course, the enclave allows Korean Americans to avoid the discrimination and racism of the larger society yet survive in an economic niche in which lack of English fluency is not a particular problem. However, the enclave has its perils and its costs. For one thing, the success of Korean enterprises depends heavily on the mutual assistance and financial support of other Koreans and the willingness of family members to work long hours for little or no pay. These resources would be weakened or destroyed by acculturation, integration, and the resultant decline in ethnic solidarity. Only by maintaining a distance from the dominant culture and its pervasive appeal can the enclave infrastructure survive.

Furthermore, the economic niches in which mom-and-pop greengroceries and other small businesses can survive are often in deteriorated neighborhoods populated largely by other minority groups. There has been a good deal of hostility and resentment expressed against Korean shop owners by African Americans, Puerto Ricans, and other urbanized minority groups. For example, anti-Korean sentiments were widely expressed in the 1992 Los Angeles riots that followed the acquittal of the policemen who had been charged in the beating of Rodney King. Korean-owned businesses were some of the first to be looted and burned, and when asked why, one participant in the looting said simply, "Because we hate 'em. Everybody hates them" (Cho, 1993, p. 199). Thus, part of the price of survival for many Korean merchants is to place themselves in positions in which antagonism and conflict with other minority groups is common (Kitano & Daniels, 1995; Light & Bonacich, 1988; Min, 1995; see also Hurh, 1998).

Filipino Americans. Ties between the United States and the Philippines were established in 1898 when Spain ceded the territory after its defeat in the Spanish-American war. The Philippines achieved independence following World War II, but the United States has maintained a strong military presence there for much of the past 60 years. The nation has been heavily influenced by American culture, and English remains one of two official languages. Thus, Filipino immigrants are often conversant in English, at least as a second language (see Exhibit 8.6, p. 356, on language acculturation).

Today, Filipinos are the second-largest Asian American group, but their numbers became sizable only in the last few decades. There were fewer than 1,000 Filipinos in the United States in 1910, and by 1960, the group still numbered fewer than 200,000. Most of the recent growth has come from increased post-1965 immigration. The group more than doubled in size between 1990 and 2007.

Many of the earliest immigrants were agricultural workers recruited for the sugar plantations of Hawaii and the fields of the West Coast. Because the Philippines was a U.S. territory, Filipinos could enter without regard to immigration quotas until 1935, when the nation became a self-governing commonwealth.

The most recent wave of immigrants is diversified, and like Chinese Americans, Filipino Americans are "bipolar" in their educational and occupational profiles. Many recent immigrants have entered under the family preference provisions of the U.S. immigration policy. These immigrants are often poor and compete for jobs in the low-wage secondary labor market (Kitano & Daniels, 1995). More than half of all Filipino immigrants since 1965, however, have been professionals, many of them in the health and medical fields. Many female immigrants from the Philippines were nurses actively recruited by U.S. hospitals to fill gaps in the labor force (Amott & Matthaei, 1991). Thus, the Filipino American community includes some members in the high-wage primary labor market and others who are competing for work in the low-wage secondary sector (Agbayani-Siewart & Revilla, 1995; Espiritu, 1996; Kitano & Daniels, 1995; Mangiafico, 1988; Posadas, 1999).

Vietnamese. A flow of refugees from Vietnam began in the 1960s as a direct result of the war in Southeast Asia. The war began in Vietnam but expanded when the United States attacked Communist forces in Cambodia and Laos. Social life was disrupted, and people were displaced throughout the region. In 1975, when Saigon (the South Vietnamese capital) fell and the U.S. military withdrew, many Vietnamese and other Southeast Asians who had collaborated with the United States and its allies fled in fear for their lives. This group included high-ranking officials and members of the region's educational and occupation elite. Later groups of refugees tended to be less well educated and more impoverished. Many Vietnamese waited in refugee camps for months or years before being admitted to the United States, and they often arrived with few resources or social networks to ease their transition to the new society (Kitano & Daniels, 1995). The Vietnamese are the largest of the Asian refugee groups, and contrary to Asian American success stories and notions of model minorities, they have incomes and educational levels that are sometimes comparable with colonized minority groups (see Exhibits 8.11 to 8.16, pp. 360–365, and the Appendix [www.pineforge.com/healeyds3e]).

Contemporary Relations

In this section, we once more use our guiding concepts to assess the situation of Chinese Americans and Japanese Americans and the other Asian groups discussed in the next chapter. This section is organized around the same concepts used in previous case study chapters.

Prejudice and Discrimination

American prejudice against Asians first became prominent during the anti-Chinese movement of the 19th century. The Chinese were castigated as racially inferior, docile, and subservient, but also cruel and crafty, despotic, and threatening (Lai, 1980; Lyman, 1974). The Chinese Exclusion Act of 1882 was justified by the idea that the Chinese were unassimilable and could never be part of U.S. society. The Chinese were seen as a threat to the working class, to American democracy, and to other American institutions. Many of these stereotypes and fears transferred to the

Japanese later in the 19th century and then to other groups as they, in turn, arrived in the United States. The social distance scales presented in Exhibit 1.7 provide the only long-term record of anti-Asian prejudice in the society as a whole. In 1926, the five Asian groups included in the study were grouped in the bottom third of the scale, along with other racial and colonized minority groups. Twenty years later, in 1946, the Japanese had fallen to the bottom of the rankings, and the Chinese had risen seven positions, changes that reflect America's World War II conflict with Japan and alliance with China. This suggests that anti-Chinese prejudice may have softened during the war as distinctions were made between "good" and "bad" Asians. For example, an item published in a 1941 issue of *Time* magazine, "How to Tell Your Friends From the Japs," provided some tips for identifying "good" Asians: "The Chinese expression is likely to be more placid, kindly, open; the Japanese more positive, dogmatic, arrogant. . . . Japanese are nervous in conversation, laugh loudly at the wrong time" (p. 33).

In more recent decades, the average social distance scores of Asian groups have fallen even though the ranking of the groups remained relatively stable. The falling scores probably reflect the society-wide increase in tolerance and the shift from blatant prejudice to modern racism that we discussed in Chapters 1 and 5. However, the relative position of Asians in the American hierarchy of group preferences has remained remarkably consistent since the 1920s. This stability may reflect the cultural or traditional nature of much of American anti-Asian prejudice.

Although prejudice against Asian Americans may have weakened overall, there is considerable evidence that it remains a potent force in American life. Stereotypical thinking about the group continues (Lin, Kwan, Cheung, & Fiske, 2005) and Asian Americans of middle and high school age, who are often seen as passive high-achievers and "curve busters," commonly experience attacks both physical and psychological (Texeira, 2005). The continuing force of anti-Asian prejudice is also marked by hate crimes against members of the group. Asian Americans of all types—citizens, immigrants, tourists—have been attacked, beaten, and even murdered in recent years.

Asian Americans have also been the victims of "positive" stereotypes. The perception of Asian Americans as a "model minority" is exaggerated and, for some Asian American groups, simply false. This label has been applied to these groups by the media, politicians, and others. It is not an image that the Asian American groups themselves developed or particularly advocate. As you might suspect, people who apply these labels to Asian Americans have a variety of hidden moral and political agendas, and we explore these dynamics later in this chapter.

Assimilation and Pluralism

Acculturation

The extent of acculturation of Asian Americans is highly variable from group to group, with Japanese Americans representing one extreme. They have been a part of American society for more than a century, and are highly acculturated. Immigration from Japan has been low throughout the century and has not revitalized the traditional culture or language. As a result, Japanese Americans are the most acculturated of the Asian American groups, as illustrated in Exhibit 8.6. Japanese Americans have the highest percentage of members who speak English "very well," versus only about half of Vietnamese Americans.

Chinese Americans, in contrast, are highly variable in the extent of their acculturation. Many are members of families who have been American for generations and are highly acculturated. Others, including many undocumented, are new immigrants who have little knowledge of English or of Anglo culture. In this dimension, as in occupations, Chinese Americans are "bipolar." This great variability within the group makes it difficult to characterize their overall degree of acculturation.

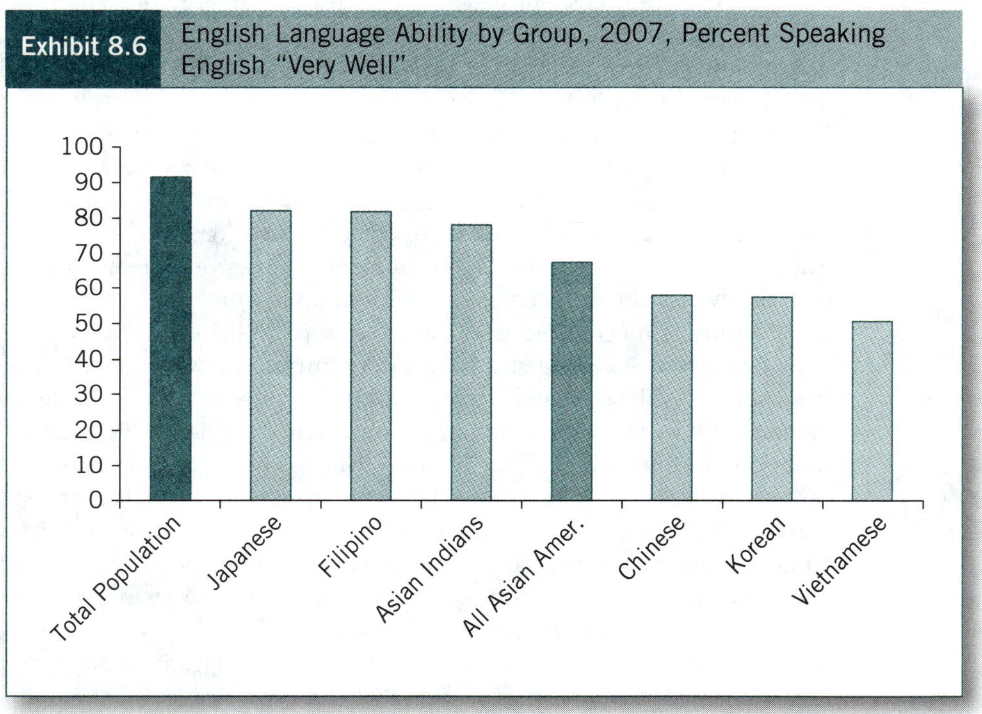

Exhibit 8.6 English Language Ability by Group, 2007, Percent Speaking English "Very Well"

SOURCE: U.S. Bureau of the Census (2007).

Secondary Structural Assimilation

We will cover this complex area in roughly the order followed in previous chapters. The Appendix (www.pineforge.com/healeyds3e) presents additional information on the relative standing of Asian American groups.

Residence. Exhibit 8.7 shows the regional concentrations of all Asian Americans. The tendency to reside on either coast and around Los Angeles, San Francisco, and New York stands out clearly. Note also the sizable concentrations in a variety of metropolitan areas, including Chicago, Atlanta, Miami, Denver, and Houston.

Exhibit 8.7 Regional Distribution of Asian Americans, 2000

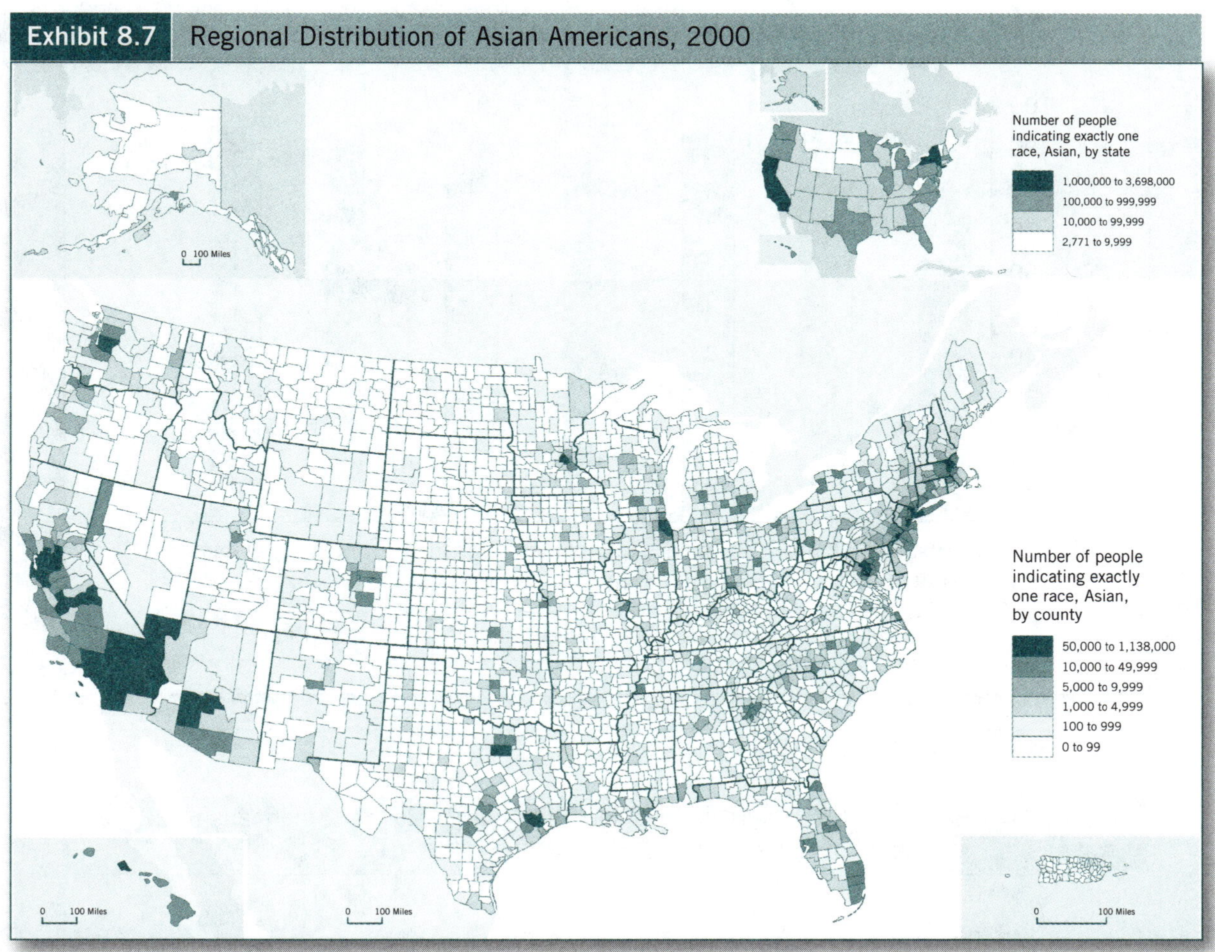

SOURCE: U.S. Bureau of the Census (2000e).

Asian Americans in general are highly urbanized, a reflection of the entry conditions of recent immigrants as well as the appeal of ethnic neighborhoods, such as Chinatowns, with long histories and continuing vitality. As displayed in Exhibit 8.8, all six Asian American groups discussed in this chapter are more than 90% urbanized, and several approach the 100% mark.

Asian Americans are much less residentially segregated than either African Americans or Hispanic American in all four regions of the nation. Exhibit 8.9 shows the average dissimilarity index for 220 metropolitan areas using the same format as in the previous three chapters. Asian Americans are not "extremely" segregated (that is, they do not have scores greater than 0.60) in any region but the level of residential segregation is holding steady or slightly rising over time, a reflection of high rates of immigration and the tendency for newcomers to settle close to other members of their group.

Exhibit 8.8 Urbanization of Six Asian American Groups, 2000

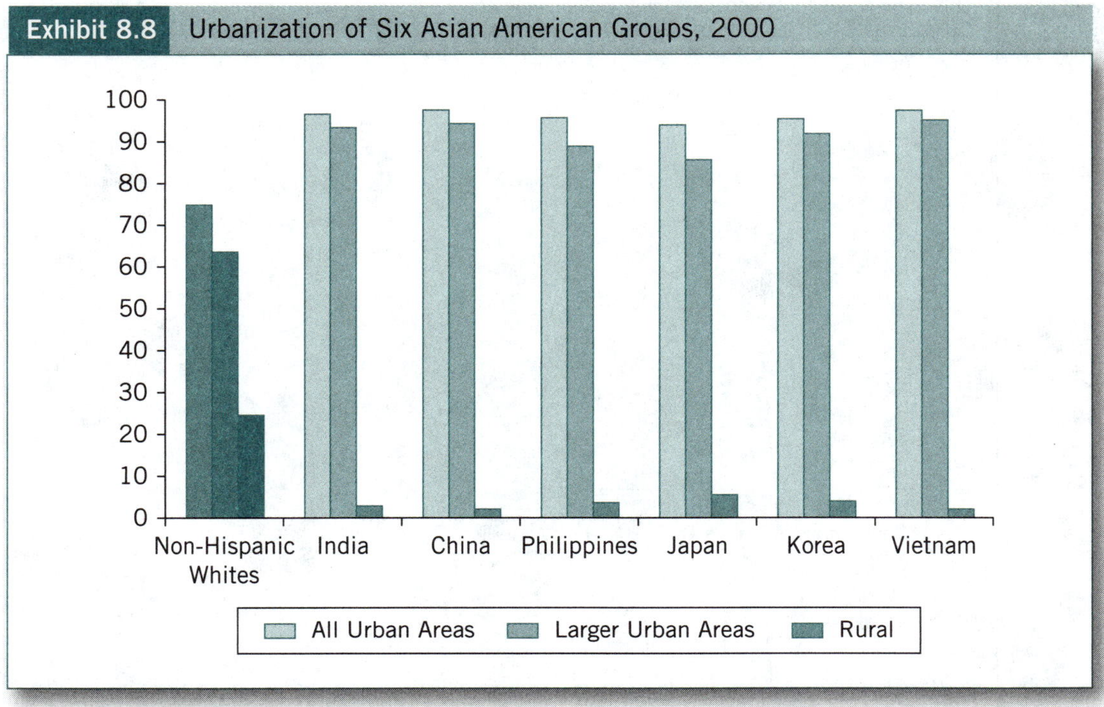

SOURCE: U.S. Bureau of the Census (2007).

Exhibit 8.9 Residential Segregation for Asian and Pacific Islander Americans in 220 Metropolitan Areas, 1980–2000

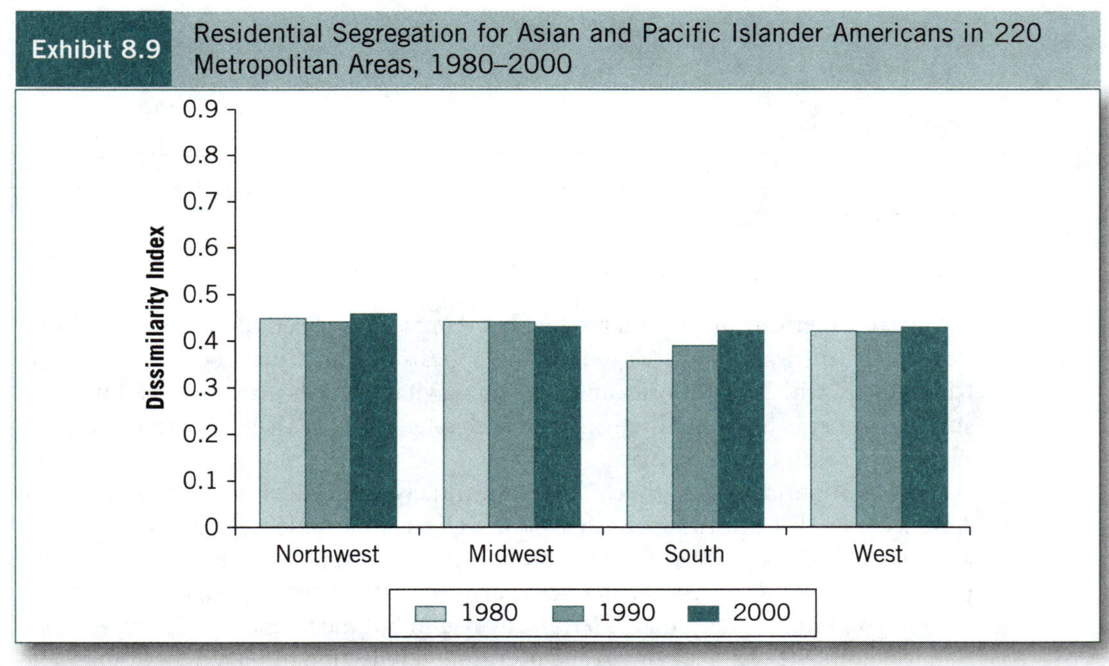

SOURCE: U.S. Bureau of the Census (2007).

Asian Americans are also moving away from their traditional neighborhoods and enclaves into the suburbs of metropolitan areas, most notably in the areas surrounding Los Angeles, San Francisco, New York, and other cities where the groups are highly concentrated. For example, Asian Americans have been moving in large numbers to the San Gabriel Valley, just east of downtown Los Angeles. Once a bastion of white, middle-class suburbanites, these areas have taken on a distinctly Asian flavor in recent years. Monterey Park, once virtually all white, is now 62% Chinese and is often referred to as "America's first suburban Chinatown" or the "Chinese Beverly Hills" (Fong, 2002, p. 49).

Education. The extent of school segregation for Asian Americans for the 1993–1994 and the 2005–2006 school years is displayed in Exhibit 8.10, as was done in previous chapters. In the 2005–2006 school year, Asian American children were much less likely to attend "majority-minority" or extremely segregated schools than either Hispanic American or African American children. However, the extent of school segregation has increased over the time period, a reflection of the pattern of residential segregation in Exhibit 8.9.

Exhibit 8.10 School Integration, 1993–1994 and 2005–2006

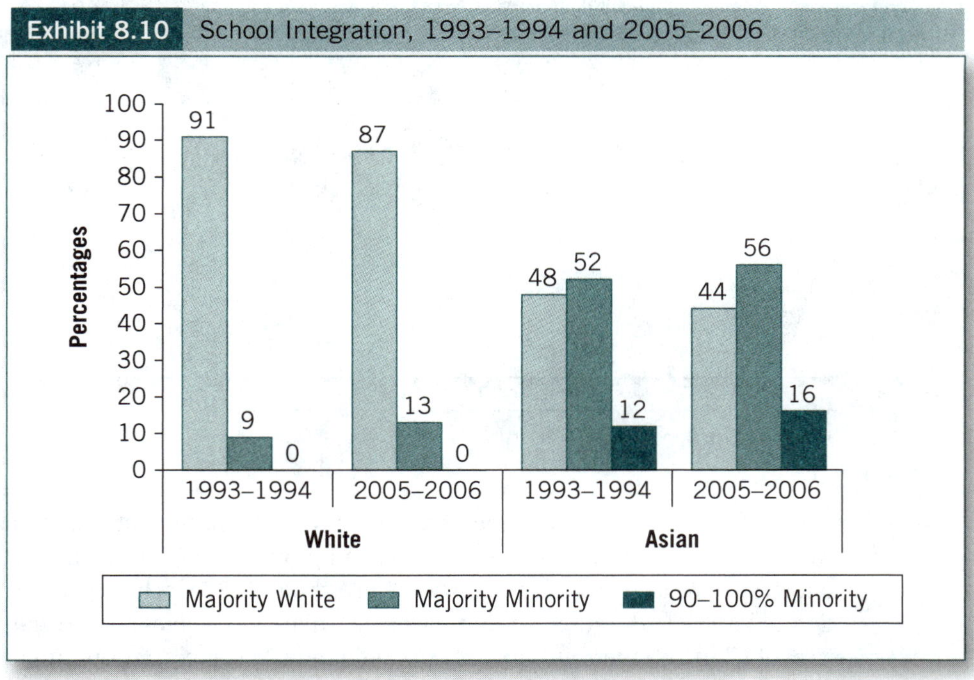

SOURCE: Fry (2007).

The extent of schooling for Asian Americans and for Chinese and Japanese Americans is very different from that for other U.S. racial minority groups. Considered as a whole, Asian Americans compare favorably with society-wide standards for educational achievement, and they are above those standards on many measures. Exhibit 8.11

shows that most Asian American groups are equal to or higher than non-Hispanic whites in high school education and far higher in college education, a pattern that has been very much reinforced by the high levels of education of many recent Asian immigrants. Four of the six Asian groups have a higher percentage of high school graduates than non-Hispanic whites, and all groups except the Vietnamese have a higher percentage of college graduates.

Exhibit 8.11 Educational Attainment for Non-Hispanic Whites, All Asian Americans, and Selected Groups, 2007

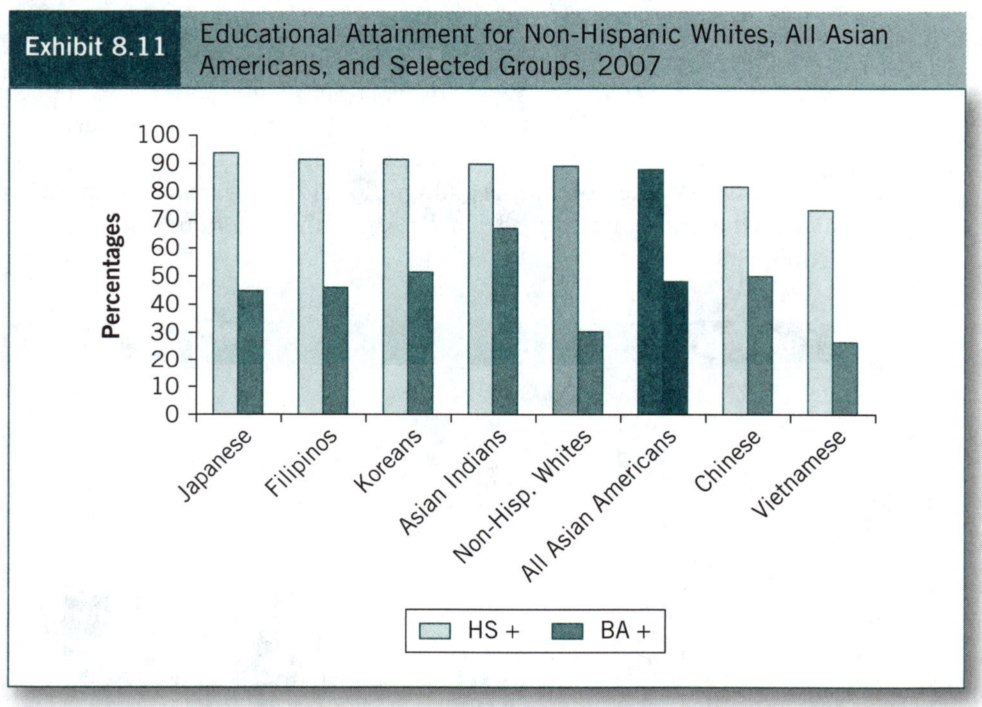

SOURCE: U.S. Bureau of the Census (2007).

Exhibit 8.11 reinforces the "model minority" image, but recall that Chinese Americans (and several other Asian American groups) are "bipolar" and have a sizable underclass group. This reality is captured in Exhibit 8.12, which compares the distribution of levels of education for non-Hispanic whites and Chinese Americans. More than 50% of Chinese Americans hold college and graduate degrees, far outnumbering whites (30%) at this level. Many of these highly educated Chinese Americans are recent immigrants seeking to pursue their professions in one of the world's most advanced economies.

Note, however, that Chinese Americans also are concentrated disproportionately at the lowest level of educational achievement. Some 18% of the group has less than a high school diploma, as opposed to 11% of non-Hispanic whites. Many of these less educated Chinese Americans are also recent immigrants (many of them undocumented), and they supply the unskilled labor force, in retail shops, restaurants, and garment industry "sweatshops," that staffs the lowest levels of the Chinatown economy.

Thus, the image of achievement and success needs to be balanced by the recognition that there is a full range of success and failure among Asian Americans and by the fact that average levels of achievement are "inflated" for Chinese Americans and some other groups by recent immigrants who are highly educated, skilled professionals.

Exhibit 8.12 Educational Levels, Non-Hispanic Whites and Chinese Americans, 2007

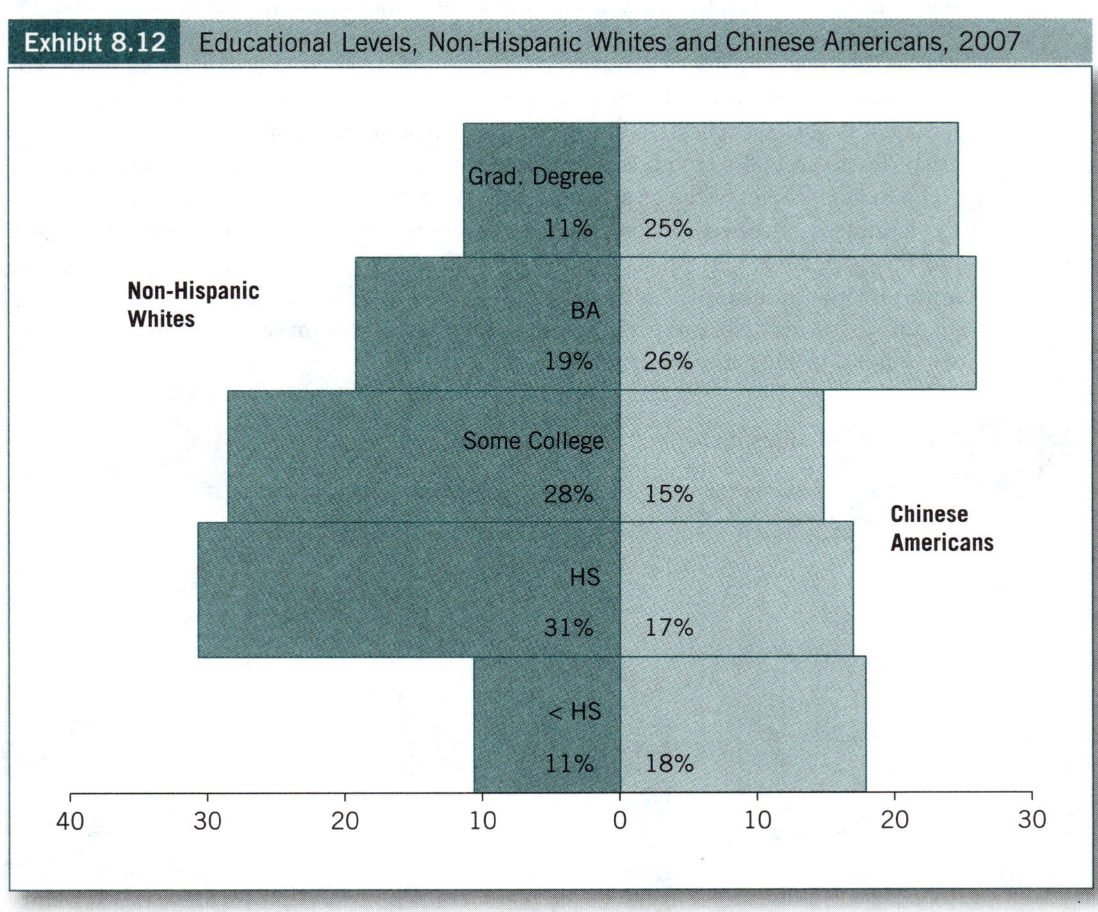

SOURCE: U.S. Bureau of the Census (2007).

Political Power. The ability of Asian Americans to pursue their group interests has been sharply limited by a number of factors, including their relatively small size, institutionalized discrimination, and the same kinds of racist practices that have limited the power resources of other minority groups of color. However, and contrary to the perception that Asian Americans are a "quiet" minority, the group has a long history of political action, including a civil rights movement in the 1960s and 1970s (Fong, 2002, pp. 273–281).

The political power of Asian Americans and Pacific Islanders today also is limited by their high percentages of foreign-born members. Rates of political participation for the group (e.g., voting in presidential elections) are somewhat lower than national norms but may rise as more members Americanize, learn English, and become citizens (Lee, 1998). Even today, there are signs of the growing power of the group, especially in areas where they are most residentially concentrated. Of course, Asian Americans have been prominent in Hawaiian politics for decades, but they are increasingly involved in West Coast political life as well. For example, in 1996, the state of Washington elected Gary Locke as governor, the first Chinese American to hold this high office. Governor Locke was reelected in 2000.

Jobs and Income. The image of success is again sustained by the occupational profiles of Asian American groups. Both males and females are overrepresented in the highest occupational categories, a reflection of the high levels of educational attainment for the group. Asian American males are underrepresented among manual laborers, but otherwise, the occupational profiles of the groups are in rough proportion to the society as a whole.

Exhibit 8.13 shows median household incomes for Asian Americans as a whole and for six Asian American subgroups. Two of the six groups are above non-Hispanic whites on this indicator of affluence and Asian Americans in general and two other subgroups are very close to parity. Only Korean and Vietnamese Americans are notably below the non-Hispanic white group.

Exhibit 8.13 Median Household Income for Non-Hispanic Whites, All Asian Americans, and Selected Groups, 2007

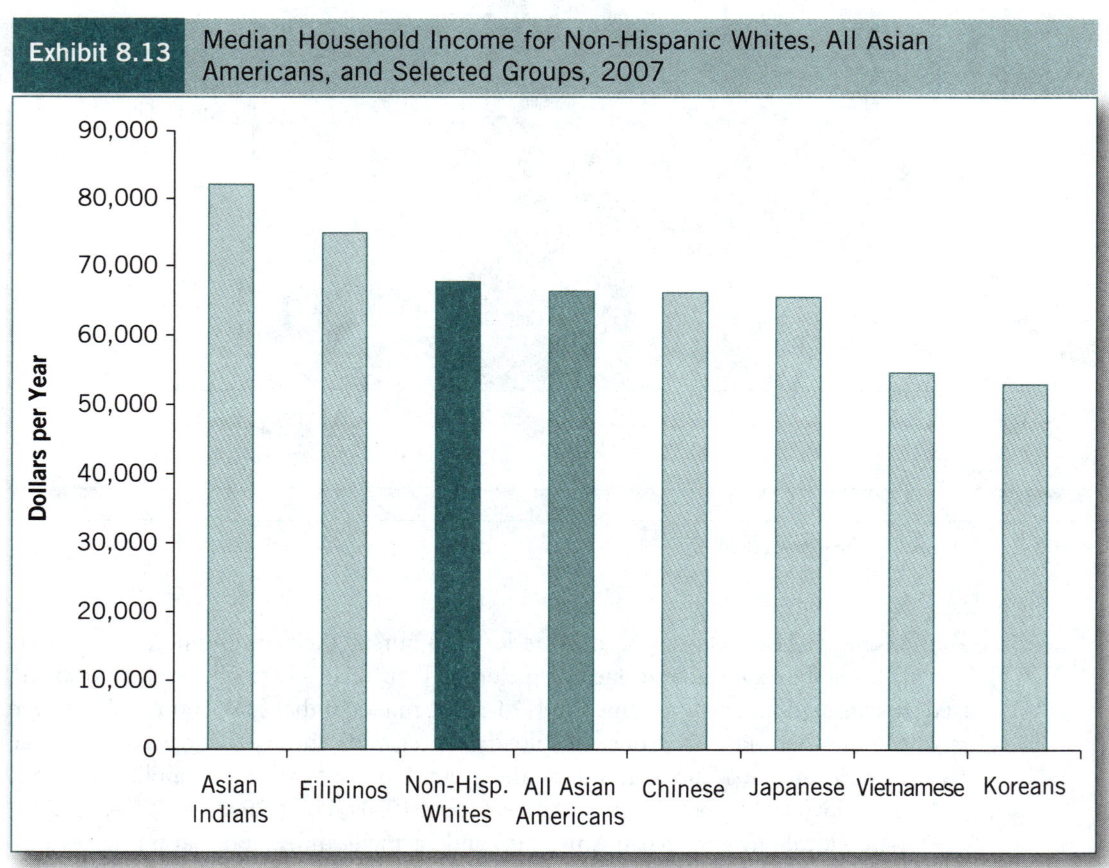

SOURCE: U.S. Bureau of the Census (2007).

Exhibit 8.13 once again sustains the notion of success and affluence. This image must be qualified, however, when we observe the distribution of income for the group as a whole (see Exhibit 8.14). Asian Americans are overrepresented in the most affluent groups but also in the lower income category, a reflection of the "bipolar" distribution of Chinese Americans and some other groups. Although 11% of both groups are in the top two income categories, 20% of Asian Americans—versus only 13% of non-Hispanic whites—are in the lowest three income categories.

Exhibit 8.14 Distribution of Household Income for Non-Hispanic Whites and Asian Americans, 2007 (in Dollars)

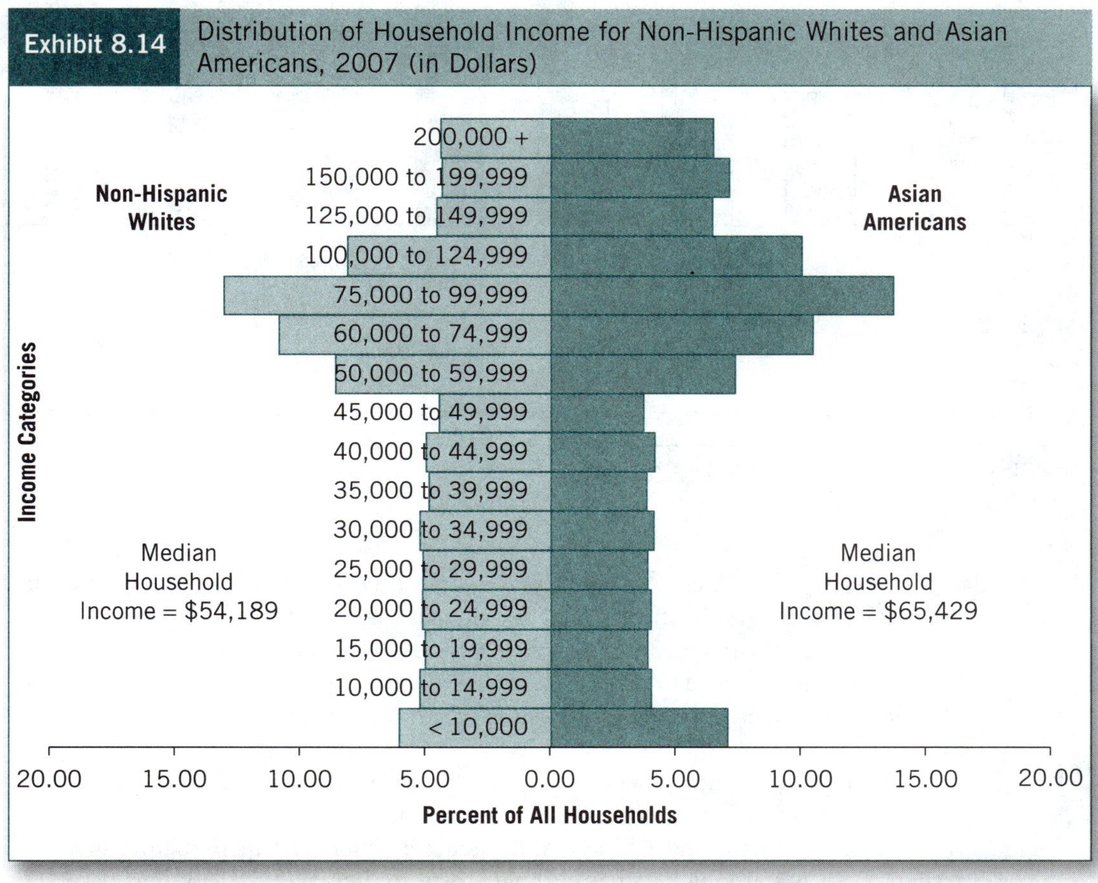

SOURCE: U.S. Bureau of the Census (2007).

Exhibits 8.15 and 8.16 display poverty rates and incomes for full-time, year round workers and return us to the picture of relative affluence for Asian Americans. As you can see in Exhibit 8.15, three Asian American groups have poverty rates below non-Hispanic whites and the rate for all Asian Americans is comparable with non-Hispanic whites. Korean and Vietnamese Americans are notably more impoverished than other Asian American groups with rates that approach the colonized racial minority groups we covered in previous chapters.

Exhibit 8.15 Percentage of Families and Children in Poverty for Non-Hispanic Whites, All Asian Americans, and Selected Groups, 2007

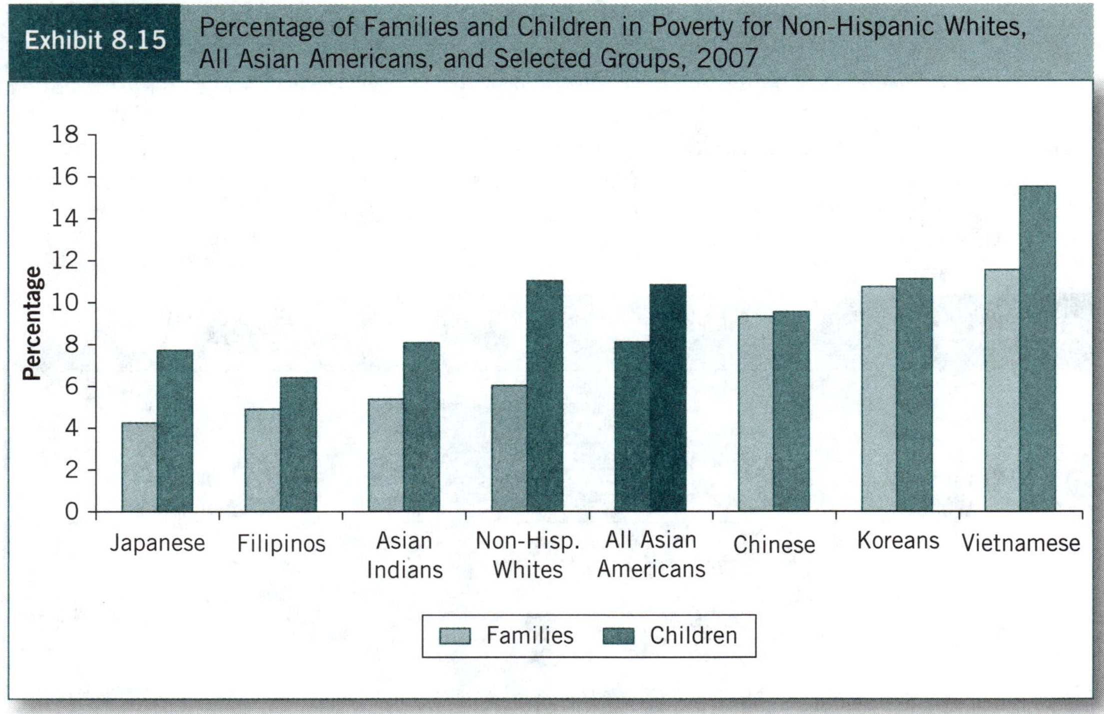

SOURCE: U.S. Bureau of the Census (2007).

The incomes of Asian American male workers are generally at or above national norms. There is a sizable income gap for men and women for some of these groups, especially Indian, Japanese, and Korean Americans. The women of these groups are much more concentrated in the service and retail sectors of the job market, and Indian American women are much less involved in professional and managerial jobs, the most lucrative occupations.

Although these data generally support the image of economic success, we must cite some additional qualifications before coming to any conclusions. First, Asian Americans in general and Chinese and Japanese Americans in particular generally reside in areas with higher-than-average costs of living (e.g., San Francisco, Los Angeles, New York); thus, their higher incomes have relatively less purchasing power. Second, they are more likely than the general population to have multiple wage earners in each household, and differences in per capita income are smaller than differences in median family income. For example, in 2007, Asian Americans as a group were only $1,500 below non-Hispanic whites in median household income (see Exhibit 8.13) but were $2,800 below non-Hispanic whites in per capita income (U.S. Bureau of the Census, 2007).

Exhibit 8.16 Median Income for Full-Time, Year-Round Workers for Non-Hispanic Whites, All Asian Americans, and Selected Groups, 2007

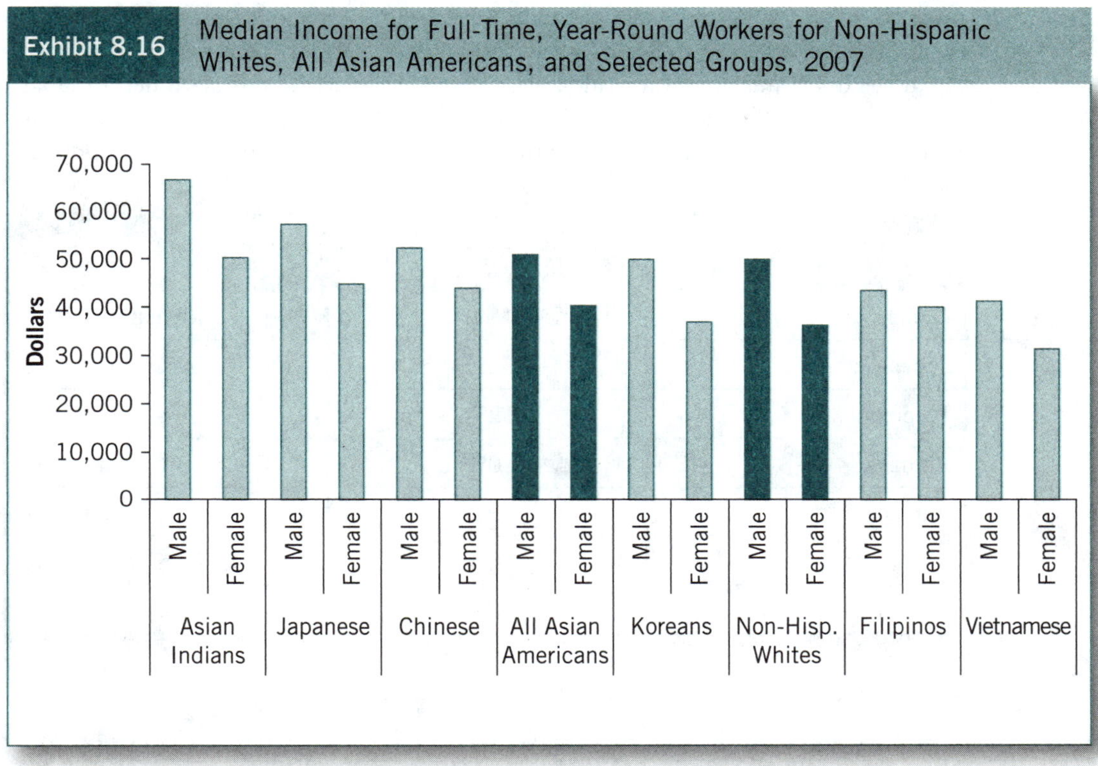

SOURCE: U.S. Bureau of the Census (2007).

Primary Structural Assimilation

Studies of integration at the primary level for Asian Americans generally find high rates of interracial friendship and intermarriage. For example, using 1980 census data, Lee and Yamanaka (1990) report higher rates of intermarriage for Asian Americans than for other minority groups. They report out-marriage rates at 2% for African Americans, 13% for Hispanic Americans, and from 15% to 34% for Asian Americans. They also found that native-born Asian Americans were much more likely to marry outside their groups than the foreign-born (see also Kitano & Daniels, 1995; Min, 1995; Sung, 1990). Some studies have found that the rate of intermarriage is decreasing in recent years in the nation as a whole and specifically in California, a pattern that perhaps reflects the high rates of immigration, the tendency for the first generation to marry within the group, and the growing number of potential partners within Asian American groups (Lee & Fernandez, 1998; Shinagawa & Pang, 1996, see also Xie & Goyette, 2004). Dr. C. N. Le, a sociologist who maintains the Asian Nation Web site (http//www.asian-nation.org) has analyzed the intermarriage patterns from the data produced by the U.S. census for 2006. His data can be found at http://www.asian-nation.org/

interracial.shtml and are summarized in Exhibit 8.17. Japanese Americans, the most acculturated group, are the most likely to marry outside of their group. Also, many Japanese Americans are "war brides" who married American GIs stationed in Japan. The groups with the highest percentage of foreign-born, Asian Indians, Koreans, and Vietnamese (see Exhibit 8.4), are also the least likely to marry outside their groups.

Exhibit 8.17 Percentage of Selected Asian American Groups Marrying Outside Their Group, 2006

Group	Men	Women
Japanese	36%	53%
Filipino	18%	39%
Chinese	10%	8%
Korean	9%	31%
Vietnamese	8%	17%
Asian Indians	8%	6%

SOURCE: Asian-Nation (http://www.asian-nation.org/interracial.shtml).

FOCUS ON CONTEMPORARY ISSUES: Explaining Asian American Success

To conclude this chapter, let's return to a question raised in the opening pages: How can we explain the apparent success of Asian Americans? Relative affluence and high status are not characteristic of the other racial minority groups we have examined, and at least at first glance, there seems to be little in our theories and concepts to help us understand the situation of Asian Americans. Even after we recognize that the "success" label is simplistic and even misleading, the relatively high status of many Asian Americans begs a closer look.

We can gain some insight into this issue by comparing Asian Americans with European immigrant groups and with colonized minority groups. What crucial factors differentiate the experiences of these groups? Can we understand these differences in terms of the framework provided by the Blauner and Noel hypotheses and the other concepts developed in this text?

The debate over the causes of Asian American success often breaks down into two different viewpoints. One view offers a cultural explanation, which accepts the evidence of Asian American success at face value and attributes it to the "good values" of traditional Asian cultures that we briefly explored at the beginning of this chapter (see Chao, 2000; Kitano, 1980).

These values—including respect for elders and for authority figures, hard work and thriftiness, and conformity and politeness—are highly compatible with U.S. middle-class Protestant value systems and presumably helped Asian Americans gain acceptance and opportunities. The cultural explanation is consistent with traditional assimilation theory and human capital theory.

The second point of view stresses the ways in which these groups entered American society and the reactions of Asian Americans to the barriers of racism and exclusion they faced. This approach could be called a "structural explanation," and it emphasizes contact situations, modes of incorporation, enclave economies, group cohesion, position in the labor market, and institutionalized discrimination rather than cultural values (Portes & Zhou, 1992; Takaki, 1993). Also, this approach questions the notion that Asian Americans are successful and stresses the realities of Asian American poverty and the continuing patterns of racism and exclusion. The structural approach is more compatible with the theories and concepts used throughout this text, and it identifies several of the important pieces needed to solve the puzzle of Asian "success" and put it in perspective. This is not to suggest that the cultural approach is wrong or irrelevant, however. The issues we raise are complex and will probably require many approaches and perspectives before they are fully resolved.

Asian Americans and White Ethnics

Chinese and Japanese immigrants arrived in America at about the same time as immigrants from Southern and Eastern Europe (see Chapter 2). Both groups consisted mainly of sojourning young men who were largely unskilled, from rural backgrounds, and not highly educated. European immigrants, like Asian immigrants, encountered massive discrimination and rejection and were also victims of restrictive legislation. Yet the barriers to upward mobility for European immigrants (or, at least for their descendants) fell away more rapidly than the barriers for immigrants from Asia. Why?

Some important differences between the two immigrant experiences are clear, the most obvious being the greater racial visibility of Asian Americans. Whereas the cultural and linguistic markers that identified Eastern and Southern Europeans faded with each passing generation, the racial characteristics of the Asian groups continued to separate them from the larger society. Thus, Asian Americans are not "pure immigrant" groups (see Blauner, 1972, p. 55). For most of the 20th century, Chinese Americans and Japanese Americans remained in a less favorable position than European immigrants and their descendants, excluded by their physical appearance from the mainstream economy until the decades following World War II.

Another important difference relates to position in the labor market. Immigrants from Southern and Eastern Europe entered the industrializing East Coast and Midwest economy, where they took industrial and manufacturing jobs. Although such jobs were poorly paid and insecure, this location in the labor force gave European immigrants and their descendants the potential for upward mobility in the mainstream economy. At the very least, these urban industrial and manufacturing jobs put the children and grandchildren of European immigrants in positions from which skilled, well-paid, unionized jobs were reachable, as were managerial and professional careers.

In contrast, Chinese and Japanese immigrants on the West Coast were forced into ethnic enclaves and came to rely on jobs in the small business and service sector and, in the case of the Japanese, in the rural economy. By their nature, these jobs did not link Chinese and Japanese immigrants or their descendants to the industrial sector or to better-paid, more secure, unionized jobs. Furthermore, their exclusion from the mainstream economy was reinforced by overt discrimination based on race from both employers and labor unions (see Fong & Markham, 1991).

(Continued)

(Continued)

Asian Americans and Colonized Racial Minority Groups

Comparisons between Asian Americans and African Americans, American Indians, and Hispanic Americans have generated a level of controversy and a degree of heat and passion that may be surprising at first. An examination of the issues and their implications, however, reveals that the debate involves some thinly disguised political and moral agendas and evokes sharply clashing views on the nature of U.S. society. What might appear on the surface to be merely an academic comparison of different minority groups turns out to be an argument about the quality of American justice and fairness and the very essence of the value system of U.S. society.

What is *not* in dispute in this debate is that some Asian groups (e.g., Japanese Americans) rank far above other racial minority groups on all the commonly used measures of secondary structural integration and equality. What *is* disputed is how to interpret these comparisons and assess their meanings. First, we need to recognize that gross comparisons between entire groups can be misleading. If we confine our attention to averages (mean levels of education or median income), the picture of Asian American success is sustained. However, if we also observe the full range of differences within each group (e.g., the "bipolar" nature of occupations among Chinese Americans), we see that the images of success have been exaggerated and need to be placed in a proper context (see Takaki, 1993). Even with these qualifications, however, discussion often slides on to more ideological ground, and political and moral issues begin to cloud the debate. Asian American success is often taken as proof that American society is truly the land of opportunity and that people who work hard and obey the rules will get ahead: In America, anyone can be anything they want as long as they work hard enough.

When we discussed modern racism in Chapters 1 and 5, I pointed out that a belief in the openness and fairness of the United States can be a way of blaming the victim and placing the responsibility for change on the minority groups rather than on the structure of society or on past-in-present or institutionalized discrimination. Asian success has become a "proof" of the validity of this ideology. The none-too-subtle implication is that other groups (African Americans, Hispanic Americans, American Indians) could achieve the same success Asian Americans have achieved but, for various reasons, choose not to. Thus, the relative success of some Asian American groups has become a device for scolding other minority groups.

A more structural approach to investigating Asian success begins with a comparison of the history of the various racial minority groups and their modes of incorporation into the larger society. When Chinese Americans and Japanese Americans were building their enclave economies in the early part of the 20th century, African Americans and Mexican Americans were concentrated in unskilled agricultural occupations. American Indians were isolated from the larger society on their reservations, and Puerto Ricans had not yet begun to arrive on the mainland. The social class differences between these groups today flow from their respective situations in the past.

Many of the occupational and financial advances made by Chinese Americans and Japanese Americans have been due to the high levels of education achieved by the second generations. Although education is traditionally valued in Asian cultures, the decision to invest limited resources in schooling is also quite consistent with the economic niche occupied by these immigrants. Education is one obvious, relatively low-cost strategy to upgrade the productivity and profit of a small-business economy and improve the economic status of the group as a whole. An educated, English-speaking second generation could bring expertise and business acumen to the family enterprises and lead them to higher levels of performance. Education might also be the means by which the second generation could enter professional careers. This strategy may have been especially attractive to an immigrant generation that was itself relatively uneducated and barred from citizenship (Hirschman & Wong, 1986; see also Bonacich & Modell, 1980; Sanchirico, 1991).

The efforts to educate the next generation were largely successful. Chinese Americans and Japanese Americans achieved educational parity with the larger society as early as the 1920s. One study found that for men and women born after 1915, the median years of schooling completed were actually higher for Chinese Americans and Japanese Americans than for whites (Hirschman & Wong, 1986). Before World War II, both Asian groups were barred from the mainstream economy and from better jobs. When anti-Asian prejudice and discrimination softened in the 1950s, however, the Chinese and Japanese second generations had the educational background necessary to take advantage of the increased opportunities.

Thus there was a crucial divergence in the development of Chinese Americans and Japanese Americans and the colonized minority groups. At the time that native-born Chinese Americans and Japanese Americans reached educational parity with whites, the vast majority of African Americans, American Indians, and Mexican Americans were still victimized by Jim Crow laws and legalized segregation and excluded from opportunities for anything but rudimentary education. The Supreme Court decision in *Brown v. Board of Education of Topeka* (1954) was decades in the future, and American Indian schoolchildren were still being subjected to intense Americanization in the guise of a curriculum. Today, these other racial minority groups have not completely escaped from the disadvantages imposed by centuries of institutionalized discrimination. African Americans have approached educational parity with white Americans only in recent years (see Chapter 5), and American Indians and Mexican Americans remain far below national averages (see Chapters 6 and 7).

The structural explanation argues that the recent upward mobility of Chinese Americans and Japanese Americans is the result of the methods by which they incorporated themselves into American society, not so much their values and traditions. The logic of their enclave economy led the immigrant generation to invest in the education of their children, who would be better prepared to develop their businesses and seek opportunity in the larger society.

As a final point, note that the structural explanation is not consistent with traditional views of the assimilation process. The immigrant generation of Chinese Americans and Japanese Americans responded to the massive discrimination they faced by withdrawing, developing ethnic enclaves, and becoming "invisible" to the larger society. Like Jewish and Cuban Americans, Chinese Americans and Japanese Americans used their traditional cultures and patterns of social life to create and build their own subcommunities, from which they launched the next generation. Contrary to traditional ideas about how assimilation is "supposed" to happen, we see again that integration can precede acculturation and that the smoothest route to integration may be the creation of a separate subsociety independent of the surrounding community.

COMPARATIVE FOCUS: Japan's "Invisible" Minority

One of the first things I did in this text was to list the five characteristics that, together, define a minority group. The first and most important of these characteristics was the disadvantage and inequality that minority groups face, and the second was visibility: Minority group members must be easily identifiable, either culturally (language, accent, dress) or physically (skin color, stature). These two traits work in tandem. Members of the dominant group must be able to determine a person's group membership quickly and easily, preferably at a glance, so that the systematic discrimination that is the hallmark of minority group status can be practiced.

Cultural and racial visibility is such an obvious precondition for discrimination that it almost seems unnecessary to state it. However, every generalization about human beings seems to have an exception, and there is at least one minority group, the Buraku of Japan, that has been victimized by discrimination and prejudice for hundreds of years but is virtually indistinguishable from the general population. That is, the Buraku are a minority and fit all parts of the definition stated in Chapter 1—except that there is no physical, cultural, religious, or linguistic difference between them and other Japanese. How could such an "invisible" minority come into being? How could the disadvantaged status be maintained through time?

The Buraku were created centuries ago, during feudal times in Japan. At that time, the society was organized into a caste system based on occupation, and the ancestors of today's Buraku people did work that brought them into contact with death (gravediggers, executioners) or required them to handle meat or meat products (leather workers, butchers). These occupations were regarded as very low in status, and their practitioners were seen as being "unclean" or polluted. In fact, an alternative name for the group, *eta,* means "extreme filth." The Buraku people were required to live in separate, segregated villages and to wear leather patches for purposes of identification (thus raising their social visibility). They were forbidden to marry outside their caste, and any member of the general population who touched a Buraku had to be ritually purified or cleansed of pollution (Lamont-Brown, 1993).

The caste system was officially abolished in the 19th century, at about the time Japan began to industrialize. The Buraku today, however, continue to suffer from discrimination and rejection, even though most observers agree that the levels of discrimination today are lower than in the past and that the overall situation of the Buraku people is improving. The Buraku still have much lower levels of education than the general population. For example, the enrollment rate of the Buraku in higher education is about 60% of the national average (Buraku Liberation and Human Rights Research Institute, 2001).

Lower levels of education in Japan, as in the United States, limit occupational mobility and lead to higher unemployment rates. The educational deficits also help to maintain gaps between the Buraku and the general population in income and poverty rates.

The Buraku are a small group, about 2% or 3% of Japan's population. About 1 million still live in the thousands of traditional Buraku areas that remain, and another 2 million or so live in non-Buraku areas, mostly in larger cities. They continue to be seen as "filthy," "not very bright," and "untrustworthy"—stereotypical traits that are often associated with minority groups mired in subordinate and unequal positions. Also, as is the case for many American minority groups, the Buraku have a vocal and passionate protest organization—the Buraku Liberation and Human Rights Research Institute (http://www.blhrri.org/index_e.htm)—dedicated to improving the conditions of the group.

The situation of the Buraku might seem puzzling. If it is disadvantageous to be a member of the group, and if the group is indistinguishable from the general population, why don't the Buraku simply blend into the larger society and avoid the discrimination and prejudice? What keeps them attached to their group? In fact, it is relatively easy for those who choose to do so to disappear into the mainstream and to "pass," as attested by the fact that two thirds of the group no longer live in the traditional Buraku areas. Why doesn't everyone in the group integrate into the larger society?

One answer to this question, at least for some Buraku, is that they are committed to their group identity and are proud of their heritage. They refuse to surrender to the dominant culture, insist on being accepted for who they are, and have no intention of trading their identity for acceptance or opportunity. For others, even those attempting to pass, the tie to the group and a subtle form of social visibility are maintained by the ancient system of residential segregation. The identity of the traditional Buraku villages and areas of residence are matters of public record, and it is this information—not race or culture—that establishes the boundaries of the group and forms the ultimate barrier to Buraku assimilation.

Japanese firms keep lists of local Buraku addresses and use the lists to screen out potential employees, even though this practice is now illegal. Also, the telltale information may be revealed when applying to rent an apartment (some landlords refuse to rent rooms to Buraku because of their alleged "filthiness") or purchase a home (banks may be reluctant to make loans to members of a group that is widely regarded as "untrustworthy"). A particularly strong line of resistance to the complete integration of the Buraku arises if they attempt to marry outside of the group. It is common practice for Japanese parents to research the family history of a child's fiancé, and any secret Buraku connections are very likely to be unearthed by this process. Thus, members of the Buraku who pass undetected at work and in their neighborhood are likely to be "outed" if they attempt to marry into the dominant group.

This link to the traditional Buraku residential areas means that this group is not really invisible. Although their social visibility is much lower than racial and ethnic minority groups, there is a way to determine group membership, a mark or sign of who belongs and who doesn't. Consistent with the definition presented in Chapter 1, this "birthmark" is the basis for a socially constructed boundary that differentiates "us" from "them" and for systematic discrimination, prejudice, inequality, and all the other disabilities and disadvantages associated with minority group status.

MAIN POINTS

- Asian Americans are diverse and have brought many different cultural and linguistic traditions to the United States. These groups are growing rapidly but are still only a tiny fraction of the total population.
- Chinese immigrants were the victims of a massive campaign of discrimination and exclusion and responded by constructing enclaves. Chinatowns became highly organized communities, largely run by the local CCBAs and other associations. The second generation faced many barriers to employment in the dominant society, although opportunities increased after World War II.

- Japanese immigration began in the 1890s and stimulated a campaign that attempted to oust the group from agriculture and curtail immigration from Japan. The Issei formed an enclave, but during World War II, Japanese Americans were forced into relocation camps, and this experience devastated the group economically and psychologically.
- Recent immigration from Asia is diverse in terms of national origins, contact situation, levels of human capital, and mode of incorporation into U.S. society.
- Overall levels of anti-Asian prejudice and discrimination have probably declined in recent years but remain widespread. Levels of acculturation and secondary structural assimilation are variable. Members of these groups whose families have been in the United States longer tend to be highly acculturated and integrated. Recent immigrants from China, however, are "bipolar." Many are highly educated and skilled, but a sizable number are "immigrant laborers" who bring modest educational credentials and are likely to be living in poverty.
- The notion that Asian Americans are a "model minority" is exaggerated, but comparisons with European immigrants and colonized minority groups suggest some of the reasons for the relative "success" of these groups.

STUDY SITE ON THE WEB

Don't forget the interactive quizzes and other resources and learning aids at **www.pineforge.com/healeyds3e**

FOR FURTHER READING

Here is an analysis of the intersections of race, class, and gender among Asian Americans.

Espiritu, Yen. 1997. *Asian American Women and Men.* Thousand Oaks, CA: Sage.

Here are two classic case studies of the Asian American groups with the longest histories in the United States.

Kitano, Harry H. 1976. *Japanese Americans.* Englewood Cliffs, NJ: Prentice Hall.

Lyman, Stanford. 1974. *Chinese Americans.* New York: Random House.

These works provide overviews of all the groups covered in this chapter.

Kitano, Harry H. L., & Daniels, Roger. 1995. *Asian Americans: Emerging Minorities* (2nd ed.). Englewood Cliffs, NJ: Prentice Hall.

Min, Pyong Gap. 1995. *Asian Americans. Contemporary Trends and Issues.* Thousand Oaks, CA: Sage.

The following are excellent studies of Chinatowns, with a behind-the-scenes look at the realities often hidden from outsiders.

Kwong, Peter. 1987. *The New Chinatown.* New York: Hill & Wang.

Zhou, Min. 1992. *Chinatown.* Philadelphia: Temple University Press.

QUESTIONS FOR REVIEW AND STUDY

1. Describe the cultural characteristics of Asian American groups. How did these characteristics shape relationships with the larger society? Did they contribute to the perception of Asian Americans as "successful"? How?

2. Compare and contrast the contact situation for Chinese Americans, Japanese Americans, and Cuban Americans. What common characteristics led to the construction of ethnic enclaves for all three groups? How and why did these enclaves vary from each other?

3. In what sense was the second generation of Chinese Americans "delayed"? How did this affect the relationship of the group with the larger society?

4. Compare and contrast the campaigns that arose in opposition to the immigration of Chinese and Japanese. Do the concepts of the Noel hypothesis help to explain the differences? Do you see any similarities with the changing federal policy toward Mexican immigrants across the 20th century? Explain.

5. Compare and contrast the Japanese relocation camps with Indian reservations in terms of paternalism and coerced acculturation. What impact did this experience have on the Japanese Americans economically? How were Japanese Americans compensated for their losses? Does the compensation paid to Japanese Americans provide a precedent for similar payments (reparations) to African Americans for their losses under slavery? Why or why not?

5. How do the Buraku in Japan illustrate "visibility" as a defining characteristic of minority-group status? How is the minority status of this group maintained?

6. What gender differences characterize Asian American groups? What are some of the important ways in which the experiences of women and men vary?

7. Describe the situation of the Chinese and Japanese Americans in terms of prejudice and discrimination, acculturation, and integration. Are these groups truly "success stories"? How? What factors or experiences might account for this "success"? Are all Asian American groups equally successful? Describe the important variations from group to group. Compare the integration and level of equality of these groups with other American racial minorities. How would you explain the differences? Are the concepts of the Noel and Blauner hypotheses helpful? Why or why not?

INTERNET RESEARCH PROJECTS

A. Updating the Chapter

1. The Asian-Nation Web site at http://www.asian-nation.org/index.html provides comprehensive coverage on a number of issues raised in this chapter. Update and expand the chapter by selecting one or two topics (e.g., the "model minority" image) and searching the Web site. Be sure to follow some of the links provided to see what additional information and perspectives you can uncover.

B. Learning More About Asian Americans

1. Select one of the Asian groups discussed in this chapter other than Japanese Americans and Chinese Americans and conduct an Internet search using the name of the group. Follow the links and see what information you can add to the profile provided in the chapter. You might focus your search by seeking answers to basic questions such as these: How large is the group? Where do the members live in the United States (region of the country, rural vs. urban)? How acculturated is the group in terms of language? How does the group compare with national norms in terms of education, occupational profile, and income? What are the major issues from the perspective of the group?

C. Mapping Immigration

1. Go to http://projects.nytimes.com/immigration/ and select (click on) the interactive map on the right side of the screen. Under "Immigration Explorer" select China and then start with the earliest year (1880) for which information is available. Where did Chinese Americans live in that year? Next, click each year on the time line and observe what happens to the Chinese American population. Compare the residential patterns in 1970 with 1880. What differences and similarities do you see? Describe the changes between 1970 and 2000.

2. Repeat this exercise with the other groups covered in this chapter: Japanese, Korean, Vietnamese, Indian, and Filipino Americans. Try to explain the changes you observe using the information and concepts presented in this chapter.

Note

1. From "Grim video lays bare Vietnamese teen violence," by Peter Stidman, January 31, 2008. Reprinted by permission of Peter Stidman, News Editor, *Dorchester Reporter.*

Part IV

Challenges for the Present and the Future

In this section, we analyze the new wave of immigration that began in the 1960s, continuing issues of assimilation and equality, inclusion and racism, and some of the most prominent issues and arguments focused on immigration and immigrants. Many of these issues—including what it means to be an American—have been discussed throughout this text, just as they have been discussed and debated throughout the history of this society. In the final chapter, we summarize the major themes of this text, bring the analysis to a close, and speculate about the future of American race and ethnic relations.

9

New Americans, Assimilation, and Old Challenges

By early 2004, Delfino [an undocumented immigrant] was armed with . . . phony papers, a car, a shared house, a job, some English. It was then that his attention turned to other things. Back in Mexico, his family's eight-by-twelve-foot shack had been the most visible sign of its . . . low social standing. The shack had dirt floors, leaked rain, and left them unprotected from the cold. A girl's family once refused Florentino's [Delfino's brother] marriage proposal because that shack was all he could offer her.

Delfino began sending extra money home every month. . . . In the middle of 2004, the family moved its shack to one side—it took only a few men to lift it. On the site where the shack once stood, Delfino built the first house in his village ever paid for with [American] dollars. It . . . had an indoor toilet, a kitchen, and concrete floors. The house was fronted by two smoked-glass windows so wide and tall that it looked as if the house wore sunglasses.

"I wanted it to look good when you pass," Delfino said, "and to have a nice view." In Xocotla, nothing like it had ever been built so quickly by a youth so poor.

A few months later, Florentino [also arranged with his father] to have a house built in the village . . . All this helped change their father [Lázaro]. He had stopped drinking and discovered Alcoholics Anonymous. He was now in his forties and tired of waking up in the pig muck. . . . His sons could now send him money for construction materials and know he wouldn't spend it on booze. So within a year of Delfino's arrival in the United States, Lázaro was not only sober but supervising construction of first Delfino's house, and then Florentino's . . .

(Continued)

(Continued)

Lázaro had never been the object of anyone's envy. He found that he liked it. He kept building those houses, telling everyone that he'd build until his sons in America told him to stop.

For a time, the Juárez brothers were the village's largest employers—spending close to forty thousand dollars on labor and supplies. As Florentino's house went up, the family of the girl who'd refused his marriage proposal let it be known that they regretted their decision. When Delfino returned to Xocotla for a few months in late 2004, older men, who'd once laughed at his mohawked hair, came to him to borrow money. "Now everyone says hello," said Delfino.

—Sam Quinones (2007, pp. 284–286)

Delfino and Florentino represent the experiences of thousands of immigrants—legal as well as undocumented—who have crossed the border into the United States over the past century. Driven by the poverty of their home village and attracted by the allure of work in el Norte, they pay thousands of dollars to their guides and often risk their lives in pursuit of the dream of earning a decent wage. Many are sojourners who remain focused on the families they have left behind. They send millions of dollars home and are the main—or even the sole—support for their kin, the hope and lifeblood for perhaps scores of relatives. Some are Mexican, such as Delfino and Florentino, and others are Chinese, Salvadoran, Filipino, Guatemalan, or Haitian. Some arrive legally, others come as tourists and overstay their visas, and still others enter illegally. Their goals and desires are as disparate as their origins, but they share the dream of being able to feed, shelter, and clothe their families.

Are they a threat to U.S. jobs or American culture? Do they threaten to bankrupt local welfare and school systems? Should the undocumented be sent to prison? What about their children? What benefits do these immigrants provide? Will they (or their children or grandchildren) enter the middle class, as immigrants have done before?

These and other issues are addressed in this chapter, but you should be aware that many of these questions will have no easy or obvious answer. The United States is once again grappling with fundamental questions about acceptance and rejection, inclusion and exclusion—about what it means to be an American. In this text, we have studied these issues academically, as intellectual matters to be discussed, analyzed, and understood. You will deal with these same issues as a citizen of this nation, probably for your entire life.

Introduction

In this chapter, we focus on the current wave of immigration to the United States and the myriad issues stimulated by this influx of newcomers. We have already addressed some new groups in American society in Chapters 7 and 8. Here, we will look at recent immigrants in general terms and then address some additional groups of new Americans: non-Hispanic groups from the Caribbean, Arab Americans and Middle Easterners, and immigrants from sub-Saharan Africa. A consideration of these groups will broaden your understanding of the wide variations of culture, motivations, and human capital in the current immigration stream to the United States. To conserve space, only groups that have at least 100,000 members are considered.

Then, the most important immigration issues facing U.S. society will be addressed and the chapter will conclude with a brief return to the "traditional" minority groups: African, Hispanic, Asian, and Native Americans—peoples of color who continue to face issues of equality and full integration and must now pursue their long-standing grievances in an atmosphere where public attention and political energy is focused on other groups and newer issues.

Current Immigration

As you are aware, the United States has experienced two different waves of mass immigration. Chapter 2 discussed the first wave, which lasted from the 1820s to the 1920s. During that century, more than 37 million people immigrated to the United States, an average rate of a little fewer than 400,000 per year. This wave of newcomers, overwhelmingly from Europe, transformed American society on every level: its neighborhoods and parishes and cities, its popular culture, its accent and dialect, its religion, and its cuisine.

The second wave of mass immigration may well prove to be equally transformative. This wave began in the 1960s and includes people from every corner of the globe. Over the past four decades, more than 30 million newcomers have arrived (not counting undocumented immigrants), a rate that far exceeds the pace of the first mass immigration. Since the 1960s, the United States has averaged about 650,000 newcomers each year, a number that has tended to increase year by year (see Exhibit 9.1). The record for most immigrants

Exhibit 9.1 Number of Legal Immigrants, 1960–2008 (Does Not Include IRCA Adjustees)

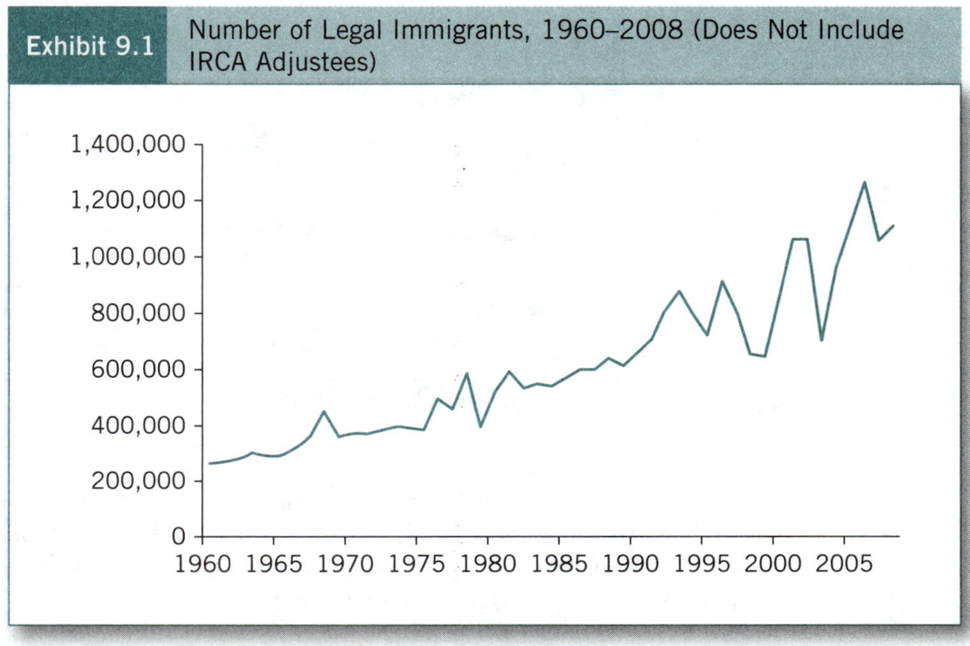

SOURCE: U.S. Department of Homeland Security (2008).

in a year was set in 1907, when almost 1.3 million people arrived on these shores. That number was almost equaled in 2006, and, if undocumented immigrants were included in the count, the 1907 record has certainly been eclipsed several times since the 1960s.

The more recent wave of immigration is much more global than the first. In 2008 alone, immigrants arrived from more than 200 separate nations, from Albania to Zimbabwe. Only about 11% of the newcomers were from Europe. A third were from North America (with 17% from Mexico alone), and another third were from Asian nations (most from China), while South America supplied another 9%. The top 20 sending nations for 2008 are listed in Exhibit 9.2. Note that Mexico accounted for more than double the number of immigrants from the next-highest sending nation.

Exhibit 9.2 Number of Legal Immigrants for Top 20 Sending Nations, 2008

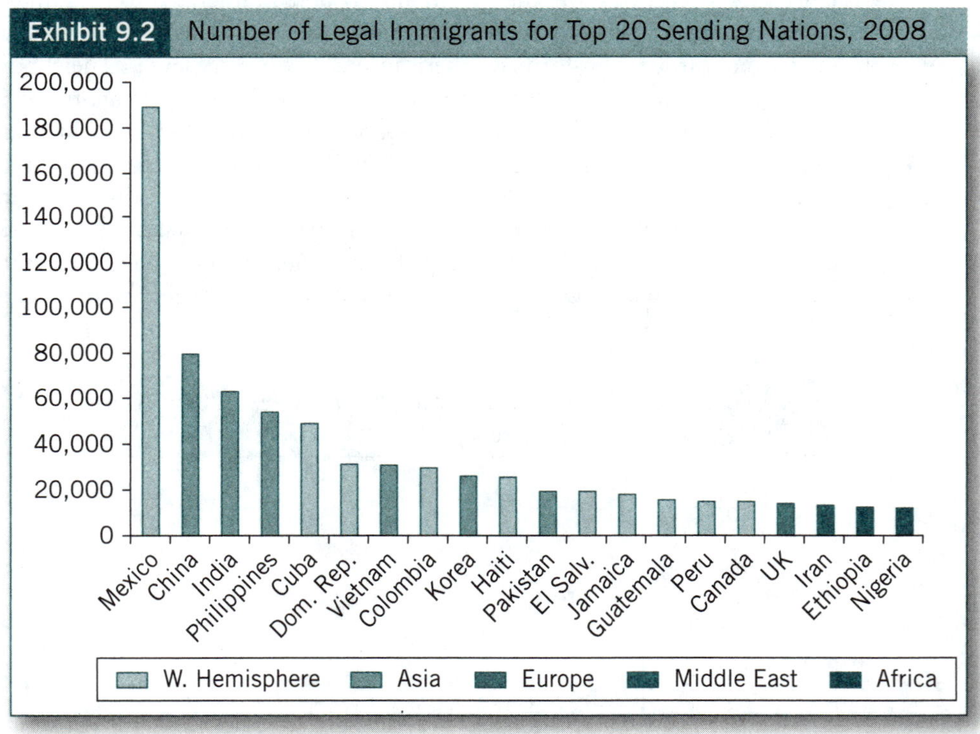

SOURCE: U.S. Department of Homeland Security (2008).

How will this new wave of immigration transform the United States? How will the immigrants be transformed by the United States? What do these new immigrants contribute? What do they cost? Will they assimilate and adopt the ways of the dominant society? What are the implications if assimilation fails?

Questions like these have been asked throughout this text, and in this chapter, these questions will be applied to the recent wave of immigrants. First, however, several more case studies of New Americans will be reviewed, focusing on information and statistics comparable with those used in Chapters 5 through 8. Also, additional data on the relative standing of these groups are available in the Appendix (www.pineforge.com/healeyds3e).

Each of the groups covered in this chapter has had some members in the United States for decades, and some for more than a century. However, in all cases, the groups were quite small until the latter third of the 20th century. Although they are growing rapidly now, all remain relatively small, and none are larger than 1% of the population. Nonetheless, some will have a greater impact on American culture and society in the future, and some groups—Arab Americans, Muslims, and Middle Easterners—have already become a focus of concern and controversy because of the events of 9/11 and the ensuing war on terrorism.

Recent Non-Hispanic Immigration From the Caribbean

We discussed immigration from Latin America and the Caribbean in Chapter 8. The groups we discussed in that chapter were Hispanic, but there are several other traditions present in the region. Here, we discuss two prominent non-Latino Caribbean groups: Haitians and Jamaicans. Haiti and Jamaica are economically much less developed than the United States, and this is reflected in the educational and occupational characteristics of their immigrants. A statistical profile of both groups is presented in Exhibit 9.3, along with non-Hispanic whites for purposes of comparison. Additional information on the relative standing of these groups is provided in the Appendix (www.pineforge.com/healeyds3e).

Exhibit 9.3 Characteristics of Two Caribbean-Origin Groups, 2007

Group	Number	% Foreign Born	% Speaking English Less Than "Very Well"	% High School Degree or More	% College Degree or More	% of Families in Poverty	% in Managerial or Professional Occupations	Median Household Income
Non-Hispanic Whites	—	4.0	1.7	89.4	30.4	6.0	38.4	54,964
Jamaica	904,501	60.2	1.3	82.1	22.9	10.3	31.9	46,964
Haiti	814,417	60.3	37.4	74.9	19.9	14.3	22.8	43,436

SOURCE: U.S. Bureau of the Census (2007).

Exhibit 9.4 Map of Caribbean Showing Haiti and Jamaica

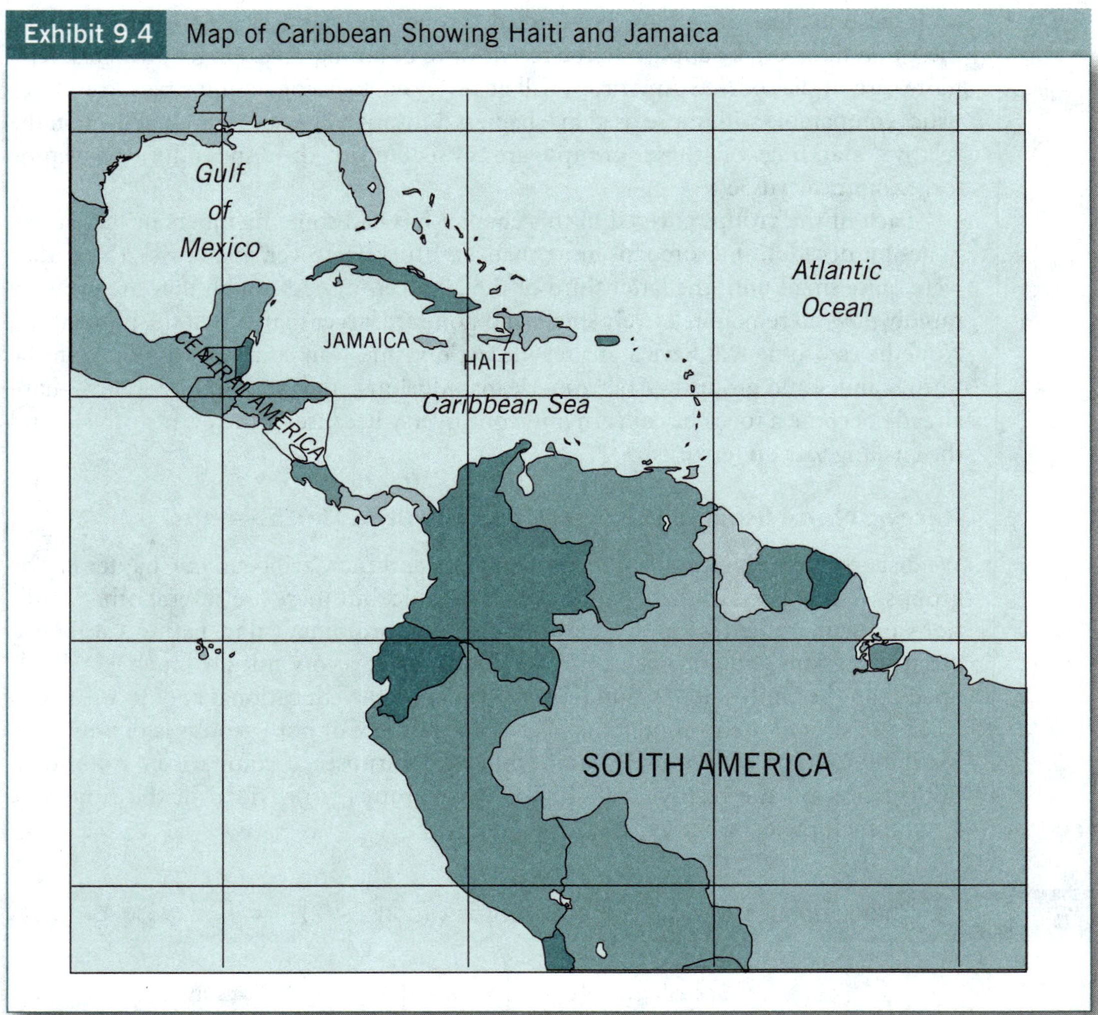

Haitians

Haiti is the poorest country in Western Hemisphere, and most of the population relies on small-scale subsistence agriculture for survival. Estimates are that 80% of the population lives below the poverty line, and fewer than one third of adults hold formal jobs. Only about half the population is literate, and Haitians average less than three years of formal education (Nationmaster.com, n.d.).

Haitian immigration was virtually nonexistent until the 1970s and 1980s, when thousands began to flee the brutal political repression of the Duvalier dictatorship, which—counting both father ("Papa Doc") and son ("Baby Doc")—lasted until the mid-1980s. In stark contrast to the treatment of Cuban immigrants (see Chapter 7), however, the United States government defined Haitians as economic refugees ineligible for asylum, and an intense campaign has been conducted to keep Haitians out of the United States. Thousands have been returned to Haiti, some to face political persecution, prison, and even death. Others have been incarcerated in the United States, and in the view of some, "During the 1970s and 1980s, no other immigrant group suffered more U.S. government prejudice and discrimination than Haitians" (Stepick, Stepick, Eugene, Teed, & Labissiere, 2001, p. 236).

What accounts for this cold, negative reception? Some reasons are not hard to identify. The first Haitian immigrants to come brought low levels of human capital and education. This created concerns about their ability to support themselves in the United States and also meant that they have relatively few resources with which to defend their self-interests. In addition, Haitians speak Creole, a language spoken by almost no one else, and a high percentage of members spoke English poorly or not at all. Perhaps the most important reason for the rejection, however, is that Haitians are black and must cope with the centuries-old traditions of rejection, racism, and prejudice that are such an intimate part of American culture (Stepick et al., 2001).

Haitian Americans today are still mostly first generation, and more than 55% of the group arrived after 1990. Overall, they are comparable with Hispanic Americans in terms of such measures of equality as level of education, income, and poverty. Still, research shows that some Haitians continue to face the exclusion and discrimination long associated with nonwhite ancestry. One important study of Haitians in South Florida found that a combination of factors—their hostile reception, their poverty and lack of education, and their racial background—combined to lead the Haitian second generation (the children of the immigrants) to a relatively low level of academic achievement and a tendency to identify with the African American community. "Haitians are becoming American but in a specifically black ethnic fashion" (Stepick et al., 2001, p. 261).

The ultimate path of Haitian assimilation will unfold in the future, but these tendencies—particularly their low levels of academic achievement—suggest that some of the second generation are less likely to move into the middle class and that their assimilation will be segmented (Stepick et al., 2001).

Jamaicans

The Jamaican economy is more developed than Haiti's, and this is reflected in the higher levels of education of Jamaican immigrants (see Exhibit 9.3). However, as is true throughout the less developed world, economic globalization has caused the Jamaican economy to falter in recent decades, and the island nation has been unable to provide full employment opportunities to its population. Jamaica is a former British colony, and immigrants have journeyed to the United Kingdom in addition to the United States. In both cases, the immigrant stream tends to be more skilled and educated and represents something of a "brain drain," a pattern we have seen with other groups, including Asian Indians. Needless to say, the loss of the more educated Jamaicans to immigration exacerbates problems of development and growth on the island.

Jamaicans typically settle on the East Coast, particularly in the New York City area. As a former British colony, they have the advantage of speaking English as their native tongue. On the other hand, they are black, and, like Haitians, they must face the barriers of discrimination and racism faced by all nonwhite groups in the United States. On the average, they are significantly higher than Haitians (and native-born African Americans) in socioeconomic standing, but poverty and institutionalized discrimination limit the mobility of a segment of the group. Like all other groups of color in the United States, the danger of segmented assimilation and permanent exclusion from the economic mainstream is very real.

Middle Eastern and Arab Americans

Immigration from the Middle East and the Arab world began in the 19th century but has never been particularly large. The earliest immigrants tended to be merchants and traders, and the Middle Eastern community in the United States has been constructed around an ethnic enclave based on small business. The number of Arab Americans and Middle Easterners has grown rapidly over the past several decades but still remains a tiny percentage of the total population. Exhibit 9.5 displays some statistical information on the group, broken down by the ancestry group with which people identify. Additional information on the relative standing of these groups is provided in the Appendix (www.pineforge.com/healeyds3e).

Middle Easterners and Arab Americans rank relatively high in income and occupation. Most groups are at or above national norms in terms of percentage of high school graduates, and all groups have a higher percentage of college graduates than non-Hispanic whites, with some (Egyptians and Iranians) far more educated. Although poverty is a problem for all groups (especially Arabs), many of the groups compare quite favorably in terms of occupation and income.

Many recent immigrants are, like Asian groups, highly educated people who take jobs in the highest levels of the American job structure. Also, consistent with the heritage of being an enclave minority, the groups are overrepresented in sales and

Exhibit 9.5 Characteristics of Middle Eastern Americans by Arab Self-Identification and by Nation of Origin (Groups Larger Than 100,000 Only)

Group	Number	% Foreign Born	% That Speak English Less Than "Very Well"	% High School Degree or More	% College Degree or More	% of Families in Poverty	% in Managerial or Professional Occupations	Median Household Income
Non-Hispanic Whites	—	4.0	1.7	89.4	30.4	6.0	38.4	54,964
Arab	266,152	48.1	24.5	83.9	37.1	21.2	32.3	45,082
Egyptian	194,932	61.7	25.4	95.8	67.4	14.6	51.2	62,089
Iranian	413,845	64.5	27.9	93.3	60.1	8.3	54.2	67,919
Lebanese	489,364	22.5	7.8	91.8	45.8	7.5	46.1	63,495
Syrians	150,527	23.8	11.1	91.3	40.2	7.0	45.9	55,461

SOURCE: U.S. Bureau of the Census (2007).

underrepresented in occupations involving manual labor. One study, using 1990 census data and a survey mailed to a national sample of Arab American women in 2000, found that immigrant Arab American women have a very low rate of employment, the lowest of any immigrant group. The author's analysis of this data strongly suggests that this pattern is a result of traditional gender roles and family norms regarding the proper role of women (Read, 2004).

Arab Americans and Middle Easterners are diverse and vary along a number of dimensions. They bring different national traditions and cultures and also vary in religion. Although Islam is the dominant religion and most are Muslim, many members of these groups are Christian. Also, not all Middle Easterners are Arabic; Iranians, for example, are Persian. (Also, about a third of all Muslims in the United States are native-born, and about 20% are African American.)

Exhibit 9.6 Map of Middle East Showing Egypt, Iran, Lebanon, and Syria

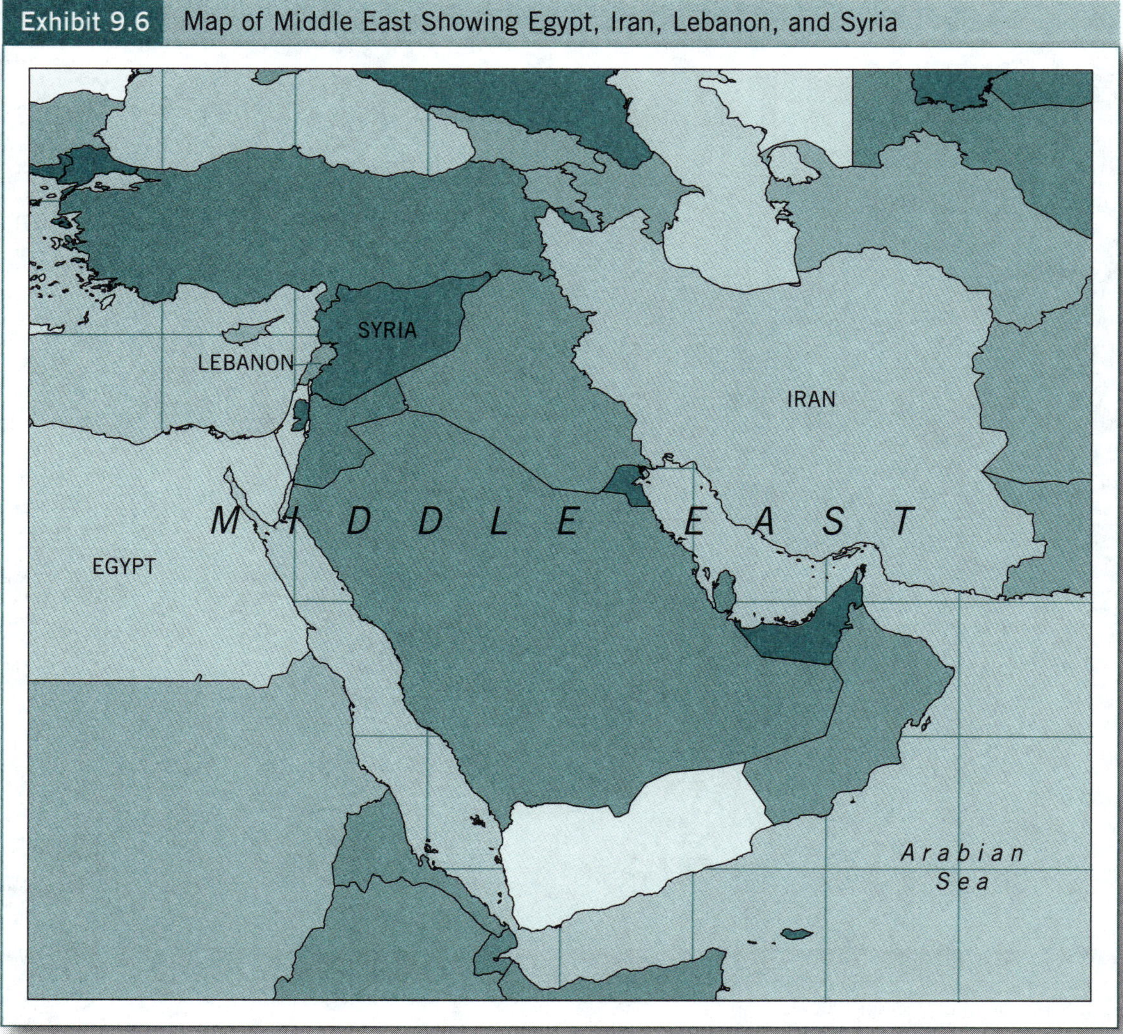

Residentially, Arab Americans and Middle Easterners are highly urbanized, and almost 50% live in just five states (California, New Jersey, New York, Florida, and Michigan). This settlement pattern is not too different from the other recent immigrant groups except for the heavy concentration in Michigan, especially in the Detroit area. Arab Americans account for 1.2% of the total population of Michigan, a far higher representation than in any other state. Arab Americans make up 30% of the population of Dearborn, Michigan, the highest percentage of any city in the nation. (Conversely, the greatest single concentration is in New York City, which has a population of about 70,000 Arab Americans.) These settlement patterns reflect chains of migration, some set up decades ago. Exhibit 9.7 shows the regional distribution of Arab Americans and clearly displays the clusters in Michigan, Florida, and Southern California.

Exhibit 9.7 Regional Distribution of Arab Americans, 2000

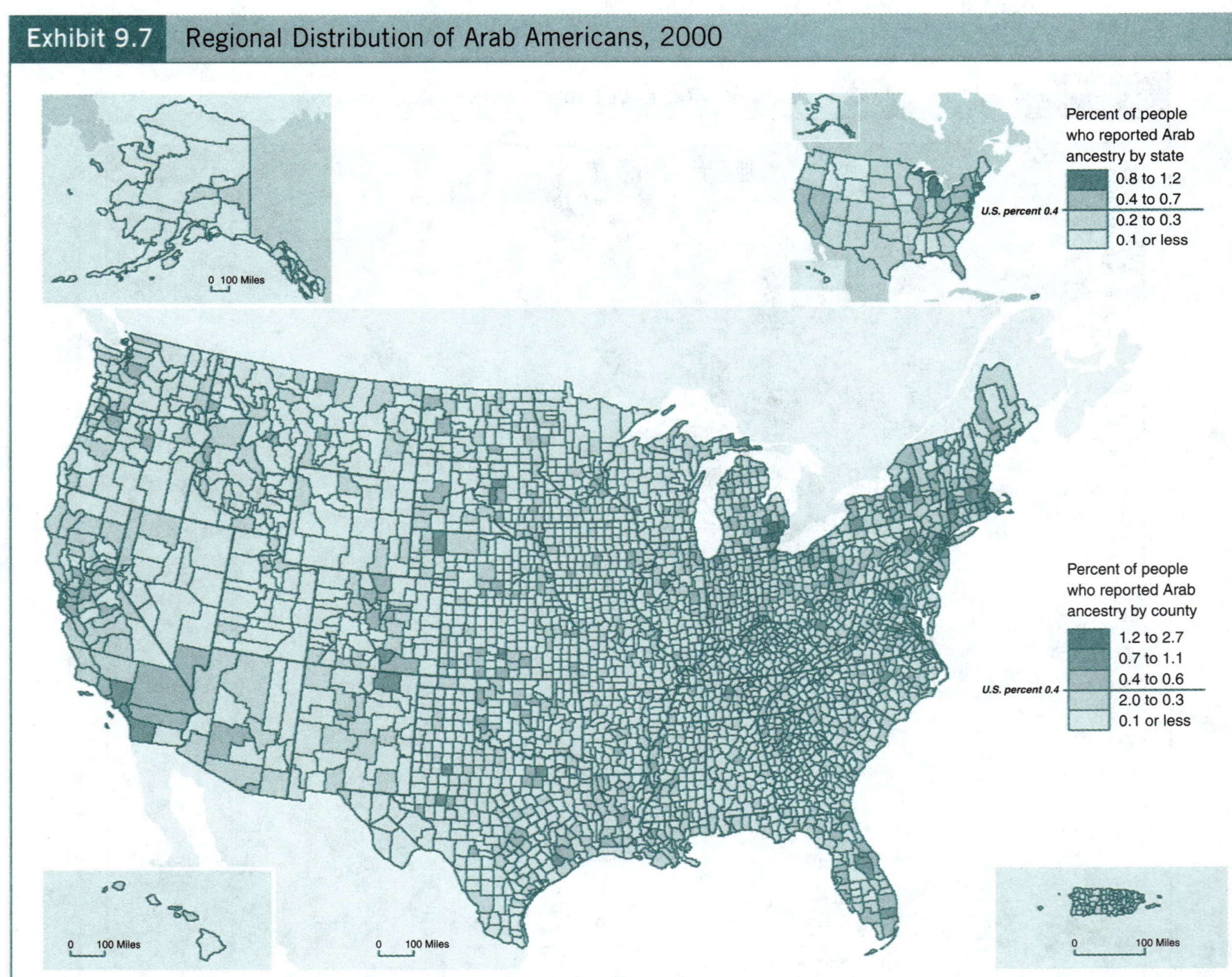

SOURCE: U.S. Bureau of the Census (2007).

9/11 and Arab Americans

There has always been at least a faint strain of prejudice directed at Middle Easterners in American culture (e.g., see the low position of Turks in the 1926 social distance scales presented in Chapter 1; most Americans probably are not aware that Turks and Arabs are different groups). These vague feelings have intensified in recent decades as relations with various Middle Eastern nations and groups worsened. For example, in 1979, the U.S. Embassy in Tehran, Iran, was attacked and occupied, and more than 50 Americans were held hostage for more than a year. The attack stimulated a massive reaction in the United States, in which anti-Arab and anti-Muslim feelings figured prominently. Continuing anti-American activities across the Middle East in the 1980s and 1990s stimulated a backlash of resentment and growing intolerance in the United States.

These earlier events pale in comparison, of course, to what happened on September 11, 2001. Americans responded to the attacks on the World Trade Center and the Pentagon by Arab terrorists with an array of emotions that included bewilderment, shock, anger, patriotism, deep sorrow for the victims and their families, and—perhaps predictably in the intensity of the moment—increased prejudicial rejection of Middle Easterners, Arabs, Muslims, and any group that seemed even vaguely associated with the perpetrators of the attacks. In the nine weeks following September 11, more than 700 violent attacks were reported to the Arab-American Anti-Discrimination Committee, followed by another 165 violent incidents in the first nine months of 2002. In this same time period, there were more than 80 incidents in which Arab Americans were removed from aircraft after boarding because of their ethnicity, more than 800 cases of employment discrimination, and "numerous instances of denial of service, discriminatory service, and housing discrimination" (Ibish, 2003, p. 7). The intensity of anti-Arab feelings were also registered by a dramatic, one-year increase in the number of hate crimes recorded by the Federal Bureau of Investigation (see Exhibit 4.9).

Anti-Arab passions may have cooled somewhat since the multiple traumas of 9/11, but the Arab American community faces a number of issues and problems, including profiling at airport security checks and greater restrictions on entering the country. Also, the USA Patriot Act, passed in 2001 to enhance the tools available to law enforcement to combat terrorism, allows for long-term detention of suspects, a wider scope for searches and surveillance, and other policies that many (not just Arab Americans) are concerned will encourage violations of due process and suspension of basic civil liberties.

Thus, although the Arab American and Middle Eastern communities are small in size, they have assumed a prominent place in the attention of the nation. The huge majority of these groups denounce and reject terrorism and violence, but, like Colombians and Italians, they are victimized by a strong stereotype that is often applied uncritically and without qualification. A recent survey of Muslim Americans, a category that includes the huge majority of Arab Americans and Middle Easterners, finds them to be "middle class and mostly mainstream." They have a positive view of U.S. society and espouse distinctly American values. At the same time, they are very concerned about becoming scapegoats in the war on terror, and a majority (53%) say that it became more difficult to be a Muslim in the United States after 9/11 (Pew Research Center, 2007).

Relations between Arab Americans and the larger society are certainly among the most tense and problematic of any minority group, and, given the continuing wars in Iraq and Afghanistan and the threat of further terrorist attacks by Al-Qaeda or other groups, they will not ease any time soon.

Immigrants From Africa

Our final group of New Americans consists of immigrants from Africa. Immigration to the United States from Africa has been quite low over the past 50 years. However, there was the usual increase after the 1960s, and Africans have made up about 5% of all immigrants in the past few years.

Exhibit 9.8 shows the total number of sub-Saharan Africans in the United States in 2007, along with the two largest national groups. The number of native Africans in the United States has more than doubled since 1990, and this rapid growth suggests that these groups may have a greater impact on U.S. society in the future. The category "sub-Saharan African" is extremely broad and encompasses destitute black refugees from African civil wars and relatively affluent white South Africans. In the remainder of this section, we will focus on Nigerians and Ethiopians rather than this very broad category. The Appendix (www.pineforge.com/healeyds3e) presents additional information on the relative standing of these groups.

Exhibit 9.8 Characteristics of Africans by Area and by Nation of Origin (Groups Larger Than 100,000 Only)

Group	Number	% Foreign Born	% That Speak English Less Than "Very Well"	% High School Degree or More	% College Degree or More	% of Families in Poverty	% in Managerial or Professional Occupations	Median Household Income
Non-Hispanic Whites	—	4.0	1.7	89.4	30.4	6.0	38.4	54,964
All Sub-Saharan Africans	2,702,367	39.0	12.8	84.7	31.3	18.0	29.6	39,451
Ethiopians	159,779	74.4	38.1	85.1	26.4	19.8	24.9	40,298
Nigerians	224,131	62.6	12.0	95.9	61.3	10.4	49.6	52,896

SOURCE: U.S. Bureau of the Census (2007).

Exhibit 9.9 Map of Africa Showing Ethiopia and Nigeria

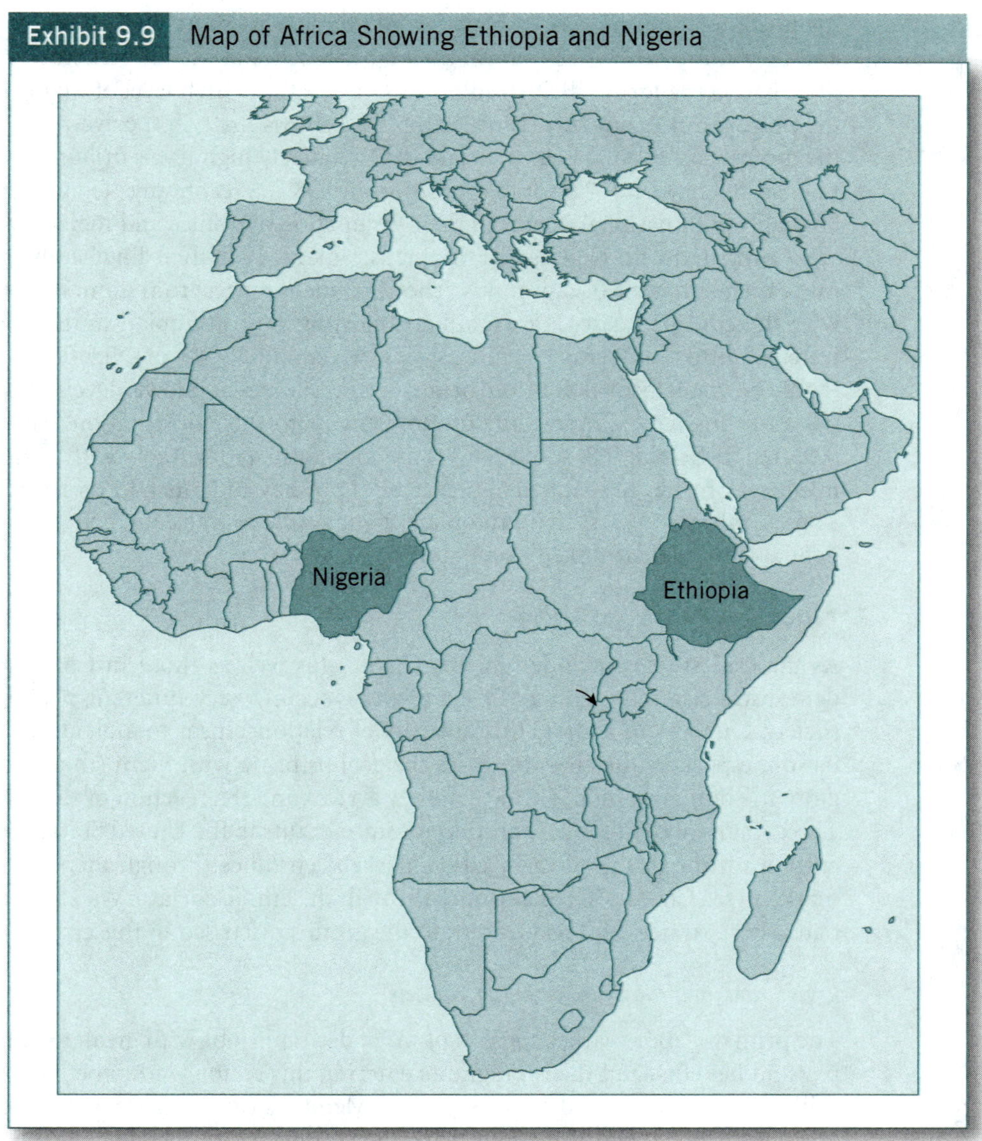

Clearly, although they may be growing, Nigerians and Ethiopians are tiny minorities: Neither group is as much as 0.1 of 1% of the total population. They are recent immigrants and have a high representation of first-generation members. They both compare favorably with national norms in education, an indication that this is another example of a "brain drain" from the countries of origin. Nigerian and Ethiopian immigrants tend to be highly skilled and educated, and they bring valuable abilities and advanced educational credentials to the United States. Like some other groups, many of the immigrants from Nigeria and Ethiopia are motivated by a search for work, and they compete for positions in the higher reaches of the job structure.

Nigeria is a former British colony, so the relatively high level of English fluency of the immigrants is not surprising. Exhibit 9.8 shows that, on the average, members of the group have been able to translate their relatively high levels of human capital and English fluency into a favorable position in the U.S. economy. They compare quite favorably with national norms in their occupational profiles and their income levels.

Compared with Nigerians, Ethiopians rank lower in their English fluency and are more mixed in their backgrounds. They include refugees from domestic unrest along with the educated elite. For example, almost 50% of Ethiopian immigrants in 2006 were admitted as "refugees and asylees" versus only 5% of Nigerian immigrants. Refugees, virtually by definition, bring fewer resources and lower levels of human capital and thus have a more difficult adjustment to their host nation. These facts are reflected in Exhibit 9.8. Although Ethiopians compare favorably with national norms in education, they have much higher rates of poverty and much lower levels of income. These contrasts suggest that Ethiopians are less able to translate their educational credentials into higher ranked occupations.

Modes of Incorporation

As the case studies included in this chapter (as well as those in Chapters 7 and 8) demonstrate, recent immigrant groups can occupy very different positions in U.S. society. One way to address this diversity of relationships is to look at the contact situation, especially the characteristics the groups bring with them (their race and religion, the human capital with which they arrive) and the reaction of the larger society. Three main modes of incorporation for immigrants in the United States seem to exist: entrance through the primary labor markets, entrance through the secondary labor markets (see Chapter 4), or entrance through the ethnic enclave. We will consider each pathway separately and relate them to the groups discussed in this chapter.

Immigrants and the Primary Labor Market

The primary labor market consists of more desirable jobs with greater security, higher pay and benefits, and the immigrants entering this sector tend to be highly educated, skilled professionals, and businesspeople. Members of this group are generally fluent in English, and many were educated at U.S. universities. They are highly integrated into the global urban-industrial economy, and, in many cases, they are employees of multinational corporations transferred here by their companies. These immigrants are affluent, urbane, and dramatically different from the peasant laborers so common in the past (e.g., from Ireland and Italy) and in the present (e.g., from the Dominican Republic and from Mexico). The groups with high percentages of members entering the primary labor market include Egyptian, Iranian, and Nigerian immigrants.

Because they tend to be affluent and enter a growing sector of the labor force, immigrants with professional backgrounds tend to attract less notice and fewer racist reactions than their more unskilled counterparts. Although they come closer to Blauner's pure immigrant group than most other minority groups we have considered, racism can still complicate their assimilation. In addition, Arab Americans must confront discrimination and prejudice based on their religious affiliation.

Immigrants and the Secondary Labor Market

This mode of incorporation is more typical for immigrants with lower levels of education and fewer job skills. Jobs in this sector are less desirable and command lower pay, little security, and few benefits and are often seasonal or in the underground or informal economy. Because working conditions in this sector are commonly unregulated by government agencies or labor unions, they are often substandard and unsafe and sometimes miserable. Workers have little or no protection from unscrupulous bosses, and workplaces that can be best described as "sweatshops" are common across the nation.

The secondary sector includes jobs in landscaping, construction, the garment industry, domestic work, and some forms of criminal or deviant activity, such as drugs and prostitution. The employers who control these jobs often prefer to hire undocumented immigrants because they are easier to control and less likely to complain to the authorities about abuse and mistreatment. The groups with high percentages of members in the secondary labor market include Haitians and the less skilled and less educated kinfolk of the higher status immigrants.

Immigrants and Ethnic Enclaves

As we have seen, some immigrant groups—especially those that can bring financial capital and business experience—have established ethnic enclaves. Some members of these groups enter U.S. society as entrepreneurs, owners of small retail shops, and other businesses; their less skilled and educated coethnics serve as a source of cheap labor to staff the ethnic enterprises. The enclave provides contacts, financial and other services, and social support for the new immigrants of all social classes. Some Arab Americans, along with Cuban Americans and Jewish Americans in the past, have been particularly likely to follow this path.

Summary

This classification suggests some of the variety of relationships between the new Americans and the larger society. The contemporary stream of immigrants entering the United States is extremely diverse and includes people ranging from the most sophisticated and educated to the most desperate and despairing. The variety is suggested by considering a list of occupations in which recent immigrants are overrepresented. For men, the list includes biologists and other natural scientists, taxi drivers, farm laborers, and waiters. For women, the list includes chemists, statisticians, produce packers, laundry workers, and domestics (Kritz & Girak, 2005).

Immigration: Issues and Controversies

In this section, we consider some of the key issues and controversies sparked by contemporary immigration. How receptive has the larger society been to the new immigrants? Is racism—modern or traditional—at work in shaping attitudes? What are the views of the immigrants? What are their goals and desires? Finally, we address the issues about which many Americans are most concerned: The costs of immigration to taxpayers and undocumented immigrants. Discussions on these issues have become very heated, particularly in the border states, and we will have to be careful to separate facts from myths as we proceed.

How Welcoming Are Americans?

One factor that affects the fate of immigrant groups is the attitude of the larger society, particularly the groups in the larger society that have the most influence with governmental policymakers. Overall, we can say that native-born Americans (even those with immigrant parents or grandparents) have never been particularly open to newcomers. The history of this nation is replete with movements to drastically reduce immigration or even eliminate it completely. We have already mentioned some of the anti-immigration movements directed against the first mass wave of immigrants from Europe (Chapter 2), Mexico (Chapter 7), and China and Japan (Chapter 8). Here we will look at attitudes and reactions to contemporary immigrants.

First, Americans have a lot of reservations about immigration; the majority of respondents in one recent poll felt that the volume of immigration should be decreased (54%) and only a small minority (11%) advocated an increase. Secondly, a report from the Pew Research Center (2006) found that an increasing percentage of Americans see immigrants as threats to their jobs and local communities. Exhibit 9.10 shows that, between 2000 and 2006, there was an increase in the percentage of respondents who viewed immigrants negatively and a corresponding decline in favorable views.

Exhibit 9.10 Increasing Immigration Worries

Immigrants today . . .	September 2000	December 2005	March 2006
Are a burden because they take jobs, housing, and health care	38%	44%	52%
Strengthen the United States with their hard work and talents	50%	45%	41%
Don't know	12%	11%	7%

SOURCE: Pew Research Center (2006). Copyright ©2006 Pew Hispanic Center, a Pew Research Center project, www.pewhispanic.org.

What factors might account for people's view of immigration? One possibility is that negative views of immigrants are linked to fear of job loss and financial insecurity. For example, one survey shows that white Americans who felt that their financial situation had worsened over the past few years were more likely to support a reduction in immigration. This relationship is displayed in Exhibit 9.11. The table shows that there is a lot of support for decreasing immigration regardless of people's perceptions of their financial situations. However, support for decreasing immigration is strongest among people who feel that their own personal financial situation has gotten worse in recent years. This relationship between a sense of threat and prejudice is consistent with the Noel hypothesis (see Chapter 3) and the outcome of Robber's Cave experiment (see Chapter 1) and should come as no surprise at this point in the text.

Exhibit 9.11 Position on Immigration by Perception of Personal Financial Situation, 2006 (Whites Only)

Do you think that the number of immigrants to America should . . .	Over the past few years, do you think that your financial situation has been getting better, worse, or stayed the same?		
	Better	**Stayed the Same**	**Worse**
Be increased	11%	9%	9%
Remain the same	35%	34%	23%
Be decreased	54%	57%	68%
	100%	100%	100%

SOURCE: National Opinion Research Council (1972-2006).

Besides a sense of personal threat, what other factors are associated with anti-immigrant attitudes? A recent study (Pettigrew, Wagner, & Christ, 2007) examined attitudes in Germany and compared these with other recent studies of European attitudes and anti-immigration feelings in Canada and the United States. The researchers found similar patterns in all locales and concluded that negative views of immigrants were highly correlated with prejudice. The same forces that produce prejudice—exposure to prejudiced norms and values during childhood, low levels of education—also produce anti-immigrant feelings. We discussed relationships of this sort in Chapter 1 when we noted that prejudice is partly cultural and is passed on from generation to generation.

However, remember that prejudice also is related to intergroup conflict. The researchers (Pettigrew et al., 2007) found that a sense of collective threat was the single strongest predictor of antiforeigner attitudes, more so than the individual-level threat examined in Exhibit 9.11. That is, the most important cause of anti-immigrant attitudes was the sense that newcomers threatened the way of life, political freedoms, and cultural integrity of the nation as a whole, not just jobs or personal financial stability. As in so many other instances we have investigated, these forms of prejudice are defensive: they are reactions to the sense that the dominant status of one's group is at risk. As we have seen on numerous occasions (e.g., the Robbers Cave experiment discussed in Chapter 1, rigid competitive relations discussed in Chapter 4), competition between groups—or even the perception of competition—can stimulate powerful emotions and extreme forms of prejudice and discrimination.

Does this mean that everyone who has reservations and questions about immigration is a racist? Emphatically not. Although anti-immigrant feelings, prejudice, and a sense of threat are linked, this does not mean that all who oppose high levels of immigration are bigots or that all proposals to decrease the flow of immigrants are racist. These are serious and complex issues, and it is not helpful to simply label people bigots or dismiss their concerns as prejudiced.

Conversely, we need to clearly recognize that anti-immigrant feelings—particularly the most extreme—*are* linked to some of the worst, most negative strains of traditional American culture: the same racist and prejudicial views that helped to justify slavery and the near-genocide of Native Americans. In popular culture, some talk radio and cable TV "news" shows, letters to the editor, and so forth, these views are regularly used to demonize immigrants, blame them for an array of social problems, and stoke irrational fears and rumors, such as the idea that Latino immigrants are aiming to return parts of the Southwest to Mexico (see the Web site for the Minutemen—an anti-immigrant, vigilante group that has taken it upon itself to help patrol the southern border—at http://www.minutemanproject.com/ for illustrations). At any rate, when American traditions of prejudice and racism are linked to feelings of group threat and individual insecurity, the possibilities for extreme reactions, hate crimes, and poorly designed policy and law become formidable.

The Immigrants

One recent survey of immigration issues (National Public Radio, 2004) included a nationally representative sample of immigrant respondents. Not surprisingly, the researchers found that their attitudes and views differed sharply from those of native-born respondents on a number of dimensions. For example, immigrant respondents were more likely to see immigration as a positive force for the larger society and more likely to say that immigrants work hard and pay their fair share of taxes.

More relevant for the ultimate impact of the contemporary wave of immigration, the survey found that only about 30% were sojourners (i.e., ultimately planning to return to their homelands), a finding that suggests that issues of assimilation and immigration will remain at the forefront of U.S. concerns for many decades.

The survey also showed that immigrants are very grateful for the economic opportunities available in the United States, with 84% agreeing that there are more opportunities to get ahead here than in their countries of origin. Conversely, the immigrant respondents were ambivalent about U.S. culture and values. For example, nearly half (47%) said that the family was stronger in their homelands than in the United States, and only 28% saw U.S. society as having stronger moral values than their homelands.

We have seen that the immigrant stream is highly diversified, but it would be helpful to keep in mind the characteristics of the "typical immigrant." The modal or most common immigrant is from Mexico, China, or other Asian or Central American nation and has decided to cross the border largely out of desperation and the absence of viable opportunities at home. They would prefer to enter legally but their desperation is such that they will enter illegally if necessary. Coming from less developed nations, they bring little human capital, education, or job skills. Many will come to the

United States for a time and then return home, circulating between nations as has been done for decades.

As is typical of the first generation, they tend to be more oriented to their home village than to the United States, and they are often less interested in acculturation or learning English. Frequently, they don't have the time, energy, or opportunity to absorb much of Anglo culture and are further hampered in their acquisition of English by the fact that they are not very literate in their native language. They are hard working and frugal, often sharing living quarters with many others so as to save on rent. They send much of their earnings home to support their family and kin and spend little on themselves. They are generally determined to find a better way of life for their children, even if the cost is to live in poverty at the margins of society.

Costs and Benefits

Many Americans believe that immigration is a drain on the economic resources of the nation. Common concerns include the idea that immigrants take jobs from native-born workers, strain institutions such as schools, housing markets, and medical facilities, and do not pay their fair share of taxes. These issues are complex and hotly debated at all levels of U.S. society, so much so that passion and intensity of feeling on all sides often compromise the objective analysis of data. The debate is further complicated because conclusions about these economic issues can vary depending on the type of immigrants being discussed and the level of analysis being used. For example, conclusions about costs and benefits can be very different depending on whether we focus on less-skilled or undocumented immigrants or the highly educated professional immigrants entering the primary job market. Also, conclusions might vary depending on the level of the analyses: national studies might lead to different conclusions than studies of local communities.

Contrary to the tenor of public opinion, many studies, especially those done at the national level, find that immigrants are not a particular burden. For example, a study conducted by the National Research Council (1997) found that immigrants are a positive addition to the economy. They add to the labor supply in areas as disparate as the garment industry, agriculture, domestic work, and college faculty (National Academy of Sciences, 1997). Other researchers have found that low-skilled immigrants tend to find jobs in areas of the economy in which few U.S. citizens work or in the enclave economies of their own groups, taking jobs that would not have existed without the economic activity of their coethnics (Heer, 1996; Smith & Edmonston, 1997). One important recent study of the economic impact of immigrants concluded that there is a relatively small effect on the wages and employment of native workers, although there do seem to be negative consequences for earlier immigrants and for less-skilled African American workers (Bean & Stevens, 2003).

Another concern is the strain that immigrants place on taxes and services such as schools and welfare programs. Again, these issues are complex and far from settled, but research tends to show that immigrants generally cost less than they contribute. Taxes are automatically deducted from their paychecks (unless, of course, they are being paid "under the table"), and their use of such services as unemployment compensation, Medicare, food stamps, and Social Security is actually lower than their proportional contributions. This is particularly true for undocumented immigrants, whose use of services is sharply limited by their vulnerable legal status (Marcelli & Heer, 1998; Simon, 1989). Bean and Stevens (2003), in their recent study, find that immigrants are not overrepresented on the welfare rolls. Rather, the key determinant of welfare use is refugee status. Groups such as Haitians, Salvadorans, and Vietnamese—who arrive without resources and, by definition, are in need of assistance on all levels—are the most likely to be on the welfare rolls.

In general, immigrants—undocumented as well as legal—pay state and federal taxes and make proportional contributions to social security and Medicare. The undocumented are the most likely to be paid "off the books" and receive their wages tax-free, but estimates are that the majority (at least 50%) and probably the huge majority (up to 75%) of them pay federal and state taxes through payroll deduction (The White House, 2005). Also, all immigrants pay sales and the other taxes (e.g., on gas, groceries, clothing, cigarettes, and alcohol) that are levied on consumers.

Far from being a drain on resources, there is evidence that the immigrant population plays a crucial role in keeping the Social Security system solvent. This source of retirement income is being severely strained by the "baby boomers"—the large number of Americans born between 1945 and 1960 who are now leaving the workforce and becoming senior citizens. This group is living longer than previous generations and, since the birth rate has stayed low over the past four decades, there are relatively fewer native-born workers to support them and replace the funds they withdraw as Social Security benefits. The high rate of immigration may supply the much needed workers to take up the slack in the system and keep it solvent. In particular, most undocumented immigrants pay into the system but (probably) will never draw any money out, because of their illegal status. They thus provide a tidy surplus—perhaps as much as 7 billion dollars a year or more—to help subsidize the retirements of the baby boomers and keep the system functioning (Porter, 2005).

Final conclusions about the impact and costs of immigration must await ongoing research, and many local communities are experiencing real distress as they try to deal with the influx of newcomers in their housing markets, schools, and health care facilities. Concerns about the economic impact of immigrants are not unfounded, but they may be confounded with and exaggerated by prejudice and racism directed at newcomers and strangers. The current opposition to immigration may be a reaction to "who" as much as to "how many" or "how expensive."

Finally, we can repeat the finding of many studies (e.g., Bean & Stevens, 2003), that immigration is generally a positive force in the economy and that, as has been true for decades, immigrants, legal and illegal, continue to find work with Anglo employers and niches in American society in which they can survive. The networks that have delivered cheap immigrant labor for the low-wage secondary job market continue to operate, and, frequently, the primary beneficiaries of this long-established system are not the immigrants (although they are often grateful for the opportunities), but employers, who benefit from a cheaper, more easily exploited workforce, and American consumers, who benefit from lower prices in the marketplace and who reap the benefits virtually every time they go shopping, have a meal in a restaurant, or purchase a home.

FOCUS ON CONTEMPORARY ISSUES: Undocumented Immigrants

Americans are particularly concerned with undocumented immigrants, and many are very frustrated with what they see as ineffective government efforts to curtail this flow of illegal aliens. For example, in a 2006 survey, 59% of the respondents said the problem of illegal immigration was "very serious," and another 30% said that they felt that the problem was "somewhat serious" (Pew Research Center, 2006).

There is no question that the volume of illegal immigration is huge. In 2000, it was estimated that there were 8.5 million people living in United States illegally, more than double the number in 1992. By 2007, the number had risen to 11.8 million but then dropped slightly in 2008 to 11.6 million (Hoefer, Rytina, & Baker, 2009).

Some undocumented immigrants enter the country on tourist, temporary worker, or student visas and simply remain in the nation when their visas expire. In 2008 alone, more than 35 million tourists, business people, temporary workers, and foreign students entered the United States (Department of Homeland Security, 2009), and these numbers suggest how difficult it is to keep tabs on this source of illegal immigrants. Others cross the border illegally in the hopes of evading the border patrol and finding their way into some niche in the American economy. The very fact that people keep coming suggests that most succeed.

A variety of efforts continue to be made to curtail and control the flow of illegal immigrants. Various states have attempted to lower the appeal of the United States by limiting benefits and opportunities. One of the best known of these attempts occurred in 1994, when California voters passed Proposition 187, which would have denied educational, health, and other services to illegal immigrants. The policy was declared unconstitutional, however, and was never implemented. Other efforts to decrease the flow of illegal immigration have included proposals to limit welfare benefits for immigrants, denying in-state college tuition to the children of illegal immigrants, increases in the size of the Border Patrol, and the construction of taller and wider walls along the border with Mexico. Over the past eight years, a variety of proposals to reform the national immigration policy have been hotly debated at the highest levels of government, but none have been passed.

Although Americans will continue to be concerned about this problem, it seems unlikely that much can be done (within the framework of a democratic, humane society) to curtail the flow of people. The social networks that deliver immigrants—legal as well as illegal—are too well established, and the demand for cheap labor in the United States is simply insatiable. In fact, denying services, as envisioned in Proposition 187, may make illegal immigrants more attractive as a source of labor by reducing their ability to resist exploitation. For example, if the children of illegal immigrants were not permitted to attend school, they would become more likely to join the army of cheap labor on which some employers depend. Who would benefit from closing public schools to the children of illegal immigrants?

Is Contemporary Assimilation Segmented?

In Chapter 2, we reviewed some of the patterns of acculturation and integration that typified the adjustment of Europeans who immigrated to the United States before the

1930s. Although their process of adjustment was anything but smooth or simple, these groups eventually Americanized and achieved levels of education and affluence comparable with national norms. Will contemporary immigrants from Latin America and the Caribbean experience similar success? Will their sons and daughters and grandsons and granddaughters rise in the occupational structure to a position of parity with the dominant group? Will the cultures and languages of these groups gradually fade and disappear?

Final answers to these questions must await future developments. In the meantime, there is considerable debate on these issues. Some analysts argue that assimilation will be segmented and that the success story of the white ethnic groups will not be repeated. Others find that the traditional perspective on assimilation—particularly the model of assimilation developed by Milton Gordon—continues to be a useful framework for understanding the experience of contemporary immigrants. We will review some of the most important and influential arguments from each side of this debate and, finally, attempt to come to some conclusions about the future of assimilation.

The Case for Segmented Assimilation

Sociologist Douglas Massey (1995) presents perhaps the most compelling argument in favor of the segmented-assimilation perspective. He argues that there are three crucial differences between the European assimilation experience of the past and the contemporary period, each of which calls the traditional perspective into question. First, the flow of immigrants from Europe to the United States slowed to a mere trickle after the 1920s because of restrictive legislation, the worldwide depression of the 1930s, and World War II. Immigration in the 1930s, for example, was less than 10% of the flow of the early 1920s. Thus, as the children and grandchildren of the European immigrants Americanized and grew to adulthood in the 1930s and 1940s, few new immigrants fresh from the old country replaced them in the ethnic neighborhoods. European cultural traditions and languages weakened rapidly with the passing of the first generation and the Americanization of their descendents.

For contemporary immigration, in contrast, the networks and the demand for cheap labor are so strong that it is unlikely that there will be a similar hiatus in the flow of people. Immigration has become continuous, argues Massey, and as some contemporary immigrants (or their descendants) Americanize and rise to affluence and success, new arrivals will replace them and continuously revitalize the ethnic cultures and languages.

Second, the speed and ease of modern transportation and communication will help to maintain cultural and linguistic diversity. A century ago, immigrants from Europe could maintain contact with the old country only by mail, and most had no realistic expectation of ever returning. Most modern immigrants, in contrast, can return to their homes in a day or less and can use telephones, television, e-mail, and the Internet to stay in intimate contact with the families and friends they left behind. According to one recent survey (National Public Radio, 2004), a little more than 40% of immigrants return to their homelands at least every year or two, and some (6%) return every few months. Thus, the cultures of modern immigrants can be kept vital and whole in ways that were not available (and not even imagined) 100 years ago.

Third, and perhaps most important, contemporary immigrants face an economy and a labor market that are vastly different from those faced by European immigrants of the 19th and early 20th century. The latter group generally rose in the class system as the economy shifted from manufacturing to service (see Exhibit 4.4). Today, rates of upward mobility have decreased, and just when the importance of education has increased, schools available to the children of immigrants have fallen into neglect (Massey, 1995).

For the immigrants from Europe a century ago, assimilation meant a gradual rise to middle-class respectability and suburban comfort, even if it took four or five generations to accomplish. Assimilation today, according to Massey and others, is segmented, and a large percentage of the descendants of contemporary immigrants—especially many of the Hispanic groups, Haitians, and peoples of color—face permanent membership in a growing underclass population and continuing marginalization and powerlessness.

A recent study reinforces some of Massey's points. Sociologists Telles and Ortiz (2008) studied a sample of Mexican Americans who were interviewed in 1965 and again in 2000. They found evidence of strong movements toward acculturation and integration on some dimensions (e.g., language) but not on others. Even fourth-generation members of their sample continued to live in "the barrio," marry within the group, and, contrary to evidence presented in Exhibits 9.12 and 9.13 from a different study, did not reach economic parity with Anglos. The authors single out institutional discrimination (e.g., underfunding of schools that serve Mexican-American neighborhoods) as a primary cause of the continuing separation, a point that is consistent with Massey's conclusion regarding the decreasing rates of upward mobility in American society.

The Case Against Segmented Assimilation

Many of the best recent studies come to a similar conclusion: the second generation is generally rising relative to their parents. This finding seems to contradict the segmented assimilation thesis and resurrects the somewhat tattered body of traditional assimilation theories. These studies (e.g., Alba & Nee, 2003; Bean & Stevens, 2003; Fernandez-Kelly & Portes, 2008; Kasnitz, Mollenkopf, Waters, & Holloway, 2008; White & Glick, 2009) argue that contemporary assimilation will ultimately follow the same course as European immigrant groups 100 years ago and as described in Gordon's theory (see Chapter 2). For example, two recent studies (Alba & Nee, 2003; Bean & Stevens, 2003) find that most contemporary immigrant groups are acculturating and integrating at the "normal" three-generation pace. Those groups (notably Mexicans) that appear to be lagging behind this pace may take as many as four to five generations, but their descendents will eventually find their way onto the primary job market and the cultural mainstream.

Studies of acculturation show that values Americanize and that English language proficiency grows with time of residence and generation (Bean & Stevens, 2003). We discussed some of these patterns in Chapter 2 (see Exhibit 2.8) and Chapter 7 (see Exhibits 7.8 through 7.11).

In terms of structural integration, contemporary immigrant groups may be narrowing the income gap over time, although many groups (e.g., Dominicans, Mexicans, Haitians, and Vietnamese) are handicapped by very low levels of human capital at the start (Bean & Stevens, 2003). Exhibits 9.12 and 9.13 illustrate this process with respect

Exhibit 9.12 Wage Differential of Mexican Workers Relative to Whites, MALES

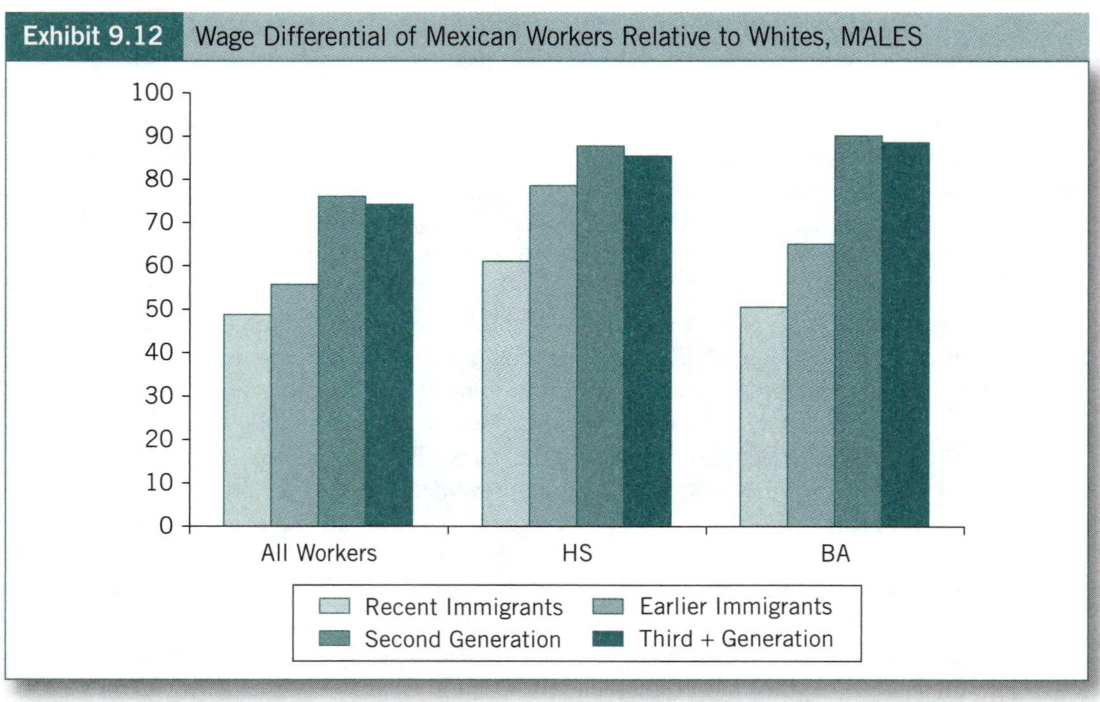

SOURCE: Bean & Stevens (2003). Copyright © 2003 Russell Sage Foundation, 112 East 64th Street, New York, NY 10021. Reprinted with permission.

Exhibit 9.13 Wage Differentials Relative to Whites, FEMALES

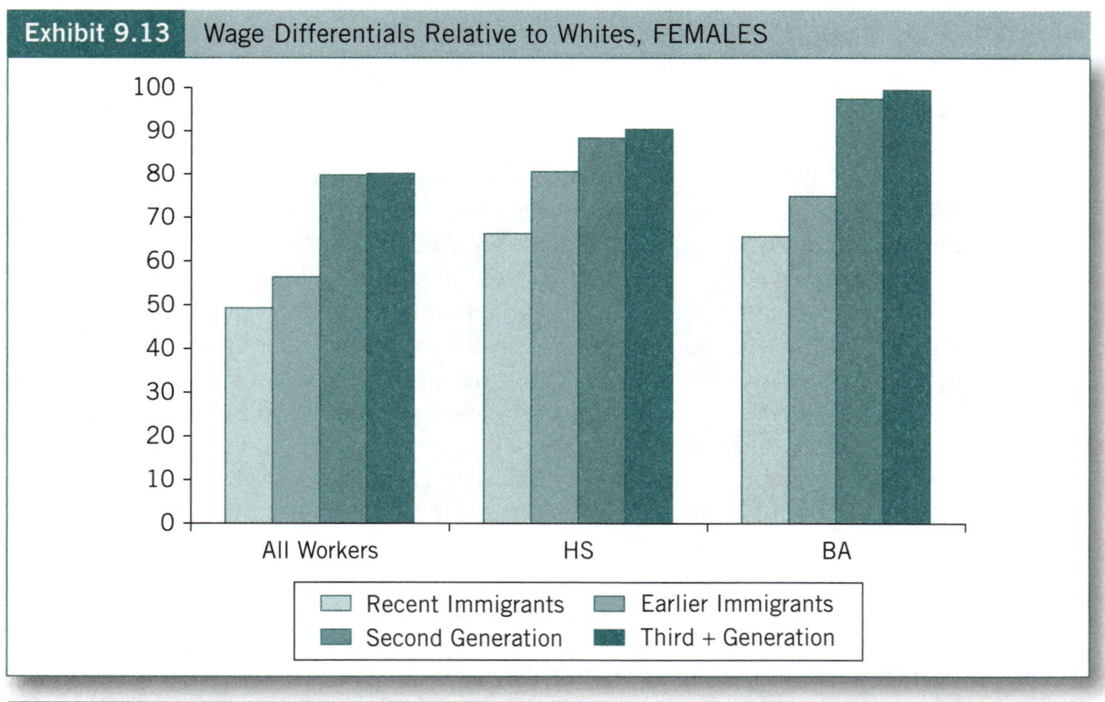

SOURCE: Bean & Stevens (2003). Copyright © 2003 Russell Sage Foundation, 112 East 64th Street, New York, NY 10021. Reprinted with permission.

to wage differentials between Mexican and white non-Hispanic males and females of various generations and levels of education. In these exhibits, complete income equality with non-Hispanic whites would be indicated if the bar touches the 100% line at the top of the graph.

Looking first at males, recent Mexican immigrants earn a little less than half of what white males earn. The difference in income is lower for earlier immigrants, lower still for Mexicans males of the second and third generation, and lowest for the most educated ("BA") members of those generations. In other words, income equality tends to increase over the generations and as education increases. Conversely, note that third-generation males do not rise relative to their parents' generation. This is contrary to the view that assimilation will proceed in a linear, stepwise fashion across the generations and is reminiscent of the findings of Telles and Ortiz (2008), cited earlier. For females, the wage differential also shrinks as the generations pass and level of education increases. Note that for third-generation, college-educated females, the wage differential shrinks virtually to zero, indicating complete integration on this variable.

These patterns generally support the traditional perspective on assimilation. The wage gap shrinks by generation and level of education, and integration is substantial by the third generation (although complete only for one group). This pattern suggests that the movement of Mexican immigrants is toward the economic mainstream, even though they do not close the gap completely. Bean and Stevens conclude that this pattern is substantially consistent with the "three-generation model": The assimilation trajectory of Mexican Americans and other recent immigrant groups is not into the urban poor, the underclass, or the disenfranchised, disconnected, and marginalized. Assimilation is not segmented but is substantially repeating the experiences of the European groups on which Gordon based his theory.

How can we reconcile these opposed points of view? In large part, this debate concerns the nature of the evidence and judgments about how much weight to give to various facts and trends. On the one hand, Massey's points about the importance of the postindustrial economy, declining opportunities for less educated workers, and the neglect that seems typical of inner-city schools are very well taken, as is the evidence supplied by Telles and Ortiz. On the other hand, it seems that even the least educated immigrant groups have been able to find economic niches in which they and their families can survive and eke out an existence long enough for their children and grandchildren to rise in the structure, a pattern that has been at the core of the American immigrant experience for almost two centuries.

Of course, this debate will continue, and new evidence and interpretations will appear. Ultimately, however, the debate may continue until immigration stops (which is very unlikely to happen, as Massey points out) and the fate of the descendents of the last immigrant groups is measured.

Recent Immigration in Historical and Global Context

The current wave of immigration to the United States is part of a centuries-old process that spans the globe. Underlying this immense and complex population movement is the powerful force of continuing industrialization, economic development, and globalization. The United States and other advanced industrial nations are the centers of growth in the global economy, and immigrants flow to the areas of greater opportunity. In the 19th century, population moved largely from Europe to the Western Hemisphere. Over the past 50 years, the movement has been from the Global South to the Global North. This pattern reflects the simple geography of industrialization and opportunity and the fact that the more developed nations are in the Northern Hemisphere.

The United States has been the world's dominant economic, political, and cultural power for much of the last 100 years and the preferred destination of most immigrants. Newcomers from around the globe continue the collective, social nature of past population movements (see Chapter 2). The direction of their travels reflects contemporary global inequalities: Labor continues to flow from the less developed nations to the more developed nations. The direction of this flow is not accidental or coincidental. It is determined by the differential rates of industrialization and modernization across the globe. Immigration contributes to the wealth and affluence of the more developed societies and particularly to the dominant groups and elite classes of those societies.

The immigrant flow also is a response to the particular dynamics of globalization, particularly since the 1980s (Sen & Mamdouh, 2008). The current era of globalization has been guided by the doctrine of neoliberalism, or free trade, which urges nations to eliminate barriers to the free movement of goods and capital. The North American Free Trade Agreement (NAFTA), which we have mentioned on several occasions, is an example of a neoliberal policy. When NAFTA went into effect in 1994, the three nations of North America became, for many purposes, a single economic unit. Corporations and capital were free to cross national borders, and many U.S. firms moved their operations to Mexico in search of cheaper workers and weaker environmental and labor regulations. Neoliberal agreements such as NAFTA also opened Mexico and other less developed nations to consumer goods manufactured and controlled by large, transnational corporations. These corporations were often able to undersell indigenous goods, driving small-scale local farmers and manufacturers out of business. Finally, the international agencies that regulate the global economy pressure states to reduce the size of their governmental sector. This often means that the national budget for health and education is slashed and that services once controlled and subsidized by the government (e.g., water, electricity) are sold to private businesses. The result of these global forces is an increasingly vulnerable population in less developed nations, unable to provide for themselves, educate their children, or afford the simplest of daily necessities.

We tend to see immigrants as individuals acting of their own free will and, often, illegally ("They chose to come to the United States and break the law"), but the picture changes when we see immigration as the result of powerful, global economic and political forces. Globalization today allows for the free movement of capital and goods but not people. As the domestic economies and social systems of less developed nations crumble, the victims of neoliberal globalization are left with few choices: they cross borders not only to the United States but to other advanced industrial nations, illegally if they have to, because "it is the best choice to achieve a dignified life—if not for themselves, then for their children" (Sen & Mamdouh, 2008, p. 7). When viewed through the lens of globalization, it is clear that this population movement will continue because immigrants simply have no choice. It is very unlikely that they can be stopped by further militarization of the border or by building bigger and taller walls. They come to the United States in their numbers, as immigrants did in the past, because the alternatives are unacceptable or nonexistent.

These thoughts suggest that the tendency of many citizens of the more developed world to reject, demonize, and criminalize immigrants is self-defeating. Punitive, militaristic policies will not stem the flow of people from the Global South to the North. Globalization, in its neoliberal form, is incomplete: It allows for the free movement of goods and capital but not of people. It benefits transnational corporations and the mega businesses that produce consumer goods but victimizes the vulnerable citizens of the less developed nations. As long as these forms of globalization hold, the population pressure from South to North will continue.

New Immigrants and Old Issues

This chapter focused on some of the issues raised by high levels of immigration since the 1960s. As these issues are debated and considered, a fundamental fact about modern American society needs to be remembered: The issues of the "traditional" minority groups—African Americans and American Indians, for example—have not been resolved. As shown in previous chapters, these groups have been a part of American society from the beginning, but they remain, in many ways, distant from achieving complete equality and integration.

Many of the current issues facing these groups relate to class as well as race. The urban underclass is disproportionately made up of peoples of color and remains marginal to the mainstream society in terms of access to education and job opportunities, decent housing, and good health care. Although it is probably true that American society is more open and tolerant than ever before, we must not mistake a decline in blatant racism or a reduction in overt discrimination for its demise. In fact, there is abundant evidence that shows that racism and discrimination have not declined, but have merely changed form and that the patterns of exclusion and deprivation that have sustained in the past continue in the present.

Similarly, gender issues and sexism remain on the national agenda. As has been shown at various points throughout the text, blatant sexism and overt discrimination against women are probably at an historic low, but, again, one cannot mistake change for disappearance. Most importantly, minority women remain the victims of a double jeopardy and are among the most vulnerable and exploited segments of the society. Many female members of the new immigrant groups find themselves in similarly vulnerable positions.

These problems of exclusion and continuing prejudice and sexism are exacerbated by a number of trends in the larger society. For example, the continuing shift in subsistence technology away from manufacturing to the service sector privileges groups that, in the past as well as today, have had access to education. The urban underclass consists disproportionately of groups that have been excluded from education in the past and have less access in the present.

The new immigrant groups have abundant problems of their own, of course, and need to find ways to pursue their self-interests in their new society. Some segments of these groups—the well-educated professionals seeking to advance their careers in the world's most advanced economy—will be much more likely to find ways to avoid the harshest forms of American rejection and exclusion. Similarly, the members of the "traditional" minority groups that have gained access to education and middle-class status will enjoy more opportunities than previous generations could have imagined (although, as we have seen, their middle-class position will be more precarious than their dominant-group counterparts).

Will we become a society in which ethnic and racial groups are permanently segmented by class, with the more favored members enjoying a higher, if partial, level of acceptance while other members of their groups languish in permanent exclusion and segmentation? What does it mean to be an American? What should it mean?

MAIN POINTS

- Since the mid-1960s, immigrants have been coming to the United States at nearly record rates. Most of these immigrant groups have coethnics who have been in the United States for years, but others are "New Americans." How will this new wave of immigration transform America? Will they assimilate? How?
- Non-Hispanic immigrants from the Caribbean include Haitians and Jamaicans. Some are driven by economic needs; others are political refugees. All face the issues of racism and institutionalized discrimination.
- Arab Americans, like other New Americans, have been growing rapidly in number, and their local communities tend to be centered in economic enclaves. The events of 9/11 make this group a special target for hate crimes and for security concerns.
- Immigrants from Africa remain a relatively small group, and many bring high levels of education and occupational skills, although others are concentrated in the lower levels of the occupational structure.
- Contemporary immigrants are generally experiencing three different modes of incorporation into U.S. society: the primary labor market, the secondary labor market, and the enclave. The pathway of each group is strongly influenced by the amount of human capital they bring, their race, the attitude of the larger society, and many other factors.
- Relations between immigrants and the larger society are animated by a number of issues, including the relative costs and benefits of immigration, concerns about undocumented immigrants, and the speed of assimilation. One important issue currently being debated by social scientists is whether assimilation for New Americans will be segmented or will ultimately follow the pathway established by immigrant groups from Europe in the 19th and 20th centuries.

STUDY SITE ON THE WEB

Don't forget the interactive quizzes and other resources and learning aids at **www.pineforge.com/healeyds3e**

FOR FURTHER READING

The following are recent, important studies of New American groups:

Alba, Richard, & Nee, Victor. 2003. *Remaking the American Mainstream: Assimilation and Contemporary Immigration.* Cambridge, MA: Harvard University Press.

Bean, Frank, & Stevens, Gillian. 2003. *America's Newcomers and the Dynamics of Diversity.* New York: Russell Sage Foundation.

Kasnitz, Phillip, Mollenkopf, John, Waters, Mary, & Holloway, Jennifer. 2008. *Inheriting the City: The Children of Immigrants Come of Age.* New York: Russell Sage.

Portes, Alejandro, & Rumbaut, Rubén. 2001a. *Ethnicities: Children of Immigrants in America.* New York: Russell Sage Foundation.

Portes, Alejandro, & Rumbaut, Rubén. 2001b. *Legacies: The Story of the Immigrant Second Generation.* New York: Russell Sage Foundation.

Telles, Edward, & Ortiz, Vilma. 2008. *Generations of Exclusion: Mexican Americans, Assimilation, and Race.* New York: Russell Sage Foundation.

White, Michael, & Glick, Jennifer. 2009. *Achieving Anew: How New Immigrants Do in American Schools, Jobs, and Neighborhoods.* New York: Russell Sage Foundation.

QUESTIONS FOR REVIEW AND STUDY

1. What differences exist between these New Americans in terms of their motivations for coming to the United States? What are the implications of these various "push" factors for their reception and adjustment to the United States?

2. Compare Arab and Middle Eastern immigrant groups with those from the Caribbean. Which group is more diverse? What differences exist in their patterns of adjustment and assimilation? Why do these patterns exist?

3. Compare and contrast African immigrants with the other groups. How do they differ? What are the implications of these differences for their adjustment to the larger society?

4. What, in your opinion, are the most important issues facing the United States in terms of immigration and assimilation? How are these issues playing out in your community? What are the implications of these issues for the future of the United States?

5. Will assimilation for contemporary immigrants be segmented? After examining the evidence and arguments presented by both sides and using information from this and previous chapters, which side of the debate seems more credible? Why? What are the implications of this debate? What will the United States look like in the future if assimilation is segmented? How would the future change if assimilation is not segmented? Which of these scenarios is more desirable for immigrant groups? For the society as a whole? For various segments of U.S. society (e.g., employers, labor unions, African Americans, consumers, the college educated, the urban underclass, and so on)?

INTERNET RESEARCH PROJECTS

A. Update and Expand This Chapter by an Internet Search

Many of the groups covered in this chapter have Web sites dedicated to them (e.g., Arab Americans are the subject of http://www.allied-media.com/Arab-American/default.htm). Select several of the groups covered in this chapter and conduct a search for relevant Web sites. See what you can learn about the concerns and situations of each group, and compare the information with what has been presented in this text. What information can you collect about their socioeconomic profiles? What can you learn about their points of view regarding the United States and their treatment by the larger society? What issues are most important for them (e.g., learning English, job discrimination, hate crimes, availability of welfare services, and so on)?

B. Update and Expand This Chapter With Data From the U.S. Census

The U.S. Bureau of the Census collects an array of information about most of the groups covered in this chapter, and the information is available online. Go to http://www.census.gov and click on "American FactFinder" on the left-hand panel of the home page. Next, click on "Data Sets" on the left-hand panel, then click on American Community Survey on the left-hand panel, and select "2007 American Community Survey 1-Year Estimates." In the next window, select "Selected Population Profiles," and then click "Add" to move the United States to the bottom window, and click "Next." Choose the "Ancestry Groups" tab and find a group covered in this text or some other group in which you are interested. Click "Show Result," and a statistical profile of the group and the U.S. population will be displayed. Extend the analysis in this chapter by selecting several variables and comparing the profile of your group with the total population.

Note

1. From *Antonio's Gun and Delfino's Dream: True Tales of Mexican Migration,* by Sam Quinones.

10

Minority Groups and U.S. Society

Themes, Patterns, and the Future

Over the past nine chapters, we have analyzed ideas and theories about dominant-minority relations and examined the historical and contemporary situations of minority groups in U.S. society. Now it is time to reexamine our major themes and concepts and determine what conclusions can be derived from our analysis. This final chapter restates the general themes of the text and raises some questions about the future. As we look backward to the past and forward to the future, it seems appropriate to paraphrase the words of the historian Oscar Handlin (1951): "Once I thought to write a history of the minority groups in America. Then, I discovered that the minority groups were American history" (p. 3).

The Importance of Subsistence Technology

Perhaps the most important sociological idea we have developed is that dominant-minority relations are shaped by large social, political, and economic forces and change as these broad characteristics change. To understand the evolution of America's minority groups is to understand the history of the United States, from the earliest colonial settlement to the modern megalopolis. As we have seen throughout the text, these same broad forces have left their imprint on many societies around the globe.

Subsistence technology is the most basic force shaping a society and the relationships between dominant and minority groups in that society. In the colonial United States, minority relations were bent to the demands of a land-hungry, labor-intensive agrarian technology, and the early relationships between Africans, Europeans, and American Indians flowed from the colonists' desire to control both land and labor. By the mid-1800s, two centuries after Jamestown was founded, the same dynamics that had enslaved African Americans and nearly annihilated American Indians made a minority group out of Mexican Americans.

The agrarian era came to an end in the 19th century as the new technologies of the Industrial Revolution increased the productivity of the economy and eventually changed every aspect of life in the United States. The paternalistic, oppressive systems used to control the labor of minority groups in the agrarian system were abolished and replaced by competitive systems of group relations. These newer systems evolved from more rigid forms to more fluid forms as industrialization and urbanization progressed.

As the United States grew and developed, new minority groups were created, and old minority groups were transformed. Rapid industrialization combined with the opportunities available on the frontier made the United States an attractive destination for immigrants from Europe, Asia, Latin America, and other parts of the world. Immigrants helped to farm the Great Plains, mine the riches of the West, and above all, supply the armies of labor required by industrialization.

The descendants of the immigrants from Europe benefited from the continuing industrialization of the economy, rising in the social class structure as the economy grew and matured. Immigrants from Asia and Latin America were not so fortunate. Chinese Americans and Japanese Americans survived in ethnic enclaves on the fringes of the mainstream society, and Mexican Americans and Puerto Ricans supplied low-paid manual labor for both the rural and the urban economy. Both Asian Americans and Hispanic Americans were barred from access to dominant-group institutions and higher paid jobs.

The racial minority groups, particularly African Americans, Mexican Americans, and Puerto Ricans, began to enter the urban working class after European American ethnic groups had started to move up in the occupational structure, at a time when the supply of manual, unskilled jobs was starting to diminish. Thus, the processes that allowed upward mobility for European Americans failed to work for the racial minority groups, who confronted urban poverty and bankrupt cities in addition to the continuing barriers of racial prejudice and institutional discrimination.

We can only speculate about what the future holds, but the emerging information-based, high-tech society is unlikely to offer many opportunities for people with lower educational backgrounds and occupational skills. It seems fairly certain that members of the racial and colonized minority groups and some of recent immigrant groups will be participating in the mainstream economy of the future at lower levels than the dominant group, the descendants of the European immigrants, and the more advantaged recent immigrant groups. Upgraded urban educational systems, job training programs, and other community development programs might alter the grim scenario of continuing exclusion. Current public opinion about matters of race and discrimination makes it unlikely that such programs will be created.

Inaction and perpetuation of the status quo likely will bar a large percentage of the population from the emerging mainstream economy. Those segments of the African American, American Indian, Hispanic American, and Asian American communities currently mired in the urban underclass will continue to compete with some of the newer immigrants for jobs in the low-wage, secondary labor market or in alternative opportunity structures, including crime.

The Importance of the Contact Situation, Group Competition, and Power

We have stressed the importance of the contact situation—the conditions under which the minority group and dominant group first come into contact with each other—throughout this text. Blauner's distinction between immigrant and colonized minority groups is fundamental, a distinction so basic that it helps to clarify minority group situations centuries after the initial contact period. In Part III, we used Blauner's distinction as an organizing principle and covered American minority groups in approximate order from "most colonized" to "most immigrant." The groups covered first (African Americans and American Indians) are clearly at a greater disadvantage in contemporary society than the groups covered last (especially immigrants from Asia with high levels of human capital) and the white ethnic groups covered in Chapter 2.

For example, prejudice, racism, and discrimination against African Americans remain formidable forces in contemporary America even though they may have softened into more subtle forms. In contrast, prejudice and discrimination against European American groups such as the Irish, Italians, and Polish Americans have nearly disappeared today even though they were quite formidable just a few generations ago. In the same way, contemporary immigrant groups that are nonwhite and bring few resources and low levels of human capital (e.g., Haitians) may experience segmented assimilation and find themselves in situations resembling those of colonized minority groups. Contemporary immigrant groups that are at the opposite end of the continuum (e.g., Asian Indians) are more likely to approximate the experiences of white ethnics and find themselves in some version of middle-class suburbia. See the Appendix (www.pineforge.com/healeyds3e) for further information on the relative standing of colonized and immigrant groups.

Noel's hypothesis states that if three conditions are present in the contact situation—ethnocentrism, competition, and the differential in power—ethnic or racial stratification will result. The relevance of ethnocentrism is largely limited to the actual contact situation, but the other two concepts help to clarify the changes occurring after initial contact.

We have examined numerous instances in which group competition—or even the threat of competition—increased prejudice and led to greater discrimination and more repression. Recall, for example, the opposition of the labor movement (dominated by European American ethnic groups) to Chinese immigrants. The anti-Chinese campaign led to the Chinese Exclusion Act of 1882, the first significant restriction on immigration to the United States. There are parallels between campaigns for exclusion in the past and current ideas about ending or curtailing immigration. Clearly, some part of the current opposition to immigration is motivated by a sense of threat and the fear that immigrants are a danger not only to jobs and to the economy but also to the cultural integrity of U.S. society.

Noel's third variable, the differential in power, determines the outcome of the initial contact situation and which group becomes dominant and which becomes minority. Following the initial contact, the superior power of the dominant group helps it sustain the inferior position of the minority group. Minority groups by definition have fewer power resources, but they characteristically use what they have in an attempt to improve their situation. The improvements in the situations of American minority groups since the middle of the 20th century have been due in large part to the fact that they (especially African Americans, who typically led the way in protest and demands for change) finally acquired some power resources of their own. For example, one important source of power for the civil rights movement in the South during the 1950s and 1960s was the growth of African American voting strength in the North. After World War II, the African American electorate became too sizable to ignore, and its political power helped pressure the federal government to take action and pass the legislation that ended the Jim Crow era.

Minority status being what it is, however, each of the groups we have discussed (with the exception of the white ethnic groups) still controls relatively few power resources and is limited in its ability to pursue its own self-interests. Many of these limitations are economic and related to social class; many minority groups simply lack the monetary resources to finance campaigns for reform or to exert significant pressure on the political institution. Other limitations include small group size (e.g., Asian American groups), language barriers (e.g., many Hispanic groups), and divided loyalties within the group (e.g., American Indians separated by tribal allegiances).

At any rate, the relative powerlessness of minority groups today is a legacy of the contact situations that created the groups in the first place. In general, colonized groups are at a greater power disadvantage than immigrant groups. Contact situations set agendas for group relations that have impacts centuries after the initial meeting.

Given all that we have examined in this text, it is obvious that competition and differences in power resources will continue to shape intergroup relations (including relations between minority groups themselves) well into the future. Because they are so basic and consequential, jobs will continue to be primary objects of competition, but there will be plenty of other issues to divide the nation. Included on this divisive list will be debates about crime and the criminal justice system, welfare policy, national healthcare policy, school integration, bilingual education, immigration policy, and multicultural curricula in schools.

These and other public issues will continue to separate us along ethnic and racial lines because those lines have become so deeply embedded in the economy, in politics, in our schools and neighborhoods, and in virtually every nook and cranny of U.S. society. These deep divisions reflect fundamental realities about who gets what in the United States, and they will continue to reflect the distribution of power and stimulate competition along group lines for generations to come.

Diversity Within Minority Groups

All too often, and this text is probably no exception, minority groups are seen as unitary and undifferentiated. Although overgeneralizations are sometimes difficult to avoid, the diversity within each of the groups that has been examined needs to be stressed. Minority group members vary from each other by age, sex, region of residence, levels of education, urban versus rural residence, political ideology, and many other variables. The experience of one segment of the group (college-educated, fourth-generation, native-born Chinese American females) may bear little resemblance to the experience of another (illegal Chinese male immigrants with less than a high school education), and the problems of some members may not be the problems of others.

This text has highlighted the importance of this diversity by exploring gender differentiation within each minority group. Study of minority groups by U.S. social scientists has focused predominantly on males, and the experiences of minority women have been described in much less depth. All the cultures examined in this text have strong patriarchal traditions. Women of the dominant group as well as minority women have had much less access to leadership roles and higher status positions and have generally occupied a subordinate status, even in their own groups. The experiences of minority group women and the extent of their differences from minority-group males and dominant-group women are only now being fully explored.

One clear conclusion we can make about gender is that minority group females are doubly oppressed and disempowered. Limited by both their minority and their gender roles, they are among the most vulnerable and exploited segments of the society. At one time or another, the women of every minority group have taken the least desirable, lowest-status positions available in the economy, often while trying to raise children and attend to other family needs. They have been expected to provide support for other members of their families, kinship groups, and communities, often sacrificing their own self-interests to the welfare of others. Jade Snow Wong (1993), a Chinese American daughter of immigrant parents, describes the subordinate role and circumscribed world of minority group females in a remembrance of her mother:

> My mother dutifully followed my father's leadership. She was extremely thrifty, but the thrifty need pennies to manage, and the old world had denied her those. Upon arrival in the new world of San Francisco, she accepted the elements her mate had selected to shape her new life: domestic duties, seamstress work in the factory-home, mothering each child in turn, church once a week, and occasional movies. (p. 50)

In their roles outside the family, minority women have encountered discrimination based on their minority group membership, compounded with discrimination based on their gender. The result is, predictably, an economic and social status at the bottom of the social structure. For example, average incomes of African American females today are lower than those of white males, white females, and black males (see Exhibit 5.4). The same pattern holds for other groups, and the women of many minority groups are highly concentrated in the low-paid secondary labor market and employed in jobs that provide services to members of more privileged groups.

The inequality confronted by minority women extends beyond matters of economics and jobs: Women of color have higher rates of infant mortality and births out of wedlock and a host of other health-related, quality-of-life problems. In short, there is ample evidence to document a pervasive pattern of gender inequality within America's minority groups. Much of this gender inequality is complexly interconnected with rising rates of poverty and female-headed households, teenage pregnancy, and unemployment for minority males in the inner city.

Gender differentiation cuts through minority groups in a variety of ways. Specific issues might unite minority women with women of the dominant group (e.g., sexual harassment in schools and the workplace), and others might unite them with the men of their minority groups (e.g., the enforcement of civil rights legislation). The problems and issues of minority women are complexly tied to the patterns of inequality and discrimination in the larger society and within their own groups. Solving the problems faced by minority groups will not resolve the problems faced by minority women and neither will resolving the problems of gender inequality alone. Women of color are embedded in structures of inequality and discrimination that limit them in two independent but simultaneous ways. Articulating and addressing these difficulties requires recognition of the complex interactions between gender and minority group status.

Assimilation and Pluralism

It seems fair to conclude that the diversity and complexity of minority group experiences in the United States are not well characterized by some of the traditional or "melting pot" views of assimilation. For example, the idea that assimilation is a linear, inevitable process has little support. Immigrants from Europe probably fit that model better than other groups, but as the ethnic revival of the 1960s demonstrated, assimilation and ethnic identity can take surprising turns.

Also without support is the notion that there is always a simple, ordered relationship between the various stages of assimilation: acculturation, integration into public institutions, integration into the private sector, and so forth. We have seen that some groups integrated before they acculturated, others have become *more* committed to their ethnic or racial identity over the generations, and still others have been acculturated for generations but are no closer to full integration. New expressions of ethnicity come and go, and minority groups emerge, combine, and recombine in unexpected and seemingly unpredictable ways. The 1960s saw a reassertion of ethnicity and loyalty to old identities among some groups, even as other groups developed new coalitions and invented new ethnic identities (for example, pantribalism among American Indians). No simple or linear view of assimilation can begin to make sense of the array of minority group experiences.

Indeed, the very desirability of assimilation has been subject to debate. Since the 1960s, many minority spokespersons have questioned the wisdom of becoming a part of a sociocultural structure that was constructed by the systematic exploitation of minority groups. Pluralistic themes increased in prominence as the commitment of the larger society to racial equality faltered. Virtually every minority group proclaimed the authenticity of its own experiences, its own culture, and its own version of history, separate from but as valid as that of the dominant groups. From what might have seemed like a nation on the verge of integration in the 1950s, America evolved into what might have seemed like a Tower of Babel in the 1960s. The consensus that assimilation was the best solution and the most sensible goal for all of America's minority groups was shattered (if it ever really existed at all).

Let's review the state of acculturation and integration in the United States on a group-by-group basis, following the order of the case studies in Part III. African

Americans are highly acculturated. Despite the many unique cultural traits forged in America and those that survive from Africa, black Americans share language, values and beliefs, and most other aspects of culture with white Americans of similar class and educational background. In terms of integration, in contrast, African Americans present a mixed picture. For middle-class, more educated members of the group, American society offers more opportunities for upward mobility and success than ever before. Without denying the prejudice, discrimination, and racism that remain, this segment of the group is in a favorable position to achieve higher levels of affluence and power for their children and grandchildren. At the same time, a large percentage of African Americans remain mired in urban poverty, and for them, affluence, security, and power are just as distant (perhaps more so) than they were a generation ago. Considering the group as a whole, African Americans are still highly segregated in their residential and school attendance patterns, and their political power, although rising, is not proportional to their size. Unemployment, lower average incomes, and poverty in general remain serious problems and may be more serious than they were a generation ago.

American Indians are less acculturated than African Americans, and there is evidence that American Indian culture and language may be increasing in strength and vitality. On measures of integration, there is some indication of improvement, but many American Indians are among the most isolated and impoverished minority groups in the United States. One possible bright spot for some reservations lies in the further development of the gambling industry and the investment of profits in the tribal infrastructure to upgrade schools, health clinics, job training centers, and so forth.

The largest Hispanic American groups also are generally less acculturated than African Americans. Hispanic traditions and the Spanish language have been sustained by the exclusion and isolation of these groups within the United States and have been continually renewed and revitalized by immigration. Cubans have moved closer to equality than Mexican Americans and Puerto Ricans but did so by resisting assimilation and building an ethnic enclave economy. Mexican Americans and Puerto Ricans share many of the problems of urban poverty that confront African Americans, and they are below national norms on measures of equality and integration.

The smaller Hispanic groups consist mostly of new immigrants who are just beginning the assimilation process. Many members of these groups, along with Mexican Americans and Puerto Ricans, are less educated and have few occupational skills, and they face the dangers of blending into a permanent urban underclass. Nonetheless, there is some evidence that these groups (or, more accurately, their descendants) may eventually find their way into the American mainstream (recall the debate over segmented assimilation in Chapter 9).

As with Hispanic Americans, the extent of assimilation among Asian Americans is highly variable. Some groups (for example, third- and fourth-generation Japanese Americans and Chinese Americans) have virtually completed the assimilation process and are remarkably successful; others (the more elite immigrants from India and the Philippines) seem to be finding a place in the American mainstream. Other Asian American groups consist largely of newer immigrants with occupational and educational profiles that resemble colonized minority groups, and these groups face the same dangers of permanent marginalization and exclusion. Still other Asian American groups (e.g., Korean Americans) have used their cohesiveness and solidarity to construct ethnic enclaves in which they have achieved relative economic equality by resisting acculturation.

Only European American ethnic groups, covered in Chapter 2, seem to approximate the traditional model of assimilation. The development even of these groups, however, has taken unexpected twists and turns, and the pluralism of the 1960s and 1970s suggests that ethnic traditions and ethnic identity, in some form, may withstand the pressures of assimilation for generations to come. Culturally and racially, these groups are the closest to the dominant group. If they still retain a sense of ethnicity, even if merely symbolic, after generations of acculturation and integration, what is the likelihood that the sense of group membership will fade in the racially stigmatized minority groups?

Assimilation is far from accomplished and, in this era of mass immigration, may be decreasing. The group divisions that remain are real and consequential; they cannot be willed away by pretending we are all "just American." Group membership continues to be important because it continues to be linked to fundamental patterns of exclusion and inequality. The realities of pluralism, inequality, and ethnic and racial identity continue to persist to the extent that the American promise of a truly open opportunity structure continues to fail. The group divisions forged in the past and perpetuated over the decades by racism and discrimination will remain to the extent that racial and ethnic group membership continues to be correlated with inequality and position in the social class structure.

Along with economic and political pressures, other forces help to sustain the pluralistic group divisions. Some argue that ethnicity is rooted in biology and can never be fully eradicated (see Van den Berghe, 1981). Although this may be an extreme position, there is little doubt that many people find their own ancestry to be a matter of great interest. Some (perhaps most) of the impetus behind the preservation of ethnic and racial identity may be a result of the most vicious and destructive intergroup competition. In other ways, though, ethnicity can be a positive force that helps people locate themselves in time and space and understand their position in the contemporary world. Ethnicity remains an important aspect of self-identity and pride for many Americans from every group and tradition. It seems unlikely that this sense of a personal link to particular groups and heritages within U.S. society will soon fade.

Can we survive as a pluralistic, culturally and linguistically fragmented, racially and ethnically unequal society? What will save us from balkanization and fractionalization? Given our history of colonization and racism, can U.S. society move closer to the relatively harmonious models of race relations found in societies such as Hawaii? As we deal with these questions, we need to remember that in and of itself, diversity is no more "bad" than unity is "good." Our society has grown to a position of global preeminence despite, or perhaps because of, our diversity. In fact, many have argued that our diversity is a fundamental and essential characteristic of U.S. society and a great strength to be cherished and encouraged. Sociologist Ronald Takaki (1993) ended his history of multicultural America *(A Different Mirror)* with an eloquent endorsement of our diversity and pluralism:

> As Americans, we originally came from many different shores and our diversity has been at the center of the making of America. While our stories contain the memories of different communities, together they inscribe a larger narrative. Filled with what Walt Whitman celebrated as the "varied carols" of America, our history generously gives all of us our "mystic chords of memory.
>
> Throughout our past of oppressions and struggles for equality, Americans of different races and ethnicities have been "singing with open mouths their strong melodious songs" in the textile mills of Lowell, the cotton fields of Mississippi, on the Indian reservations of South Dakota, the railroad tracks high in the Sierras of California, in the garment factories of the Lower East Side, the canefields of Hawaii, and a thousand other places across the country. Our denied history "bursts with telling." As we hear America singing, we find ourselves invited to bring our cultural diversity [into the open], to accept ourselves. (p. 428)

The question for our future might not be so much "Unity or diversity?" as "What blend of pluralistic and assimilationist policies will serve us best in the 21st century?" Are there ways in which the society can prosper without repressing our diversity? How can we increase the degree of openness, fairness, and justice without threatening group loyalties? The one-way, Anglo-conformity mode of assimilation of the past is too narrow and destructive to be a blueprint for the future, but the more extreme forms of minority group pluralism and separatism might be equally dangerous.

How much unity do we need? How much diversity can we tolerate? These are questions you must answer for yourself, and they are questions you will face in a thousand different ways over the course of your life. Let me illustrate by citing some pertinent issues: Is it desirable to separate college dormitories by racial or ethnic group? Is this destructive self-segregation or a positive strategy for group empowerment? Will such practices increase prejudice, or will they work like ethnic enclaves and strengthen minority group cohesion and solidarity and permit the groups to deal with the larger society from a stronger position? For the campus as a whole, what good could come from residential separation? In what ways would minority students benefit? Is there a "correct" balance between separation and unity in this situation? Who gets to define what the balance is?

How much attention should be devoted to minority group experiences in elementary and high school texts and curricula? Who should write and control these curricula? What should they say? How candid and critical should they be about America's often dismal past? How should such topics as slavery, genocide, and the racist exclusion of certain immigrant groups be presented in elementary school texts? In high school texts? Will educating children about the experiences of U.S. minority groups be an effective antidote to prejudice? Is it proper to use classrooms to build respect for the traditions of other groups and an appreciation of their experiences? If the realities of the experiences of minority groups are not addressed in school, what message will children hear? In the absence of minority-group voices, what's left? What are the limits of free speech with respect to minority relations? When does an ethnic joke become offensive? When are racial and ethnic epithets protected by the First Amendment? As long as lines of ethnicity and race divide the nation and as long as people feel passionately about these lines, the language of dominant-minority relationships will continue to have harsh, crude, and intentionally insulting components. Under what conditions, if any, should a civil society tolerate disparagement of other groups? Should the racial and ethnic epithets uttered by minority-group members be treated any differently from those of dominant-group members?

What should the national policy on immigration be? How many immigrants should be admitted each year? How should immigrants be screened? What qualifications should be demanded? Should immigration policy continue to favor the family and close relatives of citizens and permanent residents? What should be done about illegal immigrants? Should they be given the opportunity to legalize their status? Should illegal immigrants or their children receive health care and schooling? If so, who should pay for these services?

I do not pretend that the ideas presented in this text can fully resolve these issues or others that will arise in the future. As long as immigrants and minority groups are a part of the United States, as long as prejudice and discrimination persist, the debates will continue, and new issues will arise as old ones are resolved.

As U.S. society attempts to deal with new immigrants and unresolved minority grievances, we should recognize that it is not diversity per se that threatens stability but the realities of split labor markets, racial and ethnic stratification, urban poverty, and institutionalized discrimination. We need to focus on the issues that confront us with an honest recognition of the past and the economic, political, and social forces that have shaped us. As the United States continues to remake itself, an informed sense of where we have been will help us decide where we should go. Clearly, the simplistic, one-way, Anglo-conformity model of assimilation of the past does not provide a basis for dealing with these problems realistically and should not be the blueprint for the future of U.S. society.

Minority Group Progress and the Ideology of American Individualism

There is so much sadness, misery, and unfairness in the history of minority groups that evidence of progress sometimes goes unnoticed. Lest we be guilty of ignoring the good news in favor of the bad, let us note some ways in which the situations of American minority groups are better today than they were in the past. Evidence of progress is easy to find for some groups; we need look only to the relative economic, educational, and income equality of European American ethnic groups and some Asian American groups. The United States has become more tolerant and open, and minority-group members can be found at the highest levels of success, affluence, and prestige.

One of the most obvious changes is the decline of traditional racism and prejudice. The strong racial and ethnic sentiments and stereotypes of the past are no longer the primary vocabulary for discussing race relations among dominant-group members, at least not in public. Although the prejudices unquestionably still exist, Americans have become more circumspect and discreet in their public utterances.

The demise of blatant bigotry in polite company is, without doubt, a positive change. However, it seems that negative intergroup feelings and stereotypes have not so much disappeared as changed form. The old racist feelings are now being expressed in other guises, specifically in what has been called color-blind, modern, or symbolic racism: the view that holds that once Jim-Crow-type segregation ended in the 1960s, the opportunity channels and routes of upward mobility of American society were opened to all. This individualistic view of social mobility is consistent with the human capital perspective and the traditional, melting-pot view of assimilation. Taken together, these ideologies present a powerful and widely shared perspective on the nature of minority-group problems in modern American society. Proponents of these views tend to be unsympathetic to the plight of minorities and to programs such as school busing and affirmative action, which are intended to ameliorate these problems. The overt bigotry of the past has been replaced by blandness and indifference more difficult to define and harder to measure than "old-fashioned" racism, yet still unsympathetic to racial change.

This text has argued that the most serious problems facing contemporary minority groups, however, are structural and institutional, not individual or personal. For example, the paucity of jobs and high rates of unemployment in the inner cities are the result of economic and political forces beyond the control not only of the minority communities but also of local and state governments. The marginalization of the minority-group labor force is a reflection of the essence of modern American capitalism. The mainstream, higher paying, blue-collar jobs available to people with modest educational credentials are controlled by national and multinational corporations, which maximize profits by automating their production processes and moving the jobs that remain to areas, often outside the United States, with abundant supplies of cheaper labor.

We also have seen that some of the more effective strategies for pursuing equality require strong in-group cohesion and networks of cooperation, not heroic individual effort. Immigration to this country is (and always has been) a group process that involves extensive, long-lasting networks of communication and chains of population movement, usually built around family ties and larger kinship groups. Group networks continue to operate in America and assist individual immigrants with early adjustments and later opportunities for jobs and upward mobility. A variation on this theme is the ethnic enclave found among so many different groups.

Survival and success in America for all minority groups has had more to do with group processes than with individual will or motivation. The concerted, coordinated actions of the minority community provided support during hard times and, when possible, provided the means to climb higher in the social structure during good times. Far from being a hymn to individualism, the story of U.S. minority groups is profoundly sociological.

A Final Word

U.S. society and its minority groups are linked in fractious unity. They are part of the same structures but are separated by lines of color and culture and by long histories (and clear memories) of exploitation and unfairness. This society owes its prosperity and position of prominence in the world no less to the labor of minority groups than to that of the dominant group. By harnessing the labor and energy of these minority groups, the nation has grown prosperous and powerful, but the benefits have flowed disproportionately to the dominant group.

Since the middle of the 20th century, minority groups have demanded greater openness, fairness, equality, respect for their traditions, and justice. Increasingly, the demands have been made on the terms of the minority groups, not on those of the dominant group. Some of these demands have been met, at least verbally, and the society as a whole has rejected the oppressive racism of the past. Minority-group progress has stalled well short of equality, however, and the patterns of poverty, discrimination, marginality, hopelessness, and despair continue to limit the lives of millions.

As we begin the 21st century, the dilemmas of America's minority groups remain perhaps the primary unresolved domestic issue facing the nation. The answers of the past—the simple faith in assimilation and the belief that success in America is open to all who simply try hard enough—have proved inadequate, even destructive and dangerous, because they help to sustain the belief that the barriers to equality no longer exist and that any remaining inequalities are the problems of the minority groups, not the larger society.

These problems of equality and access will not solve themselves or simply fade away. They will continue to manifest themselves in myriad ways—through protest activities, rancorous debates, diffused rage, and pervasive violence. The solutions and policies that will carry us through these coming travails are not clear. Only by asking the proper questions, realistically and honestly, can we hope to find the answers that will help our society fulfill its promises to the millions who are currently excluded from achieving the American Dream.

The United States is one of many ethnically and racially diverse nations in the world today. As the globe continues to shrink and networks of communication, immigration, trade, and transportation continue to link all peoples into a single global entity, the problems of diversity will become more international in their scope and implications. Ties will grow between African Americans and the nations of Africa, agreements between the United States and the nations of Latin America will have direct impact on immigration patterns, Asian Americans will be affected by international developments on the Pacific Rim, and so forth. Domestic and international group relations will blend into a single reality. In many ways, the patterns of dominant-minority relations discussed in this text have already been reproduced on the global stage. The mostly white industrialized nations of the Northern Hemisphere have continuously exploited the labor and resources of the mostly nonwhite, undeveloped nations of the Southern Hemisphere. Thus, the tensions and resentments we have observed in U.S. society are mirrored in the global system of societies.

The United States is neither the most nor the least diverse country in the world. Likewise, our nation is neither the most nor the least successful in confronting the problems of prejudice, discrimination, and racism. However, the multigroup nature of our society, along with the present influx of immigrants from around the globe, does present an opportunity to improve on our record and to make a lasting contribution. A society that finds a way to deal fairly and humanely with the problems of diversity and difference, prejudice and inequality, and racism and discrimination can provide a sorely needed model for other nations and, indeed, for the world.

Glossary

Numbers in brackets refer to the chapter in which the term is introduced.

abolitionism [3] The movement to abolish slavery in the South.

acculturation [2] The process by which one group (generally a minority or immigrant group) learns the culture of another group (generally the dominant group).

affective prejudice [1] The emotional or "feeling" dimension of individual prejudice. The prejudiced individual attaches negative emotions to other groups.

affirmative action [4] Affirmative action programs are intended to counter the effects of institutional discrimination and the legacy of minority-group inequality.

Alien Land Act [8] Bill passed by the California legislature in 1913 that declared aliens who were ineligible for citizenship (effectively meaning only immigrants from Asia) were also ineligible to own land.

Americanization [2] The one-sided process of assimilation that occurred with many immigrant groups in the United States.

Anglo-conformity [2] The model of assimilation by which minority groups conform to Anglo-American culture.

anti-Semitism [2] Prejudice or ideological racism directed specifically at Jews.

apartheid [4] The policy of extreme racial segregation formerly followed in South Africa.

ascribed status [1] A position in society that is assigned to the individual, usually at birth. Examples of ascribed status include positions based on ethnicity, race, and gender.

assimilation [2] The process by which formerly distinct and separate groups merge and become one group.

Black Power movement [5] A coalition of African American groups that rose to prominence in the 1960s. Some central themes of the movement were black nationalism, autonomy for African American communities, and pride in race and African heritage.

black protest movements [5] *See* Black Power movement.

Blauner hypothesis [3] Minority groups created by colonization will experience more intense prejudice, racism, and discrimination than those created by immigration. The disadvantaged status of colonized groups will persist longer and be more difficult to overcome than the disadvantaged status faced by groups created by immigration.

bourgeoisie [1] Marxist term for the elite or ruling class in an industrial society that owns or controls the means of production.

Bureau of Indian Affairs (BIA) [6] The agency of the U.S. government that has primary responsibility for the administration of American Indian reservations.

capital intensive [4] Capital-intensive technology replaces hand labor with machine labor. Large amounts of capital are required to develop, purchase, and maintain the machines.

caste system [3] A closed system of stratification with no mobility between positions. A person's class at birth is permanent and unchangeable.

chattel [3] An item of personal property. In a system of chattel slavery, slaves were defined by law not as persons but as the personal property of their owners.

Chicanismo [7] A militant ideology of the Mexican American protest movement that appeared in the 1960s. The ideology took a critical view of U.S. society, made strong demands for justice and an end to racism, expressed a positive image for the group, and incorporated other pluralistic themes.

Chicanos [7] A group name for Mexican Americans. Associated with the ideology of Chicanismo, which emerged in the 1960s.

civil rights movement [5] The 1950s and 1960s effort to win the rights African Americans were entitled to under the U.S. Constitution.

cognitive prejudice [1] The "thinking" dimension of individual prejudice. The prejudiced individual thinks about other groups in terms of stereotypes.

colonized minority groups [3] Groups whose initial contact with the dominant group was through conquest or colonization.

color-blind racism [1] *See* modern racism.

competition [3] A situation in which two or more parties struggle for control of some scarce resource.

core group [1] *See* dominant group.

cultural assimilation [2] *See* acculturation.

cultural pluralism [2] A situation in which groups have not acculturated, and each maintains a distinct identity. *See also* pluralism.

culture [2] All aspects of the way of life associated with a group of people. Culture includes language, beliefs, norms, values, customs, technology, and many other components.

culture of poverty theory [5] A theory asserting that poverty causes certain personality traits—such as the need for instant gratification—which, in turn, perpetuate poverty.

de facto segregation [5] A system of racial separation and inequality that appears to result from voluntary choices about where to live, work, and so forth. Often, this form of segregation is really de jure segregation in thin disguise.

deindustrialization [4] The shift from a manufacturing economy to a service-oriented, information-processing economy.

de jure segregation [4] The system of rigid competitive race relations that followed Reconstruction in the South. The system lasted from the 1880s until the 1960s and was characterized by laws mandating racial separation and inequality.

differential in power [3] Any difference between two or more groups in their ability to achieve their goals.

discrimination [1] The unequal or unfair treatment of a person or persons based on their group membership.

dominant group [1] The group that benefits from and, typically, tries to sustain minority-group subordination.

enclave minority group [2] A group that establishes its own neighborhood and relies on a set of interconnected businesses for economic survival.

ethclass [2] The group formed by the intersection of one's religious, ethnic, and social class boundaries.

ethnic minority groups [1] Minority groups identified primarily by cultural characteristics, such as language or religion.

ethnic revival [2] The movement toward increased salience for ethnic identity, which began for European Americans in the 1960s.

ethnic succession [2] The process by which European ethnic groups affected each other's position in the social class structure.

ethnocentrism [3] Judging other groups, societies, or cultures by the standards of one's own culture.

extractive (primary) occupations [4] Jobs that involve the production of raw materials. Examples include farmer and miner.

fatalism [5] The view that one's fate is beyond one's control.

fluid competitive system [4] A system of group relations in which minority-group members are freer to compete for jobs and other scarce resources. Associated with advanced industrialization.

gender roles [1] Expectations about the proper behavior, attitudes, and personality traits for males and for females.

genocide [1] The deliberate attempt to exterminate an entire group of people.

huiguan [8] An association in Chines American society based on the region of China from which an individual or his or her family came. The huiguan performed a number of social, welfare, and business functions.

human capital theory [2] Consistent with the traditional view of assimilation, this theory considers success in the United States to be a direct result of individual efforts, personal values and skills, and education.

ideological racism [1] A belief system asserting that a particular group is inferior. Although individuals may subscribe to racist beliefs, the ideology itself is incorporated into the culture of the society and passed on from generation to generation.

immigrant minority groups [3] Groups whose initial contact with the dominant group was through immigration.

indentured servant [3] A contract laborer who is obligated to serve a particular master for a specified length of time.

intermarriage [2] *See* marital assimilation.

intersectionality [1] An approach to the study of group relations that stresses the interconnections between all forms of inequality, including class, race, ethnicity, gender, sexuality, and so forth. Especially associated with the work of sociologist Patricia Hill Collins.

Indian Reorganization Act (IRA) [6] Federal legislation passed in 1934 that was intended to give Native American tribes more autonomy.

industrial revolution [2] The shift in subsistence technology from labor-intensive agriculture to capital-intensive manufacturing.

institutional discrimination [1] A pattern of unequal treatment based on group membership that is built into the daily operations of society.

integration [2] The process by which a minority group enters the social structure of the dominant society.

Issei [8] First-generation immigrants from Japan.

Jim Crow system [4] *See* de jure segregation.

labor-intensive [2] A form of work in which the bulk of the effort is provided by human beings working by hand. Machines and other labor-saving devices are rare or absent.

level of development [1] The stage of evolution of society. The stages discussed in this text relate to agrarian and industrial subsistence technology.

machismo [7] A cultural value stressing male dominance, virility, and honor.

manufacturing (secondary) occupations [4] Occupations involving the transformation of raw materials into finished products ready for the marketplace. An example is an assembly line worker in an automobile plant.

Marielitos [7] Refugees from Cuba who arrived in the United States in 1980.

marital assimilation [2] Intermarriage between members of different groups.

means of production [1] A Marxist term that refers to the materials, tools, resources, and organizations by which the society produces and distributes goods and services.

melting pot [2] A type of assimilation in which all groups contribute in roughly equal amounts to the creation of a new culture and society.

mestizo [3] A person of mixed white and Native American ancestry.

middleman minority group [2] Group that relies on small businesses, dispersed throughout a community, for economic survival.

minority group [1] A group that experiences a pattern of disadvantage or inequality, has a visible identifying trait, and is a self-conscious social unit. Membership is usually determined at birth, and group members have a strong tendency to marry within the group.

miscegenation [1] Marriage between members of different racial groups.

model minority groups [8] A description often applied to Asian Americans. It exaggerates the relative affluence of these groups and is sometimes used as a rhetorical device for criticizing other minority groups, especially African Americans.

modern institutional discrimination [4] A more subtle and covert form of institutional discrimination that is often unintentional and unconscious.

modern racism [1] A form of prejudice that is more subtle and indirect compared to traditional, blatant prejudice. *See* also color-blind racism and symbolic racism.

mulatto [3] Person of mixed European and African descent.

multiculturalism [2] A general term for some contemporary versions of pluralism in the United States. Generally, multiculturalism stresses mutual respect for all groups and celebrates the multiplicity of heritages that have contributed to the development of the United States.

New Immigration [2] Immigration to the United States from Europe between the 1880s and the 1920s.

Nisei [8] Second-generation Japanese Americans.

Noel hypothesis [3] A theory about the creation of minority groups that asserts that if two or more groups come together in a contact situation characterized by ethnocentrism, competition, and a differential in power, some form of racial or ethnic stratification will result.

nonviolent direct action [5] An important tactic used during the civil rights movement in the South to defeat de jure segregation.

Old Immigration [2] Immigration from Europe to the United States between the 1820s and the 1880s.

Operation Wetback [7] A government program developed in the 1950s to deport illegal immigrants from Mexico.

past-in-present institutional discrimination [4] Patterns of inequality or unequal treatment in the present that are caused by some pattern of discrimination in the past.

paternalism [3] A form of dominant-minority relations often associated with plantation-based, labor-intensive, agrarian technology. In paternalistic relations, minority groups are extremely unequal and highly controlled. Rates of overt conflict are low.

patriarchy [1] Male dominance. In a patriarchal society, men have more power than women do.

plantation system [3] A labor-intensive form of agriculture that requires large tracts of land and a large, cheap labor force. This was a dominant form of agricultural production in the American South before the Civil War.

pluralism [2] A situation in which groups have separate identities, cultures, and organizational structures.

power [1] The ability to achieve goals, even in the face of opposition from others.

prejudice [1] The tendency of some individuals to think and feel negatively toward others, and to prejudge individuals on the basis of their group memberships.

prestige [1] The amount of honor or respect accorded a particular person or group.

primary labor market [4] The segment of the labor market that encompasses better-paying, higher-status, more-secure jobs. Usually in large bureaucracies.

primary occupations [4] *See* extractive (primary) occupations.

primary sector of the social structure [2] Relationships and groups that are intimate and personal. Groups in the primary sector are small.

principle of third-generation interest [2] The notion that the grandchildren of immigrants will stress their ethnicity much more than the second generation will.

proletariat [1] In Marxist theory, the workers in an industrial society.

pull [7] Factors that cause population movement out of an area. *See also* push.

push [7] Factors that cause population movement into an area. *See also* pull.

race [1] Biologically, an isolated, inbreeding population with a distinctive genetic heritage. Socially, the term is used loosely and reflects patterns of inequality and power.

racial identity [1] The part of self-image linked to racial group membership.

race relations cycle [2] A concept associated with Robert Park, who believed that relations between different groups would go through predictable cycles, from conflict to eventual assimilation.

racial minority groups [1] Minority groups identified primarily by physical characteristics such as skin color (e.g., Asian Americans).

racism [1] A belief system that asserts the inferiority of a group.

Reconstruction [4] The period of Southern race relations following the Civil War. Reconstruction lasted from 1865 until the 1880s and witnessed many racial reforms, all of which were reversed during de jure segregation, or the Jim Crow era.

relocation camps [8] The camps in which Japanese Americans were held during World War II.

repatriation [7] A government campaign begun during the Great Depression of the 1930s to deport illegal immigrants back to Mexico. The campaign also caused legal immigrants and native-born Mexican Americans to leave the United States.

revolution [2] A goal of some minority groups. A revolutionary group wishes to change places with the dominant group or create a new social order, perhaps in alliance with other groups.

rigid competitive group relations [4] A system of group relations in which the dominant group seeks to exclude minority groups or limit their ability to compete for scarce resources such as jobs.

Sansei [8] Third-generation Japanese Americans.

secondary labor market [4] The segment of the labor market that includes low-paying, low-skilled, insecure jobs.

secondary occupations [4] *See* manufacturing (secondary) occupations.

secondary sector of the social structure [2] Relationships and organizations that are public, task oriented, and impersonal. Organizations in the secondary sector can be large.

segmented assimilation [2] The idea that assimilation in the United States is now fragmented and can have a number of outcomes in addition to eventual entry into mainstream society.

separatism [2] A goal of some minority groups. A separatist group wishes to sever all ties with the dominant group.

service (tertiary) occupations [4] Jobs that involve providing services. Examples include retail clerk, janitor, and schoolteacher.

sharecropping [4] A system of farming often used in the South during de jure segregation. The sharecropper (often black), or tenant, worked the land, which was actually owned by someone else (usually white), in return for a share of the profits at harvest time. The landowner supplied a place to live and credit for food and clothing.

social class [1] A group of people who command similar amounts of valued goods and services, such as income, property, and education.

social construction [1] A perception shared by members of a society or group that reflects habitual routines or institutionalized social processes. A social construction (such as the concept of race or a stereotype of a group) becomes real to the people who share it.

social distance [1] The degree of intimacy to which a person is willing to admit members of other groups.

socialization [1] The process of physical, psychological, and social development by which a person learns his or her culture.

social mobility [1] Movement from one social class to another.

social structure [2] The networks of social relationships, groups, organizations, communities, and institutions that organize the work of a society and connect individuals to each other and to the larger society.

sojourners [2] Immigrants who intend to return to their country of origin.

stereotypes [1] Overgeneralizations that are applied to all members of a group.

stratification [1] The unequal distribution of valued goods and services (e.g., income, job opportunities, prestige and fame, education, health care) in society; the social class system.

structural assimilation [2] *See* integration.

structural mobility [2] Rising occupational and social-class standing that is the result of changes in the overall structure of the economy and labor market as opposed to individual efforts.

structural pluralism [2] A situation in which a group has acculturated but is not integrated.

subordinate group [1] *See* minority group.

subsistence technology [1] The means by which a society satisfies basic needs. An agrarian society relies on labor-intensive agriculture, whereas an industrial society relies on machines and inanimate fuel supplies.

symbolic ethnicity [2] A sense of ethnicity that is more superficial, voluntary, and changeable.

symbolic racism [1] *See* modern racism.

termination policy for Native Americans [6] A policy by which all special relationships between the federal government and American Indians would be abolished.

tertiary occupations [4] *See* service (tertiary) occupations.

tongs [8] Secret societies in Chinatowns that sometimes fought with other Chinese American groups over control of resources.

triple melting pot [2] The idea that structural assimilation for European immigrants took place within the context of the three major American religions.

urban underclass [5] The urban lower classes, consisting largely of African Americans and other minority groups of color, which have been more or less permanently barred from the mainstream economy and the primary labor market.

vicious cycle [1] A process in which a condition is assumed to be true, and forces are then set in motion to create and perpetuate that condition.

white racial identity [1] The part of the self-image that includes the perception that whites are at the top of a system of racial hierarchy.

Yonsei [8] Fourth-generation Japanese Americans.

References

ABC News. 2008, November 5. *Exit Polls: Storm of Voter Dissatisfaction Lifts Obama to Historic Win.* Retrieved March 12, 2009, from http://abcnews.go.com/print?id=6189129

Abrahamson, Harold. 1980. "Assimilation and Pluralism." In Stephan Thernstrom (Ed.), *Harvard Encyclopedia of American Ethnic Groups* (pp. 150–160). Cambridge, MA: Harvard University Press.

Acuna, Rodolfo. 1999. *Occupied America* (4th ed.). New York: Harper & Row.

Acuna, Rodolfo. 1988. *Occupied America* (3rd ed.). New York: Harper & Row.

Adarand Constructors Inc. v. Pena, 515 U.S. 200 (1995).

Agbayani-Siewert, Pauline, & Revilla, Linda. 1995. "Filipino Americans." In Pyong Gap Min (Ed.), *Asian Americans: Contemporary Issues and Trends.* Thousand Oaks, CA: Sage.

Aizenman, N. C. 2006. "Immigration Debate Wakes a 'Sleeping Latino Giant.'" *Washington Post,* April 6, p. A1.

Alba, Richard. 2004, November. "Language Assimilation Today: Bilingualism Persists More Than in the Past But English Still Dominates." *Working Paper 111,* The Center for Comparative Immigration Studies, University of California, San Diego. Retrieved May 29, 2009, from http://www.ccis-ucsd.org/PUBLICATIONS/wrkg111.pdf

Alba, Richard. 1995. "Assimilation's Quiet Tide." *The Public Interest,* 119:3–19.

Alba, Richard. 1990. *Ethnic Identity: The Transformation of White America.* New Haven, CT: Yale University Press.

Alba, Richard. 1985. *Italian Americans: Into the Twilight of Ethnicity.* Englewood Cliffs, NJ: Prentice Hall.

Alba, Richard, Logan, John, Lutz, Amy, & Stults, Brian. 2002. "Only English by the Third Generation? Loss and Preservation of the Mother Tongue Among the Grandchildren of Contemporary Immigrants." *Demography,* 39:467–484.

Alba, Richard, & Nee, Victor. 2003. *Remaking the American Mainstream: Assimilation and Contemporary Immigration.* Cambridge, MA: Harvard University Press.

Alba, Richard, & Nee, Victor. 1997. "Rethinking Assimilation Theory for a New Era of Immigration." *International Migration Review,* 31:826–875.

Aleiss, Angela. 2005. *Making the White Man's Indian: Native Americans and Hollywood Movies.* Westport, CT: Praeger.

Almquist, Elizabeth M. 1979. "Black Women and the Pursuit of Equality." In Jo Freeman (Ed.), *Women: A Feminist Perspective* (pp. 430–450). Palo Alto, CA: Mayfield.

Allport, Gordon. 1954. *The Nature of Prejudice.* Reading, MA: Addison-Wesley.

Alvarez, Rodolfo. 1973. "The Psycho-Historical and Socioeconomic Development of the Chicano Community in the United States." *Social Science Quarterly,* 53:920–942.

American Indian Higher Education Consortium. 2001. *Building Strong Communities: Tribal Colleges as Engaged Institutions.* Retrieved December 12, 2004, from http://www.ihep.com/Pubs/PDF/Communities.pdf

American Sociological Association. 2003. *The Importance of Collecting Data and Doing Social Scientific Research on Race.* Retrieved June 19, 2007, from http://www2.asanet.org/media/asa_race_statement.pdf

Amott, Teresa, & Matthaei, Julie. 1991. "I Am the Fire of Time: American Indian Women." In T. Amott & J. Matthaei (Eds.), *Race, Gender, and Work: A Multicultural History of Women in the United States* (pp. 31–62). Boston: South End Press.

Andersen, Margaret L. 1993. *Thinking About Women: Sociological Perspectives on Sex and Gender* (3rd ed.). New York: Macmillan.

Anti-Defamation League. 2000. *Anti-Semitism in the United States.* Retrieved July 12, 2002, from http://www.adl.org/backgrounders/Anti_Semitism_us.asp

Ashmore, Richard, & DelBoca, Frances. 1976. "Psychological Approaches to Understanding Group Conflict." In Phyllis Katz (Ed.), *Towards the Elimination of Racism* (pp. 73–123). New York: Pergamon.

Australian Bureau of Statistics. 2009. *Experimental Estimates of Aboriginal and Torres Strait Islander Australians, June 2006.* Retrieved June 24, 2009, from http://www.abs.gov.au/ausstats/abs@.nsf/Latestproducts/3238.0.55.001Main%20Features1Jun%202006?opendocument&tabname=Summary&prodno=3238.0.55.001&issue=Jun%202006&num=&view=

Australian Bureau of Statistics. 2002. *Australian Social Trends 2002: Population—National Summary Tables.* Retrieved from the World Wide Web on July 5, 2002, at http://www.abs.gov.au

Australian Human Rights and Equal Opportunity Commission. 1997. Bringing Them Home: Report of the National Inquiry Into the Separation of Aboriginal and Torres Strait Islander Children From Their Families. Retrieved July 5, 2002, from http://www.austlii.edu.au/au/special/rsjproject/rsjlibrary/hreoc/stolen/

Avery, Robert, & Rendall, Michael. 2002. "Lifetime Inheritances of Three Generations of Whites and Blacks." *American Journal of Sociology,* 107:1300–1346.

Bales, Kevin, & Soodalter, Ron. 2009. *The Slave Next Door: Human Trafficking and Slavery in America Today.* Berkeley: University of California Press.

Barnes, Robert. 2007, June 29. "Divided Court Limits Use of Race by School Districts." *Washington Post,* p. A1.

Barringer, Herbert, Takeuchi, David, & Levin, Michael. 1995. *Asians and Pacific Islanders in the United States.* New York: Russell Sage Foundation.

Bauer, Mary, 2008. *Close to Slavery: Guestworker Programs in the United States.* A report of the Southern Poverty Law Center. Retrieved June 2, 2009, from http://www.splcenter.org/pdf/static/SPLCguestworker.pdf

BBC. 2008. *Full Text: Apology to Aborigines.* Retrieved June 28, 2009, from http://news.bbc.co.uk/2/hi/asia-pacific/7242057.stm

Bean, Frank, & Stevens, Gillian. 2003. *America's Newcomers and the Dynamics of Diversity.* New York: Russell Sage Foundation.

Becerra, Rosina. 1988. "The Mexican American Family." In Charles H. Mindel, Robert W. Habenstein, & Roosevelt Wright (Eds.), *Ethnic Families in America: Patterns and Variations* (3rd ed., pp. 141–159). New York: Elsevier.

Bell, Daniel. 1973. *The Coming of Post-Industrial Society.* New York: Basic Books.

Bell, Derrick. 1992. *Race, Racism, and American Law* (3rd ed.). Boston: Little, Brown.

Benedict, Ruth. 1946. *The Chrysanthemum and the Sword: Patterns of Japanese Culture.* Boston: Houghton Mifflin.

Benjamin, Lois. 2005. *The Black Elite.* Lanham, MD: Rowman & Littlefield.

Bird, Elizabeth. 1999. "Gendered Construction of the American Indian in Popular Media." *Journal of Communication,* 49:60–83.

Biskupic, Joan. 1989. "House Approves Entitlement for Japanese-Americans." *Congressional Quarterly Weekly Report,* October 28, p. 2879.

Black-Gutman, D., & Hickson, F. 1996. "The Relationship Between Racial Attitudes and Social-Cognitive Development in Children: An Australian Study." *Developmental Psychology,* 32:448–457.

Blassingame, John W. 1972. *The Slave Community: Plantation Life in the Antebellum South.* New York: Oxford University Press.

Blau, Peter M., & Duncan, Otis Dudley. 1967. *The American Occupational Structure.* New York: Wiley.

Blauner, Robert. 1972. *Racial Oppression in America.* New York: Harper & Row.

Blessing, Patrick. 1980. "Irish." In Stephan Thernstrom (Ed.), *Harvard Encyclopedia of Ethnic Groups* (pp. 524–545). Cambridge, MA: Harvard University Press.

Blumer, Herbert. 1965. "Industrialization and Race Relations." In Guy Hunter (Ed.), *Industrialization and Race Relations: A Symposium* (pp. 200–253). London: Oxford University Press.

Bobo, Lawrence. 2001. "Racial Attitudes and Relations at the Close of the Twentieth Century." In Neil J. Smelser, William Julius Wilson, & Faith Mitchell (Eds.), *America Becoming: Racial Trends and Their Consequences* (Vol. 1, pp. 264–301). Washington, DC: National Academy Press.

Bobo, Lawrence. 1988. "Group Conflict, Prejudice, and the Paradox of Contemporary Racial Attitudes." In Phyllis Katz & Dalmar Taylor (Eds.), *Eliminating Racism: Profiles in Controversy* (pp. 85–114). New York: Plenum.

Bodnar, John. 1985. *The Transplanted.* Bloomington: Indiana University Press.

Bogardus, Emory. 1933. "A Social Distance Scale." *Sociology and Social Research,* 17:265–271.

Bonacich, Edna, & Modell, John. 1980. *The Economic Basis of Ethnic Solidarity: Small Business in the Japanese American Community.* Berkeley: University of California Press.

Bonilla-Silva, Eduardo. 2006. *Racism Without Racists.* New York: Rowman & Littlefield.

Bonilla-Silva, Eduardo. 2001. *White Supremacy and Racism in the Post-Civil Rights Era.* Boulder, CO: Lynne Rienner.

Booth, Alan, Granger, Douglas A., Mazur, Allan, & Kivlighan, Katie T. (2006). "Testosterone and Social Behavior." *Social Forces,* 85(1):167–192.

Bordewich, Fergus. 1996. *Killing the White Man's Indian.* New York: Doubleday.

Boswell, Terry. 1986. "A Split Labor Market Analysis of Discrimination Against Chinese Immigrants, 1850–1882." *American Sociological Review,* 51:352–371.

Bouvier, Leon F., & Gardner, Robert W. 1986. "Immigration to the U.S.: The Unfinished Story." *Population Bulletin* (Vol. 41, No. 4). Washington, DC: Population Reference Bureau.

Brace, Matthew, 2001. "A Nation Divided." *Geographical, 73:* 14–20.

Brittingham, Angela, & de la Cruz, C. Patricia. 2004. *Ancestry: 2000.* Retrieved June 29, 2007, from http://www.census.gov/prod/2004pubs/c2kbr-35.pdf.

Brodkin, Karen. 1999. *How Jews Became White Folks and What That Says About Race in America.* Piscataway, NJ: Rutgers University Press.

Brody, David. 1980. "Labor." In Stephan Thernstrom (Ed.), *Harvard Encyclopedia of Ethnic Groups* (pp. 609–618). Cambridge, MA: Harvard University Press.

Brown, Dee. 1970. *Bury My Heart at Wounded Knee.* New York: Holt, Rinehart & Winston.

Brown, Rupert. 1995. *Prejudice: Its Social Psychology.* Cambridge, MA: Blackwell.

Brown v. Board of Education of Topeka, 247 U.S. 483 (1954).

Brunsma, David. 2005. "Interracial Families and the Racial Identification of Mixed-Race Children: Evidence From the Early Childhood Longitudinal Study." *Social Forces,* 84:1131–1157.

Buraku Liberation and Human Rights Research Institute. 2001. *Discrimination Against Buraku People.* Retrieved July 10, 2002, from http://www.blhrri.org/ index_e.htm

Buriel, Raymond. 1993. "Acculturation, Respect for Cultural Differences, and Biculturalism Among Three Generations of Mexican American and Euro-American School Children." *Journal of Genetic Psychology,* 154:531–544.

Camarillo, Albert, & Bonilla, Frank. 2001. "Hispanics in a Multicultural Society: A New American Dilemma?" In Neil J. Smelser, William Julius Wilson, & Faith Mitchell (Eds.), *America Becoming: Racial Trends and Their Consequences* (Vol. 2, pp. 103–134). Washington, DC: National Academy Press.

Camarota, Steven. 2002. *Immigrants in the United States–2002.* Retrieved February 15, 2005, from http://www.cis.org/articles/2002/back1302.html

Campo-Flores, Arian. 2006. "America's Divide." *Newsweek* (International ed.), April 17, pp. 36–42.

Cancio, S., Evans, T., & Maume, D. 1996. "Reconsidering the Declining Significance of Race: Racial Differences in Early Career Wages." *American Sociological Review,* 61:541–556.

Central Intelligence Agency. 2004. *The World Factbook 2005.* Retrieved September 29, 2004, from http://www.cia.gov/cia/publications/factbook/

Central Statistics Office, Ireland. 2008. *Population and Migration Estimates, April 2008.* Retrieved August 31, 2009, from http://www.cso.ie/releasespublications/documents/population/current/popmig.pdf

Chan, Sucheng. 1990. "European and Asian Immigrants into the United States in Comparative Perspective, 1820s to 1920s." In Virginia Yans-McLaughlin (Ed.), *Immigration Reconsidered: History, Sociology, and Politics* (pp. 37–75). New York: Oxford University Press.

Chao, Margaret. 2000. "Cultural Explanations for the Role of Parenting in the School Success of Asian-American Children." In Taylor, Ronald & Wang, Margaret (Eds.), *Resilience Across Contexts: Family, Work, Culture and Community* (pp. 102–127). Mahwah, NJ: Lawrence Erlbaum Associates.

Charles, Camille Z. 2003. "The Dynamics of Racial Residential Segregation." *Annual Review of Sociology,* 29:167–207.

Chirot, Daniel. 1994. *How Societies Change.* Thousand Oaks, CA: Pine Forge.

Cho, Sumi. 1993. "Korean Americans vs. African Americans: Conflict and Construction." In Robert Gooding-Williams (Ed.), *Reading Rodney King, Reading Urban Uprising* (pp. 196–211). New York: Routledge and Kegan Paul.

Churchill, Ward. 1997. *A Little Matter of Genocide: Holocaust and Denial in the Americas, 1492 to the Present.* San Francisco: City Light Books.

Churchill, Ward. 1985. "Resisting Relocation: Dine and Hopis Fight to Keep Their Land." *Dollars and Sense,* December, pp. 112–115.

Civil Rights Act of 1964, Pub. L. 88–352 § 42 U.S.C. 2000 (1964).

Cohen, Adam, & Taylor, Elizabeth. 2000. *American Pharaoh: Mayor Richard J. Daley: His Battle for Chicago and the Nation.* New York: Little, Brown.

Cohen, Steven M. 1985. *The 1984 National Survey of American Jews: Political and Social Outlooks.* New York: American Jewish Committee.

Collins, Patricia Hill. 1991. *Black Feminist Thought.* New York: Routledge.

Conot, Robert. 1967. *Rivers of Blood, Years of Darkness.* New York: Bantam.

Conzen, Kathleen N. 1980. "Germans." In Stephan Thernstrom (Ed.), *Harvard Encyclopedia of Ethnic Groups* (pp. 405–425). Cambridge, MA: Harvard University Press.

Cornell, Stephen. 2006. *What Makes First Nation Enterprises Successful? Lessons from the Harvard Project.* Tucson, AZ: Native American Institute for Leadership, Management, and Policy.

Cornell, Stephen. 1990. "Land, Labor, and Group Formation: Blacks and Indians in the United States." *Ethnic and Racial Studies,* 13:368–388.

Cornell, Stephen. 1988. *The Return of the Native: American Indian Political Resurgence.* New York: Oxford University Press.

Cornell, Stephen. 1987. "American Indians, American Dreams, and the Meaning of Success." *American Indian Culture and Research Journal,* 11:59–71.

Cornell, Stephen, & Kalt, Joseph. 2000. "Where's the Glue? Institutional and Cultural Foundations of American Indian Economic Development." *Journal of Socio-Economics,* 29:443–470.

Cornell, Stephen, Kalt, Joseph, Krepps, Matthew, & Taylor, Johnathan. 1998. *American Indian Gaming Policy and Its Socio-economic Effects: A Report to the National Impact Gambling Study Commission.* Cambridge, MA: Economics Resource Group.

Cortes, Carlos. 1980. "Mexicans." In Stephan Thernstrom (Ed.), *Harvard Encyclopedia of Ethnic Groups* (pp. 697–719). Cambridge, MA: Harvard University Press.

Cose, Ellis. 1993. *The Rage of a Privileged Class.* New York: HarperCollins.

Curtin, Philip. 1990. *The Rise and Fall of the Plantation Complex.* New York: Cambridge University Press.

D'Angelo, Raymond. 2001. *The American Civil Rights Movement: Readings and Interpretations.* New York: McGraw-Hill.

Daniel, G. Reginald. 2006. *Race and Multiraciality in Brazil and the United States: Converging Paths?* University Park: Penn State University Press.

Daniels, Roger. 1990. *Coming to America.* New York: HarperCollins.

Debo, Angie. 1970. *A History of the Indians of the United States.* Norman: University of Oklahoma Press.

Degler, Carl. 1971. *Neither Black nor White: Slavery and Race Relations in Brazil and the United States.* New York: Macmillan.

de la Garza, Rodolfo O., DeSipio, Louis, García, F. Chris, García, John, & Falcon, Angelo. 1992. *Latino Voices: Mexican, Puerto Rican, and Cuban Perspectives on American Politics.* Boulder, CO: Westview.

de la Garza, Rodolfo, Falcon, Angelo, & García, F. Chris. 1996. "Will the Real Americans Please Stand Up: Anglo and Mexican-American Support of Core American Political Values." *American Journal of Political Science,* 40:335–351.

Deloria, Vine. 1995. *Red Earth, White Lies.* New York: Scribners.

Deloria, Vine. 1970. *We Talk, You Listen.* New York: Macmillan.

Deloria, Vine. 1969. *Custer Died for Your Sins.* New York: Macmillan.

Del Pinal, Jorge, & Singer, Audrey. 1997. "Generations of Diversity: Latinos in the United States." *Population Bulletin* (Vol. 52, No. 3). Washington, DC: Population Reference Bureau.

Department of Homeland Security. 2009. *Yearbook of Immigration Statistics, 2008.* Retrieved July 29, 2009, from http://www.dhs.gov/files/statistics/publications/YrBk08NI.shtm

Dinnerstein, Leonard. 1977. "The East European Jewish Immigration." In Leonard Dinnerstein & Frederic C. Jaher (Eds.), *Uncertain Americans* (pp. 216–231). New York: Oxford University Press.

"Dominicans Saved From Sea Tell of Attacks and Deaths of Thirst." *New York Times,* August 12, 2004, p. A13.

D'Orso, Michael. 1996. *Like Judgment Day: The Ruin and Redemption of a Town Called Rosewood.* New York: Putnam.

Doyle, Anna Beth, & Aboud, Frances E. 1995. "A Longitudinal Study of White Children's Racial Prejudice as a Socio-Cognitive Development." *Merrill-Palmer Quarterly,* 41:209–228.

Du Bois, W. E. B. 1961. *The Souls of Black Folk.* Greenwich, CT: Fawcett.

Duleep, Harriet O. 1988. *Economic Status of Americans of Asian Descent.* Washington, DC: U.S. Commission on Civil Rights.

Dyer, Richard. 2002. "The Matter of Whiteness." In Paula Rothenberg (Ed.), *White Privilege* (pp. 9–12). New York: Worth Publishers.

Eichenwald, Kurt. 1996, November 16. "Texaco to Make Record Payment in Bias Lawsuit." *The New York Times,* p. 1

Elkins, Stanley. 1959. *Slavery: A Problem in American Institutional and Intellectual Life.* New York: Universal Library.

Ellsworth, Scott. 1982. *Death in a Promised Land: The Tulsa Race Riot of 1921.* Baton Rouge: Louisiana State University Press.

Epstein, Ethan. 2006. "The New Global Slave Trade." *Foreign Affairs,* 85:104.

Espinosa, Kristin, & Massey, Douglas. 1997. "Determinants of English Proficiency Among Mexican Migrants to the United States." *International Migration Review,* 31:28–51.

Evans, Sara M. 1989. *Born for Liberty: A History of Women in America.* New York: Free Press.

Evans, Sara M. 1979. *Personal Politics.* New York: Knopf.

Espiritu, Yen. 1997. *Asian American Women and Men.* Thousand Oaks, CA: Sage.

Espiritu, Yen. 1996. "Colonial Oppression, Labour Importation, and Group Formation: Filipinos in the United States." *Ethnic and Racial Studies,* 19:29–49.

Essien-Udom, E. U. 1962. *Black Nationalism.* Chicago: University of Chicago Press.

"Europe: The Integration Dilemma: Minorities in Germany." 2007. *The Economist,* July 19, p. 39.

Evans, William, & Topoleski, Julie. 2002. *The Social and Economic Impact of Native American Casinos.* Retrieved December 5, 2004, from http://www.bsos.umd.edu/econ/evans/wpapers/evans_topoleski_casinos.pdf

Fanning, Bryan. 2003. *Racism and Social Change in the Republic of Ireland.* Manchester, UK: Manchester University Press.

Farley, John. 2000. *Majority–Minority Relations* (4th ed.). Englewood Cliffs, NJ: Prentice Hall.

Farley, Reynolds. 1996. *The New American Reality.* New York: Russell Sage Foundation.

Faux, Jeff. 2004. "NAFTA at 10: Where Do We Go From Here?" *The Nation,* February 2, pp. 11–14.

Feagin, Joe. 2001. *Racist America: Roots, Current Realities, and Future Reparations.* New York: Routledge.

Feagin, Joe, & Feagin, Clairece Booher. 1986. *Discrimination American Style: Institutional Racism and Sexism.* Malabar, FL: Robert E. Krieger.

Feagin, Joe, & O'Brien, Eileen. 2004. *White Men on Race: Power, Privilege, and the Shaping of Cultural Consciousness.* Boston: Beacon Press.

Feagin, Joe, & Wingfield, Adia. 2009. *Yes We Can? White Racial Framing and the 2008 Presidential Campaign.* New York: Routledge.

Fernandez-Kelly, Patricia, & Portes, Alejandro. (Eds.). 2008. "Exceptional Outcomes: Achievement in Education and Employment among Children of Immigrants." *The Annals of the American Academy of Political and Social Science,* 620:312–324.

Fears, Darryl. 2007, November 24. "Hate Crime Reporting Uneven." *The Washington Post,* p. A43.

Federal Bureau of Investigation. 2009. *Hate Crime Statistics.* Retrieved September 9, 2009, from http://www.fbi.gov/ucr/hc2007/incidents.htm

Fernandez-Kelly, M. Patricia, & Portes, Alejandro. (Eds.). 2008. "Exceptional Outcomes: Achievement in Education and Employment among Children of Immigrants." *The Annals of the American Academy of Political and Social Science,* 620:312–324.

Fernandez-Kelly, M. Patricia, & Schauffler, Richard. 1994. "Divided Fates: Immigrant Children in a Restructured U.S. Economy." *International Immigration Review,* 28:662–689.

Firefighters Local Union No. 1784 v. Stotts, 467 U.S. 561 (1984).

Fitzpatrick, Joseph P. 1987. *Puerto Rican Americans: The Meaning of Migration to the Mainland* (2nd ed.). Englewood Cliffs, NJ: Prentice Hall.

Fitzpatrick, Joseph P. 1980. "Puerto Ricans." In Stephan Thernstrom (Ed.), *Harvard Encyclopedia of Ethnic Groups* (pp. 858–867). Cambridge, MA: Harvard University Press.

Fitzpatrick, Joseph P. 1976. "The Puerto Rican Family." In Charles H. Mindel & Robert W. Habenstein (Eds.), *Ethnic Families in America* (pp. 173–195). New York: Elsevier.

Fong, Eric, & Markham, William. 1991. "Immigration, Ethnicity, and Conflict: The California Chinese, 1849–1882." *Sociological Inquiry,* 61:471–490.

Fong, Eric, & Wilkes, Rima. 1999. "The Spatial Assimilation Model Reexamined: An Assessment by Canadian Data." *International Migration Review,* 33:594–615.

Fong, Timothy. 2002. *The Contemporary Asian American Experience* (2nd ed.). Upper Saddle River, NJ: Prentice Hall.

Forner, Philip S. 1980. *Women and the American Labor Movement: From World War I to the Present.* New York: Free Press.

Franklin, John Hope. 1967. *From Slavery to Freedom* (3rd ed.). New York: Knopf.

Franklin, John Hope, & Moss, Alfred. 1994. *From Slavery to Freedom* (7th ed.). New York: McGraw-Hill.

Frazier, E. Franklin. 1957. *Black Bourgeoisie: The Rise of a New Middle Class.* New York: Free Press.

Fry, Richard. (2007). *The Changing Racial and Ethnic Composition of U.S. Public Schools.* Pew Hispanic Center report. Retrieved June 11, 2009, from http://pewhispanic.org/files/reports/79.pdf

Gabe, Thomas, Falk, Gene, & McCarthy, Maggie. 2005. *Hurricane Katrina: Social-Demographic Characteristics of Impacted Areas.* Congressional Research Service, U.S. Congress. Retrieved June 21, 2007, from http://www.gnocdc.org/reports/crsrept.pdf.

Gallagher, Charles. 2001. "Playing the Ethnic Card: How Ethnic Narratives Maintain Racial Privilege." Paper presented at the Annual Meetings of the Southern Sociological Society, April 4–7, Atlanta, GA.

Gallup Organization. 2007. "Americans Overwhelmingly Favor Interracial Dating." Retrieved December 5, 2007, from http://www.amren.com/mtnews/archives/2005/10/gallup_american.php.

Gans, Herbert. 1979. "Symbolic Ethnicity: The Future of Ethnic Groups and Cultures in America." *Ethnic and Racial Studies,* 2:1–20.

Garcia, Maria Cristina. 1996. *Havana USA: Cuban Exiles and Cuban Americans in South Florida, 1959–1994.* Berkeley: University of California Press.

Garvey, Marcus. 1977. *Philosophy and Opinions of Marcus Garvey* (Vol. 3). Amy Jacques Garvey & E. U. Essien-Udom (Eds.). London: Frank Cass.

Garvey, Marcus. 1969. *Philosophy and Opinions of Marcus Garvey* (Vols. 1–2). Amy Jacques Garvey (Ed.). New York: Atheneum.

Genovese, Eugene D. 1974. *Roll, Jordan, Roll: The World the Slaves Made.* New York: Pantheon.

Gerstenfeld, Phyllis. 2004. *Hate Crime: Causes, Controls, and Controversies.* Thousand Oaks, CA: Sage Publications.

Gerth, Hans, & Mills, C. Wright (Eds.). 1946. *From Max Weber: Essays in Sociology.* New York: Oxford University Press.

Geschwender, James A. 1978. *Racial Stratification in America.* Dubuque, IA: William C. Brown.

Glaeser, Edward, & Vigdor, Jacob. 2001. *Racial Segregation in the 2000 Census: Promising News.* Washington, DC: Brookings Institution.

Glazer, Nathan, & Moynihan, Daniel. 1970. *Beyond the Melting Pot* (2nd ed.). Cambridge: MIT Press.

Gleason, Philip. 1980. "American Identity and Americanization." In Stephan Thernstrom (Ed.), *Harvard Encyclopedia of Ethnic Groups* (pp. 31–57). Cambridge, MA: Harvard University Press.

Godstein, Amy, & Suro, Robert. 2000. "A Journey on Stages: Assimilation's Pull Is Still Strong But Its Pace Varies." *Washington Post*, January 16, A1.

Golash-Boza, Tanya. 2005 "Assessing the Advantages of Bilingualism for the Children of Immigrants." *The International Migration Review*, 39:721–753.

Goldberg, Steven. 1999. "The Logic of Patriarchy." *Gender Issues*, 17:53–62.

Gooding-Williams, Robert. 1993. *Reading Rodney King, Reading Urban Uprising*. New York: Routledge and Kegan Paul.

Gordon, M. 1964. *Assimilation in American Life*. New York: Oxford University Press.

Goren, Arthur. 1980. "Jews." In Stephan Thernstrom (Ed.), *Harvard Encyclopedia of Ethnic Groups* (pp. 571–598). Cambridge, MA: Harvard University Press.

Gounari, Panayota. 2006. "How to Tame a Wild Tongue: Language Rights in the United States." *Human Architecture*, 4:71–79.

Gourevitch, Philip. 1999. *We Wish to Inform You That Tomorrow We Will Be Killed With Our Families: Stories From Rwanda*. New York: Picador.

Gratz v. Bollinger, 539 U.S. 244 (2003).

Grebler, Leo, Moore, Joan W., & Guzman, Ralph C. 1970. *The Mexican American People*. New York: Free Press.

Greeley, Andrew M. 1974. *Ethnicity in the United States: A Preliminary Reconnaissance*. New York: Wiley.

Green, Donald. 1999. "Native Americans." In Antony Dworkin & Rosalind Dworkin (Eds.), *The Minority Report* (pp. 255–277). Orlando, FL: Harcourt-Brace.

Grutter v. Bollinger, 539 U.S. 306 (2003).

Gutman, Herbert G. 1976. *The Black Family in Slavery and Freedom, 1750–1925*. New York: Vintage.

Hacker, Andrew. 1992. *Two Nations: Black and White, Separate, Hostile, Unequal*. New York: Scribner.

Hakimzadeh, Shirin, & Cohn, D'Vera. 2007. *English Language Usage Among Hispanics in the United States*. Retrieved July 2, 2009, from http://pewhispanic.org/files/reports/82.pdf

Haley, Alex. 1976. *Roots: The Saga of an American Family*. New York: Doubleday.

Hamer, Fannie Lou. 1967. *To Praise Our Bridges: An Autobiography of Fannie Lou Hamer*. Jackson, MI: KIPCO.

Handlin, Oscar. 1951. *The Uprooted*. New York: Grosset & Dunlap.

Hansen, Marcus Lee. 1952. "The Third Generation in America." *Commentary*, 14:493–500.

Hanson, Jeffery, & Rouse, Linda. 1987. "Dimensions of Native American Stereotyping." *American Indian Culture and Research Journal*, 11:33–58.

Harjo, Suzan. 1996. "Now and Then: Native Peoples in the United States." *Dissent*, 43:58–60.

Harris, John F. 2004. "Bush's Hispanic Vote Dissected." *Washington Post*, December 26, 2004, p. A06.

Harris, Marvin. 1988. *Culture, People, Nature*. New York: Harper & Row.

The Harvard Project on American Indian Economic Development. 2008. *The State of the Native Nations*. New York: Oxford University Press.

Hawkins, Hugh. 1962. *Booker T. Washington and His Critics: The Problem of Negro Leadership*. Boston: D. C. Heath.

Heaton, Tim, Chadwick, Bruce, & Jacobson, Cardell. 2000. *Statistical Handbook on Racial Groups in the United States*. Phoenix, AZ: Oryx.

Heer, David M. 1996. *Immigration in America's Future*. Boulder, CO: Westview.

Herberg, Will. 1960. *Protestant-Catholic-Jew: An Essay in American Religious Sociology*. New York: Anchor.

Higham, John. 1963. *Strangers in the Land: Patterns of American Nativism, 1860–1925*. New York: Atheneum.

Hirschman, Charles. 1983. "America's Melting Pot Reconsidered." *Annual Review of Sociology,* 9:397–423.

Hirschman, Charles, & Wong, Morrison. 1986. "The Extraordinary Educational Attainment of Asian Americans: A Search for Historical Evidence and Explanations." *Social Forces,* 65:1–27.

Hirschman, Charles, & Wong, Morrison. 1984. "Socioeconomic Gains of Asian Americans, Blacks, and Hispanics: 1960–1976." *American Journal of Sociology,* 90:584–607.

Hoefer, Michael, Rytina, Nancy, & Baker, Bryan. 2008. *Estimates of the Unauthorized Immigrant Population Residing in the United States: January 2008.* Retrieved June 30, 2009, from http://www.dhs.gov/xlibrary/assets/statistics/publications/ois_ill_pe_2008.pdf

Holthouse, David. 2009, Spring. "The Year in Hate." *Intelligence Report of the Southern Poverty Law Center.* Retrieved June 4, 2009, from http://www.splcenter.org/intel/intelreport/article.jsp?aid=1027

Hostetler, John. 1980. *Amish Society.* Baltimore, MD: Johns Hopkins University Press.

"How to Tell Your Friends From the Japs." 1941. *Time,* October–December, p. 33.

Hoxie, Frederick. 1984. *A Final Promise: The Campaign to Assimilate the Indian, 1880–1920.* Lincoln: University of Nebraska Press.

Hraba, Joseph. 1979. *American Ethnicity.* Itasca, IL: F. E. Peacock.

Hughes, Michael, & Thomas, Melvin. 1998. "The Continuing Significance of Race Revisited: A Study of Race, Class and Quality of Life in America, 1972 to 1996." *American Sociological Review,* 63:785–803.

Huntington, Samuel. 2004. *Who Are We: The Challenges to America's National Identity.* New York: Simon & Schuster.

Hurh, Won Moo. 1998. *The Korean Americans.* Westport, CT: Greenwood.

Hyman, Herbert, & Sheatsley, Paul. 1964. "Attitudes Toward Desegregation." *Scientific American,* 211:16–23.

Ibish, Hussein (Ed.). 2003. "Report on Hate Crimes and Discrimination Against Arab Americans: The Post September 11 Backlash." Retrieved February 14, 2005, from http://www.adc.org/hatecrimes/pdf/2003_report_web.pdf

Iceland, John, Weinberg, Donald, & Steinmetz, Erika. 2002. *Racial and Ethnic Residential Segregation in the United States: 1980–2000.* U.S. Census Bureau, Series CENSR-3. Washington, DC: U.S. Government Printing Office. Retrieved August 17, 2006, from http://www.census.gov/prod/2002pubs/censr-3.pdf.

Ifill, Gwen. 2009. *The Breakthrough.* New York: Doubleday.

Instituto Brasileiro do Geografica e Estatica. 1999. *Distribution of the Resident Population, by Major Regions, Urban or Rural Situation, Sex, Skin Color or Race.* Retrieved on July 17, 2002, from http://www.ibge.gov.br/english/estatistica/populacao/trabalhoerendimento/pnad99/sintese/tab1_2_b_1999.shtm

Ivey, Steve. 2005, September 22. "White House Blind to Poverty in U.S." *Chicago Tribune,* p. 1.

Jackson, Beverly. 2000. *Splendid Slippers: A Thousand Years of an Erotic Tradition.* Berkeley, CA: Ten Speed.

Jibou, Robert M. 1988. "Ethnic Hegemony and the Japanese of California." *American Sociological Review,* 53:353–367.

Joe, Jennie, & Miller, Dorothy. 1994. "Cultural Survival and Contemporary American Indian Women in the City." In Maxine Zinn & Bonnie T. Dill (Eds.), *Women of Color in U.S. Society.* Philadelphia: Temple University Press.

Jones, Jeffrey. 2008. "Majority of Americans Say Racism Against Blacks Widespread." Retrieved May 20, 2009, from http://www.gallup.com/poll/109258/Majority-Americans-Say-Racism-Against-Blacks-Widespread.aspx.

Jones, Jeffrey. 2006. *Whites, Blacks, Hispanics Disagree About Way Minority Groups Treated.* Retrieved from http://www.galluppoll.com/content/?ci=23629&pg=1

Jones, Jeffrey. 2005. "Confidence in Local Police Drops to 10-Year Low." Gallup News Service. Retrieved June 11, 2009, from http://www.gallup.com/poll/19783/Confidence-Local-Police-Drops-10Year-Low.aspx

Jones, Jeffrey. 2001. "Racial or Ethnic Labels Make Little Difference to Blacks, Hispanics." Retrieved July 5, 2002, from http://www.gallup.com/poll/releases/pr010911.asp

Jordan, Winthrop. 1968. *White Over Black: American Attitudes Towards the Negro: 1550–1812.* Chapel Hill: University of North Carolina Press.

Josephy, Alvin M. 1968. *The Indian Heritage of America.* New York: Knopf.

Kallen, Horace M. 1915a. "Democracy Versus the Melting Pot, Part I" *The Nation,* February 18, pp. 190–194.

Kallen, Horace M. 1915b. "Democracy Versus the Melting Pot, Part II." *The Nation,* February 25, pp. 217–222.

Karabell, Zachary. 2009, April 20. "We Are Not in This Together." *Newsweek.* Retrieved June 7, 2009, from http://www.newsweek.com/id/193585/output/print.

Kasarda, John D. 1989. "Urban Industrial Transition and the Underclass." *Annals of the American Academy,* 501:26–47.

Kasnitz, Phillip, Mollenkopf, John, Waters, Mary, & Holloway, Jennifer. 2008. *Inheriting the City: The Children of Immigrants Come of Age.* New York: Russell Sage Foundation.

Katz, Michael, & Stern, Mark. 2006. *One Nation Divisible: What America Was and What It Is Becoming.* New York: Russell Sage Foundation.

Katz, Phyllis. 1976. "The Acquisition of Racial Attitudes in Children." In Phyllis Katz (Ed.), *Towards the Elimination of Racism* (pp. 125–154). New York: Pergamon.

Kennedy, Randall. 2001. "Racial Trends in the Administration of Criminal Justice." In Neil J. Smelser, William Julius Wilson, & Faith Mitchell (Eds.), *America Becoming: Racial Trends and Their Consequences* (Vol. 2, pp. 1–20). Washington, DC: National Academy Press.

Kennedy, Ruby Jo. 1952. "Single or Triple Melting Pot: Intermarriage Trends in New Haven, 1870–1950." *American Journal of Sociology,* 58:56–59.

Kennedy, Ruby Jo. 1944. "Single or Triple Melting Pot: Intermarriage Trends in New Haven, 1870–1940." *American Journal of Sociology,* 49:331–339.

Kephart, William, & Zellner, William. 1994. *Extraordinary Groups.* New York: St. Martin's.

Killian, Lewis. 1975. *The Impossible Revolution, Phase 2: Black Power and the American Dream.* New York: Random House.

Kim, Kwang Chung, Hurh, Won Moo, & Fernandez, Marilyn. 1989. "Intra-group Differences in Business Participation: Three Asian Immigrant Groups." *International Migration Review,* 23:73–95.

Kinder, Donald R., & Sears, David O. 1981. "Prejudice and Politics: Symbolic Racism Versus Racial Threats to the Good Life." *Journal of Personality and Social Psychology,* 40:414–431.

King, C. Richard, Staurowsky, Ellen J., Baca, Lawrence, Davis, R., & Pewardy, Cornel. 2002. "Of Polls and Race Prejudice: *Sports Illustrated*'s Errant "Indian Wars." *Journal of Sport and Social Issues,* 26:381–403.

King, Martin Luther, Jr. 1968. *Where Do We Go from Here: Chaos or Community?* New York: Harper & Row.

King, Martin Luther, Jr. 1963. *Why We Can't Wait.* New York: Mentor.

King, Martin Luther, Jr. 1958. *Stride Toward Freedom: The Montgomery Story.* New York: Harper & Row.

Kitano, Harry H. L. 1980. "Japanese." In Stephan Thernstrom (Ed.), *Harvard Encyclopedia of Ethnic Groups* (pp. 561–571). Cambridge, MA: Harvard University Press.

Kitano, Harry, & Daniels, Roger. 2001. *Asian Americans: Emerging Minorities* (3rd ed.). Upper Saddle River, NJ: Prentice Hall.

Kitano, Harry, & Daniels, Roger. 1995. *Asian Americans: Emerging Minorities* (2nd ed.). Englewood Cliffs, NJ: Prentice Hall.

Kitano, Harry, & Daniels, Roger. 1988. *Asian Americans: Emerging Minorities.* Englewood Cliffs, NJ: Prentice Hall.

Kleg, Milton, & Yamamoto, Kaoru. 1998. "As the World Turns: Ethno-Racial Distances After 70 Years." *The Social Science Journal,* 35:183–190.

Kluegel, James R., & Smith, Eliot R. 1982. "Whites' Beliefs About Blacks' Opportunities." *American Sociological Review,* 47:518–532.

Kochhar, Rakesh. 2004. *The Wealth of Hispanic Households, 1996 to 2002.* Pew Hispanic Center, Washington, DC, p. 2. Retrieved February 15, 2004, from http://www.pewhispanic.org/files/reports/34.pdf

Kraybill, Donald B., & Bowman, Carl F. 2001. *On the Backroad to Heaven: Old Order Hutterites, Mennonites, Amish, and Brethren.* Baltimore, MD: Johns Hopkins University Press.

Kritz, Mary, & Gurak, Douglas. 2005. "Immigration and a Changing America." In Reynolds Farley & John Haaga (Eds.), *The American People: Census 2000* (pp. 259–301). New York: Russell Sage Foundation.

Krysan, Maria, & Farley, Reynolds. 2002. "The Residential Preferences of Blacks: Do They Explain Persistent Segregation?" *Social Forces,* 80:937–981.

Kuperman, Diane. 2001, September. "Stuck at the Gates of Paradise." *Unesco Courier,* pp. 24–26.

Lach, Jennifer. 2000. "Interracial Friendships." *American Demographics,* January (p. n.a.).

Lacy, Dan. 1972. *The White Use of Blacks in America.* New York: McGraw-Hill.

Lai, H. M. 1980. "Chinese." In Stephan Thernstrom (Ed.), *Harvard Encyclopedia of Ethnic Groups* (pp. 217–234). Cambridge, MA: Harvard University Press.

Lamont-Brown, Raymond. 1993. "The Burakumin: Japan's Underclass." *Contemporary Review,* 263:136–140.

Landale, Nancy, & Oropesa, R. S. 2002. "White, Black, or Puerto Rican? Racial Self-Identification Among Mainland and Island Puerto Ricans." *Social Forces,* 81:231–254.

LaPiere, Robert. 1934. "Attitudes versus Actions." *Social Forces,* 13:230–237.

Lavelle, Kristin, & Feagin, Joe. 2006. "Hurricane Katrina: The Race and Class Debate." *Monthly Review,* 58:52–66.

Lee, Chungmei. 2004. *Is Resegregation Real?* Retrieved April 8, 2005, from http://www.civilrightsproject.harvard.edu

Lee, Sharon. 1998. "Asian Americans: Diverse and Growing." *Population Bulletin* (Vol. 53, No. 2). Washington, DC: Population Reference Bureau.

Lee, Sharon, & Fernandez, Marilyn. 1998. "Trends in Asian American Racial/Ethnic Intermarriage: A Comparison of 1980 and 1990 Census Data." *Sociological Perspectives,* 41:323–343.

Lee, Sharon M., & Yamanaka, Keiko. 1990. "Patterns of Asian American Intermarriage and Marital Assimilation." *Journal of Comparative Family Studies,* 21:287–305.

Lenski, Gerhard. 2005. *Ecological-Evolutionary Theory: Principles and Applications.* Boulder CO: Paradigm.

Lenski, Gerhard, Nolan, Patrick, & Lenski, Jean. 1995. *Human Societies: An Introduction to Macrosociology* (7th ed.). New York: McGraw-Hill.

Levine, Lawrence. 1977. *Black Culture and Black Consciousness.* New York: Oxford University Press.

Levy, Jacques. 1975. *Cesar Chavez: Autobiography of La Causa.* New York: Norton.

Lewis, Oscar. 1966, October. "The Culture of Poverty." *Scientific American,* pp. 19–25.

Lewis, Oscar. 1965. *La Vida: A Puerto Rican Family in the Culture of Poverty.* New York: Random House.

Lewis, Oscar. 1959. *Five Families: Mexican Case Studies in the Culture of Poverty.* New York: Basic Books.

Lewis Mumford Center. 2001. "Ethnic Diversity Grows, Neighborhood Integration Lags Behind." Retrieved July 2, 2002, from http://mumford1.dyndns.org/cen2000/report.html

Lewy, Guenter. 2004. "Were American Indians the Victims of Genocide?" *Commentary*, 118: 55–63.

Lieberson, Stanley. 1980. *A Piece of the Pie: Blacks and White Immigrants Since 1880.* Berkeley: University of California Press.

Lieberson, Stanley, & Waters, Mary C. 1988. *From Many Strands.* New York: Russell Sage Foundation.

Light, Ivan, & Bonacich, Edna. 1988. *Immigrant Entrepreneurs: Koreans in Los Angeles, 1965–1982.* Berkeley: University of California Press.

Lin, Monica, Kwan, Virginia, Cheung, Anna, & Fiske, Susan T. 2005. "Stereotype content model explains prejudice for an envied outgroup: Scale of anti-Asian American stereotypes." *Personality and Social Psychology Bulletin*, 31:34–47.

Lincoln, C. Eric. 1961. *The Black Muslims in America.* Boston: Beacon.

Ling, Huping. 2000. "Family and Marriage of Late-Nineteenth and Early-Twentieth Century Chinese Immigrant Women." *Journal of American Ethnic History*, 9:43–65.

Locust, Carol. 1990. "Wounding the Spirit: Discrimination and Traditional American Indian Belief Systems." In Gail Thomas (Ed.), *U.S. Race Relations in the 1980s and 1990s: Challenges and Alternatives* (pp. 219–232). New York: Hemisphere.

Logan, John. 2007, Winter. "The Impact of Katrina: Race and Class in Storm-Damaged Neighborhoods." *Breaking Ground.*

Logan, John, Alba, Richard, & McNulty, Thomas. 1994. "Ethnic Economies in Metropolitan Regions: Miami and Beyond." *Social Forces*, 72:691–724.

Lopata, Helena Znaniecki. 1976. *Polish Americans.* Englewood Cliffs, NJ: Prentice Hall.

Lopez, Mark, & Taylor, Paul. 2009. *Dissecting the 2008 Electorate: Most Diverse in U.S. History.* Pew Research Center report. Retrieved June 12, 2009, from http://pewhispanic.org/files/reports/108.pdf

Luciuk, Lubomyr, & Hryniuk, Stelkla (Eds.). 1991. *Canada's Ukrainians Negotiating an Identity.* Toronto: University of Toronto Press.

Lurie, Nancy Oestrich. 1982. "The American Indian: Historical Background." In Norman Yetman & C. Hoy Steele (Eds.), *Majority and Minority* (3rd ed., pp. 131–144). Boston: Allyn & Bacon.

Lyman, Stanford. 1974. *Chinese Americans.* New York: Random House.

Malcolm X. 1964. *The Autobiography of Malcolm X.* New York: Grove.

Mangiafico, Luciano. 1988. *Contemporary American Immigrants.* New York: Praeger.

Mannix, Daniel P. 1962. *Black Cargoes: A History of the Atlantic Slave Trade.* New York: Viking.

Marcelli, Enrico, & Heer, David. 1998. "The Unauthorized Mexican Immigrant Population and Welfare in Los Angeles County: A Comparative Statistical Analysis." *Sociological Perspectives*, 41:279–303.

Margolis, Richard. 1989. "If We Won, Why Aren't We Smiling?" In Charles Willie (Ed.), *Round Two of the Willie/Wilson Debate* (2nd ed., pp. 95–100). Dix Hills, NY: General Hall.

Marosi, Richard. 2005. "Death and Deliverance; The Desert Swallows Another Border Crosser, but Her Father Is Determined to Find Her Body." *The Los Angeles Times*, August 7, p. A1.

Martin, Philip, & Midgley, Elizabeth. 1999. "Immigration to the United States." *Population Bulletin* (Vol. 54, No. 2). Washington, DC: Population Reference Bureau.

Martin, Philip, & Widgren, Jonas. 2002. "International Migration: Facing the Challenge." *Population Bulletin* (Vol. 57, No. 1). Washington, DC: Population Reference Bureau.

Marx, Karl, & Engels, Friedrich. 1967. *The Communist Manifesto.* Baltimore, MD: Penguin. (Original work published 1848)

Massarik, Fred, & Chenkin, Alvin. 1973. "United States National Jewish Population Study: A First Report." In American Jewish Committee, *American Jewish Year Book, 1973* (pp. 264–306). New York: American Jewish Committee.

Massey, Douglas. 2000. "Housing Discrimination 101." *Population Today,* 28:1, 4.

Massey, Douglas. 1995. "The New Immigration and Ethnicity in the United States." *Population and Development Review,* 21:631–652.

Massey, Douglas, & Denton, Nancy. 1993. *American Apartheid: Segregation and the Making of the Underclass.* Cambridge, MA: Harvard University Press.

Mauer, Marc, & Huling, Tracy. 2000. "Young Black Americans and the Criminal Justice System." In Jerome Skolnick & Elliot Currie (Eds.), *Crisis in American Institutions* (11th ed., pp. 417–424). New York: Allyn & Bacon.

Mazzuca, Josephine. 2004. *For Most Americans, Friendship Is Colorblind.* Retrieved September 17, 2004, from http://www.gallup.com

McConahy, John B. 1986. "Modern Racism, Ambivalence, and the Modern Racism Scale." In John F. Dovidio & Samuel Gartner (Eds.), *Prejudice, Discrimination and Racism* (pp. 91–125). Orlando, FL: Academic Press.

McDowell, Amber. 2004, September 10. "Cracker Barrel Settles Lawsuit; Black Customers, Workers Reported Discrimination." *Washington Post,* p. E1.

McIntosh, Peggy. 1988. *White Privilege: Unpacking the Invisible Knapsack.* (Working Paper No. 189). Wellesley, MA: Wellesley College Center for Research on Women. Retrieved August 26, 2009, from http://www.case.edu/president/aaction/UnpackingTheKnapsack.pdf

McLemore, S. Dale. 1973. "The Origins of Mexican American Subordination in Texas." *Social Science Quarterly,* 53:656–679.

McNickle, D'Arcy. 1973. *Native American Tribalism: Indian Survivals and Renewals.* New York: Oxford University Press.

McPherson, Miller, Smith-Lovin, Lynn, & Brashears, Matthew. 2006. "Social Isolation in America: Changes in Core Discussion Networks Over Two Decades." *Social Forces,* 71:353–375.

McWilliams, Carey. 1961. *North From Mexico: The Spanish Speaking People of the United States.* New York: Monthly Review Press.

Meredith v. Jefferson County Board of Education, 915 U.S. (2005).

Min, Pyong Gap. 1995. *Asian Americans: Contemporary Trends and Issues.* Thousand Oaks, CA: Sage.

Mirandé, Alfredo. 1985. *The Chicano Experience: An Alternative Perspective.* Notre Dame, IN: University of Notre Dame Press.

Mirandé, Alfredo, & Enríquez, Evangelica. 1979. *La Chicana: The Mexican-American Woman.* Chicago: University of Chicago Press.

Moore, Joan W. 1970. *Mexican Americans.* Englewood Cliffs, NJ: Prentice Hall.

Moore, Joan W., & Pachon, Harry. 1985. *Hispanics in the United States.* Englewood Cliffs, NJ: Prentice Hall.

Moore, Joan, & Pinderhughes, Raquel. 1993. *In the Barrios: Latinos and the Underclass Debate.* New York: Russell Sage Foundation.

Moquin, Wayne, & Van Doren, Charles (Eds.). 1971. *A Documentary History of Mexican Americans.* New York: Bantam.

Moraes, Lisa de. 2005, September 3. "Kanya West's Torrent of Criticism, Live on NBC." *The Washington Post,* p. C1.

Morawska, Ewa. 1990. "The Sociology and Historiography of Immigration." In Virginia Yans-McLaughlin (Ed.), *Immigration Reconsidered: History, Sociology, and Politics* (pp. 187–328). New York: Oxford University Press.

Morgan, Edmund. 1975. *American Slavery, American Freedom.* New York: Norton.

Morin, Richard, & Cottman, Michael. 2001, June 22. "Discrimination's Lingering Sting." *Washington Post,* A1.

Morris, Aldon D. 1984. *The Origins of the Civil Rights Movement.* New York: Free Press.

"Most Blacks Say MLK's Vision Fulfilled, Poll Finds." 2009, January 19. *CNN.* Retrieved August 25, 2009, from http://www.cnn.com/2009/POLITICS/01/19/king.poll/index.html

Moynihan, Daniel. 1965. *The Negro Family: The Case for National Action.* Washington, DC: U.S. Department of Labor.

Mujica, Mauro. 2003. "Official English Legislation: Myths and Realities." *Human Events,* 59:24.

Murguia, Edward, & Foreman, Tyrone. 2004. "Shades of Whiteness." In Melanie Bush (Ed.). *Breaking the Code of Good Intentions: Everyday Forms of Whiteness* (pp. 113–122). Lanham, MD: Rowman and Littlefield.

Murguia, Edward, & Foreman, Tyrone. 2003. "Shades of Whiteness: The Mexican American Experience in Relation to Anglos and Blacks." In Ashley Doane & Eduardo Bonilla-Silva (Eds.), *White Out: The Continuing Significance of Racism* (pp. 63–72). New York: Routledge.

Myrdal, Gunnar. 1962. *An American Dilemma: The Negro Problem and Modern Democracy.* New York: Harper & Row. (Original work published 1944).

Nabakov, Peter (Ed.). 1999. *Native American Testimony* (Rev. ed.). New York: Penguin.

National Academy of Sciences. 1997. *The New Americans: Economic, Demographic, and Fiscal Effects of Immigration.* Retrieved January 23, 2005, from http://books.nap.edu/execsumm_pdf/5779.pdf

National Advisory Commission. 1968. *Report of the National Advisory Commission on Civil Disorders.* New York: The New York Times.

National Council on Crime and Delinquency. 2007. *And Justice for Some: Differential Treatment of Youth of Color in the Justice System.* Retrieved March 12, 2008, from http://www.nccd-crc.org/nccd/pubs/2007jan_justice_for_some.pdf

National Indian Gaming Commission. (n.d.). Retrieved February 9, 2005, from http://www.nigc.gov/TribalData/tabid/67/Default.aspx

National Opinion Research Center. 1972–2007. *General Social Survey.* Chicago: Author.

National Origins Act, Pub. L. 139, Chapter 190, § 43 Stat. 153 (1924).

National Public Radio. 2004. *Immigration Survey.* Retrieved February 15, 2005, from http://www.npr.org/templates/story/story.php?storyId=4062605

National Research Council. 2007. *The New Americans: Economic, Demographic, and Fiscal Effects of Immigration.,* Washington, DC: National Academy Press.

Nationmaster.com. n.d. *Education Statistics.* Retrieved June 30, 2009, from http://www.nationmaster.com/graph/edu_ave_yea_of_sch_of_adu-education-average-years-schooling-adults

Neissen, Jan, Schibel, Yongmi, & Thompson, Cressida. (Eds.). 2005. *Current Immigration Debates in Europe: Ireland.* Brussels, Belgium: Migration Policy Group. Retrieved August 31, 2009, from http://www.isp.org.pl/files/944903105003176900l129732716.pdf

Nelli, Humbert S. 1980. "Italians." In Stephan Thernstrom (Ed.), *Harvard Encyclopedia of Ethnic Groups* (pp. 545–560). Cambridge, MA: Harvard University Press.

Nishi, Setsuko. 1995. "Japanese Americans." In Pyong Gap Min (Ed.), *Asian Americans: Contemporary Trends and Issues* (pp. 95–133). Thousand Oaks, CA: Sage.

Noel, Donald. 1968. "A Theory of the Origin of Ethnic Stratification." *Social Problems,* 16:157–172.

Novak, Michael. 1973. *The Rise of the Unmeltable Ethnics: Politics and Culture in the 1970s.* New York: Collier.

Obama, Barack. 2008, March 18. "Barack Obama's Speech on Race." *New York Times.* Retrieved September 8, 2009, from http://www.nytimes.com/2008/03/18/us/politics/18text-obama.html.

Office of the United Nations High Commissioner for Human Rights. n.d. *Convention on the Prevention and Punishment of the Crime of Genocide.* Retrieved August 22, 2009, from http://www2.ohchr.org/english/law/genocide.htm

Ogunwole, Stella. 2006. *We the People: American Indians and Alaska Natives in the United States.* Retrieved March 13, 2008, from http://www.census.gov/prod/2006pubs/censr-28.pdf

Ogunwole, Stella. 2002. "The American Indian and Alaska Native Population: 2000." *U.S. Census Brief.* Washington, DC: U.S. Bureau of the Census.

O'Hare, William P. 1992. "America's Minorities: The Demographics of Diversity." *Population Bulletin* (Vol. 47, No. 4). Washington, DC: Population Reference Bureau.

O'Hare, William, Pollard, Kelvin, Mann, Taynia, & Kent, Mary. 1991. *African Americans in the 1990s.* Washington, DC: Population Reference Bureau.

Oliver, Melvin, & Shapiro, Thomas. 2006. *Black Wealth, White Wealth* (2nd ed.). New York: Taylor & Francis.

Oliver, Melvin, & Shapiro, Thomas. 2001. "Wealth and Racial Stratification." In Neil J. Smelser, William Julius Wilson, & Faith Mitchell (Eds.), *America Becoming: Racial Trends and Their Consequences* (Vol. 1, pp. 222–251). Washington, DC: National Academy Press.

Olson, James, & Wilson, Raymond. 1984. *Native Americans in the Twentieth Century.* Provo, UT: Brigham Young University Press.

Omi, Michael, & Winant, Howard. 1986. *Racial Formation in the United States From the 1960s to the 1980s.* New York: Routledge and Kegan Paul.

Organization for Economic Co-operation and Development. 2008. *Country Statistical Profiles 2009.* Retrieved August 30, 2009, from http://stats.oecd.org/Index.aspx?DataSetCode=CSP2009

Orfield, Gary. 2001. *Schools More Separate: Consequences of a Decade of Resegregation.* Cambridge, MA: Harvard University, The Civil Rights Project. Retrieved from on April 10, 2003, from http://uclawww.civilrightsproject.edu/research/deseg/separate_schools01.php

Orfield, Gary, & Lee, Chungmei. 2007. *Historic Reversals, Accelerating Resegregation, and the Need for New Integration Strategies. Civil Rights Project. Harvard University.* Retrieved September 5, 2009, from http://www.civilrightsproject.ucla.edu/research/deseg/reversals_reseg_need.pdf

Orfield, Gary, & Lee, Chungmei. 2006. *Racial Transformation and the Changing Nature of Segregation.* Cambridge, MA: The Civil Rights Project at Harvard University. Retrieved March 12, 2008, from http://www.civilrightsproject.ucla.edu/research/deseg/Racial_Transformation.pdf.

Orreniou, Pia. 2001. "Illegal Immigration and Enforcement Along the U.S.-Mexico Border: An Overview." *Economic & Financial Review,* 2002:2–11.

O'Sullivan, Eoin. 2003. *Migration and Housing in Ireland: Report to the European Observatory on Homelessness.* Retrieved February 14, 2005, from http://www.feantsa.org/files/national_reports/ireland/ireland_migration_2002.pdf

O'Sullivan, Katherine, & Wilson, William J. 1988. "Race and Ethnicity." In N. Smelser (Ed.), *Handbook of Sociology* (pp. 223–242). Newbury Park, CA: Sage.

Oswalt, Wendell, & Neely, Sharlotte. 1996. *This Land Was Theirs.* Mountain View, CA: Mayfield.

Parents Involved in Community Schools v. Seattle School District No. 1, 908 U.S. (2006).

Parish, Peter J. 1989. *Slavery: History and Historians.* New York: Harper & Row.

Park, Robert E., & Burgess, Ernest W. 1924. *Introduction to the Science of Society.* Chicago: University of Chicago Press.

Parke, Ross, & Buriel, Raymond. 2002. "Socialization Concerns in African American, American Indian, Asian American, and Latino Families." In Nijole Benokraitis (Ed.), *Contemporary Ethnic Families in the United States* (pp. 18–29). Upper Saddle River, NJ: Prentice Hall.

Parrado, Emilio, & Zenteno, Rene. 2001. "Economic Restructuring, Financial Crises, and Women's Work in Mexico." *Social Problems,* 48:456–477.

Parrillo, Vincent. 2003. *Strangers to These Shores.* (7th ed.). Boston: Allyn & Bacon.

Passel, Jeffrey S., & Cohn, D'Vera. 2009. *Mexican Immigrants: How Many Come? How Many Leave?* Retrieved August 30, 2009, from http://pewhispanic.org/files/reports/112.pdf

Pego, David. 1998. "To Educate a Nation: Native American Tribe Hopes to Bring Higher Education to an Arizona Reservation." *Black Issues in Higher Education,* 15:60–63.

Peltier, Leonard. 1999. *Prison Writings: My Life Is My Sun Dance.* New York: St. Martin's Press.

Perez, Lisandro. 1980. "Cubans." In Stephan Thernstrom (Ed.), *Harvard Encyclopedia of Ethnic Groups* (pp. 256–261). Cambridge, MA: Harvard University Press.

Petersen, Williams. 1971. *Japanese Americans.* New York: Random House.

Peterson, Mark. 1995. "Leading Cuban-American Entrepreneurs: The Process of Developing Motives, Abilities, and Resources." *Human Relations,* 48:1193–1216.

Pettigrew, Thomas. 1971. *Racially Separate or Together?* New York: McGraw-Hill.

Pettigrew, Thomas. 1958. "Personality and Sociocultural Factors in Intergroup Attitudes: A Cross-National Comparison." *Journal of Conflict Resolution,* 2:29–42.

Pettigrew, Thomas, Wagner, Ulrich, & Christ, Oliver. 2007. "Who Opposes Immigration? Comparing German and North American Findings." *DuBois Review,* 4:19–39.

Pettit, Becky, & Western, Bruce. 2004. "Mass Imprisonment and the Life Course: Race and Class Inequality in U.S. Incarceration." *American Sociological Review,* 69:151–169.

Pew Charitable Trust. 2008. *One in 100: Behind Bars in the United States.* Retrieved March 12, 2008, from http://www.pewtrusts.org/uploadedFiles/wwwpewtrustsorg/Reports/sentencing_and_corrections/one_in_100.pdf.

Pew Research Center. 2008, November 5. *Inside Obama's Sweeping Victory.* November 5. Retrieved September 8, 2009, from www.pewresearch.org/pubs/1023/exit-poll-analysis-2008

Pew Research Center. 2006. *No Consensus on Immigration Problem or Proposed Fixes: America's Immigration Quandary.* Retrieved August 26, 2009, from http://pewhispanic.org/files/reports/63.pdf

Pew Research Center. 2005. *Hispanics: A People in Motion.* Retrieved March 16, 2008, from http://pewhispanic.org/files/reports/40.pdf

Pew Research Center. 2004. *Assimilation and Language.* Retrieved July 2, 2009, from http://pewhispanic.org/files/factsheets/11.pdf

Phillips, Ulrich B. 1918. *American Negro Slavery.* New York: Appleton and Company.

Pilger, John. 2000. "Australia Is the Only Developed Country Whose Government Has Been Condemned as Racist by the United Nations." *New Statesman,* 129:17.

Pincus, Fred. 2003. *Reverse Discrimination: Dismantling the Myth.* Boulder, CO: Lynne Rienner.

Pitt, Leonard. 1970. *The Decline of the Californios: A Social History of the Spanish-Speaking Californians, 1846–1890.* Berkeley: University of California Press.

Plessy v. Ferguson, 163 U.S. 537 (1896).

Pollard, Kelvin, & O'Hare, William. 1999. "America's Racial and Ethnic Minorities." *Population Bulletin* (Vol. 52, No. 3). Washington, DC: Population Reference Bureau.

Polner, Murray. 1993. "Asian Americans Say They Are Treated Like Foreigners." *The New York Times,* March 7, p. 1.

Population Reference Bureau. 2008a. *World Population Data Sheet, 2008.* Retrieved July 1, 2009, from http://www.prb.org/pdf08/08WPDS_Eng.pdf

Population Reference Bureau. 2008b. *World Population Highlights.* Retrieved July 1, 2009, from http://www.prb.org/pdf08/63.3highlights.pdf

Porter, Eduardo. 2005. "Illegal Immigrants Are Bolstering Social Security with Billions." *New York Times,* April 5, p. A1.

Portes, Alejandro. 1990. "From South of the Border: Hispanic Minorities in the United States." In Virginia Yans-McLaughlin (Ed.), *Immigration Reconsidered* (pp. 160–184). New York: Oxford University Press.

Portes, Alejandro, & Bach, Robert L. 1985. *Latin Journey: Cuban and Mexican Immigrants in the United States.* Berkeley: University of California Press.

Portes, Alejandro, & Manning, Robert. 1986. "The Immigrant Enclave: Theory and Empirical Examples." In Susan Olzak & Joanne Nagel (Eds.), *Competitive Ethnic Relations* (pp. 47–68). New York: Academic Press.

Portes, Alejandro, & Rumbaut, Rubén G. 2001a. *Legacies: The Story of the Immigrant Second Generation.* Berkeley: University of California Press.

Portes, Alejandro, & Rumbaut, Rubén. 2001b. *Ethnicities: Children of Immigrants in America.* New York: Russell Sage Foundation.

Portes, Alejandro, & Rumbaut, Rubén. 1996. *Immigrant America: A Portrait* (2nd ed.). Berkeley: University of California Press.

Portes, Alejandro, & Zhou, Min. 1993. "The New Second Generation: Segmented Assimilation and Its Variants." In *Annals of the American Academy of Political and Social Sciences,* 530:74–96.

Posadas, Barbara. 1999. *The Filipino Americans.* Westport, CT: Greenwood.

Potter, George. 1973. *To the Golden Door: The Story of the Irish in Ireland and America.* Westport, CT: Greenwood.

Poulan, Richard. 2003. "Globalization and the Sex Trade: Trafficking and the Commodification of Women and Children." *Canadian Woman Studies,* 22:38–43.

Powlishta, K., Serbin, L., Doyle, A., & White, D. 1994. "Gender, Ethnic, and Body-Type Biases: The Generality of Prejudice in Childhood." *Developmental Psychology,* 30:526–537.

Price, S. L., & Woo, Andrea. 2002. "The Indian Wars." *Sports Illustrated,* March 4, 96:66–73.

Puzo, Mario. 1972. *The Godfather Papers and Other Confessions.* New York: Putnam.

Qian, Zhenchao, & Lichter, David. 2007. "Social Boundaries and Marital Assimilation: Interpreting Trends in Racial and Ethnic Intermarriage." *American Sociological Review,* 72:68–94.

Quillian, Lincoln, & Campbell, Mary. 2003. "Beyond Black and White: The Present and Future of Multiracial Friendship Segregation." *American Sociological Review,* 68:540–567.

Quinones, Sam. 2007. *Antonio's Gun and Delfino's Dream: True Tales of Mexican Migration.* Albuquerque: University of New Mexico Press.

Rader, Benjamin G. 1983. *American Sports: From the Age of Folk Games to the Age of Spectators.* Englewood Cliffs, NJ: Prentice Hall.

Raymer, Patricia. 1974. "Wisconsin's Menominees: Indians on a Seesaw." *National Geographic,* August, pp. 228–251.

Read, Jen'nan Ghazal. 2004. "Cultural Influences on Immigrant Women's Labor Force Participation: The Arab-American Case." *International Migration Review,* 38:52–77.

Reid, Anna. 1999. *Borderland: A Journey Through the History of Ukraine.* Boulder, CO: Westview.

Remington, Robin. 1997. "Ethnonationalism and the Disintegration of Yugoslavia." In Winston Van Horne (Ed.), *Global Convulsions: Race, Ethnicity, and Nationalism at the End of the Twentieth Century* (pp. 261–279). Albany: State University of New York Press.

Ricci v. DeStefano, 971 U.S. (2009).

Rifkin, Jeremy. 1996. *The End of Work: The Decline of the Global Labor Force and the Dawn of the Post-Market Era.* New York: Putnam.

Robertson, Claire. 1996. "Africa and the Americas? Slavery and Women, the Family, and the Gender Division of Labor." In David Gaspar & Darlene Hine (Eds.), *More Than Chattel: Black Women and Slavery in the Americas* (pp. 4–40). Bloomington: Indiana University Press.

Rockquemore, Kerry Ann, & Brunsma, David. 2008. *Beyond Black: Biracial Identity in America* (2nd ed.). Lanham, MD: Rowman & Littlefield.

Rodriguez, Clara. 1989. *Puerto Ricans: Born in the USA.* Boston: Unwin Hyman.

Rodriguez, Clara, & Cordero-Guzman, Hector. 1992. "Placing Race in Context." *Ethnic and Racial Studies,* 15:523–542.

Rosenblum, Karen, & Travis, Toni-Michelle. 2008. *The Meaning of Difference: American Constructions of Race, Sex and Gender, Social Class, Sexual Orientation, and Disability.* (5th ed.). New York: McGraw-Hill.

Rosenfield, Michael. 2002. "Measures of Assimilation in the Marriage Market: Mexican Americans 1970-1990." *Journal of Marriage and the Family,* 64:152–163.

Rosich, Katherine. 2007. *Race, Ethnicity, and the Criminal Justice System.* Washington, DC: American Sociological Association.

Ross, Brian, & El-Buri, Rehab. 2008. "Obama's Pastor: God Damn America, U.S. to Blame for 9/11." *ABC News.* Retrieved March 12, 2009, from http://abcnews.go.com/blotter/story?id=4443788

Rouse, Linda, & Hanson, Jeffery. 1991. "American Indian Stereotyping, Resource Competition, and Status-Based Prejudice." *American Indian Culture and Research Journal,* 15:1–17.

Royster, Deirdre A. 2003. *Race and the Invisible Hand: How White Networks Exclude Black Men From Blue-Collar Jobs.* Berkeley: University of California Press.

Rumbaut, Rubén. 1991. "Passage to America: Perspectives on the New Immigration." In Alan Wolfe (Ed.), *America at Century's End* (pp. 208–244). Berkeley: University of California Press.

Russell, James. 2009. *Class and Race Formation in North America.* Toronto, Ont., Canada: University of Toronto Press.

Russell, James W. 1994. *After the Fifth Sun: Class and Race in North America.* Englewood Cliffs, NJ: Prentice Hall.

Saenz, Rogelio. 2005. "Latinos and the Changing Face of America." In Reynolds Farley & John Haaga (Eds.), *The American People: Census 2000.* New York: Russell Sage Foundation.

Saenz, Rogelio. 1999. "Mexican Americans." In Antony Dworkin & Rosalind Dworkin (Eds.), *The Minority Report* (pp. 209–229). Orlando, FL: Harcourt Brace.

Sanchirico, Andrew. 1991. "The Importance of Small Business Ownership in Chinese American Educational Achievement." *Sociology of Education,* 64:293–304.

Satter, Beryl. 2009. *Family Properties: Race, Real Estate, and the Exploitation of Black Urban America.* New York: Henry Holt.

Schafer, John, & Navarro, Joe. 2004. "The Seven-Stage Hate Model: The Psychopathology of Hate Groups." *The FBI Law Enforcement Bulletin,* 72:1–9.

Schlesinger, Arthur M., Jr. 1992. *The Disuniting of America: Reflections on a Multicultural Society.* New York: Norton.

Schoener, Allon. 1967. *Portal to America: The Lower East Side, 1870–1925.* New York: Holt, Rinehart & Winston.

Schwartzman, Luisa Farah. 2007. "Does Money Whiten? Intergenerational Changes in Racial Classification in Brazil." *American Sociological Review:* 72: 940–963

Sears, David. 1988. "Symbolic Racism." In Phyllis Katz & Dalmas Taylor (Eds.), *Eliminating Racism: Profiles in Controversy* (pp. 53–84). New York: Plenum.

Sears, David, & Henry, P. J. 2003. "The Origins of Modern Racism." *Journal of Personality and Social Psychology,* 85:259–275.

Seller, Maxine S. 1987. "Beyond the Stereotype: A New Look at the Immigrant Woman." In Ronald Takaki (Ed.), *From Different Shores: Perspectives on Race and Ethnicity in America* (pp. 197–203). New York: Oxford University Press.

Selzer, Michael. 1972. *"Kike": Anti-Semitism in America.* New York: Meridian.

Sen, Rinku, & Mamdouh, Fekkak. 2008. *The Accidental American: Immigration and Citizenship in the Age of Globalization.* San Francisco: Berrett-Koehler Publications.

Shannon, William V. 1964. *The American Irish.* New York: Macmillan.

Shapiro, Thomas. 2004. *The Hidden Cost of Being African American.* New York: Oxford University Press.

Sheet Metal Workers v. EEOC, 478 U.S. 421 (1986).

Shelton, Beth Anne, & John, Daphne. 1996. "The Division of Household Labor." *Annual Review of Sociology,* 22:299–322.

Sherif, Muzafer, Harvey, O. J., White, B. Jack, Hood, William, & Sherif, Carolyn. 1961. *Intergroup Conflict and Cooperation: The Robber's Cave Experiment.* Norman, OK: University Book Exchange.

Sheth, Manju. 1995. "Asian Indian Americans." In Pyong Gap Min (Ed.), *Asian Americans: Contemporary Issues and Trends* (pp. 169–198). Thousand Oaks, CA: Sage.

Shinagawa, Larry, & Pang, Gin Yong. 1996. "Asian American Panethnicity and Intermarriage." *Amerasia Journal,* 22:127–153.

Simon, Julian. 1989. *The Economic Consequences of Immigration.* Cambridge, MA: Blackwell.

Simpson, George, & Yinger, Milton. 1985. *Racial and Cultural Minorities: An Analysis of Prejudice and Discrimination.* New York: Plenum.

Skinner, Benjamin. 2008. A World Enslaved. *Foreign Policy,* 165:62–68.

Sklare, Marshall. 1971. *America's Jews.* New York: Random House.

Slave Trade and African American Ancestry. n.d. Retrieved December 4, 2007, from http://www.homestead.com/wysinger/mapofafricadiaspora.html

Smedley, Audrey. 1999. *Race in North America: Origin and Evolution of a Worldview* (2nd ed.). Boulder, CO: Westview.

Smith, James, & Edmonston, Barry (Eds.). 1997. *The New Americans: Economic, Demographic, and Fiscal Effects of Immigration.* Washington, DC: National Academy Press.

Smith, Tom, & Dempsey, Glenn. 1983. "The Polls: Ethnic Social Distance and Prejudice." *Public Opinion Quarterly,* 47:584–600.

Snipp, C. Matthew. 1996. "The First Americans: American Indians." In Silvia Pedraza & Rubén Rumbaut (Eds.), *Origins and Destinies: Immigration, Race, and Ethnicity in America* (pp. 390–403). Belmont, CA: Wadsworth.

Snipp, C. Matthew. 1992. "Sociological Perspectives on American Indians." *Annual Review of Sociology,* 18:351–371.

Snipp, C. Matthew. 1989. *American Indians: The First of This Land.* New York: Russell Sage Foundation.

Snipp, C. Matthew. 2000. "A Sorry Tale." *The Economist,* 356:12.

Snyder, Howard, & Sickmund, Melissa. 2006. *Juvenile Offenders and Victims: 2006 National Report.* Pittsburgh, PA: National Center for Juvenile Justice.

Spicer, Edward H. 1980. "American Indians." In Stephan Thernstrom (Ed.), *Harvard Encyclopedia of Ethnic Groups* (pp. 58–122). Cambridge, MA: Harvard University Press.

Spickard, Paul. 1996. *Japanese Americans: The Formation and Transformations of an Ethnic Group.* New York: Twayne.

Spilde, Kate. 2001. *The Economic Development Journey of Indian Nations.* Retrieved July 5, 2002, from http://indiangaming.org/library/newsletters/index.html

Stampp, Kenneth. 1956. *The Peculiar Institution: Slavery in the Ante-Bellum South.* New York: Random House.

Stannard, David. 1992. *American Holocaust.* New York: Oxford University Press.

Staples, Robert. 1988. "The Black American Family." In Charles Mindel, Robert Habenstein, & Roosevelt Wright (Eds.), *Ethnic Families in America* (3rd ed., pp. 303–324). New York: Elsevier.

Stein, Nicholas. 2003, January 20. "No Way Out." *Fortune.*

Steinberg, Stephen. 1981. *The Ethnic Myth: Race, Ethnicity, and Class in America.* New York: Atheneum.

Stelcner, Morton. 2000. "Earnings Differentials Among Ethnic Groups in Canada: A Review of the Research." *Review of Social Economy,* 58:295–317.

Stepick, Alex, Stepick, Carol Dutton, Eugene, Emmanuel, Teed, Deborah, & Labissiere, Yves. 2001. "Shifting Identities and Intergenerational Conflict: Growing Up Haitian in Miami." In Rubén Rumbaut and Alejandro Portes (Eds.), *Ethnicities: Children of Immigrants in America* (pp. 229–266). Berkeley: University of California Press.

Stidman, Pete. 2008. "Grim Video Lays Bare Vietnamese Teen Violence." *Dorchester Reporter.* Retrieved August 31, 2009, from http://www.dotnews.com/beatingvideo.html

Stoddard, Ellwyn. 1973. *Mexican Americans.* New York: Random House.

Stoll, Michael. 2004. *African Americans and the Color Line.* New York: Russell Sage Foundation.

Strolovitch, Dara, Warren, Dorian, & Frymer, Paul. 2006. *Katrina's Political Roots and Divisions: Race, Class, and Federalism in American Politics.* Retrieved June 20, 2007, from http://understandingkatrina.ssrc.org

Stuckey, Sterling. 1987. *Slave Culture: Nationalist Theory and the Foundations of Black America.* New York: Harper & Row.

Stutz, Howard. 2009. "Annual Gaming Revenues Suffer Sharpest Drop in State History." *Las Vegas Review-Journal.* Retrieved June 21, 2009, from http://www.lvrj.com/news/39483742.html

Sung, Betty Lee. 1990. "Chinese American Intermarriage." *Journal of Comparative Family Studies,* 21:337–352.

Sweetman, Arthur, & Dicks, Gordon. 1999. "Education and Ethnicity in Canada." *Journal of Human Resources, 34:* 668–690.

Takaki, Ronald. 1993. *A Different Mirror: A History of Multicultural America.* Boston: Little, Brown.

Tannenbaum, Frank. 1947. *Slave and Citizen: The Negro in the Americas.* New York: Knopf.

Taylor, Jared, & Whitney, Glayde. 2002. "Racial Profiling: Is There an Empirical Basis?" *Mankind Quarterly,* 42:285–313.

Taylor, Jared, & Whitney, Glayde. 1999. "Crime and Racial Profiling by U.S. Police: Is There an Empirical Basis?" *The Journal of Social, Political and Economic Studies,* 24:485–516.

Taylor, Jonathon, & Kalt, Joseph. 2005. *American Indians on Reservations: A Databook of Socioeconomic Change Between the 1990 and 2000 Censuses.* Retrieved August 22, 2009, from http://www.hks.harvard.edu/hpaied/pubs/documents/AmericanIndiansonReservationsADatabookofSocioeconomicChange.pdf

Telles, Edward. 2004. *Race in Another America: The Significance of Skin Color in Brazil.* Princeton, NJ: Princeton University Press.

Telles, Edward E., & Ortiz, Vilma. 2008. *Generations of Exclusion: Mexican Americans, Assimilation, and Race.* New York: Russell Sage Foundation.

Texeira, Erin. 2005. "Asian Youths Suffer Harassment in Schools." *The Washington Post.* Retrieved August 17, 2009, from http://www.washingtonpost.com/wp-dyn/content/article/2005/11/13/AR2005111300385.html

Thernstrom, Stephan, & Thernstrom, Abigail. 1997. *America in Black and White.* New York: Simon & Schuster.

Thomas, Melvin. 1993. "Race, Class, and Personal Income: An Empirical Test of the Declining Significance of Race Thesis, 1968–1988." *Social Problems,* 40:328–342.

Thornton, Russell. 2001. "Trends Among American Indians in the United States." In Neil J. Smelser, William Julius Wilson, & Faith Mitchell (Eds.), *America Becoming: Racial Trends and Their Consequences* (Vol. 1, pp. 135–169). Washington, DC: National Academy Press.

Tilly, Charles. 1990. "Transplanted Networks." In Virginia Yans-McLaughlin (Ed.), *Immigration Reconsidered: History, Sociology, and Politics* (pp. 79–95). New York: Oxford University Press.

Tsai, Shih-Shan Henry. 1986. *The Chinese Experience in America.* Bloomington: Indiana University Press.

Udry, Richard. 2000. "Biological Limits of Gender Construction." *American Sociological Review,* 65:443–457.

United Nations. 2009. *Social Indicators.* Retrieved June 30, 2009, from http://unstats.un.org/unsd/demographic/products/socind/inc-eco.htm

United Nations. 2006. *The Millennium Development Goals Report 2006.* Retrieved August 8, 2007, from http://mdgs.un.org/unsd/mdg/Resources/Static/Products/Progress2006/MDGReport2006.pdf

United Nations. 2000. *United Nations Releases Most Recent Statistics on World's Women.* Retrieved June 27, 2002, from http://unstats.un.org/unsd/demographic/ww2000/ww2000pr.htm

United Steelworkers of America, AFL-CIO-CLC v. Weber, 443 U.S. 193 (1979).

U.S. Bureau of Indian Affairs. 1997. *1997 Labor Market Information on the Indian Labor Force.* Retrieved May 17, 2002, from http://www.doi.gov/bia/Labor/97 LFRCovFinal.pdf

U.S. Bureau of the Census. (n.d.-a). *Hispanic or Latino Origin.* Retrieved December 27, 2004, from http://www.census.gov/population/cen2000/atlas/censr01-111.pdf

U.S. Bureau of the Census. (n.d.-b). *Number of People, 2000: One Race: Asian.* Retrieved January 1, 2005, from http://www.census.gov/population/cen2000/atlas/censr01-108.pdf

U.S. Bureau of the Census. (n.d.-c). *Summary File 3, Table QT-P13.* Retrieved from http://factfinder.census.gov/servlet/DatasetMainPageServlet?_program=DEC&_submenuId =datas ets_0&_lang=en

U.S. Bureau of the Census. (n.d.-d). *Summary File 4.* Retrieved from http://factfinder.census.gov/servlet/DatasetMainPageServlet?_program=DEC&_submenuId=datasets_0&_lang=en

U.S. Bureau of the Census. 2009a. *American Community Survey 2007.* Retrieved September 8, 2009, from http://www.census.gov/acs/www

U.S. Bureau of the Census, 2009b. *Statistical Abstract of the United States: 2009.* Retrieved August 22, 2009, from http://www.census.gov/compendia/statab/2009edition.html

U.S. Bureau of the Census. 2009c. *Table H-5, Race and Hispanic Origin of Householder—Households by Median and Mean Income.* Retrieved September 10, 2009, from http://www.census.gov/hhes/www/income/histinc/inchhtoc.html

U.S. Bureau of the Census. 2009d. *Table P-36, Full-Time, Year-Round Workers by Median Income and Sex, 1955–2007.* Retrieved September 10, 2009, from http://www.census.gov/hhes/www/income/histinc/incpertoc.html

U.S. Bureau of the Census. 2009e. *Table 4 Poverty Status, by Type of Family, Presence of Related Children, Race and Hispanic Origin.* Retrieved September 11, 2009, from http://www.census.gov/hhes/www/poverty/histpov/famindex.html

U.S. Bureau of the Census. 2008a. *2008 National Population Projections Tables and Charts.* Retrieved May 29, 2009, from http://www.census.gov/population/www/projections/tablesandcharts.html.

U.S. Bureau of the Census. 2008b. *Historical Income Tables – People, Table p-36.* Retrieved June 4, 2009, from http://www.census.gov/hhes/www/income/histinc/p36AR.html

U.S. Bureau of the Census. 2007. *American Community Survey, 2007.* Retrieved August 22, 2009, from http://factfinder.census.gov/servlet/DatasetMainPageServlet?_program=ACS&_submenuId=datasets_2&_lang=en

U.S. Bureau of the Census. 2006. *Statistical Abstract of the United States: 2005–2006* (125th ed.). Washington, DC: Government Printing Office.

U.S. Bureau of the Census. 2005. *Statistical Abstract of the United States, 2004–2005* (124th ed.). Washington, DC: Government Printing Office.

U.S. Bureau of the Census. 2004a. *Ancestry 2000.* Retrieved August 21, 2009, from http://www.census.gov/prod/2004pubs/c2kbr-35.pdf

U.S. Bureau of the Census. 2004b. *Current Population Survey, Annual Social and Economic Supplement, 2004, Ethnicity and Ancestry Statistics Branch, Population Division.* Retrieved March 16, 2008, from http://www.census.gov/population/socdemo/hispanic/ASEC2004/2004CPS_tab19.2.pdf

U.S. Bureau of the Census. 2004c. *Poverty Status of Families, by Type of Family, Presence of Related Children, Race, and Hispanic Origin: 1959 to 2003.* Retrieved September 10, 2006, from http://www.census.gov/hhes/poverty/histpov/hstpov4.html

U.S. Bureau of the Census, 2004d. *Race and Ethnicity Data.* Retrieved March 11, 2008, from http://search.census.gov/search?q=region+race&entqr=0&ud=1&output=xml_no_dtd&oe=UTF-8&ie=UTF-8&client=default_frontend&proxystylesheet=default_frontend&site=census

U.S. Bureau of the Census. 2003a. *The Arab Population: 2000.* Retrieved from http://www.census.gov/prod/2003pubs/c2kbr-23.pdf

U.S. Bureau of the Census. 2003b. *The Black Population of the United States, March 2002.* Retrieved April 25, 2003, from http://www.census.gov/prod/2003pubs/p20-541.pdf

U.S. Bureau of the Census. 2002. *Statistical Abstract of the United States, 2001* (121st ed.). Washington, DC: Government Printing Office.

U.S. Bureau of the Census. 2001. *Profiles of General Demographic Characteristics, 2000, Florida.* Retrieved March 16, 2008, from http://www.census.gov/prod/cen2000/dp1/2kh12.pdf

U.S. Bureau of the Census. 2000a. *American Indian and Alaska Native Summary File.* Retrieved August 22, 2009, from http://factfinder.census.gov/servlet/DatasetMainPageServlet?_program=DEC&_submenuId=datasets_1&_lang=en

U.S. Bureau of the Census. 2000b. *Number of People, 2000. One Race: Asian.* Retrieved July 10, 2002, from http://www.census.gov/population/cen2000/atlas/censr01–108.pdf

U.S. Bureau of the Census. 2000c. *Population by Region, Sex, Hispanic Origin, and Race, With Percentage Distribution by Hispanic Origin and Race: March 2000.* Retrieved July 8, 2002, from http://www.census.gov/population/socdemo/hispanic/p20–535/tab19–1.txt

U.S. Bureau of the Census. 2000d. *Population, Race, Hispanic or Latino. Hawaii.* Retrieved July 12, 2002, from http://factfinder.census.gov/bf/_lang=en_vt_name=DEC_2000_PL_U_QTPL_geo_id=04000US15.html

U.S. Bureau of the Census. 2000e. *Poverty Status of Families in 1999 by Family Type, and by Hispanic Origin and Race of Householder.* Retrieved July 8, 2002, from http://www.census.gov/ population/socdemo/hispanic/p20–535/tab15–1.txt

U.S. Bureau of the Census. 2000f. *Profiles of General Demographic Characteristics, 2000.* Retrieved July 8, 2002, from http://www2.census.gov/census_2000/datasets/demographic_profile/Florida/2kh12.pdf

U.S. Bureau of the Census. 2000g. *Projections of Resident Population by Race, Hispanic Origin, and Nativity.* Retrieved September 7, 2006, from http://www.census.Gov/population/www/projections/natsum.html

U.S. Bureau of the Census. 2000h. *Summary File 4.* Retrieved August 23, 2009, from http://www.census.gov/Press-Release/www/2003/SF4.html.

U.S. Bureau of the Census. 2000i. *Pct2. Urban and Rural [7] - Universe: Total Population.* Retrieved March 11, 2008, from http://factfinder.census.gov/servlet/DTTable?_bm=y&-geo_id=01000US&-reg=DEC_2000_SF4_U_PCT002:001|002|004&-ds_name=DEC_2000_SF4_U&-_lang=en&-redoLog=true&-mt_name=DEC_2000_SF4_U_PCT002&-format=&-CONTEXT=dt

U.S. Bureau of the Census. 1998a. *Educational Attainment for Selected Ancestry Groups.* Retrieved July 11, 2002, from http://www.census.gov/population/socdemo/ancestry/table_01.txt

U.S. Bureau of the Census. 1998b. "Income and Poverty for Selected Ancestry Groups." Retrieved July 11, 2002, from http://www.census.gov/population/socdemo/ancestry/table_04.txt

U.S. Bureau of the Census. 1996. *Statistical Abstract of the United States: 1996* (116th ed.). Washington, DC: Government Printing Office.

U.S. Bureau of the Census. 1990a. *Decennial Census.* Retrieved September 4, 2009, from http://factfinder.census.gov/servlet/DatasetMainPageServlet?_program=DEC&_tabId=DEC2&_submenuId=datasets_1&_lang=en&_ts=270116530057

U.S. Bureau of the Census. 1990b. *Statistical Abstract of the United States: 1990.* Washington, DC: U.S. Government Printing Office.

U.S. Bureau of the Census. 1990c. *Summary File 3.* Retrieved March 15, 2008, from http://factfinder.census.gov/servlet/DatasetMainPageServlet?_program=DEC&_submenuId=datasets_1&_lang=en

U.S. Bureau of the Census. 1977. *Statistical Abstract of the United States: 1977* (98th ed.). Washington, DC: Government Printing Office.

U.S. Bureau of the Census, De-Navas, Carmen, Proctor, Bernadette, & Mills, Robert. 2004. *Income, Poverty, and Health Insurance Coverage in the United States: 2003.* Washington, DC: Government Printing Office.

U.S. Commission on Civil Rights. 1976. *Puerto Ricans in the Continental United States: An Uncertain Future.* Washington, DC: Government Printing Office.

U.S. Department of Homeland Security. 2008. *Yearbook of Immigration Statistics: 2008.* Washington, DC: Government Printing Office. Retrieved August 21, 2009, from http://www.dhs.gov/ximgtn/statistics/publications/LPR08.shtm.

U.S. Department of Homeland Security. 2003. *Yearbook of Immigration Statistics: 2002.* Washington, DC: Government Printing Office.

U.S. Department of State. 2008. *Trafficking in Persons Report, 2008.* Retrieved May 15, 2009, from http://www.state.gov/documents/organization/105501.pdf

U.S.English. n.d. *Official English.* Retrieved May 19, 2009, from http://www.us-english.org/view/8

U.S. Immigration and Naturalization Service. 1993. *Statistical Yearbook of the Immigration and Naturalization Service, 1992.* Washington, DC: Government Printing Office.

"Utah Supreme Court Rules That Non-Indian Members of Native American Church Can Use Peyote in Church Ceremonies." *New York Times,* June 23, 2004, p. A20.

Valentine, Sean, & Mosley, Gordon. 2000. "Acculturation and Sex-Role Attitudes Among Mexican Americans: A Longitudinal Analysis." *Hispanic Journal of Behavioral Sciences,* 22:104–204.

Van den Berghe, Pierre L. 1978. *Race and Racism: A Comparative Perspective.* New York: Wiley.

Van den Berghe, Pierre. 1967. *Race and Racism: A Comparative Perspective.* New York Wiley.

Vigilant, Linda. 1997. "Race and Biology." In Winston Van Horne (Ed.), *Global Convulsions: Race, Ethnicity, and Nationalism at the End of the Twentieth Century* (pp. 49–62). Albany: State University of New York Press.

Vincent, Theodore G. 1976. *Black Power and the Garvey Movement.* San Francisco: Ramparts.

Vinje, David. 1996. "Native American Economic Development on Selected Reservations: A Comparative Analysis." *American Journal of Economics and Sociology,* 55:427–442.

Voting Rights Act, 42 U.S.C. § 1971 (1965).

Wagley, Charles, & Harris, Marvin. 1958. *Minorities in the New World: Six Case Studies.* New York: Columbia University Press.

Wallace, Walter. 1997. *The Future of Ethnicity, Race, and Nationality.* Westport, CT: Praeger.

Washington, Booker T. 1965. *Up From Slavery.* New York: Dell.

Waters, Mary. 1990. *Ethnic Options.* Berkeley: University of California Press.

Waters, Mary, & Jimenez, Tomas. 2005. "Assessing Immigrant Assimilation: New Empirical and Theoretical Challenges." *American Review of Sociology,* 31:105–125.

Wax, Murray. 1971. *Indian Americans: Unity and Diversity.* Englewood Cliffs, NJ: Prentice Hall.

Weeks, Philip. 1988. *The American Indian Experience.* Arlington Heights, IL: Forum Press.

Weisman, Jonathan. 2008, July 10. "Rev. Jackson Apologizes to Obama." *Washington Post,* p. A4.

Weitzer, Ronald, & Tuch, Steven. 2005. "Racially Biased Policing: Determinants of Citizen Perceptions." *Social Forces,* 83:1009–1030.

Wellner, Alison. 2007. *U.S. Attitudes Toward Interracial Dating Are Liberalizing.* Population Reference Bureau. Retrieved December 5, 2007, from http://www.prb.org/Articles/2005/USAttitudesTowardInterracialDatingAreLiberalizing.aspx.

Wertheimer, Barbara M. 1979. "'Union Is Power': Sketches From Women's Labor History." In Jo Freeman (Ed.), *Women: A Feminist Perspective* (pp. 339–358). Palo Alto, CA: Mayfield.

West, Patrick. 2002. "The New Ireland Kicks Ass." *New Statesman London,* June 17, pp. 20–22.

White, Deborah Gray. 1985. *Ar'n't I a Woman? Female Slaves in the Plantation South.* New York: Norton.

White, Michael, & Glick, Jennifer. 2009. *Achieving Anew: How New Immigrants Do in American Schools, Jobs, and Neighborhoods.* New York: Russell Sage.

The White House. 2005. *Economic Report of the President.* Retrieved July 28, 2009, from http://www.gpoaccess.gov/eop/download.html

Whiting, Robert. 1990. *You Gotta Have Wa.* New York: Macmillan.

Whitlock, Craig. 2005, February 14. "As Dresden Recalls Days of Ruin, Neo-Nazis Issue a Rallying Cry." *The Washington Post*, February 14, p. A1.

Wilkins, Roger. 1992, May 3. "L.A.: Images in the Flames—Looking Back in Anger: 27 Years After Watts, Our Nation Remains Divided by Racism." *Washington Post*, p. C1.

Williams, Gregory. 1995. *Life on the Color Line*. New York: Dutton.

Willie, Charles (Ed.). 1989. *Round Two of the Willie/Wilson Debate* (2nd ed.). Dix Hills, NY: General Hall.

Wilson, George. 1997. "Payoffs to Power Among Males in the Middle Class: Has Race Declined in Its Significance?" *Sociological Quarterly*, 38:607–623.

Wilson, William J. 2009. *More Than Just Race*. New York: Norton.

Wilson, William J. 1996. *When Work Disappears*. New York: Knopf.

Wilson, William J. (Ed.). 1992. *The Ghetto Underclass*. Newbury Park, CA: Sage.

Wilson, William J. 1987. *The Truly Disadvantaged: The Inner City, The Underclass, and Public Policy*. Chicago: University of Chicago Press.

Wilson, William J. 1980. *The Declining Significance of Race* (2nd ed.). Chicago: University of Chicago Press.

Wilson, William J. 1973. *Power, Racism, and Privilege: Race Relations in Theoretical and Sociohistorical Perspectives*. New York: Free Press.

Wirth, Louis. 1945. "The Problem of Minority Groups." In Ralph Linton (Ed.), *The Science of Man in the World* (pp. 347–372). New York: Columbia University Press.

Wise, Tim. 2009. *Between Barack and a Hard Place*. San Francisco: City Lights.

Wolfenstein, Eugene V. 1993. *The Victims of Democracy: Malcolm X*. New York: Guilford.

Wong, Jade Snow. 1993. "Fifth Chinese Daughter." In Dolores LaGuardia & Hans Guth (Eds.), *American Voices*. Palo Alto, CA: Mayfield.

Wong, Morrison. 1995. "Chinese Americans." In Pyong Gap Min (Ed.), *Asian Americans: Contemporary Trends and Issues* (pp. 58–94). Thousand Oaks, CA: Sage.

Woodrum, Eric. 1979. "Japanese Americans: A Test of the Assimilation Success Story." Paper presented at the Southern Sociological Society, April, Atlanta, GA.

Woodward, C. Vann. 1974. *The Strange Career of Jim Crow* (3rd rev. ed.). New York: Oxford University Press.

Worsnop, Richard. 1992. "Native Americans." *CQ Researcher*, May 8, pp. 387–407.

Wyman, Mark. 1993. *Round Trip to America*. Ithaca, NY: Cornell University Press.

Xie, Yu, & Goyette, Kimberly. 2004. *A Demographic Portrait of Asian Americans*. New York: Russell Sage Foundation.

Yamato, Alexander. 1994. "Racial Antagonism and the Formation of Segmented Labor Markets: Japanese Americans and Their Exclusion From the Work Force." *Humboldt Journal of Social Relations*, 20:31–63.

Yancy, George. 2003. *Who Is White? Latinos, Asians, and the New Black/Non-Black Divide*. Boulder, CO: Lynne Rienner.

Yinger, J. Milton. 1985. "Ethnicity." *Annual Review of Sociology*, 11:151–180.

Zhou, Min. 1992. *Chinatown*. Philadelphia: Temple University Press.

Zhou, Min, & Logan, John R. 1989. "Returns on Human Capital in Ethnic Enclaves: New York City's Chinatown." *American Sociological Review*, 54:809–820.

Zinn, Maxine Baca, & Dill, Bonnie Thornton (Eds.). 1994. *Women of Color in U.S. Society*. Philadelphia: Temple University Press.

Zinn, Maxine Baca, & Eitzen, D. Stanley. 1990. *Diversity in Families*. New York: HarperCollins.

Index

About the Author

Joseph F. Healey is Professor of Sociology at Christopher Newport University in Virginia. He received his PhD in sociology and anthropology from the University of Virginia. An experienced, innovative teacher of numerous race and ethnicity courses, he has written articles on minority groups, the sociology of sport, social movements, and violence, and he is also the author of *Statistics: A Tool for Social Research* (8th ed., 2008).

Appendix

Selections From CQ Researcher

Census Controversy: Should Undocumented Immigrants Be Counted?

The Issues

First, the good news: When the Pew Research Center asked Americans in March for their views about the 2010 U.S. census, most respondents said they were ready to participate in the once-every-decade portrait of the national population.[1]

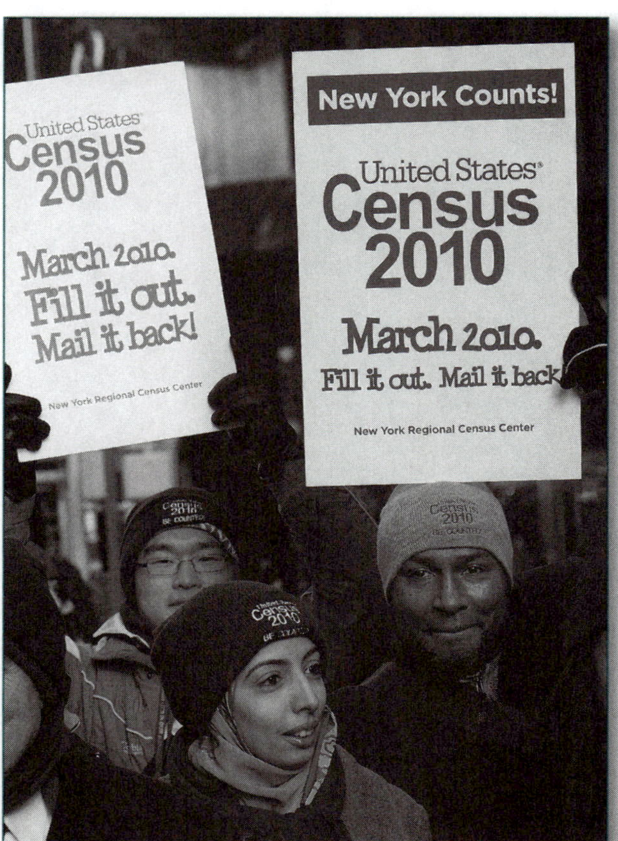

Census workers kick off the 2010 census at a rally in New York City's Times Square on Jan. 4. Censuses have been controversial since the first one in 1790, and this year's is no exception. Partisans on the right and left raised questions about a range of issues, including accuracy, invasion of privacy, counting of same-sex couples and U.S. immigration policy.

Getty Images/Mario Tama

Now the not-so-good news: The positive public response masked an angry debate over this year's census, including concerns about its accuracy. "This is probably the most polarized, political census I've seen," says Jacqueline Byers, director of research and outreach at the National Association of Counties and a veteran of four censuses.

As the census moved into full swing this spring, the decennial ritual became a lens through which partisans on both the right and left filtered their views on a range of policy issues. Ultraconservative Republicans, for example, criticized the census as an unconstitutional intrusion on privacy. Evangelical Latino pastors urged undocumented immigrants to boycott the count to protest congressional inaction on immigration reform. Liberals hailed a new census policy allowing same-sex couples to be counted as married; some conservatives called it political pandering.[2] Even the census form's question on racial background has sparked debate. (*See "At Issue," p. A-25.*)

In fact, every census — going back to the first one in 1790 — has been controversial. That's no surprise, given the political power and money at stake: Census counts are used to apportion congressional seats, redraw congressional, state and local legislative districts, and, according to a new study, allocate $447 billion in federal assistance to states and localities.[3]

From *CQ Researcher*, May 2010

The 2010 census is the most expensive ever at an estimated cost of $14.5 billion, but its impact on government outlays will be vast. "The outsized influence of census statistics on federal funding indicates the enormous return on taxpayer investment in federal statistics," Brooking Institution fellow Andrew Reamer wrote. "One way to think about this is that the $14 billion life-cycle cost of the 2010 census will enable the fair allocation of nearly $5 trillion in funds over the coming decade (not adjusting for inflation or other changes)."[4]

Yet the census has faced myriad logistical and ideological challenges.

Last year a government report said "uncertainties" surrounded the Census Bureau's readiness for the 2010 census.[5] One problem concerned a planned technical innovation: the use of special hand-held computers to verify addresses and conduct follow-up interviews with non-responding households. The devices didn't work as hoped, however, and are being used only for address verification, forcing the bureau to do pencil-and-paper follow-up interviews. And congressional squabbling over the Obama administration's appointment of a new secretary at the Commerce Department, which oversees the Census Bureau, and confirmation of a new bureau director disrupted planning.

Still, census officials are optimistic about the 2010 count and in late April were citing an encouraging sign: 72 percent of census forms had been returned by households that received them, matching the rate in the 2000 census.[6]

"Response rates in surveys have declined each year throughout the Western world," bureau director Robert M. Groves wrote in his blog. "I fully expected the census to achieve lower participation rates this decade than it did in 2000. It basically didn't happen." Even so, he added, "there is much hard work ahead to follow up on the approximately 48 million households that did not mail back a form," or didn't receive one, "and risks remain."[7]

The bureau made several significant changes this year, in part to encourage a stronger response. For example, after employing a paid advertising campaign for the first time in the 2000 census, the bureau increased its advertising and promotion efforts for the 2010 count to a total of $340 million — inviting criticism from budget hawks. As of May, a census official said the bureau spent $171 million for TV, radio, digital, print and outdoor advertising in 28 languages — including television ads before and during the Super Bowl. The bureau also sponsored a NASCAR race car and a 13-vehicle nationwide promotional road tour. The bureau also has used the Internet to boost response rates, offering, among other things, an interactive map that tracks community participation rates.[8] Certain areas of the country are receiving questionnaires in both English and Spanish.[9]

But perhaps the most far-reaching change has to do with the questionnaire itself. In another effort to encourage response, the bureau eliminated the traditional detailed "long form" survey on demographic, housing and economic factors sent to about a sixth of households since 1960. Instead, a brief 10-question form is being sent to every household. To replace the data collected by the old long form, the Census Bureau is using a separate questionnaire, the American Community Survey (ACS), which is sent to about 250,000 households each month, providing researchers with a steady flow of "rolling" socioeconomic data throughout the decade rather than a once-per-decade snapshot.

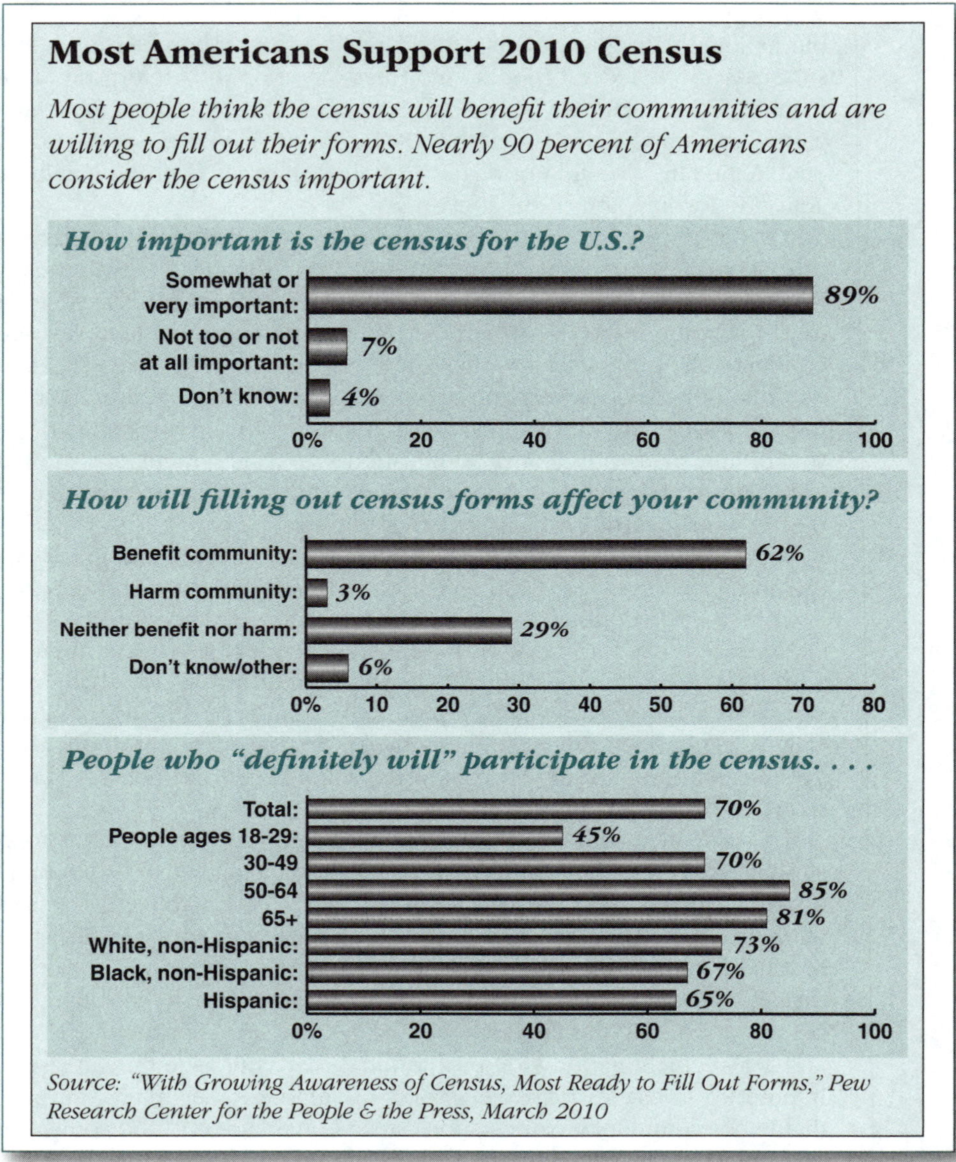

For demographers, statisticians and scholars, the change is huge — and not without some anxiety. In the short term, researchers say the switch will force them to learn how to use the rolling data and reconcile it with decennial statistics gathered by the old long form. Some worry the new ACS survey sample size may curtail the amount of useful data. But ultimately, many say, the change will be beneficial. The switch will be "extremely positive, even transforming," because it will provide more timely data, asserts Kenneth Prewitt, Census Bureau director in the Clinton administration and now a professor of public affairs at Columbia University.

Against the backdrop of operational challenges and technical change, the 2010 census has sparked bitter partisanship, raising concern that some Americans might not participate in the count even though federal law makes it mandatory to do so.

Non-cooperation costs the taxpayers heavily. The government saves $85 million for each percentage-point increase in the mail-back response rate for this year's census, Groves noted. When households don't complete a form in a timely way, the bureau must send out paid "enumerators" — some 635,000 temporary workers this year — to knock on doors and collect the information first-hand. On average, it costs 42 cents when people mail back their form, but $57 for a census taker's visit.[10]

Heightening public wariness of the census has been a tide of conservative rhetoric raising the specter of unwarranted government intrusion. U.S. Rep. Michele Bachmann, R-Minn., vowed not to provide any information except the number of people in her household, claiming last year that census questions had become "very intricate, very personal."[11] Rep. Ron Paul, R-Texas, the only House member to oppose a resolution urging census participation, opined that the census "was never intended to serve as a vehicle for gathering personal information on citizens."[12] And Republican blogger Erick Erickson, founder of the conservative website RedState.com, said he would pull out a shotgun to scare away a census worker who showed up at his house. "We are becoming enslaved by the government," he declared.[13]

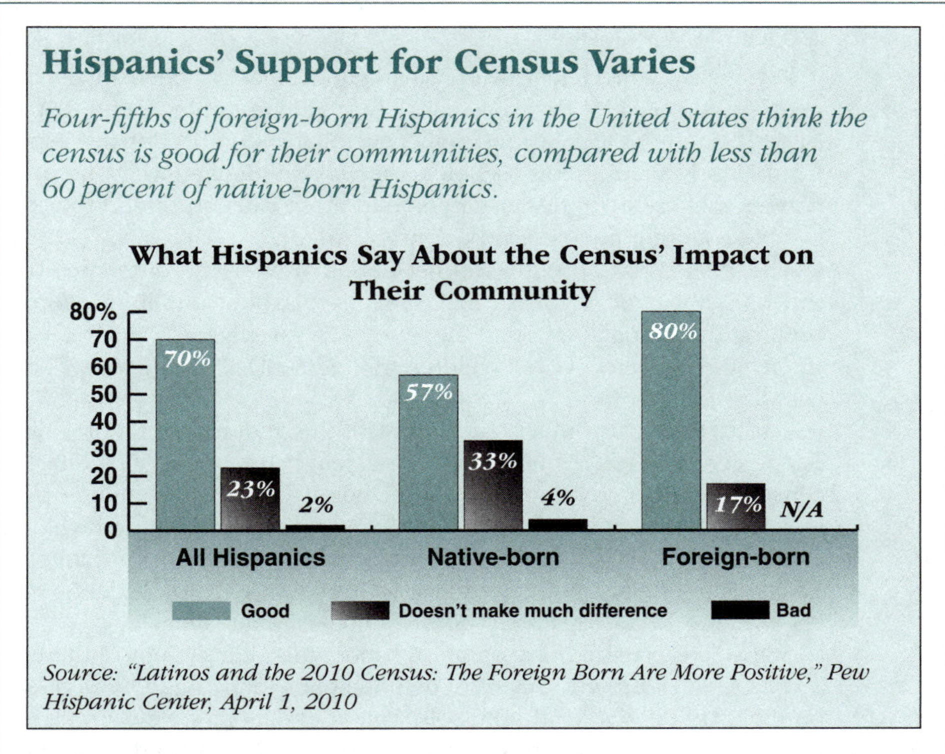

Hispanics' Support for Census Varies

Four-fifths of foreign-born Hispanics in the United States think the census is good for their communities, compared with less than 60 percent of native-born Hispanics.

Source: "Latinos and the 2010 Census: The Foreign Born Are More Positive," Pew Hispanic Center, April 1, 2010

But Rep. Patrick McHenry, R-N.C., warned against such anti-census rhetoric. Boycotting the census "offends me as an American patriot," he said, warning of potential negative consequences for the GOP. Writing on RedState.com, he said he worried about "blatant misinformation coming from otherwise well-meaning conservatives" who "are helping big-government liberals by discouraging fellow conservatives from filling out their census forms." Not responding to the census would "reduce conservatives' power in elections, allow Democrats to draw more favorable congressional boundaries and help put more tax-hiking politicians in office," he wrote.[14]

Of course, Americans of every political persuasion sometimes balk at filling out census forms. Steven Jost, associate director of communications for the Census Bureau, said the challenges in conducting the census "go across the whole demography of our country."

In researching public attitudes toward the census, he found that "about 19 percent of the people we interviewed . . . are just cynical about government. And when we looked at the makeup of that cynical fifth, it was identical to the makeup of the population as a whole — age, race, gender, education, income levels. We're in a tough environment in our country now with mistrust of government, and we happen to be the face of the government right now."[15]

As this year's census controversy heats up, here are some of the questions being asked:

Will the census be accurate?

A key goal of this year's census marketing blitz has been to persuade as many people as possible to participate. But getting an accurate count isn't easy. Undercounting is a recurring challenge for the Census Bureau, especially among minorities, low-income households, renters and immigrants.[16] The political implications of that are high, because people in those categories tend to vote Democratic. Double-counting people can be a problem, too.

The 1990 census produced a net undercount — the difference between incorrect omissions and incorrect inclusions — of about 4 million people, or 1.6 percent of the population, but the rate was far higher for blacks (4.6 percent), Hispanics (5.0 percent) and children (3.2 percent). The rate for whites was 0.7 percent.[17]

The 2000 census did a better job, with the undercount rate for blacks falling to 1.8 percent and for Hispanics to 0.7 percent.[18] But for the first time in history, the census had a net overcount. It double-counted nearly 5.8 million people, helping create a net overcount of 1.3 million.[19] Overcounts can happen when, for instance, a college student is tallied at a dorm and counted again by parents back home. This year's form warns households not to count college students, soldiers or others who are living separately but may come home later.

Many census experts are optimistic about this year's count. "I think it will be very accurate," says Brown University demographer John Logan, who directs a program on the 2010 census for the Russell Sage Foundation, a New York research center. "They've done a very professional job and are rolling with the punches," he says of the Census Bureau.

Still, the bureau faces several challenges in arriving at a reliable count. One is the nation's growing immigrant population — legal and illegal — both of which the census tallies.

To be sure, many immigrants are highly supportive of the census — foreign-born immigrants all the more so. The Pew Hispanic Center found in a March poll that 85 percent of Hispanics said they had already sent in their census form or definitely would do so. The return rate for foreign-born Hispanics was 91 percent and for native-born Hispanics 78 percent. What's more, 69 percent of foreign-born Hispanics correctly said the census can't be used to determine legal status, compared with 57 percent of native-born Hispanics.[20]

Even so, experts are concerned that many immigrants may be wary of participating. "There's a huge fear factor," says Prewitt, the former Census Bureau director. Contributing to that fear, he says, are such actions as Arizona's passage last month of a strict new law aimed at identifying and deporting illegal immigrants.[21]

"You can say over and over that the census is confidential, but in parts of the country that message is very hard to communicate," says Prewitt. He expects it to be "much, much harder to count the undocumented" this year "because of a serious change in the environment" surrounding immigration.

Angelo Falcón, president of the National Institute for Latino Policy, a New York City-based think tank, says he is sure "there will be an undercount of Latinos" —

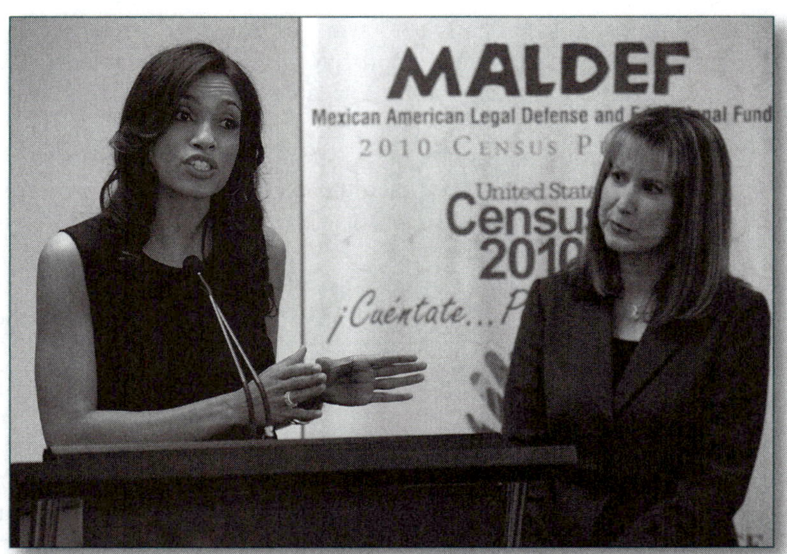

Actress Rosario Dawson announces in Los Angeles on March 10 a multimedia plan by the Mexican American Legal Defense and Educational Fund (MALDEF) and Voto Latino to encourage young California Latinos to fill out their census forms. At right is Nancy Agosto, national census director for MALDEF.

AP Photo/Chris Pizzello

due both to the fear factor and the difficulty of counting some demographic groups. "People are trying to get the word out locally" about the census, Falcón says. "We're hoping there aren't any further problems in terms of an anti-immigrant sentiment or the Department of Homeland Security doesn't have any major high-profile raids" during the census count. "Those types of things can affect whether people want to cooperate or not." And as the Census Bureau sends workers to neighborhoods to contact non-responding households, Falcón says, "it will be a test to see if the bureau did a good job in hiring people from those same neighborhoods" so residents will be willing to let the census workers into their homes.

Another roadblock to census accuracy is the difficulty of locating people in certain locales. For example, in hurricane-ravaged New Orleans, "determining how many people live [there] will not be an easy task, given the thousands who are still homeless or living with relatives as they await permanent housing," *The New York Times* noted. The newspaper added that the Census Bureau was "allowing some unconventional counting practices," such as distributing forms to people who are not at verified addresses.[22]

The fragile national economy also can upset population counts in several ways. With unemployment in the 10 percent range, some people have left home in search of work and are hard to pin down. Others may be homeless or living in temporary group quarters.

What's more, many states and localities have been short on funds for census outreach. In California, which is facing a $20 billion budget shortfall, money for census outreach was slashed to $2 million, compared with nearly $25 million in 2000. The state could lose nearly $3,000 a year in federal assistance for each resident not counted. "We need to make a push to make sure we at least stay even," said Louis Stewart, deputy director of California's census outreach. "There is a lot riding on this count."[23]

Charities and community-based groups have taken up some of the slack left by depleted state budgets. The philanthropic community poured some $15 million into census-promotion efforts, much of it directed to difficult-to-count areas and community groups serving them, according to Terri Ann Lowenthal, a census consultant and former staff director of the House census oversight subcommittee. She said the collaboration has helped push response rates above the national average in some hard-to-count areas.[24]

Deep-seated mistrust of government also can influence how people respond to the census. A new Pew Research Center survey found that only 22 percent of respondents said they could trust the government in Washington almost always or most of the time, the lowest by far since at least the Kennedy administration.[25]

Asked why he thought Republican opposition existed toward this year's census, Reamer, the Brookings Institution fellow, said "some people are using the census as a symbol of big, intrusive government, seeking to stoke fear and paranoia about government in general and the Democrats in particular." In addition, he said, "straight-up political reality is that Republicans benefit from an undercount of non-whites, who tend to vote Democratic. Democrats are the beneficiaries of a low undercount."[26]

Should the census include undocumented immigrants?

Last fall, Republican Sens. Bob Bennett of Utah and David Vitter of Louisiana proposed an amendment requiring that the census include a question on citizenship, a move aimed at removing undocumented immigrants from the count. The Senate rejected their amendment, but Bennett vowed to keep pushing for it in future censuses "so we can fairly determine congressional representation and ensure that legal residents are equally represented."[27]*

But many say such a move runs counter to the historical roots of the census. The 1790 Census Act said the decennial census "should count everyone living in the country where they usually reside," bureau director Groves told a press briefing last fall. "That applied to every census since 1790."[28]

Groves said he had "no idea how people would react" to a census question asking if a person is in the country legally or not, saying it was "really hard" to say. But experts say asking people whether they're citizens would lead many immigrants not to participate for fear of harassment or deportation. "I just want to know how you get somebody to respond to say they're citizens or not," says Byers of the National Association of Counties.

Beyond that practical consideration, many argue that given the census' key uses — to apportion congressional seats and allocate federal money — a count of all inhabitants is crucial.

"Everyone is protected by the law, so everyone should be counted in determining how many seats a state gets to write those laws," wrote Robert J. Shapiro, a

Midwest Returned Most Census Forms

The 10 areas with the best records for returning 2010 census forms are in the Midwest; Livonia, Mich., held the record, at 87 percent. Nationwide, 72 percent of American households returned forms before the May 1 deadline.

Top 10 Areas to Return Census Forms		
1.	Livonia, Mich.	87%
2.	Green Township, Ohio	86%
3.	Maple Grove, Minn.	86%
4.	Appleton, Wis.	85%
5.	Carmel, Ind.	85%
6.	Clay Township, Ind.	85%
7.	Eau Claire, Wis.	85%
8.	Frankfort Township, Ill.	85%
9.	Lakeville, Minn.	85%
10.	Macomb Township, Mich.	85%

Top Five States to Return Census Forms		
1.	Wisconsin	81%
2.	Minnesota	80%
3.	Indiana	78%
4.	Iowa	78%
5.	Michigan	77%

Source: "Take 10 Map: 2010 Census Participation Rates," U.S. Census Bureau, April 27, 2010

* Bennett, a three-term, 76-year-old Senate veteran, was denied his party's nomination for a fourth term on May 8 by the Utah GOP convention, making him one of the first congressional victims of the growing power of the conservative Tea Party movement.

former Commerce Department official who oversaw the 2000 census. "And whether or not someone has citizenship or residency papers, they still put claims on public services, which the funding for those services should reflect."

Shapiro said the implications of using the census to identify undocumented immigrants are "enormous." California "may have as many as 4 or 5 million undocumented inhabitants," he wrote. "Exclude them and the state could lose perhaps a half-dozen seats in Congress and tens of billions of dollars in federal funds. Texas and other states with large Hispanic populations would lose seats and funding as well."[29]

The controversy over citizenship goes beyond the census and flows into the country's fractious debate over immigration reform. The Rev. Miguel Rivera, leader of the National Coalition of Latino Clergy and Christian Leaders, which represents 20,000 churches in 34 states, has urged undocumented immigrants to boycott the census to protest Congress' failure to overhaul immigration laws.

As explained by National Public Radio last year, Rivera realized members of Congress have a big stake in the census because their seats and federal funding for their districts depend on the count. "So if they don't want lacking of funding for their constituents, [and] maybe losing seats at the congressional level, then what they have to do is roll [up] their sleeves and move forward with comprehensive immigration reform," Rivera said.[30]

But other Hispanic leaders who back immigration reform see it differently. "It's sad. It's unfortunate. Ultimately, it means more political power for the people who don't like immigrants," said the Rev. Luis Cortes, president of Esperanza, a faith-based network that claims more than 12,000 Hispanic congregations and other organizations.[31]

In this year's Pew Hispanic Center poll, 70 percent of Hispanics said the census is good for the Hispanic community. What's more, foreign-born Hispanics were more positive and knowledgeable about this year's census than were native-born Hispanics, Pew found.[32]

"We should be counting everybody," says Falcón of the National Institute for Latino Policy. "That's what the Constitution said. . . . It's a question of people who live here, who use the services here, who contribute here. Whether they're here legally or not, legally at a certain point becomes irrelevant. Even for reapportionment you can make the argument that these are people who require the political system to be responsive to them. They do contribute, and they are part of the body politic. Maybe they can't vote, but they might be able to contribute money or participate in campaigns. . . . I'm part of that group that would like to get a lot of these people legalized and become part of American society. By counting them you basically include them in the process."

But Mark Krikorian, executive director of the Center for Immigration Studies, a conservative think tank in Washington, is "ambivalent" on whether undocumented immigrants should be counted. He would "much rather enforce the immigration laws so it is a less salient issue in the first place," he says. A "second-best" approach would be to count everybody and use that number for dispensing federal funds, but use only a count of U.S. citizens for determining House and state legislative seats.

But that would require asking about citizenship status — a step that many say would make the census count unreliable.

States Receive Most Census-Based Federal Funds

State governments received most of the federal funds distributed on the basis of census data (top). Four major program areas — health, housing, transportation and education — received more than 90 percent of census-based funds (bottom).

Geographic Distribution of Federal Funds Based on Census Data, FY 2008

Geographic Level	Programs	Expenditures (in $ billions)	% of Total*
State	116	$386.0	86.4%
Local area	75	$78.4	17.6%
County	49	$50.3	11.3%
Metropolitan Statistical Area	45	$49.4	11.1%
School district	7	$10.3	2.3%
Census tract	7	$76.2	0.0%

Census-Guided Programs by Budget Function, FY 2008

Budget Function	Programs	Expenditures (in $ billions)	% of Total
Health	24	$272.2	60.9%
Section 8 Housing Subsidies	31	$55.3	12.4%
Transportation	11	$48.3	10.8%
Education, Training, Employment and Social Services	54	$40.0	9.0%
Community and Regional Development	34	$10.5	2.4%
Commerce and Housing Credit	13	$9.8	2.2%
Energy	4	$2.3	0.5%
Other	44	$8.0	1.8%

** Totals add to more than 100 percent because one program can use data for more than one geographic level.*

Source: "Counting for Dollars: The Role of the Decennial Census in the Distribution of Federal Funds," Brookings Institution, March 9, 2010

Should the census long form be replaced by the American Community Survey?

For decades, while most Americans filled out a regular census form, about one in six households received a more in-depth "long-form" questionnaire that asked about everything from education levels and commuting patterns to home-heating fuel and family income. The data served many purposes. Government officials used it, for example, to plan new roads, measure poverty and allocate federal funds. Demographers used it to spot social trends. Businesses used it to decide where to build everything from stores to power plants.

The Census Bureau is still asking such questions, but starting this year it is using the ongoing American Community Survey (ACS) to do so in place of the old decennial census long form. Each month the ACS is mailed to about 250,000 households — 3 million a year — and, as with the census, recipients are legally bound to fill it out.

The ACS has both pluses and minuses compared to the old long form, demographers, researchers and census scholars say. On the plus side, the flow of data will be continual and far timelier than information gleaned from the once-a-decade long form.

"With the [ACS], it's no longer necessary to rely on a single snapshot of an area that becomes increasingly dated throughout the decade," the Census Bureau says. "Instead, the survey provides a moving picture of community characteristics — a more efficient use of taxpayer dollars."[33]

Five-year data will be published on areas with fewer than 20,000 residents. Three- and five-year data will be available on areas with populations between 20,000 and 65,000. And annual data, plus three- and five-year data, will be published on areas with 65,000 or more people.

The Census Bureau began developing the ACS in the early 2000s and rolled it out in 2005. Three-year data are out now, and later this year the bureau will produce its first set of five-year ACS data, covering 2005 through 2009.

On the downside, say census experts, the ACS samples fewer households than the old long form did, though the Obama administration is seeking additional funding to increase the sample size. What's more, data on small communities won't be available as quickly as for larger cities and regions. And while multiyear data are often more useful than a 10-year snapshot, they can blur sharp economic ups and downs, presenting an unreliable picture of prevailing conditions.

"There are lots of rationales for what the Census Bureau is doing," says Byers of the National Association of Counties. Areas with 65,000 or more residents make up 82 percent of the U.S. population, she notes. But "they don't do as frequent an update of the smaller counties. And we're a nation of smaller counties."

CQ Weekly noted in December that the ACS "has been surveying a smaller and smaller portion of the population every year because its budget has remained essentially flat." In fiscal 2009, about $200 million was spent on the survey, which paid for interviews of about 3 million households, roughly the same number as in prior years, the magazine said. "That used to amount to about 2.5 percent of all the households in the United States," it said, but with population growth the same survey reaches just over 2 percent of households. Some experts say the sampling of small geographic areas or population groups, such as teen mothers or people older than 85, "is becoming too small to be statistically reliable," noted the *Weekly*.[34]

Cynthia Taeuber, a retired Census Bureau statistician who runs a consulting firm on census issues, said "this is a very big loss to businesses and to state, local and federal governments. It means that federal programs are distributing funds — say, for poverty within cities or population within rural areas — on shaky data."[35]

Reamer, the Brookings Institution scholar, says that while the ACS data will be more timely, "the tradeoff is that it's not an estimate of a point in time like the traditional long-form data." That can matter in periods when the economy is in flux, such as the one the nation has been experiencing, Reamer says. "Late in 2010, we'll get 2005-2009 data" for areas under 20,000 population, "which was the end of a boom period and the beginning and middle of recession. We're going to get somewhat of a muddled picture of economic conditions" at the neighborhood level.

For transportation planners, among the heaviest users of census data, the switch to the ACS is especially challenging. Alan Pisarski, author of a series of reports on commuting patterns published by the National Academy of Sciences, warned that the number of households surveyed in any given year will be too small to provide the kind of granular data needed to plan bus routes, traffic intersections and other needs. The old long form "gave you not only county-level detail but census tract detail — it even gave you block-group-level data," he says. With the ACS's "very small" sample, Pisarski says, "it's enough to give you good national stuff, but nowhere near as close as blocks. That means that a lot of the stuff [won't] be useful."

The ACS is "a very big change," one with "a short-term cost," says Logan, the Brown University demographer. Noting its smaller sample size, he says, "When we get Census 2010 data, we're not going to know as much, with as much accuracy and detail, about the population in neighborhoods of big cities or about small towns or smaller counties, even areas of 40,000 or 50,000 people. We're going to be dependent on the ACS, which is not a substitute for that one-time, very detailed and pretty accurate picture."

Still, Logan says, researchers will get used to the ACS. "It will be a very big contribution to see trends as they are appearing. It's something we could not do" with the 10-year snapshot provided by the long form.

Indeed, many say the switch to the ACS will be a plus in the long run. Census scholar Margo J. Anderson, a professor of history and urban studies at the University of Wisconsin-Milwaukee, points out that the long form had been spurring "increasing questions about privacy and its onerous length," dragging down response rates.

Because the ACS will provide a steady flow of timely data on local population characteristics, Anderson says it "will be very nice for local-government planning, allocation of federal money and so forth." On the downside, she notes, it'll be a different kind of data. "Users are going to have to get used to it. But in the long term it's an improvement."

Joseph Salvo, New York City's chief demographer, says the advantages of the switch outweigh the disadvantages, which include educating data users to learn to work with multiyear averages rather than data based on a fixed point in time.

But overall, the switch is clearly "positive," Salvo says. "If you go back to 2000 and look at data from the long form, a lot of it is bad," he says. "For example, the economic data in the Bronx was compromised because a whole bunch of people did not respond." The degree to which the Census Bureau had to substitute values for the missing data was "very high in a whole bunch of items in a whole bunch of communities."

Salvo also expects response rates on the ACS to be better because professional interviewers are following up with non-responders.

"The major plus is that we get data more than once a decade," Salvo says. "We get data — new estimates — every year."

Background

The First Census

This spring, a first edition of the first U.S. census, signed in 1791 by then-Secretary of State Thomas Jefferson, sold at auction for more than $122,000.[36] Jefferson's signature helped make the 56-page document a historical prize, but that first census is notable for another reason, too: Like every U.S. census that followed, the 1790 count spurred discord and doubt.

The first census, which broke out the 1790 population into free people and slaves, concluded that the new nation contained 3.9 million people. Jefferson and President George Washington both expected the count to be higher — at least 4 million if not, in Jefferson's mind, 4 to 5 million.[37]

"Washington had expected a population about 5 percent higher and blamed the 'inaccuracy' on avoidance by some residents as well as on negligence by those responsible for taking the census," former Census Bureau director Prewitt wrote. "This was not an idle irritation on Washington's part," Prewitt added. Washington "worried that a small population would tempt America's European enemies to military action."[38]

That first census was controversial for another reason, too: politics. Washington exercised the first of his two presidential vetoes on a bill to apportion House seats. Opposing sides had formed around two competing formulas, one proposed by Alexander Hamilton of New York and the other supported by Jefferson of Virginia. Washington's veto led Congress to adopt Jefferson's method.[39]

"This battle between North and South, between political parties, between geographic areas with large populations and those with small populations, or between urban and rural areas, is central to nearly all controversy over apportionment and districting from 1790 to the present," wrote census expert David McMillen.[40]

In the 1800s, the North-South battle was fought not only with Civil War cannons but also with census counts, and the slavery issue was at the heart of it.

Under an infamous compromise made during the Constitutional Convention in 1787, only three-fifths of the slave population was to be counted when apportioning seats in the House. The result was growing political power among Republican-dominated Northern states compared with the Democrat-controlled South, where most slaves lived. But in 1865, slavery was abolished through the 13th Amendment, effectively ending the three-fifths compromise. On paper, at least, that shifted more political power to the South. Even so, slavery's legacy and its relationship to the census remained an issue and became a factor in the push for civil rights in the post-Civil War South.

"Northern Republicans realized that the census and reapportionment would work to their political *dis*advantage after the Civil War and Reconstruction," wrote Anderson, the University of Wisconsin historian. With the demise of the three-fifths compromise, "the Southern states would gain a windfall of increased representation in Congress. However, since few policymakers expected the freed slaves to be able to vote initially, they realized that a disfranchised free black population would strengthen the white-led Southern states and permit the Democrats to come dangerously close to gaining control of the presidency as early as 1868. The logic of population counting and apportionment, therefore, was one of the major forces driving Congress to extend further political and civil rights to the freedmen."[41]

Rural-Urban Fight

Just as the census and reapportionment factored in Civil War-era racial tensions, they also formed a backdrop for another major battle — this one between cities and rural regions.

As a result of the 1920 census, the government announced that most Americans now lived in urban areas, a monumental shift that, as Anderson wrote, "threatened to undermine the rural states' domination of national politics and the rural towns' domination of state politics."[42] Rural legislators challenged the 1920 census count and refused to give up power, and for the only time in U.S. history Congress did not pass a reapportionment bill after a census.

The rural-urban squabble had lasting effects. As part of a reapportionment bill based on the 1930 census, Congress set aside a requirement that congressional districts be roughly equal in size. "In short, Congress redistributed political power among the states but quietly permitted malapportioned districts within states in order to preserve rural and small-town dominance of Congress," Anderson wrote. She added that malapportionment remained the norm until the 1960s.[43]

In 1962, in the landmark ruling *Baker v. Carr*, the Supreme Court held that voters could bring a constitutional challenge to a state's legislative apportionment. The decision opened the door to a series of rulings that local and state legislative bodies as well as congressional districts must be apportioned according to what became known as the "one-person, one-vote rule" — in other words, districts had to contain a roughly equal number of people as tallied in the decennial census. "Other methods of drawing legislative districts, which might use political or geographic boundaries, were invalid if those districts were not equal in population," Anderson noted.[44]

Meanwhile, the growing focus on antidiscrimination laws was helping to spotlight the issue of census accuracy and the problem of undercounting minorities. Undercounting had been a concern ever since the first census in 1790, but for 150 years demographers and census officials had little in the way of hard proof that undercounting — particularly of African-Americans — existed to any significant degree. That changed in 1940 at the advent of World War II.

As noted by the Census Bureau, demographic analysis showed that 3 percent more draft-age men, including 13 percent more blacks, registered for the World War II draft pool than were counted in the 1940 census, proving that censuses were missing part of the population.[45]

Concerns about undercounting — especially of minorities — led to major changes in modern census methods. Over the past six decades those changes

(Text continues on page A-19)

CHRONOLOGY

1790-1800s ***Constitution's mandate for a decennial census sparks political conflict over how the American population is counted.***

1790 First census puts population at 3.9 million, lower than the figure President George Washington and then-Secretary of State Thomas Jefferson hoped for; slaves counted as three-fifths of a person; Washington vetoes apportionment bill he saw as unfair.

1865 Thirteenth Amendment abolishes slavery, ending three-fifths count for African-Americans and effectively shifting more political power to the South.

1900-1950s ***Farm-to-city population shifts and undercounting of minorities cast new attention on census data.***

1902 Congress creates Census Office.

1920 Census finds that most Americans live in cities; rural legislators challenge census count, and Congress fails to pass a reapportionment bill.

1940 First hard evidence of undercounting emerges as demographic analysis shows that 3 percent more draft-age men, including 13 percent more blacks, registered for the draft pool than were counted in the 1940 census.

1951 Newly invented Univac computer used in final stages of 1950 census.

1957 Census Act allows sampling to be used in the 1960 census.

1960s-1980s ***Concern about undercounting grows among civil rights groups, cities and states.***

1969 *Ebony* magazine pushes for "accurate Black count," telling readers that census counts are important to government and industry for apportionment, program planning and analysis.

1976 In effort to address undercount, Congress amends the Census Act to require the Commerce secretary to use sampling "if he considers it feasible."

1980 Undercount reduced again, but some cities and states seek to force Census Bureau to adjust figures.

1990-Present ***Conflict arises over use of statistical adjustment of census data to reduce undercounting.***

1990 For first time since 1940 Census Bureau fails to reduce undercount; population reaches 249 million.

1991 Commerce Secretary Robert A. Mosbacher declines Census Bureau recommendation to adjust the 1990 census to deal with undercount; critics say the decision is politically driven, and several states and cities sue to force adjustment.

1996 U.S. Supreme Court, in *Wisconsin v. City of New York*, rejects cities' effort to force adjustment of 1990 census. . . . Census Bureau announces "re-engineered census" plan aimed at reducing undercount and avoiding lawsuits; congressional Republicans say the plan violates the Constitution.

1999 Supreme Court rules that the Census Act bars use of statistical sampling for reapportionment but leaves door open for using it to allocate federal funds and draw state legislative districts.

2000 Census Bureau buys ads for the first time to encourage responses.

2009 Robert M. Groves chosen to head Census Bureau, says won't use sampling to adjust the 2010 count. . . . Census Bureau cuts ties with

Association of Community Organizations for Reform Now (ACORN) after employees of the antipoverty group are filmed appearing to give advice encouraging tax fraud and prostitution.

2010 Census Bureau replaces long-form questionnaire with American Community Survey while sending all households a short 10-question form. . . . Total cost of 2010 census estimated at $14.5 billion, including $340 million promotional campaign that includes $171 million in advertising; conservative Republicans criticize census as intrusive, and some Latino advocates try to boycott it to protest lack of immigration reform; mail-back response rate of 72 percent matches 2000 rate; bureau begins effort to contact non-responders.

Gay Couples to Be Counted for First Time

But census won't provide complete count of gays in America.

With eight states and Washington, D.C., recognizing same-sex marriages, the U.S. Census for the first time this year will include data about same-sex marriages nationwide, regardless of whether they are legal.

In previous censuses, the Census Bureau considered same-sex couples who checked the "married" box as "unmarried partners."[1] But since the last census in 2000, five states and the district have legalized same-sex marriages, and three more recognize out-of-state same-sex marriages.

The Census Bureau is even encouraging same-sex couples who aren't legally married but identify themselves as such to check the "married" box. And since the census is confidential, there will be no legal repercussions for same-sex married couples who live in states in which same-sex marriages aren't legal.

"The census is a portrait of America," Che Ruddell-Tabisola, the manager of the lesbian, gay, bisexual and transgender program at the Census Bureau, told *The Kansas City Star*. "Our job is to get an accurate count. . . . One of the most important things is for same-sex couples to know that it is 100 percent safe to participate in the census."[2]

The decision to count same-sex married couples is hailed by some gay rights advocates as an important first step in getting a complete count of the lesbian, gay, bisexual and transgender (LGBT) community in the United States. "Even in the absence of federal recognition of our relationships, we have an opportunity to say on an official form that, 'Yes, we are married,' 'Yes, our relationships are every bit as equal to everyone else's,' " said Josh Friedes, executive director of the LGBT advocacy group Equal Rights Washington.[3]

Some gay rights advocates, however, say more needs to be done to recognize the U.S. LGBT community in terms of data and gathering more statistics. "[At] the moment, it's not that easy for us to answer a simple question, like 'How many LGBT people are there,' " Gary Gates, a member of Our

(Continued)

(Continued)

Families Count, a census campaign to count the LGBT community, told National Public Radio's "Tell Me More" program. In data-gathering, "When a group is essentially invisible, it's hard to make an argument that they have needs or that they are treated differently."[4]

Because the census will count only same-sex couples who live together, many say a large proportion of the community will not be counted, and the only remedy for this is to include a question on the census about sexual orientation. But the only way to add questions to the census is to get approval by Congress, so that does not appear likely anytime soon.

This year's census will include data about same-sex marriages for the first time. Rocky Galloway and Reggie Stanley, above, celebrate after applying for their marriage license in Washington, D.C., last March.

AFP/Getty Images/Mandel Ngan

Some conservative same-sex-marriage opponents worry that these new statistics will aid gay rights advocates in the fight for legal same-sex marriage in more states. Some have even said that counting same-sex couples violates the federal Defense of Marriage Act (DOMA), which defines marriage as a legal union between a man and a woman.

"Marriage is only for a man and woman. That's the law they need to follow. Somebody needs to sue the federal government to enforce the Defense of Marriage Act," said Randy Thomasson, president of SaveCalifornia.com, a pro-family advocacy group. The Family Research Council (FRC), which promotes family, marriage and human life in national policy, agrees the Census Bureau's actions may violate DOMA.

"For the Census Bureau to actually encourage same-sex couples to mark themselves as married is a clear violation of the Defense of Marriage Act," says Peter Sprigg, a senior fellow for policy studies at FRC. Sprigg says the data being collected could have been interesting because some states that have legalized same-sex marriages don't record data on how many marriages are performed. But, because the census will count *all* same-sex couples who consider themselves married — legally or not — "the data really isn't very useful."

Because Congress mandated that a marriage can be only between a man and a woman, the FRC believes the idea of same-sex marriage is an oxymoron, according to Sprigg.

And while it might be one thing for the census to simply count same-sex married couples, he said it's another thing for the Census Bureau to distribute messages encouraging same-sex couples to check the "married" box.

To promote its new way of counting same-sex couples, the Census Bureau sent a task force to reach out to the LGBT community and encourage it to be honest on its survey responses. The bureau also broadcast public service ads on the gay-oriented channel Logo about counting same-sex marriages and posted them on the Census Bureau Web site.

"We have to reach out and engage this part of the population," a Census Bureau official said. "Anything less than that is a failure."[5]

—*Julia Russell*

---

[1] "Census Form Question Stirs Controversy, U.S. Census Bureau to Acknowledge Couples Differently," KCRA (Sacramento), April 1, 2010, www.kcra.com/news/23024784/detail.html.

[2] Eric Adler, "Bureau wants same-sex couples to check the 'married' box on census form," *The Kansas City Star* (Missouri), April 6, 2010, www.kansascity.com/2010/04/06/1861880/census-bureau-seeking-count-of.html.

[3] Lornet Turnbull, "Census will count gay couples who check 'husband or wife,' " *The Seattle Times*, March 30, 2010, http://seattletimes.nwsource.com/html/localnews/2011483128_lgbtcensus31m.html.

[4] "2010 Census Will Count Same-Sex Couples," "Tell Me More," National Public Radio, Nov. 25, 2009, www.npr.org/templates/story/story.php?storyId=120816467.

[5] "Census Bureau urges same-sex couples to be counted," *USA Today*, April 6, 2010, www.usatoday.com/news/nation/census/2010-04-05-census-gays_N.htm.

have led to controversies and charges of politicization of the census — charges that persisted through the planning for Census 2010.

At the heart of the controversy has been the practice of sampling — using data on part of the population to make broader conclusions about the whole.

The 1950 census produced a net undercount of 4.4 percent of the population, but the undercount rate for blacks was 9.6 percent.[46] In 1957 Congress passed a new Census Act, which allowed sampling to be used in the 1960 census "in such form and content as" the secretary of Commerce "may determine," but the law said sampling could not be used for reapportioning House seats.[47]

By 1970, the stakes in census accuracy had grown significantly, in large part because of the passage of civil rights legislation that demanded reliable counts to monitor the application of antidiscrimination laws. In addition, big U.S. cities were under increasing financial pressure, raising the importance of census counts in the allocation of federal assistance. Judicial rulings requiring legislative districts to be equal in population also demanded accurate census counts.

In January 1969 an *Ebony* magazine editorial pushed "for an accurate Black count" and told readers that census counts were important to government and industry for apportionment, program planning and analysis. "And," the magazine claimed, "the figures they use are a lie" because about 10 percent of "non-Whites (primarily Blacks)" were "missed." The magazine noted that most census workers were white, and it advocated for black interviewers to take the census to "ghetto areas."[48]

The following year the Urban League organized a Coalition for a Black Count to monitor the 1970 census and urge participation "to assure a full and accurate minority count."[49]

Undercounts persisted, though. The 1970 census produced a net undercount of 2.9 percent of the population, but 8 percent of blacks.[50]

In 1957 Congress amended the Census Act to allow sampling, but not for apportionment. In 1976 the law was strengthened to allow the Commerce secretary to use sampling "if he considers it feasible," though again not for apportionment. The change was technical in nature and not aimed at improving the undercount.[51]

Litigation Over Sampling

But over the next quarter-century, the idea of using sampling to statistically adjust for the undercount arose repeatedly, resulting in court fights, a landmark Supreme Court ruling and charges of politicizing the census to gain a partisan edge in the apportionment of congressional seats, drawing of legislative districts and allocation of federal money to the states.

After the 1980 census, the Census Bureau stepped up its research on methods for statistically adjusting the 1990 census to correct for undercounting, but the Commerce Department subsequently decided against the idea. That led to litigation. In late 1988 New York City and a coalition of other state and local entities, joined by the NAACP and other advocacy groups, sued the Census Bureau in an effort to stop "chronic under-counting" of urban blacks and Latinos.[52]

"From a civil rights point of view, it has to do with equal voting rights," Neil Corwin, New York City's assistant corporation counsel, explained at the time. "From the federal-funding point, there are a number of programs based on population figures. If New York has more people than the Census Bureau gives it credit for, they are going to suffer in the amount of federal funds they get."[53]

In 1990 the Census Bureau failed to reduce the undercount for the first time since 1940. The overall rate was 1.6 percent, but 4.6 percent for blacks and 5 percent for Hispanics. Renters were undercounted by 4.5 percent, and many children were missed.[54]

The bureau recommended that the 1990 results be adjusted, but Commerce Secretary Robert Mosbacher, a Republican serving in the George H. W. Bush administration, declined. While conceding that minorities and some jurisdictions had been undercounted, he argued that the proposed adjustment methods, employing sampling, weren't accurate enough to improve the overall census results.[55] Critics promptly tagged his decision as without merit and politically driven. New York City Mayor David Dinkins called it "nothing less than statistical grand larceny."[56]

More litigation followed. New York City and others challenged Mosbacher's decision, but a federal district court judge ruled that it was constitutional and did not violate the Census Act. A federal appellate court overturned that decision, ruling "that because a disproportionate undercount of minorities raised concerns about equal representation, the government was required to prove that its refusal to adjust the census figures 'was necessary to achieve some legitimate goal.'"[57]

But in 1996, the Supreme Court upheld Mosbacher's decision not to adjust the 1990 count.

Using statistical means to deal with undercounting wasn't dead, however. After the string of lawsuits over the 1990 count, the Census Bureau came up with a new plan for a "reengineered census" in 2000 that it thought would correct the miscounting and avoid litigation. It was "the culmination of a four-year process of discussion and review of census plans by a broad spectrum of experts, advisors and stakeholders," according to the bureau.[58]

The plan, which became public in early 1996, called again for the use of statistical sampling. As described by *The New York Times*, the technique "was loosely similar to that of public opinion polls in that it would extrapolate information about the population from partial data. But the bureau's plans are more sophisticated. They involve using traditional methods to count everyone in 90 percent of the households in a census tract — a neighborhood of about 1,700 dwellings. Data from the 90 percent would be used to determine the number and characteristics of the remaining 10 percent, and the population would be further adjusted on the basis of a survey of 750,000 households."[59]

Congressional Republicans, who had gained control of both houses of Congress in the 1994 midterm elections, objected, saying the technique violated federal law and the Constitution. As *The Times* noted, "with House Republicans holding a razor-thin majority, both parties [were] acutely conscious of any question that might give one side an advantage."[60]

In 1998 a federal court ruled against the sampling plan, and the ruling was appealed to the Supreme Court. In 1999, in a landmark 5-4 decision, the justices barred the use of statistical sampling to arrive at population totals for the purpose of reapportionment. But the court left the door open to using sampling for other purposes, such as allocating federal funds and state districting.[61]

Political Debate

New controversies arose as the 2010 census approached. One involved last year's White House nomination of Sen. Judd Gregg, a Republican from New Hampshire, to head the Commerce Department.

"Obama's pick . . . raised alarm among some minority advocates, who noted that Gregg had opposed increases to census funding and could not be trusted to do everything necessary to reduce undercounts," *Boston Globe* correspondent James Burnett wrote. "To mollify those critics, White House spokesman Ben LaBolt indicated that for 2010 the census director would now 'work closely with White House senior management.' To some census observers — especially those observing from GOP congressional seats — this looked like a power grab."[62]

Gregg withdrew, citing the census as key among "irresolvable conflicts" with the Obama administration.[63] In picking a replacement — Washington Gov. Gary Locke, a Democrat — the White House sought to reassure critics that the census wouldn't be politicized.

But yet another controversy erupted after the Association of Community Organizations for Reform Now — a grassroots antipoverty group commonly known as ACORN — signed on as an unpaid census-promotion partner for the 2010 census. Long a target of conservative critics, ACORN had been accused by Republicans of voter-registration fraud during the 2008 presidential campaign, and its involvement in the census touched off strong GOP objections.[64]

"It's a concern, especially when you look at all the different charges of voter fraud," Rep. Lynn A. Westmoreland, R-Ga., vice ranking member of the House Oversight Subcommittee on Information Policy, Census and National Archives, told FoxNews.com. "We want an enumeration. We don't want to have any false numbers."[65]

Census Leads to Power Shift in Congress

Population migration transfers House seats to Sun Belt states.

When William Howard Taft occupied the White House in 1911, Congress set the number of seats in the U.S. House of Representatives at 435, the same as today. But every 10 years, when the census is conducted, an element of suspense surrounds that set-in-stone figure.

House seats are distributed among the states based on population figures gathered in the census, with apportionment occurring the year following the census. With every new census, some states gain seats (and the political power that goes with them) and others lose seats. Following the 2000 census, for instance, 12 seats shifted; after the 1990 count, 19 seats transferred.[1]

Political analysts often can reliably forecast winners and losers ahead of time, but some states are cliff-hangers until the Census Bureau releases its official post-census results. This year that will happen by Dec. 31.

For years, House seats and political power have been shifting toward the Sun Belt — the Southern and Western states — and away from the Midwest and Northeast, a trend expected to continue in next year's reapportionment. That trend began in earnest after World War II, spurred by the baby boom and air conditioning, says Kimball W. Brace, president of Election Data Services (EDS), a Manassas, Va., consulting firm specializing in redistricting, election administration and census analysis.

Returning veterans started families, the U.S. population grew and people moved seeking jobs — not just to the suburbs but also to warm-weather states, such as California, Texas and Florida. "With the advent of air conditioning, they ended up not feeling bad going to hot places," Brace notes.

The migratory trend continues, but with some recent twists that could have a strong impact on reapportionment, he says. "If you look at the Census Bureau's yearly studies of movement . . . since World War II, you generally find that about 17 or 18 percent of the population moves every year" whether across town or cross-country. But in the last two years, that 17 percent has dropped to 11 percent, mainly because of the housing crisis and economic upheaval, he says.

With migration slow, some states may not gain as many House seats as expected before the recent recession. According to estimates by EDS, seven states — Arizona, Florida, Georgia, Nevada, South Carolina, Utah and Washington — would each gain a seat, and Texas would gain three, based on 2009 Census Bureau population estimates, the latest available until the 2010 census is counted.[2]

Before the economy soured, Brace says, Florida was on track to gain two seats but will now be "lucky to gain one."

Texas, on the other hand, has held steady, and in fact could gain a fourth seat, depending on the 2010 census, Brace says. The migration of people to Texas from Louisiana in the wake of Hurricane Katrina in 2005 may have boosted Texas' population enough to give the state another seat, Brace says. "The issue is, have any of those people gone back? We're not sure yet."

A separate study by Polidata, a Virginia group that analyzes political data, projected that Texas could gain four seats, though the strength of that projection has decreased, it said late last year.[3]

The EDS study noted that Arizona and Nevada have both seen their population growth decline over the past decade. "Arizona's lower growth rate has impacted whether it will gain a second seat" in 2010, it said. "Nevada, on the other hand, has enough population to keep its additional seat."

Eight states — Illinois, Iowa, Louisiana, Massachusetts, Michigan, New Jersey, New York and Pennsylvania — will probably each lose a seat, according to EDS estimates, and Ohio stands to lose two.

Minnesota is an uncertainty. Based on the 2009 population data, it would not lose a seat, but if 2009 population trends continue into 2010, it will, according to EDS.

California is also a cliff-hanger — and perhaps the most consequential because of its size. Depending on the 2010 census, the state could lose a congressional seat for the first time since it achieved statehood in 1850, EDS said.

That marks a dramatic turn of events for California. Brace says when 2005 Census Bureau data were projected out to 2010, California looked to be in line to gain a seat. But then came the recession, which hit California earlier than the rest of the country, and the state's population growth rate fell behind that of some other states, he says.

If the census counted only U.S. citizens and did not include undocumented immigrants — an idea embraced by some conservatives — California could wind up losing five congressional seats, Brace says. "Immigration does have an impact."

— Thomas J. Billitteri

---

[1] Greg Giroux, "Before Redistricting, That Other 'R' Word," *CQ Weekly*, Nov. 20, 2009, p. 2768.

[2] "New Population Estimates Show Additional Changes for 2009 Congressional Apportionment, With Many States Sitting Close to the Edge for 2010," Election Data Services, Dec. 23, 2009, www.electiondataservices.com/images/File/NR_Appor09wTables.pdf.

[3] "Congressional Apportionment: 2010 Projections Based Upon State Estimates as of July 1, 2009," Polidata, Dec. 23, 2009, www.polidata.org/news.htm#20091223.

What came next all but sealed ACORN's fate. After conservative activists secretly filmed ACORN employees appearing to offer advice encouraging tax fraud to activists posing as a prostitute and her pimp, the Census Bureau cut ties with the group. "It is clear," wrote bureau director Groves, "that ACORN's affiliation with the 2010 census promotion has caused sufficient concern in the general public, has indeed become a distraction from our mission, and may even become a discouragement to public cooperation, negatively impacting 2010 census efforts."[66]

Groves himself had also stirred partisan controversy when he was nominated to the post a little over five months before the ACORN flap exploded. As a Census Bureau official in the early 1990s, he had advocated statistical adjustment to the 1990 census to deal with the undercount. After Obama nominated him to run the Census Bureau, Republicans expressed alarm.

"Conducting the census is a vital constitutional obligation," House minority leader Rep. John A. Boehner, R-Ohio, said after Groves' nomination. "It should be as solid, reliable and accurate as possible in every respect. That is why I am concerned about the White House decision to select" Groves. Rep. Darrell Issa, R-Calif., the ranking Republican on the House Committee on Oversight and Government Reform, said Groves' selection was "incredibly troubling" and "contradicts the administration's assurances that the census process would not be used to advance an ulterior political agenda."[67]

To encourage Americans to return their census questionnaires, the Census Bureau this year sponsored a NASCAR race car, above, a 13-vehicle nationwide promotional road tour and television ads before and during the Super Bowl.

U.S. Census Bureau/Public Information Office

But at his confirmation hearing in May, Groves told a Senate panel he wouldn't use sampling to adjust the 2010 census. And, he said, "there are no plans to do that for 2020."[68]

Current Situation

Redistricting

In late April the Census Bureau announced that 72 percent of 2010 census forms had been mailed back by households that received them. On his Census Web site blog, Groves expressed satisfaction with the response, calling it a "remarkable display of civic participation."[69]

But census experts cautioned that the so-called participation rate doesn't tell the full story. "[T]he measure is limited to the universe of homes to which the Census Bureau mailed . . . or hand-delivered . . . questionnaires and asked residents to mail them back," wrote Lowenthal, the census consultant and former House staffer.

"Not in the equation," she noted, are people counted separately — everyone from American Indians living on reservations and college students living in dorms to people living in migrant farm-worker camps and RV (recreational vehicle) parks. And those "additional counting operations are just part of the partial story," she said. Concluded Lowenthal, "We don't really know how many Americans have joined our decennial national portrait so far. But one conclusion is beyond doubt: The hardest part is yet to come."[70]

AT ISSUE

Should the census ask questions about race?

YES

Melissa Nobles
Associate Professor of Political Science, Massachusetts Institute of Technology

Written for *CQ Global Researcher*, September 2009

For nearly 170 years, the Census Bureau's mission in asking about race was clear: define and then distinguish who was "white" from who was "non-white, and especially from who was "black."

Today, the dismantling of formal racial segregation, the enforcement of civil rights legislation and significant increases in immigration to the United States have all introduced new purposes for racial categorization in census taking. Asking people to categorize themselves by race provides important data about our country's growing diversity and serves to support the nation's civil rights laws — especially the Voting Rights Act. Indeed, census data on race are used in a range of public policies, many of which are designed to counteract entrenched material disadvantage among minorities.

In my view, these are purposes worthy of the continued inclusion of the race question in U.S. census taking. The issue has been contentious mostly because it is impossible to disassociate the history of racial thought and politics that have fundamentally shaped census-taking from the start. For most of its history, census-taking supported a politics of racial segregation and subordination.

For example, the 1840 and 1850 censuses were directly intertwined with debates about slavery. Data from the largely discredited 1840 census purportedly disclosed higher rates of insanity among free blacks, thereby "proving" that freedom drove free black people crazy. The 1850 census first introduced the category "mulatto," at the behest of a Southern physician, in order to gather data about the presumed deleterious effects of "racial mixture." Post-Civil War censuses continued to include the "mulatto" category, reflecting the enduring preoccupation with "racial mixing."

Twentieth-century racial and ethnic census categorization remained intertwined with the century's

NO

Hans A. von Spakovsky
Senior Legal Fellow, The Heritage Foundation; former counsel to the assistant attorney general for civil rights, U.S. Justice Department

Written for *CQ Researcher*, May 2010

Americans are uncomfortable with the Census Bureau demand that everyone identify their "race" on the 2010 Census. Despite the bureau's insidious commercials urging Americans to return the form so their communities can get their "fair share" of government largesse (earmarks writ large), the constitutional reason for the census is to reapportion congressional representation. The race question invades our privacy and is part of a continuing effort to divide Americans by race and enable official discrimination.

Some justify this because the census has historically asked for racial information. That information was required prior to the Civil War because black Americans who were slaves were counted as only three-fifths of a person in reapportionment. So why must we check the race box in this day and age? Two reasons: 1) to facilitate racially gerrymandered congressional districts, a pernicious practice that segregates voters by race; and 2) to discriminate in the provision of government benefits based on race.

For Americans who chafed at the race question and either left it blank or wrote in "American," a census worker may visit their homes to get them to change their answer. If they don't, the census will impute the person's race based on what he looks like or where he lives — an offensive example of stereotyping and racial profiling in a society where so many of us are of mixed race and ancestry. Small wonder the U.S. Commission on Civil Rights recommended that this question be made voluntary — a recommendation the Census Bureau ignored.

The options given for answering the race question also reflect political correctness and half-baked, liberal social-policy theories that have

(Continued)

(Continued)

core political and social issues: racial segregation and immigration.

In regard to segregation, categories and instructions for the censuses from 1930 to 1950 largely mirrored the racial status quo in politics and law. Southern laws defined persons with any trace of "Negro blood" as legally "Negro" and subject to all of the political, economic and social disabilities such designation conferred. Southern law treated other "non-white" persons similarly. Census categories and definitions followed suit, essentially bringing the logic of racial segregation into national census taking itself.

Thus, for most of American history the census wasn't used for edifying reasons. But today it supports the political and social policies that seek to guarantee civil rights and equality.

nothing to do with biology and genetics. Although the question asks for your race, it gives you choices like "Japanese" that are nationalities, not racial categories. "Race" is a very imprecise term that scientists disagree about. Moreover, many people have no idea what their apparent racial background is for more than a few generations.

Classifying and subdividing Americans on the basis of race is repugnant. *E pluribus unum* — "out of many, one" — is both our motto and our objective. It is one we should strive for every day, and the census' continued preoccupation with race is detrimental to the great progress we've made as a nation toward achieving that goal.

In fact, in various ways, Census 2010 is only at the midpoint.

From May through July census takers will be knocking on roughly 48 million doors of households that didn't mail back their census form or didn't receive one. From August through December the bureau will conduct a separate "Coverage Measurement Survey" to evaluate the accuracy of the census count.

December 31 is the deadline for the bureau to provide the White House and Congress with the official population count by state. The individual states then use the data to apportion House seats to various congressional districts.

In March 2011 the bureau will begin providing redistricting data to the states.[71] And in 2012 the results of the Coverage Measurement Survey will become available. Census experts say that if it shows significant undercounts, states could wind up suing to press the bureau to adjust the figures because of the importance of census results to federal funding allocations and the drawing of legislative boundaries.

Counting Prisoners

As the 2010 census moves forward, advocacy groups are continuing to spotlight how certain population groups are counted, especially prison inmates.

Currently, the Census Bureau counts prison inmates where they are incarcerated. Critics argue that areas where prisons are located benefit in the allotment of political representation to the detriment of prisoners' home communities.

"Most people in prison in America are urban and African-American or Latino," Rep. William Lacy Clay, D-Mo., chairman of the House census subcommittee, wrote to the Census Bureau. But, he added, the 2010 census "will again be counting incarcerated people as residents of the rural, predominantly white communities that contain prisons."[72]

Some change on the issue is coming. In May 2011, a few months earlier than in the past and in time for redistricting in most states, the Census Bureau will identify the location and population counts of prisons and other group quarters, according to Aleks Kajstura, legal director at Prison Policy Initiative, a Massachusetts-based group pushing for change in the way prisoners are counted. States can choose whether they want to collect the home addresses of prisoners and adjust the census counts before redistricting, she says.

Ultimately, advocates want the Census Bureau to change the way prisoners are counted in time for the 2020 census. But some states are acting on their own. In April, Maryland became the first state to pass legislation requiring inmates to be counted in the jurisdiction of their last permanent address rather than where they are incarcerated.[73] Similar legislation is pending or under consideration in eight other states, including New York, Florida, Illinois and Pennsylvania, Kajstura said.

"In a lot of states the trend has been to build new prisons at locations far removed from the home community of incarcerated persons, which means a shift in political and representation power and representation away from these home communities to generally more rural areas where prisons are located," says Brenda Wright, director of the Democracy Program at Dēmos, a liberal research and advocacy group in New York that also is pushing for a change in how prisoners are counted. "At the same time, we emphasize it's not just a rural versus urban problem at heart, because the issue of how prisoners are counted affects local county and city redistricting as well."[74]

How the Census Bureau counts prisoners also "inflates the weight of the vote of any district where a prison happens to be located at the expense of all other districts that do not have a prison," Wright says.

Doling Out Funds

Prisoner counts are just one part of the larger census picture, of course, and the stakes for states and localities in the ability of the Census Bureau to produce an accurate count are huge — not only for legislative districting and congressional seats but also for allocations of federal money.

A new study by the Brookings Institution's Reamer found that in fiscal 2008, 215 federal domestic-assistance programs used census-related data to guide $447 billion in distributions to the states, local governments and other recipients, mostly for Medicaid and other aid for low-income households and highway programs.[75]

Census accuracy is especially important to low-income recipients of federal help, the study notes. Based on 2000 census data, it said, "each additional person included in [that census] resulted in an annual additional Medicaid reimbursement to most states of between several hundred and several thousand dollars."

In an interview, Reamer notes the census' widespread importance — to apportionment and redistricting, enforcement of antidiscrimination laws, distribution of federal funds and the information needs of business, for example. "To the extent the census is inaccurate, we have a less efficient economy if businesses are making decisions based on faulty data," he says.

His study notes that the decennial census is the basis for 10 other data sets that help shape federal-assistance funding, including a Bureau of Economic Analysis series on per capita income.

The effectiveness of the decennial census depends, of course, in no small part on how seamlessly it is planned and executed. In Congress a bipartisan group of legislators want to see that future censuses run more smoothly than many past ones have, including the 2010 census.

A bill called the Census Oversight, Efficiency and Management Reform Act would, among other things, make the Census Bureau directorship a five-year appointment so census planning isn't disrupted by a presidential election.[76] The 10-year decennial cycle would be split into two five-year phases — the first for planning and the second for operations, fostering consistency across administrations. Under the current system, every president appoints a new director.

In addition, the bill would give bureau directors more independence by having them report directly to the Commerce secretary and letting them give recommendations or testimony to Congress that represents their views and not necessarily those of the administration. It also would keep directors from having to testify on census issues they didn't agree with.[77]

Seven former Census Bureau directors endorsed the bill in March, stating that "the time has come for the Census Bureau to be much more independent and transparent."[78]

They said that after 30 years in "which the press and Congress frequently discussed the Decennial Census in explicitly partisan terms, it is vitally important that the American public have confidence that the census results have been produced by a nonpartisan, apolitical and scientific Census Bureau."

In addition, they said the importance of the Census Bureau "waxes and wanes, peaking as the decennial approaches but then drifting down the [Commerce] Department's priority list," but that the bureau "needs to more efficiently focus on [its] continuous responsibilities," which include not only the decennial census but other measurement projects.

And third, the former directors noted, "each of us experienced times when we could have made much more timely and thorough responses to congressional requests and oversight if we had dealt directly with the Congress."

Outlook

Changing Times

As census experts look beyond the completion of the 2010 count, they see prospects for important changes in the way the government creates its every-10-year national portrait. Social and cultural shifts are likely to make census taking more challenging in 2020 and beyond, yet technology could also make it cheaper, easier and more effective.

In 1970, 78 percent of households receiving a census form mailed it back. That rate fell to 65 percent in 1990, rose modestly in 2000 — thanks in part to heavy spending on advertising — and remained largely flat in 2010. Some of the long-term decline in response no doubt reflects growing concerns about privacy and a wariness of how information collected by the census might be used, experts say. That wariness may grow, particularly in the nation's expanding immigrant communities — especially if Congress fails to pass comprehensive immigration reform before the next census.

Lifestyle changes also have made it more challenging — and costly — for the Census Bureau to do its work. The growth of same-sex unions and inter-racial marriages, increases in joint custody of children, the expansion of second-home purchases among the nation's aging baby-boom population and other trends may make it more difficult for the Census Bureau to get a firm fix on population and demographic trends.

But other developments may work in the Census Bureau's favor. One is the growth of communications technology, which could make census taking cheaper for the government and more convenient for households.

An online data-collection option is a probable evolution in 2020. The bureau said an Internet option was deemed feasible from a technical standpoint. But "without time to fully test the entire system, security concerns led the Census Bureau to decide to not offer the 2010 census questionnaire online," it said. The bureau said it plans to introduce an Internet option in the next census.[79]

One thing seems likely: Criticism of the census will be around in future decades much as it has been in the past.

After the bureau announced the 72 percent mail response to this year's census, Rep. Jason Chaffetz, R-Utah, phoned *The Washington Post* to point out that while this year's mail-back rate matched the 2000 figure, the cost of the 2010 count was more than double that of the 2000 census. And, he criticized the amount the bureau spent on advertising, saying "they're getting poor results in the places we know we have problems."

However, Jost, the bureau communications official, told *The Post* the 2010 advertising budget was the same as for 2000 on an inflation-adjusted basis. "We spent just 5 percent more in equivalent dollars this year on a population that was 10 percent bigger."[80]

Notes

1. "With Growing Awareness of Census, Most Ready to Fill Out Forms," Pew Research Center, March 16, 2010, http://people-press.org/report/596/census-forms.

2. See Michelle Malkin, "True Confessions from America's Census Workers," April 7, 2010, http://news.yahoo.com/s/uc/20100407/cm_uc_crmmax/op_1913518.

3. Andrew D. Reamer, "Counting for Dollars: The Role of the Decennial Census in the Geographic Distribution of Federal Funds," Brookings Institution, March 2010, www.brookings.edu/reports/2010/0309_Census_dollars.aspx.

4. Andrew Reamer, "Census Brings Money Home," April 6, 2010, www.brookings.edu/opinions/2010/0315_census_reamer.aspx?p=1.

5. "2010 Census: Fundamental Building Block of a Successful Enumeration Faces Challenges," U.S. Government Accountability Office (GAO), March 5, 2009, www.gao.gov/new.items/d09430t.pdf.

6. Rate achieved by April 27.

7. Robert M. Groves, "A Surprise Reaction," The Director's Blog, U.S. Bureau of the Census, April 23, 2010, http://blogs.census.gov/2010census/.

8. "Take 10 Map," http://2010.census.gov/2010census/take10map/.

9. See "How the 2010 Census is Different," Population Reference Bureau, www.prb.org/Articles/2009/changesin2010.aspx.

10. Robert M. Groves, The Director's Blog, U.S. Bureau of the Census, entries for April 14, 15 and 16, 2010, http://blogs.census.gov/2010census/.

11. Stephen Dinan, "Exclusive: Minn. Lawmaker vows not to complete Census," *The Washington Times*, June 17, 2009.

12. Naftali Bendavid, "Republicans Fear Undercounting in Census," *The Wall Street Journal*, April 5, 2010, p. 4A. Paul's comment appeared in a weekly column in April 2010.

13. Andy Barr, "Erickson's census 'shotgun' threat," *Politico*, April 2, 2010, www.politico.com/news/stories/0410/35338.html.

14. Patrick McHenry, "Returning the Census is Our Constitutional Duty," *RedState.com*, April 1, 2010, www.redstate.com/rep_patrick_mchenry/2010/04/01/returning-the-census-is-our-constitutional-duty/.

15. Transcript, "The 2010 Census," "The Diane Rehm Show," National Public Radio, March 3, 2010.

16. For background, see the following *CQ Researcher* reports: David Masci, "Latinos' Future," Oct. 7, 2003, pp. 869-892; Kenneth Jost, "Census 2000," May 1, 1998, pp. 385-408, and R. K. Landers, "1990 Census: Undercounting Minorities," *Editorial Research Reports*, March 10, 1989, pp. 117-132.

17. "What is the 1990 Undercount?" U.S. Census Bureau, www.census.gov/dmd/www/techdoc1.html.

18. "Technical Assessment of A.C.E. Revision II," U.S. Census Bureau, March 12, 2003, www.census.gov/dmd/www/pdf/ACETechAssess.pdf.

19. *Ibid.*

20. Mark Hugo Lopez and Paul Taylor, "Latinos and the 2010 Census: The Foreign Born Are More Positive," Pew Hispanic Center, April 1, 2010, http://pewhispanic.org/files/reports/121.pdf.

21. Randal C. Archibold, "Arizona Enacts Stringent Law on Immigration," *The New York Times*, April 23, 2010, www.nytimes.com/2010/04/24/us/politics/24immig.html?scp=5&sq=arizona%20and%20immigrants&st=cse.

22. Campbell Robertson, "Suspense Builds Over Census for New Orleans," *The New York Times*, April 7, 2010, www.nytimes.com/2010/04/08/us/08orleans.html?ref=us.

23. The Associated Press, "State, local government budgets hamper census outreach," *The Washington Post*, April 12, 2010, www.washingtonpost.com/wp-dyn/content/article/2010/04/11/AR2010041103832.html.

24. *Ibid.*

25. "Distrust, Discontent, Anger and Partisan Rancor," Pew Research Center, April 18, 2010, http://pewresearch.org/pubs/1569/trust-in-government-distrust-discontent-anger-partisan-rancor.

26. Reamer, "The Scouting Report Web Chat: 2010 Census," *op. cit.*

27. Matt Canham, "Bennett's census-immigration amendment rejected," *Salt Lake Tribune*, Nov. 5, 2009, www.sltrib.com/news/ci_13721132.

28. "2010 Census Operational Briefing Transcript," U.S. Census Bureau, Sept. 23, 2009, www.census.gov/Press-Release/www/releases/pdf/2010CensusBriefing_Transcript.pdf.

29. Rob Shapiro, "The Latest Attack on the Census is an Attack on All of Us," New Policy Institute, Oct. 1, 2009, www.newpolicyinstitute.org/2009/10/the-latest-attack-on-the-census-is-an-attack-on-all-of-us/.

30. Jennifer Ludden, "Hispanics Divided Over Census Boycott," National Public Radio, July 13, 2009, www.npr.org/templates/story/story.php?storyId=106555313.

31. *Ibid.*

32. Lopez and Taylor, *op. cit.*

33. "An Introduction to the American Community Survey," U.S. Census Bureau, summer 2009, www.census.gov/Press-Release/www/2009/pdf/09ACS_intro.pdf.

34. Clea Benson, "The Data Catch: Not Enough Information," *CQ Weekly*, Dec. 7, 2009, p. 2810.

35. Quoted in *ibid.*

36. The Associated Press, "Thomas Jefferson Signed Census Sells for $122,500," *The Huffington Post*, April 15, 2010, www.huffingtonpost.com/2010/04/15/thomas-jefferson-signed-c_n_538634.html.

37. "A Century of Population Growth: From the First Census of the United States to the Twelfth, 1790-1900," 1909, Bureau of the Census, Department of Commerce and Labor, p. 48, www.archive.org/details/centuryofpopulat00unit. On Jan. 23, 1791, Jefferson wrote: "The census has made considerable progress, but will not be completed till midsummer. It is judged at present that our numbers will be between four and five millions."

38. Kenneth Prewitt, "The American People: Politics and Science in Census Taking," Russell Sage Foundation and Population Reference Bureau, 2003, p. 6, accessed at www.thecensusproject.org/factsheets/PrewittSAGE-PRBCensus2000Report.pdf.

39. David McMillen, "Apportionment and districting," in Margo J. Anderson, ed., *Encyclopedia of the U.S. Census* (2000), pp. 34-35.

40. *Ibid.*, p. 34.

41. *Ibid.*, p. xiii.

42. *Ibid.*

43. *Ibid.*, p. xiv.

44. *Ibid.* The case is *Baker v. Carr*, 369 U.S. 186 (1962).

45. "United States Census 2000: Press Briefing Background Documents," U.S. Census Bureau, June 14, 2000, p. 6, www.census.gov/Press-Release/www/background.pdf.

46. Margo J. Anderson and Stephen E. Fienberg, *Who Counts? The Politics of Census-Taking in Contemporary America* (1999), p. 60. Figures are estimated net census undercounts as measured by a technique called Demographic Analysis, in which the best estimate of the previous census count is updated with various kinds of administrative statistics on births, deaths and net immigration, along with Medicare data, to produce an estimate of the population separately from the current census count. The authors cite Robert E. Fay, *et al.*, *The Coverage of the Population in the 1980 Census*, Bureau of the Census, 1988.

47. "United States Census 2000," U.S. Census Bureau, *op. cit.*

48. Anderson and Fienberg, *op. cit.*, p. 38.

49. *Ibid.*, p. 39.

50. *Ibid.*, p. 60. Figures are estimated net census undercounts as measured by demographic analysis.

51. "United States Census 2000," U.S. Census Bureau, *op cit.*

52. Sam Burchell, "Big Cities Sue for Changes in '90 Census," United Press International, Nov. 3, 1988, *Los Angeles Times*, http://articles.latimes.com/1988-11-03/news/mn-1041_1_census-bureau. See also U.S. Bureau of the Census, "1990 Overview," www.census.gov/history/www/through_the_decades/overview/1990.html.

53. Quoted in Burchell, *op. cit.*

54. "United States Census 2000," U.S. Census Bureau, *op. cit.*

55. Anderson, "Litigation and the census," in Anderson, ed., *Encyclopedia of the Census*, *op. cit.*, p. 270.

56. Anderson and Fienberg, *op. cit.*, p. 128. The authors attribute the Dinkins quote to *The New York Times*, July 16, 1991.

57. Linda Greenhouse, "High Court Hears Arguments For Census Alteration by Race," *The New York Times*, Jan. 11, 1996, www.nytimes.com/1996/01/11/us/high-court-hears-arguments-for-census-alteration-by-race.html?pagewanted=1.

58. "2000 Overview," U.S. Census Bureau, www.census.gov/history/www/through_the_decades/overview/2000.html.

59. Steven A. Holmes, "Court Voids Plan to Use Sampling for 2000 Census," *The New York Times*, Aug. 25, 1998, www.nytimes.com/1998/08/25/us/court-voids-plan-to-use-sampling-for-2000-census.html?scp=1&sq=2000%20census%20and%20sampling&st=cse.

60. *Ibid.*

61. Linda Greenhouse, "Jarring Democrats, Court Rules Census Must Be by Actual Count," *The New York Times*, Jan. 26, 1999, www.nytimes.com/1999/01/26/us/jarring-democrats-court-rules-census-must-be-by-actual-count.html?scp=1&sq=census%20and%20sampling%20and%20supreme%20court&st=cse.

62. James Burnett, "Night of the census taker," *The Boston Globe*, Oct. 18, 2009, www.boston.com/bostonglobe/ideas/articles/2009/10/18/look_out_obama_is_sending_his_minions_to_your_house_the_deep_history_of_a_conspiracy_theory/.

63. Joseph Curl and Kara Rowland, "Census battle intensifies; GOP leader threatens lawsuit," *The Washington Times*, Feb. 13, 2009, www.washingtontimes.com/news/2009/feb/13/gregg-withdrawal-foreshadows-census-debate/.

64. "Times Topics: Acorn," *The New York Times*, http://topics.nytimes.com/top/reference/timestopics/organizations/a/acorn/index.html.

65. Cristina Corbin, "ACORN to Play Role in 2010 Census," FOXNews.com, March 18, 2009, www.foxnews.com/politics/2009/03/18/acorn-play-role-census/.

66. The Associated Press, "Census Bureau Drops Acorn from 2010 Effort," *The New York Times*, Sept. 12, 2009, www.nytimes.com/2009/09/12/us/politics/12acorn.html.

67. Quoted in David Stout, "Obama's Census Choice Unsettles Republicans," *The New York Times*, April 3, 2009, www.nytimes.com/2009/04/03/washington/03census.html? scp=6&sq=gary%20locke%20and%20judd%20gregg%20and%20census&st=cse.

68. Timothy J. Alberta, "Census Nominee Rules Out Statistical Sampling in 2010," *The Wall Street Journal*, May 15, 2009, http://online.wsj.com/article/SB124241977657124963.html.

69. "A Surprise Reaction," *op. cit.*

70. Terri Ann Lowenthal, "Taking Stock: A Mid-Census Reality Check," The Census Project Blog, April 20, 2010, http://censusprojectblog.org/.

71. For background see Jennifer Gavin, "Redistricting," *CQ Researcher*, Feb. 16, 2001, pp. 113-128.

72. Sam Roberts, "New Option for the States on Inmates in the Census," *The New York Times*, Feb. 11, 2010, www.nytimes.com/2010/02/11/us/politics/11census.html.

73. Erica L. Green, "Baltimore will gain residents in prison count shift," *The Baltimore Sun*, April 24, 2010, http://articles.baltimoresun.com/2010-04-24/news/bs-md-inmate-census-20100425_1_prison-towns-state-and-federal-inmates-census-bureau.

74. See also Dēmos, "A Dilution of Democracy: Prison-Based Gerrymandering," www.demos.org/pubs/prison_gerrymand_factsheet.pdf.

75. Reamer, "Counting for Dollars," *op. cit.*

76. "Count Us in Favor," *The New York Times*, March 29, 2010, www.nytimes.com/2010/03/29/opinion/29mon2.html?scp=1&sq=count%20us%20in%20favor&st=cse. The bill is HR 4945 and S 3167.

77. "Statement in Support of The Census Oversight, Efficiency and Management Reform Act," The Census Project, March 25, 2010, www.thecensusproject.org/letters/cp-fmrdirs-bill-25march2010.pdf.

78. *Ibid.*

79. "Census on Campus: Students' Frequently Asked Questions," U.S. Bureau of the Census, http://2010.census.gov/campus/pdf/FAQ_CensusOnCampus.pdf.

80. Ed O'Keefe, "Was 2010 Census a Success?" Federal Eye blog, *The Washington Post*, April 26, 2010, http://voices.washingtonpost.com/federal-eye/2010/04/was_2010_census_a_success.html.

Bibliography

Books

Anderson, Margo J., ed., *Encyclopedia of the U.S. Census*, CQ Press, 2000.
An expert on the census who is a professor of history and urban studies at the University of Wisconsin, Milwaukee, offers dozens of articles on topics ranging from redistricting to government use of census data, plus an appendix with historical data.

Anderson, Margo J., and Stephen E. Fienberg, *Who Counts? The Politics of Census-Taking in Contemporary America*, Russell Sage Foundation, 1999.
Census expert Anderson and a professor of statistics and social science at Carnegie Mellon University examine how well the census counts the U.S. population.

Nobles, Melissa, *Shades of Citizenship: Race and the Census in Modern Politics*, Stanford University Press, 2000.
An MIT political scientist examines issues surrounding race during U.S. and Brazilian censuses and argues that "census-taking is one of the institutional mechanisms by which racial boundaries are set."

Articles

Farley, Rob, "Census takers contend with suspicion and spin over the 2010 count," *St. Petersburg Times*, April 11, 2010, www.tampabay.com/incoming/census-takers-contend-with-suspicion-and-spin-over-the-2010-count/1086739.
The newspaper examines three assertions about the census designed to quell Republican fears that the census is intrusive and cumbersome.

Roberts, Sam, "New Option for the States on Inmates in the Census," *The New York Times*, Feb. 11, 2010, www.nytimes.com/2010/02/11/us/politics/11census.html?scp=1&sq=new%20option%20for%20the%20states%20on%20inmates%20in%20the%20census&st=cse.
In time for congressional and legislative reapportionment, the Census Bureau in May 2011 will give states more flexibility on how to count prison inmates.

Robertson, Campbell, "Suspense Builds Over Census for New Orleans," *The New York Times*, April 7, 2010, www.nytimes.com/2010/04/08/us/08orleans.html?scp=1&sq=suspense%20builds%20over%20census%20for%20new%20orleans&st=cse.
The final census count for hurricane-battered New Orleans "will go far in determining how [the city] thinks about itself, whether it is continuing to mount a steady comeback or whether it has sputtered and stalled," says *The Times*.

Santos, Fernanda, "Door to Door, City Volunteers Try to Break Down Resistance to the Census," ***The New York Times*****, March 31, 2010, www.nytimes.com/2010/04/01/us/01count.html?scp=1&sq=Door%20to%20Door,%20city%20volunteers%20try%20to%20break%20down&st=cse.**

The work of volunteers in helping to encourage participation is crucial, as demonstrated by their efforts in New York City, a reporter finds.

Williams, Juan, "Marketing the 2010 census with a conservative-friendly face," ***The Washington Post*****, March 1, 2010, www.washingtonpost.com/wp-dyn/content/article/2010/02/28/AR2010022803364.html.**

The Census Bureau has responded to challenges from conservatives with "unprecedented outreach," including putting the bureau's name on a NASCAR auto.

Reports and Studies

"Preparing for the 2010 Census: How Philadelphia and Other Cities Are Struggling and Why It Matters," Pew Charitable Trusts, Oct. 12, 2009, www.pewtrusts.org/uploadedFiles/wwwpewtrustsorg/Reports/Philadelphia-area_grantmaking/Census%20Report%20101209_FINAL.pdf?n=8566.

Most of the 11 cities studied had less money and smaller staffs for local census preparation than they did a decade ago, raising concerns about undercounting in urban areas.

Prewitt, Kenneth, "The American People, Census 2000: Politics and Science in Census Taking," Russell Sage Foundation and Population Reference Bureau, 2003, www.thecensusproject.org/factsheets/PrewittSAGE-PRBCensus2000Report.pdf.

A former Census Bureau director writes in this lengthy and useful analysis that while the census may sound "dull and technical," it "is a drama at the very center of our political life."

Williams, Jennifer D., "The 2010 Decennial Census: Background and Issues," Congressional Research Service, April 27, 2009, http://assets.opencrs.com/rpts/R40551_20090427.pdf.

"Far from being simple . . . , the attempt to find and correctly enumerate 100 percent of U.S. residents is increasingly complicated and expensive," declares this overview.

On the Web

The Census Bureau (www.census.gov) offers extensive data and other information on the U.S. population, households, business, congressional districts and more. A separate Web site for Census 2010 (www.2010.census.gov) includes details, in multiple languages, about this year's decennial census, plus a blog by Census Bureau Director Robert M. Groves.

For More Information

Brookings Institution, 1775 Massachusetts Ave., N.W., Washington, DC 20036; (202) 797-6000; www.brookings.edu. Centrist think tank that studies a wide range of policy issues.

Center for Immigration Studies, 1522 K St., N.W., Suite 820, Washington, DC 20005-1202; (202) 466-8185; www.cis.org. Conservative nonprofit research organization that provides information on immigration.

Dēmos, 220 5th Ave., 5th Floor, New York, NY 10001; (212) 633-1405; www.demos.org. Liberal research and advocacy group that follows economic, voter-participation and other policy issues.

Election Data Services, 6171 Emerywood Ct., Manassas, VA 20112; (202) 789-2004; www.electiondataservices.com. Political consulting firm specializing in redistricting, election administration and analysis and presentation of census and political data.

Heritage Foundation, 214 Massachusetts Ave., N.E., Washington, DC 20002-4999; (202) 546-4400; www.heritage.org. Conservative think tank that studies wide range of policy issues, including the census.

National Association of Counties, 25 Massachusetts Ave., N.W., Washington, DC 20001; (202) 393-6226; www.naco.org. National organization representing county governments.

National Institute for Latino Policy, 101 Avenue of the Americas, Suite 313, New York, NY 10013; (800) 590-2516; www.latinopolicy.org. Nonprofit think tank that focuses on policies affecting the Latino community.

Pew Research Center, 1615 L St., N.W., Suite 700, Washington, DC 20036; (202) 419-4300; www.pewresearch.org. Nonpartisan group that provides information on issues, attitudes and trends shaping the United States and world.

Prison Policy Initiative, P.O. Box 127, Northampton, MA 01061; www.prisonpolicy.org. Nonprofit group that researches impact of Census Bureau policy that counts people where they are incarcerated rather than in their home communities.

Russell Sage Foundation, 112 East 64th St., New York, NY 10065; (212) 750-6000; www.russellsage.org. A research center on the social sciences that performs scholarly analysis of census results.

U.S. Census Bureau, 4600 Silver Hill Rd., Washington, DC 20233; (301) 763-4636; www.census.gov. Federal agency that conducts the decennial census.

Women in the Military: Should Combat Roles Be Fully Opened to Women?

The Issues

Army Spec. Shannon Morgan came home from Iraq changed by war. When she enlisted at age 20 and left rural Arkansas, shortly after Sept. 11, 2001, she hoped to help defend her country against more terrorist attacks while earning money for college. Eight years later, she's back home, hoping for a nursing career but diagnosed with post-traumatic stress disorder.[1]

Morgan enlisted as a vehicle mechanic and never expected to kill anyone in Iraq. Instead, she became one of the first women in U.S. history to take part in direct ground combat and killed at least one Iraqi. Even though military policy bars women from participating in such missions, Morgan was recruited into the first Lioness team — an ad hoc group of Army women who supported male front-line troops in both the Army and the Marines by dealing with women and children in houses where soldiers were pursuing potential insurgents.

Then-President-elect Barack Obama and former U.S. Army helicopter pilot Tammy Duckworth, who lost both legs in combat in Iraq, prepare to place a wreath at The Bronze Soldiers Memorial in Chicago on Veterans' Day in 2008. Duckworth now serves as an assistant secretary of the Department of Veterans Affairs.

AFP/Getty Images/Stan Honda

In April 2004 she accompanied a Marine unit searching for insurgents in the central Iraqi city of Ramadi. Unfamiliar with Marine signals and commands, she suddenly found herself alone on a street — and being fired at — when the squad abruptly withdrew from a neighborhood after walking into an ambush.

Morgan hesitated at first and then began returning fire with her light machine gun.

"For that second, I was like, 'God, is this right?' . . . I don't want to go to hell someday because I killed somebody," she recalls. "Then I realized, 'I betcha he's not caring over there, or he wouldn't be shooting at me.' " Today, she says she doesn't regret what she did but wishes it had never happened.[2]

The quiet use of women in ground-combat roles from which they are officially barred is not the only evidence that women's role in the U.S. military is growing more prominent. In September, Command Sgt. Maj. Teresa L. King, the 48-year-old daughter of a sharecropper near Fort Bragg, N.C., became the Army's top drill sergeant, the first woman to be named commandant of the Fort Jackson, S.C., school that trains all of the Army's drill instructors.

"When I look in the mirror, I don't see a female. I see a soldier," said Sgt. Maj. King. Recruiting more women into the school is one of her top priorities.[3]

From *CQ Researcher,* November 2009

Women Are 14 Percent of U.S. Military

Women make up 14.3 percent of the 1.3-million-member U.S. military and 15.1 percent of the officer corps. The Air Force has the highest percentage of women overall as well as the highest percentage of female officers. The Marine Corps has the lowest percentages.

Active Duty by Branch of Service, September 2007

Branch of Service and Status*	Number of Women	Number of Men	Total	Women as Percentage of Total
Department of Defense **				
Officer	33,567	187,952	221,519	15.1%
Enlisted	162,424	981,628	1,144,052	14.2%
Total	**195,991**	**1,169,580**	**1,365,571**	**14.3%**
Army				
Officer	12,983	71,699	84,682	15.3%
Enlisted	58,117	374,984	433,101	13.4%
Total	**71,100**	**446,683**	**517,683**	**13.7%**
Air Force				
Officer	11,835	53,887	65,722	18.0%
Enlisted	52,595	210,777	263,372	20.0%
Total	**64,430**	**264,664**	**329,094**	**19.6%**
Navy				
Officer	7,611	43,820	51,431	14.8%
Enlisted	41,144	239,694	280,838	14.6%
Total	**48,755**	**283,514**	**332,269**	**14.7%**
Marine Corps				
Officer	1,138	18,546	19,684	5.8%
Enlisted	10,568	156,173	166,741	6.3%
Total	**11,706**	**174,719**	**186,425**	**6.3%**
Coast Guard				
Officer	1,160	6,891	8,051	14.4%
Enlisted	3,790	28,809	32,599	11.6%
Total	**4,950**	**35,700**	**40,650**	**12.2%**

* *Officers include warrant officers*

** *Does not include the Coast Guard, which in peacetime is part of the Department of Homeland Security*

Source: U.S. Department of Defense, Defense Manpower Data Center, unpublished data. Compiled by the Women Research & Education Institute, January 2008

In 2008, another so-called brass ceiling was broken when Gen. Ann E. Dunwoody, a master parachutist and logistics and supply specialist, became the first female four-star general. "Her issue is, when are people going to stop being surprised?" said a friend, retired Maj. Gen. Jeanette Edmunds.[4]

Still, some military analysts are not only surprised but chagrined at the pace of women's integration into the armed forces and particularly at the Army's surreptitious moves to place women in frontline ground-combat areas.

Elaine Donnelly, president of the Center for Military Readiness, a Michigan-based think tank opposed to both ground-combat roles for women and gays serving openly in the military, says that as women have moved into more and more military jobs over the years, double standards for women's and men's physical performance have weakened overall military standards and sown seeds of discord among the ranks.[5]

Furthermore, the Army has "defied logic in retaining co-ed basic training" and setting different standards of physical achievement for men and women, Donnelly wrote. Such "gender-normed standards emasculate" the military's "warrior training" when they "[assure] 'success' for average female trainees" by setting the bar lower. "Soldiers know that there is no gender-norming on the battlefield."[6]

For example, for a 1.5-mile run, the Navy awards a "satisfactory" physical-readiness rating to a man who runs the distance in 13 minutes and 15 seconds, while a woman gets the same rating — and earns the same number of points toward boot-camp graduation — for a 15-minute, 15-second time, she said.[7]

A sure path to a weaker military is favoring women's interest in total workplace equality over military-readiness concerns, Donnelly said, and, "Right now we're favoring women's desire for careers over everything else."

But Melissa Sheridan Embser-Herbert, a professor of sociology at Hamline University in St. Paul, Minn., and a former captain in the Army Reserve, says "the argument over combat is ridiculous." Women, who comprise 14 percent of the overall military workforce, make up about 11 percent of those who have served in Iraq and Afghanistan, where combat is all around, she says. Yet the high number of women has not harmed the mission.

More than 120 female soldiers have been killed in those conflicts — 66 of them killed in combat. "Regardless of whether we label a job as a combat job, people are in harm's way" because of how wars are fought today, she says. Women should be recognized — and trained — for the combat roles they occupy today, she says.

As philosophical struggles persist over how aggressively full gender-integration of the military should be pursued, so do practical difficulties with creating a harmonious gender-integrated force.

For example, early this year the Department of Defense (DoD) released 2008 data on sexual assaults involving military victims or military perpetrators, showing that reported assaults increased by 8 percent overall from the previous year — and by a whopping 26 percent in Iraq. Sexual-assault rates generally run much higher in combat zones than in non-combat areas or in peacetime.

"I had one woman tell me, 'You just expect it. That's why we go to the latrine in pairs,' " or "create a brother/sister relationship with a male soldier," says Francine D'Amico, an associate professor of international relations at Syracuse University, who's studied female military officers. "I heard that from at least six different women."

However, the military is working much harder to crack down on sexual violence and harassment and will continue to do so, partly because it has become a "resource issue," says Darlene M. Iskra, program coordinator for the University of Maryland's Leadership Education and Development Center and a retired Navy commander who in May 1990 became the first woman to command a Navy ship. With an all-volunteer force, the military must compete with the civilian economy for good, skilled workers and spend significant resources to train enlistees, "so they can't allow them to leave" because of fear of a hostile environment, something that could be corrected, she says.

"The Pentagon has made some efforts to manage this epidemic — most notably in 2005, after the media received anonymous e-mails about the high rate of sexual assaults at the U.S. Air Force Academy," said Rep. Jane Harman, D-Calif. "The press scrutiny and congressional attention that followed led DoD to create the Sexual Assault Prevention and Response Office (SAPRO)," which initiated training and improved reporting of assaults.[8]

As Congress, military leaders and an interested public debate the issue of integrating women into military service, here are some questions being debated:

Are efforts to fully integrate women into the armed services harming military readiness?

Over the past 40 years, the number of women in the U.S. armed forces has grown from under 2 percent to more than 14 percent today. The range of military jobs women may hold and the number of females who become high-ranking officers also have grown substantially. Supporters of these trends say there's no evidence that military readiness has suffered, but critics say they have resulted in lower standards and morale problems that have been swept under the rug.

Setting unequal standards to allow women to succeed despite their physical differences from men damages unit cohesion by creating a backlash against the women, says Donnelly of the Center for Military Readiness. "Women say, 'I get resentment because my high scores aren't as high as the men's,' " she says.

In order to gender-integrate training, the military has had to reduce standards for physical performance because experiments in the early 1980s "found that women got injured trying to keep up with the men," said Stephanie Gutmann, author of *The Kinder Gentler Military: Can America's Gender Neutral Fighting Force Still Win Wars?*[9]

"I'm not sure people are aware of how little similarity there is between men and women" when it comes to physical characteristics such as upper-body strength. "Ninety-nine percent of the time a man is stronger," says Kingsley Browne, a law professor at Wayne State University in Detroit and author of *Co-Ed Combat: The New Evidence that Women Shouldn't Fight the Nation's Wars.* These strength differences matter greatly in many situations, such as when a ship suffers damage from a missile or other weapon and all sailors — including the cooking staff, for example — must seal off compartments and carry injured people to safety.

Moreover, "what happens when you take a cohesive group of men and introduce women into the group? The men begin to compete for the women," to the detriment of their bonds of trust with one another, says Browne. In addition, a

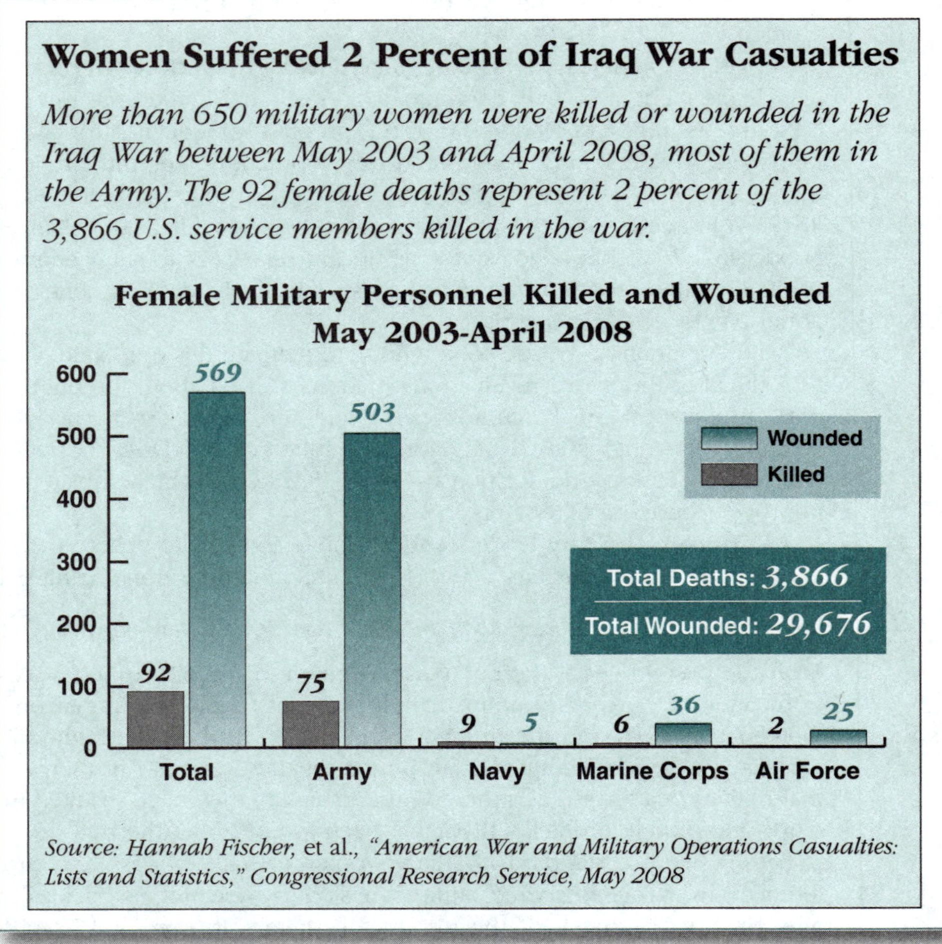

"ready" military depends on having all workforce positions filled so the force can immediately respond when it's needed. But with women making up a larger portion of the forces, pregnancy may get in the way, say many analysts.

When she was doing pre-deployment processing of soldiers on their way to Iraq, Army Sgt. Erica Crawley found that "many women became pregnant to get out of deploying," according to Laura Browder, an English professor at Virginia Common wealth University in Richmond, who interviewed Crawley for a forthcoming book, *When Janey Comes Marching Home: Portraits of Women Combat Veterans.*[10]

Retired Army Maj. Lori Sweeney told Browder that when she was serving in Iraq she saw women getting pregnant. It could have been done deliberately in order to cut their deployments short, said Sweeney, or accidentally, since military doctors are not allowed to prescribe birth control because sex is prohibited.[11]

Deliberate or not, pregnancies that allow women to escape difficult jobs cause a "major morale problem" for the troops who remain on duty, says Browne. "Other people have to pick up the slack, and that can cause a lot of resentment."

Women typically join the military for career purposes rather than a desire to go to war, says Browne. Evidence of that appeared in the early 2000s, when previously rising numbers of new female recruits began dropping off. That was "probably because prior to that they weren't subjected to the possibility of being blown up," Browne says.

Men are much more likely to enlist because they wish to fight, Browne says. "The eagerness of many men to go to war" is well known, he wrote. In the early stages of World War I — before the United States went to war — "Americans crossed the border into Canada to join the Canadian army before the 'fun' was over," he wrote.[12]

However, James Martin, a retired Army colonel and professor of social work at Bryn Mawr College near Philadelphia, says that, critics notwithstanding, "The question has been answered about whether women will ruin the military. They haven't, as demonstrated by, among other things, the senior roles women occupy, extending even to commanding troops in combat operations."

Twenty years ago, Martin says, there were "questions about women being successful on ships, and today they are" — an achievement made more striking because the first women didn't have senior female mentors. Today "we have women integrated throughout the Navy, becoming captains."

Martin says exactly the same arguments were made against fully integrating black soldiers into all-white units. "Just substitute the word 'women' for the word 'black,'" he says.

"The conspicuous 'femaleness' of women presents some challenges to group cohesion in the military, especially insofar as sexual friction . . . result[s] from their presence," acknowledged Regina M. Titunik, a professor of political science at the University of Hawaii in Hilo. However, these factors "do not seem to preclude the type of bonding that is such an essential part of military service." A major 1997 analysis from the RAND Corporation think tank, for example, found that, among members of the military, "gender integration is perceived to have a relatively small effect on readiness, cohesion and morale," Titunik wrote.[13]

Many military women point out that once their male colleagues see them in action, they quickly gain respect, says Browder. One convoy gunner she interviewed said that she could not win the respect of older men in her unit until she ended up in charge during a tense situation and "was the one who had to radio for help and decide who to kill," says Browder. "After that she had no difficulty getting respect."

Browder says she was surprised by "how many women talk about being soldiers and Marines first, not about being mothers and wives." Women "are in the military for all the same reasons as men," including a desire to blow things up, she says. "I heard over and over again that bonds in the [military] unit became stronger than family bonds," shedding doubt on the idea that gender-integrated units lack cohesion.

Furthermore, many women Browder spoke with "were really looking forward to going to war," including one young Marine who was excited to learn that the post she was headed to "had been blown up the night before." And a B-52 bomber pilot she interviewed "wished she could have dropped more bombs." Like many male soldiers, many women thought of this as "the ultimate existential challenge," Browder says.

For some observers, there remains little doubt that some women can be as aggressive and persistent as men in the face of violence. For example, Army Lt. Gen. Bob Cone singled out two women as performing with special heroism in the Nov. 5 mass shooting at Fort Hood, in Texas. Civilian Fort Hood police officer Kimberly Munley sought out and shot the gunman four times despite being shot herself, in "an amazing and an aggressive performance," said Cone. Another "amazing young lady," 19-year-old Pfc. Amber Bahr, a nutritionist, put a tourniquet on a wounded fellow soldier and carried him to get medical care before realizing that she, too, had been shot, Cone said.[14]

"Look at the facts. There have been an increasing number of women in our military" over the past two decades, "and our military is not weak. Women have not diluted our readiness," says Iskra of the University of Maryland.

"Our young people today are used to seeing women in authority, in and out of the military," she says. "They are working with women and going to school with women," so "this selective segregation doesn't make sense to the new generation. They see differences, but they don't see them as negative."

Should combat roles be fully opened to women?

More than 90 percent of armed-services jobs are open to women. The largest remaining all-male job category is ground-combat units — infantry troops that directly seek out and engage the enemy in fire.

In interviews with military officers and analysts, "we were told repeatedly that, if relevant and realistic tests existed so that only qualified women (and men) were assigned to these positions, gender integration would not be an issue," said analysts from the RAND Corporation think tank in an influential 1997 analysis.[15]

"Women are already engaged in combat" because under today's conditions, "combat is everywhere," says Martin of Bryn Mawr. So the old distinctions between front-line positions that are barred to women versus more secure rear areas — where women are allowed — are no longer relevant and should be scrapped, he says.

"Units comprised of women and men have bonded . . . and maintained good order for centuries — or did they have separate-sex wagon trains pioneering the West?" wrote blogger and retired Air Force Capt. Barbara A. Wilson. "I have known some pretty weak men who wouldn't protect the back of their own mother in a crisis or combat situation and some strong women who would go to the wall for a total stranger in the trenches — and vice versa."[16]

Arguments against women in combat sometimes rest on "the military's mission to make professional killers" of its combat soldiers and women's supposed unsuitability for that role, says Iskra of the University of Maryland. But, in fact, "everybody recognizes that women can kill," she says. "It's just not the cultural norm," so it's easy to ignore.

Furthermore, there's now proof that "women in the combat area tend to defuse explosive situations just by their presence," says Iskra. The evidence comes from the Lioness groups of women soldiers who accompany male Army and Marine Corps units on counterinsurgency missions, she says. With the women there, gaining control of explosive situations in hostile territory becomes mainly a matter of separating women and children out and "talking rather than shooting," she says.

Command Sgt. Maj. Teresa L. King became the Army's top drill sergeant in September when she was named commandant of the Fort Jackson, S.C., school that trains all of the Army's drill instructors. "When I look in the mirror, I don't see a female" she says. "I see a soldier." Recruiting more women into the school is one of her top priorities.

AP Photo/Mary Ann Chastain

"Imagine if somebody broke into your home. Of course the Iraqi men are shouting, panicking." But "with the women there they know that their wives won't be raped," and that confidence helps defuse the danger, she says.

Nevertheless, "the type of ground combat that involves directly attacking the enemy, actively rooting out enemy forces — not simply being in harm's way," still exists, and there's no guarantee such aggressive missions won't be needed in the future, says Donnelly.

That being the case, "the strongest argument and the one that research backs up is that female soldiers do not have an equal opportunity to survive or help others survive" in situations requiring them to "go out and seek out the enemy," Donnelly says. "Nobody questions the bravery of our women soldiers," she continues, but "it's not fair to the women and not fair to the men" to put women in jobs serving directly with ground-combat troops because most women can't carry out required duties, such as carrying a wounded soldier from the front.

In combat areas toilet and washing facilities are rudimentary at best and, often, nonexistent, and some studies have found that, for women soldiers, "unmet basic hygiene needs affect morale" and their ability to cope in combat circumstances, says Browne of Wayne State. In such situations, some women "retained urine and stool and limited their water intake to reduce the number of times they would have to go to the bathroom," which both increased their risk of urinary-tract infections and dehydration and decreased their ability to work at top efficiency.[17]

Though the military is not willing to discuss the topic, sexual attraction would be inevitable in a mixed-gender combat unit and would quickly damage the required atmosphere of life-or-death trust, says a former infantry officer and West Point graduate who did three tours of duty in Iraq, including as a ground-combat officer in the August 2004 battle to control the city of Najaf in southern Iraq.

Women served in one supply company for his unit, and "when you'd go back there, you'd start looking at those girls and thinking, 'My goodness,' " says the officer. If the women had served alongside the men in combat, "you would be distracted. A woman there would just get prettier and prettier every day," he says. "I wouldn't do anything inappropriate, but I would worry because I know there'd be guys in my platoon who would act on their feelings, whether the woman wanted them to or not" — an extra concern for an officer already bearing the burden of leading troops in battle.

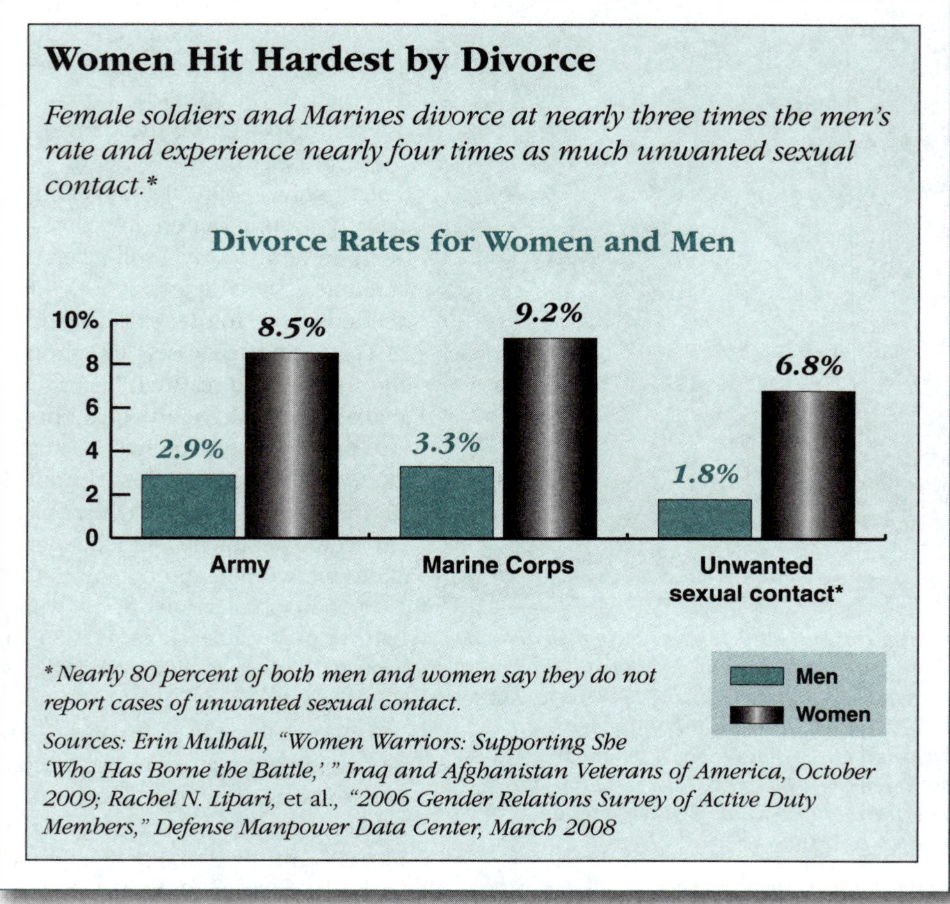

*Nearly 80 percent of both men and women say they do not report cases of unwanted sexual contact.

Sources: Erin Mulhall, "Women Warriors: Supporting She 'Who Has Borne the Battle,'" Iraq and Afghanistan Veterans of America, October 2009; Rachel N. Lipari, et al., "2006 Gender Relations Survey of Active Duty Members," Defense Manpower Data Center, March 2008

Is enough being done to reduce sexual violence in the military?

Allegations of sexual assault of women service members have been a feature of military life as long as the military has been gender integrated. But many factors complicate efforts to stamp out such problems.

For one thing, because most military personnel are 18-to-20-somethings, many away from home for the first time, the armed forces must struggle with "all the issues of any college-age population, including binge drinking and reckless behavior," including assault and date rape, "which are normative in that age group," says Martin of Bryn Mawr.

"Research shows that there's a much lower incidence [of sexual assault] in noncombat zones, and higher rates in combat areas," says D'Amico of Syracuse.

When men and women in the same unit "are counting on each other to watch their backs" in potentially deadly situations, there are many opportunities for miscommunication, says Embser-Herbert of Hamline University. "You're having to create a situation of trust, but you're also hoping that everyone understands boundaries" and that cues meant to signify "we trust each other" aren't misread as invitations to make unwanted sexual moves, she says.

In previous military occupations, sex industries quickly grew up around U.S. military bases, but in the Middle East that's happened much less, "so you have a lot of displaced sexual energy" in young people "who are also frustrated because they're being told they're going to go home, and then they don't get to go home," says D'Amico. The military had not been doing a good job of managing those tensions, including sexual tensions, she says.

But over the past five years, the military has stepped up its efforts to combat sexual assault.

High-ranking defense leaders, including Defense Secretary Robert Gates and Joint Chiefs of Staff Chairman Adm. Mike Mullen, now express "real concern" about the issue, and the Army, in particular, "is making strides," said Rep. Harman.[18]

The Department of Defense also has required every major defense installation to appoint a Sexual Assault Response Coordinator to monitor care for victims and organize prevention, education and outreach campaigns, said Rep. Louise Slaughter, D-N.Y.[19]

Mullen "has come out with a new strategy for preventing harassment," focusing on men's responsibility, says the University of Maryland's Iskra. "Before it was, 'Don't dress provocatively,' directed at women, but now the focus is on the men, where it should be. People need to be held accountable." A similar approach worked for stopping racial harassment, she notes. "You don't hear racist statements anymore."[20]

The DoD also is working to develop a database for complaints about abusive or harassing behavior, Iskra says. "So if you see patterns of complaints about a person," even if the separate reports are of a slightly different character or occur at different posts, commanders can become aware of a potential problem, she says.

Nevertheless, sexual violence against military women persists, despite numerous congressional hearings on the subject and recent DoD attempts at reform, said Helen Benedict, a journalism professor at Columbia University and author of a 2009 book on women soldiers serving in Iraq.[21] At least 41 percent of female veterans treated at the West Los Angeles Veterans Affairs Health Center said they had experienced sexual assault in the military, and 29 percent say they were raped, said Harman.[22]

"At the heart of this crisis is an apparent inability or unwillingness to prosecute rapists in the ranks," Harman said. Only 181 out of 2,212 subjects — or 8 percent — investigated for sexual assault in 2007 were referred to courts martial, she said, and they generally only received "slaps on the wrist . . . even for convicted offenders." By contrast, in the civil justice system, 40 percent of those arrested for rape are prosecuted, she pointed out.[23]

Military language, charged Benedict, reveals an "unabashed hatred of women," which creates a rape-friendly culture. Drill instructors "routinely denigrate recruits by calling them pussy, girl, bitch, lady and dyke," and military men still sing misogynist rhymes that have been around for decades. So the message sent from the top is "that women are second-class soldiers," fit mainly to serve as "sexual prey."[24]

Background

Forgotten Amazons?

Throughout history women have participated in wars, frequently as victims but often by supporting troops with farm or industrial labor on the home front. And in smaller numbers but persistently through time women have served as spies, saboteurs and armed combatants, especially when military manpower was in short supply. When wars end, however, women's involvement often is written out of the history books as too minimal to matter.[25]

"Women have not engaged in warfare at all times and in all places, but they have fought bravely and well in many times and in many places," wrote Robert B. Edgerton, a professor of anthropology at the University of California, Los Angeles.

Throughout time, some cultures have claimed to have had warrior women — ranging from the Amazons of Greek mythology and France's legendary Joan of Arc to the Scythian women of southern Russia. But historians today disagree on whether these women played as big a role in physical combat as their legends portray.

However, one culture in which the role of warrior women has not been disputed was the West African Kingdom of Dahomey, which existed in the 18th and 19th centuries in the area where modern-day Benin is located. "Full-time professional women soldiers fought so ferociously and successfully for so many years that they eventually became the elite force of Dahomey's professional, highly successful standing army," according to Edgerton.[26]

In one 1864 battle, Dahomean male and female troops, led by the king's corps of elite fighting woman, attacked the stronghold of a neighboring people — the Egba, who possessed much better, more modern weaponry. As the Egba opened fire with cannon and muskets, the poorly armed Dahomeans "led by Amazons screaming, 'Conquer or die,' sprinted toward the city," wrote Edgerton. "One woman lost her arm in the attack but shot an Egba with her other hand before being killed with a sword. . . . One woman sat on the wall for some time smoking her pipe and contemptuously staring at the Egba before she was shot down."[27]

Virtually every war has had some female combatants. At least 400 women are known to have fought in the American Civil War, for example, many dressed as men. Some women whose gender was discovered while they were on active duty were jailed or assigned to traditional female jobs, such as laundress or seamstress, wrote Lisa Tendrich Frank, author of *Women in the Civil War*. Others were discharged and sent home, but "some determined female combatants reenlisted in other units and continued to fight until they were discovered again," according to Frank.[28]

In 1901, the U.S. Army established an official nurse corps for women, and the Navy established a nurse corps in 1908. In World War I, about 34,000 American women worked for the U.S. military. Most were nurses, but others filled noncombat jobs such as clerk, translator, telephone operator, radio electrician and camouflage designer. The War Department resisted calls to establish specific women's corps in the armed services, except for the nurses' corps, and even the nurses did not have full military status. After the war the non-nurses were demobilized, and while some military analysts argued that a women's corps would be needed if another war occurred, the War Department and Congress resisted making any plans for that.

Women and Manpower

In World War II, European and American armed forces saw the greatest influx of women ever. When the war began, most governments were reluctant to enlist women even into auxiliary, home-front roles in the armed forces. As manpower shortages appeared, however, attitudes changed.

Initially, "many negative stereotypical images of women" existed among top military leaders and in written policies, said Patricia M. Shields, a professor of political science at Texas State University in San Marcos. "Prior to World War II women were considered more costly" for the military, regardless of the job. For example, "two women typists were calculated to be needed to replace one male typist" when, "in fact, the reverse was true," said Shields.[29]

Early in the war, British Prime Minister Winston Churchill was reluctant to bring women into auxiliary military roles, such as support and technical jobs in air defense units, says Bernard Cook, a professor of European history at Loyola University in New Orleans. "But when someone told [Churchill] that doing it would save 40,000 men who could then be deployed overseas," he quickly changed his mind, says Cook.

The hard-pressed Soviet army employed the most women in the widest range of jobs, says Cook. Between 800,000 and 1 million Soviet women fought — about 8 percent of the total force — filling roles from tank driver to pilot. About 400,000 women were drafted, and the rest volunteered. Some were awarded medals for heroism, and many served in front-line areas, including during the fall of Berlin in spring 1945, the last great battle of the war, says Cook.

Meanwhile, because Hitler held an ultra-traditional view of women as embodying an idealized femininity, Germany held out as long as it could against allowing women to help the war effort, says Cook. Unlike in other nations, Hitler even insisted that German factories continue producing consumer goods like cosmetics during the war, rather than turning out war goods. Eventually, however, women took air-defense posts — looking out for and providing technical help to soldiers trying to shoot down or deflect incoming enemy airborne attacks — and finally, as Germany grew more desperate, some received weapons training.

In the United States, the nation's first peacetime draft for men was implemented in 1940, with war already raging in Europe. Even so, military workforce shortages reached crisis proportions shortly after the country's December 1941 entry into the war.

At that point, many argued that women should be officially brought into the armed services. "Men who would have filled positions in combat units were being siphoned out . . . to fill jobs in non-combat units" that many believed could be performed by women, observed retired Air Force Maj. Gen. Jeanne Holm.[30]

Women also ate less than men — and thus would cost the government a bit less money to feed — increasing the government's interest in recruiting them, said Titunik of the University of Hawaii.[31]

But some military analysts maintain deep skepticism, even today, about whether the armed forces should have opened their doors to women in the 1940s.

(Text continues on page A-51)

CHRONOLOGY

1800s-1930s ***Some American women serve in military support roles, such as nurses, cooks, clerks, telephone operators and translators (World War I), but during the Civil War, some sneaked into combat, most dressed as men.***

1940s-1960s ***Wartime personnel shortages lead to recruitment of women for support roles.***

1942 First official female Navy and Army units are established; women fill labor shortages in support jobs like control-tower operators, parachute riggers and navigation instructors.

1943 American Medical Association drops objection to recruiting female physicians.

1948 Women officially become eligible for membership in all military branches, with their numbers capped at 2 percent.

1967 Two percent cap on female enlisted personnel is dropped; all but top officer ranks open to women.

1970s-1980s ***Armed forces recruit more women, but not for combat jobs.***

1973 Draft ends; recruitment of women increases.

1976 Service academies open to women.

1978 Navy assigns women to non-combatant ships for first time.

1980 Congress rejects President Jimmy Carter's proposal to register women for future drafts.

1981 Supreme Court rules in *Rostker v. Goldberg* that a male-only draft does not violate Constitution's "equal protection" clause.

1989 All Coast Guard and Air Force jobs open to women, along with 59 percent of Navy jobs, 52 percent of Army jobs and 20 percent of Marine jobs. . . . For first time, female officers command Marine Corps units: a recruiting station and a reserve support unit.

1990s ***Women take on more military roles, but sexual-assault scandals cast doubt on whether gender integration works.***

1990 Cmdr. Darlene Iskra is first woman to command a Navy ship, the rescue and salvage vessel *USS Opportune*.

1991 Congress lifts ban on women flying combat missions.

1994 Army women join men at boot camps. . . . Jobs on combat ships and aircraft are opened to women. . . . Lt. Kara Hultgreen, the Navy's first female fighter pilot, dies when her F-14 crashes on approach to a carrier landing.

1995 Air Force Lt. Kelly Flinn becomes the first female B-52 bomber pilot. She later resigns to avoid a court martial stemming from an affair with a married civilian.

1996 Female recruits at Aberdeen Proving Grounds in Maryland charge male drill sergeants with harassment, rape. A company commander and three drill sergeants are sent to prison.

2000s ***Iraq and Afghanistan wars see record numbers of women in wartime service.***

2003 Manpower shortages in Iraq lead Army to send women on counterinsurgency missions, against regulations.

2005 Bill to ban women in land combat fails to advance in Congress.

2008 Ann E. Dunwoody, commander of the Army Materiel Command, becomes first female four-star general, the highest rank attained by a woman.

2009 Navy announces plans to put women on submarines. . . . Sgt. Maj. Teresa L. King becomes first female chief of Army drill-sergeant training. . . . Uptick in sexual-assault reports seen as evidence that more women are reporting crimes. . . . Navy inspector general reports ships face serious labor shortages as more pregnant women leave their deployments.

Can Women Handle Combat?

"Most guys discover women are just like everybody else."

Critics of opening military combat roles to women often argue that while men tend to be enthusiastic warriors by temperament, women generally are not, which makes combat an unsuitable and unhealthy place for women.

Proponents of women in combat, however, say that while women respond to some situations differently from men, they, too, have a great capacity for aggression, loyalty to comrades and other traits traditionally associated with warriors.

Citizens who try to stop crimes provide a concrete measure of the difference between men and women, such as physical aggressiveness and risk-taking, according to Kingsley Browne, a law professor at Wayne State University in Detroit. For example, "a study of individuals intervening to thwart violent crimes, such as muggings, armed robberies and bank holdups, found that only one of 32 individuals in the sample was a woman," Browne wrote.[1]

The importance of mothers to children's survival means that women have likely "evolved to rate the costs of physical danger higher than men do," which explains women's lower levels of aggression and risk-taking, Browne said.[2]

Moreover, Browne says some female officers' zeal for career advancement has led to myth-making about women's zest for war. "When Demi Moore's character in [the 1997 movie] 'G.I. Jane' claimed that wanting to 'blow shit up' was her motivation for joining the [Navy] SEALs, we already knew enough about her character to realize that she was not telling the truth," Browne wrote. "She wanted a combat assignment to further her career, which . . . is the principal motivation of women seeking to serve in combat units."[3]

In recent years, largely due to workforce shortages, the Army has circumvented official military policy to put women into ground-combat situations in Iraq and Afghanistan. Predictably, the experience has proved difficult for many women, who generally don't desire such roles, says Elaine Donnelly, president of the Center for Military Readiness, the Michigan think tank she founded that advocates for military personnel policies such as barring women from ground combat.

Donnelly cites the case of Spec. Stephanie Filus, who attempted suicide when she realized she faced deployment in a unit required to be all-male — due to its combat-related mission — even though her recruiter had assured her that she would not see close combat. "I certainly do not approve of her choice of action, but it is regrettable that she felt that she had no recourse," says Donnelly. "Our young women should not be kept in the dark about the obligations they will face if they enlist, mistakenly believing that they will not be assigned or placed in a direct ground-combat unit that used to be all-male."

Awareness that women are serving in combat roles today hasn't hit home with the public or even with military institutions, such as the Veterans Affairs health-care system. Unlike with men, women's combat-related post-traumatic stress disorder (PTSD) is often overlooked and underestimated by their families and others, including health workers, because, unlike men, "they're not supposed to punch a wall, they're not supposed to get aggressive with their spouse," said Carri-Ann Gibson, director of the Trauma Recovery Program at the James A. Haley Veterans' Hospital in Tampa, Fla.[4]

(Continued)

(Continued)

Other analysts argue that, while many women do respond differently to their wartime experiences than men, their responses in no way make them liabilities.

Women have the same level of devotion to their military mission as men, not less, says Erin Solaro, author of the 2006 book *Women in the Line of Fire*. "Some women volunteered for Lioness* missions, others didn't, but I never met a woman who felt free to decline one, because that meant someone else would have to go in her place, and if no women went, the mission was more dangerous than it otherwise would have been."[5]

A female Italian paratrooper is one of 2,800 Italian soldiers serving in the North Atlantic Treaty Organization's (NATO) peacekeeping mission in Afghanistan. Italy is one of 12 NATO countries — out of the 28 — that allow females to serve in combat. Most began allowing it in the late 1980s and early '90s.

Getty Images/Laura Lezza

Capt. Anastasia Breslow, a member of one of the original Lioness teams, recalled, "I still can't believe that I was in a firefight. Me, a female signal officer, someone expected to support from a desk was out there. . . . They needed a Lioness team so badly . . . that even as a support officer I was pulled in. I hope I don't have to do them very often, but I will never try to get out of it."[6]

"I don't think my experiences [in combat] were any different than my male counterparts," said another Lioness member, Maj. Kate Guttormsen. "I think some of my coping mechanisms were different. For example, I'm sure I cried more . . . behind closed doors."[7]

In fact, some women do enter the military with a desire to "blow things up," just like men, says Laura Browder, a professor of English at Virginia Commonwealth University in Richmond, who has interviewed many women who've served in Iraq.

"I grew up in New Jersey in the ghetto. I was always getting in trouble, getting into fights," Marine Sgt. Jocelyn Proano told Browder. "I did Army boot camp. And I loved it so much. . . . It was just awesome, marching and all that . . . And then I started hearing about the Marines. . . . They're the most hard core. . . . I chased the recruiter down. . . . I just wanted to go out, get some adventure, travel, go out to war, do the whole nine [yards]."[8]

Her first night in Al-Asad, Iraq, she was awakened by a mortar strike on a fuel storage area, said Proano. "It exploded. Smoke everywhere," she recalls. "And I wasn't even scared — I was pretty excited. I was like 'holy crap — we're at war. This is going to be good.' "[9]

"Most guys I know discover, once they have worked with women, that women are just like everybody else," said Brig. Gen. Rhonda Cornum, who was taken prisoner during the first Gulf War, in 1991, and is now director of Comprehensive Soldier Fitness for the Army. "There are some [women] that are just awesome, some that are absolutely worthless, and most of them are just in between. And I think the percentage of males who are that way is the same."[10]

---

* Lioness teams are ad hoc groups of Army and Marine women who support male ground combat troops by dealing with the women and children in Iraqi and Afghan homes where soldiers are pursuing potential insurgents.

"In reality, women have always been capable of killing," wrote Linda Grant De Pauw, a historian and founder of the Maryland-based Minerva Center, an education foundation on women and warfare. "Even a small woman catching a man unaware or able to add poison when she prepared his food could end his life." But most cultures, including our own, have "profound, complex and emotionally charged" reasons — involving human psychology and societies' mythical images of themselves — for drawing a veil over this reality, she argued. For one thing, "when combat serves as a puberty ritual for boys, girls cannot participate without destroying its meaning. If girls could qualify as both mothers and warriors, there would be no unique identity for boys."[11]

— Marcia Clemmitt

---

[1] Kingsley Browne, *Co-Ed Combat: The New Evidence that Women Shouldn't Fight the Nation's Wars* (2007), p. 35.

[2] *Ibid.*, p. 52.

[3] *Ibid.*, p. 119.

[4] Quoted in Damien Cave, "Women at Arms: A Combat Role, and Anguish, Too," *The New York Times*, Oct. 31, 2009, p. A1.

[5] Erin Solaro, *Women in the Line of Fire: What You Should Know About Women in the Military* (2006), p. 77.

[6] "Interview with Capt. Anastasia Breslow, Team Lioness," Public Broadcasting System, www.pbs.org.

[7] "Interview with Maj. Kate Guttormsen, Team Lioness," Public Broadcasting System, www.pbs.org.

[8] Quoted in Laura Browder, *When Janey Comes Marching Home: Portraits of Women Combat Veterans* (forthcoming), p. 23.

[9] *Ibid.*, p. 30.

[10] "War Story: Rhonda Cornum," "PBS Frontline: The Gulf War," Public Broadcasting System, www.pbs.org, January 1996.

[11] Linda Grant De Pauw, *Battle Cries and Lullabies: Women in War from Prehistory to the Present* (2000), p. 12.

"The duties women performed for the War and Navy departments in Washington, D.C., where most military women were stationed, could just as easily have been performed by the men who were not drafted or by civilian men and women," said Brian P. Mitchell, author of *Women in the Military: Flirting With Disaster*. "Their other uses hardly justified the trouble of establishing and maintaining separate women's components of the Army, Navy, Coast Guard and Marines."[32]

Seeing women performing war work around the world changed many minds, however. "Until my experience in London I had been opposed to the use of women in uniform," said President Dwight D. Eisenhower, a five-star general who served as Supreme Commander of the Allied Forces in Europe during the war. "But in Great Britain I had seen them perform so magnificently in various positions, including service in active anti-aircraft batteries, that I had been converted."

In fact, said Eisenhower, women proved so effective that by the end of the war even the "most stubborn diehards" were convinced that they could be useful to the war effort "and demanded them in increasing numbers."[33]

A bill to establish a Woman's Army Auxiliary Corps was introduced in Congress in May 1941, but it languished until manpower shortages in 1942 finally compelled its passage. Congress also established a Navy Women's Reserve in 1942, and in June 1943 lawmakers established the Women's Army Corps, in which the enlistees enjoyed full military status, unlike those who had enlisted in the auxiliary corps.

Services for Military Women Lagging Behind

Many don't seek health care, even when eligible.

With thousands of women now serving in the military, including in combat roles, and the number of female veterans poised to double over the next decade, military policy makers are struggling to develop appropriate responses to issues ranging from child care to post-traumatic stress disorder (PTSD).[1]

For example, while around 22 percent of male veterans use Veterans Affairs (VA) health-care facilities in a given year, "utilization rates" for female veterans range from 11 to 19 percent. Research shows that many women veterans don't even think of themselves as bona fide veterans whose service makes them eligible for benefits like health care, even when they've served in combat zones, so many don't apply for benefits, said Joy J. Ilem, deputy national legislative director of Disabled American Veterans. To make matters worse, said Ilem, nearly 19 percent of women veterans who reported they had no access to health care actually have service-connected disabilities that would fully qualify them for VA health services.[2]

Because many women who do use VA health facilities suffer from PTSD connected to sexual assaults in the military, the VA is promising to make its facilities more woman-friendly. But progress is slow. For example, the Government Accountability Office found earlier this year that women's exam-room tables in some VA facilities still faced doors rather than walls, raising privacy concerns, and that women sometimes had to walk through waiting rooms to get to restrooms.[3]

Another concern is the growing number of homeless women vets.

"I had a young woman Air Force veteran come in initially asking for help finding a job, but at the end of our conversation it became evident she was homeless," Tia Christopher, women veterans coordinator for Swords to Plowshares, told a Senate Committee in July. "It broke my heart that this sister veteran" who "honorably served her country . . . was now selling her body just to get by." The story makes clear that "services are insufficient for women veterans," but when a veterans' assistance organization connected the woman with another woman veteran, "she felt comfortable asking for help," and relieved not to have to confront the VA's notorious bureaucracy, Christopher said.[4]

As of September, the VA estimated there were 13,100 homeless female veterans, many with serious mental-health problems and about 40 percent of whom say they were sexually assaulted by a fellow service member. Moreover, many homeless women vets are parents of young children, complicating the situation. Among women vets who participate in one of the VA's homelessness programs, 23 percent have children under age 18, according to Iraq and Afghanistan Veterans of America. And since the VA is legally barred from providing "direct care to children or spouses of veterans, this becomes a huge unmet need," says the group.[5]

"Motherhood complicates everything" for service members, says Laura Browder, a professor of English at Virginia Commonwealth University in Richmond, who has conducted extensive interviews with active-duty female soldiers. For example, "while many, many soldiers have talked to me about PTSD, no mothers have," says Browder. She surmises that mothers' silence may stem from the fact that "being a bad mother is the ultimate taboo" in our society, which may intensify pressures on military women.

"I feel that the Army should have something like a sabbatical for dual military couples, when it comes . . . to deployments," Army Spec. Rebecca Nava told a PBS television interviewer. Currently, military couples, as well as single parents, must present detailed plans for how their children will be cared for if they're deployed overseas, but in families where both parents are military, that difficulty could be overcome if spouses' deployments were timed so that "one parent goes . . . and then when that one gets back the other one goes," Nava said. "If one parent is with the child at all times, they don't have to worry" so much about the family's well-being.[6]

"Twenty years ago, when I was a young lieutenant, I felt I was committed to a career and could not have a family," says Darlene M. Iskra, program coordinator for the University of Maryland's Leadership Education and Development Center and a retired Navy commander who was the first woman to command a U.S. Navy ship. "Now women think they can have it all, and many are managing it, although the attrition rate is higher for women."

And the armed forces are looking at some family-friendly policies, says Iskra. For example, "The Navy has started a pilot program of sabbaticals offering up to three years off for men and women" to care for children or elderly parents, go to grad school or other purposes. People on sabbatical would remain on Navy rolls so they could have health insurance, and they would retain their rank when they returned. Currently, the program is open to 40 people, she says. Such programs — utterly unheard of in the past — are becoming important today, says Iskra. "Both women and men are becoming more family oriented. That's a sea change."

Unintended pregnancies also are a problem for military women, in part because of strict federal policies on abortion and emergency contraception. The so-called Hyde Amendment, attached to government spending bills each year, has barred federal funding for abortions since 1976. The Department of Defense currently allows women to pay for their own abortions at military facilities overseas — but only if their pregnancies endanger their lives or resulted from rape or incest. In addition, under current rules military facilities are not required to stock emergency contraception.[7]

As a result, women stationed overseas "face two unpalatable choices: Fly elsewhere for a safe, legal abortion, or seek a risky abortion off-base in the country where they are stationed," wrote Caitlin Borgmann, a professor of law at the City University of New York, in an August letter to *The New York Times*.[8]

— Marcia Clemmitt

---

[1] Genevieve Chase, testimony before Senate Committee on Veterans Affairs, July 14, 2009, http://veterans.senate.gov.

[2] Testimony before Senate Committee on Veterans Affairs, July 14, 2009, http://veterans.senate.gov.

[3] Erin Mulhall, "Women Warriors: Supporting She Who Has Borne the Battle," Iraq and Afghanistan Veterans of America, October 2009, http://media.iava.org/IAVA_WomensReport_2009.pdf.

[4] Testimony before Senate Committee on Veterans Affairs, July 14, 2009, http://veterans.senate.gov.

[5] Mulhall, *op. cit.*

[6] "Interview with Spec. Rebecca Nava, Team Lioness," Public Broadcasting System, www.pbs.org.

[7] "Military Women Should Have Full Access to Reproductive Health Care," National Women's Law Center, Women's Research & Education Institute, and Alliance for National Defense, December 2008.

[8] Caitlin Borgmann, letter to the editor, *The New York Times*, Aug. 17, 2009.

More than 1,000 female pilots also served, primarily ferrying planes from manufacturing facilities to military bases. However, despite several legislative attempts to extend military status to the pilots, the Women Airforce Service Pilots organization — WASP — was never militarized. Its members were considered civil servants and denied military benefits.

All told, more than 350,000 American women served in military roles in World War II.

At war's end, most who'd seen military service — men and women — returned to civilian life. In most countries, the late 1940s saw a nearly complete exodus of women from the armed forces, says Cook. In the Soviet Union, for example, where women had made up a full 8 percent of the wartime service, "the women were decommissioned and got veterans' benefits. But very few stayed on," Cook says. By 1959, out of a Soviet army of more than 4 million, only 659 were women, he says.

In the United States, however, a 1948 law established a legitimate place for women in the military, but also strictly limited their participation. The Women's Armed Services Integration Act, signed into law by President Harry S. Truman on June 12, 1948, gave permanent status to women in the regular and reserve branches of all the services. It capped women's participation at 2 percent in each service branch and set a 10-percent limit on female officers, who could advance in rank no further than lieutenant colonel or Navy commander. Women could enlist at age 18 but needed parental permission until age 21, while men could enlist at 17 and only needed parental permission until age 18.[34]

The law barred women from combat aircraft and from all Navy ships except hospital ships and transports. From the outset, different services had different levels of gender integration, with Air Force women generally governed by the same organization structure as men but the Army maintaining a separate Women's Army Corps for training, promotions and other management functions.[35]

Over time, the military jobs that had been open to women during the war were trimmed back, and the services went out of their way to emphasize a traditionally feminine image for women in uniform, said Maj. Gen. Holm. In the Air Force, for example, "beginning in 1958 . . . enlisted women were phased out of fields where their representation had been small," such as intelligence, control-tower operation and some equipment-maintenance jobs, and were moved into desk jobs.[36]

Furthermore, "all basic training programs were heavily sprinkled with courses to enhance feminine appearance," said Holm. Female Marines, for example, "were told their lipstick and nail polish had to match the braid on their uniform hats, which was Marine Corps scarlet," while Air Force women were told to use lipstick and nail polish in a "natural shade."[37]

Volunteers All

In 1973, women accounted for 1.6 percent of military personnel. And, after years of growing public distaste for the Vietnam War, the United States ended the draft, opting to move forward with an all-volunteer military. Then, as public opposition to the war limited the number of men who enlisted, recruitment of women was stepped up to help fill the gap.[38]

But, points out Titunik, of the University of Hawaii, the increased use of women in the military between 1973 and the early 1990s "was connected primarily with military necessity, not direct feminist pressure."[39]

Economics also played a role in increasing the number of female recruits, says Linda Grant De Pauw, a historian and founder of the Maryland-based Minerva Center, an education foundation on women and warfare. "The economy declined so much that one man could no longer support a family," leaving more women seeking careers, including new ones provided by the volunteer military.

Women joined the armed forces rapidly during the 1970s. In 1975, President Gerald Ford signed legislation officially admitting women to the Army's military academy (West Point) and the Naval and Air Force academies at Annapolis and Colorado Springs. The first women matriculated in the fall of 1976, and the first co-ed classes graduated in 1980.

With an aggressive push by President Jimmy Carter, the percentage of women recruited swelled from under 2 percent to 8.9 percent by September 1981, for a total of 184,651 women across all service branches. The Carter administration announced a recruitment goal of 254,300 women — 12.5 percent of the force — by 1985.[40]

In early 1981, however, "military leaders asked the incoming Reagan administration to hold down the number of women enlistees until their impact on force readiness could be determined. In August 1982, the administration announced it would lower goals for female recruitment, make 23 additional job categories male-only, and establish new strength tests for other jobs that would close or nearly close them to women.[41]

Recruitment of women slowed somewhat but continued, and by 1985, women made up 10 percent of the military and, by 1990, 11 percent. In the 2000s, the percentage has hovered at about 14 percent.[42]

In the past two decades, more military jobs have opened to women, with more than 90 percent of jobs now open to women, including as ship commanders and bomber pilots.

In 1993, after the successful performance of women in the first Persian Gulf War, Congress repealed its previous ban on women serving on combat aircraft and on permanent duty on combat ships, noted scholars from the University of Maryland's Center for Research on Military Organization. (However, military policies continued to exclude women from serving in ground-combat positions, Special Operations forces, submarines and some other positions.)[43]

By now, more than 120 women have been killed in the Iraq and Afghanistan wars, but the expected public recoil from the death of women soldiers has not materialized, says Browder of Virginia Commonwealth University. "The American public is able to handle mothers getting killed."

During the last eight years of war, women have proven their value to the military mission. "They're attaining Silver Stars for valor," says Iskra of the University of Maryland.

But other analysts argue that women's desire for equal opportunity has swamped considerations about military missions.

"The overwhelming focus of integrationists has been the argument for equal rights rather than national security," wrote Wayne State's Browne. Putting women into ground combat roles risks potential loss of public support for a war if civilians at home react badly to seeing women — whom they may view as being like their mothers, daughters and sisters — taken captive in combat zones. It also risks requiring men in gender-integrated combat units to pick up some of the slack for women when it comes to heavy lifting, since the overwhelming majority of women have less upper-body strength than men, he says.[44]

For those reasons, "the exclusion of women from combat aviation should also be reinstated," said Browne. "Combat aviation crews may end up fighting for survival on the ground," and physical strength can also become "a critical factor in maintaining control" of aircraft hit by enemy fire. Pilots flying over enemy territory risk being shot down, "and it is in the national interest not to have women taken prisoner, even if individual women are willing to take the risk."[45]

Nevertheless, military workforce needs have opened more positions to women, including real — though ostensibly unofficial — roles in units serving with ground-combat forces. Beginning around 2003, U.S. military commanders began adding women to units engaged in direct ground combat, skirting the rule that women cannot be "assigned" to such units by having records state that they are only "attached" to the units.

For example, in 2004 and 2005, retired Lt. Col. Michael A. Baumann commanded 30 enlisted women and six female officers in a unit patrolling Baghdad's Rashid district, a hotbed of violence at the time and officially off-limits to female soldiers. But "we had to take everybody," said Baumann. "Nobody could be spared to do something like support." Moreover, he added, "I saw them with my own eyes. I had full trust and confidence in their abilities."[46]

"When they need boots on the ground, they'll put women where they need them," says D'Amico of Syracuse University.

But that is exactly the problem, says Donnelly of the Center for Military Readiness. The Army has assigned women to new roles in combat areas surreptitiously and without consulting Congress or the public about what amounts to a major — and, in her view, ill-advised — change in policy, she says.

Back in 1994, then-Secretary of Defense Les Aspin announced the "collocation rule" — declaring that women could be barred not only from ground-combat units but also from other units, such as supply units, that are "required to physically collocate and remain with direct ground combat units."[47]

Aspin's statement is valid and should stand, says Donnelly. "If the Army wants to change that, they're supposed to notify Congress 30 days earlier — come in and talk about it," so Congress can weigh in with legislation if they object, she says. "Instead, the Army has tried to redefine this, without going to Congress."

In 2005, congressional Republicans, led by Rep. Duncan Hunter, Calif., Chairman of the House Armed Services Committee, sponsored a bill to codify women's exclusion from ground combat. The provision was approved by committees in both the House and Senate, but lawmakers ultimately abandoned it. President Bush's Defense Secretary, Donald Rumsfeld, also expressed opposition to the legislation.[48]

"President George W. Bush immediately after [September 11, 2001] should have issued a call for young men, especially, to volunteer for the combat Army," says Donnelly. "He never did that, so instead we've got single mothers out there" because of heavy recruiting of young women to make up the workforce slack, she says. "I think the president missed the big picture here."

Current Situation

Woman Submariners?

In 2009, arguments over what military jobs should be open to women have heated up, following statements by Joint Chiefs Chairman Mullen and other Navy leaders that they hope to begin integrating women into submarine crews.[49]

AT ISSUE

Should military combat roles be fully opened to women?

YES

Melissa Sheridan Embser-Herbert
Professor of Sociology, Hamline University, and Army veteran

Written for *CQ Researcher,* November 2009

Combat positions should be open to those who are qualified, regardless of sex. Note that the question is not whether women should be permitted to *serve* in combat. That's because people are finally realizing that women already *are* in combat. Their job may not be "coded for combat," but improvised explosive devices (IEDs) don't know that. Snipers don't know that. The question is whether, acknowledging that women play vital roles in today's military and do serve in combat, the country will make more occupational categories and assignments available to women.

Those opposed to such a move claim, among other things, that women complain of being lied to by recruiters when they end up in combat-support units, and that men instinctively try to protect women. But while those entering the military do receive training in a particular occupation, in the Army everyone is a soldier first. There's a reason that even truck drivers complete Basic Combat Training, the "nine-week journey from civilian to soldier." No matter the career field or assignment coding, everyone knows — including women — that they may end up taking, and returning, fire. As for chivalry, the Army, as one example, would not have had to establish a Sexual Harassment/Assault Response & Prevention (SHARP) program if male military personnel were "predisposed to protect" female colleagues.

The military needs qualified personnel. If a woman demonstrates that she meets the requirements to perform a job, she should be allowed to do it. The requirements should include physical ability, and if this means that few women make the cut, so be it. Physical-fitness tests should be tied to the demands of one's military occupation,

NO

Elaine Donnelly
President, Center for Military Readiness

Written for *CQ Researcher,* November 2009

In March 2003 an aggressive ground assault by infantry, armor, Special Operations Forces and Marines liberated Baghdad. In November 2004 the same forces cleaned out Fallujah, an enemy stronghold. Both battles involved brutal street-to-street, door-to-door fighting — the very definition of "direct ground combat." Despite assurances that today's wars "have no front lines," missions of close combat troops remain unchanged. All deployed personnel serve "in harm's way," but that is not the same as direct ground combat: closing with and destroying the enemy with deliberate *offensive action* under fire.

For many reasons, under current regulations battalion-level units in or near direct ground-combat battalions must be all-male. Infantrymen routinely must carry weapons, ammunition, electronic equipment and protective/survival gear weighing more than 100 pounds. All are prepared to lift and evacuate an injured fellow soldier in order to save his life. Female soldiers and Marines face hazardous duty inspecting female civilians in war zones, but in direct ground combat women do not have an "equal opportunity" to survive or to help fellow soldiers survive.

Current law requires the Defense Department to notify Congress well in advance of proposed changes in regulations affecting women. Instead, Army officials have redefined regulations unilaterally, without authorization. The result has been "anything goes" policies, combined with misguided recruiting priorities that attract single mothers and create problems for families left behind.

Navy officials now are pushing for women on submarines, despite irresolvable health risks identified by experts in undersea medicine. Elevated trace elements in the constantly recycled atmosphere,

(Continued)

(Continued)

not one's sex. An infantry soldier *should* have higher physical-fitness standards than a cook. If the military is serious about wanting the strongest military possible — truly ready to defend the nation — it needs to start thinking about *people*, not reproductive organs and archaic ideas regarding the ability of women and men to work together.

Since 2001, more than 200,000 women have served in Iraq and Afghanistan. More than 100 have died, thousands have sustained serious physical injuries and an untold number suffer from post-traumatic stress disorder. To continue to deny women the right to serve honorably — and in combat — is insulting and disingenuous. Moreover, refusing the service of women who are willing and capable of serving in an expanded combat role is detrimental to the military mission.

such as carbon monoxide and carbon dioxide, are safe for adults but not for a developing embryo in the earliest weeks before a sailor knows she is pregnant. Life-threatening ectopic pregnancies, which are not statistically rare, would require immediate, extremely hazardous mid-ocean evacuations that compromise undersea missions. Submarine habitability standards are difficult enough, and 100 percent manning requirements are incompatible with enlisted pregnancy rates that jumped from 12 to 19 percent in only two years.

Pride in our courageous military women and their impressive accomplishments should not deter questions about flawed policies that encourage social problems affecting discipline, deployability, morale and readiness. Congress should provide responsible oversight, holding Pentagon officials accountable. Equal opportunity is important, but if there is a conflict, the needs of the military must come first.

U.S. Navy Lt. Kara S. Hultgreen — the nation's first woman combat pilot — was killed off the coast of San Diego when her F-14 crashed on approach to the aircraft carrier USS Abraham Lincoln *in 1994.*

Reuters/STR New

Mullen, formerly chief of naval operations, wrote to the Senate Armed Services Committee that, "as an advocate for improving the diversity of our force . . . one policy I would like to see changed is the one barring their service aboard submarines."[50]

In interviews with the *Navy Times* newspaper, the heads of the Navy Submarine Force and Fleet Forces Command — the organization in charge of the Atlantic fleet — described near-term plans for integrating women into the submarine fleet. Top Navy and Pentagon leaders still must sign off on the plan, and Congress must be given 30 days' notice of the Navy's intentions before money can be spent implementing the change. The process of seeking those approvals is just beginning, Vice Adm. Jay Donnelly of the Submarine Force recently told the *Navy Times*.[51]

Female junior officers — ensigns and lieutenants — will be the first women onboard because their smaller numbers mean that modifications to accommodate them will be cheaper, Vice Adm. Donnelly said. Sub officers share three-person or two-person staterooms, some of which would be reserved for the women. Female officers would share a bathroom — each of which has just a single shower, sink and toilet — with male officers, using a sign to indicate whether men or women are using the facility. Initially, the Navy would add women only to the crews of 18 large subs, the so-called *Ohio*-class subs, which launch ballistic and guided missiles, not to the smaller, "fast-attack" subs, like the *Seawolf* class.[52]

The women would require 15 to 16 months of training, putting the earliest possible date for the integration in 2011 or 2012, Donnelly said.[53]

For proponents of fully integrating women into the military, the news is welcome.

Sub duty is a traditional path to career advancement, says Hillman of the University of California. Top officers are generally chosen from among infantry and submarine officer pools — not from the military police or other job categories where most women serve today.

Many of the arguments against women serving on submarines are similar to those expressed against integrating women onto surface ships, said the University of Maryland's Iskra, who in 1990 became the first woman to command a Navy vessel. "Issues such as fraternization and sexual harassment" can be "dealt with as disciplinary issues," and "shipboard pregnancy is related to negative command climate and leadership," she argued. Moreover, she pointed out, "Since women serve on submarines in Australia, Canada, Norway and Sweden, it may be assumed that necessary privacy can be achieved."[54]

But other analysts argue that life on a submarine is different enough from shipboard conditions to make including women on subs dangerous both to the sub's mission and to some of the women. "The biggest mistake the Navy could make would be to gender-integrate the submarine force," says Donnelly of the Center for Military Readiness.

If a woman became pregnant, both she and her fetus would face serious medical risks by staying aboard a submarine, according to retired Rear Adm. Hugh P. Scott. "One of the more serious problems . . . in the sealed environment of a submarine is the off-gassing of several thousand organic trace contaminants" that escape from construction and maintenance operations, as well as "exposures to increased levels of carbon monoxide and carbon dioxide" arising from cigarette smoking, overheated insulation and other sources in a closed atmosphere, Scott said.[55]

Although the pollution poses no more danger to non-pregnant women than to men, it would be very dangerous to a fetus during the first trimester of pregnancy, Scott wrote. It could interfere with fetal oxygen supply during critical stages of development and could cause ectopic pregnancies — pregnancies that occur outside the uterus and are not survivable by an embryo, he argued.[56]

"If a woman discovers she's pregnant, the captain has only two choices," says Donnelly. One would be to "surface and evacuate her," a very complicated and potentially dangerous process in some conditions, such as if the sub is under the polar ice cap. Alternatively, she says, the captain could "keep the woman there and risk birth defects. Women are not being told about these risks."

Sexual Assault

Whether one favors or opposes it, no one argues that harmonious gender integration of the armed forces comes without problems.

Early this year the Defense Department released 2008 data on sexual assaults involving military personnel, showing that reported assaults increased by 8 percent overall from the previous year and by 26 percent in Iraq, a combat zone. But while that may strike some as bad news, the Pentagon said the rise is just what it wanted to see.[57]

Increased reports mean "the department's policy of encouraging victims to come forward is making a difference," said Kaye Whitley, director of SAPRO, the Pentagon's Sexual Assault and Prevention Office. "We're getting the victims in to get care." In both civilian and military life, sexual assault is the least-reported crime, and what's not reported can't be remedied, she pointed out.[58]

Of the 2,908 reports, 643 were made as "restricted" reports — an option the Pentagon began offering in 2005 in order to allow victims to report an assault to get care without reporting the incident to law enforcement or military commanders. Of the 2,265 "unrestricted" reports, 1,594 victims were armed-forces members, while the other 671 were civilians.[59]

Some members of Congress called the data alarming. "While the report shows modest improvement, we're far from 'Mission Accomplished,' " said Rep. Harman. "Military women are more likely to be raped by a fellow soldier than killed by enemy fire in Iraq.[60]

In February, Rep. Slaughter introduced the Military Domestic and Sexual Violence Response Act, which would establish an Office of Victims' Advocate in the DoD to help those reporting assaults get care, establish a sexual-assault care team at each military medical facility, require commanders who receive reports of violence to investigate and report them and establish a Director of Special Investigations to refer cases for prosecution. No action has occurred on the bill, however.[61]

Meanwhile, advocates of limiting gender integration argue that maintaining some gender-segregated units is the best way to cut down on all kinds of sexual misconduct, including sexual assault. "Sexual misconduct is a problem in a gender-mixed force even though we've tried everything," says Donnelly. The best approach is probably to "separate genders as much as possible," she says. "The Marines have separate-gender training, and the Army should return to it."

But others say the future does not lie in gender segregation. Policy makers are moving forward to integrate women into roles such as the submarine service despite problems and significant dissent from both inside and outside the military, says Bryn Mawr's Martin. "Policies drive public understanding and perception," not the other way around, he says. "If you waited to get everybody on board, it would never happen."

Moreover, with the Army bringing women into ground-combat positions in Iraq and Afghanistan — even in advance of official policy changes — "we might be up for more action on the policy level" once the current wars have ended, says Rosemarie Skaine, author of the 1998 book *Women at War*. That would open positions that have been opened de facto already.

"The reality is that the women are already there," she says.

Outlook

Gender Roles

For those who believe women should participate fully in the armed services, recent events like the Navy's push to open submarine duty to women suggest that it's mainly a matter of time before all military roles are gender-neutral.

But skeptics say focusing on the armed services as a necessary step in achieving equal workplace opportunity is likely to backfire, potentially opening the door to abuse of some valuable female soldiers by forcing them into combat roles they have no wish to enter and for which they are unsuited.

Time alone may work much of the change, says D'Amico of Syracuse. "The new generations — generations X, Y and the ones that follow — look really differently at every sort of institution. My students tend to ask, 'Why should women not be in the military? What's the problem?' " and that sentiment includes many politically conservative students, she says.

"We aren't going to go back," and "the barriers will fall," including the barrier to serving in ground combat, says Virginia Commonwealth's Browder.

Furthermore, social expectations outside the military play a major role in holding women back from military advancement, and, while gender expectations are shifting throughout society, such change occurs slowly, says Bryn Mawr's Martin. "For example, we still define women as having significant responsibility for caring for elderly parents," a cultural norm that keeps military women — like women in some other professions, notably academic science — from "reaching certain benchmarks required for promotion."

But "the campaign to force young women into or near the violence of close combat" flies in the face of some traditional — and important — American values, requiring "psychological acceptance of the idea that men can and should place women in physical or mortal danger," said Donnelly of the Center for Military Readiness.[62]

There's a deep disconnect between efforts to protect military women believed to be victims of sexual violence or harassment and the simultaneous movement to push them into super-dangerous combat roles, said Donnelly. "Many officials in Congress, the Pentagon and the service academies are eager to establish ubiquitous 'victim advocate' offices, staffed by professionals who vow to protect military women from the slightest form of harassment, real or imagined." Meanwhile, "the same officials simultaneously promote the deliberate exposure of military women to extreme abuse and violence in close, lethal combat, where females do not have an equal opportunity to survive."[63]

Furthermore, "indications are . . . that many female recruits are not being informed, prior to enlistment, that regulations no longer exempt women from assignments known to involve a 'substantial risk of capture,' " Donnelly said. "Nor are the female recruits being told that their 'job description' might involve involuntary placement in ground-combat-collocated units, despite regulations requiring those units to be coded for men only."[64]

Rather than trying to establish a completely equal career playing field for women within the armed services, a fairer regime for the many women who currently enter the military as a career move might be to expand government benefits like health insurance and education currently available only to armed-forces members to a much wider range of public-service jobs, says Marie De Young, a former Army chaplain and operations officer and co-author of *Women in Combat: Civic Duty or Military Liability?*

"We predicted in the early 1990s that we'll be short 10 million teachers," and other public-service roles also need filling, such as emergency first-responders, she says. "So why are we valorizing only the military? The people who are really going in for the benefits — why not let them do civil service and community service in other ways?"

Notes

1. For background, see David Koon, "A New Soldier Story," *Arkansas Times*, May 15, 2008, www.arktimes.com.

2. Quoted in "Lioness: There for the Action, Missing from History," a documentary film by Meg McLagan and Daria Sommers, 2008, www.lionessthefilm.com.

3. Quoted in James Dao, "First Woman Ascends to Top Drill Sergeant Spot," *The New York Times*, Sept. 22, 2009, p. A1.

4. Rachel L. Swarns, "Commanding a Role for Women in the Military," *The New York Times*, June 30, 2008, p. A17.

5. See Peter Katel, "Gays in the Military," *CQ Researcher*, Sept. 18, 2009, pp. 765-788.

6. Elaine Donnelly, "The Army's Gender War," *National Review Online*, Jan. 7, 2005, www.nationalreview.com.

7. Elaine Donnelly, "Constructing the Co-Ed Military," *Duke Journal of Law and Gender Policy*, June 18, 2007, p. 881.

8. Jane Harman, testimony to the House Oversight and Government Reform Subcommittee on National Security and Foreign Affairs, July 31, 2008.

9. Transcript, "Ben Wattenberg's Think Tank," PBS, Sept. 16, 2000, www.pbs.org/thinktank/transcript895.html.

10. Laura Browder, *When Janey Comes Marching Home: Portraits of Women Combat Veterans*, forthcoming, p. 4.

11. *Ibid.*

12. Kingsley Browne, *Co-Ed Combat: The New Evidence that Women Shouldn't Fight the Nation's Wars* (2007), p. 115.

13. Regina F. Titunik, "The First Wave: Gender Integration and Military Culture," *Armed Forces & Society*, winter 2000, p. 248.

14. "Military Hails Two Heroes from Ft. Hood Rampage," MSNBC.com, Nov. 6, 2009, www.msnbc.msn.com.

15. Margaret C. Harrell and Laura L. Miller, "New Opportunities for Military Women; Effects Upon Readiness, Cohesion, Morale," RAND, 1997, p. xvii.

16. Barbara W. Wilson, "Women in Combat: Why Not," Military Women Veterans blog, http://userpages.aug.com/captbarb/combat.html.

17. Browne, *op. cit.*, p. 259.

18. Harman, *op. cit.*

19. Louise Slaughter, testimony to the House Oversight and Government Reform Subcommittee on National Security and Foreign Affairs, July 31, 2008.

20. For background, see Craig Donegan, "New Military Culture," *CQ Researcher*, April 26, 1996, pp. 361-384.

21. Helen Benedict, testimony before the House Oversight and Government Reform Subcommittee on National Security and Foreign Affairs, June 25, 2009, http://nationalsecurity.oversight.house.gov.

22. Harman, *op. cit.*

23. *Ibid.*

24. Benedict, *op. cit.*

25. For background, see Bernard Cook, ed., *Women in War: A Historical Encyclopedia from Antiquity to the Present* (2006).

26. Robert B. Edgerton, *Warrior Women: the Amazons of Dahomey* (2000), p. 3.

27. *Ibid.*, p. 100.

28. Lisa Tendrich Frank, "American Women Combatants During the Civil War," in Cook, *op. cit.*, p. 118.

29. Patricia M. Shields, "Women as Military Leaders: Promises and Pitfalls," Faculty Publications — Political Science, eCommons@Texas State University, http://ecommons.txstate.edu/polsfacp/42.

30. Jeanne Holm, *Women in the Military: An Unfinished History* (1993), p. 23.

31. Titunik, *op. cit.*, p. 229.

32. Brian P. Mitchell, *Women in the Military: Flirting With Disaster* (1998), p. 4.

33. Quoted in Titunik, *op. cit.*, p. 229.

34. Holm, *op. cit.*, p. 120.

35. *Ibid.*, p. 120.

36. *Ibid.*, p. 184.

37. *Ibid.*, p. 181.

38. For background, see Marc Leepson, "Women in the Military," *Editorial Research Reports*, July 10, 1981, and Rodman D. Griffin, "Women in the Military," *CQ Researcher*, Sept. 25, 1992, pp. 833-856.

39. Regina F. Titunik, "The Myth of the Macho Military," *Polity*, April 2008, p. 140.

40. Ellen C. Collier, "Women in the Armed Forces," Issue Brief No. IB79045, Congressional Research Service, 1982, http://digital.library.unt.edu/govdocs/crs/permalink/meta-crs-8513:1.

41. *Ibid.*

42. Jake Willens and Daniel Smith, "Women in the Military: Combat Roles Considered," Center for Defense Information, 1998, www.cdi.org/issues/women/combat.html.

43. Michelle Sandhoff, Mady Wechsler Segal and David R. Segal, "Gender Issues in the Transformation to an All-Volunteer Force: A Transnational Perspective," http://papers.ccpr.ucla.edu/papers/PWP-MPRC-2008-027/PWP-MPRC-2008-027.pdf.

44. Browne, *op. cit.*, p. 295.

45. *Ibid.*, p. 296.

46. Quoted in Lizette Alvarez, "G.I. Jane Breaks the Combat Barrier," *The New York Times*, Aug. 16, 2009, p. A1.

47. Les Aspin, "Memorandum from the Office of the Secretary of Defense," Jan. 13, 1994, Center for Military Readiness Web site, http://cmrlink.org/CMRNotes/LesAspin%20DGC%20DefAssign%20Rule%20011394.pdf.

48. For background, see "Hunter Admonishes Army on Women in Land Combat," Center for Military Readiness Web site, June 1, 2005, http://cmrlink.org, and "House Drops Limitation on Women in Combat Bill," News Insider Web site, May 25, 2005, www.newsinsider.org.

49. For background, see Andrew Scutro and Mark D. Faram, "Female Sailors Could Join Sub Crews by 2011," *Navy Times*, Oct. 12, 2009, www.navytimes.com, and "Mullen Wants Females on Subs," *Defense Tech*, Sept. 24, 2009, www.defensetech.org.

50. Quoted in *ibid.*

51. Scutro and Faram, *op. cit.*

52. *Ibid.*

53. *Ibid.*

54. Darlene M. Iskra, "Attitudes Toward Expanding Roles for Navy Women at Sea: Results of a Content Analysis," *Armed Forces & Society*, January 2007, p. 203.

55. Hugh P. Scott, letter to Rep. Floyd D. Spence, June 12, 2000, http://cmrlink.org/CMRNotes/HPScott%20061200.pdf.

56. *Ibid.*

57. William H. McMichael, "DoD: Sexual Assault Reports Increased in 2008," *Army Times*, March 17, 2009, www.armytimes.com.

58. Quoted in *ibid.*

59. *Ibid.*

60. Quoted in *ibid.*

61. For text and status of legislation, see http://thomas.loc.gov.

62. Donnelly, "Constructing the Co-Ed Military," *op. cit.*, p. 930.

63. *Ibid.*, p. 931.

64. *Ibid.*

Bibliography

Books

Browne, Kingsley, *Co-Ed Combat: The New Evidence that Women Shouldn't Fight the Nation's Wars*, Penguin, 2007.

A law professor at Wayne State University in Detroit lays out the arguments against integrating women fully into the military and into combat roles.

Cook, Bernard A., ed., *Women and War: A Historical Encyclopedia from Antiquity to the Present*, ABC-CLIO, 2006.

A professor of European history at Loyola University in New Orleans assembles expert-written articles on the extent and nature of women's participation as both victims and combatants in wars around the world, including guerrilla warfare, terrorism and the current wars in the Middle East.

Holm, Jeanne M., *Women in the Military: An Unfinished Revolution*, Presidio, 1993.

A retired Air Force major general who became the first female two-star general in the armed services and who championed women's full integration into the military describes women's changing military roles from the American Revolution through the Persian Gulf War.

Articles

Alvarez, Lizette, "G.I. Jane Breaks the Combat Barrier," *The New York Times*, Aug. 16, 2009, p. A1.

Due to personnel shortages, women regularly have been seeing combat in Iraq and Afghanistan, in defiance of official policy.

Cave, Damien, "A Combat Role, and Anguish, Too," ***The New York Times*****, Nov. 1, 2009, p. A1.**

Female soldiers suffer from post-traumatic stress disorder and other combat-related mental and physical problems just like men, but they get less sensitive treatment at Veterans' Affairs hospitals, which sometimes treat them as if they don't believe they have combat-related conditions.

Donnelly, Elaine, "The Army's Gender War," ***National Review Online*****, Jan. 7, 2005, www.nationalreview.com.**

Some women soldiers feel betrayed by the Army when they're assigned — counter to military policy — to accompany front-line ground-combat troops, according to a leading opponent of women's participation in ground combat.

Koon, David, "A New Soldier Story: 'Lioness' Tracks an All-Woman Combat Unit," ***Arkansas Times*****, May 15, 2008, www.arktimes.com.**

A soldier who was profiled in the documentary film "Lioness," about women soldiers serving on offensive missions in combat zones in Iraq, has struggled to come to terms with taking an enemy life.

Lubold, Gordon, "Army 'Lionesses' Hit Streets with Marines on Combat Ops," ***Marine Corps Times*****, Aug. 4, 2004, www.militaryphotos.net/forums/showthread.php?t=18513.**

Team Lioness, staffed by women from the Army's 1st Engineer Battalion, has accompanied Marines on offensive operations in Iraq's hottest combat zones, provoking both admiration and skepticism.

McMichael, William H., and Andrew Scutro, "SecNavy, CNO: Women Should Serve on Subs," ***Navy Times*****, Sept. 27, 2009, www.navytimes.com/news/2009/09/navy_roughead_subs_092409w.**

The Navy plans to open submarine duty to women.

Tilghman, Andrew, "Report Outlines Pregnancy Policy Concerns," ***Navy Times*****, Oct. 19, 2009, www.navytimes.com.**

In 2007, the Navy extended shore leave for new mothers from four months to 12 months, thus expanding the entire limited-duty period for pregnant women to 21 months. Apparently as a result, pregnancies in the Navy have increased, leaving many units deployed at sea with manpower shortages.

Yeager, Holly, "Soldiering Ahead," ***The Wilson Quarterly*****, summer 2007, www.wilsoncenter.org.**

More women are gaining acceptance on the battlefield and as military leaders, but the jury is still out about how their growing numbers will alter traditional military culture.

Reports and Studies

"Military Personnel: DoD's and the Coast Guard's Sexual Assault Prevention and Response Programs Face Implementation and Oversight Challenges," Government Accountability Office, Aug. 29, 2008, www.gao.gov/products/GAO-08-924.

Congress' nonpartisan auditing agency finds that Department of Defense programs to prevent and respond to sexual-assault problems apparently undercount the number of assaults that occur and may not have enough resources to fulfill their responsibilities.

Burrelli, David F., "Women in the Armed Forces," Congressional Research Service, Sept. 29, 1998, www.fas.org/man/crs/92-008.htm.

Congress' nonpartisan research arm provides a history of the U.S. military's recruitment and job-assignment policies for women from the end of the draft in 1973 through the late 1990s.

For More Information

Center for Military Readiness, P.O. Box 51600, Livonia, MI 48151; (202) 347-5333; www.cmrlink.org. Think tank and advocacy organization concerned with how personnel policies, such as assigning women to ground-combat units, could adversely affect military readiness.

Center for Women Veterans, Department of Veterans Affairs, 810 Vermont Ave., N.W., Washington, DC 20420; (800) 827-1000; www.va.gov/WOMENVET. Provides services for and information about female veterans.

Defense Department Advisory Committee on Women in the Services, OUSD (P&R) DACOWITS, Room 2C548A, 4000 Defense Pentagon, Washington, DC 20301-4000; (703) 697-2122; http://dacowits.defense.gov. Civilian panel appointed by the Secretary of Defense to conduct research and provide recommendations on recruitment and retention of women in the military.

Defense Equal Opportunity Management Institute, 66 Tuskegee Airmen Dr., Patrick Air Force Base, FL 32925-3399; www.deomi.org. Department of Defense office that educates military leadership about diversity issues, including gender relations.

MilitaryWoman.org, 6574 N State Rd. 7, Suite 110, Coconut Creek, FL 33073; (877) 282-6620; www.militarywoman.org. Web site providing information, assistance and a gathering place to communicate on all issues affecting women who are in the military or are considering enlistment.

Service Women's Action Network, 123 William St., 16th Floor, New York, NY 10038; (646) 602-5621; www.servicewomen.org. Nonprofit providing assistance and advocacy for women veterans.

Sexual Assault Prevention and Response, Department of Defense; (703) 696-9422; www.sapr.mil. Provides information and coordinates the armed forces' response to sexual-assault reports in the military.

Women in Military Service for America Memorial Foundation, Dept. 560, Washington, DC 20042-0560; (703) 533-1155; www.womensmemorial.org. Web site associated with the Women's Memorial at Arlington National Cemetery; provides historical information on women's roles in the U.S. military.

Future of Globalization: Is the Recession Triggering Deglobalization?

The Issues

In a two-bedroom Mumbai apartment in 1982, young entrepreneurs Ashank Desai and two partners launched Mastek, one of India's first software companies. Today, its nearly 4,000 employees handle information-technology operations for firms around the world, many in the United States and the United Kingdom.

If Mastek is a symbol of the outsourcing phenomenon sweeping the global workplace, Caterpillar embodies the traditional, heavy manufacturing that first made America an economic powerhouse. Catepillar's big, yellow "Cats" — backhoes, bulldozers and loaders — are still ubiquitous in the United States, but these days two-thirds of Caterpillar's business comes from foreign sales.

Vietnamese workers in Vietnam's Mekong Delta region process shrimp bound for American dinner plates. International trade has tumbled dramatically since the current recession began, declining by margins not seen since the Great Depression. Some economists suggest international trade is entering an era of "deglobalization" — a sustained retreat from global trade and economic integration fed by increasingly nationalistic policies and rising protectionism.

AP Photos/Richard Vogel

Mastek and Caterpillar, in fact, are both examples of modern, highly globalized firms. And both companies are dealing with a world economy that looks far different than it did two years ago.

In the wake of the global recession, international trade has fallen off a cliff, tumbling by margins not seen since the Great Depression. The falloff, combined with other factors, has led some economists and historians to suggest international trade is entering an era of "deglobalization" — a sustained retreat from global trade and economic integration fed by increasingly nationalistic policies and rising protectionism.

The result, they say, will increase not only economic stress but also political tensions around the world. International sales and profits have tumbled at both Mastek and Caterpillar in the last year. But as officials at the two firms contemplate the future, they see two scenarios. From India, where the economy has continued growing despite the downturn, Desai is optimistic the "Great Recession," will end within a year.

"If that happens," he says, "I don't think things will change much. We'll get back to where we were."

But from his office in Washington, Bill Lane, Caterpillar's director of governmental affairs, sees more cause for concern. "There's increasing evidence that the world could be turning inward," Lane says, "and where you will see that first is in countries embracing protectionist measures. Some of that's already happening."

Analysts who believe deglobalization lies ahead say it is being driven by more than just the recession. "Two phenomena are overlapping," says Harold

From *CQ Global Researcher*, September 2009

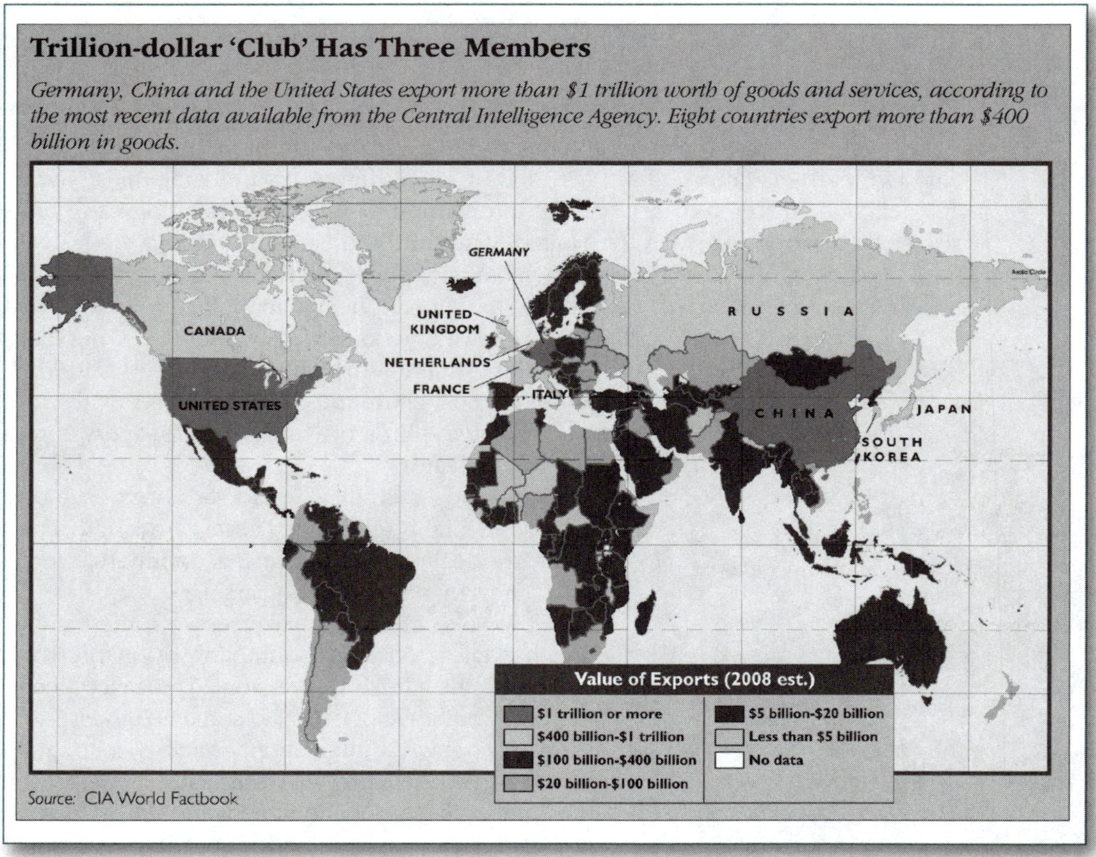

Trillion-dollar 'Club' Has Three Members

Germany, China and the United States export more than $1 trillion worth of goods and services, according to the most recent data available from the Central Intelligence Agency. Eight countries export more than $400 billion in goods.

Source: CIA World Factbook

James, a British professor of history and international affairs at Princeton University. "One is a crisis in the financial system that drove global integration over the past four decades; the other is worry about the character of globalization itself and a backlash against it. I think the financial crisis is the tipping point that moved things in the direction of deglobalization, but there were already substantial pressures pushing in that direction."

In a recent article James became one of the first scholars to suggest the trade collapse heralds something more lasting.[1] Other economic analysts support his view, as do many longtime critics of globalization, but for different reasons.

James' theory — also laid out in his soon-to-be published book *The Creation and Destruction of Value: The Globalization Cycle* — has its skeptics. "If you see globalization as primarily a matter of trade flows, then, yes, it has slowed down," says Moisés Naím, editor of *Foreign Policy* magazine. "But it's really a web of interactions between institutions and individuals in a whole variety of arenas. I see it as a political and technological revolution that's essentially irreversible."

Deglobalization undoubtedly would represent a sea change in the course of history. Since World War II, global trade has grown steadily, spurred by a Western political consensus that trade promotes both peace and prosperity. In the last two decades, this process has accelerated dramatically, with China, India and other emerging economies becoming aggressive players in global markets.

But the World Trade Organization (WTO), which monitors world trade, is now predicting global trade will contract by 10 percent in 2009.[2] Other forecasts are even bleaker. The Organisation for Economic Co-operation and Development (OECD), a group of 30 nations working to promote democracy and open markets, predicts a 16 percent falloff in world trade this year.[3] (*See graph, p. A-71.*)

Global trade is declining faster than at the beginning of the Great Depression, according to Kevin O'Rourke, a professor of economics at Trinity College in Dublin, Ireland, and Barry Eichengreen, a professor of economics and political science at the University of California, Berkeley.

They examined a host of factors, such as industrial output and stock market levels, and concluded that the downturn is, in fact, another depression.[4] Of all the indicators, "the one that really stands out is the world trade index. It is clearly falling more rapidly than world trade in the Great Depression," says O'Rourke. "It's really the most alarming aspect of the day."

The Depression was the last great era of deglobalization, with disastrous worldwide economic and political consequences. But while O'Rourke sees many similarities between the Great Depression and today's collapse, he is careful to point out that the current governmental responses have been very different.

In the 1930s, countries around the world retreated behind tariffs and other trade barriers, led by the protectionist Smoot-Hawley Tariff Act of 1930 in the United States. (*See "Background," p. A-78.*) "There have been some protectionist actions here and there, but there's nothing dramatic like what happened in the '30s," says O'Rourke, who considers it an "open question" whether a period of deglobalization is coming.

Economists are perhaps most alarmed by the fact that world trade has fallen more precipitously than the overall global economy has contracted, suggesting strongly that something more fundamental is occurring.

However, an analysis by Joseph Francois, an economics professor at Johannes Kepler University in Linz, Austria, indicates the decline is not as out of line as it appears. Rather, Francois says, trade has fallen off most sharply in those sectors that have been hardest hit by the recession, such as automobiles, machinery and tools.[5]

Leaders of the industrialized nations, known as the G-20, met in Washington in November and vowed not to repeat the protectionist mistakes made during the Great Depression.[6] By February, however, a World Bank study found that between October 2008 and February 2009 at least 17 of the G-20 nations had implemented 47 protectionist measures at the expense of other countries, and more were proposed.[7] (*See graph, p. A-73.*)

Still, protectionist impulses have been largely contained so far, most economists note. "Even if you look at the 'surge' in trade remedies, they don't really cover a lot of trade," says Francois. "These actions are like steam valves, allowing governments to blow off some of the protectionist pressure they're feeling, while still maintaining the basic system."

But to globalization's longtime critics, the world economic order is collapsing from the weight of its own excesses and inequities. "The whole idea that we've got

The World's Top 20 Exporters

Rank	Country	Exports In $billions (2008 est.)
1	Germany	$1,500.0
2	People's Republic of China	$1,400.0
3	United States	$1,300.0
4	Japan	$776.8
5	France	$761.0
6	Italy	$566.1
7	Netherlands	$537.5
8	Russia	$476.0
9	United Kingdom	$468.7
10	Canada	$461.8
11	South Korea	$419.0
12	Belgium	$372.9
—	Hong Kong*	$362.1
13	Saudi Arabia	$311.1
14	Mexico	$294.0
15	Spain	$292.8
16	Republic of China (Taiwan)	$255.7
17	Singapore	$235.8
18	United Arab Emirates	$207.7
19	Brazil	$200.0
20	Malaysia	$195.7

* *Listed separately from mainland China*

Source: CIA World Factbook

a free market is a misnomer, because it's actually bound by rules that protect corporate power and not the rights of people," says David Korten, author of the new book *Agenda for a New Economy: From Phantom Wealth to Real Wealth*.

Until now the anti-globalization movement — a loose coalition of disparate groups, ranging from anarchists to union members seeking labor protections in international trade agreements — has been unable to derail the political consensus favoring expanded trade. Now, however, those who see deglobalization on the horizon worry that anti-globalization sentiment and other political pressures could usher in a new world order characterized by greater international tension and conflict.

"I'm absolutely convinced that eras of deglobalization are much more destructive and difficult for people living in them than periods of globalization," says Princeton's James. He doesn't see the world economy getting back to normal anytime soon.

As analysts study the global economy, here are some of the questions they are trying to answer:

Does rising protectionism threaten global economic recovery?

Some analysts worry that recently adopted protectionist measures may signal that more protectionism is on the way.

James says last November's G-20 meeting reminded him of the World Economic Conference organized by the League of Nations in 1927, in which the major industrial nations pledged to reduce tariffs — a proclamation that proved empty after the global economy crashed. He sees a similar hollowness to the G-20 declaration.

The G-20 "vowed to stand by free trade, and within a day or so Russia imposed a whole series of tariffs on automobiles, and India imposed a whole set of protectionist regulations," he says. "It was a kind of political verbiage that was disconnected from what immediately happened."

But Douglas Irwin, a Dartmouth College professor specializing in trade history, believes international structures now in place will prevent a tariff war like the one that broke out in the 1930s. "We have the World Trade Organization," he says, "and in previous times, most notably the Depression, there wasn't such an organization, and it wasn't clear you'd be retaliated against if you took protectionist action. Today, it's very clear that if you violate a rule, you are going to be penalized."

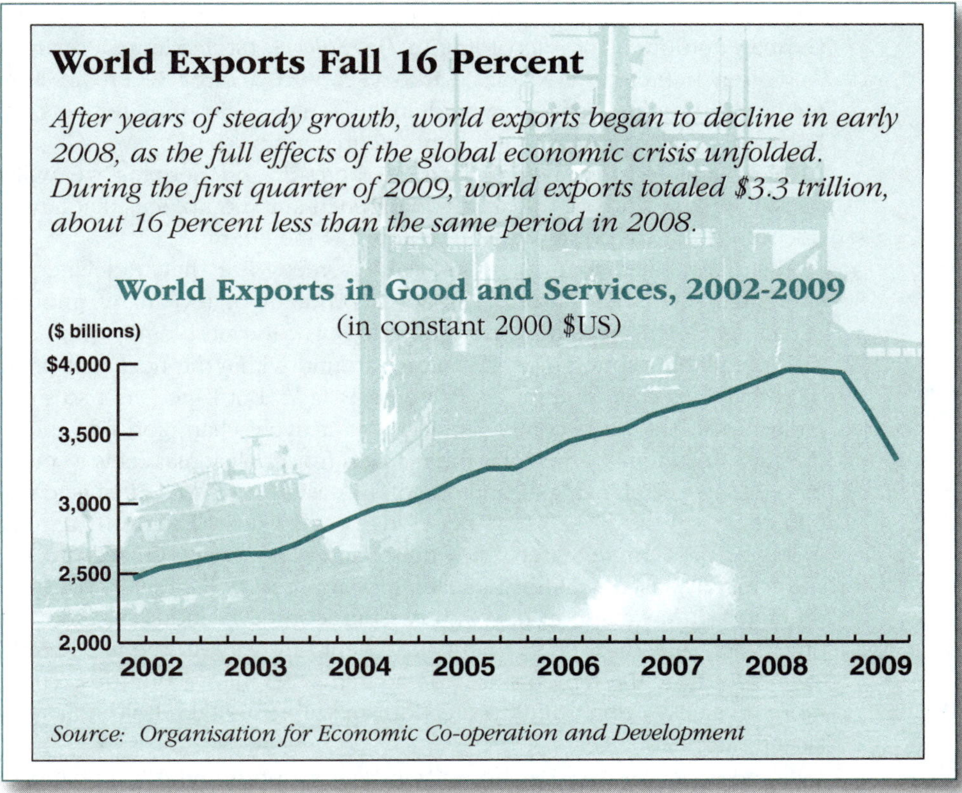
World Exports Fall 16 Percent
After years of steady growth, world exports began to decline in early 2008, as the full effects of the global economic crisis unfolded. During the first quarter of 2009, world exports totaled $3.3 trillion, about 16 percent less than the same period in 2008.
World Exports in Good and Services, 2002-2009
(in constant 2000 $US)
($ billions)
$4,000
3,500
3,000
2,500
2,000
2002
2003
2004
2005
2006
2007
2008
2009
Source: Organisation for Economic Co-operation and Development

Jaime Daremblum, a Costa Rican author of several works on economics and a former ambassador to the United States, notes that much of world trade nowadays is governed through regional pacts, such as the North American Free Trade Agreement (NAFTA).[8] Although trade issues can still flare up, he says, larger trading blocs created through regional agreements like the European Union or NAFTA have "taken a lot of trade off the table," when it comes to retaliatory battles.

But other analysts see a threat from so-called soft, or indirect, protectionism. "It's protectionism with a smile," says Caterpillar's Lane. "In today's world, no one will give a speech openly promoting protectionism and isolationism, but they will support policies that have the same effect." Soft protectionism includes industrial policies that favor domestic companies or shield them from larger economic forces, such as the original "Buy American" provisions in the U.S. stimulus package, which mandated that U.S. materials be used for any public-works projects funded by the act.[9]

Nearly all of the stimulus packages passed by Western industrial nations in response to the recession included some protectionist measures, notes Austin Hughes, chief economist for KBC Bank Ireland. He considers indirect protectionism one of the threats to economic recovery. "It's almost inevitable, really," Hughes says, "that as governments get more involved in bailing out sectors of their economy, they become more susceptible to this sort of thing."

The German stimulus plan, for example, is "designed to primarily benefit the German auto industry," according to *Der Spiegel*, the leading German newspaper.[10] And French President Nicolas Sarkozy caused a furor when he announced his country's stimulus benefits would include nationalist requirements at odds with European Union principles of economic integration.

"We want to stop moving factories abroad, and perhaps we will bring them back," Sarkozy said, specifically citing French auto companies that have moved production to the Czech Republic, a fellow EU member.[11]

But Irwin believes most world leaders recognize that trade inequities did not cause the Great Recession. "It's not a problem of too many imports," he says. "Cracking down on trade is not going to solve the problem."

If the global economy begins to turn around within the next year or so, Irwin predicts that protectionist impulses will quickly fade. But Lane is not so sure, noting that political leaders are becoming reluctant to actively champion free trade. "Normally, during an economic downturn, the reaction from policy makers is to promote exports by opening foreign markets, and one of the easiest ways to do that is to negotiate trade barriers away," he says. "That's not going on right now. The bilateral free-trade agreements before Congress aren't moving forward, and the WTO talks are stalled."[12]

In India, Mastek's Desai believes globalization will prevail, since he's seen the difference it has made in his country's burgeoning IT industry. "Maybe there was a time when globalization's benefits just went one way, to the wealthier nations," he says. "But now the benefits are spread across so many countries. There's so much more diversity, I don't think protectionism will really take hold unless the recession lasts three or four years."

Some economists see a shorter window of opportunity. If global economic conditions continue to deteriorate for another year, says Irish economist O'Rourke, "not only would protectionism be likely, it would be almost inevitable. I don't think you could expect political leaders not to succumb to the pressure that would ensue."

Are some protectionist measures appropriate in today's economy?

Arvind Panagariya, an Indian economist at Columbia University who has worked for both the World Bank and the World Trade Organization, notes that WTO rules allow "countries, in certain situations, to safeguard domestic companies from foreign competition" during times of economic distress.

The so-called safeguard provisions allow restrictions on certain imports if they threaten serious injury to a domestic industry. But the restrictions must be temporary, providing the domestic industry time to adjust to new conditions. Countries also may restrict imports if they believe a foreign company is "dumping" goods into their market at subsidized or unfairly low prices.[13]

In 2002 when the U.S. steel industry sought protection from foreign imports, President George W. Bush used the safeguard provisions to impose temporary tariffs on imports.[14] Some critics said the action betrayed the administration's free-trade principles.[15] But Kevin Dempsey, senior vice president for public policy and general counsel for the American Iron and Steel Institute, says Bush made the right choice. "The U.S. industry worked hard during that period to become more competitive," he says, "It gave us time to restructure."

Crisis Triggers Protectionist Measures

Developed and developing nations implemented 47 protectionist measures during the height of the global economic crisis last winter. Developed countries adopted subsidies totaling $48 billion worldwide. Developing countries adopted a variety of measures, including import duties and subsidies. Russia raised tariffs on used autos, and Argentina used non-tariff measures, such as imposing licensing requirements on textiles, TVs, toys and shoes.

Types of Trade Protections Implemented
(October 2008-February 2009)

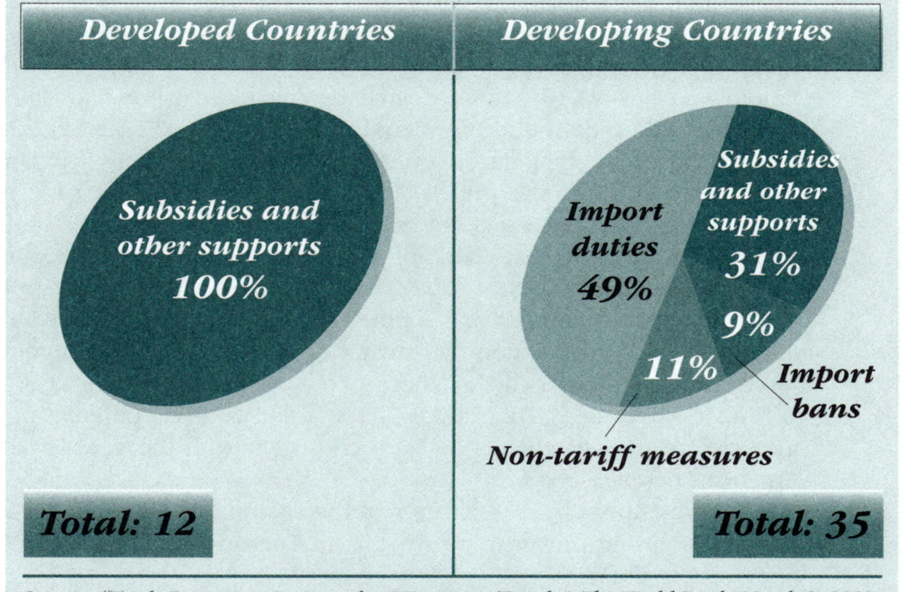

Source: "Trade Protection: Incipient but Worrisome Trends," The World Bank, March 2, 2009

In the current recession, the U.S. automobile tire industry has applied for similar relief from Chinese imports. Manufacturers of several different steel products also have brought dumping charges against Chinese competitors, which the Commerce Department is reviewing.[16]

Dempsey believes such actions are necessary and legitimate, particularly in today's economic climate. "Unfortunately, when companies invoke their rights under WTO law to insure that other countries' actions don't harm them, a lot of people refer to this as protectionism," he says. "But bringing an anti-dumping case or a safeguard case can be an important way to make sure we have fair competition."

Panagariya is skeptical, noting "a big surge in anti-dumping actions" since the economic crisis began. "There are signs people may be abusing the privilege." Even if these actions meet the WTO definition of a legal action, he believes they are usually counterproductive. "In the end, two can play the same game," he says. "You're simply inviting retaliation, and it's ultimately detrimental to everyone."

The Obama administration moved aggressively early in its term to back the U.S. auto industry, believing its survival was essential to the nation's economic health. The industry's troubles were, in part, the result of the financial crisis, which dried up credit, and not of the industry's making, Dempsey notes. "We support the efforts to help the U.S. auto industry to restructure," he says. "It's critical to give them breathing room to adjust, and under these circumstances, it's warranted."

But Panagariya believes subsidized loans and other aid provided to domestic auto industries by the United States, Germany, France, Australia and Brazil were protectionist, discriminating against foreign manufacturers selling cars in those countries. The actions "will almost certainly be challenged and found to break WTO rules," he predicted.[17]

Other analysts, however, think even stronger measures are needed to protect domestic industries. The Trade Reform, Accountability, Development and Employment (TRADE) Act, supported by organized labor and other U.S. interest groups, would require the president to renegotiate NAFTA and other trade agreements with more stringent environmental, labor and safety standards for nations exporting goods into the United States. The legislation, which has more than 100 House cosponsors, also sets out what could not be included in trade agreements, such as requirements that economic sectors be privatized or deregulated.

Lori Wallach, director of Global Trade Watch for Public Citizen, a U.S. consumer advocacy organization that has lobbied for legislation to dramatically revamp U.S. trade law, rejects the notion that such measures will hurt global commerce.

"The question isn't whether there's going to be trade," she says. "The question is 'Under what rules?' The TRADE Act is about taking a different approach, fixing the rules to get agreements that are consistent with the goals and values of the American people."

But Boris Kozolchyk — director of the National Law Center for Inter-American Free Trade at the University of Arizona in Tucson — believes the effort is protectionist and will fail.

"In today's global economy, there's always going to be a replacement buyer or seller to take your place," he says. "It would be a loss economically for whoever tries it."

Will globalization survive the world economic crisis?

The recession, by numerous measures, is the worst economic crisis since the Great Depression. But economists disagree over what impact the recession will have and whether globalization will be one of its casualties. Those who believe deglobalization could worsen see political and economic conditions combining to create a fundamental breakdown in the existing order.

"It is now clear that the global economic crisis will be deep and prolonged and that it will have far-reaching geopolitical consequences," former U.S. Deputy Treasury Secretary Roger Altman wrote recently. "The long movement toward market liberalization has stopped, and a new period of state intervention, re-regulation and creeping protectionism has begun.

Does a 'Level Playing Field' Exist in Global Trade?

Critics say rules often favor competitors.

American critics of free-trade policies often say they only want to establish "a level playing field" so U.S. and foreign businesses all compete under the same rules.

When American companies compete with Chinese manufacturers, for instance, the Chinese companies have an advantage because of exploitative government labor policies, argues Sen. Byron Dorgan, D-N.D. In his book *Take this Job and Ship It: How Corporate Greed and Brain Dead Politics are Selling Out America*, Dorgan writes that government policies in China allow "for children to work, or for workers to be put in unsafe workplaces, or for companies to pollute the air and water, or jail [for] those who try to start a union. Manufacturing is less expensive in China precisely because workers are exploited."[1]

But what constitutes a "level" playing field in trade, and are U.S. companies really being forced to compete at a disadvantage? The answers aren't as simple as they may seem.

Free-trade policies today are based on the classical economic theory of "comparative advantage," developed by 19th-century English political economist David Ricardo. The theory states that each nation has natural advantages and disadvantages when it comes to producing different crops and goods. Prosperity, Ricardo argued, is achieved if each nation concentrates on its strengths by producing crops and products it can create the most efficiently (cheaply) and selling them in the international marketplace.

Cotton farmers in Burkina Faso gather cotton bolls for market. Farmers in the West African nation and other developing countries say they can't compete with cotton farmers in industrialized countries, particularly those in the United States, who receive hefty government subsidies.

AFP/Getty Images/Issouf Sanogo

For example, Ricardo noted, England's lush, cool landscape was perfect for raising sheep, while Portugal enjoyed other natural advantages for growing grapes. While wine could be made in England and sheep raised in Portugal, the economic efficiency and thus the wealth of both nations would increase if each nation played to its strength and traded its key product for the other's country's specialty.

Trade today is vastly more complicated than exchanging wine and wool, encompassing services and complex manufactured goods made from raw materials that can come from dozens of countries. But Ricardo's theory remains at the heart of free-trade ideology, particularly the idea that free trade allows a country to concentrate on areas in which the field is tilted decidedly in its favor. The concept of a level playing field is largely irrelevant under Ricardo's theory, say some economists.

"The idea of competitive or uncompetitive applied to a country is problematic," says Arvind Panagariya, a former economist at the World Bank, the Asian Development Bank and the World Trade

(Continued)

(Continued)

Organization.[2] "In an industry, you can be competitive or uncompetitive, but as a nation you can't be." Nations can always find areas where a trading partner seems to have an unfair advantage, he says. For instance, while U.S. free-trade critics cite a lack of safety and labor standards in competing nations, "If you are India or China, you could say, 'There's no level playing field because America has so much money to invest in new technology, and we've got such limited capital, it's not fair.'"

Likewise, cotton farmers in a developing country who don't receive government subsidies say it's unfair for them to have to compete with cotton farmers in industrialized countries, particularly the United States, who get hefty government subsidies.

But critics of globalization believe the theory of comparative advantage isn't working. As proof, critics like Dorgan cite the $673 billion U.S. trade deficit, the result of U.S. imports exceeding exports.[3] "Yes, they can create an economic advantage," Dorgan writes. "But it is not a *natural* competitive advantage."[4]

However, Jaime Daremblum, former Costa Rican ambassador to the United States, says trade agreements can help reduce such disparities. "Free-trade agreements like CAFTA [Central American Free Trade Agreement] are not just about trade," Daremblum says. "They're also plans for governance, in terms of improving the judiciary, improving the enforcement of labor laws and labor standards, improving transparency and accountability. The field is being leveled as we speak."

But many free-trade critics see such trade rules as unfair intrusions into national policies. If CAFTA, NAFTA (North American Free Trade Agreement) and other trade pacts are leveling the playing field, they are doing so by encouraging a "race to the bottom," forcing wages and standards in the wealthier nations down to those in the poorest nations, according to Lori Wallach, head of Global Trade Watch for Public Citizen, a U.S. advocacy group.

Farmers halt traffic in Zagreb, Croatia, on June 10, 2009, to protest plummeting milk and wheat prices. Such well-organized resistance from farm groups in developed countries prevents officials from lowering agricultural subsidies that harm Third World farmers.

Getty Images/Hrvoje Polanafp

Wallach claims advocates of free trade cite the wrong statistic to prove it's working. "They look at the volume of trade flows between countries, but that is not the measure of the success of a trade agreement," she says. Instead, the question should be: "Did it raise incomes?" U.S. median wages have now declined to 1972 levels, and income inequality has drastically increased since NAFTA and the World Trade Organization accords were adopted, she says.

To Wallach and other critics of current trade policy, the increase in income inequality helps prove the playing field remains far from level.

[1] Byron Dorgan, *Take this Job and Ship It: How Corporate Greed and Brain Dead Politics are Selling Out America* (2006), pp. 42-43.

[2] Panagariya is now an economics professor at Columbia University.

[3] Christopher Rugaber, "U.S. Trade Deficit Fell Sharply in 2008," The Associated Press, March 18, 2009.

[4] Dorgan, *op. cit.*

Farmers — Both Rich and Poor — Demand Protection

European milk producers seeking protection from falling milk prices clash with police outside European Commission headquarters in Brussels, Belgium, on July 22, 2009 (top). As economic stress increases, farmers in poor countries are also flexing their political muscle. In New Delhi, thousands of protesting Indian farmers on Dec. 16, 2008, demand help in competing in global markets (bottom). Among other things, they were seeking higher subsidies, lower diesel prices and interest-free agricultural loans.

AFP/Getty Images/Dominique Faget
AFP/Getty Images/Raveendran

Indeed, globalization itself is reversing. The long-standing wisdom that everyone wins in a single world market has been undermined."[18]

Altman and others see deglobalization as the start of a new geopolitical era that will be accompanied by escalating conflicts over key natural resources and the ascendancy of China to a position of greater worldwide influence. In effect, they say, the world's economic problems and geopolitical tensions will create a feedback loop of growing distrust and disagreement, pushing the world into the deglobalized era. In this scenario, countries with a smaller economic base, particularly developing nations, will be especially hard hit. (*See "Outlook," p. A-90.*)

In Honduras, however, former trade minister Norman García sees nothing so severe in his crystal ball. Despite the severity of the recession, he says, "We haven't really felt that much effect in our trade with the United States. We're still maintaining the same levels." Honduras' primary exports are clothing and agricultural goods, and its primary markets are the United States and Europe, he says.

Indeed, García says that while trade is down overall, "No trading partner has enacted any protectionist measures that have had any effect on us," thanks mostly to the Central American Free Trade Agreement (CAFTA). The pact includes the United States, Honduras and five other countries.[19] The Honduran government was determined to sign CAFTA for that very reason, García says.

"What we were doing is guaranteeing that that market was here to stay for good," he says. Because of such agreements, including the WTO, he says, "I don't think this so-called deglobalization will get any momentum."

But David Smick, an economic policy strategist and author of the 2008 book *The World Is Curved: Hidden Dangers to the Global Economy*, has less faith. "The whole economic model under which the world has operated in the last two decades is crash landing," he says. "The global emerging-market export model is in real trouble."

In that model, he explains, less developed nations such as China promoted rapid growth by setting up their economy "as an export platform, heavily dependent on the U.S. consumer." The model depended on several factors, including a favorable rate of currency exchange with the dollar to keep exports relatively inexpensive.[20] But most critically, it depended on Americans' voracious consuming habits and their willingness to pile up debt as they kept buying. The debt habit was fed by easy credit, underwritten by ever-appreciating home equity.

But the housing bubble has burst, and Americans appear to have changed their buying habits, at least for the moment. "There are surveys showing Americans are pulling back, and they're finding pleasure in pulling back," Smick says. "A large part of the world is in denial about this. They think the U.S. consumer is coming back. Well, the U.S. consumer is never coming back in the same way because U.S. regulators are never going to allow that kind of over-leveraging again."

The contraction of that export market, he believes, will significantly strain export-dependent countries such as China, Germany and Korea, along with many smaller developing nations. "I really think we are entering a period of deglobalization," Smick says. "The question is just how fast and to what extent."

But Alan Winters, an economist at the University of Sussex in the United Kingdom, is more optimistic about the future, citing the G-20's April pledge of additional aid to help developing nations weather the crisis.[21] "There's certainly room to do more, but we have avoided a meltdown," he says.

Moreover, he says, the world's two rising economic powers, China and India, have tremendous incentives to avoid a retreat from globalization. "When people ask me, 'Is this the end of capitalism as we know it?' I say, 'No, capitalism is safe in the hands of the Chinese. They know they've done incredibly well out of the global markets, and the Indians know that, too.'"

But after considerable time in China, Smick believes China's ability to adjust to the changing trade picture is complicated by an authoritarian political structure, an aging population and a bureaucratic culture that can still discourage individual innovation.

The United States remains the engine of the global economy, he says, and American political leaders are losing their determination to resist Americans' rising protectionist sentiment. But without U.S. leadership, he warns, the global consensus in favor of free trade could splinter.

"Today there are just so many parallels to where we were in the '30s, when every country paid attention to their own bilateral priorities," Smick says. "I'm afraid that's the world we're moving in again."

Background

Ancient Traders

Globalization is either a modern phenomenon or nearly as old as civilization itself — depending on one's viewpoint.

Many economists see globalization as the unprecedented level of worldwide economic and financial integration, fueled by technological advances, witnessed in the last 30 years. Others view globalization as the age-old exchanging of goods and ideas by people from different parts of the world. As financial historian William J. Bernstein puts it: Globalization "is a process that has been slowly evolving for a very, very long time."[22]

In his 2008 book *A Splendid Exchange, How Trade Shaped the World*, Bernstein traces the role of trade in world affairs since the dawn of recorded history, depicting a surprising range and diversity of trading in the ancient world.

Bronze-age Mesopotamians actively traded grain, metals and goods across southern Arabia. The Roman Empire traded across Europe, much of Africa and as far away as India and China. In 30 B.C., "Rome was flooded with pepper, exotic animals and precious jewels from the Orient," Bernstein writes. "Chinese silk was the most famous and coveted of these commodities."[23]

In more recent times, the disruptive impacts of international trade were felt long before modern treaties like the North American Free Trade Agreement sought to promote open trade between nations. More than 200 years ago, for example, a flood of cheaper tanned hides from the Americas undercut Europe's leather industry. "If *The New York Times* columnist Thomas Friedman had been writing in 1800, he would have had little trouble explaining the flattening of world commerce to European tanners," Bernstein observes.[24] (Friedman, *The New York Times* columnist and author of *The World Is Flat, A Brief History of the Twenty-first Century*, embraces globalization as a nearly unstoppable revolution brought forth by a convergence of new technologies and an emerging world order.)

"Globalization is such a diverse, broad-based, and potent force that not even today's massive economic crash will dramatically slow it down," writes *Foreign Policy* editor Naím. "Love it or hate it, globalization is here to stay."[25]

But historians such as Bernstein and Princeton's James believe the longer view reveals many eras of globalization, usually followed by periods in which trade and other contacts declined significantly. In the period around 30 B.C., for example, trade expanded within the Roman Empire, followed by a period in which it slowed to a trickle, Bernstein notes, as Rome fell into decline following the death of Emperor Marcus Aurelius.[26] And other periods of robust globalization — including the era of trade expansion that occurred during the Renaissance and the emergence of French and English colonial empires in the 18th century — also eventually slowed or ended dramatically, James observes.

"All of these previous globalization episodes came to an end, almost always with wars . . . accompanied by highly disruptive and contagious financial crises," he writes.[27]

Depression and Protection

Whether globalization is an old story or uniquely modern, the contemporary chapter clearly begins about 80 years ago, with a worldwide economic disaster.

Contrary to popular belief, the Great Depression of the 1930s wasn't started by protectionist tariffs and other trade barriers rising around the globe. The economic debacle was well under way when President Herbert Hoover signed the 1930 Smoot-Hawley act, which increased nearly 900 different import tariffs on foreign goods.

Authors Rep. Willis Hawley, R-Ore., and Sen. Reed Smoot, R-Utah, reaped political infamy for their efforts, but the measure reflected lawmakers' widespread protectionist sentiments. Thomas Hall, a professor of economics at Miami University in Ohio and co-author of *The Great Depression: An International Disaster of Perverse Economic Policies*, believes it was more the Depression that caused Smoot-Hawley, rather than the reverse. "Smoot-Hawley had been kicking around in Congress for some years," he says. "What the Depression did was align the political forces to get it passed."

The measure became law despite desperate opposition from financial and economic circles, remarkably including 1,028 economists who signed an open letter calling on Hoover not to sign the bill. Thomas Lamont, a partner at J. P. Morgan and an economic adviser to the president, recalled: "I almost went down on my knees" to beg Hoover to veto the bill.[28]

Hoover, however, had long harbored protectionist sentiments and signed the bill into law. As opponents had predicted, the act led to a trade war, with nations around the world raising their own import barriers in retaliation.

Economists differ on how much responsibility Smoot-Hawley bears for the calamitous collapse in world trade in the 1930s. U.S. imports from Europe declined from a 1929 high of $1.3 billion to just $390 million in 1932 — a precipitous 69 percent drop. U.S. exports to Europe declined 65 percent — from $2.3 billion to $784 million — over the same period. Overall, world trade fell a breathtaking 66 percent from 1929 to 1934.[29]

But many historians have noted that the real impact of Smoot-Hawley was to turn nations inward at a time of international political and economic crisis. In its 1941 obituary for Hawley, *Time* went so far as to call Smoot-Hawley "one of the most enormous acts of isolationism in U.S. history." The magazine even suggested that the act set the world on course for the worst war in history. "Economic nationalism, forced into full flower by the Smoot-Hawley Tariff, became the physical basis for the ideology of fascism," *Time* intoned. "The lines were written, the stage was set for World War II."[30]

Whether that verdict was too harsh — and most historians would argue the conditions that gave birth to fascism ranged beyond isolationist trade policies — it reflects postwar convictions. The democracies of the West, led by the United States, emerged from World War II convinced that protectionist tariffs had not only exacerbated the worst economic collapse in modern history but also helped lead to a catastrophic war.

For the rest of the 20th century, trade policy would be seen through the lens of the negative impact of protectionism. With only occasional demurrals, the Free World agreed that trade must be kept open to maintain peace and prosperity. In the aftermath of the war, the West would go about setting up the international structures to make that happen.

From GATT to WTO

The years immediately after World War II produced watershed events in international integration. The United Nations held its first General Assembly in 1946.[31] The North Atlantic Treaty Organization (NATO) set up its collective defense agreement in 1949. And the forerunner of the European Economic Community was formed in 1951.

But before the war had even ended, representatives of the 44 Allied nations met in tiny Bretton Woods, N.H., in July 1944, to hammer out the postwar economic order, establishing the International Monetary Fund (IMF) and the International Bank for Reconstruction and Development (the World Bank).

The delegates also established a new global monetary system. Because the United States had become far and away the world's most powerful economy and also held most of the world's gold reserves, Bretton Woods tied the world's currencies to the dollar, which the delegates agreed should be convertible into gold at $35 per ounce. The goal was to prevent the wild currency fluctuations that had contributed to instability in the 1930s. The IMF was charged with maintaining the system of exchange rates.[32]

Guiding all these efforts was the belief that a stable global economic system, allowing a free exchange of goods and services, was essential to world order. "Unhampered trade dovetailed with peace. High tariffs, trade barriers and unfair economic competition with war," U.S. Secretary of State Cordell Hull later wrote in his autobiography.[33]

Three years after Bretton Woods, 23 nations met in Geneva, Switzerland, to finalize work on a General Agreement on Tariffs and Trade (GATT). It established basic trade rules and included 45,000 tariff concessions, eliminating or reducing duties on $10 billion worth of products being traded at the time — about one-fifth of the worldwide total.[34]

GATT membership would grow dramatically through the years, as would its scope, which was expanded in a series of negotiations known as "trade rounds," named after the cities in which they were convened. For nearly half a century, GATT would provide the basic framework for world trade.

Dartmouth trade historian Irwin notes that GATT didn't always succeed in boosting trade. For instance, its inability to eliminate agricultural subsidies, still widely protected around the globe, is considered one of the treaty's largest failings. And its provisions are often ignored by some countries during economic stress, such as in the late 1970s and early '80s, when sluggish growth again led to a rise in protectionism.[35]

But overall the picture has been positive. "There's been a demonstrable lowering of trade barriers over the last 60 or so years, and GATT was largely responsible," says Irwin. World trade has expanded dramatically in the 60 years since GATT was first signed, growing 8 percent a year through the 1950s and '60s.[36]

"It added stability to the system," he notes, making people "more willing to make investments in other countries, which has helped the developing world, in particular."

But GATT was only meant to be a stop-gap measure. The architects of the postwar world order envisioned an International Trade Organization (ITO), operating as a U.N. agency, which would serve as a third pillar of the world economy alongside the IMF and the World Bank. The draft charter for the ITO included rules on employment, business practices, international investment and services.[37] Eventually, ITO negotiations foundered on the sheer magnitude of the concept. However, nearly half a century later, the international community would return to the idea, creating the World Trade Organization in 1995 as the successor to GATT.

CHRONOLOGY

1920s ***Trade flourishes until Great Depression hits.***

October 1929 U.S. stock market crashes.

1930s ***Protectionism worsens the Depression.***

1930 Smoot-Hawley Tariff Act in U.S. raises more than 900 import duties; other nations later follow suit.

1929-1934 World trade drops 66 percent.

1940s ***Nations seek to build postwar international economic relationships.***

1944 Allied nations meet in Bretton Woods, N.H., to create international monetary and financial structure.

1947 General Agreement on Tariffs and Trade (GATT) encourages free trade by reducing tariffs.

1950s-1960s ***Growing economic and political cooperation expands ties among Western nations.***

1951 Six countries form European Coal and Steel Community, the precursor of the Common Market.

1957 European Economic Community, or Common Market, expands economic cooperation and cross-border trade.

1962 Trade Expansion Act empowers President John F. Kennedy to negotiate major tariff reductions. . . . European Union gives members joint control over food production and prices.

1967 Kennedy round of trade talks, honoring the slain president, conclude.

1970s-1980s ***Open markets and political changes in West appear to reverse economic stagnation, while dramatic reforms unleash China's economy. Soviet Union and former satellite nations embrace free markets, open trade.***

1973 Arab oil embargo causes gas shortages and worsens economic malaise known as "stagflation."

1978 China initiates free-market reforms.

1985 Soviet leader Mikhail Gorbachev initiates reforms that lead to the USSR's collapse in 1991.

1989 U.S. and 11 Pacific nations form Asia Pacific Economic Cooperation forum to discuss free trade.

1990s ***Global trade grows, but backlash develops.***

1992 A European Union treaty moves toward a common currency. Union eventually grows to 27 nations.

1994 North American Free Trade Agreement eliminates most trade barriers between U.S., Canada and Mexico.

1995 The 123-member World Trade Organization (WTO) replaces GATT.

1999 Anti-globalization protesters shut down WTO Seattle meeting.

2000s ***Recession undercuts global trade.***

2001 Trade talks begin in Doha, Qatar, to lower remaining trade barriers.

2007 U.S. housing prices begin to collapse, rattling U.S. financial institutions.

2008 Worst recession in nearly 80 years hits world economy. Banking institutions worldwide face insolvency. . . . Doha round talks collapse.

2009 Global trade plummets in the first two quarters and is expected to drop 10 percent or more for the year. . . . China and Western nations initiate massive stimulus spending to revive their economies. By mid-summer signs of recovery are mixed with economic difficulties, prompting some experts to predict deglobalization will fracture the global status quo.

The WTO represented the culmination of the original postwar vision of a new level of international commerce. But at the end of the millennium the world was a much different place than in the years immediately after World War II. And since its inception, the WTO has attracted ardent critics and supporters.

But on one thing they all agree: the WTO in the 21st century faces a series of challenges that reflect the stresses of the global economic and political order.

Governing Trade Today

In recent years, countries have focused more on crafting regional and bilateral trade agreements, while international trade talks have languished. In fact, regional free-trade agreements have proliferated so rapidly they've become an alphabet soup of acronyms: NAFTA, CAFTA, SAFTA (the South Asia Free Trade Agreement) and more.

Bilateral free-trade agreements have also proliferated. The United States, for example, now has trade agreements — both bilateral and multilateral — with 17 countries, and three more are pending in Congress.[38] Many other countries have similar agreements with neighboring countries or important trading partners.

As the number of trade agreements has multiplied, the size of global markets has grown dramatically. Before the collapse of the Soviet Union in 1991 and the opening up of the Chinese and Indian economies, a large share of the world's population was essentially shut off from international trade. As a result of political changes in those countries, however, more than 1.5 billion people joined the competitive global work force.[39] Many smaller, developing nations also turned to low-cost global exports in an attempt to raise living standards.

Simultaneously, the World Trade Organization has expanded its reach into areas such as the trade in services and intellectual-property rights. The expanded authority, however, required new rules that reach much farther into the internal practices and regulation of national economies.

"Until the mid-1990s, trade rules were about trade. They set tariffs, that sort of thing," says Wallach at Global Trade Watch. "Now you have a whole bunch of policies that have nothing to do with how goods move between countries. They have to do with domestic policies."

WTO rules on intellectual property, for instance, have been particularly controversial because they can involve patents for lifesaving drugs and can restrict or increase the cost of medicine in many parts of the world. Proponents view the WTO's intellectual-property-rights provisions as essential to boosting trade, encouraging innovation and promoting the adoption of best practices around the globe. Opponents see them as a form of exploitation by multinational corporations.

Trade agreements and other WTO policies have caused job losses in certain economic sectors in participating countries, such as the U.S. textile industry, and have contributed to downward pressure on wages, particularly in developed nations.

Not surprisingly, a backlash developed against the WTO and the whole idea of globalization. The scope of the anti-globalization movement and the depth of its frustration became apparent during the 1999 WTO meeting in Seattle, where a massive, largely peaceful protest was marked by violent outbursts that so rattled officials they ended the conference early.[40]

Rejecting Globalization Produces Winners and Losers

Developing nations could suffer economically and politically.

For two decades, Ireland flourished as "the poster child for globalization," in the words of Irish economist Austin Hughes. Today, the country's battered economy reflects the sharp reversal of fortune that can come with a collapse in world trade.

Ireland's embrace of policies that opened the island to global markets and international investment had turned its economy into the "Celtic Tiger." But the global economic downturn sent Ireland's property values plummeting, its banks required a government bailout and unemployment has soared to close to 12 percent.

"There was a sense that we had discovered the crock of gold at the end of the rainbow," Hughes says. "Now there's this fatalism that says it was just a crock."

Some desperate economies that once embraced globalization are now beginning to turn inward, in a trend called deglobalization, in which they adopt restrictive tariffs and other protective policies. If the trend continues, experts say, there will be winners and losers on both the global and national stages. The losers will far outnumber the winners, according to many mainstream economists, but in anything as vast and complicated as the global economy, some industries and even nations will find themselves with a relative advantage in the new status quo.

Ireland is hardly the only nation that will face a significant economic adjustment if the recession triggers an era of deglobalization. Several smaller Western nations, including Iceland and Latvia, are in similar straits, and many of the world's successful economies are highly export dependent, notes David Smick, an international economic strategist. Exports provide more than 40 percent of the gross domestic product (GDP) in China, Germany and Korea, among other nations, he says.

Boris Kozolchyk, director of the National Law Center for Inter-American Free Trade in Tucson, Ariz., believes developing countries would be big losers in an era of deglobalization. Many Latin American countries, for example, have staked their economic and political development on free trade.

Kozolchyk says the banking crisis that sparked the recession illustrates intertwined global relationships. "There was a chain of finance: you had Wells Fargo Bank providing financing to Banco Atlántida in Honduras, which was financing local businesses," he says. "Now it's all come to a halt."

Kozolchyk also fears developing nations could lose politically, as their economic struggles lead them to turn away from democracy in search of other solutions. "This has already started happening," he says, citing the influence of Venezuelan President Hugo Chávez. "You definitely have a return to demagoguery and authoritarian government, all in the name of false economic development."

Large and economically diverse nations will be hurt less. Only 11 percent of the U.S. GDP is tied to exports, according to Smick. "We will be hurt," he says, "but we will be less vulnerable than most of the rest of the world."

Within the U.S. economy, however, certain industries would be disproportionately affected by deglobalization. Exports in medical equipment, industrial engines and aircraft engines all grew significantly last year.[1] Other industries, however, were already heavily export driven. For example, nearly 40 percent of the computer and electronics-industry jobs in the United States are dependent upon exports, according to government statistics. Heavy manufacturing, the chemical industry and the U.S. leather goods trade also count on exports for a substantial share of their business.[2]

Even distinctly American industries are global enterprises these days and could suffer if the world deglobalizes. Hollywood made nearly twice as much money on its movies overseas as it did in the United States.[3] If deglobalization triggers a rise in economic and cultural nationalism, the entertainment industry could be a big loser.

The winners? It depends on your perspective on globalization. David C. Korten — a long-time critic of "corporate globalization" and author of *Agenda for a New Economy: From Phantom Wealth to Real Wealth* — sees a retreat from international markets sparking a more sustainable lifestyle in the United States and abroad. The trend would embrace smaller-scale, local agriculture and green technologies, including alternative-energy production and more efficient building practices. In the view of anti-globalists like Korten, the final winners would include Americans, who would enjoy better-quality lives.

Others take a more cynical view of how winners would be determined. "It really depends on which industries have the political clout to get the best protectionism," says Douglas Irwin, a specialist in trade policy at Dartmouth College.

---

[1] "U.S. Export Fact Sheet," International Trade Administration, U.S. Department of Commerce, Feb. 11, 2009, http://trade.gov/press/press_releases/2009/export-factsheet_021109.pdf.

[2] "Total Jobs Supported by Manufactured Exports, 2006," Office of Industry and Trade Information, U.S. Department of Commerce, www.trade.gov/td/industry/otea/jobs/Reports/2006/jobs_by_industry.html.

[3] "Entertainment Industry Market Statistics 2007," Motion Picture Association of America, p. 3, www.mpaa.org/USEntertainmentIndustryMarketStats.pdf.

Globalization's critics cite the economic crisis that hit in 2007 and '08 as proof of its failure, while supporters urged that eight-year-long trade negotiations, known as the Doha round, be concluded to help lift the world out of the recession.

Although these debates reflect modern tensions, Bernstein points out that anti-globalization protests have occurred for centuries. "Today's debates over globalization repeat, nearly word for word in some cases, those of earlier eras," he writes. "Wherever trade arrives, resentment, protectionism and their constant companions — smuggling, disrespect for authority and occasionally war — will follow."

Yet Bernstein also notes, "The instinct to truck and barter is part of human nature; any effort to stifle it is doomed to fail in the long run."[41]

Current Situation

Clouded Forecast

Several analysts say evidence suggests the recession in the United States, China and other nations could be coming to an end. In early August, the U.S. government said the nation's economic output shrank only 1 percent in the second quarter of the year, a dramatic improvement over the 6.4 percent contraction in the previous quarter [42]

Moreover, the U.S. stock market recorded its best July in 20 years, and home prices appeared to be creeping upward.[43] A number of major banks also have recorded profits, leading some to predict the financial system has stabilized. Since the United States is the largest driver of the global economy, these signs indicate a recovery may be in the cards for the last half of 2009 or early 2010.

In one of the most protectionist responses to the global economic crisis, Ecuador's government in February imposed restrictions on most imported items. Now many imports — like this hair conditioner and deodorant being sold in a store in Quito — are more expensive.

AP Photo/Dolores Ochoa

Two of the world's emerging economic powerhouses, India and China, also offer reason for optimism. In June, the World Bank raised its 2009 growth forecast for China from 6.5 percent to 7.2 percent.[44] In July, Chinese manufacturing expanded at its fastest rate in a year, according to a survey.[45] Also in July, the IMF revised its projection for India's economic growth for 2009 upward to 5.4 percent while forecasting an overall global contraction of 1.4 percent.[46]

"My take is that the U.S. will come out of this in another six months to a year, and the large majority of nations will start pulling out once the U.S. economy does," says Panagariya, the former World Bank and WTO economist.

But for every patch of blue sky visible on the economic horizon there remains a cloud. U.S. consumer spending, which comprises 70 percent of economic activity, has continued to fall. And with U.S. unemployment not expected to peak until later this year or early in 2010, a consumer-driven recovery will be delayed. The Obama administration's $787 billion stimulus package now accounts for 20 percent of U.S. output, but federal officials acknowledge that the current level of deficit spending is unsustainable in future years.[47]

Meanwhile, credit markets remain tight, both globally and in the United States, limiting money for new investments, particularly in riskier economies. Conditions continue to look bleak in many leading Western industrial nations. The IMF predicts continued contraction of 4 percent or more this year in Germany, Japan, the United Kingdom, Russia and Italy — among other nations — with negative or only negligible growth seen in 2010.[48]

"There's all this talk right now about 'green shoots' [signs of economic recovery] and the end of the recession, and I understand why people feel this way: They hope they can get back to normal very quickly," says James, the Princeton University economic historian, "but I just don't think they're going to be able to do that."

Indeed, the overall world economy looks remarkably grim by any historical measure. As of June, the declines in world industrial output and other key indicators were slightly worse than during the Great Depression at the same point in its history, according to one analysis.[49] In a late June assessment, the World Bank noted that "unemployment continues to rise throughout the world, housing prices in many countries are still falling . . . bank balance sheets are fragile."[50]

AT ISSUE

Will a period of deglobalization disrupt world trade?

YES

Harold James
Professor of History and International Affairs, Princeton University
Author, The Creation and Destruction of Value: The Globalization Cycle

Written for *CQ Global Researcher,* September 2009

Globalization is a very old phenomenon. It has also produced tremendous benefits in terms of poverty reduction in many countries. But historically, globalization is also vulnerable to terrible and costly backlashes, as in the late 18th century, when it was interrupted by wars and revolutions, or in the early 20th century, when the very integrated world of the late 19th century was pulled apart by the First World War and by the Great Depression. We might think of the globalization phenomenon as cyclical.

Because so much recent globalization was driven by financial flows, the financial meltdown is a very serious setback. The most immediate impact of the financial collapse of September 2008 was on world trade, with a 30 percent decline in the last quarter of 2008, and only very fragile signs of recovery in 2009. The World Trade Organization estimates that global trade will be 10 percent lower in 2009 than in 2008.

Fiscal stimulus packages have a similar effect, in that they are intended to benefit domestic producers and involve the assumption of additional debt, which constitutes a long-term liability of domestic taxpayers. In consequence, many of the large stimulus packages are accompanied by more or less explicit provisions ("Buy America" or "Buy China") that attempt to ensure domestic, not foreign, producers are stimulated.

The reactions against globalization are as much driven by a new psychology as by economic reality or a precise weighing of the costs and benefits of globalization. Crises give rise to conspiracy theories, often directed against foreigners or foreign countries. Many Americans argue that the mess is the fault of Chinese surpluses. Many people in other countries already argue that they are being

NO

Moisés Naím
Editor in Chief, Foreign Policy
Author, Illicit: How Smugglers, Traffickers and Copycats Are Hijacking the Global Economy

Excerpted with permission from *Foreign Policy* #171 (March/April 2009) www.foreignpolicy.com

Rumors of globalization's demise — such as Princeton economic historian Harold James' recent obituary for "The Late, Great Globalization" — have been greatly exaggerated. . . .

All kinds of groups are still connecting, and the economic crisis will not slow their international activities. . . . It might even bolster them. Global charities, for instance, will face soaring demand for their services. . . . At a time when cash is king and jobs are scarce, globalized criminals will be one of the few . . . sources of credit, investment and employment in some places. . . .

It's true that private flows of credit and investment across borders have temporarily plummeted. . . . But as private economic activity falls, the international movement of public funds is booming. Last fall, the U.S. Federal Reserve and the central banks of Brazil, Mexico, Singapore and South Korea launched $30 billion worth of currency arrangements for each country designed to stabilize their financial markets. Similar reciprocal deals now tie together central banks throughout Asia, Europe and the Middle East.

Yes, some governments might be tempted to respond to the crisis by adopting trade-impairing policies, imposing rules that inhibit global financial integration or taking measures to curb immigration. The costs of doing so, however, are enormous and hard to sustain in the long run. What's more, the ability of any government to shield its economy and society from outside influences and dangers has steadily evaporated in the past two decades. . . .

Globalization is such a diverse, broad-based and potent force that not even today's massive economic crash will dramatically slow it down or permanently reverse it. . . .

But claims about the return of strong governments and nationalism are equally overstated. Yes, China might team up with Russia to counterbalance the United States in relation to Iran, but meanwhile the

(Continued)

(Continued)

hit by a U.S. crisis made in America. We will see trade protectionism and massive and powerful xenophobic sentiment. Perhaps many former so-called "globalization critics" will see just how good the integration was when it starts to fall apart.

Chinese and U.S. economies will be joined at the hip (China holds more than a trillion dollars of U.S. debt, and the United States is the main destination for its exports). . . .

The bottom line: Nationalism never disappeared. Globalization did not lessen national identities; it just rendered them more complex. . . . Globalization and geopolitics coexist, and neither is going anywhere.

Several factors could derail the beginnings of a recovery, analysts say, especially rising energy costs. In early August, Fatih Birol, chief economist for the International Energy Agency, warned that rising oil prices — which had reached $73 a barrel — threaten economic recovery. Sustained oil prices above $70 a barrel could strangle a recovery, he says.[51]

Even if the recession is ending, the recovery is widely expected to be feeble, barely relieving public suffering or discontent. "While the global economy is likely to begin expanding again in the second half of 2009, the recovery is expected to be subdued as global demand remains depressed, unemployment remains high and recession-like conditions continue until 2011," Hans Timmer, director of the World Bank's Development Prospects Group, said recently.[52]

In this environment, the determination of the world's political leaders to maintain global trade could be critical. But the latest signals can be read both ways.

Trade Policy Pressure

In July, U.S. Trade Representative Ron Kirk addressed workers at a steel plant outside Pittsburgh, Pa. The steel industry continues to be hit hard by foreign imports and has been pushing the administration to act against what it considers unfair competition from China. Kirk's language was as combative as any heard from a White House trade official in some time.

The United States will get tough on foreign governments that ignore trade rules, he said, and would no longer wait for a complaint to be filed but would proactively identify and investigate potential violations of labor rules in countries with free-trade agreements with the United States.

"We will take new steps to protect the rights of American farmers and small-business owners. We will hold our trading partners to their word on labor standards," Kirk said. "And we will use work we're already doing to fight even harder for the men and women who fuel our economy and support their families."[53]

Kirk's speech could be read as a tilt toward the wing of the Democratic Party that has pushed for more aggressive action to level the playing field in trade. Even before Kirk spoke, some free-trade supporters worried the Obama administration was less committed to the idea of free trade than its predecessors.

"I do not believe the current administration is at all protectionist," says Lane, the governmental affairs director for Caterpillar. "But by the same token, there's been a reluctance to engage their core constituencies on these measures. What's missing so far is advocacy. So far, they haven't made it a priority."

Yet some observers saw the speech as an attempt to reassure labor unions and other Democratic Party interest groups before a push by the administration for ratification of bilateral trade agreements with Panama, Colombia and South Korea.[54] The deals, signed by the Bush administration, are pending in Congress but have been put on hold by a wary Democratic leadership.

The G-20 will meet again later this month in Pittsburgh, where President Obama is expected to discuss his administration's trade agenda.

Doha Stalls

More than eight years after negotiators began working on the latest international trade agreement, known as the Doha round, the adjective most commonly attached to the negotiations is "stalled."

In mid-summer, WTO Director-General Pascal Lamy laid out what he described as a road map for negotiations to be completed in 2010. But his plan was met with only muted responses from the world's leading industrial nations.

Yet finishing Doha is critical in helping the world economy recover and preventing deglobalization, says Winters, the economist at Sussex University in the U.K., who studies the problems of developing nations. "If the Doha round fails, it's not clear that we can maintain the status quo," he says. "Doha helps us head off a big increase in protectionism that could occur if we don't get it."

The Doha impasse centers on disagreements between developed and developing nations, which believe they were promised certain concessions in return for opening up their economies in the last round. Perhaps the most highly publicized dispute is over EU and U.S. agricultural price supports. Many developed nations use price supports, import quotas and other programs to protect producers of some farm commodities from cheaper foreign imports.

For example, government programs in the United States subsidize politically powerful cotton producers, helping to depress the world price for cotton and hurting producers in Africa and India. The African nations, in particular, have been pushing for reduced cotton price supports in the developed nations. A 2007 study by Oxfam, a London-based nongovernmental organization dedicated to fighting global poverty, estimated that if the United States — the world's largest cotton-exporting nation — eliminated its cotton subsidies, the price for West African cotton would increase by 5 to 12 percent, dramatically improving the lives of the region's cotton farmers.[55]

Winters believes the disagreement over agricultural policy in developed countries has come to carry more weight than it should. Rather than pressing the developed nations to make politically difficult reforms, Winters thinks developing nations should concentrate on getting rid of quotas, tariffs and other more traditional agricultural trade barriers. "Most African nations are net food importers," he says. "For a good part of the developing world, it's really far more important that the West open up its markets than it is that they lower their agricultural subsidies."

While most analysts are pessimistic that Doha will move forward anytime soon, others remain hopeful. Jagdish Bhagwati, a professor at Columbia University who has been an adviser for both GATT and the WTO, notes that no trade round has ever failed.

"They often break down, are often thought to be in intensive care where the pessimists predict that they will expire," he wrote with Panagariya, "and they come back like the proverbial cat and are concluded. Doha will be no exception."[56]

But others see a watershed moment. Smick, the author and global economic policy strategist, sees the economic crisis combining with existing tensions to splinter the international political consensus in favor of continuing trade liberalization, even though globalization has lifted millions of people around the world out of poverty.

"You're seeing the collapse of world trade authority with Doha, unless there's a miracle," Smick says, "and it doesn't look like that's going to happen."

Outlook

Era of Deglobalization?

Experts who fear the world is headed into a period of deglobalization paint a gloomy picture of increased international tensions, conflict and nationalist fervor. Great Power politics — specifically the United States and China — will predominate, and governments will aggressively intervene in their national economies as state power grows.

Princeton professor James says a drop in international commerce combined with growing demand for limited resources such as oil is a recipe for increased international hostility. "Issues like the fuel supply or the supply of food — countries have and may again go to war about exactly this," says James.

Developing countries will be hit particularly hard, according to former Clinton Deputy Treasury Secretary Altman. "Already unstable nations, such as Pakistan, could disintegrate. And poverty will rise sharply in a number of African nations," he wrote in a recent issue of *Foreign Affairs*.[57]

Like James, Altman sees one nation in particular emerging in a more powerful position. "The one clear winner is China, whose unique political-economic model has come through unscathed," he wrote.

A recent report of the U.S. National Intelligence Council considers it a "relative certainty" that the global tensions predicted by James and Altman lie ahead. The report, "Global Trends 2025: A Transformed World," concludes that the world population — expected to increase by 1.2 billion people by 2025 — will put increasing pressure on energy, food and water resources. But the council is less certain that the world will retreat from global markets, calling it one of the "key uncertainties" of the next 16 years.[58]

Deglobalization would be a welcome development for globalization's longtime critics. Walden Bello, a sociology professor at the University of the Philippines and a leading critic of globalization, called the current crisis proof that globalization has "ended in massive failure." The crisis is an opportunity for developing nations to build regional relationships that go beyond trade to shared economic and social goals, promoting greater equity and justice, he says, citing recent efforts by Venezuelan President Hugo Chávez to build regional economic relationships.[59]

Chinese factory workers in Huaibei manufacture clothes for export to the United States. China's rapid growth has been based on an export-driven economy that heavily depended on Americans' voracious consuming habits. U.S. demand for Chinese products declined during the recession, however, prompting China to protect its textile and other labor-intensive industries with tax rebates.

AP Photo/Imaginechina

Other globalization critics see the crisis as the end of an unsustainable system of corporate economic domination and excessive consumption. Korten, the author and longtime critic of "corporate globalization," thinks the world will eventually embrace a radically different approach. "Food sources would be primarily local," he says. People would rely more on renewable energy, including solar and wind. "It would mean much more energy-efficient buildings and a far greater attention to . . . sustainable development."

In Korten's vision, global prosperity would depend not on what a country sells abroad but what it produces close to home. "The economy would be much more based on what our real needs are," he says.

But other experts predict a less calamitous or revolutionary future. Panagariya, the Columbia University economist, says under the most pessimistic scenario the U.S. economy would follow the route of the Japanese in the 1990s, with a lost decade of little or no economic growth. But he considers that unlikely.

"The U.S. is a lot more proactive policywise," Panagariya says. "It's willing to take a lot more risks, and the U.S. markets are a lot more flexible."

He also doesn't expect any significant changes in habits, among nations or individuals. "If housing prices go up," he says, "I think we'll go on a spending spree again."

Ireland did as well as any nation under globalization, but its crash has been as severe as any in Europe. Looking ahead, Irish economist Hughes hopes the future is found in the middle ground.

"I don't think the question is whether globalization is the right thing or not, but whether you can have a trajectory that's more sustainable and deals with the downsides of globalization," he says. "I'm suggesting that wise counsel prevails and people realize they have to learn to move it forward at a walking pace, rather than just rocket forward."

Notes

1. Harold James, "The Late Great Deglobalization," *Current History*, January 2009.
2. Jonathan Lynn and Kazunori Takada, "World trade to shrink 10 pct, Asia leads recovery: WTO," Reuters, July 22, 2009, www.reuters.com/article/businessNews/idUSSP48113720090722.
3. Angel Gurría and Jørgen Elmeskov, "Economic Outlook No. 85," Organisation for Economic Co-operation and Development, June 24, 2009, www.oecd.org/dataoecd/36/57/43117724.pdf.

4. Barry Eichengreen and Kevin O'Rourke, "A Tale of Two Depressions," at VoxEU.org, Centre for Economic Policy Research, June 4, 2009, www.voxeu.org/index.php?q=node/3421.

5. Joseph Francois, "The Big Drop: Trade and the Great Recession," *The Random Economist*, May 2, 2009, www.intereconomics.com/blogs/jff/2009/05/big-drop-trade-and-great-recession.html.

6. "Statement from G-20 Summit," Nov. 15, 2008. The complete text can be found at www.cfr.org/publication/17778/.

7. Elisa Gamberoni and Richard Newfarmer, "Trade Protection: Incipient but Worrisome Trends," *Tradenotes*, No. 37, The World Bank, March 2, 2009, www.voxeu.org/index.php?q=node/3183.

8. For background, see Mary H. Cooper, "Rethinking NAFTA," *CQ Researcher*, June 7, 1996, pp. 481-504.

9. Those provisions were subsequently modified, at the insistence of the Obama administration, to include a stipulation that they must comply with WTO rules.

10. Wolfgang Münchau, "Europe and the Protectionism Trap," Spiegel Online International, Feb. 13, 2009, www.spiegel.de/international/europe/0,1518,607457,00.html.

11. *Ibid.*

12. The latest round of WTO-sponsored trade talks, known as the Doha round, have been stalled over disagreements between developing and developed countries.

13. "Anti-dumping, subsidies, safeguards: contingencies, etc," "Understanding the WTO: the Agreements," www.wto.org/english/theWTO_e/whatis_e/tif_e/agrm8_e.htm.

14. "President Announces Temporary Safeguards for Steel Industry," White House press release, March 5, 2002, http://georgewbush-whitehouse.archives.gov/news/releases/2002/03/20020305-6.html.

15. Daniel J. Ikenson, "Sordid Steel Shenanigans," Fox News Online, Sept. 18, 2002, www.cato.org/pub_display.php?pub_id=3608.

16. Daniel Lovering, "Steel Product Makers Claim China Dumping Goods," *Manufacturing .net*, June 9, 2009.

17. Jagdish Bhagwati and Arvind Panagariya, "Legal Trade Barriers Must Be Kept in Check," *The Financial Times*, June 11, 2009, www.ft.com/cms/s/0/bcdf98c8-56b2-11de-9a1c-00144feab dc0.html.

18. Roger Altman, "Globalization in Retreat, Further Geopolitical Consequences of the Financial Crisis," *Foreign Affairs*, July/August 2009, p. 2.

19. The agreement is formally known as the CAFTA-DR, and the other signatories are Costa Rica, El Salvador, Guatemala, Nicaragua and the Dominican Republic.

20. For background, see Peter Behr, "The Troubled Dollar," *CQ Global Researcher*, October 2008, pp. 271-294.

21. For background, see Peter Behr, "Fixing Capitalism," *CQ Global Researcher*, July 2009, pp. 177-204.

22. William Bernstein, *A Splendid Exchange, How Trade Shaped the World* (2008), p. 14.

23. *Ibid.*, p. 8.

24. *Ibid.*, pp. 13-14.

25. Moisés Naím, "Think Again: Globalization," *Foreign Policy*, March/April 2009, www.foreign policy.com/story/cms.php?story_id=4678.

26. Bernstein, *op. cit.*, p. 8.

27. James, *op. cit.*, p. 21.

28. "The Battle of Smoot-Hawley," *The Economist*, Dec. 18, 2009, www.economist.com/displayStory.cfm?story_id=12798595.

29. Statistical information on U.S. and international trade volumes from the U.S. Department of State Historical Timeline, http://future.state.gov/when/timeline/1921_timeline/smoot_tariff.html.

30. "The Congress: Death of a Woodcutter," *Time*, Aug. 4, 1941.

31. "Milestones in United Nations History, a Selective Chronology," www.un.org/Overview/milesto4.htm.

32. "The Bretton Woods Conference," from the U.S. Department of State Timeline of U.S. Diplomatic History, www.state.gov/r/pa/ho/time/wwii/98681.htm. For background, see Behr, "The Troubled Dollar," *op. cit.*

33. Cordell Hull, "The Memoirs of Cordell Hull: Vol. 1" (1948), p. 81.

34. "The GATT Years: From Havana to Marrakesh," Understanding the WTO, World Trade Organization, www.wto.org/english/thewto_e/whatis_e/tif_e/fact4_e.htm.

35. Douglas Irwin, "GATT Turns 60," *The Wall Street Journal*, April 9, 2007, http://online.wsj.com/article/SB117607482355263550.html.

36. "The GATT Years: From Havana to Marrakesh," *op. cit.*

37. *Ibid.*

38. For a list see Office of the United States Trade Representative, www.ustr.gov/trade-agreements/free-trade-agreements.

39. Tom Friedman, *The World Is Flat: A Brief History of the Twenty-first Century* (2007), p. 212.

40. For background, see Brian Hansen, "Globalization Backlash," *CQ Researcher*, Sept. 28, 2001, pp. 761-784.

41. Bernstein, *op. cit.*, p. 367.

42. Catherine Rampell and Jack Healy, "In Hopeful Sign, Output Declines at Slower Pace," *The New York Times*, Aug. 1, 2009, p. A1, www.nytimes.com/2009/08/01/business/economy/01econ.html.

43. Nick Timraos and Kelly Evans, "Home Prices Rise Across U.S.," *The Wall Street Journal*, July 29, 2009, p. A1.

44. *China Quarterly Update*, The World Bank, June 2009, http://go.worldbank.org/9FV11IHMF0.

45. Joe McDonald, "Survey: China manufacturing improved in July," The Associated Press, Aug. 3, 2009.

46. "World Economic Outlook Update," International Monetary Fund, July 8, 2009, www.imf.org/external/pubs/ft/weo/2009/update/02/pdf/0709.pdf.

47. Rampell and Healy, *op. cit.* U.S. Treasury Secretary Timothy Geithner, speaking on ABC's "This Week," Aug. 2, 2009.

48. "World Economic Outlook Update," *op. cit.*

49. Eichengreen and O'Rourke, *op. cit.*

50. "Global Development Finance 2009: Outlook Summary," The World Bank, June 22, 2009, http://go.worldbank.org/HCR2ABQPX0.

51. Kate Mackenzie, "Global economy at risk from oil price rise," *The Financial Times*, Aug. 3, 2009, www.ft.com/cms/s/0/1281aad6-8049-11de-bf04-00144feabdc0.html.

52. "The Financial Crisis: Charting a Global Recovery," The World Bank, June 22, 2009, http://go.worldbank.org/KUG53HWZY0.

53. A complete text of Kirk's speech can be found at www.ustr.gov/about-us/press-office/speeches/transcripts/2009/july/ambassador-kirk-announces-new-initiatives-trade.

54. Ian Swanson, "Kirk Sooths on Trade," *The Hill*, July 16, 2009, http://thehill.com/the-executive/kirk-soothes-on-trade-2009-07-16.html.

55. Julian M. Alston, Daniel A. Sumner and Henrich Brunke, "Impacts of Reductions in US Cotton Subsidies on West African Cotton Producers," Oxfam America, 2007.

56. Jagdish Bhagwati and Arvind Panagariya, "Doha: The Last Mile," *The New York Sun*, Aug. 21, 2008, www.nysun.com/opinion/doha-the-last-mile/84314/.

57. Altman, *op. cit.*

58. "Global Trends 2025: A Transformed World," National Intelligence Council, www.dni.gov/nic/PDF_2025/2025_Global_Trends_Final_Report.pdf.

59. Walden Bello, "Challenges of Regional Integration," presented July 21, 2009, to the Universidad de Deportes, Asunción, Paraguay, reprinted by Focus on the Global South, http://focusweb.org/index.php.

Bibliography

Books

Bernstein, William, *A Splendid Exchange, How Trade Shaped the World*, Grove Press, 2008.

An American financial theorist comprehensively examines how trade has influenced world events throughout history.

Dorgan, Byron, *Take This Job and Ship It: How Corporate Greed and Brain-dead Politics are Selling Out America*, Thomas Dunn Books, St. Martin's Press, 2006.

The populist Democratic senator from North Dakota takes on what he considers the misguided political choices and false perceptions about world trade that have cost Americans jobs and income.

Ferguson, David, and Thomas Hall, *The Depression: An International Disaster of Perverse Economic Policies*, University of Michigan Press, 1998.

Two economists examine policy decisions that helped to create the Great Depression and then make it worse.

Friedman, Thomas, *The World Is Flat: A Brief History of the Twenty-first Century*, Picador, 2007.

The New York Times columnist's international best-seller presents a largely optimistic take on the globalization phenomenon.

James, Harold, *The Creation and Destruction of Value, The Globalization Cycle*, Harvard University Press, forthcoming, September 2009.

The British professor of history and international affairs at Princeton University who started the current debate about deglobalization puts the current crisis into historical context.

Korten, David, *Agenda for a New Economy: From Phantom Wealth to Real Wealth*, Berrett-Koehler, 2009.

An intellectual leader of the opposition to what he terms "corporate globalization" offers a radically different view of economic prosperity, focused not on corporate profits but on quality of life.

Smick, David, *The World Is Curved, Hidden Dangers to the Global Economy*, Portfolio, 2008.

In what amounts to a response to Friedman's book, a global economic policy strategist and free-trade proponent presents reasons to worry about globalization's future.

Articles

"The Battle of Smoot-Hawley," *The Economist*, Dec. 18, 2009.

The article examines how Congress passed and President Herbert Hoover signed one of the world's most disastrous anti-trade measures.

Altman, Roger, "Globalization in Retreat: Further Geopolitical Consequences of the Financial Crisis," *Foreign Affairs*, July/August 2009.

A former deputy U.S. Treasury secretary under President Bill Clinton sees a "new period of state intervention, re-regulation and creeping protectionism" under way.

Irwin, Douglas, "GATT Turns 60," *The Wall Street Journal*, April 9, 2009.

A Dartmouth College professor who specializes in trade history traces the beginnings of modern globalization from the GATT negotiations after World War II.

James, Harold, "The Late, Great Globalization," *Current History*, January 2009.

A Princeton history professor suggests a period of deglobalization is beginning in which trade will decline and tensions between nations will rise as they compete for critical resources.

Naím, Moisés, "Think Again: Globalization," *Foreign Policy*, March/April, 2009.

The magazine's editor, a former minister of trade and industry in Venezuela, argues that globalization is more than an economic phenomenon but an unstoppable cultural and technological transformation.

Reports and Studies

Eichengreen, Barry, and Kevin O'Rourke, "A Tale of Two Depressions," VoxEU.org, June 4, 2009.

Irish and American economists examine a series of key economic indicators that reveal how closely the current economic downturn tracks the first years of the Great Depression.

Gameroni, Elisa, and Richard Newfarmer, "Trade Protection: Incipient but Worrisome Trends," *Tradenotes*, No. 37, The World Bank, March 2, 2009.

The authors examine protectionist measures taken since the economic downturn started.

Gurría, Angel, and Jørgen Elmeskov, "Economic Outlook No. 85," Organisation for Economic Co-operation and Development, June 24, 2009.

The OECD's secretary general (Gurría) and the head of its Economics Department examine major trends in the world economy.

Mattoo, Aaditva, and Arvind Subramian, "Multilateralism Beyond Doha," "Working Paper No. 153," Center for Global Development, October 2008.

The authors contend the international trading system has failed to adapt to changing world economic conditions and suggest what should be done.

For More Information

Focus on the Global South, http://focusweb.org. An anti-globalization research and activist group with offices in Thailand, the Philippines and India, which aims to transform the global economy "from one centered around the needs of transnational corporations to one that focuses on the needs of people, communities and nations."

Organisation for Economic Co-operation and Development, 2, rue André Pascal F-75775 Paris Cedex 16, France; +33 1.45.24.82.00; www.oecd.org. Organization made up of 30 industrialized countries that provides economic research and advises governments on handling the economic, social and governance challenges associated with a globalized economy.

Peterson Institute for International Economics, 1750 Massachusetts Ave., N.W., Washington, DC 20036-1903; (202) 328-9000; www.iie.com. A private, nonpartisan research institution devoted to the study of international economic policy; advocates expanded global trade.

Public Citizen's Global Trade Watch, 1600 20th St., N.W., Washington, DC 20009; (202) 588-1000; www.citizen.org/trade. Nongovernmental organization that promotes democracy "by challenging corporate globalization, arguing that the current globalization model is neither a random inevitability nor 'free trade.' "

World Trade Organization, Centre William Rappard, Rue de Lausanne 154, CH-1211 Geneva 21, Switzerland; (41-22) 739 51 11; www.wto.org. A 153-member international organization established to set global trade rules and manage disputes.